Anybody's Business

Barbara Van Syckle
Jackson Community College

Brian Tietje
Cal Poly State University, San Luis Obispo

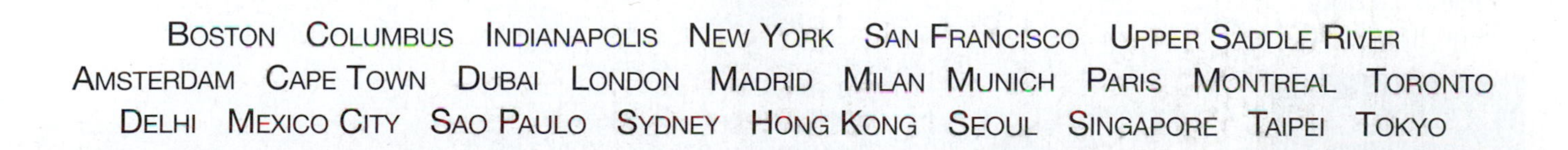

Boston Columbus Indianapolis New York San Francisco Upper Saddle River
Amsterdam Cape Town Dubai London Madrid Milan Munich Paris Montreal Toronto
Delhi Mexico City Sao Paulo Sydney Hong Kong Seoul Singapore Taipei Tokyo

VP/Publisher: Natalie E. Anderson
AVP/Executive Editor: Jodi McPherson
Director, Product Development: Pamela Hersperger
Editorial Project Manager: Melissa Arlio
Development Editor: Shannon LeMay-Finn
Editorial Assistant: Christina Rumbaugh
AVP, Executive Editor, Media: Richard Keaveney
Director of Digital Development: Lisa Strite
Senior Marketing Manager: Maggie Moylan-Leen
Marketing Assistant: Justin Jacob
Editorial Media Project Manager: Ashley Lulling
Media Development Managers: Cathi Profitko and Robin Lazrus
Development Editor, Media: Gina Huck Siegert
Production Media Project Manager: John Cassar
Senior Managing Editor: Cynthia Zonneveld
Production Project Manager: Lynne Breitfeller
Senior Operations Supervisor: Natacha Moore
Design Development Manager: John Christinia
Director of Marketing: Kate Valentine
Text and Cover Designer: Blair Brown
Manager, Visual Research: Beth Brenzel
Photo Researcher: Manager, Rights and Permissions: Zina Arabia
Image Permission Coordinator: Cynthia Vincenti
Cover, Visual Research and Permissions: Karen Sanatar
Cover Photos: Corbis/Colin Anderson; istockphoto
Text Illustrations: Sproutin Up Designs, Inc. LLC and Blair Brown
Full-Service Project Management: Words & Numbers, Inc.
Composition: Absolute Service
Printer/Binder: Courier/Kendallville
Cover Printer: Phoenix Color
Text Font: Gill Sans/Light 10/12

Credits and acknowledgments borrowed from other sources and reproduced, with permission, in this textbook appear on appropriate page within text (or on page 383).

Library of Congress Cataloging-in-Publication Data

Van Syckle, Barbara.
Anybody's business / Barbara Van Syckle, Brian Tietje.
p. cm.
ISBN 0-13-608634-9
1. Business enterprises—Finance. 2. Finance. I. Tietje, Brian C. II. Title.

HG4026.V363 2010
658—dc22

2009032661

10 9 8 7 6 5 4 3 2 1

Prentice Hall
is an imprint of

www.pearsonhighered.com

ISBN 10 digit: 0-13-608634-9
ISBN 13 digit: 978-0-13-608634-5

Dedication

To Phil, Fritz, Chivy, Calli, Rachael, and Thunder Lake for believing in me.
To Jodi for believing in AB.
God bless America, Blair, Brian, Jodi, Maggie, Melissa, Shannon, and the Hiawatha National Forest.
And to each of you for whom *Anybody's Business* makes a difference in your standard of living and quality of life.

Barbara Van Syckle

To my Lord who saved me; Debbie, whose love inspires me; Summer, who delights me; my parents, who sacrificed for me; and Hunter, our adventure on the horizon. Also to Jodi and Barbara, for inviting me into the AB family.

Brian Tietje

About the Authors

Barbara Van Syckle

Never one to stand still for too long, Barbara spends much of her time travelling, working, and studying stateside and abroad—a passion that has led her to China, Cyprus, British Columbia, Alberta, Kenya, France, the Czech Republic, Tanzania, Belgium, Germany, Poland, Switzerland, the Netherlands, Newfoundland, and Russia. She's received innumerable awards and accolades, including a Fulbright to Eastern Europe, the first National Teaching Excellence award in Business (recognized by President Clinton and Michigan Governor Engler), a position as the board of director's president for the Association of Collegiate Business Schools and Programs, and the honor of conducting an economic analysis for the Russian government. Barbara has also owned three small businesses along the way and holds a full-time faculty position at Jackson Community College.

A true follower of the work hard, play hard life code, Barbara, her husband, Phil, and their black and chocolate Labrador Retrievers split their time between homes in Chicago, Grand Rapids, Thunder Lake in the Hiawatha National Forest, and Jackson, Michigan, when they're not busy on the road. Passionate about art, antiques, and animals, Barbara and her husband spend their time snowshoeing, canoeing, hiking, and primitive camping. The couple volunteers with a variety of start-up companies, working with entrepreneurs to get their ventures "up and running," and are deeply committed to multiple environmental issues. Barbara can be reached at barbaravansyckle@yahoo.com.

Brian Tietje

Brian is a left-handed farm boy from Ohio who ventured his way through a business degree at Bowling Green State University to a sales career with Johnson & Johnson. He later returned to academics, earning an MBA from the University of Hawaii and a Ph.D. in Marketing from the University of Washington. Brian has been a marketing professor at Cal Poly State University, San Luis Obispo, since 1999 and is currently the Associate Dean of the Orfalea College of Business. He has published articles in a variety of academic journals and has won several teaching awards for his contributions to sales and marketing courses and executive education seminars. Brian and his wife, Debbie, their daughter, Summer, and son, Hunter, reside in Atascadero, California. He can be reached at btietje@calpoly.edu.

Acknowledgments

Anybody's Business is much more than a book. It's an approach to business and life that harnesses the best of people and how they work together to produce a transformation in perspective and purpose. It only makes sense, then, that the people who were involved in the development of *Anybody's Business* reflect those same values.

The vision of *Anybody's Business* has been faithfully shepherded by our executive editor Jodi McPherson. Her leadership, tenacity, and uncanny ability to pull together a team from around the country and keep them on the same rhythm are truly remarkable. *Anybody's Business* would have no life without her. Thank you, Jodi, and go Red Sox!

With any visionary, there needs to be a faithful manager who makes sure that the right work gets done at the right time by the right people. Development Editor Shannon LeMay-Finn was instrumental in moving every detail of this project forward. Along the way, she displayed the rarest of synergies—the ability to manage every detail of the project, ensure the editorial quality of every word in the text, and accommodate the constant flow of new ideas and concepts that seemed to continually spring forth throughout the project, and doing all of this with patience, understanding, and sensitivity. Thank you, Shannon, for putting up with us!

Melissa Arlio brought contemporary freshness, unbridled enthusiasm, and the unparalleled ability to keep track of details and responsibilities for the development of the complementary media and learning tools that are as critical to the success of *Anybody's Business* as the book itself. As Editorial Project Manager/Assistant Editor, Melissa kept us focused on the student's perspective, and she somehow managed to be everywhere at once as different phases of the project moved forward simultaneously.

Anybody's Business is so much more than just a book of words, and designer Blair Brown was the translator who took the time to patiently listen to our ideas and intentions, and somehow was able to express those ideas through visualizations that always managed to go beyond what we could have ever imagined. We thank Blair for the aesthetic distinctiveness and intentionality toward learning that are captured by the illustrations and designs in *Anybody's Business*, and for his unpredictable sense of humor that continually reminded us that this project was fun.

The success of any academic textbook rests largely on the support it receives from the publisher's marketing and sales force. We are indebted to Marketing Manager Maggie Moylan for putting her full support behind this project and inspiring her marketing and sales force to catch the vision of *Anybody's Business* so that its impact could extend across the country. Maggie always managed to bring her panache to this project even amidst an intense travel and project schedule. Maggie, we still don't know how you do it!

Of course, no text can find success without someone working behind the scenes to make sure all the pieces come together in the final product. Production Project Manager, Lynne Breitfeller, worked tirelessly to ensure that every word, illustration, and photograph you now see on these pages appeared seamlessly, essentially taking all of our ideas and concepts and literally giving them life.

Every word, paragraph, and chapter was an experiment for us, and any experiment first needs to be tested before the ideas can be publicly communicated. We enlisted a team of elite reviewers—our Top Hats—who are listed on the next page. These reviewers generously shared their expertise and passion for a high-impact learning experience and tirelessly repeated the "read-edit-repeat" process time and again for every chapter. We are so grateful for their help.

This project would never have seen the light of day without the support of Jerome Grant and Natalie Anderson, who were willing to take risks and invest resources on a project that tended to break the rules of traditional publishing in almost every aspect of its design. Thank you for taking the chance on us. Remember, high risk, high reward!

There are so many more individuals who invested themselves in this project. We are deeply indebted to them, and we hope that they can share our satisfaction of a job well done. *Anybody's Business* has been born! Now, we invite you to join us as we embark on a learning experience where business truly comes to life.

Reviewers

Top Hats

Like any well-oiled machine, the *Anybody's Business* team often needed to enlist the help of talented verbal mechanics to fine tune the writing process and make sure we never veered off course. Without the invaluable feedback, suggestions, and ideas of these passionate reviewers, this text may have never been able to plow through the weeds, and if it did, it certainly wouldn't have been so shiny.

Thomas Christian

Louann Cummings, University of Findlay

Patrick Greek, Macomb Community College

LaShon Harley, Durham Technical Community College

Lisa Pierce, Northwestern College

Gerald Pierri, Villanova University

Phyllis Shafer, Brookdale Community College

Susan Sieloff, Northeastern University

Rachael Snyder

Brian Stetler

Henry Velarde, Malcolm X College

Timothy Whited, National College

Ned Young, Sinclair Community College

Market Reviewers

We'd also like to extend our gratitude to the reviewers below whose time, hard work, and passion helped shaped *Anybody's Business.*

Michael Aubry, Cuyamaca College
April Bailey, Shippensburg University of Pennsylvania
Felicia Baldwin, Richard J. Daley College
Michael Baran, South Puget Sound Community College
Richard Bartlett, Columbus State Community College
Gayona Beckford-Barclay, Community College of Baltimore County
Connie Belden, Butler Community College
George Bernard, Seminole Community College
Patricia Bernson, County College of Morris
Laurel Berry, Bryant & Stratton College
Robert Berwick, Heritage Institute
Judy Boozer, Lane Community College
Chuck Bowles, Pikes Peak Community College
Malcolm Bowyer, Montgomery Community College
Mike Bowyer, Montgomery Community College
Steven Bruenjes, Dover Business College
Barry Bunn, Valencia Community College
Patrick Burke, Ivy Tech Community College
Patrice Burleson, Winthrop University
Marian Canada, Ivy Tech Community College of Columbus
Bonnie Chavez , Santa Barbara City College
William Chipman, Kankakee Community College
Desmond Chun, Chabot Community College
Michael Cicero, Highline Community College
Subasree Cidambi, Mount San Antonio College
David Clifton, Ivy Tech Community College - Southern Indiana
Paul Coakley, Community College of Baltimore County
Rachna Condos, American River College
Solveg Cooper, Cuesta College
Shawna Coram, Florida Community College at Jacksonville
Douglas Crowe, Bradley University
Dana D'Angelo, Drexel University
Thomas D'Arrigo, SUNY-Maritime College
James Darling, Central New Mexico Community College
Jamey Darnell, Durham Technical Community College
Helen Davis, Jefferson Community College
Kate Demarest, Carroll Community College
Gerard Dobson, Waukesha County Technical College
Kathleen Dominick, Bucks County Community College
Michael Drafke, College of DuPage
Allison Duesing, Northeast Lakeview College
Steve Dunphy, Indiana University Northwest
Timothy Durfield, Citrus College
Robert Edmonds, State University of New York-Maritime College
Karen Edwards, Chemeketa Community College
Russ Edwards, Valencia Community College
James Emig, Villanova University
Mary Ewanechko, Monroe Community College
Thom Foley. Kent State University - Geauga
Mark Fox, Indiana University South Bend
Leatrice Freer, Pitt Community College
Theresa Freihoefer, Central Oregon Community College
William Furrell, Moorpark College
Mary Beth Furst, Howard Community College
George Gannage Jr., West Georgia Technical College

Wayne Gawlik, Joliet Junior College
Larisa Genin, Saint Mary's College of California
Paul Gerhardt, Pierce College
Vanessa Germerot, Ozarks Technical Community College
Gerald GeRue, Rock Valley College
Katie Ghahramani, Johnson County Community College
Lucia Gheorghi, Passaic County Community College
David Gillis, San Jose State University
Robert Goldberg, Northeastern University
Connie Golden, Lakeland Community College
Carol Gottuso, Metropolitan Community College
Madeline Grant, Santa Ana College
Lawrence Green, Salt Lake Community College
Maurice Greene, Monroe College
Gary Guidetti, Northampton Community College
Lynn Halkowic, Bloomsburg University of Pennsylvania
Karen Halpern, South Puget Sound Community College
Roxanne Hamilton, Landmark College
LaShon Harley, Durham Technical Community College
Helen Marie Harmon, Indiana University Northwest
Linda Hefferin, Elgin Community College
Charlane Held, Onondaga Community College
Kathleen Hess, Salem State College
Dorothy Hetmer-Hinds, Trinity Valley Community College
Linda Hoffman, Ivy Tech Community College-Northeast
Phil Holleran, Mitchell Community College
William Huisking, Bergen Community College
Kimberly Hurns, Washtenaw Community College
Holly Hutchins, Central Oregon Community College
Marc Hyman, Cascadia Community College
Channelle James, University of North Carolina at Greensboro
Pam Janson, Stark State College of Technology
Dennis Johnson, Delaware County Community College
Gwendolyn Jones, The University of Akron
Ken Jones, Ivy Tech Community College
Lillian Kamal, University of Hartford
Todd Korol, Monroe Community College
Jack Kraettli, Oklahoma City Community College
Christine Kydd, Universtiy of Delaware
Kim Lamb, Stautzenberger College
Marie Lapidus, Oakton Community College
Angela Leverett, Georgia Southern University
Peter Lippman, Santa Monica College
Lori Long, Baldwin-Wallace College
Ivan Lowe, York Technical College
John Mago, Anoka Ramsey Community College
Mike Magro, Mt. Sierra College
Jan Mangos, Valencia Community College
Suzanne Markow, Des Moines Area Community College
Stacy Martin, Southwestern Illinois College
Marian Matthews, Central New Mexico Community College
Kelli Mayes-Denker, Carl Sandburg College
Lee McCain, Valencia Community College, East Campus
Patrick McCormick, Ivy Tech Community College Fort Wayne
Lisa McCormick, Community College of Allegheny County
Edward McGee, National Technical Institute for the Deaf at Rochester Institute of Technology
Bruce McLaren, Indiana State University
Robert McNutt, University of Delaware
Bill McPherson, Indiana University of Pennsylvania
Juan Meraz, Missouri State University
John Miller, Pima Community College Downtown
Mark Nagel, Normandale Community College
Rachna Nagi-Con, American River College
Mark Nygren, Brigham Young University-Idaho
Akira Odani, State University of New Yok-Delhi
Mary Padula, City University of New York Borough of Manhattan Community College
Esther Page-Wood, Western Michigan University
Rose Pollard, Southeast Community College
Lana Powell, Valencia Community College
Sally Proffitt, Tarrant County College, Northeast Campus
Michael Quinn, James Madison University
Lori Radulovich, Baldwin-Wallace College
Carlton R. Raines, Lehigh Carbon Community College
Greg Rapp, Portland Community College
Robert Reck, Western Michigan University
Delores Reha, Fullerton College
Gloria Rembert, Mitchell Community College
Reina Reynolds, Valencia Community College
Lynn Richards, Johnson County Community College
Tim Rogers, Ozarks Technical College
June Roux, Delaware Technical & Community College
Carol Rowey, Community College of Rhode Island
Carolyn Seefer, Diablo Valley College
Patricia Setlik, William Rainey Harper College
Phillis Shafer, Brookdale Community College
Dennis Shannon, Southwestern Illinois College
Carole Shook, University of Arkansas
Steven Skaggs, Waubonsee Community College
Maria Sofia, Bryant and Stratton College, North Campus
Frank Sole, Youngstown State University
Ray Sparks, Pima College
Rieann Spence-Gale, Northern Virginia Community College Alexandria Campus
Keith Starcher, Indiana Wesleyan University
Shallin Suber, Tri-County Technical College
Deanna Teel, Houston Community College
Alexis Thurman, County College of Morris
Frank Titlow, Saint Petersburg College
Kristin Trask, Butler Community College
Joyce Twing, Vermont Technical College
Shafi Ullah, Broward College
Bob Urell, Irvine Valley College
Ezgi Uzel, State University of New York Maritime
Richard Vaughan, Durham Technical Community College
Dom Visco, Bucks County Community College
Louis Watanabe, Bellevue College
Tim Whited, National College
Les Wiletzky, Pierce College - Puyallup Campus
George Williams, Bergen Community College
Richard Williams, Santa Clara University
Doug Wilson, University of Oregon
Colette Wolfson, Ivy Tech Community College - South Bend
Kim Wong, Central New Mexico Community College
Wanda Wong, Chabot College
Mark Zorn, Butler County Community College

Letter from the Authors

This book is different, in many ways, from other texts in the Introduction to Business landscape. But because *different* isn't necessarily a guarantee for *better*, we know that the distinctiveness of this book needs to deliver on some important promises. We make these promises to the students who will be learning from this book, the instructors who are the facilitators of that learning, and the organizations who will be hiring students who have experienced business in a distinctively "AB" way.

AB is relevant to today's business environment. Although some students may enjoy long, successful careers with a single employer like a Fortune 500 corporation, other students are more likely to work for private firms, nonprofit organizations, and not-just-for-profit organizations, or they might launch their own venture now or in the future. AB is relevant for the entire spectrum of organizations in our global economy. You won't find traditional terms like "corporate finance" in AB, because the core concepts of cash flow and profitability are far more relevant and adaptive to the diverse business landscape students face.

Students: you'll be able to use what you learn from AB in any career direction you take.
Instructors: we've prepared concepts, skills, and examples that you can use for any audience, any age, on any career path.
Employers and investors: the AB student you hire will be ready to contribute to your organization, regardless of its ownership structure, size, mission, or industry.

AB delivers learning that lasts a lifetime. We intentionally focus on the higher levels of learning—application, synthesis, and evaluation—that equip students to use important business concepts to solve problems, make decisions, and improve their quality of life and standard of living. We only use terminology if it's essential to help the reader learn how to do something well, like a SWOT analysis, and our writing always emphasizes the "how to" aspect of a concept. Students won't forget a five-step process if they use that process daily. AB equips students with skills that they can use now, in the business of life, and the memory of these skills will last a lifetime. A student who understands how to evaluate a decision's impact on cash flow will be able to apply that knowledge throughout his or her personal and professional life.

Students: you will use what you learn from AB for the rest of your life.
Instructors: AB will help you achieve high levels of learning
(and the corresponding assessment) in your course and program.
Employers and investors: the AB student you hire will not only be able to tell you what he or she **learned** from this course, that student will also be able to tell you what he or she **can do** to impact your bottom line today.

AB meets students where they are. The writing style is clear and concise, classic and contemporary, approachable and encouraging, and its tone is seasoned with sassiness. As a result, this book will not be perceived as pages of content that have to be endured, but rather experiences that students won't want to miss. Throughout AB, we draw upon real events in a student's life and reveal how these experiences demonstrate important business concepts for personal and professional success. A trip to the doctor's office, filing an auto accident claim, or paying the tab at the restaurant—all of these events become AB internships as business concepts are brought to life.

Students: you're doing business already (but maybe you don't always see it that way), and AB will show you how to take the skills you already have and leverage them for personal and professional success.
Instructors: AB triggers student motivation and engagement by making the personal connection between business and life.
Employers and investors: you need a workforce that "gets" business and is passionate about it. AB triggers an enthusiastic business sense by helping students see business in their lives and appreciate business excellence when they see it.

AB Positive,
Barbara and Brian

Made **for Students, by Students**

On a constant quest to breathe even more life and a young, fresh voice into *Anybody's Business*, the team decided there was no better resource for insight and creativity than those who were closest to the college experience. After all, when building a text intentionally designed to come to YOU, the student, why not go back to the source?

As you look through *Anybody's Business*, take note of the photos that appear throughout it. They were taken by a student just like you. **Aaron Binaco**, the photographer and artist whose work fills these pages, was born in Massachusetts. Surrendering to the pull of bright lights and urban living, Aaron made his way to New York City to attend the School of Visual Arts with a focus in photography. In the past four years, he has worked alongside high-end celebrity photographers, noted documentarians, and fine artists, as well as his talented and success-bound classmates. His work can be seen in many magazines and galleries throughout the United States. Aaron truly is his own business and a real-life example of what *Anybody's Business* can do for you.

It was during a first-grade project where the class was asked to create a storybook out of a cereal box, construction paper, and crayons that advertising copywriter **Janine Lucas** realized she wanted to be a writer. What she didn't know at the time was how her desire to write would one day translate into a career in business. Years later, with a bachelor's degree in English and creative writing from SUNY New Paltz, and several freelance writing projects under her belt, Janine has found herself writing advertising copy as well as descriptive content for Pearson textbooks, including *Anybody's Business*. Eager to help other students turn their passion into business careers, Janine has used her love of writing to show you what this text, and the study of business, is all about.

Curiosity may have killed the cat, but it's what helped **Melissa Arlio** land a central role on the AB team and the title of Editorial Project Manager/Assistant Editor at Pearson Education. Her first word reportedly, "Why?" Melissa set out to Rutgers University, where she turned her endless inquisitions into a bachelor's degree in journalism. An internship at Pearson later turned into a full-time Editorial Assistant's spot and, one year into the gig, led to a promotion to her current position. It was here that Melissa changed the focus of her questions from "Why?" to "Why not?" and aided the team in pushing the envelope and essentially changing the way business is taught and learned. Melissa was involved in every aspect of the project from vision to creation and beyond, and her aim throughout the process was to offer a unique student perspective. After all, she, too, in the not-so-distant past, once sat in those lecture hall chairs wondering what it all meant to her life—a life that goes beyond papers and final exams. She now hopes that her hard work on *Anybody's Business* will provide students like you with the answer.

Brief **Contents**

Contents

5: Tech Insight Available at mybizlab.com

6: Beyond Business Available at mybizlab.com

This course won't be like other courses where you daydream your way through class and try to memorize terms the night before the test. This is YOUR course—a course that's about YOUR life from day one. And, as you can see, ***Anybody's Business*** isn't like all your other books either. This text is your very own Business Road Map—minus all the stuffy, boring material that's usually crammed onto every page. Why? Well, it's because understanding business is about understanding things that really matter, in business and in life. Everything you learn with ***Anybody's Business*** will affect your standard of living and quality of life, starting right now and lasting well into the future. So, whether you want to start your own business, be a manager, or become some big, hot shot executive, this Business Road Map will prepare you for your professional and personal journey—starting today.

So, are you ready to hear about important business concepts that will help you develop the skills to solve problems, make decisions, and improve the quality of your life and standard of living? It starts now!

Let's start with the first page of Chapter 1. Now **STOP!** You don't want to skip over this section like you would in all your other textbooks. The opening page of each chapter shows you how you are already doing business in your life. Have you ever negotiated more time out on a Saturday night? Have you ever had your own credit or debit card? If you have, then you already have some of the business skills that you'll be building throughout this course. Reading these opening sections will help you see the personal connection between business and your life.

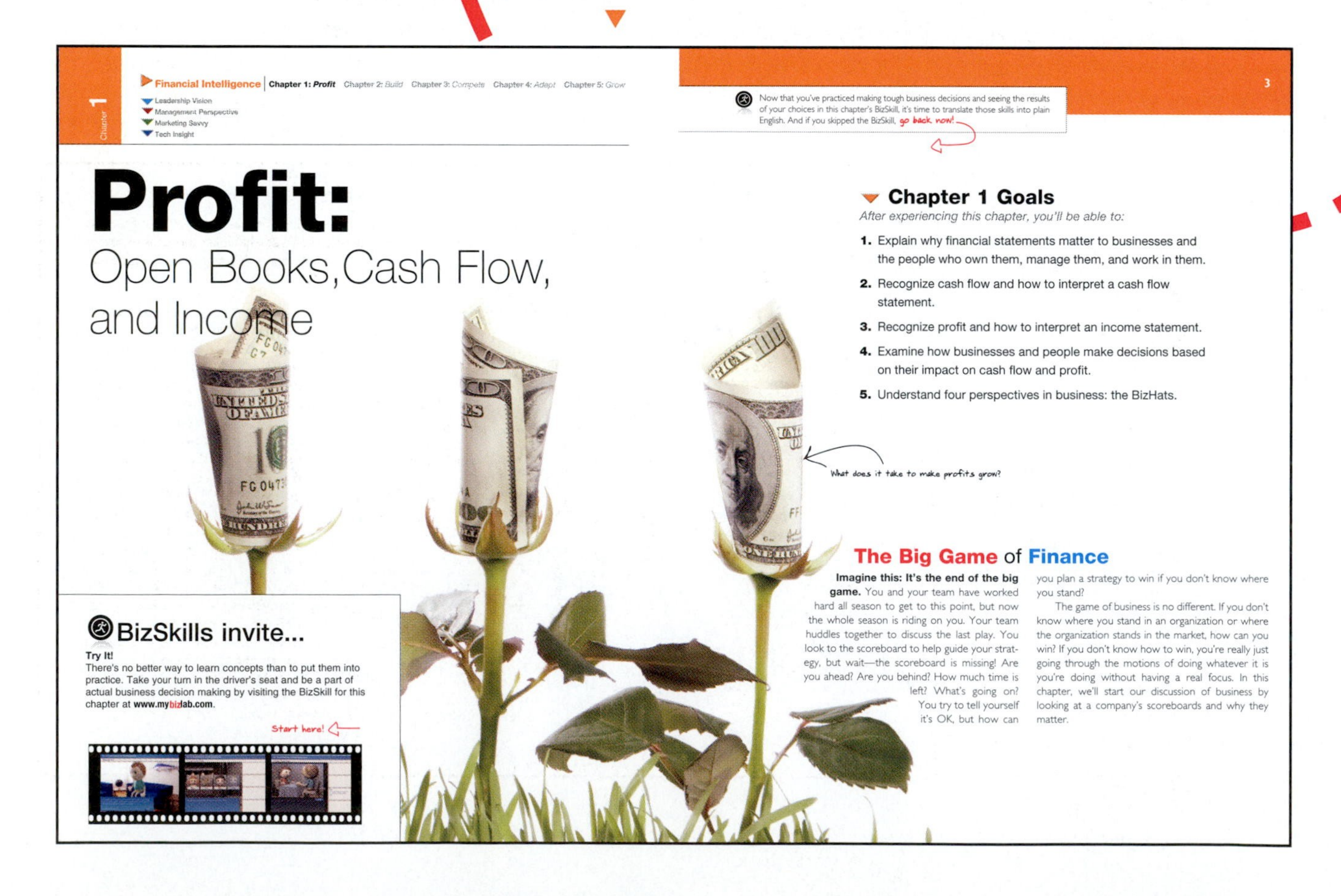

Chapter 1

Financial Intelligence | Chapter 1: *Profit* Chapter 2: *Build* Chapter 3: *Compete* Chapter 4: *Adapt* Chapter 5: *Grow*

Leadership Vision
Management Perspective
Marketing Savvy
Tech Insight

3

Now that you've practiced making tough business decisions and seeing the results of your choices in this chapter's BizSkill, it's time to translate those skills into plain English. And if you skipped the BizSkill, go back now!

Profit:
Open Books, Cash Flow, and Income

Chapter 1 Goals

After experiencing this chapter, you'll be able to:

1. Explain why financial statements matter to businesses and the people who own them, manage them, and work in them.
2. Recognize cash flow and how to interpret a cash flow statement.
3. Recognize profit and how to interpret an income statement.
4. Examine how businesses and people make decisions based on their impact on cash flow and profit.
5. Understand four perspectives in business: the BizHats.

What does it take to make profits grow?

The Big Game of Finance

Imagine this: It's the end of the big game. You and your team have worked hard all season to get to this point, but now the whole season is riding on you. Your team huddles together to discuss the last play. You look to the scoreboard to help guide your strategy, but wait—the scoreboard is missing! Are you ahead? Are you behind? How much time is left? What's going on? You try to tell yourself it's OK, but how can you plan a strategy to win if you don't know where you stand?

The game of business is no different. If you don't know where you stand in an organization or where the organization stands in the market, how can you win? If you don't know how to win, you're really just going through the motions of doing whatever it is you're doing without having a real focus. In this chapter, we'll start our discussion of business by looking at a company's scoreboards and why they matter.

BizSkills invite...

Try It!
There's no better way to learn concepts than to put them into practice. Take your turn in the driver's seat and be a part of actual business decision making by visiting the BizSkill for this chapter at **www.mybizlab.com**.

Start here!

BizSkills invite...

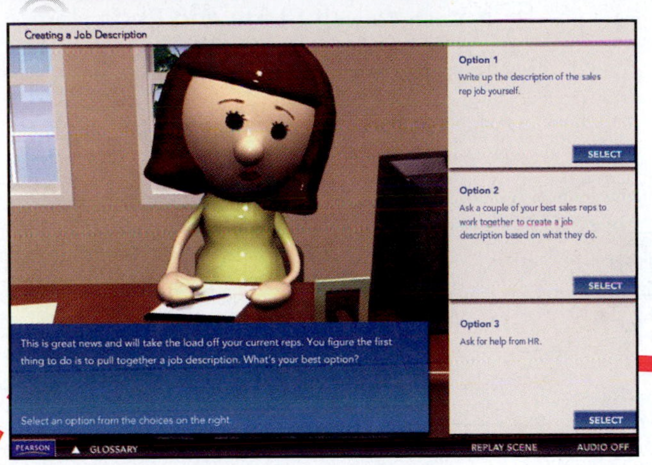

See the **BizSkill invite**? It's signaling you to go to **www.mybizlab.com** and complete a BizSkill. BizSkills are brief, four-minute animated simulations that let you play the role of a decision maker in a business scenario. There's no better way to learn concepts than to put them into practice. So go ahead, take your turn in the driver's seat and be a part of an actual business decision!

OK, let's flip through a few pages. By now you are probably noticing that this text looks different. Did you happen to see those **illustrations**? Those hand-drawn pictures are there to help you get certain concepts that might not be understood with words alone. And rather than feature random pictures of Starbucks or an iPod like you'll see in other texts, each of these illustrations has a purpose—and its not just to fill pages—so they'll be worth checking out.

Cash Flow Versus Profit

The illustration on page 18 shows a visual way to compare the difference between cash flow and profit. As you know, profit is a very specific calculation that looks at what is left over after expenses are subtracted from an organization's income. In contrast, cash flow looks at the bigger picture and shows you the in- and outflow of cash.

The bill payer, let's call him Bill, is putting the table's lunch on his credit card, and then he's going to take everyone's cash. He thinks he's making money, but he's not. In fact, he'll probably lose money in the end. When the waitress charges his credit card, he's creating an expense. Now he owes that money back to the credit card company. However, because he's getting a fistful of cash, he thinks he's making money. He'll probably use some of that cash for additional expenses, like coffee or tomorrow's lunch, and when his credit card bill comes, he won't be able to pay it off. In this case, Bill is confused about the difference between cash flow and profit—just because he has cash on hand doesn't mean he has a profit. This is clearly a case of someone who doesn't understand the importance of considering both cash flow and net profit in his financial decision making.

2. Cash Flow: It Starts and Ends Here

The first—and arguably the most important—aspect of business is managing the inflow and outflow of cash, which is known as the **cash flow**. Without cash, there is no business. Imagine trying to do something as simple as run a lemonade stand without cash. How would you buy supplies? How would you make change for your customers? And say you expanded. How would you pay your employees? Because having cash is so important, the management of that cash should be the top concern of any business owner. Improper management of cash flow can destroy a business, no matter how profitable the business may be.

Cash Flow
Customer
Employee
Company
Company's Cash Flow
Why is cash flow so important to a business?

Cash Flow: Important from Any Perspective

Let's look at an example of the importance of cash flow. Say you've decided to start your own online business selling T-shirts. You're creative and like designing clothes, so you figure this is a good way to start. To get started, you borrowed money from your family with the promise to pay the money back after you start receiving orders. This money helped you order materials and other items to create the shirts.

You now have little money left over, and you still need to pay for and create a Web site. Once the Web site is up and running, the orders start coming in, but your cash is already tapped out. There's another problem, too: you made equal numbers of sizes S-XL, but most of your customers are ordering medium and large. You've already sold out of those sizes and need to order more. You *should* order more shirts, but unfortunately you need to pay your vendor upfront. You haven't received all of the payments for the sold shirts, so you don't have any cash. Even though you were supposed to pay your family back, you end up having to borrow more money from them just to keep your business up and running.

Alright, go ahead and read a paragraph. You'll see that the people who wrote this book are talking directly to you. Do you like how the material is clear and concise, approachable and encouraging, and at times even bold and a bit edgy? Trust me, you won't be falling asleep while reading this text for class.

Do It...

1.2: Create a Personal Cash Flow Statement Create and analyze a simple cash flow statement for your personal finances. If you have a checking account or debit card, you might refer to your bank statement to trace the ins and outs of your cash from that. Where does your money come from (what are your inflows)? What are you spending your money on (what are your outflows)? Where can you cut back? Where could you save?

But I know just reading about a topic isn't always enough—sometimes you have to actually practice. The **Do It** feature is designed for exactly that—it gives you a shot at applying the information, rather than just reading about it.

Right after the Do It is a section called **Debrief**. These are short, simple bulleted lists that wrap up the section. Make sure you read these to stay on track throughout the chapter.

Now Debrief...

- **Cash flow** is the inflow and outflow of cash. Most business ideas and decisions start and end with cash. Lack of cash flow is one of the main reasons businesses fail.
- To manage their cash, businesses review **cash flow statements**, which report cash-in and cash-out transactions, as well as beginning and ending cash balances.
- A **budget** is helpful in managing cash because it quantifies the expected cash inflows and outflows, and this enables business owners to determine whether they have enough cash to keep their business running.
- It's also useful to monitor your own personal cash flow. Once you figure out the inflow and outflow of your personal finances, you can create a way to pay yourself first and start saving and investing.

See the section called **Translation Guide**? These will help you really understand some of the more out-there, challenging material. The Translation Guide is where we take commonly misunderstood concepts or vocabulary and explain them in plain English. Read these to make sure that you are truly grasping the concepts.

Translation Guide

In Conversation: The terms *shareholder* and *stakeholder* are often used interchangeably.

In Business Terms: A shareholder is someone who owns a share, or part, of a company, and has a vested interest in the company's profits. A **stakeholder** is any person or group that is affected by the organization's activities and has a stake in the way the organization conducts itself.

Example: A *shareholder* of Dow Chemical Co. wants the business to make profits and increase the value of its stock. A *stakeholder*, on the other hand, might live near one of Dow's chemical plants and may be interested in how the company protects the community from being contaminated with toxic chemicals.

Now, do you see those sentences that don't line up with the rest of the text? No, those aren't mistakes, they're **notes** that sum up the main take-away point of the section. When you go back to review a chapter to prepare for the test, you can see the main points at a glance.

Profit is a necessary part of business. There is no way a business can continue without making a profit.

There are other reasons that the profitability of a business is important. Of course we want to take care of ourselves, but what about our kids or our future kids? As John Friedman, board member of the Sustainable Business Network of Washington, says, "Financial success is one of the needs of the current generation that cannot be sacrificed or the business will not be around to provide for future generations."[7] So, profitable businesses also benefit us all by using profits to expand their business and create new products, which means that they are also creating opportunities to improve the quality of life and standard of living of their stakeholders.

For-Profit Versus Not-for-Profit

A **business model** is an organization's plan for creating value for its stakeholders. Most of us are aware of the for-profit business model. In a **for-profit business,** the goal of the company (among other things) is to make a profit for its owners. Huge companies like Bank of America and small companies that you find in your hometown are typical for-profit companies.

What about not-for-profit organizations? The defining difference between a for-profit and a not-for-profit is the goal of the organization. The goal of a for-profit company is to earn a profit for its owners, whereas the goal of a **not-for-profit** (or **nonprofit**) **organization** is to use any money it makes to further the cause or association it promotes rather than distribute those profits to shareholders. A not-for-profit organization may support a charitable cause that aims to serve and improve the community, such as the Boys and Girls Club of America, or it may support an institution or association such as the University of Notre Dame or the American Dental Association. The types of organizations that can be considered for not-for-profit status are clearly defined by the United States Internal Revenue Code, a document that defines the tax law in the United States.

4. Examine how businesses and people make decisions based on impact on cash flow and profit. **(pp. 19–23)**

- Income statements and cash flow statements are useful in making decisions.
- Analyzing income statements helps managers figure out areas that need improvement and identify trends.
- Cash flow analysis lets managers know if cash is available, and it also shows how the cash level has changed compared to the previous month. This helps organizations figure out if there is enough cash on hand to pay all necessary expenses.

Summary: By understanding the information contained in income and cash flow statements, owners, managers, and employees can make informed decisions about the future of an organization.

After you have worked through all of the sections of the Business Road Map, it's time to review and make sure you understand what you just read. The **Visual Summary** sums up the main topics and illustrations to keep you on track and help you begin preparing for your test.

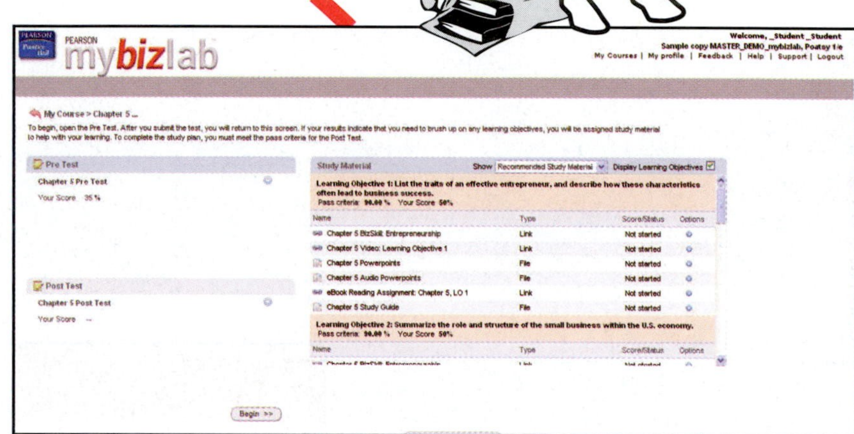

Once you have worked through the chapter, you'll have the opportunity to interact with the material! Jump on your computer and check out **www.mybizlab.com**.

Here are some of the resources available:

- Apply your skills in an interactive environment with more **BizSkill experiences**...and see if you have what it takes
- Talk with your peers about hot business topics in **BizChats**
- Flex your business communication skills and build your own portfolio with the **Communication Plan exercises**
- Watch the chapter material come to life with **Just Plain Business** videos
- Study on-the-go with **Audio Chapter Summaries in MP3 format**
- Brush up on the lecture and content with **Audio PowerPoints**
- Discover how well you are doing and see what areas you need to improve on with **Pre-Tests and Post-Tests**, which generate a personalized study plan to help you earn an A!

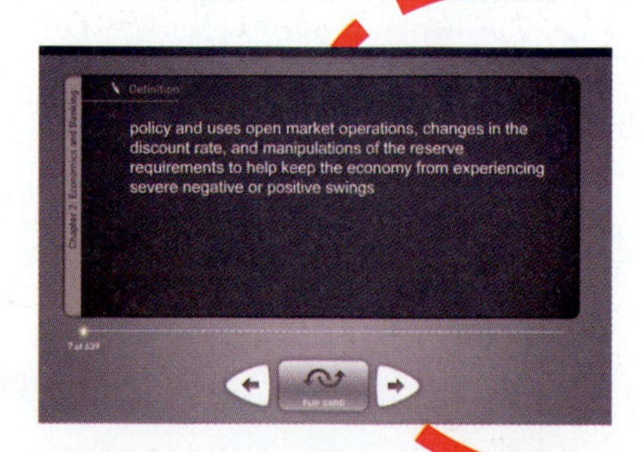

There is a lot of new vocabulary in this course. To make sure you are up to speed on the language of business, review these terms. You can also flip through the chapter **flashcards** in **mybizlab** to make sure you really nailed it.

Ending the chapters are sections called **Prove It**. These are just like the Do Its but they cover the full chapter, not just a section. You are asked to answer questions by looking at a scenario from a certain perspective. Let's say you're a manager, how would you deal with a new employee who continues to show up late for work?

Prove It...

Owner/Investor

Now, let's put on one of the BizHats. With the **Owner/Investor BizHat** squarely on your head, look at the following exercise:

The cash flow statement and the income statement provide two very different, but very critical pieces of information. We've talked about the differences between the statements, as well as some analysis of the statements. Now it's time to put your knowledge to use. You are going to research a company to determine whether you should invest in it.

1. Choose a publicly traded company that you like, for whatever reason.
2. Go to the company's Web site and search for the annual report. If you can't locate the annual report there, check out Google Finance (http://www.google.com/finance) or Yahoo! Finance (http://finance.yahoo.com).
3. Locate the income statement and cash flow statement for the company.
4. What do you see with respect to the financial statements of the company? Is it making a profit? Have its revenues increased or decreased since the previous year? Have its expenses increased or decreased? Does it bring in enough cash to cover all of its expenses?
5. Based on your review of the financial statements, would you invest in this company? How many shares would you purchase?
6. Optional: Regardless of whether you choose to invest, record the current stock price as of the day you make your decision. At the end of this course, look back and see whether you would have made a good choice.

Come up with a solution for that new employee? Now it's time to **Flip It**. Imagine you're the employee who is coming in late. How would you handle the confrontation with your manager? Looking at all sides of a business scenario will help you gain a full and complex understanding of common business experiences.

Flip It...

Customer

After you've decided whether you want to invest in the company you chose above, **flip over to the Customer BizHat.** As a customer, consider whether the company's financial statements give you confidence to spend your hard-earned money on their products. Is the company likely to be around in a few years if you need customer service? If the company is spending a great deal on investing activities and research and development, what might this mean for you?

Owner/Investor

Ready to get started?

With ***Anybody's Business*** and **mybizlab**, you'll see the personal connections between business concepts and your everyday life. Immediately useful and relevant, this Business Road Map equips you with crucial business skills that you can use from the moment you leave class and throughout your professional journey.

Because this is ***Anybody's Business***, you should look at this course as YOURS. So...

Live Life. Learn Business.

Profit:
Open Books, Cash Flow, and Income

BizSkills invite...

Try It!
There's no better way to learn concepts than to put them into practice. Take your turn in the driver's seat and be a part of actual business decision making by visiting the BizSkill for this chapter at **www.mybizlab.com**.

Now that you've practiced making tough business decisions and seeing the results of your choices in this chapter's BizSkill, it's time to translate those skills into plain English. And if you skipped the BizSkill, go back now!

Chapter 1 Goals

After experiencing this chapter, you'll be able to:

1. Explain why financial statements matter to businesses and the people who own them, manage them, and work in them.
2. Recognize cash flow and how to interpret a cash flow statement.
3. Recognize profit and how to interpret an income statement.
4. Examine how businesses and people make decisions based on their impact on cash flow and profit.
5. Understand four perspectives in business: the BizHats.

What does it take to make profits grow?

The Big Game of Finance

Imagine this: It's the end of the big game. You and your team have worked hard all season to get to this point, but now the whole season is riding on you. Your team huddles together to discuss the last play. You look to the scoreboard to help guide your strategy, but wait—the scoreboard is missing! Are you ahead? Are you behind? How much time is left? What's going on? You try to tell yourself it's OK, but how can you plan a strategy to win if you don't know where you stand?

The game of business is no different. If you don't know where you stand in an organization or where the organization stands in the market, how can you win? If you don't know how to win, you're really just going through the motions of doing whatever it is you're doing without having a real focus. In this chapter, we'll start our discussion of business by looking at a company's scoreboards and why they matter.

1. How Financial Statements Matter... And Not Just to the Boss

Every organization has scoreboards that let people know what's going on. These are financial statements: the *cash flow statement*, the *income statement*, and the *balance sheet*. **Financial statements** act as scoreboards because they summarize the financial information for a company during a given period. They are used throughout a company to drive many decisions, such as how much money to invest in different resources and in hiring new employees, among others. Financial statements let managers and others know where a company has been, know where it is now, and help anticipate where it's going.

But what do financial statements have to do with you? By the end of this chapter, you'll know just how important understanding these statements can be, both to you personally and to you as a current or future employee. Let's start by looking at two important factors at play in our discussion: standard of living and quality of life.

Your Standard of Living and Quality of Life

Quick question: What's the difference between your standard of living and your quality of life? Is there a difference? Your **standard of living** is defined by many factors, but essentially it's based on tangible things such as how much money you make and what you can afford to buy with that money. For example, if you make enough money to have a nice home, buy nice things, and go out whenever you want, you have a high standard of living. On the other hand, if you struggle from paycheck to paycheck to get your bills paid, you have a much lower standard of living. Standard of living is also based on how much money the people in your community make and how much they can afford to buy, which affects the quality of goods and services available for you to purchase. For example, U.S. residents on the whole enjoy a high standard of living compared to citizens of some countries who can't afford indoor plumbing or electricity.

However, even if you have a low standard of living, that doesn't mean you don't have a satisfying life. Your **quality of life** is an expression of the *intangible* aspects of life, such as having plenty of leisure time, having good relationships with family and friends, feeling fulfilled and safe—in short, your well-being. There are probably people living off the land in a Central American jungle who are more satisfied and content than some millionaires living in Los Angeles. Money doesn't necessarily improve your quality of life.

How does this discussion on standard of living and quality of life tie into a discussion on financial statements? Imagine this: The economy is struggling, companies are closing left and right, but for some reason your company seems to be doing well. How can you take this financial information from your workplace and apply it to your personal life? Well, first off, you can see that with so many companies closing, the economy is on shaky ground. Because of this, you may take extra precautions and start budgeting your finances more and cutting back on unnecessary spending. Just because your company is doing well, you never know what might happen in the future. Adjusting your standard of living may be a good step to take, and doing so may also improve your quality of life. Since your employer is doing well, you're not worried about losing your job, and you feel good about saving more money every month. Basically, because you're aware of your company's finances, you're able to translate that into your personal life and be more secure about where you stand.

Translation Guide

In Conversation: The terms *standard of living* and *quality of life* are sometimes used interchangeably in conversation. Although the terms are somewhat related, they do not mean the same thing.

In Business Terms: Standard of living and quality of life both affect how we live, but they affect different aspects of our lives. *Standard of living* is generally measured by consumption, or how much you can buy, whereas *quality of life* is generally measured by your feeling toward life, or how content you are.

Example: A person who makes less than minimum wage and lives in a small apartment may have a low standard of living, but if that person is content with his or her situation and is in good mental and physical health, that person probably has a high quality of life.

The Importance of Understanding Financial Statements

Understanding financial information can personally help you in other ways, too. For example, you can make wiser investment decisions. People who don't know how to read financial statements may invest in a company that isn't doing well. Just look at investors in the financial services firm Lehman Brothers, which filed for bankruptcy in 2008. After that debacle, many people were left scratching their heads and asking, "What happened?"

Chances are not many investors could tell you what went wrong. Lehman Brothers was a huge *publicly traded company*, meaning a company that issues stock available for the public to buy on a stock exchange or other markets, so by law its financial statements were available for the public to review. In fact, most financial statements from publicly traded companies like Lehman Brothers are available in an *annual report*—a description of a firm's financials, which is distributed to all people who own stock and is typically available through a firm's Web site or other public postings. However, what's not readily available is the knowledge to *interpret* the meaning of that financial information. A savvy investor can interpret financial statements not only to determine the current state of a company, but also to predict how the company will perform in the future.

In the case of Lehman Brothers, an educated potential investor could have reviewed the company's past and current financial statements and discovered that the firm had a lot of funds invested in home mortgages, a market that was very volatile at the time. That cautious investor could have then understood that investing in Lehman Brothers would be a very risky venture and would therefore invest his or her money elsewhere. Likewise, if the Lehman Brothers shareholders, who were already invested in the company, would have interpreted the financial statements well and had a clear understanding of the mortgage market, they may have demanded different investment strategies from management, or perhaps they would have sold their shares and bought different investments.

What If There Was a Better Way? Open Book Management

In 1983, a small group of employees found themselves in a situation in which the owners of their company were facing bankruptcy. The owners offered the company for sale to this group of employees, and the group took the owners up on the offer and bought it.

With a company swimming in debt, the new employee-owners decided to try something different. They felt that to make a turnaround, the entire attitude of the company would need to be altered—a culture shift. They asked themselves the questions, "What if all of the employees understood the company's finances? What if all of the employees had input and a stake in the success of that company?" The company was SRC Holdings, headed by Jack Stack. The employee-owners didn't just ask these questions, though, they actually followed through on them and opened the books to *all* employees, not just those at the top. By doing so, the employee-owners wanted to give everyone an opportunity to review the financial numbers, see how their performance affected those numbers, and suggest ways to improve them. This policy of giving employees access to financial statements and information is the model of **open book management (OBM)**.[1] OBM is one method that companies use to help employees connect their individual jobs to the overall success of the company.

Reactions to Opening the Books When faced with the idea of opening the books to all employees, many owners bring up one obvious, but major, problem—you have to show employees the numbers! Most companies prefer to keep financial numbers confidential. Some managers become concerned that if the numbers are made available to all employees, they could get into the hands of competitors. The new owners of SRC Holdings decided the risk of exposure was worth the benefit. The employees were shocked and surprised when the books were opened but also felt a sense of respect and trust. Many employees felt that if the employee-owners were going to trust them with this information, then the employee-owners must respect the thoughts and opinions of every employee.

What are the pros and cons of opening the books?

But just because a company doesn't utilize OBM, that doesn't mean it keeps its employees completely in the dark; OBM isn't the only way to share financial information and make the connection between individual employees and a business. OBM is just one way for a company to be transparent. OBM and transparency are investments in the overall financial education of employees. These investments are intended to:

- affect the employees' understanding of both company and personal financial matters;
- create a culture of trust and openness between management and employees; and
- educate the employees on what they can do to improve the financial health of the company.

A great example of the positive effects of OBM can be seen in the cohesive work environment at Boston's Beth Israel Deaconess Medical Center. In 2002, CEO Paul Levy realized the hospital was faced with a huge financial problem. Instead of trying to conjure up a solution with a select group of high-level managers, Levy turned to the entire staff of the hospital for some much-needed advice. In an e-mail to the staff, who did not yet know about the financial problems of the organization, Levy bluntly explained the hospital's financial problems and asked the staff to share their ideas on how to solve them. Over the following few months, employees offered information that helped the organization become more efficient, and employees of all levels worked together to find methods to avoid mass layoffs. Levy's open management methods made his staff become more like a team and essentially saved the hospital from bankruptcy.[2]

This form of management style rescued the hospital, but it helped the employees as well. The overall success of a company can help improve an employee's standard of living by ensuring the employee has a steady paycheck. In addition, a successful company has the opportunity to reward employees' hard work with raises, which allows them to buy more goods and live more comfortably. It might also improve an employee's quality of life because an open and honest work environment could lead to less stress and more enjoyment during work hours.

Reading the Language Versus Understanding It Have you ever had that experience where you read an entire page of a difficult subject and then stopped and realized you had no idea what you just read? For example, here's part of the opening paragraph of a Ph.D. dissertation in astrophysics:

I present results of a campaign to find and identify counterparts to X-ray sources in the Galactic Center (GC), searching for accretion disk signatures in the form of Br° line emission via Infrared

(IR) spectroscopy.... Follow-up observations of the source, CXO J174536.1-285638 (hereafter, Edd-1), revealed a 189 ± 6 day periodicity.[3]

OK, we can all read what it says—it's English (mostly)—but what does it *mean*? There is a clear difference between *reading* something and *understanding* it. The same goes for reading financial information. We can all see and read the numbers on the page, but it's a different thing entirely to understand what these numbers mean to the company, its employees, investors, and customers—and to make decisions based on that information.

This is another problem business owners have with open book management: Employees must *understand* what they are reading for this policy to be effective. This was certainly an issues at SRC Holdings. Being a machine remanufacturing company, people were trained to operate machines, not analyze numbers.[4] When faced with terms like *cash flow*, *income statement*, and *balance sheet*, most people's eyes glazed over. The new employee-owners realized that in order for the employees to really get on board, all of the employees would need to know the basics of "looking at the numbers."

A large investment of time and effort is needed by the owners to educate all employees. In fact, Jack Stack indicates that OBM is 70 percent working and 30 percent learning. Although OBM does require a large time commitment from owners and employees, it ultimately creates a completely transparent company culture that is free of secrets and generally appreciated by employees. Often, companies who follow the OBM model are the kinds of companies many people want to work for and with.

Defining the Bottom Line(s)

Once you understand how to read financial statements, which we'll go over later in more detail, what do you do with this knowledge? As noted earlier, part of reading financial statements is knowing whether we as employees are hitting our target (e.g., knowing what the bottom line is). So, what is the "bottom line"? Is there more than one way to measure it?

In accounting, the "net profit" is always presented at the bottom of a financial report with a line both above and below the figure. You will learn later what exactly net profit is, but for now, just know the term "**the bottom line**" is an accounting calculation that figures out financial performance based on net profit. The problem is that measuring the success of an entire company based on one figure presents an incomplete picture. Net profit alone can't show the overall bigger picture—the true health of a company. There are many more factors than just net profit.

Understanding your bottom line, whether at work or at home, can help you figure out and ultimately reach your goals. Figuring out your goals is important; if you don't have a goal, how will you know when you get where you want to be? To be successful, you cannot just define a goal and shoot for it; you must make that goal measurable and track your progress. Goals have to have quantifiable results that can be measured at each point to determine whether the company is improving. For example, if you wanted to become a faster runner, you would not just define your goal as "running faster"; you would set a goal of improving your per mile speed, or more specifically improving your per mile speed by, say, 45 seconds.

When the employee-owners of Jack Stack's company were trying to figure out their goals, they needed the help of professionals. The employee-owners utilized the help of some very sharp financial planners, accountants, and managers and narrowed the numbers down to the *critical number*,[5] a bottom line number that clearly showed the success or failure in realizing the goal. The company then set up a brightly colored scorecard, which simply and clearly displayed the results of the critical number on a regular basis.

During training sessions, employees learned more and more about the numbers on the scorecard and were able to realize how their work affected these numbers. People then learned what they could do in their day-to-day duties to improve the numbers on the scorecard, and they were expected to take action to improve those numbers. But why would employees want to be responsible for the numbers?

Motivating Employees to Be Responsible for the Bottom Line

It seems to make sense that if you want people to perform better, you should offer an incentive, right? Indeed, many methods have been tried to entice employees to excel—one of the most common is *bonuses*. For example, the top five performing sales reps for a company may be promised a trip to a major resort in the Bahamas. This may sound like it makes sense, but this method of incentivizing employees—like many other methods—has problems. The vacation may be a great incentive for some sales reps, but:

1. It doesn't bring them any closer to understanding the financial situation of the company or to understanding financial matters in general, and;
2. It only gives employees a motive to work toward the *reward*—not a guarantee that they care about the ongoing success of the company.

Also, incentives such as a trip to the Bahamas may only pique the interest of some employees. Those who do not enjoy traveling may find little reason to compete for this perk, and therefore little reason to improve their job performance.

This is where open book management comes in. Most (though not all) OBM companies have profit-sharing programs, such as bonuses, or equity-sharing programs, such as an *Employee Stock Ownership Program (ESOP)*. An ESOP sets up a trust fund with individual employee accounts and periodically deposits cash or stock in it. When the employee leaves the company, he can take the trust or sell its contents back to the company for its market value. So, by understanding the numbers and their role in improving the bottom line, and being provided with an incentive tied to the bottom line, employees are motivated to perform.

The next section will take a more in-depth look at the financial workings of a company, starting with cash flow.

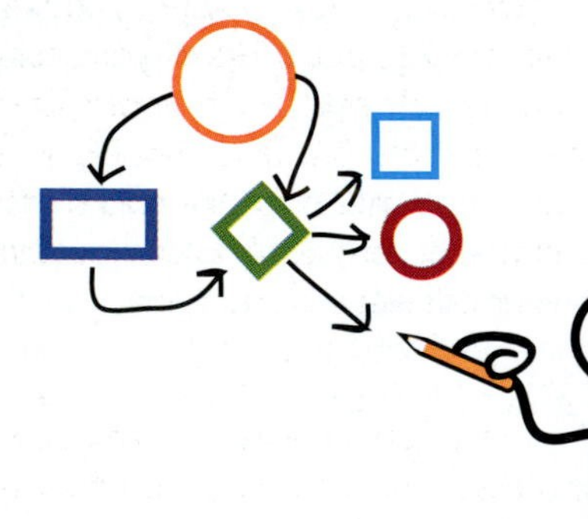

Do It...

1.1: Consider Open Book Management Consider how open book management could be applied to a company you've heard of or worked for. What reaction would it likely get from employees? What about management? What could be the possible benefits to the company? Limit your response to one page, and be prepared to submit it electronically or present it to your class.

Now Debrief...

- **Financial statements** act as a company scoreboard because they summarize the financial information for a company. There are three types of financial statements: the *cash flow statement*, the *income statement*, and the *balance sheet*. Financial statements let managers and others know where a company has been, know where it is now, and help anticipate where it's going.
- People who understand financial statements can use that knowledge to benefit their personal situations, including their standard of living and quality of life. **Standard of living** is a measurement of material or tangible things, whereas **quality of life** is the expression of intangible aspects of life (such as leisure time). When you understand how to read financial statements, you'll know how they can help benefit these aspects of your life.
- **Open book management** is a management style that gives all employees access to the company's financial information. This helps employees know the organization's bottom line and how their jobs are connected to the overall success of the business.

2. Cash Flow: It Starts and Ends Here

The first—and arguably the most important—aspect of business is managing the inflow and outflow of cash, which is known as the **cash flow**. Without cash, there is no business. Imagine trying to do something as simple as run a lemonade stand without cash. How would you buy supplies? How would you make change for your customers? And say you expanded. How would you pay your employees? Because having cash is so important, the management of that cash should be the top concern of any business owner. Improper management of cash flow can destroy a business, no matter how profitable the business may be.

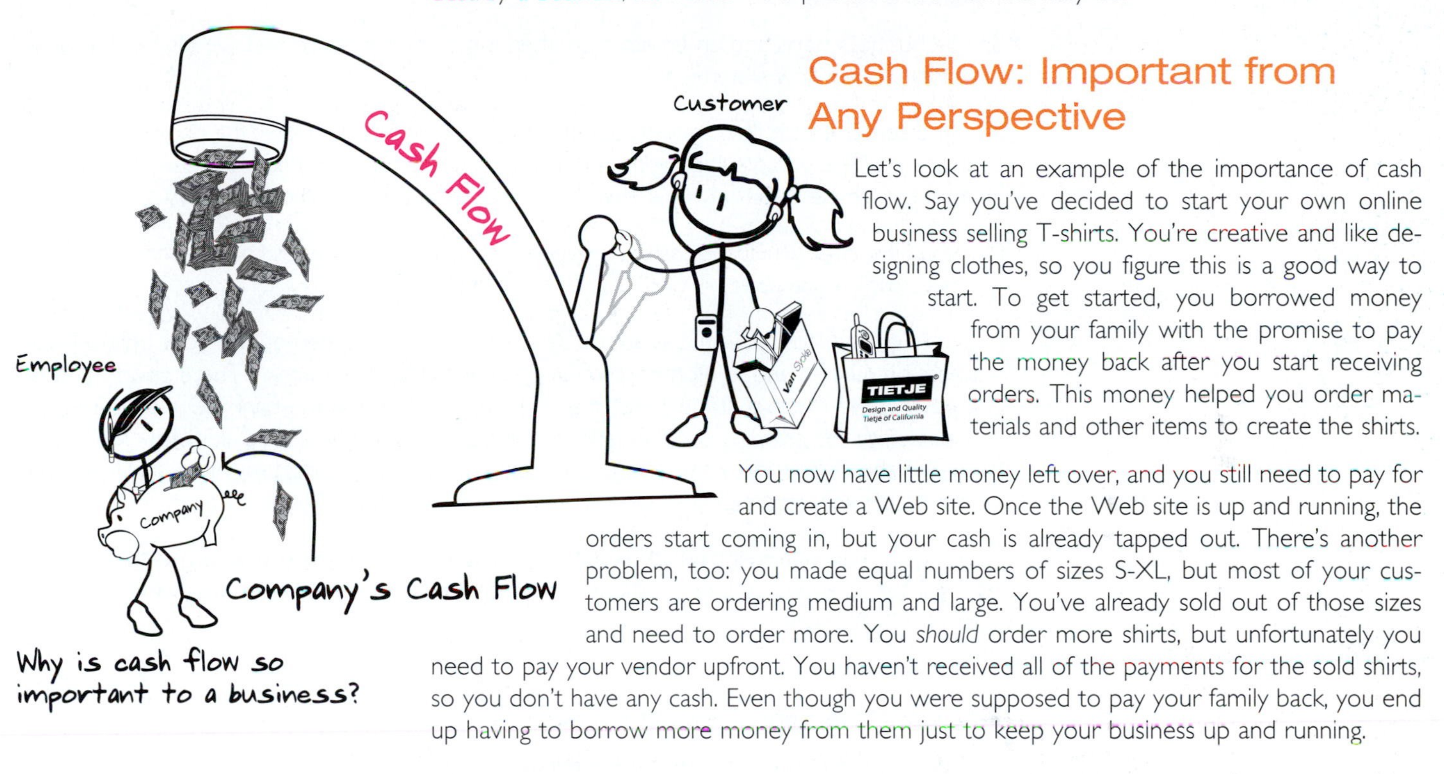

Cash Flow: Important from Any Perspective

Let's look at an example of the importance of cash flow. Say you've decided to start your own online business selling T-shirts. You're creative and like designing clothes, so you figure this is a good way to start. To get started, you borrowed money from your family with the promise to pay the money back after you start receiving orders. This money helped you order materials and other items to create the shirts.

You now have little money left over, and you still need to pay for and create a Web site. Once the Web site is up and running, the orders start coming in, but your cash is already tapped out. There's another problem, too: you made equal numbers of sizes S-XL, but most of your customers are ordering medium and large. You've already sold out of those sizes and need to order more. You *should* order more shirts, but unfortunately you need to pay your vendor upfront. You haven't received all of the payments for the sold shirts, so you don't have any cash. Even though you were supposed to pay your family back, you end up having to borrow more money from them just to keep your business up and running.

Cash Flow Statement The cycle of lack of planning and running out of cash ensnares many businesses. The main problem that new businesses run into with cash flow is that there are often many upfront costs that must be paid before the company receives cash from customers. The owner will need to be able to cover these costs until the money comes from customers. The **cash flow statement** reports these cash-in and cash-out transactions, as well as beginning and ending cash balances. The cash flow statement shows the company's management just how much cash is currently on hand to spend on immediate needs. As you can see, cash flow is the lifeblood of any business. Even if you have the best customer service, the best product, the best everything, none of it will matter if your company can't pay the bills.

Budgeting and Business The problem with your T-shirt business is that you went in without a plan and without any cash of your own. Without a plan, you were surprised by how many costs popped up just to get the business running and keep it going. This resulted in your not having the cash when it came time to pay back your family.

> "If you can't pay for a thing, don't buy it. If you can't get paid for it, don't sell it. Do this, and you will have calm and drowsy nights, with all of the good business you have now and none of the bad."
> **—Benjamin Franklin**[6]

To be able to meet cash demands, both businesses and individuals must carefully monitor their cash flows. An important tool for monitoring cash flow is a budget. A **budget** quantifies all of the expected cash inflows (what you're getting paid) and cash outflows (what you're paying to others). Once a budget is calculated, people reading the cash flow statement will be able to determine whether the inflow and outflow are sufficient to keep the business in operation or if changes need to be made. For example, if a company knows it lost a big customer last year, the budget for the following year should reflect this decrease in cash inflow.

Once the budget is made, users will compare the actual results to the budget and discuss any items that stray from the budget. These items can be indications of many issues that the users should be aware of, positive or negative.

Reading a Cash Flow Statement

So, if a business starts and ends with cash, then it only makes sense that we discuss the basics of reading a cash flow statement.

In essence, a cash flow statement aims to tell you one thing: either the company has cash or it doesn't. The complexities both in detail and analysis of a cash flow statement extend far beyond this simple question. However, the concept can be simplified as follows:

> *You have cash, you spend cash, you receive cash, and then at the end of the month, you either have cash or you don't.*

Let's go back to the T-shirt example. You read your bank statement for your online T-shirt business on July 31, and it informs you that you have $70 in the bank. "That's good," you tell yourself. "I have money, although last month there was $100 in the bank." During the month you paid $80 for shipping supplies and T-shirts. Also, customers paid you $50 for orders. Figure 1.1 shows how cash flows from operating your T-shirt business might be summarized in a simple cash flow statement.

A cash flow statement will show you where cash came from and where cash went, but let's focus on the two simple questions cash flow statements should answer when compared from month to month:

1. Do we have cash?
2. Do we have more or less cash than last time?

In Figure 1.1, it's important to note two things:

1. There is cash in the bank, and
2. There is less cash in the bank than last month.

The fact that there is cash in the bank is important—you hope it's enough to pay your upcoming bills. However, what about the change in cash? There is less cash than last month (or

Figure **1.1** | **Simple Cash Flow Statement**

Your T-Shirt Business, Inc. **Cash Flow Statement** **July 31, 20xx**	
At the beginning of the month, there is this much cash in the bank	**$100**
Subtract the cash you spent on bills	**−80**
Add the money people paid you	**+50**
At the end of the month, there is this much cash in the bank	**70**
Difference in beginning and ending balance	**−30**

a negative cash flow). In this case, you have $30 less than last month. If you continue on this path, you could potentially have $30 less each month and eventually run out of cash to pay your bills.

Based on these results, you'd likely want to take action to improve your cash flow statement. You know there are two factors that build the numbers on the cash flow statement: 1) how much cash you have coming in (your inflows), and 2) how much cash you have going out (your outflows). Therefore, to take action, you have to address one or both of these items. Possible solutions include increasing inflows by selling more T-shirts, raising the price of your T-shirts, or any other method of generating extra money for our business you can think of. Another solution is to decrease outflows by cutting expenses, holding off on paying bills, reducing bill payment amounts when possible, or any other method of cutting back you can think of. No matter which method you choose, you must take some action to show an increase in your cash balance. No business can continue indefinitely with a negative cash flow.

Cash Flow for Anybody

The advantages of reviewing a cash flow statement extend beyond business uses. Every individual has his or her own personal cash flow statement. Have you taken the time to look at your own? Do you have cash at the end of each month? Is your cash increasing or decreasing each month? How do you bring in money, or cash inflows? What are your expenses, or cash outflows? Businesses aren't the only ones that need to know the answers to these questions. The results may surprise you—and they'll certainly guide you in your decision making.

In looking at your cash flow statement, it may also be helpful to treat yourself like a business and create a budget for yourself. When you do this, you're figuring out a financial game plan. Ask yourself questions a business would also consider: Are you spending more than you make? Are there expenses you could cut? Could you make better choices regarding how to spend your money?

Another key to figuring out and improving your financial situation is to focus on the things you can control. You can't control external factors, like the direction of the stock market or the price of crude oil, but you can control how much of your investments are placed in the stock market, and you can control how much gas you need by changing your driving patterns or taking public transportation. Making the best decisions you can within your means is the best way to maintain peace of mind, and this peace of mind can add to your quality of life.

Want to Have a Million Dollars?

Somehow you find money every month to pay your bills such as your rent and credit card bill. But do you know the secret to having a million dollars by the time you retire? It's by treating *yourself* as a bill and paying yourself every month. This concept, referred to as "**paying yourself first**," means that every time you get paid, you immediately take a set amount and transfer it somewhere else, perhaps to a savings account or a 401(k) plan (a long-term investment account with special tax incentives), and *do not touch* that money unless you're using it to make more money.

The money you save each month will then create a personal cash inflow by earning **interest**, the fee that a bank or other institution pays you for the use of your money. Although it may be difficult at first to set aside a certain amount of money every month to pay yourself first (especially if you're a student), most people find that they get used to living off less money and don't even realize the absence of the other money.

The Rule of 72

OK, so you understand that you can increase your cash inflow by paying yourself first every month. But how can you make a million dollars?

By contributing money to a savings, 401(k), or other account with a decent interest rate over a long period of time and not touching it, you can end up with a lot of money in the bank. It all boils down to a simple equation. It's called the **Rule of 72** and it goes like this:

$$\frac{72}{\text{Interest rate}} = \text{The number of years it will take to double your money}$$

If we say the interest rate is 8 percent, then this formula shows that your money will double every 9 years (72/8 = 9). "OK, that's great." you say, "but what does it mean to me?"

Let's say you have $2000 and you're 20 years old. The Rule of 72 tells you that if you invest that money at 8 percent interest, you'll have $4000 when you're 29, and by the time you're 65, you'll have $64,000—and all you had to do was wait. The Rule of 72 is a handy tool that demonstrates the power of **compound growth**, which is what happens when the interest you earn is added to your savings and earns even more interest.

You might also be interested in finding out the interest rate you would need to be paid to double the money you have in a certain period of time. Good news—the Rule of 72 can help you with that, too:

$$\frac{72}{\text{The number of years you have to save}} = \text{The interest rate needed to double your money}$$

So if you're 29 and want that $4000 to turn in to $8000 by the time you're 35, the Rule of 72 quickly tells you that you'll need to get a 12 percent rate of return (72/6 = 12) to reach your goal. Or, consider this. If you invest $4000 at 12 percent when you're 20, you can be a millionaire by the time you're 66. Now, that's not a bad investment.

Do It...

1.2: Create a Personal Cash Flow Statement Create and analyze a simple cash flow statement for your personal finances. If you have a checking account or debit card, you might refer to your bank statement to trace the ins and outs of your cash from that. Where does your money come from (what are your inflows)? What are you spending your money on (what are your outflows)? Where can you cut back? Where could you save?

Now Debrief...

- **Cash flow** is the inflow and outflow of cash. Most business ideas and decisions start and end with cash. Lack of cash flow is one of the main reasons businesses fail.
- To manage their cash, businesses review **cash flow statements**, which report cash-in and cash-out transactions, as well as beginning and ending cash balances.
- A **budget** is helpful in managing cash because it quantifies the expected cash inflows and outflows, and this enables business owners to determine whether they have enough cash to keep their business running.
- It's also useful to monitor your own personal cash flow. Once you figure out the inflow and outflow of your personal finances, you can create a way to pay yourself first and start saving and investing.

3. Net Profit and the Income Statement

It doesn't matter if you're going to run a business or run your personal finances, you need to know how to make money and how to figure out if you're *really* making money. We just discussed the importance of cash, but how does a company know if it will have enough cash in the future to pay its bills?

To figure this out, management closely analyzes profit. But what exactly is profit, and how do we measure it? What if a customer pays you $100 for your product—have you made a profit? What if you were selling T-shirts? What if you were selling a car? What if you were paid for your time preparing a tax return? Have you made a profit? What if it cost you four years of college to become a tax preparer? Then have you made a profit? More specifically, have you made a net profit? **Net profit** (or *net income*) is the amount of money remaining after all expenses have been paid. As you can see, the net profit can't simply be the cash received from customers; there are expenses involved, such as utilities and rent.

The Income Statement

So, how do businesses analyze their net profit? An **income statement** (also known as a *profit and loss statement*) measures the net profit of a company by tracking the company's income and expenses during a given period. The income statement is perhaps the most frequently used of the three financial statements, and net profit is one of the most well-known indicators used to decide whether a company is doing well or not. Basically, an income statement reads as follows:

Revenue − Expenses = Net Profit (or Net Income)

Now let's take a minute to clarify the financial terms that are being thrown around.

It doesn't matter if you're going to run a business or run your personal finances, you need to know how to make money and how to figure out if you're *really* making money.

Income is the amount of money a company generates during a period of time. **Revenue** is the total amount of money received by a company for a good, service, or experience. Revenue is not the same thing as income because revenue is recorded when a sale is made, but not necessarily when payment for that sale is received. As you can see in the equation above, net profit is calculated when all expenses (the cost of sales, operating costs, and other expenses such as taxes) are subtracted from revenue.

Sources of Revenue Sources of revenue are as varied as the businesses that are out there. For example, revenue may come from:

- the sale of a car,
- the sale of services to fix a car, or
- the rental of a luxury sports car for your vacation.

As this list indicates, revenue can come from the sale of tangible items, or **goods**, as well as the sale of your time, effort, or knowledge—intangibles known as **services**. **Experiences** also provide an intangible value to customers, but they can comprise both goods and services, and they directly involve customer participation. So, revenue can come from any type of **product**, whether it's a good, service, or experience that is available for purchase.

Looking at Expenses Look back at the equation for calculating net profit above. In it, **expenses** refer to the amount of money spent on something during a certain time. That may sound a lot like an outflow of cash, but there is an important difference. Like revenues, expenses are recorded when bills are received, but that doesn't mean that the money is going out right then

Translation Guide

In Conversation: The terms *product* and *good* are often used interchangeably.

In Business Terms: Products are goods, services, and experiences that a business makes or offers. Goods are products that are tangible and take up physical space. Services are products that are intangible and involve an action. Experiences are a mixture of goods and services in which customers immerse themselves.

Example: Goods are pieces of clothing you might buy at a mall. Services are the tailoring or dry cleaning you might have done to those pieces of clothing. An experience might be the service offered by a clothing retailer combined with a hip garment that makes you feel like you are taking part in a hot new trend.

and there. It's common for businesses to wait 30 to 60 days to pay expenses, so *an expense doesn't become an outflow of cash until it is paid.* Expenses are usually further divided into *cost of revenue* and *operating expenses.*

- As the name implies, **cost of revenue** (also referred to as **cost of goods sold** when dealing with a manufacturing business) is any amount incurred by the company for expenses directly related to the sale of the product. For example, the cost of revenue for a car dealer could be purchasing cars for resale.
- On the other hand, **operating expenses** are amounts paid for expenses *not* directly related to the sale of the car. For example, money paid for administrative salaries, rent, and utilities would be operating expenses.

So did we make any money? That is the question of the day. To calculate this, Revenue − Expenses = Net Profit. There are many more details to analyzing an income statement, but in general the goal is to report a positive net profit. Companies can't continue without profit, and who would want to go through the trouble of starting a business in the first place if there's no profit? And as we'll discuss later, even not-for-profit organizations need net income to reinvest in their growth.

The Importance of Profit and Business

Of course, profit benefits the business owner, but what about the rest of us? Some people have negative associations with the profits of a business, especially if the profit is large. They feel profits only benefit the people who own the company (its **shareholders**), or that profit is made by treating employees and other **stakeholders**, the people that have an interest in an organization such as suppliers and the community, unfairly. However, this isn't necessarily the case. Although profits make many people rich, profits also allow the business to employ workers and keep operations running smoothly.

Translation Guide

In Conversation: The terms *shareholder* and *stakeholder* are often used interchangeably.

In Business Terms: A shareholder is someone who owns a share, or part, of a company, and has a vested interest in the company's profits. A stakeholder is any person or group that is affected by the organization's activities and has a stake in the way the organization conducts itself.

Example: A *shareholder* of Dow Chemical Co. wants the business to make profits and increase the value of its stock. A *stakeholder*, on the other hand, might live near one of Dow's chemical plants and may be interested in how the company protects the community from being contaminated with toxic chemicals.

The reality is profit is a necessary part of business. There is no way a business can continue without making a profit. The financial success of businesses affects all of us, even if indirectly. When businesses succeed or fail, there is a ripple effect throughout the community; the ripple may be weak or strong, and the community may be local or global, but every decision, no matter the size, has an impact. On a personal level, a successful and profitable business will pay our paychecks if nothing else. And this contributes to our standard of living and possibly our quality of life. For this reason alone, it's important for businesses to be profitable.

Profit is a necessary part of business. There is no way a business can continue without making a profit.

There are other reasons that the profitability of a business is important. Of course we want to take care of ourselves, but what about our kids or our future kids? As John Friedman, board member of the Sustainable Business Network of Washington, says, "Financial success is one of the needs of the current generation that cannot be sacrificed or the business will not be around to provide for future generations."[7] So, profitable businesses also benefit us all by using profits to expand their business and create new products, which means that they are also creating opportunities to improve the quality of life and standard of living of their stakeholders.

For-Profit Versus Not-for-Profit

A **business model** is an organization's plan for creating value for its stakeholders. Most of us are aware of the for-profit business model. In a **for-profit business,** the goal of the company (among other things) is to make a profit for its owners. Huge companies like Bank of America and small companies that you find in your hometown are typical for-profit companies.

What about not-for-profit organizations? The defining difference between a for-profit and a not-for-profit is the goal of the organization. The goal of a for-profit company is to earn a profit for its owners, whereas the goal of a **not-for-profit** (or **nonprofit**) **organization** is to use any money it makes to further the cause or association it promotes rather than distribute those profits to shareholders. A not-for-profit organization may support a charitable cause that aims to serve and improve the community, such as the Boys and Girls Club of America, or it may support an institution or association such as the University of Notre Dame or the American Dental Association. The types of organizations that can be considered for not-for-profit status are clearly defined by the United States Internal Revenue Code, a document that defines the tax law in the United States.

Translation Guide

In Conversation: The terms *business*, *company*, and *organization* are often used interchangeably to refer to the same thing.

In Business: *Organization* is used to refer broadly to both for-profit and not-for-profit organizations. The terms *business* and *company* are generally used to refer specifically to a for-profit organization.

But not-for-profit organizations need to generate some funds to keep the doors open. Like for-profit companies, not-for-profit organizations have bills that must be paid—rent, administrative supplies, and, in some not-for-profit organizations, salaries for employees. To encourage people to run organizations that benefit society, not-for-profit organizations are given many benefits through the Internal Revenue Code that are not given to for-profit companies, such as tax-exempt status, tax-deductible contributions for donors, and eligibility for public and private grants. In exchange for these benefits, not-for-profits face additional regulatory restrictions as well as restrictions on excess profits. Unlike for-profit companies, any excess profits do not belong to the organizers of the not-for-profit organization (i.e., the employees), but to the organization itself. This means that the excess profits must be reinvested in the organization or used to provide goods and services to the groups the organization was formed to help or support.

Cash Flow Statements Versus Income Statements

What's the difference between a cash flow statement and an income statement? Well, that depends on what kind of income statement you're talking about.

Cash Versus Accrual-Based Accounting In accounting, the rules for preparing these statements are outlined by a set of guidelines known as *Generally Accepted Accounting Principles*, or GAAP. There are two types of income statements allowed under GAAP: *cash* and *accrual*. The main difference between the two rests in how a company records the comings and goings of cash.

A **cash basis of accounting** records revenue when cash is received, and it records expenses when cash is paid out. If this sounds similar to a cash flow statement, you're right. Very small businesses that do most of their business in cash use this kind of income statement.

Larger businesses that have a lot of **accounts receivable**—unpaid bills for products they've sold—and **accounts payable**, or unpaid bills for expenses they've incurred, can't use the cash basis of accounting because it doesn't give them an accurate picture of their net profits for a certain period.

To see why, think back to the T-shirt company example. The cash flow statement in Figure 1.1 showed that you lost a net total of $30 in July, and using cash-based accounting, so would your income statement. You might think your T-shirt business was in the red, or losing money. But what if you actually sold $100 worth of merchandise, but only got paid $50? In that case, you would actually be making a profit on July's activity—you just won't get to *realize* that profit until your customers pay the outstanding $50 in bills.

To give you an accurate picture of whether your T-shirt business is profitable, you need a different accounting method: the **accrual basis of accounting**. Accrual-based accounting records income when a good is delivered or a service is provided. Expenses are treated the same way; they are recorded when the expense is incurred (or accrued, which is where the name comes from), regardless of whether the service which resulted in that expense was actually paid for.

The accrual basis of accounting keeps revenue from the service provided and expenses incurred from that service together so that the net profit from that service can be clearly determined. The terms "services provided" and "expenses incurred" may sound a bit formal, but those are the technical accounting terms for income and expense and are extremely important in determining what is income (or an expense) and when to count each as such.

An Example

This is complicated stuff, so let's look at an example. Say you invested in FedEx. Share prices of such large companies are usually based on certain numbers, one of which is net profit. To calculate net profit, what do we need? Think back to the equation for net profit. In order to determine net profit, you need to know your revenue and subtract your expenses.

But when exactly does FedEx record revenue? Is it when the company takes an order for a delivery? Is it when the driver picks up the delivery? Is it when the delivery is actually made? These determinations can have a huge impact on the revenue record and therefore the net profit for FedEx. What if FedEx recorded everything as income the minute an order was taken? What would happen to the income statement? Of course, income would be recorded at that moment. Well, what if orders are cancelled, changed, or lost? Or, what's worse, what if there was no clear definition of when to record something as income? Then FedEx management could change the definition whenever they wanted so that the company could report certain numbers that look better than they would have with a standard definition.

Taking this example further, imagine what could happen to FedEx's share price if people learned that income was being reported inconsistently or in a way to make the company appear more profitable. What if it was to hide the unpleasant realities of the company's numbers? As a stakeholder, a person who is affected by the company's actions, you want to know that a company has guidelines when reporting income so that shareholders aren't stuck with shares with declining value. This is why it's important to clearly and consistently define terms like "services provided."

An Important Distinction

In accrual-based accounting, a sale is usually considered revenue the day the services are provided or goods are delivered in full. As you probably already know, this day is very rarely the day the company is actually paid. However, for the purposes of analysis, management needs to know that the money was made that day and that they expect payment for the good or service in the future. Furthermore, even though the payment hasn't arrived, the company is due that money and should count it as income.

The same idea applies to expenses. Expenses are recorded when they are incurred. This means that the day the company receives a good or service from another company and uses that good or service in a business transaction, the expense is recorded. Even if the company hasn't paid for the expense yet, that product is still used and needs to count as an expense.

Comparing the Statements

As we said before, the important difference between the cash flow statement and the income statement is when certain transactions are recorded. Revenue recorded "when provided" is not the same as cash recorded "when received" and expenses recorded "when incurred" is not the same as expenses recorded "when paid." Let's look at your T-shirt company. When you provide (or sell) a T-shirt to someone, this does not mean it's the same moment you receive payment for the shirt. You may have received the payment the week before or the week after you sold the shirt. Similarly, if you order supplies and incur (or become responsible for) an expense, you have not necessarily already paid for the supplies.

Take this example: Last month you had $310 in the bank. Let's say your computer guy needs to be paid right away (he has rent to pay, after all) and so does the T-shirt manufacturer, but only half of your customers have paid as of now because you are waiting on payments by mail.

Cash Flow Statement	
Money in the bank to start	**$310**
Cash paid for expenses	**−800**
Cash received from customers	**+500**
Money remaining in the bank	**10**
Difference	**−300**

As you can see by the large negative difference, your T-shirt company has used a relatively large amount of cash this month and may not have the cash to pay the bills next month. It is in this way that a company can be profitable but still run into a cash flow crisis.

Now let's look at your income statement. Your online T-shirt company sold $1000 worth of T-shirts this month. You also paid $700 to the T-shirt manufacturer (cost of sales) and $100 to a computer guy to keep the Web site running and updated (operating expenses). The income statement is pretty straightforward in this case:

Income Statement	
Revenue	**$1000**
Cost of sales	**−700**
Operating expenses	**−100**
Net profit	**200**

The advantage of the income statement is that it lets you know what revenues and expenses you have incurred in the current month, no matter when you actually received the money from your customers or paid the money to your computer guy. It also shows if your company is making enough income to continue in the future. In this example, your company appears healthy. There is a significant net profit, right?

Let's look at your friend's car washing company. Let's say he collected all the money from his customers upfront, but he is only required to pay half of the expenses during this period.

Cash Flow Statement	
Money in the bank to start	$50
Cash paid for expenses	−450
Cash received from customers	+800
Money remaining in the bank	400
Difference	350

In this case your friend's company has a large amount of cash in the bank at the end of the period even though his company shows a net loss. This is because all of the money is due immediately, but the expenses are not paid until later.

Now let's look at your friend's income statement. As you can see, your friend's company shows a negative net profit, which is called a **net loss**, because the company has incurred more expenses than it has provided services.

Income Statement	
Revenue	$800
Cost of Sales	−500
Operating expenses	−400
Net loss	−100

As you can see, the difference between the cash flow and income statement can be dramatic, and each statement can show different aspects of the company that the other doesn't show.

Cash Flow Versus Profit

The illustration on page 18 shows a visual way to compare the difference between cash flow and profit. As you know, profit is a very specific calculation that looks at what is left over after expenses are subtracted from an organization's income. In contrast, cash flow looks at the bigger picture and shows you the in- and outflow of cash.

Do you ever confuse cash flow with profit?

The bill payer, let's call him Bill, is putting the table's lunch on his credit card, and then he's going to take everyone's cash. He thinks he's making money, but he's not. In fact, he'll probably lose money in the end. When the waitress charges his credit card, he's creating an expense. Now he owes that money back to the credit card company. However, because he's getting a fistful of cash, he thinks he's making money. He'll probably use some of that cash for additional expenses, like coffee or tomorrow's lunch, and when his credit card bill comes, he won't be able to pay it off. In this case, Bill is confused about the difference between cash flow and profit—just because he has cash on hand doesn't mean he has a profit. This is clearly a case of someone who doesn't understand the importance of considering both cash flow and net profit in his financial decision making.

Do It...

1.3: Compare Income Statements Together with a teammate, find annual reports for a publicly traded company from the last two years. (You can usually find annual reports on a company's Web site.) Compare the year-end income statements found within the annual reports for each year and analyze the differences between them. What elements recorded on the income statements seem to be affecting the differences in the company's bottom line from one year to the next?

Now Debrief...

- The **income statement** summarizes the revenues from goods and services provided and expenses incurred by a business in a set period of time and reports net profit. **Income** is money generated during a period of time. **Revenue** is money received for a good, service, or experience.
- Profit is important for both **shareholders** (people who own a company) and **stakeholders** (people that have an interest in a company, such as employees, suppliers, and the community).
- Net profit is important to both **for-profit companies,** but it is also important to **not-for-profit companies**, which are given special privileges by the government for promoting social causes or supporting associations but still need to make money.
- Net profit is an important indicator of financial health of a company; however, it's not the only indicator. Companies also use cash flow to assess the health of a company. The income statement is asking the question, "Is the company making money?" whereas the cash flow statement is asking the question, "Do we have any cash?"
- The timing of cash received and paid reported on the cash flow is critical to a company, as is the profitability of a company, reported on the income statement. To make effective financial decisions, management will use the cash flow statement and income statement together.

4. Making Decisions: The Tools Available to Anybody

We've discussed the income statement and the cash flow statement; now let's talk about what the numbers in those statements are saying. If we know what the statements are telling us, this information can help owners, managers, employees, investors, and even creditors make better decisions about what's next.

A key point to remember is that the statements answer different questions:

- The cash flow statement addresses the question "Do we have any cash?"
- The income statement addresses the question "Are we making any profit?"

The different nature of these two reports makes the analysis of *both* reports critical.

Analyzing the Cash Flow Statement The simple cash flow statement that we discussed earlier only covered cash flows from the day-to-day activities of a T-shirt business, but those aren't the only ways that cash can flow in to and out of a company. A cash flow statement for a big company like Apple tracks three main sources of cash flow:

1. *Operating activities* measure the cash used or generated by the daily business of a company. For example, Apple's cash from operating activities would include the revenue from selling computers, as well as the amount of money spent buying and assembling the components to make those computers.
2. *Investing activities* represent the cash used in investments or the purchase of assets that could increase the company's profitability. For Apple, that could be a state-of-the-art manufacturing facility, which allows the business to operate more efficiently and sell more products.
3. *Financing activities* show the cash exchange between owners, shareholders, and creditors. For Apple, cash from financing activities could be issuing and selling, or buying shares of company stock.

Understanding the different sources of cash flows can help managers and others isolate which activities are helping (or hurting) a business's bottom line. Figure 1.2 shows Apple's actual cash flow statement from 2008. Note that figures in parentheses indicate negative numbers.

Figure **1.2** | **Cash Flow Statement for Apple Inc.**

Apple Inc.
Summary Cash Flow Statement
as of September 27, 2008
(in thousands of dollars)

Net Income (or Net Profit)	**4,834,000**
Operating Activities, Cash Flows Provided By or Used In	
Depreciation	473,000
Adjustments To Net Income	170,000
Changes in Accounts Receivables	(785,000)
Changes in Liabilities	7,517,000
Changes in Inventories	(163,000)
Changes in Other Operating Activities	(2,540,000)
Total Cash Flow From Operating Activities	**9,596,000**
Investing Activities, Cash Flows Provided By or Used In	
Capital Expenditures	(1,091,000)
Investments	(6,760,000)
Other Cash Flows from Investing Activities	(338,000)
Total Cash Flows From Investing Activities	**(8,189,000)**
Financing Activities, Cash Flows Provided By or Used In	
Dividends Paid	0
Sale Purchase of Stock	483,000
Net Borrowings	0
Other Cash Flows from Financing Activities	633,000
Total Cash Flows from Financing Activities	**1,116,000**
Effect of Exchange Rate Changes	0
Change in Cash and Cash Equivalents	**$2,523,000**

Apple's net profit from 2008. (→ Net Income)

Assets like manufacturing plants and equipment wear out and lose value over time. The loss of this value is recorded as an expense each period and is referred to as a depreciation. (→ Depreciation)

Liabilities are debts that Apple owes to suppliers and creditors. (→ Changes in Liabilities)

Capital expenditures refers to cash that Apple spent to buy, improve, or maintain the resources it uses to run its business. (→ Capital Expenditures)

Dividends are cash payments to shareholders. Like many fast-growing companies, Apple does not pay out dividends, preferring instead to invest in the company's growth. (→ Dividends Paid)

Source: Based on Apple Inc. Cash Flow Statement, September 28, 2008, *Yahoo! Finance*, at http://finance.yahoo.com/q/cf?s=AAPL&annual (accessed May 13, 2009).

Take a look at Figure 1.2 and examine Apple's cash flow. What business activity seems to be making the most cash for the company? If you look at the totals for each category, you will see that the majority of Apple's change in cash came from operating activities (the production and sale of computers, software, or other Apple products), rather than from its investing or financing activities.

Creditors can use the information recorded on the cash flow statement to measure a company's short-term health, particularly its ability to pay its bills, and Apple's employees can view this information and feel confident that the company makes enough money to pay their salaries and possibly provide raises.

Apple's cash flow statement can also be useful to you if you're interested in buying shares in the company. Because Apple's operating activities bring in a substantial net cash gain, you can be confident that the company has enough money to stay in business for a while. You can also see that Apple has a great deal of cash going toward investments. Those reinvested funds could help grow or streamline operations, eventually making the business more profitable. And the positive gain from financing activities indicates that Apple is not getting buried paying back interest on loans, which shows that the company is not taking on an excessive amount of risk to keep running.

So, understanding a cash flow statement and knowing how efficiently management generates and uses cash can give each party involved better insight into the financial health of the company, and help a person judge whether being involved with Apple's business will contribute to improving that person's quality of life or standard of living.

Analyzing the Income Statement

If you're thinking about investing in a company like Apple, the cash flow statement is not the only financial information you're going to want to look at it to make an informed decision. You'll also want to analyze the company's income statement to get a more complete picture of the company's finances.

As we noted earlier in the chapter, on the most basic level, the income statement provides a summary of a company's income, expenses, and net profit (or loss). Often, people focus entirely on the bottom line and ignore everything else, but the income statement is packed with information that can help managers and others diagnose the overall health of a business.

For example, did sales increase this month? How about last month? Are these changes a trend or a one-time event? How much does the company spend on research and development for new products, and is that investment paying off? The income statement can help answer all of these questions and more. Let's take a look at Figure 1.3, which shows Apple's income statement for 2008.

The income statement is not just useful for investors and creditors. A company's management can also use this information to make smart business decisions. If a company uses a budget as an analysis tool, managers can create a goal based on the income statement. For example, if management wants to increase the company's revenue by 5 percent in the next 12 months, they would base their target on the current income statement. Then, when six months have passed, they can compare these goals to the actual results shown on the next income statement. This way, they can evaluate whether the strategies and tactics they've used to boost sales were effective, or if they need to go back to the drawing board and come up with a new plan. If expenses are too high in one area, they may try to cut costs. If sales aren't where they want them to be, they may hire additional salespeople, provide more training, or create sales incentives, such as discounts, for customers.

Figure 1.4 compares Apple's 2007 performance with its 2008 performance. As you can see, setting a goal to increase revenue by just 5 percent over the course of one year would be big step backward for Apple based on their 2008 performance. In addition to increasing *gross profit*, the amount left over after all the costs of creating and delivering products for sale have been subtracted from revenue (this does not include overhead expenses), by almost

Figure **1.3** | **Income Statement for Apple Inc.**

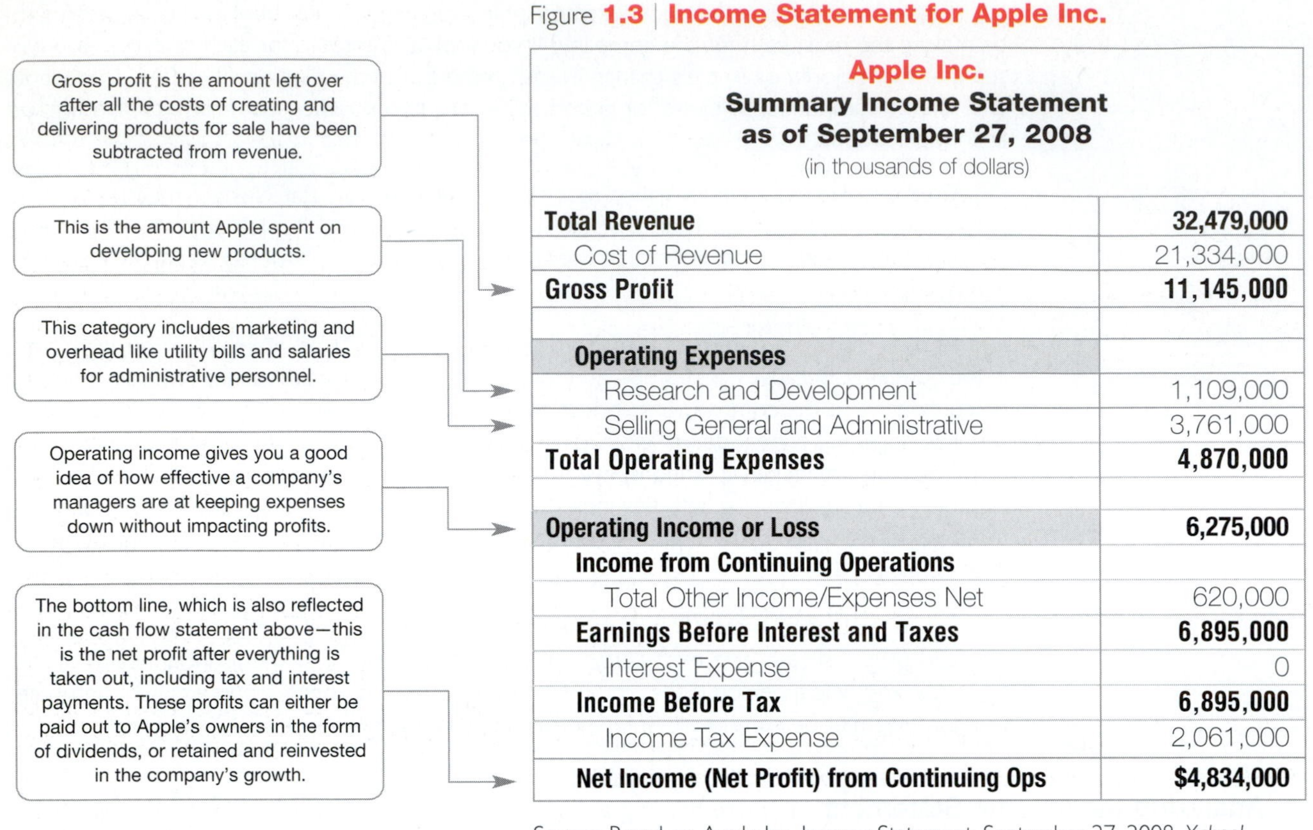

Apple Inc.
Summary Income Statement
as of September 27, 2008
(in thousands of dollars)

Total Revenue	**32,479,000**
Cost of Revenue	21,334,000
Gross Profit	**11,145,000**
Operating Expenses	
Research and Development	1,109,000
Selling General and Administrative	3,761,000
Total Operating Expenses	**4,870,000**
Operating Income or Loss	**6,275,000**
Income from Continuing Operations	
Total Other Income/Expenses Net	620,000
Earnings Before Interest and Taxes	**6,895,000**
Interest Expense	0
Income Before Tax	**6,895,000**
Income Tax Expense	2,061,000
Net Income (Net Profit) from Continuing Ops	**$4,834,000**

Source: Based on Apple Inc. Income Statement, September 27, 2008, *Yahoo! Finance*, at http://finance.yahoo.com/q/is?s=AAPL&annual (accessed May 13, 2009).

Figure **1.4** | **Comparative Income Statement for Apple Inc.**

Apple Inc.
Income Statement
Year Ended September 27, 2008 and September 29, 2007
(in thousands of dollars)

	2007	2008	Amount Increase	Percentage Increase
Revenues	**24,006,000**	**32,479,000**	**8,473,000**	**35.3%**
Cost of Revenues	15,852,000	21,334,000	5,482,000	34.6%
Gross Profit	**8,154,000**	**11,145,000**	**2,991,000**	**36.7%**

Source: Based on Apple Inc. Income Statement, *Yahoo! Finance,* at http://finance.yahoo.com/q/is?s=AAPL&annual (accessed May 13, 2009).

37 percent. The company managed to keep costs from growing faster than revenues—never an easy task when a company is growing quickly. Apple's management will almost certainly set the bar even higher in the future, and they can feel pretty confident knowing that their business strategies are working well.

What the Decisions Mean to the Rest of Us

Throughout this section we have discussed why the cash flow statement and the income statement are important to companies. But if decisions are made by someone else based on financial statements and you don't have a say in the decisions, what difference does it make to you if you can read financial statements or not?

If you are currently working for a company, understanding its financial statements will help you determine its financial health, and that will allow you to judge whether your job is secure. If the financial statements are not as good as they should be, you'll know that it might be time to take action. Maybe you'll work smarter in your position to be more effective and more profitable. Maybe you'll get the whole department to worker smarter and be more profitable. You may be able to make an impact on the company as a whole to improve the situation. If all hope is lost, at least you won't be caught surprised when the axe starts to fall, and you can start making other employment arrangements. And even if you work for a company that doesn't share its financial information with its employees or the public, just knowing what kinds of things impact the bottom line can help you make smarter decisions on the job.

When a company is successful, all employees reap the rewards, whether it uses OBM or not and whether the employee is involved in profit sharing or not. Successful companies generally offer yearly raises, which directly contribute to your standard of living. With this financial reward, you can upgrade your belongings, or your house, or start putting more money away. And as we discussed earlier, if you start saving now, you'll have a pretty good chunk of money working for you before you know it. Along with an increased standard of living, you may also experience a higher quality of life. If you're working for a profitable company with great benefits, you can feel confident because you'll have job security and good heath care. A comfortable financial position may offer you other things you're looking for, such as extra leisure time, or working part-time to spend more time with your family. These are just some of the benefits of having financial knowledge.

Do It...

1.4: Determine Profitability You are the chief financial officer (CFO) of your own business, and that business is you. Review your bank statements, bills, and pay stubs and create an income statement for a specific period of time, such as one month. Use this statement to determine whether you were profitable during that time period.

Now Debrief...

- Cash flows recorded on the cash flow statement are split into three categories: operating, investing, and financing activities. Knowing where cash is coming from and going to helps owners and managers make and evaluate business strategies and tactics, and this knowledge helps creditors and investors evaluate the risk of doing business with the company.
- The income statement shows the net profit after costs of generating revenue, operating expenses, and payments on interest and taxes are taken out. Comparing these numbers to the total revenue can help owners and managers, as well as interested parties outside the company, judge how efficiently the business can turn resources and effort into profit.
- As an employee, understanding the cash flow and income statements of your company and the factors that affect the bottom line on these statements can help you do your job more effectively, as well as give you an idea of whether your job is secure and how likely it is that you'll be able to get a raise or a promotion.

5. The Four BizHats

Many businesses may look the same to you, but depending on whose eyes you look through, they can look totally different. Let's say you visit a farm, and while you're there, you notice someone riding a horse. In fact, she's been riding horses all morning—this is her job. She comes in every day to exercise the horses. Along with her, there are a few people who care for the other animals—cleaning stalls, filling water buckets, and making sure the animals have enough food. In the afternoon, the manager of the farm arrives to speak to some of the workers about financial arrangements.

This farm is a business, like any other. To the visitor (or customer), the farm may be a serene place to visit. To the employees, the farm probably looks a little different. Since they're working, the word "serenity" is probably replaced with the word "work." The manager may enjoy the serenity, but he also has to make sure people are doing their jobs and that the finances are in order. The owner of the farm has to make sure her money is being put to good use and will eventually make a profit.

These are the four hats of business—the **BizHats**: the customer, the employee, the manager, and the owner/investor. It is smart for all employees to put on all of these hats when looking at every aspect of business, such as when examining cash flow and income statements, so that they can view the logistics of the business from multiple vantage points. Throughout this book, you'll be asked to look at business from the perspective of these four hats as well.

The Customer BizHat

We've all worn this hat. Any person who purchases goods, services, or experiences from a company wears the **Customer BizHat**. The perspective of the customer may be varied. Sometimes, customers may not need to know the financial status of the company if they're making a small purchase. For example, customers purchasing a single item from your T-shirt company may not care how profitable your company is as long as they get the shirts. But let's say a customer is in the market to buy a car and he hears in the news that car dealers are going through tough financial times. Do you think this will make her more wary of purchasing a car from a struggling dealer? If the company goes bankrupt, will there still be parts to fix her new car? What about warranties? What about resale value? As you can see, if they're spending a lot of money or making a long-term investment, customers want to know the company they are buying from is stable.

The Employee BizHat

Those who wear the **Employee BizHat** do the day-to-day work of a business. These jobs are essential to the operations of businesses, as these employees may be responsible for performing administrative work, educating students, providing health care for the community, serving food to hungry customers, or maintaining the Web site for your online T-shirt company. There is no end to the types of tasks performed by employees, and their importance is not to be underestimated. Without such employees, there would be no business!

When employees understand how their actions impact their organization's bottom line, they can be more effective in supporting the organization's vision and mission. Just think back to Jack Stack's former company, SRC Holdings. If the employees hadn't stepped up to the challenge and bought the company, it would have gone bankrupt and left many people unemployed.

Manager

The Manager BizHat

In business, as you know, effective employees are often promoted to jobs where they supervise other employees—these people wear the **Manager BizHat**. Managers are still employees of the company and perhaps still hold this view of the company where they show up for work and collect a paycheck. However, instead of performing the day-to-day tasks, managers are responsible for guiding others in their day-to-day tasks. The manufacturer that supplies the T-shirts for your small company probably has multiple managers that make sure the shirts are produced and delivered on time.

A manager's primary job is to point the employees in the right direction and make sure that the work meets certain criteria. However, managers can directly affect an organization's bottom line by motivating employees and developing more efficient business processes.

Owner/Investor

The Owner/Investor BizHat

Those who wear the **Owner/Investor BizHat** come from a variety of backgrounds. Owners may have started as an entry-level employee and then moved up, eventually purchasing the company from the prior owner, or they can be first-time entrepreneurs like you with your T-shirt company. An investor may be a person who had some extra cash and wanted to put that money to good use, so she became an investor in a company. No matter the path, the owner and investor both have a vested interest in the financial success of the company, but may or may not have active day-to-day responsibilities in the company. These are people who are closely examining a company's financial statements to gauge the overall health of the company.

These four perspectives of business define the lens through which people look, and the business looks very different depending on whose perspective you're using. We'll return to these hats throughout the book as we look at situations from different perspectives. In the next chapter, we'll continue our discussion of financial statements by looking at the balance sheet.

Do It...

1.5: Wear the BizHats Imagine a situation in which a major employer like Wal-Mart announces that it will provide free, comprehensive health care to all of its employees, full- and part-time. Take turns putting on each of the hats and describe how you might view this decision from that perspective. Limit your response to one page, and be prepared to submit it electronically to your instructor.

Now Debrief...

- In business, there are four perspectives that shape how a person sees a situation. These four perspectives, the **BizHats**, are the **Customer**, **Employee**, **Manager**, and **Owner/Investor BizHats**.
- The Customer BizHat is worn by anyone who purchases a good, service, or experience.
- The Employee BizHat is worn by anyone who participates in the day-to-day work of a business.
- The Manager BizHat is worn by anyone who guides employees and makes sure that the work meets certain criteria.
- The Owner/Investor BizHat is worn by anyone who has a vested interest in the financial success of a company, without necessarily participating in day-to-day responsibilities.

Chapter 1 Visual Summary

Financial Intelligence | **Chapter 1: *Profit*** Chapter 2: *Build* Chapter 3: *Compete* Chapter 4: *Adapt* Chapter 5: *Grow*

1. Explain why financial statements matter to businesses and the people who own them, manage them, and work in them. (pp. 4–8)

- **Financial statements** act as scoreboards for the company by summarizing financial information.
- **Standard of living** is a measurement of tangible things, such as income, whereas **quality of life** is a measurement of intangible aspects of life, such as well-being.
- **Open book management** is a style of management that gives employees access to a company's financial statements and information. This is also generally known as being transparent.
- Open book management helps employees learn about company finances and sometimes shares the profits. Giving the employees the whole story and rewarding them is much more effective than just giving out rewards without knowledge of finances. When rewards are given without financial knowledge, it doesn't give the employees vested interest in the company.
- **The bottom line** is also known as the **net profit**, which is the amount of income left over after all expenses have been paid.

Summary: Understanding financial statements can help people make good financial decisions, such as investing in a financially sound company. People who use this knowledge have the tools to improve their standard of living and quality of life.

2. Recognize cash flow and how to interpret a cash flow statement. (pp. 9–12)

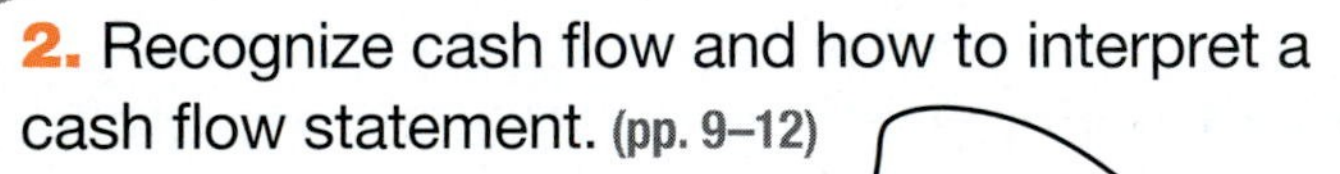

- One of the most important aspects of business is managing **cash flow**, which means managing the inflow and outflow of cash.
- One of the biggest problems businesses have is running out of cash due to poor planning. A **budget** can help monitor cash flow by quantifying all of the expected inflows and outflows of cash.
- **Cash flow statements** report cash-in and cash-out transactions as well as the beginning and ending balances.
- Budgeting is a good way to come up with a financial game plan. Part of that plan should be saving, which is easy if you pay yourself first. "**Paying yourself first**" means that every time you get paid, you immediately take a predetermined amount and transfer it into a savings account.

Summary: Understanding and managing cash flow is crucial for a successful business because without cash, there is no business to run. Mismanaging cash flow can ruin a business no matter how successful it is.

3. Recognize profit and how to interpret an income statement. (pp. 13–19)

- An **income statement** measures the net profit of a company by tracking the revenue and expenses during a given period.

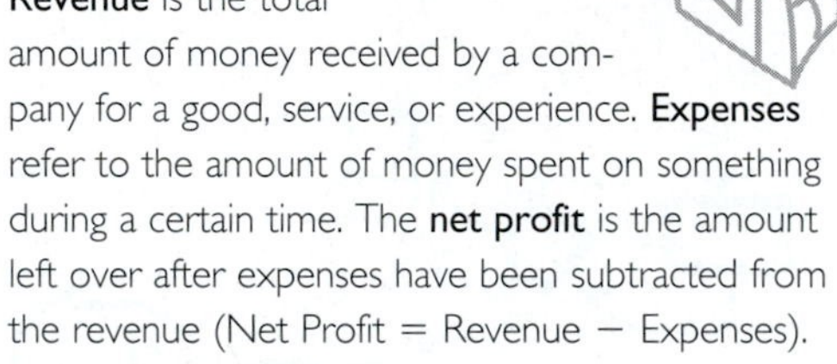

- **Income** is the amount of money generated by a company during a given time period. **Revenue** is the total amount of money received by a company for a good, service, or experience. **Expenses** refer to the amount of money spent on something during a certain time. The **net profit** is the amount left over after expenses have been subtracted from the revenue (Net Profit = Revenue − Expenses).
- Basic types of business models include for-profit and not-for-profit companies. The difference between the two is business goals: In a **for-profit company**, the goal is to make a profit for the owners. In a **not-for-profit (or nonprofit) organization** the goal is to serve and improve the community or support associations or institutions.
- In accounting, there are two types of income statements: cash basis of accounting and accrual basis of accounting. A **cash basis of accounting** records cash flows (income) and cash flows (expenses) when they happen. It answers the question, "Do we have any cash?" The **accrual basis of accounting** records income when a service is provided and the expense when the expense is incurred. It answers the questions, "Is the company making money?"

Summary: In order to understand whether or not you or your business is making money, it's important to understand profit. However, profit can get confused with cash flow. This is why it's important to analyze income and cash flow statements to determine the net profit, or bottom line.

4. Examine how businesses and people make decisions based on impact on cash flow and profit. (pp. 19–23)

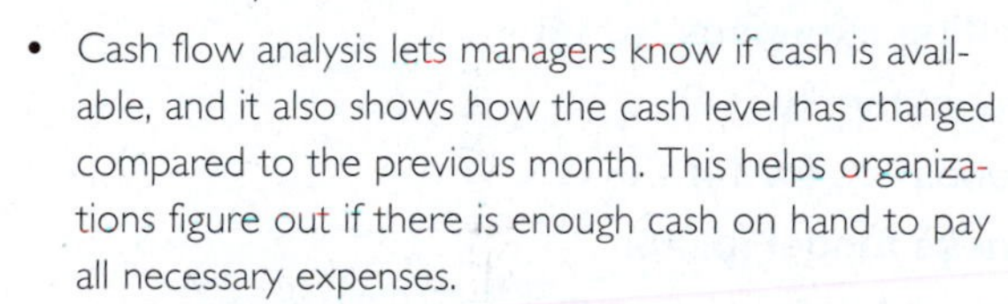

- Income statements and cash flow statements are useful in making decisions.
- Analyzing income statements helps managers figure out areas that need improvement and identify trends.
- Cash flow analysis lets managers know if cash is available, and it also shows how the cash level has changed compared to the previous month. This helps organizations figure out if there is enough cash on hand to pay all necessary expenses.

Summary: By understanding the information contained in income and cash flow statements, owners, managers, and employees can make informed decisions about the future of an organization.

5. Understand four perspectives in business—the BizHats. (pp. 24–25)

- Four perspectives in business include the customer, the employee, the manager, and the owner/investor.
- The **Customer BizHat** is worn by anyone who purchases a good or service from a company.
- Those who wear the **Employee BizHat** perform the day-to-day work of a business.
- Those who wear the **Manager BizHat** are responsible for guiding employees in their day-to-day tasks.
- Those who wear the **Owner/Investor BizHat** have a vested interest in the company's financial success even though they may not participate in its day-to-day operations.

Summary: By looking at a situation from different perspectives—the BizHats—we are able to figure out the logistics of a situation from different perspectives.

Get the most out of what you just read by practicing your skills and actually DOING something with the material! The best place to do this is at **www.mybizlab.com**. Here's just some of what is available to you there:

- Apply your skills in an interactive environment with more **BizSkill** experiences...and see if you have what it takes
- Think critically and talk with your peers on hot business topics in **BizChat**
- Flex your business communication skills and build your own portfolio with the **Communication Plan exercises**
- Watch the chapter material come together with **Just Plain Business** videos
- Study on-the-go with **Audio Chapter Summaries** in MP3 format
- Brush up on the lecture and content with **Audio PowerPoints**
- Discover how well you are doing and see what areas you need to improve on with the **Pre-Tests** and **Post-Tests**

Key Words

These key words and more are also available as flash cards to practice with at **www.mybizlab.com**.

1. Explain why financial statements matter to businesses and the people who own them, manage them, and work in them. **(pp. 4–8)**

Financial statements (p. 4)
Standard of living (p. 4)
Quality of life (p. 4)
Open book management (OBM) (p. 5)
The bottom line (p. 7)

2. Recognize cash flow and how to interpret a cash flow statement. **(pp. 9–12)**

Cash flow (p. 9)
Cash flow statement (p. 9)
Budget (p. 9)
Paying yourself first (p. 11)
Interest (p. 11)
Rule of 72 (p. 12)
Compound growth (p. 12)

3. Recognize profit and how to interpret an income statement. **(pp. 13–19)**

Net profit (p. 13)
Income statement (p. 13)
Income (p. 13)
Revenue (p. 13)
Good (p. 13)
Service (p. 13)
Experience (p. 13)
Product (p. 13)
Expenses (p. 13)
Cost of revenue (p. 14)
Cost of goods sold (p. 14)
Operating expenses (p. 14)
Shareholders (p. 14)
Stakeholders (p. 14)
Business model (p. 15)
For-profit business (p. 15)
Not-for-profit (or nonprofit) organization (p. 15)
Cash basis of accounting (p. 16)
Accounts receivable (p. 16)
Accounts payable (p. 16)
Accrual basis of accounting (p. 16)
Net loss (p. 18)

4. Examine how businesses and people make decisions based on their impact on cash flow and profit. **(pp. 19–23)**

5. Understand four perspectives in business—the BizHats. **(pp. 24–25)**

BizHats (p. 24)
Customer BizHat (p. 24)
Employee BizHat (p. 24)
Manager BizHat (p. 25)
Owner/Investor BizHat (p. 25)

Prove It

Prove It...

Now, let's put on one of the BizHats. With the **Owner/Investor BizHat** squarely on your head, look at the following exercise:

The cash flow statement and the income statement provide two very different, but very critical pieces of information. We've talked about the differences between the statements, as well as some analysis of the statements. Now it's time to put your knowledge to use. You are going to research a company to determine whether you should invest in it.

1. Choose a publicly traded company that you like, for whatever reason.
2. Go to the company's Web site and search for the annual report. If you can't locate the annual report there, check out Google Finance (http://www.google.com/finance) or Yahoo! Finance (http://finance.yahoo.com).
3. Locate the income statement and cash flow statement for the company.
4. What do you see with respect to the financial statements of the company? Is it making a profit? Have its revenues increased or decreased since the previous year? Have its expenses increased or decreased? Does it bring in enough cash to cover all of its expenses?
5. Based on your review of the financial statements, would you invest in this company? How many shares would you purchase?
6. Optional: Regardless of whether you choose to invest, record the current stock price as of the day you make your decision. At the end of this course, look back and see whether you would have made a good choice.

Flip It...

After you've decided whether you want to invest in the company you chose above, **flip over to the Customer BizHat.** As a customer, consider whether the company's financial statements give you confidence to spend your hard-earned money on their products. Is the company likely to be around in a few years if you need customer service? If the company is spending a great deal on investing activities and research and development, what might this mean for you?

Now Debrief It...

Compare the perspectives of the two BizHats described above. Did taking the perspective of the Customer change your Owner/Investor opinion about the company? How were the two perspectives different?

Build:

Balance Sheet, Risk, Financing, and Diversification

BizSkills invite...

Try It!
There's no better way to learn concepts than to put them into practice. Take your turn in the driver's seat and be a part of actual business decision making by visiting the BizSkill for this chapter at **www.mybizlab.com**.

Now that you've practiced making tough business decisions and seeing the results of your choices in this chapter's BizSkill, it's time to translate those skills into plain English. And if you skipped the BizSkill, go back now!

Chapter 2 Goals

After experiencing this chapter, you'll be able to:

1. Differentiate an asset from a liability, recognize assets that generate income, and evaluate an organization's financial position by its balance sheet.
2. Appreciate the value and necessity of risk in business by conducting a SWOT analysis and considering opportunity costs.
3. Use the concept of diversification to not only manage risk, but also thrive in it.
4. Make short-term and long-term financing decisions based on risk and diversification.
5. Become a wise investor who makes decisions based on risk and diversification.

How do you build a profitable business?

Making Money Work for You

Do you want to be a millionaire? "Who doesn't?" you might say. But for most people, *wanting* a million dollars isn't enough—you have to *earn* it. So, what's your plan for making that first million? Get a good education, get a good job, and wait for the bucks to roll in? Good luck with that! It might seem like a six-figure salary will get you to millionaire status pretty quickly, but the local, state, and federal governments all take their cut, and you still have to worry about paying off your mortgage, car, and student loans. The more money you earn, the more you have to pay in taxes and expenses.

Most of the people whom you would consider wealthy today didn't get that way by spending a lot of money. What's their secret? Most wealthy people know that you can't put all your eggs in one basket, and if you're counting on just your salary to make you wealthy, that's exactly what you're doing. The rich get richer because they own a lot of valuable items—like stocks, property, or their own businesses—that make them more money. They ensure that their money is working for *them*, instead of for the government, banks, and credit card companies.

The great thing about owning items that make you money is that you can use that money to acquire *more* items that make you *more* money, and before you know it, that cash flow (remember that term from Chapter 1?) can snowball into big bucks. If you've ever paid yourself first and used it to invest in stocks or some other type of investment, then you already have *some* money working for you. This chapter will show you how to really get the ball rolling and how you can apply these same principles to any organization that you might work for, invest in, or own.

1. Here's to Good Health... Financial Health

Do you hire a limousine to chauffeur you around town every day? Do you eat every meal at an expensive restaurant? Of course not. You know that if you were to live such an expensive life, you'd be spending more money than you'd be taking in, and soon you'd be in pretty bad financial shape. For businesses, finding the right balance between revenues and spending can mean all the difference between success and failure. We discussed in Chapter 1 the effects that properly balanced revenues and spending can have on the income and cash flow statements. Now we'll take a look at how to balance the things you own with the money you owe, and how businesses do the same.

What are your assets and liabilities?

Establishing Value: Assets

Anything you own or control that you can exchange for some value is an **asset**. Your car is an asset, as well as your college degree. Just as you have assets, so do companies. A company uses its assets to run its business. We discussed the most obvious asset to a company in Chapter 1: cash. As you learned there, cash is king for every organization; without it, there is no business.

Another important asset is **accounts receivable**. This is any money that you or a business are owed. For example, suppose you worked 40 hours last week but you haven't been paid yet. This unpaid money would be your accounts receivable. Remember the T-shirt company you started in Chapter 1? The money you're waiting to be paid from customers is your accounts receivable. For a business, accounts receivable include any money owed by customers or vendors.

Another important asset is **notes receivable.** This is any money that you or a business is owed and that has a written promise for payment, or *promissory note*. Suppose your brother borrows $50 from you until payday. You don't have the money in your hand, but he writes you an IOU for $50 that will be made good (hopefully) on payday. Likewise, a business may sell a product to a trusted customer in return for a written pledge that the customer will pay for the product by a certain date.

> Finding the right balance between revenues and spending can mean all the difference between success and failure.

Other types of assets are described as **fixed assets**. Fixed assets include property, manufacturing plants, and equipment. For a manufacturing company, fixed assets might include the land and the building in which the products are made, the machinery used to make the products, and any vehicles used to transport materials associated with the business. For your T-shirt company, the place where you make your T-shirts and your screen-printing equipment would be fixed assets.

Intangible assets, like intellectual property or patents, are also important fixed assets. Ownership of an idea can be just as important as a manufacturing facility.

Many small businesses have much of their money tied up in **inventory,** which is considered another asset. Inventory consists of all merchandise, raw materials, and products that have not yet been sold. Managing the appropriate amount of inventory can be a crucial business decision. Too little inventory means not having enough items to sell or not having the materials needed to manufacture a product. Too much inventory means the company will have less money to use for daily operations or other investments.

Current vs. Long-Term Assets

"There are plenty of ways to get ahead. The first is so basic I'm almost embarrassed to say it: spend less than you earn."
—Paul Clitheroe,
Chairman of *Money Magazine*[1]

Assets can be divided into two major categories: *current assets* and *long-term assets*. This means that assets are classified according to how quickly they can be turned into cash. The ability of an asset to be converted into cash is known as its **liquidity**. The more liquid an asset, the faster and easier it can be converted into cash. What is the most liquid type of asset? Cash, for obvious reasons, is the most liquid of all assets (it doesn't need to be converted at all). Any assets that can be easily converted into cash within one calendar year are known as *current assets*. Checking accounts as well as accounts receivable or notes receivable that are due within one year's time are considered current assets.

If you needed cash right away, would you look to sell your home? What if your restaurant needed cash, would you sell your ovens? Probably not. It takes time to find a buyer for a major purchase such as real estate or machinery. Even when you find a buyer, the processes of completing the sale and obtaining the cash are not like immediate ATM withdrawals. This is why fixed assets are considered *long-term assets,* which are expected to be held for more than one year. It takes a long time for them to be converted into cash.

Another Way to Evaluate Assets

There is another way to evaluate assets. Some assets *earn money while you have them*. In other words, they generate income. To understand this, begin by thinking small. Suppose you buy a television. The TV is an asset that you own. Down the road, if you tried to sell your TV, you wouldn't be able to sell it for more than what you paid for it. You may enjoy watching the TV, but you don't gain money by owning it.

Now suppose instead, you buy a townhouse that you rent out throughout the year. Renters pay you to stay in your townhouse. The townhouse is an asset that generates income for you. Likewise, if a business were to purchase a new piece of equipment that doubled the efficiency of production, the increase in production would begin paying dividends almost immediately.

Other assets do not generate income immediately. Imagine, for example, you buy a painting from an up-and-coming artist. The painting may not be worth much now, but as the artist becomes famous, the value of the painting rises. In time, with any luck, you can sell the painting for more than you paid for it. The same is true for other investments, including stocks and bonds (which we'll discuss later in this chapter). The famous saying, "Buy low, sell high" is true when it comes to assets that generate income. Likewise, if a business decides to invest in an up-and-coming technology company, it might not see much in the way of financial gains in the first year, but it could benefit greatly from the investment in the long term.

Just as assets can gain value, they can also lose value, or simply retain the same value. You know this if you've ever owned a stock that took a nosedive. Individuals and companies can quickly find themselves in a tough position when assets lose value.

Payback Time: Liabilities

Do you have a student loan? The bank expects you to pay your student loan over time (and with interest), making it a liability. A **liability** is a legal obligation that an individual or company has to pay back a debt—basically, a liability is something you *owe*.

Liabilities for a company aren't very different than those for individuals, although they are usually for much larger amounts of money. For a company, liabilities are claims by creditors against the assets of the business. **Accounts payable** are one type of liability. Accounts payable consist of credit that is extended to a business for necessary purchases. For example, your T-shirt company may order fabric to create its T-shirts, but it may not have to pay for the fabric for 30, 60, or 90 days. The amount you owe to the fabric supplier is considered an account payable.

Another type of liability is related to unpaid employee salaries. Suppose a company pays its employees once a month. Before the payments are actually made, they are owed by the company. Therefore, the amount owed by the company to its employees is considered a liability. Any taxes that a business must pay on its earnings are also considered a liability.

Current vs. Long-Term Liabilities Just as assets are current or long term, so are liabilities.

- A *current liability* must be paid within one year. An example of a current liability would be a purchase of raw materials on credit that needs to be paid within the next year.
- A *long-term liability* can be paid over a longer period of time. An example of a long-term liability would be a mortgage payment on a building that a company purchased, with the terms of the mortgage lasting more than a year—possibly even decades.

What's It Worth? Net Worth and Owners' Equity

If you've ever read *Fortune* magazine, you may have seen its list of the wealthiest companies or people in the world. But how, exactly, do you measure the worth of a company or even a person?

At any given time, you usually have some money that's neither coming nor going—money that's yours and isn't promised to anyone else. The assets you keep after you've paid off all your liabilities make up your **net worth**, which is the figure you hear when *Fortune* reports that American investor and businessman Warren Buffett is worth $37 billion.

In business, net worth is usually referred to as **owners' equity** (or **shareholders' equity**). This is the amount of money initially invested into a company, plus any net profits that the company retains from a specific period. **Retained earnings** are earnings that are reinvested into a company (or *retained*) rather than paid out to its shareholders. So, if you invested $50,000 to start your T-shirt company, this is your owners' equity before the company generates any retained earnings.

A Balancing Act: The Balance Sheet

Now that you understand the concept of assets and liabilities, you're ready to learn how organizations account for them. We looked at the cash flow and income statements in Chapter 1. In this chapter, we'll look at the financial statement that compares assets and liabilities: the balance sheet. A **balance sheet** is a record of a company's assets and liabilities at a fixed point in time. It weighs the relationship between what a company has or expects to get soon (its assets), what it owes to others (its liabilities), and what it owes to the owners (owners' equity). Balance sheets are therefore based on what is known in business as the **fundamental accounting equation**:

Assets = Liabilities + Owners' Equity

The fundamental accounting equation says that your assets (what you own) should equal your liabilities (what you owe) plus owners' equity (what is owed to the business's owners). Recording these amounts is the purpose of the balance sheet. Figure 2.1 shows a simple example of a balance sheet.

Figure **2.1** | **Simple Balance Sheet**

Your T-Shirt Business, Inc. Balance Sheet July 31, 20xx	
Assets	
Cash	$100
Accounts Receivable	$50
Inventory	$50
Total Assets	$200
Liabilities and Owners' Equity	
Accounts Payable	$100
Owners' Equity	$100
Total Liabilities and Owners' Equity	$200

You see right away that the balance sheet in Figure 2.1 is divided into sections. The top part of the sheet lists assets. The bottom part lists liabilities and owners' equity. Some balance sheets separate the sections by columns. Notice that the total assets equal the total liabilities plus the owners' equity. That's the fundamental accounting equation in action.

Balance sheets are usually more detailed than the simple one shown in Figure 2.1. For example, look at the sample balance sheet from Apple Inc. shown in Figure 2.2.[2]

Apple's balance sheet shows that its net worth (or owners' equity) is quite high—over $21 billion. Its current assets are more than enough to pay off all of its liabilities, which is good news for the company, because if worse comes to worse, Apple would not

Figure **2.2** | **Apple Inc. Balance Sheet**

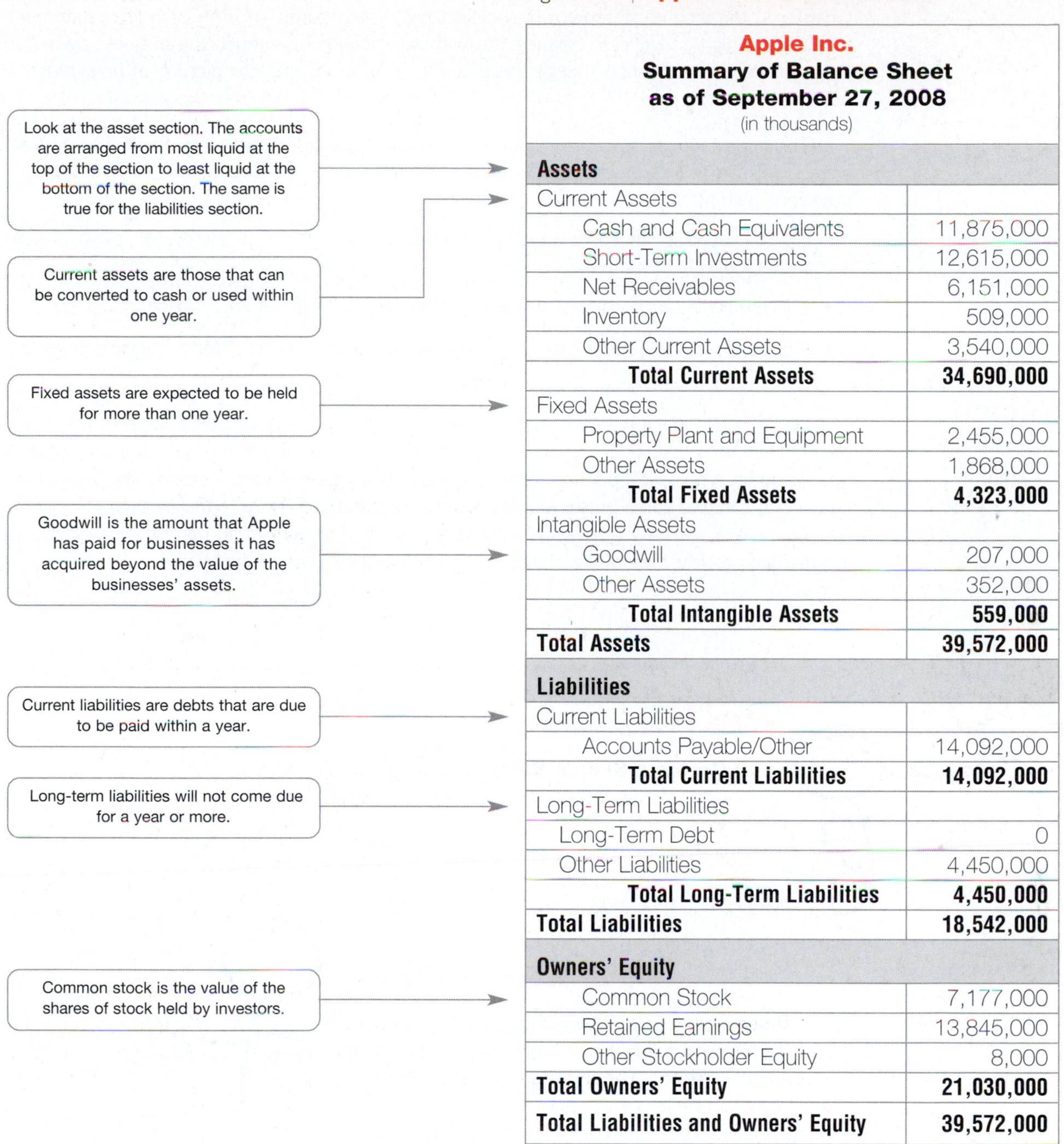

Apple Inc.
Summary of Balance Sheet
as of September 27, 2008
(in thousands)

Assets	
Current Assets	
Cash and Cash Equivalents	11,875,000
Short-Term Investments	12,615,000
Net Receivables	6,151,000
Inventory	509,000
Other Current Assets	3,540,000
Total Current Assets	**34,690,000**
Fixed Assets	
Property Plant and Equipment	2,455,000
Other Assets	1,868,000
Total Fixed Assets	**4,323,000**
Intangible Assets	
Goodwill	207,000
Other Assets	352,000
Total Intangible Assets	**559,000**
Total Assets	**39,572,000**
Liabilities	
Current Liabilities	
Accounts Payable/Other	14,092,000
Total Current Liabilities	**14,092,000**
Long-Term Liabilities	
Long-Term Debt	0
Other Liabilities	4,450,000
Total Long-Term Liabilities	**4,450,000**
Total Liabilities	**18,542,000**
Owners' Equity	
Common Stock	7,177,000
Retained Earnings	13,845,000
Other Stockholder Equity	8,000
Total Owners' Equity	**21,030,000**
Total Liabilities and Owners' Equity	**39,572,000**

have to try to sell fixed assets to cover its debts. And the majority of its current assets are held in cash and other short-term investments, which is helpful if any unexpected expenses come up. Liquidating inventory and collecting on accounts receivable can be time-consuming, so it's good to have plenty of cash on hand for emergencies.

Another plus for Apple is that it carries no long-term debt. This indicates that Apple is financing its business from the sale of stock and retained earnings, which is a secure and therefore enviable position for any company to be in.

Why the Balance Sheet Matters

So, why does the balance sheet matter? How is it different from the income statement and cash flow statement we discussed in Chapter 1? Businesses actually use all three financial statements to get a complete picture of how well a business is performing. As we discussed in Chapter 1, the income statement may reflect high sales figures, and the cash flow statement may show a high ending cash balance, but without knowing how much the business owes (or the liabilities on its balance sheet,) these figures give an incomplete picture of how much a business is worth.

This information is obviously important to financial managers and accountants, but the balance sheet can also help company leaders, employees, and investors answer many important questions such as:

- Can the business afford to expand, such as buy a new store or factory or invest in new technology?
- Can the business afford to pay its immediate bills?
- How is the balance sheet changing over time, and what do these trends suggest about the future of the business?

You can also use a balance sheet on a personal level. If your personal liabilities are much greater than your assets—if you owe more than you have—then you're in a precarious position. From an employee's point of view, understanding the assets and liabilities that your company holds can give you a better idea of how to contribute to improve the balance sheet. And as noted above, the balance sheet is extremely important to current and potential investors, as it gives them a clear idea of the status of the company they are investing in.

Do It...

2.1: Create a Simple Balance Sheet Use the following sample assets, liabilities, and owners' equity to generate a simple balance sheet.

Accounts Receivable: 5,500
Accounts Payable: 8,000
Owners' Equity: 17,000
Inventory: 4,500
Cash: 15,000

Now Debrief...

- An **asset** is anything you own or control that you can exchange for some value. For a business, cash, **accounts receivable, notes receivable,** and **inventory** are examples of assets.
- If an asset can be converted into cash within a year, it is considered a *current asset. Long-term assets* take more than one year to be converted into cash.
- The opposite of an asset is a **liability**, which is a legal obligation to pay a debt within a certain period of time. For a business, **accounts payable** and unpaid employee salaries are examples of liabilities.
- *Current liabilities* must be paid within one year. Materials purchased on credit are an example of a current liability. *Long-term liabilities* are paid off over a period of time longer than a year. A mortgage or piece of property are examples of long-term liabilities.
- **Owners' equity** (or **shareholders' equity**) is the amount of money initially invested into a company, plus any net profits that the company retains from a specific period.
- A **balance sheet** is a financial statement that records a company's assets and liabilities at a fixed point in time. It displays the **fundamental accounting equation**: Assets = Liabilities + Owners' Equity.

2. Risky Business: Assessing and Balancing Risk

"Every business and every product has risks. You can't get around it."
—Lee Iacocca,
President and CEO
of Chrysler, 1978–1992[3]

If a business is profitable and generates positive cash flow, it will begin to accumulate items of value. Leaders recognize that the value of items can change or be lost, so risk is a reality of business. Many people, from investors to employees to customers, want to avoid risk at all costs. But should they? The answer is no. Almost everything in business involves some kind of risk. Just as in your personal life, with risk often comes reward. ■ The goal is to seek opportunities, assess threats, and enjoy rewards.

Identifying Risk

When you decide whether to take a risk in your life, you consider all the pros and cons. Sometimes, you can do this quickly—*Is it worth the risk to dart across this busy four-lane highway to catch the bus? No. I'll just catch the next one.* Sometimes, you need to spend more time weighing your options. *It's certainly a risk to move across country, away from all my friends and family, but it could pay off in the end.* In business, a **risk** is any circumstance in which the outcome of a decision or action is uncertain. The greater the risk, the larger the difference between a favorable or unfavorable outcome. You might evaluate a risk differently from another person. Likewise, what may be a small risk for a large company might have the potential to destroy the livelihood of the owner of a small business.

Think about a risk you might face. For instance, let's say your friend wants to borrow your car. He will pay you to borrow the car, but how do you figure out whether it's a risk worth taking? The first step is to consider what might go wrong versus the payoff you'll receive. In this case, the risk is that your friend might not be careful with your car. Maybe he'll forget to lock the doors and the car will get stolen. Maybe he'll get in a fender bender that leaves your car dented, and you'll end up paying for repairs. Are these risks worth the money your friend is willing to pay you to rent the car?

In business, companies face a variety of risks, such as natural disasters that will affect supplies, advances in technology that will make a product obsolete, or a change in political power or legislation that will prevent a product from reaching the marketplace. Other risks involve such things as interest rate changes, cost overruns, and damage to a company's reputation.

Once you identify what you're risking, you need to estimate the probability that an event will happen. How likely is your friend to be negligent of your car? A business asks similar questions. How likely is it that a financial investment is going to pay off? How likely is it that the product will cost far more to produce than anticipated?

Now think about what it will cost if the event actually occurs. What costs will the company have to pay if a new investment ends up being a bust? What will it cost the company if interest rates rise? In the case of your friend, what will it cost to repair or replace the car if it's damaged or stolen?

■ The goal is to seek opportunities, assess threats, and enjoy rewards.

Many financial risks are reflected on the balance sheet. Too much debt, not enough cash, and excess inventory that is collecting dust instead of revenue are all financial risks that businesses face. A company therefore wants to know its business risks so it can plan a strategy for reducing them or dealing with them.

SWOT Analysis: Assessing Risk

In today's business climate, risk isn't about just surviving risk. It is about assessing risk and using it to your advantage whenever possible. That's where SWOT analysis comes in. SWOT stands for

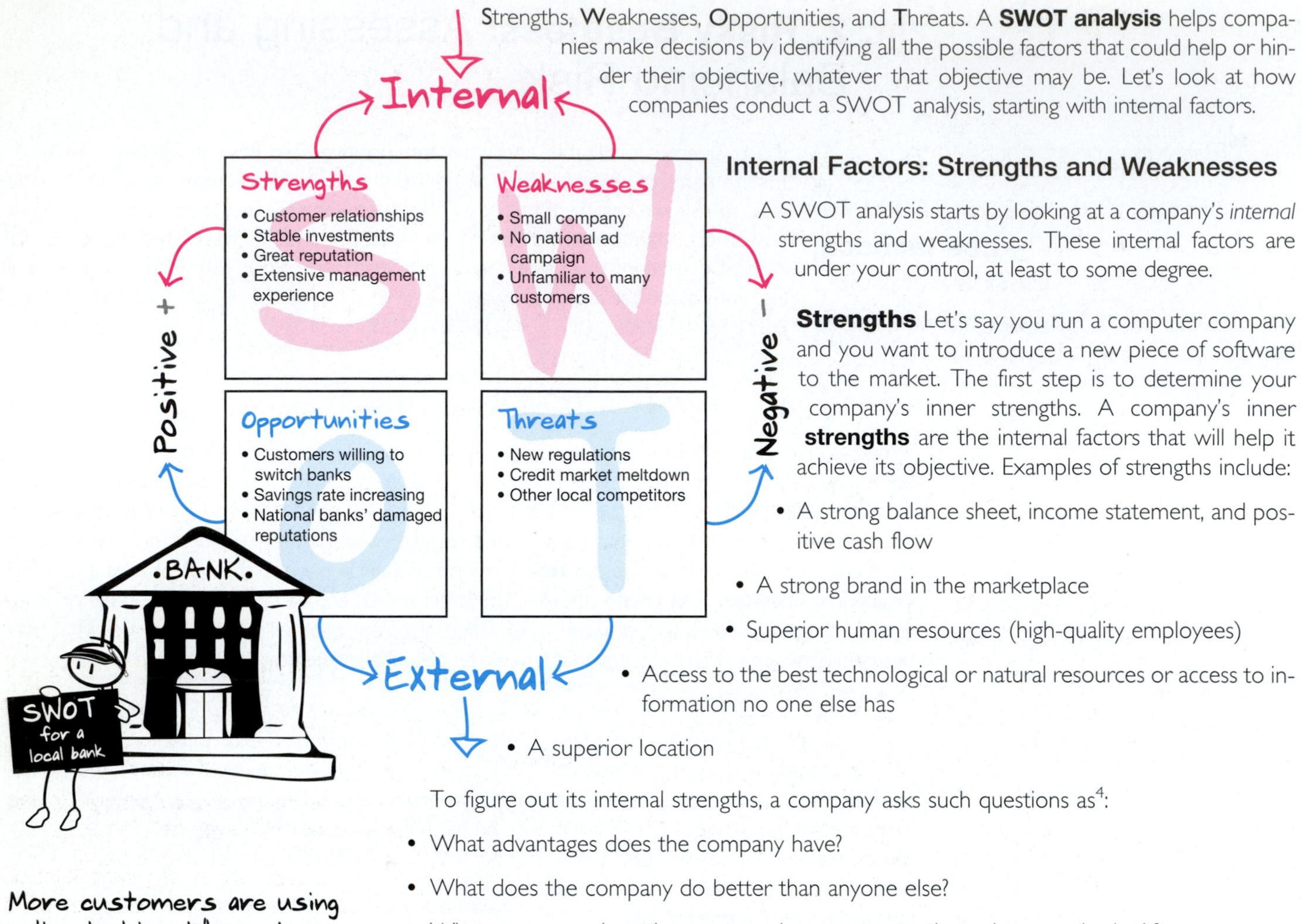

Strengths, Weaknesses, Opportunities, and Threats. A **SWOT analysis** helps companies make decisions by identifying all the possible factors that could help or hinder their objective, whatever that objective may be. Let's look at how companies conduct a SWOT analysis, starting with internal factors.

Internal Factors: Strengths and Weaknesses

A SWOT analysis starts by looking at a company's *internal* strengths and weaknesses. These internal factors are under your control, at least to some degree.

Strengths Let's say you run a computer company and you want to introduce a new piece of software to the market. The first step is to determine your company's inner strengths. A company's inner **strengths** are the internal factors that will help it achieve its objective. Examples of strengths include:

- A strong balance sheet, income statement, and positive cash flow
- A strong brand in the marketplace
- Superior human resources (high-quality employees)
- Access to the best technological or natural resources or access to information no one else has
- A superior location

To figure out its internal strengths, a company asks such questions as[4]:

- What advantages does the company have?
- What does the company do better than anyone else?
- What resources does the company have access to that other people don't?

More customers are using online banking. Where does that fact belong in the SWOT figure above?

Weaknesses A company's **weaknesses** are the internal factors that may stop it from achieving its objective. What kind of weaknesses does your computer company have that will prevent you from creating new software? Examples of weaknesses include:

- A weak balance sheet, income statement, or negative cash flow
- An unknown brand in the marketplace
- Inferior human resources
- Inadequate access to resources or information
- A poor location

To figure out its internal weaknesses, a company asks such questions as[5]:

- What does another company do better than we do?
- What could our company do better internally?
- What resources is our company lacking?

Sometimes, a strength is also a weakness. For example, a huge company may have a cost advantage because it can buy in bulk, but it may also have a weakness because it may not be as flexible or provide the same quality of customer service that a small company can.

As you can see, some of the internal strengths and weaknesses are financial. A company must therefore interpret its financial statements to make effective strategic decisions. By looking at your computer company's financial statements and the state of your company, you should be able to determine how appropriate it is to release a new product. Is the necessary cash flow available? Do you already have too many liabilities? Do you have an adequate staff to take on the new responsibility? If the internal environment says that moving forward with a new product is a go, it is time to consider factors *outside* your control.

External Factors: Opportunities and Threats

External factors include opportunities and threats. These are factors outside your company's control, including economic, political, regulatory, social, and technological factors affecting your industry. Any one of these factors can make or break a business venture.

Opportunities A company's **opportunities** are external conditions that can assist the company in achieving its objective. External opportunities offer growth and possibility to businesses. Examples of external opportunities include:

- A major customer looking for a new company for its advertising campaign
- A discovered need that other companies are not servicing
- New technology that allows the company to be more productive
- A promising new investment that looks like it will pay off
- An improvement in accounting practices that will improve cash flow in the short-term

What kind of opportunities can your computer company take advantage of in producing this new software? To determine its external opportunities, a company asks such questions as[6]:

- What is happening in the industry that is favorable for our company?
- What is the status of other companies in the industry, and how does this affect our company?
- Are there any new resources, such as new technology or new markets opening up, that other companies are not taking advantage of?
- Are there regulatory changes, such as decreased taxes or lowered trade restrictions, that may help the company?
- What are the biggest customer complaints/desires for the industry?

What kinds of strategic decisions might a company make based on the information shown here?

Threats In contrast, **threats** are external conditions that may deter a company from achieving its objective. What outside conditions might prevent your computer company from doing well with its new software venture? Examples of threats include:

- A powerful competitor who has entered the company's market
- Strict government regulations proposed in the industry that would significantly add to the company's costs
- A weak economic environment in which customers cannot pay on time or at all

To determine its external threats, a company asks such questions as[7]:

- What obstacles do we face?
- What are our competitors doing that could hurt our business?

- Is the regulatory environment changing in a way that does not benefit our company?
- Is the economic environment affecting our company?
- What are customers' complaints about current products?

SWOT Strategy The answers to questions like these can help companies like your fictional computer company determine how risky it is to enter into a new venture, and what the potential payoffs may be. Releasing a new product into a weak economy might be a bad decision, but releasing a product that competitors have not yet thought of could give a company the financial boost it needs. ■ Companies use SWOT to analyze risks and benefits and create effective strategies to drive their business objectives. They capitalize on the strengths and opportunities and minimize or protect against the weaknesses and threats.

■ Companies use SWOT to analyze risks and benefits and create effective strategies to drive their business objectives.

Opportunity Cost: Evaluating the Cost of Each Option

Part of conducting a SWOT analysis is considering the cost of every option. Not only the direct cost of the potential action, but also the cost of missing out on a different option.

Just like a lot of decisions, many situations do not have a clear best option. For example, if you're about to get money back on your tax return, do you pay down your credit card or do you put the money in savings? Both are important goals, so how do you identify which is better?

This is the concept behind opportunity costs. If you put the money in the bank, you've lost the opportunity to pay down your credit card bill, which would save you money. The cost for making this decision is that you must pay the interest charges on your credit card. This is known as **opportunity cost**, and it refers to the cost of passing up another option when making a decision.

Has anyone every told you that "There's no such thing as free lunch"? They were really talking about opportunity costs. Think about it—even if someone offers you a totally free sandwich for lunch, you still have to sacrifice your time to eat that lunch, as well as the opportunity to eat something totally different (and potentially tastier). In business, the choices are often complex, as are the financial calculations. Financial statements provide the information necessary to determine the actual cost of each opportunity.

Sometimes, one choice is clearly the better choice when looked at through the opportunity cost method. For example, let's say that your business could make a 5 percent profit on an investment in a partner company. The money going into this investment could be put into a savings account, but it would only generate a 2 percent profit in the same period of time. The cost of missing out on the high-yield savings account is outweighed by the greater profit from the investment.

Which option has more opportunity costs?

However, opportunity costs are not limited to purely financial factors. Opportunity costs can be non-financial, such as lost time, effort expended, or any other non-financial benefit. Let's say you decided to go to an art show tonight that has an admission of five dollars. However, the cost of going is more than five bucks. The opportunity cost is two hours of your time, mileage put on your car to get there, and missing out on the possibility of hanging out with other friends not attending the show, going to the movies, studying, and so on.

Do It...

2.2: Apply SWOT and Opportunity Cost Apply the concepts of SWOT and opportunity costs to a high school senior's decision whether to (a) attend college or (b) immediately pursue the work force instead. (Assume the student could get a job, but one that pays less than a job he or she could get after earning a college degree.) Limit your response to one page and be prepared to submit it electronically or present it to your class.

Now Debrief...

- In business, a **risk** any circumstance in which the outcome of a decision or action is uncertain. The greater the risk, the larger the difference between a favorable or unfavorable outcome. It is necessary to take risks to succeed, and figuring out how serious a risk is part of making any decision.
- One tool that helps companies assess risk is a **SWOT analysis**, which helps companies make decisions by identifying all possible factors that could help or hinder their objectives.
- SWOT stands for **strengths**, **weaknesses**, **opportunities**, and **threats**. Companies use SWOT to analyze risks and benefits and create effective strategies to drive their business objectives.
- **Opportunity cost** is the cost of passing up another option by making a decision.

3. Managing Risk: Diversification, Mergers, and Acquisitions

You've heard the expression "Don't put all your eggs in one basket." You don't put all your eggs in one basket because if you drop the basket or it gets lost, you lose all your eggs at once. But what if you spread your eggs among different baskets? Or put some eggs in a basket, some in a bucket, and a few in a box? Or give some eggs to your friends to hold on to? That way, if something happens to one basket, the other eggs should still be fine. We have discussed risk, SWOT analysis, and opportunity cost. Now we'll go into detail about smart financial strategies to help manage the necessary risks of doing business.

Diversification

What do eggs in a basket have to do with business? Well, like eggs in a basket, a company can't put all of its money and resources in one place. If something went wrong, it would lose everything at once. That's why businesses use an approach known as **diversification**, which means spreading resources out over several different areas. Investing all of a company's money in one stock or one venture would be risky and probably not the best use of that money. Diversification is a method of managing risk.

Diversification

Low

What is the risk of putting all your eggs in one basket?

Most employees have one source of income. If you're an employee, then, what happens if you get laid off? Suddenly, you have no source of income. If instead you have a second job, income from a rental property, or maybe income from a hobby, then you still have a source of income after the layoff. (You might also consider ways to diversify your skills so if a layoff should occur, you'll be more attractive to other employers.)

"Take calculated risks. That is quite different from being rash."
—George S. Patton, United States Army General[8]

Just as you can benefit from diversifying your income, so can companies. For example, in 2007, Google showed that it was diversifying its sources of income when it announced it was developing software for cell phones.[9] A little over a year later, in February 2009, Google announced that it was again diversifying by providing to software to make 1.5 million books available on mobile devices such as the iPhone.[10] Basically, Google was expanding its options. Even if one of these software applications failed, Google would still have plenty of other technologies that provide a platform for the advertising that brings money into the company.

Sometimes, businesses diversify their income because they perceive risks to their future success. For instance, the Philip Morris Companies (now known as the Altria Group) anticipated that the cigarette industry would start to decline as early as the 1960s. So, it began to look for ways to make money other than from tobacco sales. Over the next few decades, Philip Morris bought several other companies, including Miller Brewing, General Foods, Kraft, and Oscar Meyer. By 1989, tobacco products accounted for only 40 percent of sales for Philip Morris.[11]

Mergers and Acquisitions

It seems that major headlines about deals between companies that are worth hundreds of millions of dollars are in the news on a weekly basis. Should you cheer or boo at these headlines? To answer this question, you need to understand the different types of deals. Although the terms are often used interchangeably, mergers and acquisitions are not exactly the same.

- A **merger** takes place when two companies agree to go forward as a single new company. For example, both Daimler-Benz and Chrysler ceased to exist when the two firms merged, and a new company, DaimlerChrysler, was created.[12]
- An **acquisition** occurs when one company takes over another company and sets itself up as the new owner. You might think of an acquisition of one company swallowing up another. Earlier you read about some of the acquisitions of Philip Morris.

So, why do companies join together? For one, mergers and acquisitions are sometimes methods through which companies diversify and manage their risk.

For example, companies may join with other companies that offer different types of products, thus increasing the diversity of their product lines. Yum brands, a large fast-food company, owns KFC, Taco Bell, Pizza Hut, Long John Silver, and A&W, among others.[13] This company has covered pretty much all fast-food bases with its diverse offerings.

Other reasons companies join together include:

- entering other geographical areas, and
- taking over a competitor to get a competitive advantage, a specialized piece of information, or a patent.

Let's say you own a regional grocery store. Your store is becoming increasingly popular in the tri-state area where it is located, and it feels like it's time to expand. By purchasing another regional chain that is spread out across a different area, you'd be entering a new market that could bring major new business. Purchasing a major competitor can also be a huge step in eliminating competition.

Mergers and acquisitions do carry risks, however, and performing a SWOT analysis and calculating opportunity costs are necessary in determining whether a merger or acquisition is wise.

Thriving in Diversification: When Less Can Be More

Many companies churn out huge numbers of products each year. It may seem, then, that to succeed in business you must find a way to sell millions of each of your products. But that is not always the case. Some companies thrive in diversification—they offer many different products to choose from, even though some products will sell in very small amounts.

Business journalist and *Wired* editor Chris Anderson[14] recognized that instead of selling millions of a single product, successful companies are selling a few units of millions of products. It makes sense if you consider a few examples. Think about the online music retailer Rhapsody, which has a library of about 1.5 million songs. It carries about 1,000 very popular songs, which are each downloaded more than 10,000 times in an average month.

However, in addition to those songs, Rhapsody also offers about 1,499,000 other ones. These less popular songs sell some, although the numbers are considerably lower than for the top songs. A store that sells a physical product would have to limit its inventory to only the most popular music. An online retailer, however, can offer the complete library. Every song added to the library will find some audience, even if it consists of just a handful of people. Anderson named this phenomenon *the long tail*.

You're probably familiar with this concept. Have you ever wanted to rent a cult classic movie you couldn't find in a traditional video store? You might have relied on an online retailer, such as Netflix. Anderson points out that a traditional video store with only a storefront can only offer the most popular movies. Netflix, however, can maintain a library of tens of thousands of titles. Many of those titles may be considered obscure or unpopular, but the demand for them doesn't simply disappear. Stores just can't afford to offer them, so they are often phased out. Netflix takes advantage of these niche markets by offering those movies to the people who want them.

Do It...

2.3: Identify How Diversification Reduces Risk Symantec, a computer software security company, recently acquired Mi5 Networks, a privately held Web security company. How do you think Symantec has reduced its risk by purchasing Mi5? Research both companies online and explain how this acquisition reduces Symantec's risk. Limit your response to one page, and be prepared to submit it electronically or present it to your class.

Now Debrief...

- One way that companies manage risk is through **diversification**, which is a method of spreading out resources over several different areas.
- Two ways companies diversify is through mergers and acquisitions. A **merger** involves two companies agreeing to go forward as a single new company, whereas an **acquisition** involves one company taking over another company and setting itself up as the new owner.
- Other reasons companies join together include entering a new geographical area, gaining a competitive advantage, and gaining specialized information.
- Companies can also diversify be selling a wide variety of products in small quantities. These are known as *long-tail companies*.

4. Making Financing Decisions

You've heard the clichés a hundred times. *Money doesn't grow on trees. Nothing in life is free. Money makes the world go round.* These sayings may be trite, but there's a lot of truth to them. Almost everyone will encounter situations in their life in which they have to make tough financial decisions. Paying for college is one of them. Should you take out student loans? Get a part-time job? To figure out your best choice, you need to know your options.

The same goes for any business. To build a business and make good strategic decisions, company leaders need to know their financing options and the risks associated with each. In this section, we discuss the financing options available to businesses, both for short-term and long-term needs.

Financing for the Short Term

Sometimes, businesses find themselves in a position where money is needed right away. An imbalance in cash flow, often caused when a company must wait for late payments from customers, can be a major disaster if the company has large bills coming due. What does a company do when it needs money now that it doesn't have?

One option is to borrow money. When a business borrows money, it pays a fee (called *interest*) for the use of that money. The amount is said to be *financed*. Over time, the amount borrowed is repaid plus the interest.

Which tools do you think are used most often? Which ones carry the most risk?

Financing for a period of one year or less is generally known as **short-term financing**. Funds such as these are usually borrowed so a company can run day-to-day operations. The company might need inventory or supplies, or it might need to pay wages to its employees. Short-term financing might also be used if work has to be interrupted for some reason. For example, a pool contractor might be out of work for a few weeks if there is a concrete shortage and would therefore require short-term financing to stay afloat.

Where do companies go for short-term financing? Deciding which type of financing to use depends on the company's particular situation and the flexibility it wants to maintain.

Friends, Family, and Credit Cards

One resource many small business owners tap is family and friends. The problem with this option is that there is a risk of damaging relationships if something goes wrong.

1. Family, Friends, and Credit Cards

Another source of short-term financing is credit cards. A credit card is issued by a financial company and allows the holder to borrow funds at the moment of sale. When you swipe your credit card, you're borrowing the amount of money needed to make a purchase. That money must be paid back at a later time. Credit cards charge interest and are therefore primarily used for short-term financing. Interest usually begins one month after a purchase is made, and the company sets borrowing limits on the card based on a set credit rating. Credit cards have higher interest rates than most loans, so they can become very expensive if not paid off in full every month.

Bank Sources

There are several types of short-term loans that banks grant to businesses.

2. Bank Sources

- A **secured loan** is backed by something of value, such as property or inventory. The valuable item(s) backing the loan are known as *collateral*. If the loan isn't paid back, the bank can seize the collateral. If a business were to put up its office building as collateral and fail to repay the loan, the bank could claim ownership of the office building.
- A less common type of loan is an **unsecured loan**. This is exactly what it sounds like: The bank lends money with no collateral backing it up. These kinds of loans are generally only given to trusted customers or to companies perceived to be extremely financially stable.
- Another arrangement for businesses with good relationships with the bank is a **line of credit**. This allows a business to borrow short-term funds, up to a set amount, whenever it is necessary without having to apply for a new loan every time.

Bank loans are a great way for businesses to get quick money to cover short-term expenses.

Pledging or Factoring Accounts Receivable

Companies can also use accounts receivable to generate short-term funding if necessary. For example, businesses can use accounts receivable as collateral for a bank loan; this is known as **pledging**. The company can

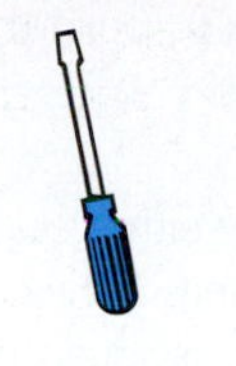

borrow an amount that is less than the receivables. The bank takes into account that some receivables may never be paid, especially those that have been owed for longer periods of time. The advantage to the borrowing company is that this type of financing frees up money that is stuck in accounts receivables.

Suppose it takes 30, 60, or even 90 days for customers to pay their bills for the T-shirts your company sells. At any given time, you might have done a lot of business, but you're still waiting for the payment from the customers to roll in. This type of loan gives your company money to spend while you're waiting for your customers to pay.

Another option for generating short-term funds with accounts receivable is **factoring**. This is the sale of accounts receivable to a third party at a discounted rate in exchange for immediate cash. The rate depends on how old the accounts receivable are, the kind of business, and the current condition of the economy.

Let's say you've sold a lot of T-shirts but not many customers are paying up, and now you're hard up for cash to keep the business running. You have $1,500 in invoices (your accounts receivable), but you're worried that you're not going to get paid. To get some cash fast, you could find someone willing to buy these invoices for less than what they're worth. After you sell the invoices, that person is now responsible for collecting money from your customers. That person can still make a profit on the exchange since it has bought the accounts receivable for less than they're worth.

Financing for the Long Term

Not all financing needs are short term in nature. If you have a mortgage or a student loan, you're already familiar with long-term financing. **Long-term financing** involves repaying a loan over periods longer than one year. Companies use long-term financing to pay for fixed assets such as property, manufacturing facilities, and equipment that will be used over the course of many years. Long-term financing can also be used to pay for major acquisitions of other companies.

Businesses have several ways of obtaining long-term financing; the method they choose depends on the level of risk, and the company's finances and strategic goals.

Debt Financing

When a company borrows money that it has a legal obligation to repay, the company is using **debt financing**. There are two main debt-financing options: long-term bank loans and bonds.

1. A company can raise money by taking a *long-term bank loan*, which is typically paid off in three to seven years, but sometimes extends 15 to 30 years. Banks are willing to make these types of loans because of the potential payoff. The greater the risk of issuing a long-term loan, the higher the interest rate the bank charges to the business.
2. When the rates for bank loans are too high or the amount of financing needed exceeds what a bank is willing to offer, issuing bonds is another option. A **bond** is basically an agreement to lend money that will be repaid at a later date.

Companies typically issue bonds in order to finance a business venture, and investors in these bonds might be individuals or institutions. In return for lending the money, the individuals or institutions become creditors. As a result, they receive a promise that the company will repay them their money, with interest. There are secured bonds, which are backed with collateral of some kind, and unsecured bonds, which are backed only by the company's promise and reputation.

Before a company decides to issue bonds, it needs to consider the overall cost of issuing the bonds. For example, it may not be a good move to issue bonds if the interest rate is too high for the company to afford. The length of the bond is also important to consider. Generally, the longer the bond term, the riskier the venture. It's hard to predict the future, so agreeing to pay back the bond at a certain time may not be realistic for a company.

Companies that rely on debt to finance aggressive growth or acquisitions are known to be *highly leveraged*. Their strategy is to use other people's money to build their business. It's risky, but it sometimes pays off.

Equity Financing

In **equity financing**, a company raises money by either selling stock to investors, or withdrawing it from the owners' retained earnings (which we discussed earlier). *Stock* is a share of ownership in a company. Investors can be individuals or institutions that become known as *shareholders*, and in return for the money they paid, they receive ownership interests in the company.

If a company wants to expand without taking on more debt, selling stock may be an option. The major downside of selling stock is giving up some control of the company. Holders of stock become partial owners of a company, and they often have voting rights on company decisions. This is risky for the company because even though shareholders don't manage the company's day-to-day operations, they do have a say in the board of directors, which is the group of people who manage a company.

Also, stock prices fluctuate according to the whims of investors. For example, bad publicity can cause some investors to sell a company's stock, which will cause the stock's price to fall. If a company's stock price were to drop too much, investors might sell all their stock for fear of further losses, which can put the company at risk by affecting its net worth.

Offering stock is not an easy matter, as a company must meet requirements set by the Securities and Exchange Commission as well as state agencies. The public also has to be interested in buying stock, as no one wants partial ownership of a company that is going to fail.

When a company first makes stock available to the public it is known as an *initial public offering (IPO)*. The company gets the money from the stock purchase, but then part of the company is in the hands of the public to be bought, sold, and traded. Smaller, younger companies that are looking for money to expand often issue IPOs, but they can also be offered by large, privately owned companies that want to become publicly traded.

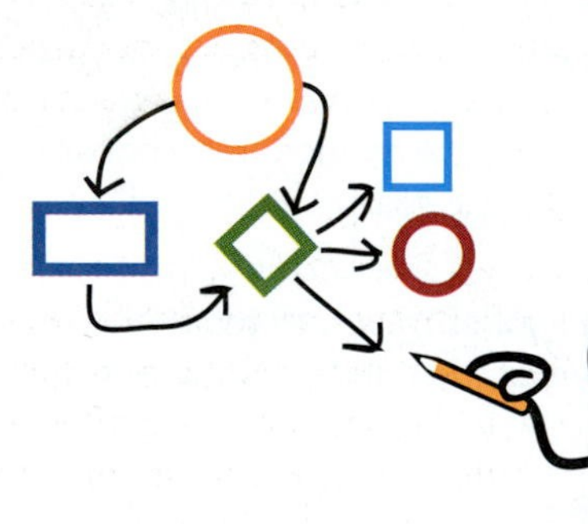

Do It...

2.4: Rank Financing Options Below is a list of the short- and long-term financing options that we discussed in this section. Which of the options do you think would have the highest interest rate? Second highest? Rank them all and then explain the trade-offs between the options that you think have the highest interest rates and those with the lowest. Why would any business owner choose to use the options that have relatively high interest rates?

- Short-term financing options: *family/friends, credit cards, unsecured loans, secured loans, line of credit, pledging/factoring*
- Long-term financing options: *long-term bank loans, issuing bonds, selling stock*

Now Debrief...

- **Short-term financing** is financing for a period of one year or less. It is usually used by companies to cover immediate expenses. Short-term financing options include friends and family, credit cards, trade credit, bank sources (**secured loans**, **unsecured loans**, and a **line of credit**), **pledging**, and **factoring**.
- **Long-term financing** is financing that lasts for a period of more than a year. Two types of long-term financing include **debt financing** and **equity financing**.
- **Debt financing** involves borrowing money from outside sources to finance business operations. Long-term loans and issuing bonds are two options for long-term financing.
- **Equity financing** involves raising money from either retained earnings or the sale of stock.

5. Wise Investing

"The poor and middle class work for money. The rich have money work for them."

—Robert Kiyosaki, author of *Rich Dad, Poor Dad*[15]

As you've seen, putting all your eggs in one basket probably isn't the best way to manage your finances. It makes more sense to spread your investments out over a wide variety of options. ■ Measuring risk versus return is the key to any investment decision. If the company you've invested all your money in goes bust, your savings will go down the tubes along with the company.

In this section, you'll learn about making intelligent investments with a high potential for reward. As you'll see, if you make wise investments in the stock market, you'll find yourself in much better financial shape over time, with greater assets and fewer liabilities. (And for more information about personal finance, check out Chapter 20 at **www.mybizlab.com**.)

Investment Options

You know that companies often rely on selling stocks and bonds to finance operations. People invest in these companies in hopes of making a profit from their investments. A **portfolio** is a collection of these investments. There are several different types of investments that can make up a portfolio.

What comes to mind when you see the New York Stock Exchange floor?

Stocks Investing in stocks can be a risky proposition—it can pay off big, or it can blow up in your face. As you've learned, when you buy stock, you're essentially buying a small slice of ownership in the company. Stock is purchased through a stock exchange, which is an organization where members can buy and sell securities for companies and individual investors. You may be paid a **dividend** on your stock, which is a portion of the company's earnings. For example, if you own stock in CSX Corp, you might receive a dividend of $0.22 for each share you own. *Big deal*, you might be thinking. *Twenty-two cents doesn't seem like much.* But if you have thousands of shares and then you use your dividends to buy more stock, you can make a lot of money over the years.

Bonds Bonds are another investment that are part of your portfolio. As you learned earlier, companies issue bonds to investors to generate money. Bonds must be paid back in full by a set date, with interest. The advantage of purchasing bonds compared to stocks is that a return is more secure than with a stock, as bonds are often issued with collateral. A disadvantage of bonds when compared to stocks is that the bondholder does not have any ownership of the company and has no say in company decisions.

Mutual Funds **Mutual funds** are a somewhat different investment option. These are organizations that collect investors' money, pool it, and buy a variety of stocks and bonds. Some mutual funds purchase only government securities, whereas others specialize in specific industries, foreign companies, or high-risk, high-return investments.

A major advantage of investing in mutual funds is that the fund managers do the hard work of research and diversification, so if one investment fails, the losses should be balanced by gains among other investments in the fund. The disadvantage is that you have to trust someone else's financial judgment, and there is always the possibility that the fund manager's judgment is wrong. In addition, a portion of the money you invest in mutual funds is collected as fees to pay the money managers who make the investment decisions on behalf of the fund.

■ Measuring risk versus return is the key to any investment decision.

Your Portfolio Choices

The sum total of your investments—stocks, bonds, and mutual funds—makes up your investment portfolio. What are the best types of investments to keep in your portfolio?

Figure **2.3** | **Bear Markets Over the Past 50 Years**

Start	End
1. 12/12/1961	6/26/1962
2. 2/9/1966	10/7/1966
3. 11/29/1968	5/26/1970
4. 1/11/1973	10/3/1974
5. 11/28/1980	8/12/1982
6. 8/25/1987	12/4/1987
7. 7/16/1990	10/11/1990
8. 3/27/2000	7/18/2002

The answer probably depends on whom you ask. Every asset has the potential to make money, but it also runs a risk of losing money. Stocks tend to fluctuate over time. You've probably seen the terms *bull market* and *bear market* on the news. Simply put, a bull market happens when the stock market rises for an extended period of time. A bear market happens when the stock market falls for an extended period of time. Figure 2.3 displays eight bear markets over the last 50 years. Bull and bear markets can greatly affect the value of your assets. A bear market, for example, can greatly reduce your returns.

One way you might manage these risks is to have a mix of investments. You might have some long-term investments, but you could also have assets that won't fluctuate as much as stocks do. That way, even if your long-term investments aren't making money at the moment, your other assets will help balance them out.[16] The mix of investments in a portfolio is called **portfolio diversification**.

There is no one ideal way to diversify—it's something every investor does a little bit differently. The mix must be appropriate for a specific investor, and it will change throughout the investor's lifetime. You might be willing to take on more risk when you're younger because you have more time before retirement to make back any money you lose. As you get older, you might shift to less volatile investments to make sure you don't lose your retirement fund.

On the flip side, the more money you have to invest, the more likely you will be willing to tolerate higher risk in continuing to build wealth. After all, the idea is to continually increase the amount of money you have to invest, which should lead to a more diverse portfolio, which will hopefully continue to generate more wealth.

There are two general types of portfolio diversification: vertical and horizontal.

- *Vertical diversification* spreads your money between different types of assets. You might hold government bonds, corporate bonds, property, and stocks. They each behave slightly differently, so no matter how conditions change, you should have some return from your investments.
- *Horizontal diversification* is the situation in which you have assets that address different aspects of the same situation. A classic example describes a company that makes ice cream and a company that makes umbrellas. If the weather is hot and sunny, customers will flock to the company that makes ice cream. If the weather is rainy and gloomy for weeks, people will rely on the company that sells umbrellas. If you own stock in both companies, you will have a return no matter what the conditions are.

The investment choices and diversification strategies are plentiful and are entirely your choice, but it is important to remember not to put all your eggs in one basket.

Don't Forget the Cash: Liquidity

Earlier in this chapter, you learned that the term *liquidity* describes how easily an asset can be converted into cash. For example, money in a checking account is said to be very liquid. You have instant access to money in your checking account. You can withdraw funds any time you need—even online. Now that you know more about investments, you can better appreciate the importance of liquidity.

When you open a savings account at a bank, you're told the current interest rate. Interest on a savings account is the amount the bank pays you to use your money. The money you get back for putting your money in a savings account is the return on your investment. For a simple savings account, the interest rate is generally low—less than 2 percent. A certificate of deposit (CD), a bank account that is insured, but with a fixed interest rate for a short period of time, usually offers a somewhat higher rate of return. The drawback can be that you're not allowed to withdraw the money before a specified date without a penalty. Although the CD provides a higher rate of return, it is less liquid than the savings account because the money is tied up for a certain period of time.

Despite the small difference, bank accounts, CDs, and savings bonds are considered liquid because they can be quickly converted to cash even if there is some penalty. Even common stocks are basically liquid because they can usually be sold within a short period of time. The actual liquidity of a stock depends on how often it is traded, which determines how easy it will be for you to sell it.

Investments in objects, such as coins, stamps, and art, are less liquid. You would need to find another collector or a dealer who agrees to purchase them from you. Depending on how quickly you want the cash, you may need to accept a lower return. Real estate is considered the least liquid asset because it can take weeks, months, or even years to sell. Again, your rate of return will depend on how quickly you want to sell the asset.

Why is liquidity important? Understanding liquidity can help companies and individuals make decisions about investing. When you invest in assets, you want to keep liquidity levels in mind. If you underestimate the amount of cash you need, you'll find yourself having to convert assets to cash. This can be time-consuming, expensive, and inefficient.

Here's the bottom line. When you make investment decisions, you need to think about both the short term and the long term. You need to consider risk and liquidity. In the end, investing is a personal process that changes over time. If you know what you're doing and make good decisions, you'll find yourself making money.

Do It...

2.5: Invest Your Money Imagine you have $100,000 to invest across stocks, bonds, and mutual funds. How would you split your investment money up assuming that you won't need the actual cash from it for 20 years? How would you change the portfolio if you needed the money in five years? What made the difference in the two portfolios?

Now Debrief...

- A **portfolio** is the sum total of your investments, including stocks, bonds, and mutual funds.
- A mix of investments in a portfolio is called **portfolio diversification**. Two types of portfolio diversification include *vertical* and *horizontal diversification*.
- The liquidity, or ease with which an asset can be converted to cash, is a consideration in making investments. If you need funding that can be immediately available, more liquid assets are necessary.

Chapter 2 Visual Summary

1. Differentiate an asset from a liability, recognize assets that generate income, and evaluate an organization's financial position by its balance sheet. (pp. 32–36)

- An **asset** is anything owned or controlled that can be exchanged for some value.
- Assets include cash, **accounts receivable, notes receivable, inventory,** and **fixed assets** such as property, plant, and equipment.
- **Liquidity** is the ability of an asset to be converted to cash.
- A **liability** is a legal obligation to pay a debt within a certain period of time.
- Liabilities include **accounts payable** and unpaid employee salaries.
- **Owners' equity** (or **shareholders' equity**) is the amount of money initially invested into a company plus any net profits that the company retains from a specific period.
- A **balance sheet** is a financial statement that records a company's assets and liabilities at a fixed point in time. The **fundamental accounting equation** seen on the balance sheet is Assets = Liabilities + Owners' Equity.

Summary: The balance sheet is a physical representation of a company's assets, liabilities, and owners' equity. In order to be financially healthy, a company's liabilities should not exceed its assets.

2. Appreciate the value and necessity of risk in business by conducting a SWOT analysis and considering opportunity costs. (pp. 37–41)

- In business, a **risk** is any circumstance in which the outcome of a decision or action is uncertain. The greater the risk, the larger the difference between a favorable or unfavorable outcome. Businesses take risks all the time; the important thing is to make sure that the risks are calculated and will pay off.
- A **SWOT analysis** helps companies make decisions by identifying all possible factors that could help or hinder their objectives. SWOT stands for **strengths, weaknesses, opportunities,** and **threats.** Conducting a SWOT analysis is a good idea before making any financial decision.

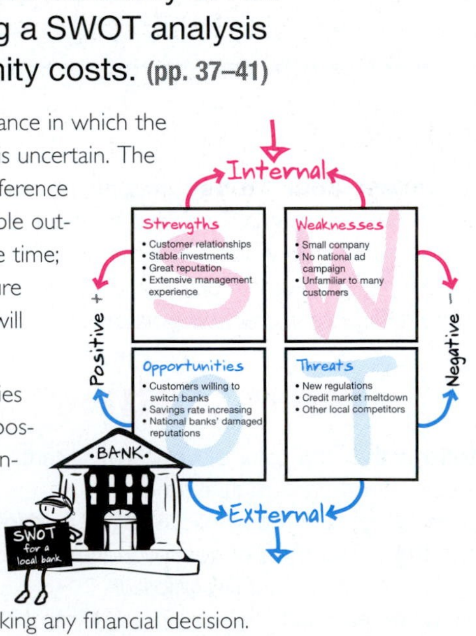

- **Opportunity cost** is the cost of passing up the next best option by making a decision. Every decision has an opportunity cost.

Summary: Business is full of risks, and learning to make the right choice in a risky situation is crucial. Conducting a SWOT analysis can help determine whether a risk is worth taking.

3. Use the concept of diversification to not only manage risk, but also thrive in it. (pp. 41–43)

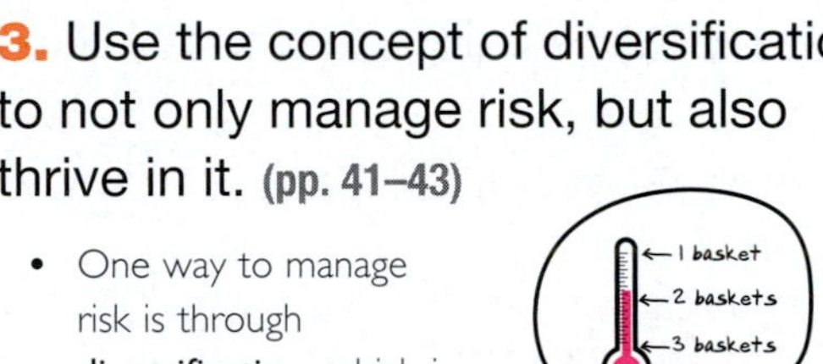

- One way to manage risk is through **diversification,** which is a method of spreading resources over several different areas.
- Mergers and acquisitions are two types of diversification. A **merger** involves two companies agreeing to go forward as a single new company. An **acquisition** involves one company taking over another company and setting itself up as the new owner.
- Companies also diversify by selling a wide variety of products in small quantities, which are known as *long tail companies.*

Summary: Not putting all your money and resources in one place is an excellent strategy to manage risk. That way if one venture fails, your business will still have others going that can support it.

4. Make short-term and long-term financing decisions based on risk and diversification. (pp. 43–46)

- Companies and individuals can finance purchases and investments by borrowing money from individuals and banks that is to be paid back with interest.
- **Short-term financing** is financing for a period of one year or less and includes friends and family, credit cards, **pledging**, and **factoring**. Banks are also a good source of short-term financing that includes **secured loans, unsecured loans**, and a **line of credit**.
- **Long-term financing** lasts for a period of more than a year and includes **debt financing** and **equity financing**.

Summary: Companies often have great expenses that cannot be covered outright with cash. Borrowing allows companies to function better in the meantime, which makes it possible to pay off debt in the long run.

5. Become a wise investor who makes decisions based on risk and diversification. (pp. 47–49)

- A **portfolio** is the sum total of your investments, including stocks, bonds, and **mutual funds.**
- A return is an amount you earn from an investment.
- A **dividend** is a portion of a company's earnings that is paid to stockholders.
- **Portfolio diversification** describes the mix of investments in a portfolio. Two types of portfolio diversification include vertical and horizontal diversification.
- Liquidity should be considered when making investments. If you need funding that can be immediately available, more liquid assets are necessary.

8 Bear Markets

Start	End
1. 12/12/1961	6/26/1962
2. 2/9/1966	10/7/1966
3. 11/29/1968	5/26/1970
4. 1/11/1973	10/3/1974
5. 11/28/1980	8/12/1982
6. 8/25/1987	12/4/1987
7. 7/16/1990	10/11/1990
8. 3/27/2000	7/18/2002

Summary: Regardless of the types of investments you make, it is always important to maintain a diverse portfolio so that all your eggs are not in the same basket.

Get the most out of what you just read by practicing your skills and actually DOING something with the material! The best place to do this is at **www.mybizlab.com**. Here's just some of what is available to you there:

- Apply your skills in an interactive environment with more **BizSkill** experiences...and see if you have what it takes
- Think critically and talk with your peers on hot business topics in **BizChat**
- Flex your business communication skills and build your own portfolio with the **Communication Plan exercises**
- Watch the chapter material come together with **Just Plain Business** videos
- Study on-the-go with **Audio Chapter Summaries** in MP3 format
- Brush up on the lecture and content with **Audio PowerPoints**
- Discover how well you are doing and see what areas you need to improve on with the **Pre-Tests** and **Post-Tests**

Key Words

These key words and more are also available as flash cards to practice with at **www.mybizlab.com**.

1. Differentiate an asset from a liability, recognize assets that generate income, and evaluate an organization's financial position by its balance sheet. **(pp. 32–36)**

asset (p. 32)
accounts receivable (p. 32)
notes receivable (p. 32)
fixed assets (p. 32)
intangible assets (p. 32)
inventory (p. 32)
liquidity (p. 33)
liability (p. 33)
accounts payable (p. 33)
net worth (p. 34)
owners' equity (or shareholders' equity) (p. 34)
retained earnings (p. 34)
balance sheet (p. 34)
fundamental accounting equation (p. 34)

2. Appreciate the value and necessity of risk in business by conducting a SWOT analysis and considering opportunity costs. **(pp. 37–41)**

risk (p. 37)
SWOT analysis (p. 38)
strengths (p. 38)
weaknesses (p. 38)
opportunities (p. 39)
threats (p. 39)
opportunity cost (p. 40)

3. Use the concept of diversification to not only manage risk, but also thrive in it. **(pp. 41–43)**

diversification (p. 41)
merger (p. 42)
acquisition (p. 42)

4. Make short-term and long-term financing decisions based on risk and diversification. **(pp. 43–46)**

short-term financing (p. 44)
secured loan (p. 44)
unsecured loan (p. 44)
line of credit (p. 44)
pledging (p. 44)
factoring (p. 45)
long-term financing (p. 45)
debt financing (p. 45)
bond (p. 45)
equity financing (p. 46)

5. Become a wise investor who makes decisions based on risk and diversification. **(pp. 47–49)**

portfolio (p. 47)
dividend (p. 47)
mutual funds (p. 47)
portfolio diversification (p. 48)

Prove It

Prove It...

Now, let's put on one of the BizHats. With the **Owner/Investor BizHat** squarely on your head, look at the following exercise:

You are an owner of a local housekeeping company that has steadily grown over the past 10 years. You primarily work with businesses in your area, but your company also provides housekeeping services for local residents. Your most recent balance sheet indicates that many of your assets are in accounts receivable and that these are taking longer and longer to collect. The customers of your company form a small but loyal base. You've known many of them for years and wouldn't want to lose them. Identify various financing options that would help keep your business running.

Flip It...

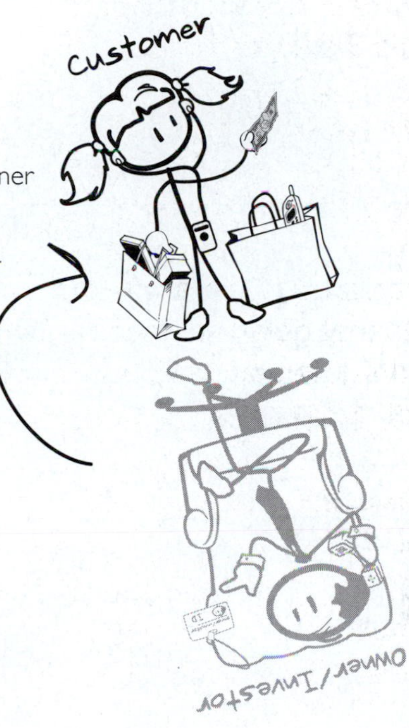

After you've decided on your financing options as the owner above, **flip over to the Customer BizHat**.

You are now the CEO of a local office that uses the housekeeping company described above. You haven't paid for housekeeping services for the past two months, and now you owe $3000. Based on the balance sheet below, why haven't you been able to pay up? What kind of financing options can you use to pay back the housekeeping company?

Assets	
Cash	$15,000
Accounts Receivable	7,000
Inventory	5,000
Total Assets	$27,000
Liabilities and Owners' Equity	
Accounts Payable	$25,000
Owners' Equity	15,000
Total Liabilities and Owners' Equity	$40,000

Now Debrief It...

Compare the perspectives of the two BizHats described above. Did taking the perspective of the customer change your perspective of the owner's situation? How did the balance sheet help you better understand the customer's perspective?

Compete: Economics and Competition

BizSkills invite...

Try It!
There's no better way to learn concepts than to put them into practice. Take your turn in the driver's seat and be a part of actual business decision making by visiting the BizSkill for this chapter at **www.mybizlab.com**.

Start here!

Now that you've practiced making tough business decisions and seeing the results of your choices in this chapter's BizSkill, it's time to translate those skills into plain English. And if you skipped the BizSkill, go back now!

Chapter 3 Goals

After experiencing this chapter, you'll be able to:

1. Describe why and how companies compete in a capitalist economy, and how a focus on sustainability and the triple bottom line keeps companies competitive.
2. Identify the economic principles that dictate how competition occurs.
3. Identify different market structures, and understand how companies in each market structure form competitive business strategies.
4. Explain how the life cycle of an industry, product, or business affects its competitive strategies.

Do you have what it takes to beat the competition?

It's All About Competition

For months, you've trained. You've stretched. You've carbo-loaded. And now, at last, your toe is on the starting line, and you're ready to compete in the marathon. You look around you at the other runners. On an ordinary day, they might be your friends, but today they're your competitors: the people you'll be strategizing against, pushing past for a cup of water, and, ideally, leaving in the dust. Why? To be honest, you're not just running a marathon to see the sights and get some exercise. You want to win (or at least beat your personal best). And you're hardly alone. You're well aware that each of your competitors shares your dream of crossing the finish line fast and first.

Like a marathon, the world of business isn't exactly a jog in the park. You might find yourself acting a lot like a marathoner when you size up your competitors, strategize about ways to get ahead, and give everything you've got—your time, your money, and your talents—to cross the finish line first in your field, whether that means building the best laptop, serving the most customers, or simply making the most money. In the business world, in short, the name of the game is competition. In this chapter, we'll look at competition and the economic principles that dictate how competition occurs. We'll start by examining capitalism.

1. Capitalism: Competing in a Free Market

Competition doesn't suddenly disappear from your life when you finish the marathon, quit the football team, or refuse to play another game of Rock Band. You can't even go out for fast food without running into competition: McDonald's competes with Burger King, Coca Cola competes with PepsiCo. Whether you're ordering a chicken sandwich or working in the back flipping burgers, those companies' competitive relationships shape your fast food experience by affecting how much customers pay for their meals, how much the burger-flipper is paid, which items are on the menu, what the quality of the food is, and many other details. If you live in a **capitalistic economy**—an economic system in which the means to produce goods and services are owned by private interests—you can't avoid competition.

So the United States is a capitalist economy, right? Well, not exactly. It's more of a *mixed market economy*. This just means that the United States borrows elements from different economic systems, like capitalism or socialism, to create an ideal system. You'll learn more about this in Chapter 4. For now just remember that in both capitalistic and mixed market economies, competition plays a very big role.

For example, let's say you decide to open a business installing swimming pools. You'll get the materials you need, hire employees, and prepare advertising. In return, any profits you make belong to you. But can you charge as much as you want to install a new pool? Of course not. If your prices are too high, nobody will buy your product. If your prices are too low, you won't earn a profit. In a capitalistic economy, the types of goods and services produced, the prices charged, and the amount of income received are all determined through the operation of the **free market**.

Of course, the free market doesn't mean that everything is free of cost. In this case, the word *free* refers to people's freedom to choose what they buy and sell. For example, when you buy a DVD, you voluntarily exchange your money for a copy of the latest Oscar-winning film; no one is forcing you to buy that particular movie from that particular store. An employee voluntarily exchanges his or her time and labor for money. In return, a company voluntarily

What does it mean to cross the finish line first?

"A business that makes nothing but money is a poor kind of business."
—Henry Ford[1]

exchanges money for employees' time and labor. Both parties take part in an exchange because they have something to gain. If they didn't expect to gain, they wouldn't agree to the exchange.

Competing in the 21st Century: Sustainability and the Triple Bottom Line

Think about that swimming pool company you started in the last section. You're competing with other swimming pool builders for customers and money in order to make your business a financial success. But how, exactly, do you *measure* success? Is a company successful if it earns a profit for six months, one year, or maybe 10 years?

Often, if people see profits early on for a new company, they may call the company a success. However, focusing on short-term profitability doesn't give you the big picture. Today, a better measure of success is *sustainability*. In 1987, the World Commission on Environment and Development defined sustainable development as meeting "the needs of the present without compromising the ability of future generations to meet their own needs."[2]

What does that mean exactly? **Sustainability** is the capacity for an organization to create profit for its shareholders today while making sure that its business interests are also in the best interests of the environment and other stakeholders for the future. As we noted in Chapter 1, *stakeholders* are all people who have an interest in an organization. This may include employees, suppliers, and the community. *Shareholders* are the people who actually own a company and directly benefit from its profits. The good news about a sustainable business is that it stands an excellent chance of beating out the competition, being more successful tomorrow, and remaining successful for generations.

The Triple Bottom Line

One way companies can measure their own sustainability is by looking not just at their bottom line, but at their **triple bottom line**.[3] The triple bottom line approach to sustainability suggests that when organizations benefit, this benefit echoes throughout society—people have jobs and money to buy goods, establish a home, and ensure a high standard of living. When this happens, it's an indicator that the economy is going strongly, which is good for the overall economic health of society. In essence, ■ the triple bottom line focuses on three aspects of the corporate bottom line: social, environmental, and economic—people, planet, and profits.

Let's take a look at the first of those three "Ps"—people. Triple bottom line companies employ fair business practices toward their employees and their communities. These businesses don't use child labor, they maintain safe work environments, and they pay fair salaries. But true triple bottom line companies take things a step further by contributing to the growth of their communities through initiatives like health and education programs. One company walking the talk is TOMS Shoes. For every pair of shoes the company sells, it donates a pair to a child in need. To date, the company has given away 140,000 pairs of shoes to children around the world.[4]

■ The triple bottom line focuses on three aspects of the corporate bottom line: social, environmental, and economic—people, planet, and profits.

Companies that follow the triple bottom line approach also work to reduce their impact on the planet. For example, they might manage their consumption of energy, reduce their waste, and dispose of that waste in a way that minimally impacts the environment. Take 3M, the company that makes Scotch tape and Post-It notes. In 2005, 3M celebrated the 30th anniversary of its Pollution Prevention Pays (3P) program.[5] Rather than cleaning up pollution once it's been created, the 3P program aims to prevent pollution before it's made. Since the 3P program's inception, it has prevented more than 2.9 billion pounds of pollutants from being released into the environment—and it's saved 3M nearly $1.2 billion. The company has been able to do this through product reformulation, equipment redesign, and recycling and reuse of waste materials.[6] Clearly, 3M's program is good for the environment, good for the people who live in the environment, and good for the profits of its shareholders.

This whole sustainability discussion might make you feel warm and fuzzy about seemingly selfless companies, but a triple bottom line approach actually *makes a company more competitive*. In fact, authors Andrew Savitz and Karl Weber[7] argue that sustainable development is not simply an activity added onto a business plan; it *is* the business plan. Unlike traditional business models, which focus solely on profits, the triple bottom line approach recognizes that a company needs profits, but also needs to keep its employees happy and healthy and to protect the environment.

So, organizations following the triple bottom line approach do still think about profit. They just think about it in a different way compared to other companies. Followers of the triple bottom line see profit as the economic benefit enjoyed by all stakeholders involved. This belief has worked out pretty well, too. In fact, over the past three years, companies listed on the Dow Jones Sustainability Index (www.sustainability-index.com), which tracks the performance of sustainable businesses, have outperformed similar companies on national stock exchanges by 15 to 25 percent.[8] We'll discuss other steps companies take to become socially responsible in Chapter 8.

Sustainability and You It's clear that following a sustainable business plan can make companies competitive, but what does this mean for you? As a customer, you can personally support sustainability by, for example, seeking out sustainably fished seafood the next time you buy fish. Some fisheries use wasteful and destructive practices by overfishing a region of the ocean. Although overfishing may lead to short-term profits, these fisheries are threatening the future of the fishing industry as well as the people who depend on fishing for their livelihood.

In 1996, the World Wildlife Fund and Unilever, one of the biggest buyers of frozen fish, started an initiative to ensure the future of the world's fisheries. By carefully choosing the fisheries from which it purchases resources, Unilever is focusing on the sustainability of its **supply chain**—the chain a product travels through from raw materials to the consumer.[9] Decisions like these are good news for the planet, but they also keep companies like Unilever competitive. Unilever ensures that it can remain in the fish business for years to come, and eco-conscious customers might vote with their wallets and loyally purchase the Unilever brand.

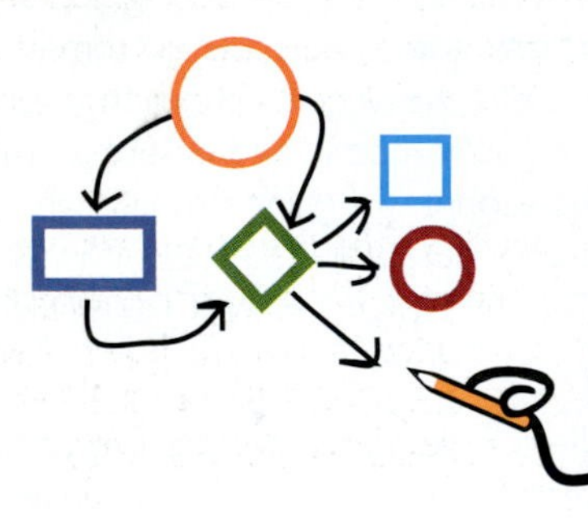

Do It...

3.1: Consider a Triple Bottom Line Strategy A company that supplies meat to a major fast-food restaurant recently changed its farming methods so that it now provides a larger living area for its animals. Together with two teammates, put on the Customer, Owner/Investor, and Manager BizHats (one to each team member), and describe how this decision might affect the hat you have been assigned. Limit your response to one page, and be prepared to submit it electronically or present it to your class.

Now Debrief...

- Companies compete in order to succeed in a **capitalistic economy**—an economic system in which the means to produce goods and services are owned by private interests.
- Customers determine which goods and services are supplied, and prices for those goods and services are set through voluntary exchanges that individuals and businesses make in the **free market**.
- The success of a modern company is no longer measured by monetary profits alone. Instead, companies use the ideas of **sustainability** and the **triple bottom line** to provide social value, environmental value, and economic value—paying attention to people, the planet, and profits.

2. The Rules of Competition

When you're running a marathon, you're willing to do whatever it takes to win. However, you're not exactly *allowed* to do whatever it takes. You can't trip your fellow racers, you can't hop in a cab halfway through and ride to the finish line, and you can't use steroids to gain an advantage. Unless you're Superman, the laws of physics also govern you; your body can only move at certain speeds and in certain ways. No matter how much you'd love to fly to the finish line, it's just not going to happen.

"The most important single central fact about a free market is that no exchange takes place unless both parties benefit."

—Nobel Prize winning economist Milton Friedman[10]

Every competition has rules, and business competition is no exception. If you want your company (or your personal bank account) to succeed, you'll need to know a few things about economics, which dictates many of the rules of the game. Once you're familiar with some basic economic concepts, you'll be able to use them to your advantage.

Economics: What Are You Buying Today?

This may surprise you, but economics is the study of *you*. More specifically, economics is the study of how you get the things you want and the things you need. That is, **economics** aims to understand and predict how people behave as they try to fulfill their wants and needs.

■ The field of economics tries to describe how both individuals and nations behave in response to certain material constraints.

Economics makes the assumption that we humans generally try to fulfill our self-interests. It also assumes that we're rational in our efforts to fulfill our wants and needs. Take a moment to think about this from your own perspective. You have limited resources, or money, with which to fulfill your wants and needs. As a result, you need to make choices with your money. You might spend some money on rent and utilities. Then you'll have to decide what to do with what you have left. You obviously need to eat. Will you buy food at the grocery store and cook your own meals, or eat out? You probably need some form of transportation. Will you buy a new car, a used car, or a subway token?

Economists are truly interested in the choices you make, and they want to know why you make them. They're also interested in predicting what choices you'd make if conditions changed. They want to know whether you'd still go the movie theater if the price of a movie ticket rose by five dollars. In essence, ■ the field of economics tries to describe how both individuals and nations behave in response to certain material constraints.

Limited Resources

You probably know all too well that you don't have all the time in the world. In other words, time is a limited resource. And, unless you have a money tree in your backyard, so is income. Companies have limited resources, too—not only time and money, but also employees, machinery, natural resources, and so on.

In fact, all resources are scarce—that is, there's not an infinite supply of anything. The concept that resources are limited is known in economics as **scarcity**. Because resources are scarce, not everyone can have everything they want or even what they need. Just think about gasoline. Cars are just about everywhere, and most need gas to work. However, gas is made from oil, which is not plentiful or cheap. This means that not everyone can have as much gas as he or she would like. If gas was free and people could get all of it they *wanted*, the oil supply would run out quickly—and most likely permanently. Sometimes—in fact, most of the time—people can't have it all.

Because resources are scarce, they have to be rationed, and in a free market economy, resources are rationed through prices. What does this mean exactly? Prices are determined by the relationship between supply and demand. We'll explain how prices are based on the balance between supply and demand in a bit, but for now, let's talk about how the supply and demand of a product are determined.

Supply and Demand

Even if you're not a video game aficionado, chances are good that you've heard of the popular game console, the Nintendo Wii. Maybe you even waited in line for hours when Nintendo released the first Wii in November 2006. And you weren't alone: Demand for the Wii was tremendous. Shipments disappeared from stores before new consoles could even be stocked on shelves. Plenty of people who'd been planning to buy a Wii as a holiday present ended up on "Wii waiting lists" instead.

What, then, was so different about the Wii? The difference between the Wii and other consoles, like the Xbox 360 or the Playstation 3, was that the Wii had a low price and advertised itself as focusing on family-friendly games. Because of this, there were more people who wanted to purchase a Wii than there were consoles available. The number of Wii game systems that people wanted to buy at the price offered is the **demand**. The number of Wii game systems offered by Nintendo is the **supply**. In this case, the demand for Wii game systems was greater than the supply.

If business is a competition, supply and demand are two of the most important terms in the rulebook. In fact, following the rules of supply and demand can actually give you a substantial leg up in your race to the finish line by helping your company turn a profit or allowing you to save a few dollars when it's time to purchase that next big game system.

The Quantity Demanded

Let's say that, in November 2006, you were among the millions of adoring Wii fans—or wanted to join their ranks. The Wii cost $250 at that point, and you were happy to fork over the money. But what would you have done if the Wii had cost more—say, $1,000? Your answer would probably depend on what you'd have to give up in order to buy a Wii. Maybe you'd still make the purchase if the price was raised to $300, but if it went higher than that, you'd decide you had other purchases you'd rather make. You could put that extra money toward next month's rent or dinner at a fancy restaurant . . . or you could even decide to spend it on a different video game system, like an Xbox 360 (which costs about $300).

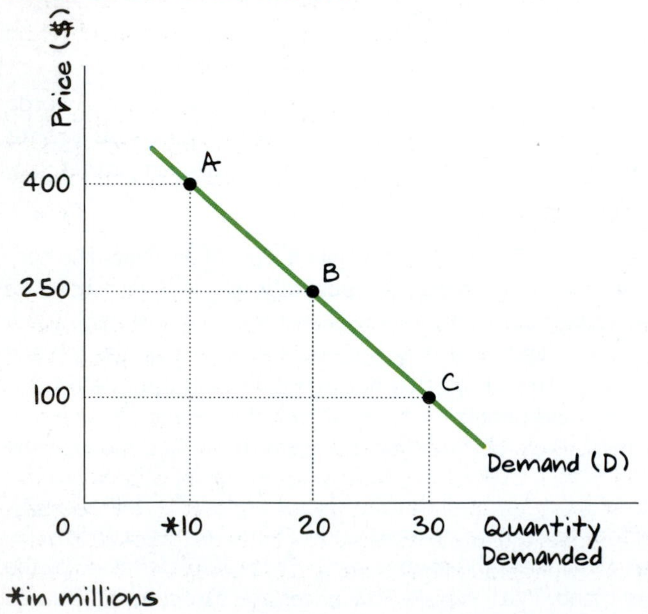

To sum things up, if the price of the Wii had gone up, you might have decided not to buy it. Plenty of other potential customers would have felt the same way, and far fewer people would have been clamoring for a $1,000 Wii. In other words, the price increase would have caused demand for the product to go down. When prices go up, demand generally goes down; when prices go down, demand generally goes up.

Figure **3.1** | **Hypothetical Demand Curve for the Wii**

You can see this relationship between price and demand for yourself on the graph in Figure 3.1. The horizontal axis on the graph tells you how many Wii consoles the general public is willing to buy, and the vertical axis tells you how much the Wii costs. (The numbers on the graph are only hypothetical, but they should give you some idea of what actually goes on in the "real world.") You can see that when the Wii is priced at $250, the public is willing to buy a whopping 20 million Wiis. Things get even rosier for potential Wii buyers when the price drops to $100; now the quantity demanded rises to 30 million consoles. But if the price rises to $400, people aren't as interested, and the demand drops to 10 million consoles. It's worth knowing that a graph representing demand isn't always an exact straight line. More often, it's a curve, which is why it's known as the *demand curve*.

Factors that Influence Demand

Like everything else in economics, the demand curve depends on the customers who are demanding (or not demanding) the product. If their situation changes in some way, the entire demand curve may also change, or shift. Imagine that you get a raise at work. As a result, your income is higher, and you can afford to spend more on a Wii. If enough other people also get raises, they'll also be willing to splurge on a pricier game system, and Nintendo can afford to make the Wii more expensive without fear of losing profit.

Figure **3.2** | **A Shift in the Demand Curve for the Wii**

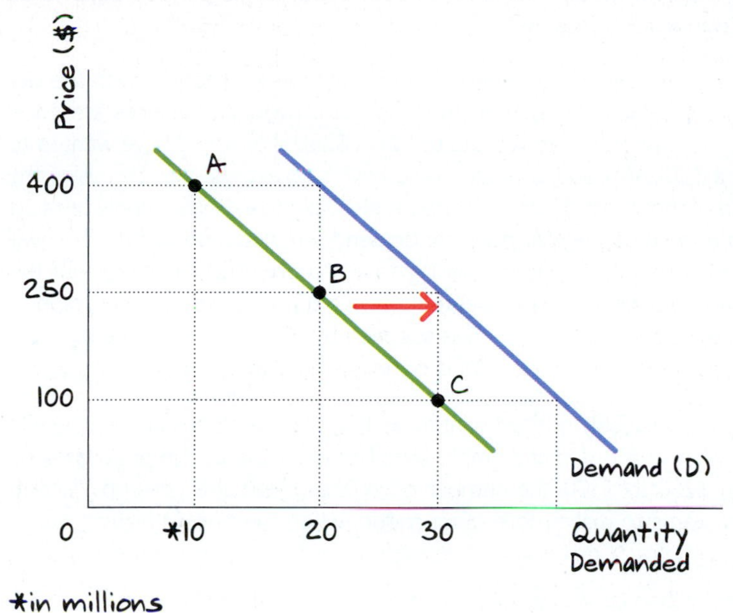

But what happens to Wii prices in a *recession*, when economic times are tough? It is no surprise that when people lose their jobs or have their salaries cut, they're less willing to make purchases. People who'd previously been able to afford a $250 Wii might decide that a new game system is a luxury they just can't afford. As a result, Nintendo would have to lower the price of Wii game systems to retain demand for the product.

So, you understand that a demand curve illustrates the relationship between prices and how much of a product is demanded in the market. As prices change, demand for the product changes as well. Sometimes, changes occur that actually shift the entire demand curve. As illustrated in Figure 3.2, when a shift occurs in the demand curve, the *relationship* between prices and quantity demanded changes. The following are some of the reasons why a shift in the demand curve might occur:

- *Changes in customer preference:* Customer preferences change constantly, and there are a wide variety of ways this can happen. Just think about endorsements or scientific studies. When actress Nicole Kidman became the face of Chanel No. 5, perfume sales increased by 30 percent.[11] The perfume didn't change; it was the celebrity endorsement that created higher demand.
- *Increases in the number of potential buyers:* The size of a market can directly affect demand. For example, the coffee shop near your campus may be very busy during the spring and fall semesters. However, during the summer when most students are gone, demand may go down.
- *The prices of related products:* Related products relate to one another or help complete each other. Related products are also known as *complementary goods*. A classic example is hot dogs and hot dog buns. As the price for hot dogs rises and falls, so does the demand for hot dog buns. Often around the Fourth of July, hot dogs go on sale, so it shouldn't be a surprise that during this time demand for hot dog buns also increases.
- *The prices of substitute products:* A substitute product is similar to the product you want, and it can be purchased in place of the desired product without much effect. Let's go back to the Wii and the Xbox. If the price of the Wii rose dramatically, you may consider the Xbox an equal substitute and buy it instead.

The Amount Supplied

By this point, you should have a pretty good idea of the rules that determine demand for a product like the Wii, but what determines the supply? How does a company like Nintendo know how many Wiis it should make—and how can Nintendo use the rules of supply to its advantage?

In an ideal world, Nintendo would have seen the mad rush for its new game console and immediately increased its supply. After all, if millions of people *want* to buy your product, you should make sure that each of those people can *actually* buy your product. If Wii devotees can't find a Wii to buy, none of their money will make its way into Nintendo's pockets. If more Wii consoles are available, though, more people will buy them and Nintendo will earn greater profits.

Figure 3.3 | **Hypothetical Supply Curve for the Wii**

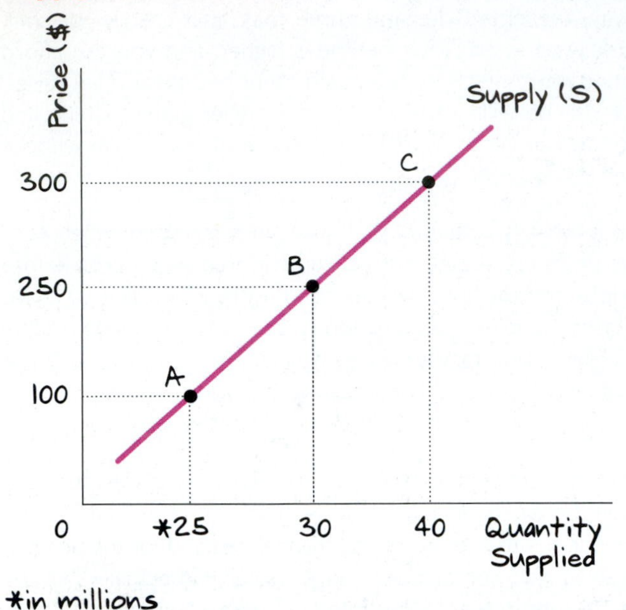

There's only one problem with this plan. In late 2006, Nintendo simply didn't have the capacity to increase its supply to meet the demand. Why not? Unfortunately, Nintendo had planned its production based on the demand it expected, which turned out to be significantly lower than the actual demand. The company probably thought the Wii would be successful, but it had no idea it would be as popular as it became.

In situations like this, where the supply cannot keep up with the demand, a company may raise the price of a product. Chances are good that many people who wanted to buy a $250 Wii would have wanted to buy a $300 Wii, so Nintendo could have boosted its sales by raising the price of the Wii to $300. Nintendo is also able to increase supply because as the price of the Wii goes up, demand will decrease slightly. This will leave more Wiis for people willing to pay more. You can check out this relationship between price and supply, a *supply curve*, on the graph in Figure 3.3. The number of Wiis supplied by Nintendo is on the horizontal axis, and the price per Wii is on the vertical axis.

You probably noticed right away that the line slopes in the opposite direction of the demand graph. Why? In this case, as the price goes up from $250 to $300, the number of Wiis supplied also goes up. A company wants to make more of a product when the price is higher.

Factors that Influence Supply

Like the demand curve, the supply curve can also shift, as shown in Figure 3.4. What if Nintendo hired extra manufacturing staff or developed a more efficient method for producing Wiis? The available supply of Wiis would increase, and the supply curve would shift to the right. Other factors that influence supply include the following:

- *Changes in prices of substitute products:* If a company is presently using its resources to make red trash cans and the price of blue trash cans increases, the company would want to reduce the number of red trash cans it makes and increase how many blue trash cans it makes. Why? Acting in its own self interests, the company will want to produce items whose prices are increasing because higher prices means higher profits (if everything else stays constant). This means that the supply of an item will decrease when the price of a substitute product increases.
- *Changes in price expectations:* Price expectations refer to what the company thinks the future price for a product will be. If Nintendo thinks that the Wii's price will increase in the future, it would limit the supply of Wiis now and increase supply in the future when prices are higher. Why? To maximize profits due to higher prices. Conversely, if Nintendo expects the price of Wiis to drop in the future (perhaps because of a competitive entry from another game maker), Nintendo would increase its supply of Wiis to maximize profits now.

Figure 3.4 | **Shift in the Supply Curve for the Wii**

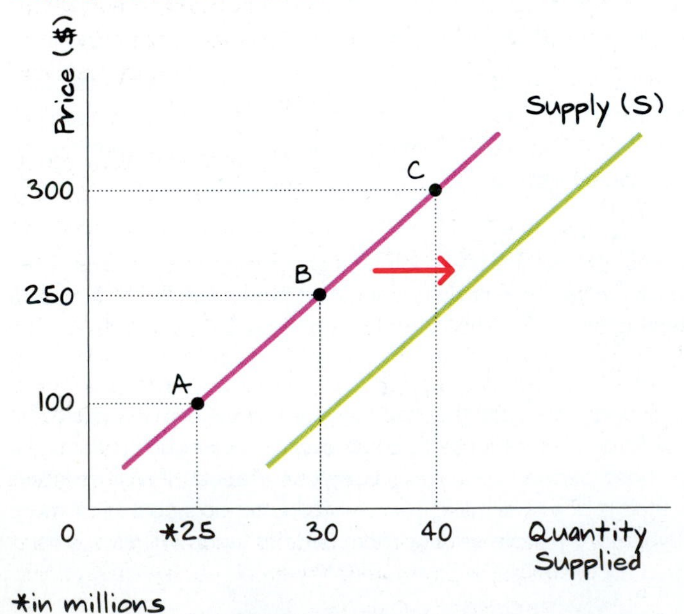

- *Changes in production costs:* When the cost of producing a particular item increases, producers will make less of that item. Why? Because the producer is making less profit on the item and, acting in the company's own self-interest, will naturally choose to make less of the item. If the cost of rubber goes up, making it more expensive for Reebok to make shoes, Reebok will make fewer shoes, assuming that everything else (retail prices, competitor prices, consumer demand) stays the same.
- *Changes in technology:* A technological innovation that allows a product to be made more efficiently—and therefore, cheaply—will encourage a producer to increase supply at each price, because the producer will be making a larger profit off of each product. So, for example, if a technological innovation in an assembly process allowed Nintendo to make the Wii more cheaply, Nintendo would be encouraged to increase the

Figure **3.5** | **Equilibrium Price for the Wii**

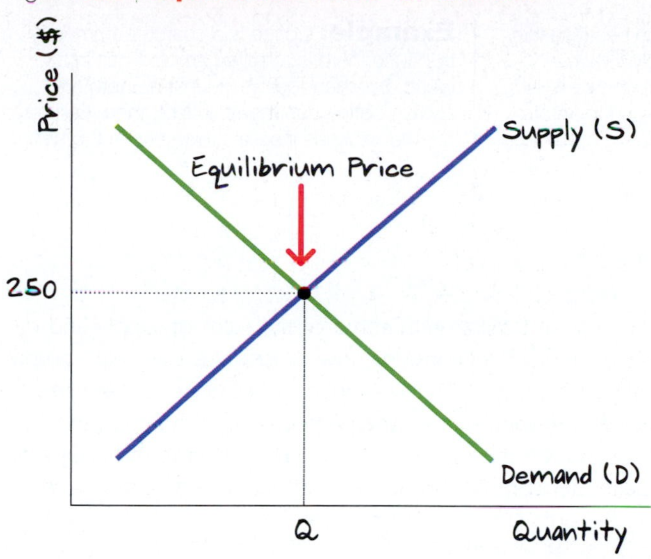

amount of Wiis it supplies, as it would be able to make a greater number of Wiis for the same price as before, and the profit on each Wii sold would be greater, since the costs to make each one have been cut.

- Changes in the number of competitors: When a profitable idea takes off, competitors soon follow, and as more sellers enter the market, the supply of similar products will increase.

Equilibrium Price

It wasn't until the spring of 2009, almost three years after its introduction, that the Wii's supply finally met its demand.[12] In other words, every person willing to buy a Wii game system at the price offered was able to get one. This point of balance, where the supply is equal to the demand, is called **equilibrium price**. When equilibrium price is achieved, suppliers are selling all the goods they've produced and consumers are getting all the goods they demand. Take a look at the graph in Figure 3.5: You can see that equilibrium price occurs at the point where the graphs of supply and demand intersect.

Although this graph can help you understand the rules of supply and demand, it doesn't tell the entire story. In the real marketplace, equilibrium price can't be completely achieved. Instead, the prices of goods and services are constantly changing as a result of fluctuations in demand and supply. For example, sellers might not exactly know what the demand is, or buyers may not be aware that they have other choices. This might lead to prices being artificially low or high. One important rule of competition is that if either the supply or the demand changes, the equilibrium price will shift, too.

Surpluses and Shortages

What happens if a company produces more of a product than people buy? This might happen, for example, if a company sets the price for a good too high. Think about the theoretical thousand-dollar Wii; the Wii is fun, but there's plenty of other fun to be had for less than $1,000. Most customers would probably not purchase super-expensive Wiis, leaving already manufactured game consoles sitting on stockroom shelves. At that point, the supply exceeds the demand. When a company makes more of a product than people want to buy, that company has a **surplus**.

Now let's flip things around. What happens when a company hasn't made enough of a product and it can't meet customer demand? We already examined a situation like this when we talked about how the Wii sold out quickly in November 2006. When demand for a product exceeds supply, there is a **shortage** of that product. Sometimes, a shortage occurs because the supplier underestimated the demand of the product. Other times, suppliers purposely limit the supply to drive up demand.

Surpluses and shortages aren't limited to goods. In fact, it's perfectly possible to have a surplus or a shortage of *people*. Think about the future plans of people you know: If a lot of them are going to medical school and not many of them are specializing in childhood education, there may be a surplus of doctors and a shortage of teachers a few years down the line. Knowing about shortages and surpluses in the workforce can actually help you in the job market: If you choose to enter a field in which there's a shortage of workers, you could end up with a higher salary. Just as customers are willing to pay more for a Wii if there are only a few consoles available, managers are willing to pay more for an employee if workers are in short supply.

demand
supply
Demand for IT employees
Supply of people with IT majors

How would IT salaries have to change to balance supply and demand?

Translation Guide

In Conversation: A *shortage* may seem like the same thing as *scarcity*, but they are fundamentally different concepts.

Why: All resources are scarce because they do not exist in an endless supply. However, *scarcity* does not imply that a resource is *rare*, or available in small quantities, and therefore difficult to find, as is the case during a *shortage*. A shortage occurs when a supplier produces less of a product than is demanded.

Example: Coffee is a scarce commodity because there is a limited amount of it in the world, but that doesn't mean that there are always coffee shortages. In fact, there can be a coffee surplus if sellers raise prices too high.

Competition, Supply, and Demand

Now that you're familiar with some of the rules of supply and demand, you can start to consider how those rules can help companies compete in the marketplace. If you're creating a new product, you'll want to strategize to make sure that you price that product appropriately. Set the price too high, and you'll wind up with a surplus and no customer demand; set the price too low, and you won't make a profit. Either way, you won't be able to beat your competitors. If you find that perfect price, however, you'll please your customers and come out on top of the competition.

It's worth knowing the rules of the game if you're a customer, too. Rather than buying a hot new product when customer demand is at its peak, if you wait a few months for the enthusiasm to die down, prices will probably drop. Companies often lower their prices if initially strong demand starts to slip.

Economies of Scale

You probably know that if you go to a large store such as Sam's Club or Costco, you can get some of the same items you'd find at a small store, but the big-box stores have lower prices. This happens because several additional factors in real economies affect supply, demand, and choices. In this example, the larger store sells more of the same item; therefore, its suppliers make more of the same item. For most items, the average cost of producing an item goes down as production increases, allowing raw materials to be purchased in larger quantities, machinery to be used at capacity, and so on. Why? **Fixed costs**, which are expenses that remain constant and do not depend on the level of business being generated, are spread out over more customers, and larger stores can demand better pricing from their suppliers. This concept is known as **economies of scale**.

Think about the fixed costs for a magazine publisher. To print one magazine, the publisher needs a building and the necessary machinery. It also needs labor and equipment to write and design an issue of the magazine. Aside from the additional paper and ink, there are no major costs required to print the second copy of the magazine. In fact, the cost of printing the magazine is spread out over the number of copies printed. If the publisher prints 10,000 copies, each copy of the magazine costs less than it would if the publisher printed only 100 copies.

Economies of scale can also involve services provided. Imagine you're a freelance writer who's writing a magazine article about women's health. You have the fixed costs of your office equipment, and you'll probably invest a number of hours in researching your article topic. Then, however, you might use that same research to write different, but related, articles for other magazines. Although that first article may take you days to complete, the related articles might take only a few hours. Once you make an initial investment of time and resources to write the first article, your subsequent articles will be "cheaper"—they will require less of your time and fewer resources.

As a result of economies of scale, large businesses can pass lower costs on to customers through lower prices, enabling those businesses to increase their market share and undercut smaller businesses. Alternately, large businesses can maintain their existing prices and earn a higher profit. Although each company must make that strategic decision for itself, it's clear that using economies of scale can give larger businesses a competitive edge.

How do self interests promote a greater benefit through the invisible hand?

The Invisible Hand

You know by now that competition in a free market economy is the result of the complex interaction of many forces. So, who's in charge of keeping that competition going? In the 18th century, philosopher Adam Smith (known as the "father of economics") used the term *invisible hand* to describe the natural force that guides free market capitalism through competition for scarce resources.[13]

Smith looked at it this way: There are two ways you can get people to think about the needs of others. You can appeal to their goodwill (that is, their desire to do good), which is often a tough sell, or you can appeal to their own self-interest, which is a much easier task. When you offer someone an exchange, you show that person what good or service you have to offer that can be of use to them. When the exchange is carried out, you gain something in return. A chain of such exchanges makes the participants—and the entire society—better off than they would have been alone. Even though a person might have no concern for the society as a whole, he or she contributes to society just by acting in his or her own self-interest.

The invisible hand of self-interest guides buyers and sellers to make decisions about how much of something they produce and how much they buy and consume, and the relationship between these two decisions determines the price for a product. The competitive marketplace produces a remarkable outcome: a combination of buyers and sellers acting in their own individual self-interests, creating a balance of supply, demand, and prices that is optimal for everyone in the market as a whole. As depicted in the illustration to the left, when buyers and sellers act in their own self-interest, their interests support each other and guide the dominoes of the market to fall in place.

Do It...

3.2: Examine Supply and Demand In 100 words or less, explain why a hurricane in the Gulf of Mexico this week could cause you to pay more for gas at the pump next week.

Now Debrief...

- When you study **economics**, you're trying to understand and predict how people behave as they try to fulfill their wants and needs.
- Companies try to gain competitive advantages by making decisions about pricing and production based on principles of **supply** and **demand**.
- Factors that affect demand include changes in customer preferences, increases in the number of potential buyers, the prices of related products, and the prices of substitute products. Factors that affect supply include changes in prices of substitute goods, changes in price expectations, changes in production costs, and changes in the number of competitors.
- When a product's supply equals its demand, that product has found its **equilibrium price**.
- Competition in the business world can also be affected by **economies of scale**, in which larger companies can afford to sell products for lower prices.
- Market competition is guided by a force known as the *invisible hand*, in which people work to advance their own self-interests and, in the process, advance the free market economy.

3. Levels of Competition

We've been talking about marathons, in which individuals compete against each other; but not all running competitions are created equal. There's a big difference between a small-town foot race that anyone can enter and a high-stakes international contest that gives only elite runners the chance to compete.

You can probably see where this metaphor is heading: Some types of competition in the business world are more like the small-town races, and others are more like the Boston Marathon. And you could even argue that some dominant companies are the business equivalent of Michael Phelps, the Olympic swimmer who won eight gold medals in 2008. In a capitalist society, competition is a way of life, but depending on the type of work you do, that competition may look very different.

If you're going to win the race, you have to know the competition and the rules of the game. This knowledge helps you evaluate your strengths and weaknesses. This is true in business, too. Once you know whom you're competing against and the rules you're abiding by, you'll be better equipped to win.

Perfect Competition

Imagine you're working on a farm, and you've just harvested your first crop of red, ripe tomatoes. Now you can sell them for five dollars each, right?

Not so fast—you're hardly the only farm in town. In the agriculture industry, there are so many sellers of virtually identical vegetables, fruits, and grains that no single seller can set the price for the products. This makes the agriculture industry the closest thing we have to a real-life example of **perfect competition**. Perfect competition exists in a market in which there are many sellers that all produce a virtually identical product. Sellers can easily enter and exit the market, and there are many buyers. If a single seller decided to raise its selling price for the product, consumers would simply turn to the nearest competitor for the lower price. (No matter how delicious your tomatoes may be, you'd be hard-pressed to find someone who'd spend five dollars on one.)

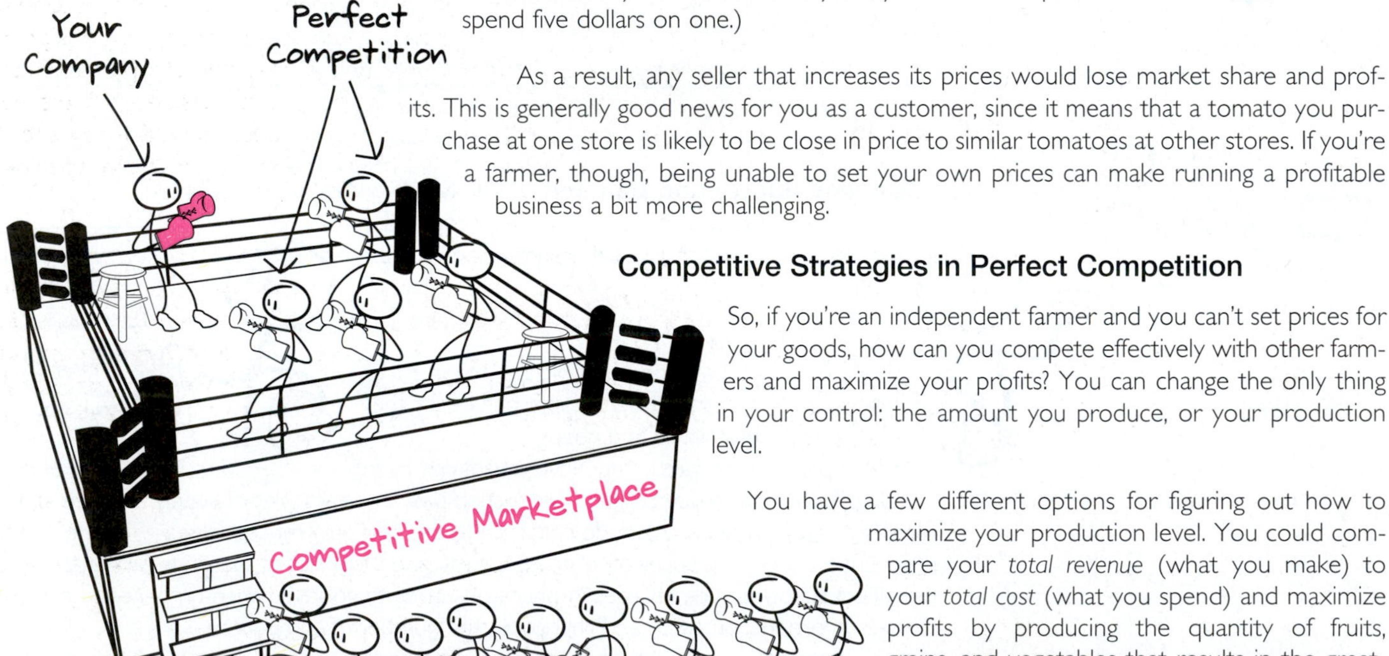

As a result, any seller that increases its prices would lose market share and profits. This is generally good news for you as a customer, since it means that a tomato you purchase at one store is likely to be close in price to similar tomatoes at other stores. If you're a farmer, though, being unable to set your own prices can make running a profitable business a bit more challenging.

Competitive Strategies in Perfect Competition

So, if you're an independent farmer and you can't set prices for your goods, how can you compete effectively with other farmers and maximize your profits? You can change the only thing in your control: the amount you produce, or your production level.

You have a few different options for figuring out how to maximize your production level. You could compare your *total revenue* (what you make) to your *total cost* (what you spend) and maximize profits by producing the quantity of fruits, grains, and vegetables that results in the greatest difference between total revenue and total cost. You want to figure out how you can make as much money as possible while spending the least amount of money possible.

Alternately, you could compare your marginal revenue and marginal cost. What does this mean? *Marginal revenue* is simply the additional revenue you would gain by producing one additional unit. In other words, how much more money will you earn by selling one more item? *Marginal cost* is simply how much it will cost to produce one more unit. The marginal revenue might be the price you earn on one more bushel of corn, while the marginal cost might be the expense of producing that one additional bushel of corn. When the marginal revenue is greater than the marginal cost, the revenue is increasing faster than the costs. So, if as a farmer you make more money than you spend on that additional unit, you should increase production.

Now think about the opposite situation. If marginal revenue is less than marginal cost, you spend more than you make on that additional unit, and you should decrease production. In this example, you can earn the greatest profit by identifying the amount you need to produce for marginal revenue to equal marginal cost.

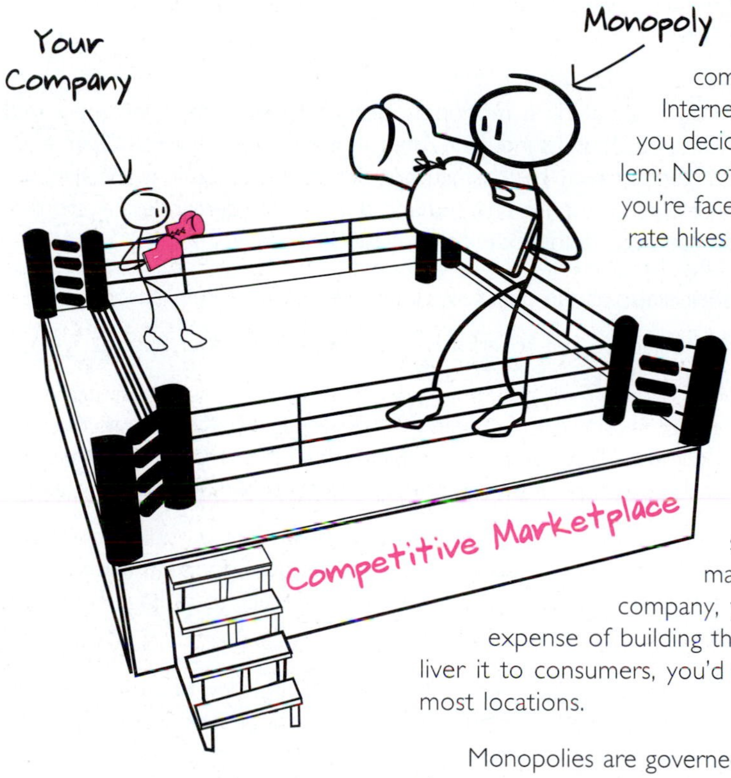

Monopoly

Your Company
Monopoly
Competitive Marketplace

There are other levels of competition out there besides perfect competition. Let's say the company that provides your cable TV and Internet raises its rates. Your budget is stretched tight enough as it is, so you decide to switch to a different cable company. There's just one problem: No other company offers cable services in your area. As a customer, you're faced with an unpleasant choice: You can give in to the company's rate hikes or abandon cable TV and Internet entirely.

How can one company have so much control over your quality of life? The cable company in this example is a monopoly. The opposite of perfect competition, a **monopoly** exists when there is only one provider for a product or service and there are no substitutes. In other words, a single business *is* the industry.

High costs or other barriers, which may be economic, social, or political, prevent businesses from entering this type of market. If you suddenly decided you wanted to open an electric company, you'd face some pretty large obstacles. Aside from the huge expense of building the facilities that you'd need to produce the electricity and deliver it to consumers, you'd face government regulations preventing you from opening in most locations.

Monopolies are governed by laws that can be traced back to the 19th century. At that time, some corporations organized themselves into large units known as *trusts*. Through sheer size and strength, they began to control the markets. They set the prices, crushed any business that tried to compete with them, and even worse, they lowered the quality of goods and services they provided. In 1890, the U.S. government passed the *Sherman Anti-Trust Act*, which forbade businesses from establishing trusts, monopolies, or other plans that would oppose free trade.

This legislation was quickly used to break apart several major monopolies. The American Tobacco Company and the Standard Oil Company were both broken up in the early 1900s. More recently, the Department of Justice filed a group of civil actions against Microsoft, accusing the company of abusing monopoly power in its sales of operating systems and Web browsers. When the case was settled in 2001, Microsoft was required to share its application programming interfaces with third-party companies.[14] The government also has the right to block corporate mergers if the merger would create a monopoly.

Before you get the idea that monopolies should be avoided at all cost, consider this: some goods have high design costs associated with them.[15] It might cost $500 million to create the first pill of a new drug, such as Plavix, but it costs only pennies to produce the second pill. Because there was no such drug as Plavix on the market when the U.S. Food and Drug Administration (FDA) approved it in 1998, Bristol-Myers Squibb and Sanofi-Aventis had an instant monopoly with its introduction. These companies had a patent that prevented other companies from copying the drug. If they hadn't, other businesses would have quickly entered the market. Competition would have driven down the prices and the partnership between Bristol-Myers Squibb and Sanofi Aventis would have never recouped its expenses. If this were the case, the partnership would have had no incentive to develop the drug in the first place. You might say, then, that monopoly can be the engine of invention. Businesses work toward developing a monopoly by producing a new good or service and driving out the competition.

Some monopolies are actually protected by the government. Utilities of water, natural gas, and electricity are typically monopolies in most regions. When you move into a new home and want to turn on your water, do you have many choices about who to call? Not likely. Why does the government let this happen? The reason, as mentioned earlier, is that there are obstacles to entering this type of industry. Delivering water, for example, requires connecting every building to the main facility. It wouldn't make sense to have several companies making these connections throughout a community.

Competitive Strategies in a Monopoly You might think a monopoly doesn't have to be concerned with competition in its industry. After all, it *is* the industry. However, even a monopoly can drive its customers away by making poor decisions. Monopolies are still controlled by the relationship between the price charged and the quantity demanded. A monopoly can also mismanage its resources to the extent that it cannot survive.

Monopolies achieve their status as the only seller in an industry for three reasons:

1. *Government ruling.* As noted above, the government can give a single seller, such as an electric company, the rights to a market.
2. *Ownership of a resource.* If a company has complete control over a resource, then no one else has the opportunity to compete. This can occur through control over materials (such as petroleum or iron ore) or through control over information (such as patents and copyrights).
3. *Economies of scale.* Economies of scale involve a company being able to reduce costs as it expands service. When this happens, a business can provide more goods at a lower cost and can thus eliminate the competition. Often, public services, such as garbage collection, are able to create monopolies this way.

Perhaps the greatest problem a monopoly needs to avoid is inefficiency. Because a monopoly can produce less output and charge a higher price than perfect competition would allow, the business can become inefficient. Monopolies also need to avoid the temptation to abuse their power, such as trying to prevent potential competitors from entering the market. Monopolies may not have to play the game of business in the way that most other companies do, but they still need to come up with competitive strategies for keeping you, their customer, happy.

As a customer and an individual citizen, there's not much you can do about monopolies, but think back to the example of the cable company that raised its rates. You *could* choose to live without cable. Unless you go entirely "off the grid," it's unlikely that you'd choose to live without water or heat, or the U.S. Postal Service but you can keep yourself informed about the government policies that regulate these industries, and you can get involved by contacting your local or state representatives if there's a law you'd like to see changed.

Monopolistic Competition

If you've ever decided between a sweater from Old Navy and one from Kohl's, you're already familiar with **monopolistic competition**. In this type of competition, businesses compete against each other to sell similar (but not identical) products at prices that are usually higher than the lowest possible price. As in perfect competition, sellers are able to enter and exit the market freely.

Translation Guide

In Conversation: Monopoly may seem similar to monopolistic competition, but these concepts are very different.

In Economic Terms: A *monopoly* implies that there is only one seller of a specific good. *Monopolistic competition* means that there are many sellers, with similar goods.

Example: When you go out to eat Italian food, there are a large number of restaurants to choose from, but they all serve basically the same thing. This is monopolistic competition.

Competitive Strategies in Monopolistic Competition Do you feel that New Balance sneakers fit you better than Nike sneakers do? If so, you understand that in monopolistic competition, small differences between similar products can guide customers' purchasing decisions. Although it can be hard to tell one farmer's tomato from another farmer's tomato, it's often significantly easier to distinguish between MP3 players or kitchen appliances. Companies are well aware that buyers make preference choices among products, and they try to compete by designing products that most customers will like best. How do businesses make their products stand out?

Your Company

Monopolistic Competition

Competitive Marketplace

1. They make their products physically different. For example, many restaurants sell sandwiches, but Subway differentiates its product by focusing on more healthy choices. It has developed an advertising campaign to point out that many of its sandwiches have six grams of fat or less.[16]
2. They use a brand name or packaging to create *perceived* differences. In other words, they attempt to convince customers that two very similar products are actually significantly different. Have you ever ordered a Coke and been asked, "Is Pepsi OK?" Coke and Pepsi are similar products. However, each company has made an effort to establish a difference among customers. Coca-Cola, for example, has established a loyalty program called MyCokeRewards, in which customers find codes on Coca-Cola products and earn points that they can exchange for prizes. Although some customers consider Coke and Pepsi interchangeable products, others have established brand loyalty. They will choose only one or the other.
3. They provide customers with first-class customer service. Have you ever called customer service only to be left hanging on the line for what seems like hours at the whim of a robotic voice? A company can stand out from its competitors by offering timely e-mail responses, establishing a reasonable return policy, and treating its customers fairly. It's more than politeness; it's a smart business strategy. Just ask companies like Wegman's Food Markets and Enterprise Rent-a-Car, both of which have been recognized for superior customer service[17]—and have earned a devoted customer base as a result.

As a customer, you might want to think about these three competitive strategies when you're shopping for a particular product. Is that $100 sweater substantially different from the $30 sweater, or is one company using branding and packaging to create a perceived difference? And if you have to return the sweater, will the company make things easy for you, or will it (inadvertently) drive you around the bend?

Oligopoly

You have dozens of choices when you're looking for a new pair of jeans, but if you need to fly from Minneapolis to Baltimore, your choices are more limited. When only a few businesses make up an industry, those businesses are known as an **oligopoly**. As in a monopoly, there are barriers to entry into the market, such as the potential for substantial lost costs if the venture doesn't succeed. The small group of businesses in an oligopoly has control over the price of their product, whether that product is automobiles, airplane flights, or semiconductors.

Competitive Strategies in an Oligopoly

Businesses in an oligopoly are characterized by their interdependence. Just as marathon runners adjust their pace in response to their competitors' actions, businesses react to changes in their competitors' pricing, production, or advertising policies. If one business in an oligopoly lowers its prices, it will gain a greater share of the market. In turn, other businesses will have to lower their prices as well or sacrifice market share. Maybe you live in a region in which Publix and SweetBay are the main supermarkets. If SweetBay advertises lower prices on strawberries, you might make the switch to SweetBay, at least when it comes to strawberries. In response, Publix may lower its prices on strawberries as well.

This means that lowering prices doesn't increase market share; it only lowers profits, and that's not a recipe for competitive success. Members of oligopolies therefore tend to keep prices relatively constant, so much of the competition happens in areas other than price. The following strategies are used to help a business in an oligopoly be competitive:

1. **Advertising.** Oligopolistic businesses use commercial advertising to attract customers from competitors and to prevent competitors from attracting their customers.
2. **Product differentiation.** As in the case in monopolistic competition, oligopolistic businesses often compete by offering a product that is somehow newer, bigger, better, or faster than another.
3. **Prevention.** Finally, businesses try to keep others from entering the competition in the first place. They seek to get patents or other legal protection for a product in order to prevent other businesses from entering the oligopoly.

Since oligopolistic businesses offer similar products for similar prices, you don't need to focus too much on finding the best price when you're shopping for one of these products. Your buying choices will probably depend more on other factors. Which airline offers free baggage? Which gas station is most environmentally friendly? You can do a little research to figure out what these companies are offering to entice customers, and take advantage of those offers if you think they're worthwhile.

Pricing: Takers and Makers

In elementary school, were you always the first one to have the cool new toy? In fact, was that toy cool simply *because* you owned it? Or were you more of a follower who waited for other kids to set trends before you followed them?

If you were an influential trendsetter, you'd be known in business terms as a price maker. **Price makers** are businesses that are influential enough to affect the price of an item. For example, a company that holds a monopoly is a price maker because it lacks competition. However, when you look at oligopolies and monopolistic competition, each of the competitors affect prices to a different extent, so it's not easy to identify just one price maker. In terms of individuals, an investor who owns enough shares in a business to affect its price is also considered a price maker.

If, on the other hand, you were a trend-follower as a kid, you'd be better described in business terms as a price taker. **Price takers** are businesses that don't have enough influence to affect a product's price. Take a look at Pizza Hut, for example: aside from promotions and specials, it can only charge what the market generally charges for pizza. If it were to raise its prices substantially, consumers would go to one of the myriad other pizza places in town. In terms of individuals, unless you're a millionaire buying large quantities of stock, you're a price taker when you invest. Your individual action is not enough to change the price of a stock. When you buy an item in a store, you're also a price taker. An individual consumer is a price taker because their individual purchases don't affect the price a business determines for its products.

Table **3.1** | **Levels of Competition**

Market Structure	Number of Sellers	Type of Product	Ease of Entry	Examples
Perfect Competition	Many	Homogenous	Very easy	Agriculture
Monopoly	One	Unique	Almost impossible	Public utilities
Monopolistic Competition	Many	Differentiated	Easy	Retail trade
Oligopoly	Few	Homogenous or differentiated	Difficult	Autos, airlines, steel

Even if you don't own a business, you can apply the principles of price making and price taking to your own life. Let's say you're a candidate for a job, and your potential boss asks you what your salary requirements are. If you're the only candidate being considered and the company can't survive without you, you might be able to act like a monopoly and name whatever salary you'd like. You're a price maker because you're influential enough that the company is willing to shift its usual pay scale to hire you. However, if there is a lot of competition for the position, the company will only be willing to pay you as much as they pay other people in similar positions—the market price. In this situation, you're a price taker; you'll settle for an average salary for your position because if you don't, you probably won't get the job. Knowing whether you're a price maker or a price taker can help you compete effectively against those other hopeful new hires.

Do It...

3.3: Make a Choice Imagine having three job offers sitting in front of you, either for an internship or a full-time job: One company has a monopoly, one is part of an oligopoly, and the third is in an industry that is as close to perfect competition as you can get. If all other elements of the job offers were identical, which offer would you prefer, and why?

Now Debrief...

- The type of competition a business faces often determines the strategies it uses to become and remain profitable.
- **Perfect competition** exists in a market with many buyers and sellers. Sellers can enter and exit the market freely, and no single seller is a price maker.
- A **monopoly** exists when a single provider of a product or service controls the market. In the United States, government regulation prevents monopolies in some industries and regulates them in others.
- In **monopolistic competition**, many buyers and sellers offer products that are similar. Buyers make choices based on perceived differences among the products.
- An **oligopoly** is similar to a monopoly in that it exists in a market with substantial barriers to entry. However, it consists of a few competitors that are interdependent.
- **Price makers** are businesses that can affect the price of an item, while price takers are businesses that cannot.
- The levels of competition are summed up briefly in Table 3.1.

4. Industry, Product, and Business Life Cycles: Ups and Downs

Maybe you've been competitive your whole life. You were the first baby in the nursery to learn how to crawl; you were the first of your toddler friends to learn your ABCs. As a kid, though, it wasn't easy to compete against adults. If you'd entered a race as a 10-year-old, you might have had some good sprinting speed, but you probably wouldn't have expected to beat your competition.

Then you grew up. Your muscles and your stamina developed, you became more familiar with the rules of the game, and you started to win some races. Pretty soon, you found yourself at the peak of your physical fitness, and competing against others became much easier. As you get older, though, you may find that you can't run as fast as you once could, and although you'll still have that drive to compete, you may have to adjust your strategies in your athletic endeavors.

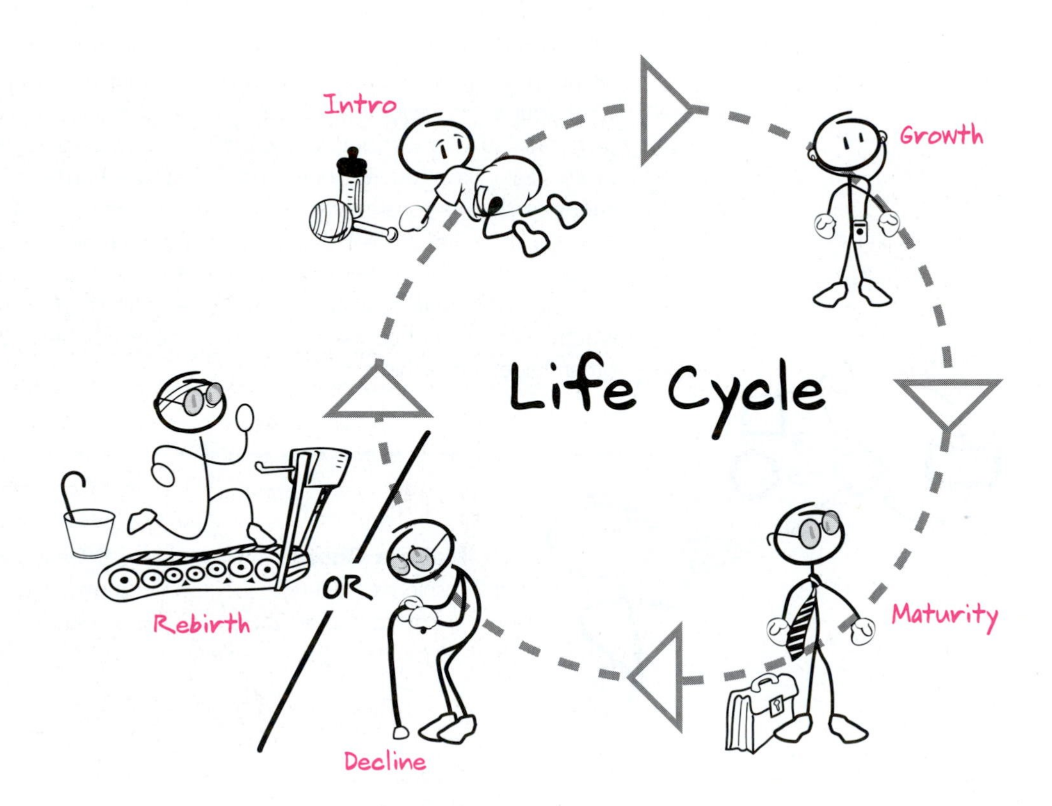

Like humans, industries, products, and businesses go through "life cycles," and each stage in the life cycle requires companies to develop a new set of skills and strategies to remain competitive. How, then, do companies change over time, and what do these changes mean for you as a customer and a potential employee?

The Introductory Stage

When Apple introduced the iPhone, a new industry was born: an industry of mobile phones that could also play music and movies, navigate the Web, edit photos, and send text messages. An industry is born when someone—either an existing, established company or a new start-up—develops a new product or service. As a result, most often that one business is alone in the industry during the *introductory stage*.

■ Industries, products, and businesses go through "life cycles," and each stage in the life cycle requires companies to develop a new set of skills and strategies to remain competitive.

So, if there's just one business in an industry, it doesn't have to worry about competition, right? Not exactly. At this stage of the game, the single business is essentially competing for the right to exist, and it needs a strategy that will build awareness and name recognition among customers and present its new product or service as unique. For example, the iPhone got a lot of buzz before it was released, so by the time it was available in stores, customers couldn't wait to get their hands on it.

If you get hired to work in a new industry, or if you end up starting your own business launching a new product, you should know right away that you shouldn't expect to make a lot of money, at least at first. You might think that because you are offering a unique product or service, it will make huge profits in the introductory stage. However, this isn't usually the case. New ventures generally spend a large amount of money creating the product, testing prototypes, and marketing. As a result, the company might be operating at a loss. Any profits that might be earned are usually invested back into developing the product or service.

That's not to say that it's a bad idea to start something new; it's just a bit risky. On the other hand, a business that enters an industry early on gets a significant chance to establish its brand in customers' minds before too many competitors show up to the game.

The Growth Stage

If a new industry or company starts to be successful, it won't take long for the competition to heat up. If you're embarking on a job search and you're trying to find companies that are actively hiring, you might want to check out companies in relatively new industries that have entered the *growth stage* of the life cycle. Sales are increasing throughout the industry, production is becoming more efficient, new companies are popping up left and right, and businesses are actually making a profit, so they're probably looking to hire more staff and expand their scope.

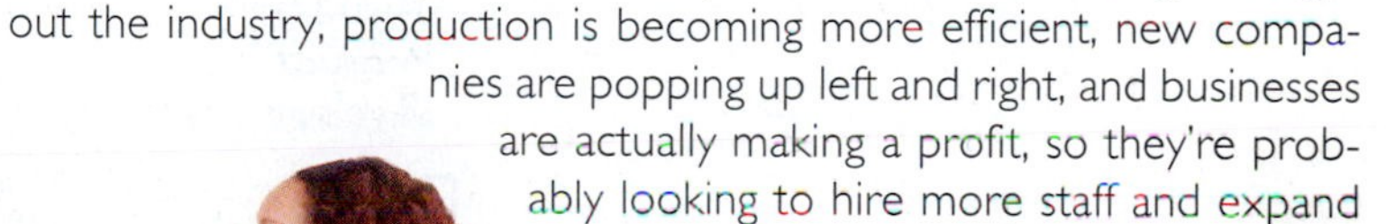

As the industry grows, it's good news for employees looking for jobs, but business owners have to shift their strategies if they want to remain competitive. This is key because oftentimes many firms never go through an introductory phase. Instead they launch a "me-too" product and try to start growing immediately. This is why businesses work to differentiate their product from those of their competitors. At first, the iPhone was popular simply because there wasn't anything else like it, but as other companies developed similar phones, Apple had to explain to customers why the iPhone was different from and (in Apple's opinion) better than those other phones. By employing creative advertising strategies, developing a sleek design, and adding unique features to a product, companies can make their goods stand out from their competitors. By doing this, they create demand for their products.

Industries tend to spread out geographically during the growth stage. If you want to work in the computer business, you aren't required to move to California; if you want to make cars, you don't necessarily have to go to Detroit. Although your job search may be confined to one geographic area during an industry's introductory stage, you'll have a lot more freedom to decide where you live if your industry of choice has grown up a little.

The Maturity Stage

If you want a job in a stable industry with a proven record of growth, you'll want to look for industries that have entered the *maturity stage* of the life cycle. At this stage, companies' sales expand and earnings grow. And there's good news for you investors out there: during the maturity stage, a business may have excess funds to pay its shareholders.

The competition doesn't let up, though. Additional competitors may still join the market and try to steal some market share. That means businesses must continue to stress the unique features of their product to consumers. In addition, businesses may try to differentiate themselves by lowering their prices. If a business can differentiate itself as the better product while also being priced more competitively, it can continue to have a strong presence in the market during its maturity stage. Businesses may make some changes to improve their product at this stage, too, but those changes probably won't be radical.

The Decline Stage

The music industry is alive and well today, but how about the gramophone industry? The telephone industry is hanging in there, but the tele*graph* industry didn't fare so well. Almost every

Figure **3.6** | **Industry and Product Life Cycle**

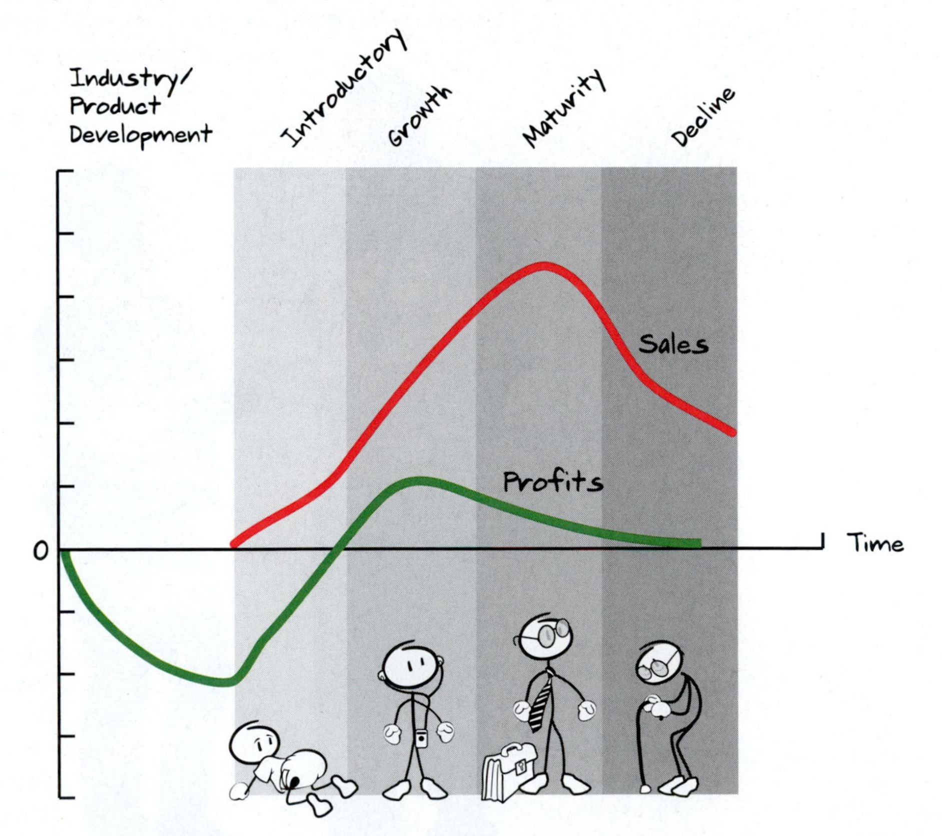

industry experiences decline at some point or, in these cases, the industry has simply died. Often, technological changes make an entire industry obsolete.

Sometimes, a company can adapt to customers' changing needs: Kodak, for example, transitioned from analog to digital photography and remains a successful business. Sometimes, though, companies can't adapt, and they'll find themselves caught in the *decline stage* of the industry life cycle. In the decline stage, sales decrease at an accelerating rate. Profits, however, may continue to rise because little expense is invested in the product.

Some competitors will drop out of the market at this point, while others remain to compete in the smaller market that remains behind. It's still a competition, but the field is smaller, the pace is slower, and it's clear to owners, shareholders, employees, and customers that this race won't last too much longer.

It's important to note that companies in some industries are able to prolong the life cycle by, for example, revitalizing an existing brand. A familiar example is Arm & Hammer baking soda, produced by Church & Dwight Co.[18] The founders first introduced their product in 1846. Although the logo, packaging, and advertising have changed over the years, the product itself hasn't changed much at all. In the 1960s, baking soda sales were falling due to an overall decline in home baking. Rather than letting the product leave the maturity stage, though, the company started promoting even more uses for baking soda as a deodorizer, laundry additive, toothpaste additive, and carpet freshener.

The growth of an industry or product's sales over time is often used to chart its life cycle. You can see this for yourself in Figure 3.6.

Do It...

3.4: Understand the Life Cycle If you wanted to buy a product that was clearly in the introduction phase of its life cycle, what kind of pricing would you expect a company to offer you? Why do profits peak in the growth stage, but sales peak in the maturity stage?

Now Debrief...

- Industries and products move through a life cycle that includes introduction, growth, maturity, and decline or rebirth.
- During the introduction stage, profits are small or negative because of the expense of development and marketing.
- In the growth stage, other businesses enter the market. Businesses work to differentiate their products from those of their competitors. Sales expand and profits become positive.
- In the maturity stage, sales continue to expand and earnings grow. Changes to products are minimal, and funds become available to pay shareholders.
- At the end of the life cycle, industries and produces reach decline. A business may still earn profits, but many businesses exit the market. However, companies in some industries are able to prolong the life cycle by, for example, revitalizing an existing brand.

Chapter 3 Visual Summary

1. Describe why and how companies compete in a capitalistic economy, and how a focus on sustainability and the triple bottom line keeps them competitive. (pp. 56–58)

- Businesses are limited by competition in any **capitalistic economy**, an economic system in which the means to produce goods and services are owned by private interests.
- The types of goods and services produced and the prices charged for them are determined by the **free market**.
- A good measure of a company's success is **sustainability**, which means that the company can operate today without destroying the ability of future generations to meet their own needs.
- Sustainable businesses can evaluate their success using the **triple bottom line**, which focuses on three aspects of the corporate bottom line: people, planet, and profits.

Summary: Competition is a key factor in business and is unavoidable in a capitalistic economy. Two ways to stay competitive are to be sustainable and to follow the triple bottom line approach.

2. Identify the economic principles that dictate how competition occurs. (pp. 59–65)

- **Economics** is the study of choices that are made as businesses and consumers compete for scarce goods.
- **Scarcity** describes the situation in which goods and services are not limitless. There are not enough resources to meet all wants and demands for goods or services.
- The quantity of an item that businesses or people are willing to pay for at a given price is the **demand**. The number of items available is the **supply**.
- Demand is affected by customer preferences, market size, the price of related products, and the price of substitute products. Supply is affected by the prices of substitute products, changes in price expectations, changes in production costs, and the number of competitors.
- **Equilibrium price** occurs when the supply is equal to the demand.
- A **surplus** occurs when the supply is greater than the demand. A **shortage** occurs when the demand is greater than the supply.
- Some sellers are affected by **economies of scale**, which allows them to spread out fixed costs, in turn lowering their price per unit or to take advantage of growth in the industry.
- All the activities of the free market are driven by what Adam Smith described as an *invisible hand*, which guides competition for scarce resources by allowing participants to exchange goods and services freely.

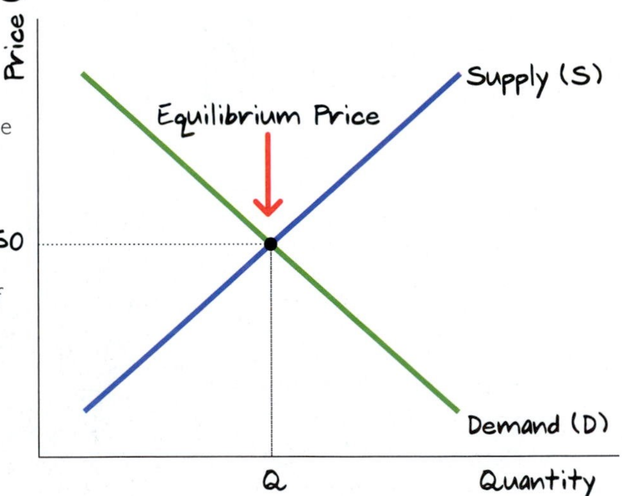

Summary: To successfully compete in any market, an organization needs to know the rules of competition. Economic concepts are what make up the rules of business.

3. Identify different market structures, and understand how companies in each market structure form competitive business strategies. (pp. 66–71)

- **Perfect competition** exists when there are many buyers and sellers who can enter and exit the market easily. No single seller can determine the price of a product.
- In a **monopoly**, only one seller makes up the market. Other sellers are barred from the market by barriers such as high costs or government regulations.
- **Monopolistic competition** occurs when there are many buyers and sellers that can enter the market easily. Sellers produce similar products that are differentiated by buyer preferences.
- In an **oligopoly**, a few businesses make up the market and determine prices. Each one reacts to the strategies of the others.
- Depending on the level of competition, businesses can act as **price makers** by setting prices for products or **price takers** by accepting prices set by the market.

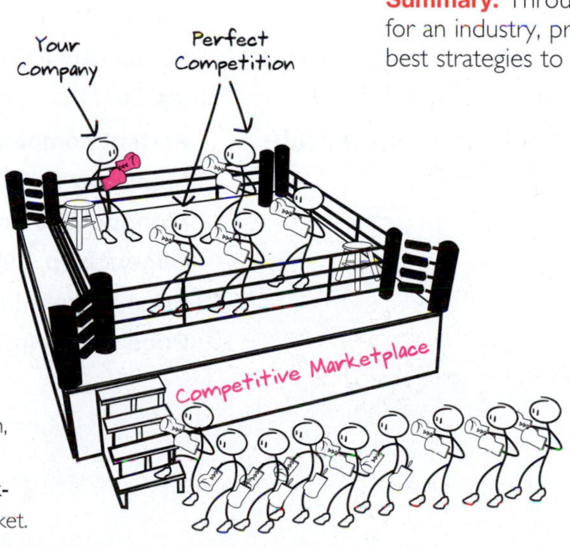

Summary: Not all businesses face the same level of competition. However, once a business figures out its competition, it can determine strategies to become profitable.

4. Explain how the life cycle of an industry, product, or business affects its competitive strategies. (pp. 72–75)

- Industries, products, and businesses go through a four-stage life cycle.
- In the introductory stage, an industry is formed. Businesses focus on developing recognition for their product among consumers.
- In the growth stage, sales increase at a steady rate. Other businesses see opportunities and enter the market.
- In the maturity stage, sales expand and earnings grow.
- In the decline stage, the product is no longer changed or updated. Sales are decreasing and little investment is made in the product. In time, the business may drop out of the industry.
- Companies in some industries are able to prolong the life cycle by, for example, revitalizing an existing brand.

Summary: Throughout a life cycle, it's important for an industry, product, or business to identify the best strategies to remain competitive

Get the most out of what you just read by practicing your skills and actually DOING something with the material! The best place to do this is at **www.mybizlab.com**. Here's just some of what is available to you there:

- Apply your skills in an interactive environment with more **BizSkill** experiences...and see if you have what it takes
- Think critically and talk with your peers on hot business topics in **BizChat**
- Flex your business communication skills and build your own portfolio with the **Communication Plan exercises**
- Watch the chapter material come together with **Just Plain Business** videos
- Study on-the-go with **Audio Chapter Summaries** in MP3 format
- Brush up on the lecture and content with **Audio PowerPoints**
- Discover how well you are doing and see what areas you need to improve on with the **Pre-Tests** and **Post-Tests**

Key Words

These key words and more are also available as flash cards to practice with at **www.mybizlab.com**.

1. Describe why and how companies compete in a capitalist economy, and how a focus on sustainability and the triple bottom line keeps them competitive. (pp. 56–58)

Capitalistic economy (p. 56)
Free market (p. 56)
Sustainability (p. 57)
Triple bottom line (p. 57)
Supply chain (p. 58)

2. Identify the economic concepts that dictate how competition occurs. (pp. 59–65)

Economics (p. 59)
Scarcity (p. 59)
Demand (p. 60)
Supply (p. 60)
Equilibrium price (p. 63)
Surplus (p. 63)
Shortage (p. 63)
Fixed costs (p. 64)
Economies of scale (p. 64)

3. Identify different market structures, and understand how companies in each market structure form competitive business strategies. (pp. 66–71)

Perfect competition (p. 66)
Monopoly (p. 67)
Monopolistic competition (p. 68)
Oligopoly (p. 69)
Price makers (p. 70)
Price takers (p. 70)

Prove It

Prove It...

Now, let's put on one of the BizHats. With the **Owner/Investor BizHat** squarely on your head, look at the following exercise:

The Toyota Prius is a hybrid vehicle that was introduced in the United States in 2000. It uses electricity along with conventional gasoline, and it can be powered by either source separately or together. The car is not only fuel-efficient but also releases less pollution than conventional cars. Since its introduction, suppliers have been unable to keep up with the demand. Customers wanting to buy a Prius have to get on a waiting list that can be six months or longer.[19]

1. As the owner of a Toyota Prius dealership, explain how the supply relative to the demand leads to a shortage.
2. Explain how the supply and demand for the car affects the price you can charge for the Prius. Draw a graph to support your answer.
3. Toyota chose not to raise prices despite the increased demand. Suggest reasons for this strategy.
4. New hybrids are entering the market and providing competition to the Prius. Explain how this might affect your pricing strategy. What might this indicate about the industry life cycle?

Flip It...

After you've looked at the supply and demand data from the Owner's perspective, **flip over to the Customer BizHat.** Consider the purchase of a Prius by comparing it with several conventional cars.

Explain how the equilibrium price for the Prius is determined by the market. Draw a graph to support your answer.

Now Debrief It...

Compare the perspectives of the BizHats described above. Did looking at the situation from the Customer BizHat change your original perspective of the Owner/Investor BizHat?

Adapt: Monetary and Fiscal Policy, the Economic Cycle, and Economic Systems

BizSkills invite...

Try It!
There's no better way to learn concepts than to put them into practice. Take your turn in the driver's seat and be a part of actual business decision making by visiting the BizSkill for this chapter at **www.mybizlab.com**.

Now that you've practiced making tough business decisions and seeing the results of your choices in this chapter's BizSkill, it's time to translate those skills into plain English. And if you skipped the BizSkill, go back now!

Chapter 4 Goals

After experiencing this chapter, you'll be able to:

1. Use economic indicators to characterize the current business cycle you're living in, and identify the opportunities it offers for business and your personal success.
2. Explain how fiscal and monetary policy decisions can affect a business.
3. Describe how companies have adapted and continue to adapt to changing economic environments.
4. Explain how companies scan their environment to adapt effectively.
5. Predict how a business's strategy would change in a different economic system.

How do you adapt to keep your head above water?

Adapting to the Weather

You wouldn't plan a trip to the ski slopes without checking on the conditions. And obviously, even though you can't control whether you'll have good snow, you *can* decide how warmly you'll dress, whether you'll postpone your trip, or whether you'll buy an all-day ticket. You adapt. After all, skiing in the rain is nobody's idea of a good time.

The same is true of businesses; they have to adapt to what's going on outside. Although companies can't control external factors, they can pay attention, try to predict what will happen next, and strategize accordingly. Are consumers hanging onto their money instead of spending it? Are prices on the rise? And what about that new piece of technology that might just make life easier for employees? In this chapter, we'll step outside for a look at the forces that businesses have to contend with, how they adapt, and what it all means for you.

1. The Business Cycle: Riding the Roller Coaster

In November of 2008, newspapers across the country announced that Circuit City, the second-largest electronics retailer in the United States, filed for bankruptcy protection. Just two months later, after repeated attempts to boost sales and a fierce battle to find a buyer, the store declared it would be going out of business. The casualties totaled 722 store closures, leaving around 40,000 employees out of work.[1] Going out of business had become a trend; within a period of about a year, popular retail companies Sharper Image, Bombay Co., Mervyn's, and Linen's 'N Things had closed their doors. If those closures hadn't scared investors and consumers enough, Circuit City's failure certainly did.

So, why did businesses start dropping like flies in 2008? Clearly, it was not coincidence, and clearly, these well-known retailers weren't the only ones suffering. Beginning in December 2007, the U.S. economy was entering a **recession**, which is characterized as at least two successive quarters of economic decline in the gross domestic product (or GDP, the total amount of all goods and services produced in a country in one year).[2] This simply means there were two successive quarters during which there was a decline in the value of all the products produced in the United States.

The market began to look grim for everyone; small businesses, large corporations, employees, consumers, and investors were face-to-face with loss of income, loss of productivity, and loss of employment. Companies that only months earlier were making money and increasing production found that they had in fact been poised at the top of an economic peak and were now sliding—in some cases careening—down the other side.

Although nobody likes a recession, they're a recurring part of the **business cycle**—the cycle of fluctuations in the economy that occur at irregular intervals. As shown in Figure 4.1, the business cycle can be a lot like a roller coaster ride.

- Think about a roller coaster: once you get to a certain point, there's only one place to go: down. Eventually, employment, output, and stock prices decline, which can lead to a recession; this is the heart-pounding ride to the bottom, or the **trough**. It's safe to say there's screaming involved in going down this hill. On a roller coaster, you know you're only going to be at the bottom for a second or two, but no one knows how long or deep the trough will be in the business cycle. The average length of time for a recession is one year.
- Recessionary periods are generally followed by a **recovery** period, during which the economy once again expands.
- Very rarely, recovery takes longer to occur than expected, leading to a **depression**, or a long recession with more severe consequences.[3] Although there isn't a clear dividing line between recession and depression, most people agree that the Great Depression (1929–1944) was the U.S. economy's only real depression during the 20th century.
- During recovery, if the economy continues to grow beyond former peak levels, this period is known as an **expansion**. Although in theory the economy could expand indefinitely, in practice, the economy has never been able to sustain such growth beyond a certain point. Once the economy reaches its peak, it's only a matter of time before it starts heading down again.

Figure **4.1** | **The Business Cycle Roller Coaster**

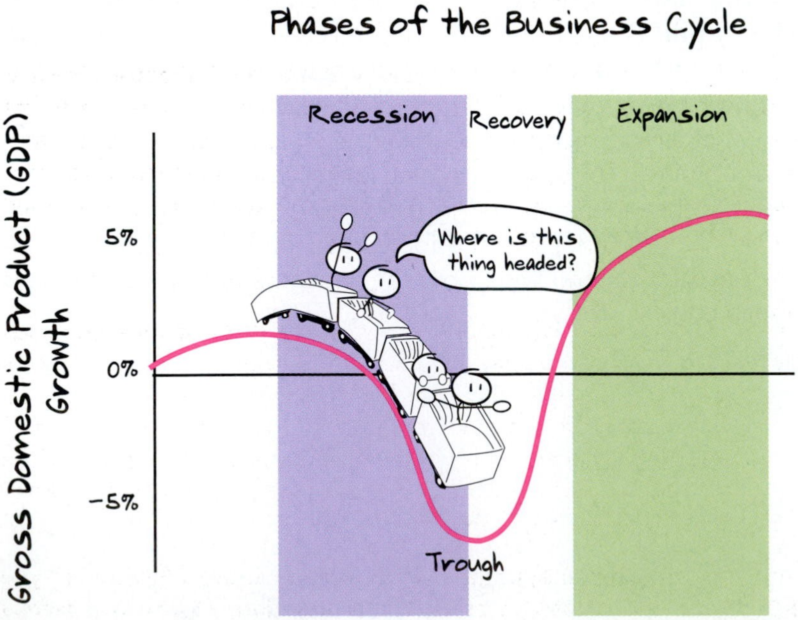

So, why do periods of recession occur? Well, just as meteorologists sometimes predict sun on a day that turns out to be rainy, so too do business developers and investors sometimes misread economic indicators and make the *wrong* adjustments to their strategies. This happens on a small scale often enough—we all know of people who have lost money in the stock market or failed at a business venture—but what happens when this same thing happens on a large scale? You may have already guessed: recession.

■ Businesses may adapt their business practices to external forces in the economy. By reading various signs, they can forecast future trends in spending, consumer preferences, and economic growth and adjust their plans accordingly.

Finding Opportunities Along the Ride

You've seen how the business cycle roller coaster ride can be a dangerous one for companies like Circuit City. But it can also create opportunities. How? When the economy takes a nosedive, people aren't spending as much, and businesses struggle. This struggle comes from a lack of demand, and as you learned in Chapter 3, suppliers must often reduce their prices when demand decreases. People who have made good financial decisions and saved money have opportunities all around them—prices for homes, cars, and food all fall. Stocks and other investments also become affordable to people looking to invest.

For example, let's say you're interested in a certain stock, but at $20 a share, it's too expensive for you. During an economic downturn, that stock may fall to $3 a share. If you feel that this is a temporary situation, you can grab up a bunch of shares, sit back, and see what happens. If you know this, you can do things that can significantly improve your standard of living and just maybe your quality of life. You can now see how our current economic downturn may offer a silver lining to those who have the resources to capitalize on investment bargains.

■ Businesses may also adapt their business practices to external forces in the economy. By reading various signs, they can forecast future trends in spending, consumer preferences, and economic growth and adjust their plans accordingly. Those who are able to adapt the best, succeed.

Economic Indicators: How Are We Doing?

Sometimes, it's pretty clear to everyone, without much consideration, where the market hangs in the business cycle. In 1933, at the lowest point of the Great Depression, for example, when one in four Americans was out of work, there was no question about the state of the market.

But most of the time, analysts rely on a number of **economic indicators** (such as the GDP and unemployment rate) to read the pulse of the economy and measure its rate of growth against other years. The goal of the National Bureau of Economic Research (NBER) is to follow economic indicators for signs of recession or expansion, which they release to the public so that investors, homebuyers, and business owners—anyone who might benefit from understanding current economic trends—can make use of them.

Gross Domestic Product The clearest measure of economic growth is the **gross domestic product (GDP)**, which is the sum you'd have if you added the dollar values of *all* goods and services—from manicures to concert tickets to college tuition to kitchen tables—*produced in a country in one year.* If a company like Nike manufactures some of its shoes in China, then the Nike shoes produced in China would *not* be counted as part of the United States' GDP, even though Nike is a U.S. company. Instead, the shoes would factor into China's GDP.

It also bears mentioning that when analysts use GDP to measure economic growth, they're using *real GDP*, which is the GDP measure that adjusts for **inflation**. Inflation is a general increase in the level of prices. Inflation decreases the spending power of the dollar, since one dollar can buy fewer products. You'll learn more about inflation and how it is measured later in this chapter.

The average increase of real GDP in the United States is about 3 percent per year; so the total income generated within the United States should increase by about 3 percent from one year to the next (although, of course, the increase may be higher when the economy is in a period of expansion). When the GDP stays level or drops, that's a pretty good indicator of an economic recession. Businesses are producing less, consumers are purchasing less, and service providers are unable to sell as many of their services. For example, during the recession of the 1970s, real GDP fell by over 6 percent at the recession's worst.

Productivity On the other hand, an *increase* of the GDP can be caused by higher **productivity**, or the amount of goods and services produced per hour of labor. If businesses can produce more with the same input of labor, their overall output will rise. One way to do this is through technology and innovation.

Let's look at an example. Take someone who starts a lawn care business with two friends. With all three employees working full-time, the company is able to mow 70 lawns each week. A year later the company is mowing more than 100 lawns each week. Has it hired more employees? No. It's the same three employees. Are they working longer hours? No. They're all still working 40-hour weeks.

Instead, they've been able to improve their productivity with technology. Before, the employees were using push mowers to cut grass, but now the company has riding mowers. Same input, higher output, which is great news for everyone. More income for the company means better wages, and maybe even better prices for customers. Even the government benefits from the higher tax revenues.

You can probably see where this is going. When productivity increases for a huge number of businesses at once—that is, in the *aggregate*—this generally leads to a healthy, expanding economy.

Gross National Product

Another indicator similar to GDP is **gross national product (GNP)**—the total value of goods and services produced by citizens of a country during a one-year time period. For this measurement, it does not matter where citizens are living. For example, U.S. citizens living in Italy would have their production totals added to the United States' GNP, not Italy's. Basically, the GDP measures a country's production, whereas the GNP measures a country's citizens' production. Even though the GNP is an important economic indicator, GDP is the preferred figure among analysts because it measures the economic activity generated within a specific geographical region.

The Unemployment Rate

In the first half of 2009, it seemed like businesses were laying off employees left and right. In May 2009, the overall **unemployment rate**, which is the percentage of people in the labor force who are unemployed, was 9.4 percent, or 14.5 million people.[4] Considering that the official unemployment rate only measures joblessness among people who have been *actively* looking for work for four weeks, it's clear that the actual number of people suffering from job loss in May 2009 was higher.[5] That 9.4 percent didn't factor in the people who had simply *stopped* looking for work, gone back to school, or were forced to a part-time workweek.

So, how is unemployment tied to the business cycle? Sometimes, unemployment is the result of price inflation. When almost everyone who wants to work has a job (when there is low unemployment), businesses have to offer higher wages to compete for employees. Eventually, these increases in salaries may mean that businesses have to start charging more for their goods and services, which eventually drives down demand. As demand goes down, businesses need to cut costs to make up for lost income, which means that some employees may find themselves out of work. In turn, businesses start producing less.

A Vicious Cycle As you can probably predict, unemployment has the potential to become part of a vicious cycle. An economic downturn may lead to failure in certain sectors of the economy more than others, in which case large numbers of people in those sectors will lose their jobs at once. This then hurts other sectors of the economy.

Consider the housing industry in early 2008. Because of the collapse of the housing market, banks and other financial institutions that were heavily invested in this market took massive losses and became less willing to extend credit to businesses as they had in the past. Without lines of credit from the financial industry, many businesses weren't able to cover operating expenses and had to reduce their workforce. In turn, these unemployed workers could not pay their own debts to the financial industry. This further weakened the banks' position, hurting more businesses and resulting in more layoffs.

Do you know the current unemployment rate in the United States?

To see the effect this downward spiral can have on a particular business, let's look at Microsoft. Not only did fewer consumers buy new PCs in 2008, but businesses cut their spending on Microsoft operating systems as well. Many individuals and businesses that *did* buy PCs that year were switching to cheaper versions of the operating systems or opting for substitute goods, which, if you recall from the previous chapter, affects demand.

The rationale went something like this: *I'm struggling to make ends meet, and I have the choice of paying to use Microsoft products or to use free open-source systems and software (like Open Office or Linux).* The free, substitute good seemed like a more attractive option to a lot of people at that time. As a result, Microsoft felt the effects in loss of income. To cut back on costs, the company announced in January 2009 that it would be laying off 5,000 employees.[6]

A Planning Tool Generally, business owners try to use the unemployment rate as a planning tool. If the level of unemployment seems to be increasing in some industries, chances are business owners in other industries will be affected, too. The problem is that laying off workers and then rehiring them when the economy improves is expensive—not to mention a hassle and an unpleasant thing to do. If businesses can compensate for this by decreasing everyone's workload (thereby decreasing salaries as well), or by encouraging older employees to retire, or by some other less painful/expensive means, that's generally preferable, but it also requires careful planning.

The unemployment rate can be a planning tool for you, too. Let's say you're about to graduate from college and enter the workforce. You hear on the news that the unemployment rate is the highest it's been in the past five years. What does this mean for you? If more people are looking for work, job hunting can be competitive (remember the basics behind supply and demand). Companies that are hiring can be choosy about people they hire and may lower starting salaries simply because they can—when times are tough, many people are willing to take a pay cut.

So, what do you do with the information? You need to make yourself as attractive as possible to potential employers. If you have trouble finding a job, you could take this time to improve yourself. Maybe go back to school and get a higher degree. Or, take a class to work on a weakness. You might also want to look for industries that are growing, even in the midst of economic declines. For example, the health care industry continues to need skilled employees, even as other industries are reducing their workforce.[7] Volunteer. Network. Do whatever you can to make yourself a better prospect.

Price Indexes: What Would You Pay for a Basket Of... It hits you one day when you're standing in line for a movie. *When did the cost of a movie ticket get to be $9? Wasn't it just $7 a year or two ago?* The price may have been $9 for a while now, but you notice it today because you don't have enough money to pay for your ticket in cash. You thought you'd have enough, but that coffee you just bought cost more than you were expecting, too. You notice regretfully that everything you buy lately seems to cost a little more.

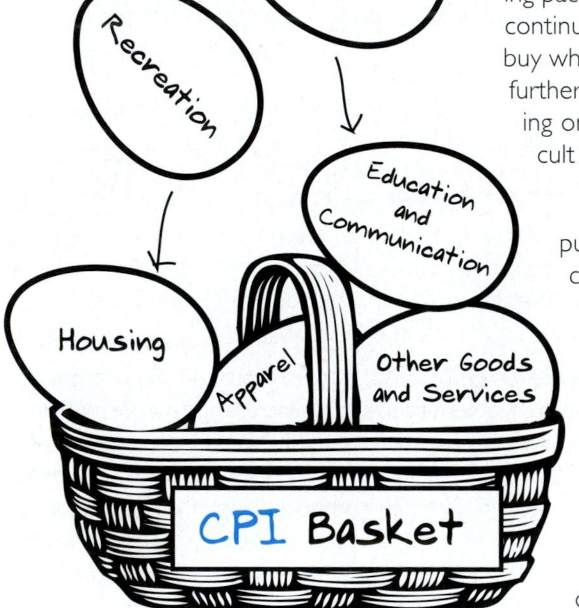

What items do you put in your basket most often?

The CPI What you've noticed is an increase in the **consumer price index (CPI)**, which measures changes to the average cost of the coffee, groceries, health care, and other goods and services the average urban consumer buys on a regular basis. Every month, the Bureau of Labor Statistics releases the CPI data for a representative "basket" of consumer purchases that it tracks in comparison to other months. Economists use the CPI more than anything else to calculate the inflation rate.

Ideally, inflation should be increasing at about the same rate as the GDP—historically about 3 percent a year. Remember that inflation is a decrease in the spending power of the dollar. Some inflation is a normal part of economic growth. For example, if you bought something for $20 in 2000, the same item would cost $25.37 in 2009.[8] The problem is that when inflation rises faster than economic growth (i.e., faster than the increase in GDP), consumers' buying power is not keeping pace with the cost of the products they consume. If this cycle continues, workers demand higher wages so they can afford to buy what they need. Businesses must then raise their prices even further to compensate for the additional money they are spending on wages. This triggers a cycle of inflation that can be difficult to reverse.

The flip side of inflation is **deflation**, in which a dollar's purchasing power *increases* because of a continuous decrease in prices. The trouble with deflation is that it tends to become a downward spiral. When the economy is flagging, companies have to work harder to attract customers, which can lead to a price-dropping competition. ("Quick—the breakfast joint across the street's selling pancakes for $2! Let's advertise eggs and bacon for a buck fifty." And so on.) And *that* becomes a sticky situation when consumers decide to wait for costs to drop further. Why buy a new sound system *now* when the price might be lower in another month? When spending decreases, businesses consequently bring in less revenue, which forces them to lay off workers to save money. The people laid off then spend less, which cuts even further into businesses' revenues, and so the cycle continues.

Translation Guide

In economic terms: Inflation means a decrease in the purchasing power of the dollar. You may also look at inflation as an increase in the price of products.

Example: If the inflation rate has consistently stayed at 3 percent for the past few years, then it's possible that the $1 cup of coffee you enjoy so much will cost $1.03 next year.

Breaking free of this trap can be very difficult, as neither individuals nor businesses are able to spend enough money to stop the cycle. At this point, the government has to step in to stop the spiral of deflation. You'll learn more about the tools the government has to fight deflation when we talk about fiscal policy later in this chapter.

PPI The **producer price index (PPI)**, as the term implies, looks at the costs of goods and services from the *producer's* perspective. This index tracks the average change of the prices that producers pay for the goods and services they purchase for their business operations. Let's say Milo has a sandwich shop. The price Milo pays the bakery for the bread it delivers—the *wholesale price*—would factor into the PPI. But, assuming this is a bakery that also operates a storefront and sells its bread directly to customers, the price *you* pay when you stop in for a fresh loaf of sourdough would fall under the CPI. As you can see, there is a strong relationship between CPI and PPI.

Economic indicators are informative, but they aren't always perfect, nor are those who interpret them.

The CPI and PPI are both important measurements for business owners to track. If an increasing PPI means the bakery suddenly starts charging Milo 50 cents more per loaf of bread, Milo will probably have to increase the price of his sandwiches, thus impacting CPI. On the other hand, a decreasing PPI (often driven by reduced demand for products that producers use) will translate to lower costs for producers, who can either pass those lower costs on to their customers in the form of lower prices, or keep prices steady and reap higher profits. The latter option may be difficult to maintain, however, because customers may find other producers who choose to lower their prices. That competitive pressure, motivated by the invisible hand we mentioned in Chapter 2, maintains a predictable relationship between consumer and producer prices.

Economic Indicators: Driving Strategy

Economic indicators are informative, but they aren't always perfect, nor are those who interpret them. For example, when the economy was on the rise in 2004, gambling was good, and the Las Vegas-based MGM Mirage was buying and selling properties like a Monopoly player on a roll. In late 2006, when the economy was still expanding, the company took a shot at forecasting and dumped $8.6 billion into the construction of a "67-acre vertical city" on the Vegas Strip.[9]

With an economic recession following close on the heels of MGM's massive investment, construction was underway when tight times started taking a toll on gambling revenues. Consumers were opting to save their money rather than gambling it away as they had in years of greater economic bounty, and scores of potential travelers to Vegas were canceling their vacations. As a result, MGM Mirage experienced billions in losses, jeopardizing the company's loans and the City Center project in the process.[10] Clearly, it hadn't seen this coming. To adapt, the company was forced to scale back on City Center in addition to selling some of its individual properties.

At the same time, a strained economy can be a boom for some businesses that adapt wisely. Let's turn to Amazon.com, the Seattle-based online retailer, for a look at its response to the recession in 2008. As we already know about economic downturns, overall spending levels fall; when people do spend, they're only willing to do so at significantly lower prices than they might have purchased at before. Keeping this in mind, Amazon chose to deeply discount the prices on many of its goods, realizing the discounts would hurt the company's profit margins, but predicting that the number of loyal customers it gained would produce positive growth overall. The company was right. While businesses were reporting losses across the board at the end of that year, Amazon's profits actually rose 9 percent. Most of this was due to savvy business strategy—taking advantage of recession spending habits to actually draw business away from many traditional retail stores.[11]

Do It...

4.1: Understand Economic Indicators Watch a news program, such as those on CNN and MSNBC, or read an article from a magazine, newspaper, or the Internet that focuses on the economy. Find two economic indicators that were discussed. For each, explain what these indicators might predict, and how you might personally benefit from knowing what is happening in the business environment. Limit your response to one page, and be prepared to submit it electronically or present it to your class.

Now Debrief...

- The **business cycle** refers to fluctuations in the economy that occur at irregular intervals: recession → trough → recovery → expansion.
- **Recessions** are economic downturns—companies experience decreased profits, consumer spending falls, and unemployment rises, which leads to **troughs**, the lowest points in the cycle.

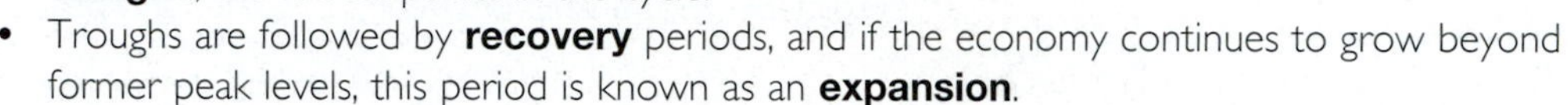

- Troughs are followed by **recovery** periods, and if the economy continues to grow beyond former peak levels, this period is known as an **expansion**.
- When businesspeople want to get a reading on the health of the economy, they look to **economic indicators**: **gross domestic product (GDP)**, **gross national product (GNP)**, **unemployment rates**, the **consumer price index (CPI)**, and the **producer price index (PPI)**.
- The GDP is the most commonly watched indicator because it reflects the monetary value of all goods and services produced within a country in a year.

2. Fiscal and Monetary Policy: To the Rescue?

> "There are risks and costs to a program of action. But they are far less than the long-range risks and costs of comfortable inaction."
>
> **—John F. Kennedy**[12]

Quick question: If the economy's in trouble, what should you do to help fix it? Spend money or save money? This is actually a trick question—you need to do both wisely. If you're spending money on capital goods such as a house or a car or you're saving money in a bank, this makes money available for banks to loan to others. When this happens, banks can loan money to businesses, which creates new jobs and money for builders to build houses. Of course, getting the economy back on course isn't up to you. In this section, we'll examine the tools the government uses to regulate the economy.

Fiscal Policy: The Government Steps In

When President Obama took office in January 2009, businesses and consumers were hoping for a change in **fiscal policy**—that is, government actions directed at stabilizing the economy—to help the weakened economy. Economists argued over how the new administration should use its fiscal policy tools of *government spending* and *taxation* to jump-start the market most effectively.

Government Spending

One of the first actions of the Obama administration was to propose the American Recovery and Reinvestment Act,[13] which aimed to stimulate the economy through increased government spending on public works projects. You may be thinking, "If the economy is in trouble, why are we spending money?" Well, the rationale of this—and similar fiscal policy decisions of the past—is that in times of recession, **aggregate demand**, or overall demand, for goods and services is low. People are afraid to spend money because they're afraid they won't be able to get more of it.

For example, if you're running low on money, you probably think twice before buying something you don't need. In fact, you may start economizing—making your own lunch, carpooling, and so on. Business owners go through this, too. Since they don't know when sales might pick up again, they may cut back on capital (large-scale) investments and unnecessary expenses, order fewer supplies, and lay off employees.

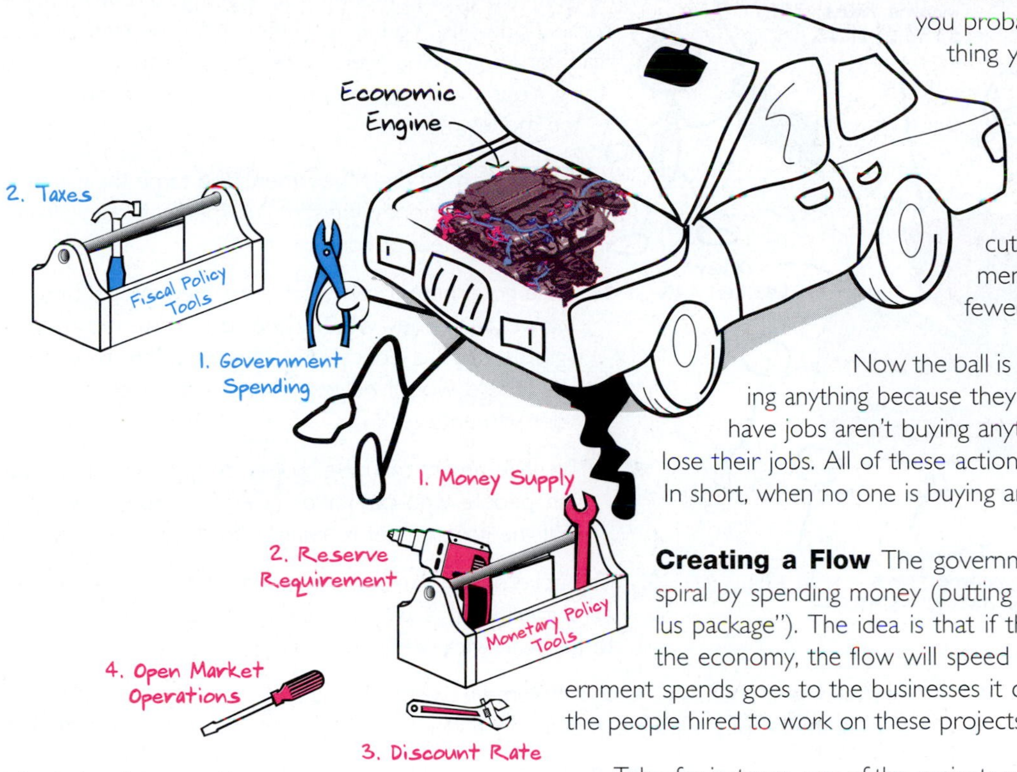

Now the ball is rolling. Laid-off employees aren't buying anything because they can't afford to. And people who still have jobs aren't buying anything because they're afraid they may lose their jobs. All of these actions cause the cash flow to slow down. In short, when no one is buying anything, everyone gets poorer.

What tools can the government use to rev up the economic engine?

Creating a Flow The government can help break the deflationary spiral by spending money (putting the *stimulus* in the "economic stimulus package"). The idea is that if there is more money flowing through the economy, the flow will speed up. Here's how: the money the government spends goes to the businesses it contracts for stimulus projects and to the people hired to work on these projects.

Take, for instance, one of the projects approved for government spending, the improvement of airport runways in Fayetteville, Arkansas.[14] Now let's take a hypothetical Arkansan, Stu, the owner of Stu's Steamrollers, whose company is one of those selected for the project. Stu's Steamrollers suddenly has a greater demand for business and consequently more money to invest in capital—more workers and maybe even more steamrollers. Perhaps in a couple of months, one of Stu's new employees, who happily has a job again, will be able to go out and buy a new car for her family, which also helps improve business in the auto industry.

Spending Money to Boost the Economy Just like jump-starting a car, the government uses the power of government spending to get the economy's engine running on its own again. But where does this money come from? Take a minute and look at the illustrations on pages 90 and 91 to see where government money comes from and where it goes.

In economic terms, the government spends taxpayer money to increase the aggregate (or overall) demand for products back to a healthy level, so that the economy can start growing again. But, realistically, the government's spending strategy only works as a means to growth if it boosts consumer spending on a larger level. Even though Stu's employee decides to buy a new car, the auto industry won't actually benefit unless a number of other people also decide to go out and buy new cars. If people are afraid to spend because they're afraid they won't be able to get more money, the government's strategy falls flat.

To have its desired effect, fiscal policy needs to be far-reaching enough that people won't feel like they're taking a risk by spending. For this to happen, people need to feel secure and feel like their investments are making money. When people believe their income is increasing, they have a tendency to increase their spending; this is known as the *wealth effect*. This may help explain why even when you're making more money, your bank account balance stays the same because you spend more.

Coming Up with the Money However, fiscal policy is a very complex subject, and decisions like increasing spending have drawbacks, too. Imagine you're struggling financially and you

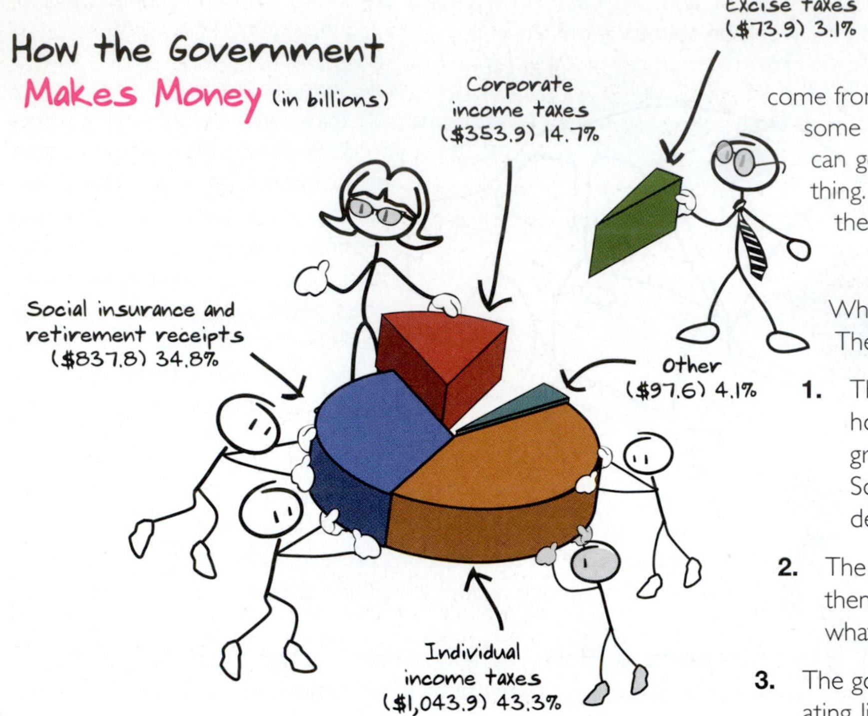

have the opportunity to make an investment that may pay off big time. However, to get started, you need $5,000. But where is that $5,000 going to come from? To get this money, you're going to have to make some trade-offs. You may tighten your budget, or you can get a loan. However, there's no such thing as a sure thing. Your investment may not pay off even if you can get the money.

In terms of the government, the same thing is true. Where does money for stimulus spending come from? There are a few options:

1. The government can work with the national budget; however, money would have to be taken from programs such as education, transportation, or energy. So, there would be less money for these or other departments.
2. The government can raise money by increasing taxes, but then people who pay taxes have less money, which is what the government is trying to fix.
3. The government can borrow money, but then it's just creating liabilities that will increase future taxes and will have to be dealt with later.
4. The government could also just print some new money, but that has its drawbacks, too. Increasing the money supply can cause inflation.

Finally, if the government does go through with increased spending, it doesn't have a crystal ball to predict the future or even to see what's going to happen with the economy day to day. The stimulus spending might not be enough to jump-start the economy because of the time it takes to implement projects for roads, schools, and bridges—or, it may turn out that the spending was excessive or unnecessary. But because economic indicators only show what *has* happened, rather than what is happening or what will happen, it's impossible to know whether aggregate demand is getting weaker or stronger at any given moment.

Taxation

Taxation, another fiscal policy tool that the government can use, can also influence aggregate demand. As noted above, when the government raises taxes—often because it needs more money to fund its spending commitments—businesses and consumers have less money in their pockets to spend. Thus, higher taxes might decrease demand but also potentially reduce inflation.

On the other hand, if the federal government *lowers* taxes, in theory, consumers and businesses will have more to spend, thereby increasing demand and fueling the economy. However, fiscal policy is always simpler in theory than in practice. Lowering taxes doesn't increase demand directly the way spending on government projects does. If people take the extra money they're bringing home after taxes and put it in their savings accounts or hide it under their mattresses, the tax break didn't trigger greater demand.

Consider the economic stimulus payment you may have received in 2008. What did you do with that extra money? If you saved the stimulus money rather than spending it, the tax rebate didn't have its intended effect. But it may have increased the amount of money banks have from savings accounts, so it's not an entirely bad thing. As you can see, every decision the government makes at a broad—or macro—level triggers a complex series of effects.

Fiscal Policy and You

The trick for businesses is to predict how fiscal policy in combination with monetary policy (which we discuss next) and other environmental factors will influence

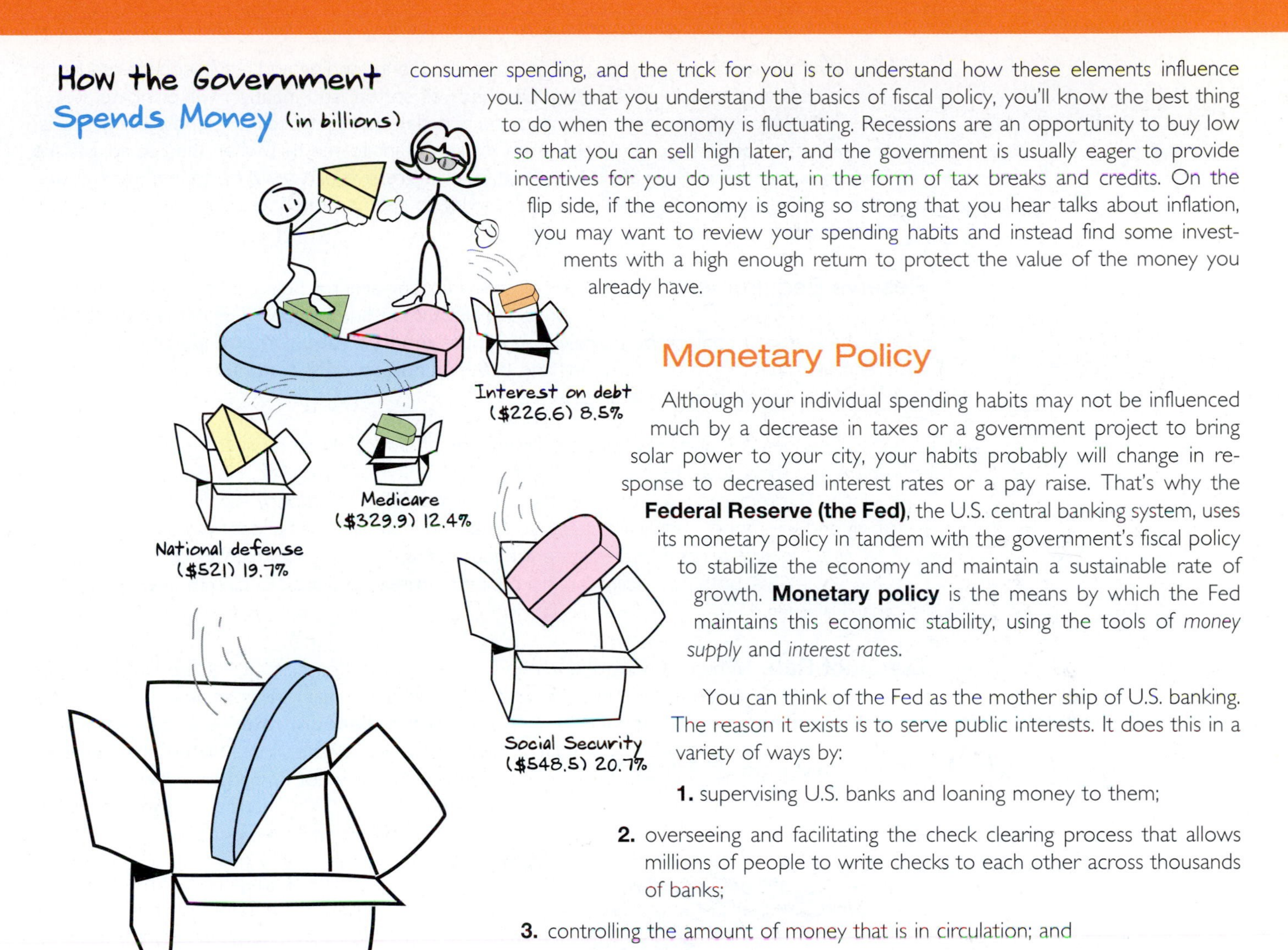

consumer spending, and the trick for you is to understand how these elements influence you. Now that you understand the basics of fiscal policy, you'll know the best thing to do when the economy is fluctuating. Recessions are an opportunity to buy low so that you can sell high later, and the government is usually eager to provide incentives for you do just that, in the form of tax breaks and credits. On the flip side, if the economy is going so strong that you hear talks about inflation, you may want to review your spending habits and instead find some investments with a high enough return to protect the value of the money you already have.

Monetary Policy

Although your individual spending habits may not be influenced much by a decrease in taxes or a government project to bring solar power to your city, your habits probably will change in response to decreased interest rates or a pay raise. That's why the **Federal Reserve (the Fed)**, the U.S. central banking system, uses its monetary policy in tandem with the government's fiscal policy to stabilize the economy and maintain a sustainable rate of growth. **Monetary policy** is the means by which the Fed maintains this economic stability, using the tools of *money supply* and *interest rates*.

You can think of the Fed as the mother ship of U.S. banking. The reason it exists is to serve public interests. It does this in a variety of ways by:

1. supervising U.S. banks and loaning money to them;
2. overseeing and facilitating the check clearing process that allows millions of people to write checks to each other across thousands of banks;
3. controlling the amount of money that is in circulation; and
4. studying the economy carefully and developing plans to keep the economy strong and stable.[15]

You may be thinking, "What does this have to do with me?" Well, if you have a student loan or are thinking about buying a home, this is the bank that sets the range of interest rates that banks can charge you for loans. That's the annual percentage rate in the fine print in many financial statements. We'll go over interest rates more later on in the chapter, but first let's take a look at the money supply.

Money Supply

The value of money is directly related to the **money supply**, the amount of money in circulation at one time. This is why controlling the supply is so crucial. When economic growth has slowed, the government, but more specifically the Fed, takes actions to increase the money supply so that more will be available for consumers and businesses to spend and invest. The Fed is able to increase the money supply by adjusting the *reserve requirement* and the *discount rate* and by engaging in *open market operations* (all of which we'll discuss next). Such *expansionary monetary policy* is designed to stimulate the economy, whereas *tight monetary policy* is intended to slow economic growth by reducing the money supply.

The Money Supply and Value When the Fed tinkers with money supply, its primary effect is on lending. When money supply increases, banks and other lending institutions are more willing to lend money to businesses and consumers, who in turn use that money to buy stuff.

The increase in the money supply will thus increase demand for products, but if the demand grows too quickly, so will prices, and inflation will occur. The Fed might respond by lowering the money supply, thus triggering a decline in lending and a subsequent reduction in business and consumer spending. Demand will soften, and inflation will dissipate. But, if the Fed reduces the money supply too much, deflation might occur. See how tricky this is? For you as a consumer or businessperson, it's important to see that when the Fed adjusts the money supply, it will likely affect how hesitant or aggressive banks will be to lend money, and that could affect your job, the loans you're trying to get, and the prices you pay for the products you buy.

Reserve Requirement With billions of dollars floating around, how can the Fed monitor this money and use it to affect the money supply? One of the tools the Fed might tweak to control the money supply is the **reserve requirement**, the amount of currency a bank is required to keep on hand, based on how much its customers deposit—in a vault or on deposit with the Federal Reserve.

The idea is that by lowering the reserve requirement, the Fed will increase a bank's willingness to make loans by providing it with more money to do so. And this expands the money supply. The requirement is one way the Fed helps stabilize the money supply. When the economy and the money supply are stable, you may find it easier to get a loan with terms you agree to or to receive a good interest rate on your savings account. Ultimately, you're able to get more with less, both personally and in a business context, and *this* can directly affect your standard of living.

Discount Rate When scanning the economic news, you often hear about the Fed raising or lowering commercial interest rates. What's actually going on when you hear this news is that the Fed has decided to raise or lower the **discount rate**—the reduced interest rate the Fed charges private banks when they borrow money. Although this may not immediately affect you, it ultimately affects the interest rate *you* pay when you borrow from your bank.

Interest Rate Domino Effect

Fed
changes discount rate
Banks
lend to businesses and consumers
Businesses
borrow and invest
building
inventory
AB card
house
Consumers
borrow and spend
car

How do you participate in the domino effect?

The Fed acts as the bank for commercial banks; when a bank temporarily needs additional money, it generally turns to the Fed for a loan. Controlling the discount rate is therefore another means of controlling the money supply. When the discount rate is high, making it more expensive for banks to borrow money, the money supply decreases; banks are less willing to borrow and therefore less willing to loan money out. To regulate the number of people coming in for loans, your bank will raise its interest rates because high interest rates deter people from taking out loans.

For you this means that if the Fed raises the discount rate, the interest rate for that loan you need will probably rise, too. However, if the Fed lowers the discount rate, you may want to celebrate because your interest rate should decrease as well. This isn't to say that if the discount rate is lowered, run out and get a loan. What you can do is take what you know about monetary policy and use it to make smart decisions about your money.

Open Market Operations The most commonly used monetary policy tools are the Fed's **open market operations** by which it once again *indirectly* controls commercial interest rates through purchasing or selling government bonds. If the Fed wants banks to lower their interest rates, it puts a process into motion that begins with buying large quantities of government bonds on the open market.

The dealers who purchase the government bonds then turn around and deposit the money from these sales with private banks, which now have a greater supply of money to lend. In order to attract more borrowers, the banks lower their interest rates—both the interest they charge other banks (which is known as the **federal funds rate**) and the interest they charge businesses and individuals.

As you saw with the discount rate, this can directly affect people who need loans. The hope is that with lower interest rates, the Wilson family might decide to borrow the money they need to remodel their house, the local plant nursery might borrow the funds to invest in a new species of tropical shrub, and a national chain restaurant might take out a loan to open new storefronts across the country. In other words, the Fed lowers interest rates to help promote economic growth.

Do It...

4.2: React to Changes in the Money Supply How might the Owner/Investor and Customer BizHats react to the following situations?

- The Fed raises the discount rate from 4 percent to 6 percent
- The Fed lowers the reserve requirement

Limit your response to one page, and be prepared to submit it electronically or present it in class.

Now Debrief...

- Government actions directed at stabilizing the economy comprise **fiscal policy**. To help jump-start a slow economy, the government can stimulate the economy through increased spending and lowering taxes. On the flip side, government can slow down the economy through decreased spending and higher taxes.
- **Monetary policy**, which is the means by which the **Federal Reserve (the Fed)** maintains economic stability, is also useful by working with the **money supply**, **reserve requirement**, and **discount rate**, and by engaging in **open market operations**. By working with all of these tools, the Fed has the ability to help encourage or discourage spending.

3. Adapting to Economic Environments: Beyond the Farm and Factory

It's hard to imagine, but at one time in our history, it took half the working population of the United States to keep everyone fed. That's not "putting food on the table" in a figurative sense; we're talking about going out there and literally producing food from the soil. By contrast, these days, only 2.5 percent of the U.S. population works in agriculture. Clearly, it's a long way from then to now, and the story of that journey has to do with the changing importance of the **factors of production**, how businesses have adapted to these changes, and how our economy was transformed in the process. Economists generally use four categories to label the factors that go into production: *land*, *labor*, *capital*, and *entrepreneurship*.

At one point in our history, land was the most essential factor of production. A farmer could feed his family and maybe a few other folks, if he had enough land and if the land was productive. (Generally speaking, *land* includes not only the plot of ground itself, but the natural resources that come from it.)[16]

During the second half of the 19th century, all that changed as people began flocking to the cities, where machine-based manufacturing, coal fuel, steam power, and the railways were increasing productivity. Our nation was developing into a manufacturing economy, and more than anything else, businesses that wanted to make a profit in this economy needed *labor*—in this case, most specifically factory workers[17]—and *capital*, money and equipment that allowed laborers to churn out products so much more efficiently.

An experience economy doesn't focus on producing a product; instead, it expands the idea of what a product is: a good, service, and now also an experience.

Gradually, as new technology allowed manufacturers to produce the same output with a smaller input of labor, business again adapted. Around the middle of the last century, *entrepreneurship*—organization, innovation, and risk-taking—combined with technological advancements to become the greatest source of profit.[18]

In turn, the U.S. economy shifted from a manufacturing economy to a service-based economy: think phone companies, utilities providers (such as the gas or water company), educational institutions, and accounting firms.

Knowledge: The New Factor of Production

As times have changed, the economy has shifted yet again. Within the last 20 years or so, the most important factor of production has been *knowledge* (sometimes considered a form of human capital). Businesses have responded by increasingly employing experts—people with specialized knowledge—and by dealing in information.[19] In a **knowledge economy**, like the one we have today, the economy is based on producing information and ideas. This is a sharp contrast to an economy based on goods and services. Workers in a knowledge economy are forced to apply ideas, concepts, and information to their jobs instead of physical labor or skill.

A Real-Life Case of Adaptation In 1896, while the U.S. economy was still invested in manufacturing, the son of a German immigrant invented a tabulating machine to help the U.S. Census Bureau keep track of the country's mushrooming population. Soon after, the immigrant's son started a manufacturing business, the Tabulating Machine Company (TMC), and sales took off. Over the next decade, in order to expand business and adapt to consumer demands, TMC began manufacturing other gadgets, from meat slicers and coffee grinders to commercial scales and time recorders.

Eventually, as times and demands changed, the company focused its efforts on developing time- and labor-saving technology. During the Great Depression, it contracted to provide the Social Security Administration with innovative accounting services, and later, during World War II, it went on to contribute innovations to early computing. This company succeeded where many other businesses did not because what it offered was a blend of technology with "services and solutions." Today, the company, which is now called IBM, has focused its goals on "integrated business solutions," offering products, services, and information to consumers.[20]

The Experience Economy

But, hold on, IBM's transition to offering information isn't where economic transitions stop. Another big shift, which we are in the midst of, is to an *experience economy*. This is different from

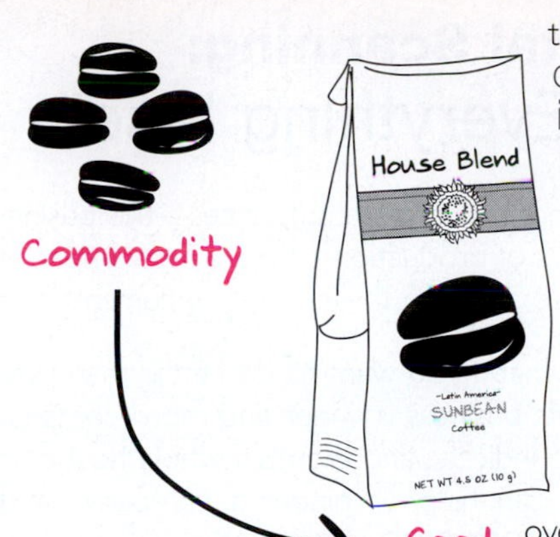

the factors of production mentioned above. ■ An experience economy doesn't focus on producing a product; instead, it expands the idea of what a product is: a good, service, and now also an experience. What kinds of experiences? People want to party in Vegas. They want to have lasagna prepared by Mario Batali or they want their children to meet Mickey Mouse. In an experience economy, people are paying for events that will leave a lasting memory. Why else would a family travel halfway across the country to go to Disneyland? It usually isn't the rides that get them there; it's the memories the trip will hopefully create.

Creating an Experience Shift Many businesses in the game of selling an experience don't happen overnight. Most products originate with a consumer need or problem. Once this has been identified, businesspeople look for ways to fulfill this need. The business may start off by acquiring a *commodity*, which is something that people find useful or valuable, like coffee beans. After the business gets a hold of the beans, it sets out to make an attractive good. This means roasting the beans at the perfect temperature or maybe even grinding them. Once the coffee is packaged, it's ready to be shipped and sold.

Once the business owner has a handle on selling a good, the next step may be selling a service. The owner works on brewing the best cup of coffee, but as you know, that's usually not enough. Coffee shops are just about everywhere, so what makes this one better than the next? To help gain a competitive edge, the shop may try to provide better service with friendly employees or by making drinks to order. However, the company may lose its edge again because other businesses catch on and follow suit.

So, if every other coffee shop has good coffee, friendly service, and makes your drink to order, what can you do to keep your edge? Well, you give them something no one else can: the ultimate *experience*. This is exactly what Starbucks did. Starbucks differentiates itself from others coffee shops by providing a European coffeehouse experience. This may help explain why certain businesses, like Starbucks or Disney, dominate in their field. You can ride a roller coaster or grab coffee at any number of places, but it's the experience that brings you back.

What factors of production are used to produce each of these?

Do It...

4.3: Figure Out What You Consume One of the experience components of Starbucks is its European coffeehouse atmosphere. Together with a teammate, list 10 products you consume or buy regularly. Looking at this list, how many are based on the experience, and how? Limit your response to one page, and be prepared to submit it electronically or present it in class.

Now Debrief...

- The most important factors of production in the U.S. economy have shifted from land to labor and capital to entrepreneurship to knowledge. The United States is a **knowledge economy**, that is, the economy is based on producing information and ideas.
- Many businesses have also adapted by expanding the idea of product to keep customers interested. Now the stages of a product model include commodity, good, service, and experience.

4. Environmental Scanning: Tuning into "Everything Else"

All right, so by now we can agree that external circumstances—the business cycle, monetary and fiscal policies, and changing factors of production—have a hefty impact on business operations. It's clear that companies need to adapt to these changing currents to stay afloat.

But what if you want to do better than stay afloat? The world that affects business is wider and more complex than tidy models like to indicate, and there's a whole host of outside factors that can help or hinder a company. ■ Environmental scanning is a way of keeping your radar tuned to the forces of change in the outside world, forces that could signal opportunity or be red flags for a business.

People who practice environmental scanning learn to notice ideas, trends, and triggers for change: What's new? Where's it coming from? What does it mean for my business? Environmental scanning has always been good business strategy, but these days, with technology changing in the blink of an eye, and new ideas spreading over the Internet like fires through dry brush, it's more relevant than ever.

To get a better handle on environmental scanning, it might help to remember PEGSET: **P**olitical/Legal, **E**conomic, **G**lobal, **S**ociocultural, **E**nvironmental, and **T**echnological. These are the factors businesses consider as they scan the changing business landscape. We'll discuss each of these factors in detail below.

Which plane in the picture is probably moving the fastest?

Political/Legal Factors

One important step in environmental scanning is to keep up with political and legal factors that might affect a business. In scanning this aspect of the environment, businesses look for changes to such things as: copyright laws, environmental protection legislation, minimum wage regulations, union ordinances, licensing laws, tax policies, trade restrictions, and litigation costs.

For example, consider the television networks that several years ago were suing file-sharing networks. The networks claimed that the public release of TV episodes on these Web sites was a major copyright violation, which it was, under the Digital Millennium Copyright Act (1998). The trouble is that these file-sharing sites tend to spring back like the mythical hydra's heads—cut one off, and three others take its place.

Somewhere along the way, the networks wised up and figured, *If you can't beat 'em, join 'em.* These days you can go to the Fox Network's Web site or NBC.com and download your favorite TV episodes right there—legally. By scanning the environment and adapting to it, the networks cut back on unauthorized downloading (as well as spending on lawsuits) and brought more viewers to the network Web sites. Sure, the non-network download sites are still out there, but plenty of people turn to the network sites now, and in the process they get a look at all the paid advertisements tucked into the margins of the pages. (Interested in learning more about legal issues affecting businesses? Check out Chapter 18 at **www.mybizlab.com**.)

Economic Factors

In this chapter, we've discussed many economic factors businesses must adapt to in order to compete. As you've learned, in scanning the economic environment, business must look for changes to such things as: monetary and fiscal policy, economic growth rates, inflation and deflation, consumer and producer prices indexes, and unemployment.

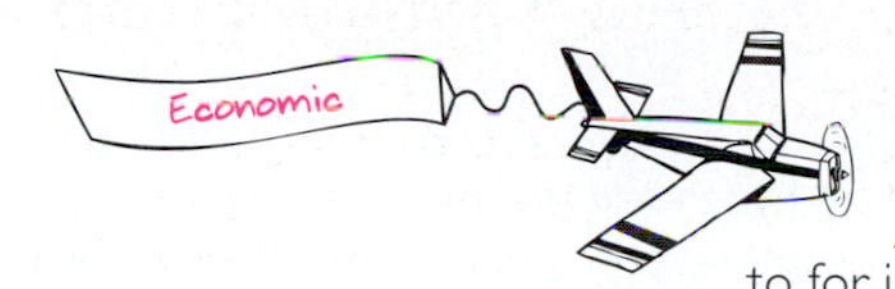

Where do businesses go to get such information? In addition to government and Internet sources, there are many different publications dedicated to economics, such as *Fortune*, *The Wall Street Journal*, *Business Week*, and *The Economist* that business leaders turn to for information. Understanding such economic indicators can make a big difference in whether a business will adapt to the changing marketplace successfully.

Global Factors

Keeping up with trends in the global market by scanning the global environment is hugely important these days, as companies around the world practice an increasing exchange of goods, services, and ideas across international borders. Globalization is providing companies with new ways to cut costs and expand their business in new marketplaces, which in turn generates a larger profit.

On the other hand, globalization can also raise potential issues for businesses as well. For example, there's concern that moving businesses overseas could be a threat for U.S. companies. Because of the globalized market, businesses also increasingly face issues such as: competition from overseas companies, threats to information security and patent protection, and political instability in partner nations.

All businesses are involved in a global market to some degree. These days, the marketplace *is* global, and businesses need to scan the global environment and adapt their strategies to compete effectively. We'll go over the global environment and what factors companies must keep on their scanning horizons in much more detail in Chapter 5.

■ Environmental scanning is a way of keeping your radar tuned to the forces of change in the outside world, forces that could signal opportunity or be red flags for a business.

Sociocultural Factors

To successfully market their products, businesses often examine who their customers are and what their customers want and need. These businesses therefore scan the *sociocultural* features of their customers; that is, they examine the social and cultural aspects of their customers. Scanning the sociocultural environment therefore includes looking at such factors as: gender, age demographics, income distributions, education levels, ethnicity, religious beliefs, and values.

How do twenty-somethings feel about family values? Which groups are providing the greatest contributions to charity? What do older, well-educated people buy when they go to the grocery store? These are the types of questions businesses pose as they scan the sociocultural environment.

Consider Sunflower Market, a natural foods grocery chain started by Mike Gilliland, the founder of Wild Oats. In scanning the sociocultural environment, Gilliland discovered an untapped niche. He noticed:

1. a growing interest in natural and organic foods and good nutrition;
2. the high costs of popular natural foods retailers like Whole Foods, or even of independent retailers and farmers' markets.

Together, these trends mean that middle- to low-income shoppers, while they might be attracted to the idea of natural foods, are turned away by the unaffordable prices. Gilliland adapted a solution: "Serious Foods, Silly Prices." Sunflower was designed to specialize in natural meats and organic produce, but to use cost-cutting methods to offer the products at reasonable prices. The result? Business took off: the store now operates in 21 locations and plans to open another 20 to 30 locations in the next five years.[21]

Environmental Factors

Ecological concerns have become hyper-relevant these days with the rise of the Green movement and recent legislation to promote a green economy. Businesses find that it pays to keep up with attitudes about climate change and environmental protection, to stay current on laws and regulations directed at emissions controls and consumption, and to keep ahead of the curve by reducing their carbon footprint.

And real-life examples have demonstrated that scanning the environment and adapting to environmental concerns can be the key to survival for some companies. For example, luxury-goods makers have been promoting their "green credentials" to today's consumers who place a higher value on caring for the environment than luxury consumers used to. Firms such as LVMH Moët Hennessy Louis Vuitton, Tiffany & Co., and Hermès have implemented several changes to both their operations and marketing to reflect a stronger emphasis on the environmental impact of their activities. Even executive bonuses at some of these firms are now tied to environmental goals such as reducing carbon emissions.[22]

Technological Factors

With the rapid growth of the IT industry these days, most businesses' survival—their ability to compete—depends to some extent on their ability to scan the technological environment and adapt to technological advancements. Recall that technological advancements are often the source of increased productivity. Considering that software can become obsolete in mere months and that computers need to be replaced every few years, technology has become a huge capital expense for almost any business.

On the other hand, technology can also reduce costs for businesses. Think of the "virtual workforce," or telecommuters who can work from almost anywhere. Not only do these employees allow companies to more easily find the ideal employee for a position, but telecommuters also cut back on the costs of business travel—no plane tickets or hotel rooms necessary. And if fewer employees are actually present in the workplace, businesses don't need as much space to operate, which again saves on costs.

Another technological phenomenon businesses must consider is e-commerce—buying and selling products through the Internet. Recall the example of Amazon's increased sales during a time of economic recession. Because the company doesn't operate out of a storefront, it has fewer overhead costs than traditional retail stores do. In addition, buying groceries, shoes, or books with a few clicks of the mouse is a heck of a lot more convenient than actually going to the store in person. And the store is accessible from anywhere in the world, at any time of day. By the end of 2007, 3.5 percent of total retail sales were conducted online, and that number continues to grow.

There are numerous examples of businesses successfully scanning the technological environment. Take GlobalGarageSale.net based in Winooski, Vermont. Erik Holcomb and Peter Becker started the company in 2003, after a friend asked them to sell some things for him on eBay. The partners tapped in to the market for used goods online and the philosophy that one man's trash is another man's treasure. Within two years the company's gross sales went from $76,000 to $680,000.[23] We'll discuss the technical environment in much more detail in Chapters 15 and 16.

Do It...

4.4: Scan the Environment Read a recent copy of a major business publication and locate two articles that apply to various elements of PEGSET. For each article, list the PEGSET element(s) it relates to, and identify a company or industry that could be affected by this PEGSET factor. Limit your response to one page, and be prepared to submit it electronically or present it in class.

Now Debrief...

- **Environmental scanning** is a way of keeping your radar tuned to the forces of change in the outside world.
- There are six main factors businesses scan in the environment: Political/Legal, Economic, Global, Sociocultural, Environmental, and Technological (PEGSET).
- By examining PEGSET headlines on a daily basis, businesspeople are able to notice new ideas, trends, and triggers, and prepare themselves for change.

5. Adapting to Different Economic Systems: The Challenge of a Global Economy

We've talked a lot about how businesses must adapt in order to succeed. Let's broaden our scope and take a look around the world. With the rise of globalization, businesses are increasingly operating with partners, suppliers, and customers from other countries. However, these countries aren't all U.S. look-a-likes. As you'll remember from Chapter 3, the United States has a (mostly) *free market economy*. This means that the government does not control businesses, so these businesses determine what is produced and the amount something costs. ■ When taking business overseas, these companies have to adapt to cultural differences, but they also have to understand how to operate within the framework of different economic systems. The tried and true techniques from a strongly capitalist economy may not apply.

Think back to Chapter 1 and how business was compared to "the big game." When you start a business or expand into a new market, you need to understand how your new market (in this case, a new country) plays the game and how to adapt accordingly. Let's look at some different economic systems and how businesses may adapt in order to operate within them.

■ When taking business overseas, these companies have to adapt to cultural differences, but they also have to understand how to operate within the framework of different economic systems.

Adapting to Socialist Economies

You may remember the controversy surrounding Michael Moore's 2007 documentary *Sicko*, in which Moore heatedly argues that the American health care system needs to be overhauled and remade into the image of the government-run systems in Canada, France, or even Cuba. The film was drawing a comparison between capitalist and socialist models of health care. A **socialist economy** is an economy in which the government uses taxes to redistribute wealth throughout the country. This redistribution is achieved through government programs like health care, transportation, education, utilities, and other social services.

Regardless of whether you prefer capitalism or socialism, the free market dominates health care and many other social services in the United States. This means you'll pay more to visit the doctor's office, but you'll also pay less in taxes each year than you would if you lived in, say, Denmark, where social services are provided through a socialist economic model. To fund social programs like universal health care, the taxes levied on Denmark's citizens can be as high as a whopping 60 percent![24] On the other hand, citizens in Denmark are supposedly some of the happiest people in the world,[25] which either means Danes love giving their money away, or they're getting something in return for all that money.

To help figure out why Danes are so happy, let's take a minute to look at Denmark's culture. Danes obviously pay a lot in taxes, but in return they get pretty good benefits. Aside from health care, benefits usually also include extensive paid time off for vacation and holidays and a significantly longer maternity leave than mothers in the United States usually enjoy. Generally, Danes get up to (and sometimes more than) 30 days of paid leave a year.[26] As far as maternity leave, women are entitled to 22 weeks or more at 90 percent of their previous pay. Men are also given the option of taking time off after their wives have a baby.[27] Danes also work fewer hours per week; for many, a full workday is seven hours.

Let's say you wanted to run a business in Denmark. What should you expect? Well, you probably can't afford to hire many workers because taxes and benefits are so high. In addition, the unemployment rate in Denmark is around 2 percent, so finding skilled workers may be difficult.[28] However, these potential drawbacks have not deterred U.S. companies from expanding into Denmark. The General Manager of Dell Denmark, Guy Auger, thinks that Denmark has a competitive edge because of its flexible labor laws and high quality of life. In addition, the cost of employee benefits, such as social security, unemployment, and health insurance, are transparent, so companies have a good idea of the cost of running a business before they even enter the Danish marketplace. In fact, business for Dell Denmark has been so strong that in less than 10 years the branch has gone from 6 to 600 employees.[29]

Adapting to Communist Economies

How would you like to live in a classless society where the people own everything? Well, if you said, "Great! I'll take it," welcome to the world of communism. This goal of a classless society has pretty much always been a pipe dream, and most of the communist governments established during the 20th century have more or less collapsed (such as the Soviet Union).

There are still a few communist countries that have managed to hang on (though their economies are not doing well), including Cuba, North Korea, and North Vietnam. In this present-day form of a **communist economy**, the government controls all things economic, from the factors of production to the distribution of wealth. The government decides what gets produced, in what quantities, and how.

You may be wondering, "Where's China?" Well, because of China's economic policies, its economy is considered more of a mixed market, even though the country is run by a communist government.

What does this mean for businesses? If you wanted to start a business in a communist country, you should expect a lot of government interference. In addition, should your idea catch on, the business would not be yours; it would be considered government property. This type of economic system does not embrace private businesses. What other issues would you need to consider before operating a business in a communist land?

Mixed Market Economies

What do you get when you take capitalism and add a dash of socialism? As we discussed in Chapter 2, you'd get the United States. Many people think the United States is a purely capitalistic country, but in reality, the United States has a mixed market economy. For the most part, countries aren't purely capitalist or socialist, but fit somewhere in between. These **mixed market economies** borrow elements from various economic models to create an "ideal" system.

The United States provides government-run welfare, the U.S. postal system, public education, and other programs. Under this system, both government and individual people produce goods and services. So, the government might control some social services, but other industries are left to their own devices.

The reason that the government runs some services is that public goods, like the police and fire department, are *non-excludable*, meaning that everyone, whether they pay for them or not, can enjoy these services. And when that's the case, there's not much incentive for a private business to offer them—after all, staffing and running the fire and police departments is an expensive business, and most companies can't afford to offer services that they can choose not to pay for. That's why the government has to step in and run these services—unlike a private business, the government can force the people who enjoy the protection of firefighters and police to pay for them through taxes.

Another mixed market economy would be China. Although China is run by a communist government, the economic system in the country may resemble the U.S. system more than you'd expect. Now privately held businesses, like Wal-Mart, are allowed in China, and they are thriving. The private sector has helped boost China's economy to the third largest in the world (behind the European Union and the United States).[30]

What does this mean for businesses? Opening and operating a business in a mixed market economy shouldn't be much of a problem (provided you have money and a plan). You'll have fewer taxes to worry about and more personal freedom compared to purely socialist and communist economies. But of course, opening and operating a business in another country is never an easy undertaking. We'll discuss global business in more detail in the next chapter.

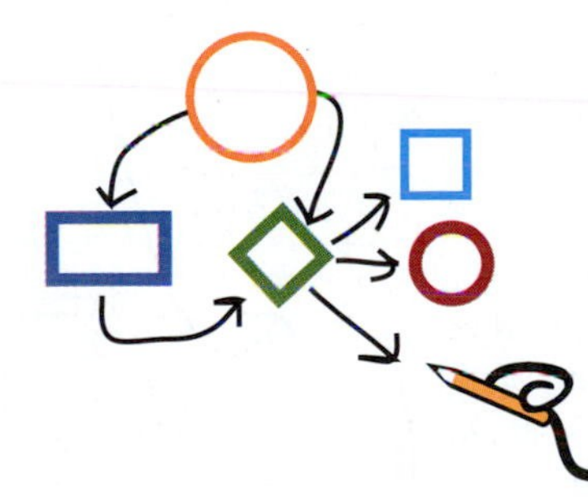

Do It...

4.5: Identify Economic Challenges Pick a country other than the United States and research which aspects of its economy are socialized and which are not. If you were a U.S. corporation planning to move a sector of your business to this country, what challenges and differences would you have to adapt to? Limit your response to one page, and be prepared to submit it electronically or present it in class.

Now Debrief...

- As the world grows closer and closer due to globalization, U.S. businesses must learn to adapt to the economic systems of other nations in which they might conduct operations.
- In **socialist economies**, the government controls certain industries, particularly the social services: education, welfare, health care, and others. The goal in socialist economies is to even out the distribution of wealth through taxation.
- **Communist economies** operate on more extreme principles of having a classless society. In modern communist countries, the government plans and controls the economy. The government allocates wealth and regulates all industry, as well as the factors of production.
- In **mixed market economies**, countries borrow elements from various economic models to create an "ideal" system. Almost all countries today operate under mixed economies, in which some sectors of the economy are planned, or government run, and others function independently through competition.

Chapter 4 Visual Summary

1. Use economic indicators to characterize the current business cycle you're living in, and identify opportunities it offers for business and your personal success. (pp. 82–88)

- The **business cycle**, which refers to economic fluctuations that occur at irregular intervals, is a recurring part of the economy. The business cycle is generally characterized by the following fluctuations: recession → trough → recovery → expansion.
- **Recessions** are economic downturns that feature decreased profits and consumer spending, and increased unemployment. During recovery periods, consumer spending increases, the demand for goods and services grow, and profits increase.
- Business experts can get a reading on the economy using economic indicators, such as the **gross domestic product (GDP)**, the **gross national product (GNP)**, the **unemployment rate**, the **consumer price index**, and the **producer price index**.
- Price indexes help gauge inflation. **Inflation** occurs when the price of goods and services increase. This causes the spending power of the dollar to decrease.

Summary: Because the business cycle is a recurring cycle full of ups and downs, businesses must evaluate economic indicators to read the pulse of the economy, measure its rate of growth, and then adapt their strategies accordingly.

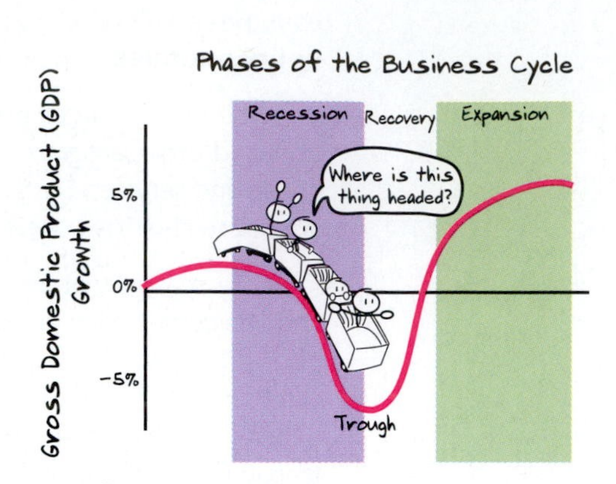

2. Explain how fiscal and monetary policy decisions can affect a business. (pp. 88–93)

- Government actions directed at stabilizing the economy comprise **fiscal policy**. To help jump-start a slow economy, the government can stimulate the economy through increased spending and lowering taxes. On the flip side, government can slow down the economy through decreased spending and higher taxes.
- The **Federal Reserve** is the central banking system in the United States. It works with the government to stabilize the economy and maintain a sustainable rate of growth through monetary policies.
- The Fed uses monetary policies, such as working with the **money supply**, **reserve requirement**, and **discount rate**, and by engaging in **open market operations**, to help encourage or discourage spending.

Summary: The federal government has two tools to help control the economy: fiscal policy and monetary policy.

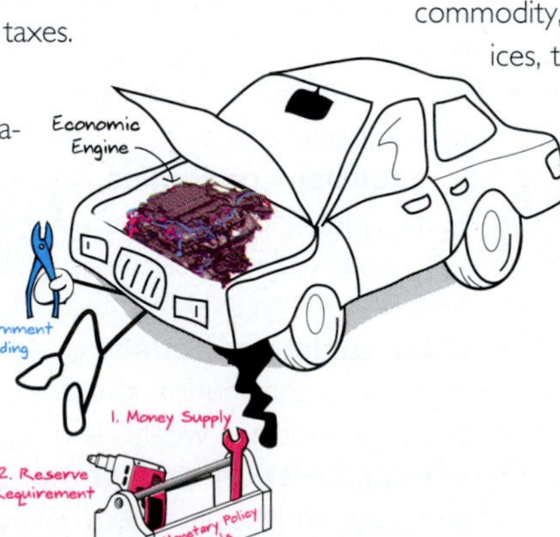

3. Describe how companies have adapted and continue to adapt to changing economic environments. (pp. 93–95)

- You can see how businesses adapt to **factors of production** throughout history, such as going from the farm to the factory.
- Businesses have shifted from focuses on land, to labor and capital, to entrepreneurship, to knowledge. This also expanded the idea of what a product is: from a commodity, to goods, to services, to experiences.

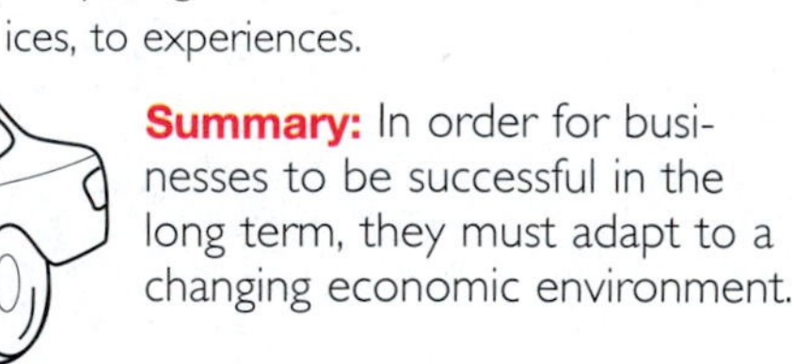

Summary: In order for businesses to be successful in the long term, they must adapt to a changing economic environment.

5. Predict how a business's strategy would change in a different economic system. (pp. 99–101)

- When taking business overseas, businesses have to adapt to cultural differences, but they also have to understand how to operate within the framework of different economic systems.
- A **socialist economy** is an economy in which the government uses taxes to redistribute wealth throughout the country.
- In a **communist economy**, the government controls all things economic, from the factors of production to the distribution of wealth.
- **Mixed market economies** borrow elements from different economic systems to create a more "ideal" system. The United States is a mixed-market economy that incorporates elements of capitalism and socialism.

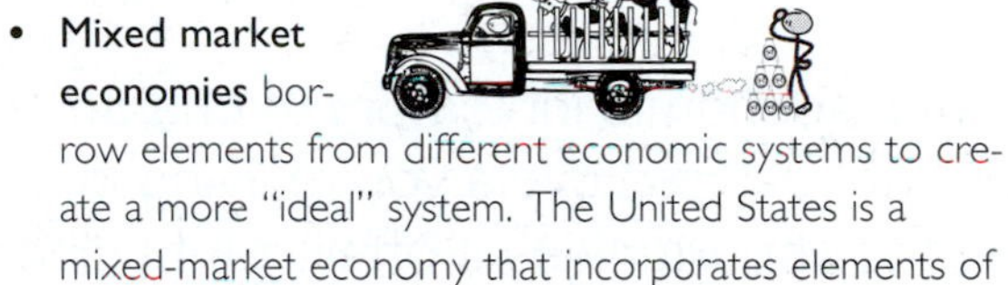

Summary: When operating in another country, businesses must have a clear understanding of the economic system in place and what implications this system may have for the business.

4. Explain how companies scan their environment to adapt effectively. (pp. 96–99)

- **Environmental scanning** is a way of keeping your radar tuned to the forces of change in the outside world, forces that could signal opportunity or be red flags for a business.
- Businesses scan for information involving political/legal, economic, global, sociocultural, environmental, and technological (PEGSET) factors.

Summary: In order to adapt, companies must scan their environment for political/legal, economic, global, sociocultural, environmental, and technological factors that may affect how they do business.

Get the most out of what you just read by practicing your skills and actually DOING something with the material! The best place to do this is at **www.mybizlab.com**. Here's just some of what is available to you there:

- Apply your skills in an interactive environment with more **BizSkill** experiences...and see if you have what it takes
- Think critically and talk with your peers on hot business topics in **BizChats**
- Flex your business communication skills and build your own portfolio with the **Communication Plan exercises**
- Watch the chapter material come together with **Just Plain Business** videos
- Study on-the-go with **Audio Chapter Summaries** in MP3 format
- Brush up on the lecture and content with **Audio PowerPoints**
- Discover how well you are doing and see what areas you need to improve on with the **Pre-Tests** and **Post-Tests**

Key Words

These key words and more are also available as flash cards to practice with at **www.mybizlab.com**.

1. Use economic indicators to characterize the current business cycle you're living in, and identify opportunities it offers for business and your personal success. **(pp. 82–88)**

recession (p. 82)
business cycle (p. 82)
trough (p. 82)
recovery (p. 82)
depression (p. 82)
expansion (p. 82)
economic indicators (p. 83)
gross domestic product (GDP) (p. 83)
inflation (p. 83)
productivity (p. 84)
gross national product (GNP) (p. 84)
unemployment rate (p. 84)
consumer price index (p. 86)
deflation (p. 86)
producer price index (p. 87)

2. Explain how fiscal and monetary policy decisions can affect a business. **(pp. 88–93)**

fiscal policy (p. 88)
aggregate demand (p. 88)
taxation (p. 90)
Federal Reserve (the Fed) (p. 91)
monetary policy (p. 91)
money supply (p. 91)
reserve requirement (p. 92)
discount rate (p. 92)
open market operations (p. 92)
federal funds rate (p. 93)

3. Describe how companies have adapted and continue to adapt to changing economic environments. **(pp. 93–95)**

factors of production (p. 93)
knowledge economy (p. 94)

4. Explain how companies scan their environment to adapt effectively. **(pp. 96–99)**

environmental scanning (p. 96)

5. Predict how a business's strategy would change in a different economic system. **(pp. 99–101)**

socialist economy (p. 99)
communist economy (p. 100)
mixed market economy (p. 101)

Prove It

Manager

Prove It...

Now, let's put on one of the BizHats. With the **Manager BizHat** squarely on your head, look at the following exercise:

In recent months the market has begun to grow. The Fed has announced their intention to lower the federal funds rate by purchasing more government bonds. In addition, Congress has just passed a bill to issue tax rebates, urging consumers and investors to put their stimulus payments back into the economy.

A couple of years ago you opened a small sandwich shop that has been fairly profitable. Now, you'd like to expand your business, but are having trouble deciding whether to do so. You'd love to expand the menu to include hot food options. However, to do this, you'd need to remodel the kitchen and extend the storefront to accommodate more tables. Expanding the shop also means you'd need to hire a cook and wait staff.

You think the remodeling would really get customers' interest if you advertised more aggressively, perhaps purchasing commercial time on a local TV or radio station. To cover these expenses, you would need to take out a loan of $250,000. Consider the economic situation and explain whether it would be wise to take out a loan now or to wait. You should take into account not only interest rates, but also the impact current fiscal and monetary policy will have on consumer spending and prices and how these things will impact how you manage your business.

Flip It...

After you've decided whether or not it's a good idea to remodel and expand your shop, **flip over to the Owner/Investor BizHat.**

You are an investor who specializes in small businesses. A local restaurant owner/manager has applied for a loan of $250,000 in exchange for equity—partial ownership of the business. Consider the business plan the owner has outlined for you (above) in addition to the current economic situation and possible investment alternatives. Would you choose to invest in the restaurant at this time? Is there additional information that would help you make your decision?

Now Debrief It...

Compare the perspectives of the two BizHats described above. Did taking the perspective of the Owner/Investor change your opinion about the loan? How did the current information regarding the market shape your opinion for each perspective?

Grow: Global

BizSkills invite...

Try It!
There's no better way to learn concepts than to put them into practice. Take your turn in the driver's seat and be a part of actual business decision making by visiting the BizSkill for this chapter at **www.mybizlab.com**.

Now that you've practiced making tough business decisions and seeing the results of your choices in this chapter's BizSkill, it's time to translate those skills into plain English. And if you skipped the BizSkill, go back now!

Chapter 5 Goals

After experiencing this chapter, you'll be able to:

1. Describe the trends in globalization and how businesses can capitalize on them.
2. Analyze a company's strategies for reaching global markets.
3. Scan the global economic environment and identify trends and opportunities based on what you discover.
4. Scan the trading environment of a particular region or culture and identify trends and opportunities based on what you discover.
5. Scan the cultural, legal, political, and ethical environment of a particular region or culture and identify trends and opportunities based on what you discover.

Do you know what it takes to go global?

Globalization Here, There, Everywhere

Rachel gets up at 6:30 a.m., turns off her alarm clock (Timex, made in China), and heads downstairs to make coffee. She opens a package of Colombian dark roast and smells the rich aroma of the beans that have traveled 4,000 miles to arrive in her kitchen. If she looked underneath her espresso machine, she would see a label reading "Made in China." She fills her mug (also made in China) and starts up her computer (microprocessor: Philippines; memory: Germany; motherboard: Taiwan; keyboard: China; display: South Korea; wireless card: Malaysia; hard drive: Thailand; power cord: India.)[1]

In the next 20 minutes, Rachel uses shampoo made in the United States from imported products. She puts on jeans (made in Mexico), a T-shirt (made in Cambodia), and shoes (made in England), and rushes to school. On the way, she stops to fill her tank. She swipes her credit card, using technology developed in India and the Czech Republic. She pumps her gas (processed from crude oil, imported from the Persian Gulf region), and away she goes.

Like many of us, within the first hour of her day, Rachel will touch objects and use services that have traveled thousands of miles to reach her. In an increasingly global market, 100 percent U.S.-made products are becoming less common. In this chapter, you'll read about the increasingly global marketplace and its effect on businesses around the world.

1. Globalization: The Connected, Borderless Globe

Let's take a minute to revisit where we are in the book, and how globalization fits in. In Chapters 1 and 2, you learned that the income statement, the cash flow statement, and the balance sheet measure how we keep score in business, and that the triple bottom line is how we measure success. In Chapter 3, you learned how the principles of economics such as supply and demand help us predict and explain how customers and businesses act in a competitive marketplace. In Chapter 4, you learned how companies have to scan, anticipate, and react to the external environment outside their sphere of influence. In many cases, this external environment is a product of global forces, so it's important to understand those forces and how to navigate and capitalize on them. As we dive into the international waters, keep in mind that there are two primary elements of global business:

1. international business strategies that can be used to pursue global markets; and
2. cross-cultural considerations that are essential for building relationships with international firms and customers.

Now let's get started on our global voyage.

Globalization and Improved Technology

Would it surprise you to know that an average of 1 billion Google searches are performed each day? That's more than three times the population of the United States. What may be more surprising is the fact that fewer than one-third of those searches are performed by users in the United States,[2] or that the United States ranks only 20th in the world for broadband Internet coverage.[3]

How much of what you are wearing and carrying right now comes from outside the United States?

With the Internet becoming increasingly available worldwide, now a person living in rural Mali, a stockbroker in New York, and you all have access to the same information. And all of you, despite the geographical and sociocultural differences that may separate you, can connect online with as much effort as it takes to pick up the phone and call your neighbor. Yet despite this high level of online connectivity, using the Internet is a task that each of us generally performs alone, and it's easy to forget how connected we really are.

It's not just the Internet that connects people across borders. For instance, the number of text messages exchanged in the last 24 hours has far exceeded the population of the planet.[4] Communications technologies are shrinking the world and changing the way we relate, including the way we do business. *Telecommuting* allows people to collaborate on work from virtually anywhere, and workflow software allows a large number of people to contribute seamlessly to a single project, whether they're working in the same building or from opposite sides of the planet.

Richard N. Haass, president of the Council on Foreign Relations, describes this phenomenon, **globalization**, as encompassing the flow of ideas, knowledge, people, business, and culture across borders.[5] Globalization also involves the integration of countries' economies, usually through trade. Regardless of whether businesses decide to expand their operations overseas, this global marketplace is the world in which businesses operate, in terms of competition, suppliers, collaborators, and customers.

Meanwhile, transportation technologies are moving products around the world at greater speeds and lower costs. Trade barriers have also been reduced, helping to open borders and allow for a freer exchange of products. The **World Trade Organization (WTO)**, established in 1995, has set standards that allow member nations to exchange goods across borders with fewer restrictions.[6] Additionally, the **European Union**, established in 1993, now has 27 member states and functions as a single market, allowing the free flow of goods, services, workers, and capital between European countries. As you can see, the world is a very different place to do business than it was even 15 years ago.

Global Business Trends and How Technology Is Taking Us There

The global economy has begun to change at a rapid pace, which can catch businesses off guard. In whatever capacity you participate in the global economy—whether as a customer, an owner, an investor, or an employee—it's important to understand the impact of globalization and the growing trends in the global market to make informed decisions. In this section we'll consider three global business trends and what they mean for businesses and you.

Trend #1: More Customers in Emerging Economies In 2008, Finnish telecommunications giant Nokia released a new model of the Nokia 1209 phone, which allows up to five users to store their contact lists in a single device. The phone was developed in response to a growing trend among cell phone customers in *emerging economies*—non-industrialized nations that are achieving vast economic growth through the use of new technologies, such as telecommunications, energy, and information technologies.[7] Nokia surveyed customers in India, China, Brazil, Pakistan, Vietnam, Russia, and Egypt and found that people in these countries commonly shared a single phone among family members or friends.[8] Sharing a phone makes sense for customers who would benefit from communications technologies but can't afford to own a single phone themselves.

Why would Nokia want to encourage phone sharing? Wouldn't the company profit more if everyone bought his or her own phone? To provide some perspective, for every baby that's born in the United States this year, almost six babies will be born in India and four will be born in China.[9] In other words, when you consider the population density of these emerging markets, one phone for every five consumers is still quite a few phones. By adapting to consumer preferences in these ever-expanding markets, some companies are hitting the jackpot.

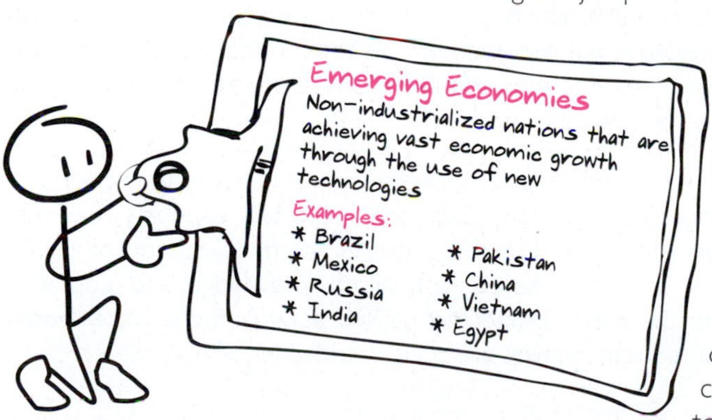

In fact, a new trend has taken place recently in which innovation has started to flow in the opposite direction. Rather than a product appearing in the United States first, then migrating to Europe and Japan and finally winding up in emerging markets a year or more later, some technology developed specifically to meet demand in India, Morocco, or Vietnam is finding its eventual way to the U.S. and European markets.

Technological innovation is flowing in both directions now, and the demand for technology is growing in emerging markets. Businesses that can keep in touch with this demand—and the varied needs of customers—in emerging markets have a competitive advantage, but the competitive field is also growing. Now companies have to keep up with competitors not only within their borders, but around the world as well.[10]

What does this mean for you? Employers are now choosing from a global workforce, so your competition is not only coming from people in your area, but from around the globe. You must prove your value to an organization relative to the value that someone else—often someone who's willing to work for less—can deliver. After all, if you're willing to buy a stereo from

China because it has comparable features and a lower price compared to a U.S. brand, why wouldn't a major employer consider the same option the next time it needs accountants or programmers?

Trend #2: The Shift of Economic Activity Within and Between Regions Now that trade barriers have been reduced, economic activity is beginning to shift within regions. For example, because the countries of the European Union basically work as a single market, it makes sense for France to focus more of its efforts on agriculture, which it excels at, and to shift some of its financial services and workers to the United Kingdom, which excels in the financial service industry.

Similarly, now that China has joined the World Trade Organization, businesses from many developed economies are practicing *offshore outsourcing.* You've probably heard of outsourcing. *Outsourcing* simply means that a company contracts with another company or individual to handle specific tasks. For example, a company might outsource its accounting functions to another company. In **offshore outsourcing** (or **offshoring**), a company outsources tasks such as manufacturing to a foreign location, usually one that is less expensive, such as China. Because workers are plentiful and wage expectations are lower in countries like China, companies can cut costs and keep up with competitors in the global market. In the process, China benefits from the greater foreign investments and the influx of technologies into its economy.[11]

For many businesses, the shift to a global economy means working overtime to keep up. If other companies are finding cheaper ways to get the job done, then your company must figure out how to cut costs, too. For customers, the costs of certain products are dropping as companies collaborate overseas to produce more efficiently. As an employee, it means that you may have to work extra hard to earn your keep against your foreign competitors. As a manager, it means that you have more options for labor and getting work done. And for investors, who attempt to predict which sectors of the economy will take off and when, these shifts open up new investment opportunities.

Trend #3: Greater Know-How and Easy-to-Access Info Chances are if you want to try something new for dinner, you'll look online to find a recipe. Twenty years ago, you would have looked in a cookbook. The wealth of information that's now available to anyone with a computer and a network connection is a recent phenomenon that has changed not only the way we learn, but also the way we communicate and do business. Easier access to information means better-informed consumers and an increased ability for businesses to get their product's name into more markets.

"Globalization has changed us into a company that searches the world, not just to sell or to source, but to find intellectual capital—the world's best talents and greatest ideas."
—Jack Welch,
former Chairman and CEO of General Electric[13]

Think back to Chapter 4, where we talked about the notion of a knowledge-based economy. Not only is the U.S. economy now centered on knowledge, but the global economy is also becoming increasingly knowledge-based. Specialized knowledge and education levels set the most competitive nations above others, while literacy rates and education levels are rising worldwide.[12]

Consider that in 2006, there were 1.3 million new U.S. college graduates. But India had 3.1 million college grads that year, and China had 3.3 million.[14] Both India and China are strong global competitors, not because of abundant natural resources, but because of their knowledge base (or human capital), and both governments are pushing to grow this knowledge base, particularly in the science and technology sectors. Additionally, phone and Internet access is becoming a greater reality in developing nations so that more people have access to the technology that can propel them forward in terms of knowledge and competitiveness.

Do It...

5.1: Survey Your Possessions Generate a list of at least 10 items that you're wearing, have in your purse or wallet, or carry in your car or backpack. Identify the country where each item is manufactured. Are there are any patterns you notice? Be prepared to submit your list and discussion electronically or present it in class.

Now Debrief...

- **Globalization** encompasses the flow of ideas, knowledge, people, business, and culture across borders. Globalization also involves the integration of countries' economies, usually through trade. Regardless of whether businesses decide to expand their operations overseas, they are operating in a global economy.
- Not only is technology making the flow of information and labor a greater reality, but reduced trade barriers are opening up trade options. The **World Trade Organization** has helped promote freer trade worldwide, and regional trade agreements such as the **European Union** have helped reduce trade barriers between neighboring countries.
- It's important to understand the impact of globalization and the growing trends in the global market, such as:
  1. More customers in emerging economies.
  2. A shift of economic activity within and between regions (some of which is related to **offshore outsourcing**).
  3. Greater ease of obtaining information and developing knowledge.

2. How Companies Reach Global Markets

Businesses need to lay some groundwork before going global. If a company doesn't know how it measures up in the global marketplace, what sorts of advantages it has relative to companies in other nations, or how it might collaborate in overseas markets, how will it know how to proceed? In this section, we'll look at the advantages and disadvantages that companies face both at home and abroad, and the options they have for expanding internationally.

Competitive Advantage

Suppose you're given an assignment that requires artistic skills. Although you're not a trained artist, you're better at drawing than your classmates. When you compare your skills to your friends, you have a **competitive advantage**. In other words, you're in a better position than your friends. A company has a competitive advantage in relationship to its competitors if it does something better than those competitors. To remain competitive on a global scale, businesses must figure out the advantages their home country has in relation to other countries. For example, differences in the availability of natural resources, work force, geographical and climate differences, and many other factors contribute to give countries advantages and disadvantages relative to one another.

Comparative Advantage

A common form of advantage that drives trade is **comparative advantage**. According to the theory of comparative advantage, countries should specialize in producing the goods or services they can produce at a lower opportunity cost compared to other countries. They should then trade those goods and services with other countries for products whose opportunity costs are too high for them to produce.

For example, because of its large amount of arable land, the United States has a comparative advantage in producing corn and wheat as compared to, for example, Japan, a country with less arable land. The opportunity costs to Japan of trying to grow all of its own corn and wheat would be prohibitively high, as it would have to devote land that could be better used manufacturing products that have a comparatively low opportunity cost, such as consumer electronics. The United States would therefore focus on trading corn and wheat with Japan in exchange for electronics. If all countries produce those goods and services for which they have a comparative advantage, more high-quality goods and services are produced, more profit is made, fewer resources are used, and everyone benefits.

Collaborative Advantage It's a Boeing like none before: An extra-wide interior gives the cabin a feeling of spaciousness. The windows can be dimmed by a central control panel, and a seamless, carbon fiber body cuts down on resistance. Named the Dreamliner, the U.S. company had a record 900 orders from airlines around the world months before its 2009 release. And, unlike any Boeing plane before, more than 70 percent of the airframe was offshored; parts came from workers in China and engineers in India. A team of more than 1,000 aerospace engineers in Russia helped develop the titanium parts. Japanese and Italian engineers designed the wings and sections of the fuselage.

Six countries involved in the creation of a single plane? Isn't it better competitive strategy to outsource the manufacturing tasks and save the design work for in-house engineers? Not necessarily. In the 787 project, Boeing was looking to a *long-term* competitive strategy and sustainability, in which case collaboration was a mutually beneficial option.

Consider the collaboration with China, for instance. Boeing and the Chinese government agreed to swap aircraft sales in the Chinese market in exchange for manufacturing work; you give us a share in the world's largest airplane market, and we'll give you jobs.[15] Boeing is tapping into **collaborative advantage**, an approach that seeks mutual gains through collaboration between equal partners. Collaborating on development can help companies achieve their goals more efficiently, by pooling resources.

Entering the Global Market

So, once you've figured out your company's competitive position in the global marketplace, how do you carry out your operations? One of the deciding factors in how to go global is the level of risk the company is willing to take. In this section, we'll consider the ways in which companies can enter the global market and examples of businesses that have found successful ways to compete globally.

Foreign Direct Investment We've discussed how some companies test the waters of the global marketplace by offshoring. Other companies are practicing what's known as **foreign direct investment (FDI)**, investing resources in a foreign country to expand a business and increase profits. Traditionally, FDI simply meant building a factory in the foreign host country (the way Boeing did in China). Although this still describes most FDI, companies are increasingly finding other ways to invest—through joint ventures, strategic alliances, licensing, and franchising, which we'll discuss here.

International Joint Ventures It may sound like an odd match, but in 2009, Japanese automaker Mitsubishi and French automaker Peugeot cut a deal to collaborate on the development of a hybrid vehicle with plans to release the product to the European market the following year. Mitsubishi had already developed the hybrid technology when the two companies struck the deal, and the partners agreed that the new car would be released under the Peugeot brand.

Why would Mitsubishi allow a competitor not only to use its hard-earned technology, but use it under the competitor's name? Collaborative advantage. Peugeot benefited by tapping into a valuable technology that it wouldn't have had access to otherwise, while Mitsubishi benefited by borrowing the Peugeot name (trusted and respected by Europeans) to ease its cars into the

European marketplace.[16] This type of collaboration is known as a **joint venture**: teaming up with another individual or company in an effort to create a product. The Peugeot-Mitsubishi partnership is an example in which the two companies joined together to create a new entity, much like a corporation. This collaboration helps both companies expand the influence of their businesses and creates a more powerful presence in the market.

There are other reasons joint ventures can make good economic sense for a business: companies can reduce competition with each other, gain access to a foreign market that was off-limits to one of the partners, and diversify the risks associated with a particular venture.

Strategic Alliances

Another option for a company to enter the global market is to form a **strategic alliance**. Like joint ventures, strategic alliances are agreements between business partners. Unlike joint ventures, however, both companies remain separate entities while working together. In addition, a strategic alliance does not usually involve creating a product; rather, a strategic alliance is a relationship between two companies in which both agree to work toward a specific set of long-term goals.

Consider the partnership between 20 international airline companies that make up the Star Alliance. Although the airline carriers work together, each carrier remains an independent entity. The alliance was formed in 1997 as a way for the companies to cut costs and to consolidate travel options to compete with other, non-affiliated airlines.[17]

Licensing

When Sony Entertainment's James Bond film *Quantum of Solace* was released in 2008, Coca-Cola entered into a global licensing agreement with Sony, temporarily renaming its Coke Zero product Coca-Cola Zero Zero 7 in an effort to connect its brand with the edgy 007 image of the films. The product came out in sleek bottles featuring the 007 logo and a picture of the film's star, Daniel Craig.[18]

Coke, the most widely recognized brand name in the world, is famous for licensing its brand to other companies that want to borrow Coke's image to promote their own products. In this case, **licensing** simply means that one party grants another party permission to use a copyright or patent. In a global economy, licensing can be an increasingly valuable form of collaboration, as companies who want to expand into overseas markets work to establish brand recognition. Often, a company that's new to a market will license internationally recognized brands—or brands specific to a certain area—to help promote its products with new customers.

Franchising

In 2008, before the Beijing Olympic Games, InterContinental Hotels Group (IHG), the United Kingdom-based hotel giant, began franchising its Holiday Inn Express hotels in China. The company planned to use franchising as a way to expand business, opening 50 new hotels in China in the coming year.[19] A **franchise agreement** allows individuals or businesses to use the franchisor's (in this case IHG's) products, strategies, and trademarks in exchange for a royalty fee, plus a percentage of overall sales. Franchising provides yet another option for a company to enter the global market.

Let's say a Chinese family that owns a hotel has been struggling against competition from large hotel chains. The family may decide to sell their hotel and sign a franchise agreement with IHG instead. The family will benefit from Holiday Inn Express's brand, and Holiday Inn will benefit from the expertise—particularly the cultural connectedness—of its local management. For a business that wants to expand globally, franchising can be a way of mobilizing the host country's resources toward the growth of the company.

Importing and Exporting

Think back to the beginning of this chapter, where you read about the origins of the products that an average American might use in a single hour. If you completed Do It 5.1, you undoubtedly found that a majority of the products you use didn't originate in the United

States. **Importing**, or buying products that were designed or manufactured outside the country, is nothing new, but with greater reductions in trade barriers, it's becoming more common.

The Effects of Importing Take, for example, blue jeans, which are seen the world over as an iconic American product. Given this status, it's a little ironic that in 2001, Levi Strauss—the U.S.-based company that actually *invented* the blue jean in 1873—closed its last U.S. factory because it could no longer compete with low-cost labor from foreign manufacturers.[20] Companies like Wal-Mart and Target were importing foreign-manufactured jeans and selling them at a fraction of the cost of U.S.-made jeans.

For customers, this was great news. Let's say you buy a pair of jeans from Target. The quality will be fine, and you'll probably only pay around $30, but the jeans won't be made in the United States; maybe in Mexico or Cambodia, but definitely not in Arkansas or Illinois. On the other hand, you could head to True Religion and pick up a pair of jeans manufactured in the United States from all-American materials. Undoubtedly, the quality will be excellent, but you'll be paying upward of $300. Chances are, if you're a middle-class customer, you won't be willing to pay so much for a pair of jeans.

Protecting Against Foreign Competition But Levi's were never pricey jeans. So, how was Levi Strauss able to compete with foreign manufacturers until 2001? As you can see, imports are generally good for customers; if another nation is able to produce a product of better quality at lower costs, then customers have options when they're considering which products to buy. On the flip side, imports are generally bad news for producers; if customers have more inexpensive options, demand for your products will drop. As a producer, you have to either find a way to make better, less expensive products than the foreign manufacturers, or you have to find a way to reduce the foreign competition.

Say you're a blue jeans manufacturer and you know factories in Mexico can produce jeans at a much lower cost than your U.S. plant can. So, you find a politician and you talk her into implementing some form of import restriction on blue jeans from Mexico. Maybe she'll pass a bill to place **import quotas** on blue jeans from Mexico, limiting the number of shipments they can send across the border. Or maybe she'll find a way to raise **tariffs**—import taxes—on blue jeans, thereby raising the overall retail cost of foreign-manufactured jeans so that they aren't cheaper than your brand. As a final option, you might convince the politician to come up with some other law to restrict or limit imports; maybe some of the materials or some part of the manufacturing process will be required to be performed in the United States. (Politicians are often convinced to implement these trade barriers because they face pressure from their constituents to protect jobs in the home country.)

NAFTA In fact, up until 1994, this was exactly the case when it came to blue jeans manufacturing. In the early 90s, laws were in place that required blue jeans sold in the United States to use U.S.-manufactured buttons, trim, and labels. Import quotas and tariffs also helped limit foreign competition. However, in 1994, the **North American Free Trade Agreement (NAFTA)** did away with these import restrictions. NAFTA is a trade agreement between the United States, Canada, and Mexico, reducing tax tariffs and making trade between the three countries easier. As a result, within a few years, many U.S.-based jeans manufacturers, like Levi Strauss, closed shop, and companies began importing their products from places like Torreon, Mexico, a textile-manufacturing hub.[21]

Why would a country want to do away with trade restrictions? Won't free trade across borders hurt a country's economy overall? Well, that depends. If a country's imports double, for instance, but its **exports**—the products it sells to other nations—triple, then overall the country has gained. Although imports are generally hard on producers, exports are cause for rejoicing. Consider the way Mexico's increased exports have benefited producers in the city of Torreon. Since NAFTA was signed, apparel employment in that region of Mexico has increased 600 percent. Wages have

Top 10 Countries the U.S. IMPORTS FROM
2008 Imports (Goods)
(in billions)

1. China $337.8
2. Canada $335.6
3. Mexico $215.9
4. Japan $139.2
5. Germany $97.6
6. United Kingdom $58.6
7. Saudi Arabia $54.8
8. Venezuela $51.4
9. South Korea $48.1
10. France $44.0

also increased, working conditions have improved, and the textile companies are able to invest in better technology to raise productivity.[22]

The Effect of NAFTA on the United States But what about manufacturers in the United States? Haven't they been hurt as a result? The pro-free traders point out that U.S. employment increased 24 percent between 1993 and 2007.[23] Folks on the other side of the argument point out the growing U.S. trade deficit with Mexico and Canada and highlight the United States' loss of manufacturing jobs to Mexico.[24]

People in certain industries will suffer job loss as imports increase, but according to free trade advocates, this job loss will cause workers to find better, higher-paying jobs, either from going back for more education or switching to another industry.[25] Advocates of keeping industry domestic disagree and say that the job losses will weaken the domestic economy in the long run.

Multinational Corporations What would you guess is the second most published book in the world today after the Bible? According to one source, it's the IKEA catalogue. The Swedish-based, Dutch-owned home furnishings company has as many visitors to their stores worldwide each year as there are people in the United States.[26] Increasingly in a global economy, *multinational corporations* like IKEA, companies that have assets in at least one country outside their home country, often generate most of their revenue from sources outside their home country. Keep in mind, however, that creating a multinational corporation tends to be the most expensive option for entering the global market. Organizations that capture the title "multinational" have vast resources to support operations across the globe.

Do It...

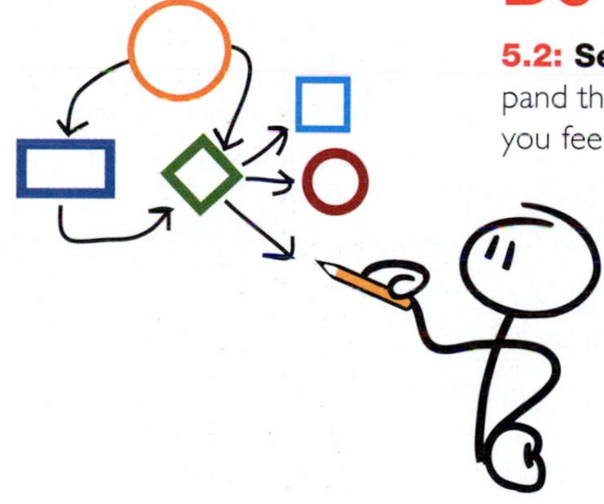

5.2: Select a Mode of Entry Below are descriptions of companies that want to expand their operations to international customers. For each, select the mode of entry that you feel would be the best choice, and justify your answer in 25 words or less.

1. A small producer of homemade spaghetti sauce wants to expand her sales to other countries. Her company is a sole proprietorship.
2. A technology firm develops a patented approach to design computer chips and wants to expand it internationally.
3. A home repair franchise wants to apply its business concept in other countries.

Now Debrief...

Concept A
Concept B
Concept C
Concept D

- Businesses must consider the **competitive advantages** of their home country in relation to other countries to compete on a global scale.
- Most countries rely on their **comparative advantage** to produce certain goods and services at a lower opportunity cost compared to other countries. These products are then traded to other countries for products that those countries have a comparative advantage in producing.
- What trade arrangements and partnerships will give your business the greatest advantage overall? Strategists have begun to talk about **collaborative advantage**, an approach to global business that seeks mutual gains through equal partnerships.
- There are a variety of ways for a company to enter and compete in the global market, including **foreign direct investment**, international **joint ventures**, **strategic alliances**, **licensing**, **franchising**, **exporting** and **importing**, and forming a multinational corporation. Companies must carefully consider the risks and rewards of each mode of entry and build a strategy that fits their business.

3. Scanning the Global Economic Environment

In Chapter 4, we discussed how in order to adapt and remain successful, businesses must participate in environmental scanning, focusing on political/legal, economic, global, sociocultural, environmental, and technological factors, or PEGSET. It's now time to take a closer look at the G in PEGSET, the global factors that affect businesses. Let's start by discussing the global economic environment—what your money can buy here, there, and anywhere, how trade between countries is measured, and what it all means to businesses and customers like you.

Exchange Rates

As a graduation gift, your uncle offers to send you and one of your friends on a vacation anywhere in the world. There's one catch, though. He'll pay for your airfare, but he's only going to give you a fixed amount of money to spend while you're on the vacation. How would you decide where to go?

You might take into consideration the exchange rate of the U.S. dollar with the currency in the countries you wanted to visit. The **exchange rate** is the amount of any currency you receive when you trade it for another currency. For example, in July 2009, one U.S. dollar equaled roughly 0.71 Euros. Exchange rates fluctuate constantly based on a wide range of factors.

Exchange rates are incredibly important to businesses that operate globally. Let's look at an example. In 2008, due to a weakened economy and rising inflation rates in the United States, the exchange rate of the U.S. dollar fell in the international marketplace. The dollar's value fell so far, in fact, that the exchange rate of one U.S. dollar dipped below 100 Japanese yen for the first time since 1995.[27]

It might seem like this would be cause for rejoicing in Japan; after all, now Japanese consumers could get more dollars for their yen when they traveled to the United States. However, the weakened dollar was actually a cause for alarm in the Japanese economy. Why? Japan's economy relies heavily on exports. For exporters, when the local currency is weak in comparison to foreign currencies, business is actually better: When the value of your currency decreases, your products sell for less in the global marketplace, so demand for your products goes up.

Let's say Toyota makes a car and ships it overseas at a cost of 2 million yen. The company then sells the car for 3 million yen, or $20,000 in the U.S. market. In this case, the exchange rate is 150 yen to the dollar. But what happens to the price of the Toyota if the dollar weakens against the yen, for an exchange rate of 1:100? Suddenly, the price of the car increases to $30,000. Consequently, Toyota will have to lower the price of the car, or the demand for the car in the U.S. market will decline.

On the other hand, if Toyota keeps the price low, ensuring that demand remains constant, a car they can sell for $20,000 in the United States will generate zero net profit. To compensate, the actual price of the car on the U.S. market will probably end up somewhere in the middle of the two extremes; in either case, Toyota suffers.

Although this particular scenario is hypothetical, it's a realistic illustration of the way exchange rates affect earnings and revenues for multinational companies. In fact, every time the value of the dollar drops by just one yen, Toyota actually loses about $350 billion dollars in revenue![28]

On the other side of the coin—or dollar—when exchange rates decreased in 2008, U.S.-based multinationals profited. For example, Hewlett-Packard reported a 5 percent increase in sales due to the dollar's decline in foreign markets.[29] Knowing the impact fluctuating exchange rates have on sales and profits, investors and business strategists try to anticipate how these exchange rates will affect the bottom line and the growth of a company overseas and plan their investments accordingly.

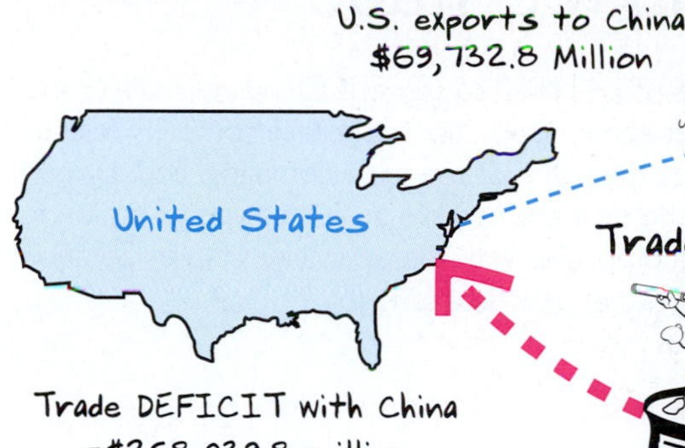

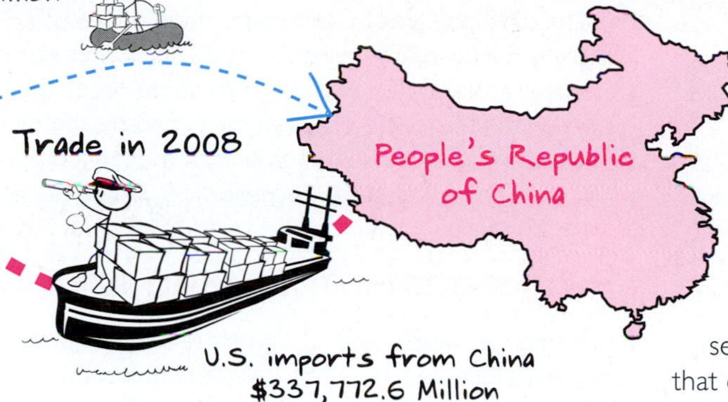

Why do you think the United States has a trade deficit with China? Do you think this will always be so?

Balance of Trade

Earlier in the chapter, we talked about the surprising number of products and services in the United States that come from other parts of the world. And while the United States *does* export products and services to sell in foreign countries, the U.S. **balance of trade**, the value of everything exported minus the value of everything imported, has got some people worried. Sure, the United States might export corn, wheat, software, and airplanes, earning money that flows into the economy. On the other hand, the parts (and now even significant portions of the engineering) involved in making those airplanes come from outside the country. U.S. companies are increasingly offshoring research and development tasks to places where engineers work for less. Since the early 90s, the United States has had an increasingly large **trade deficit**—it spends more on imports more than it makes on exports.

But trade deficit doesn't tell the whole story. Say Wal-Mart orders a shipment of DVD players from a factory in China. The money Wal-Mart spends on those DVD players will go into the Chinese economy. Meanwhile, China has a **trade surplus**; overall, it exports more than it imports. Additionally, Chinese consumers may not turn around and use their money to buy U.S. imports. This means that U.S. trade with China registers as a deficit.

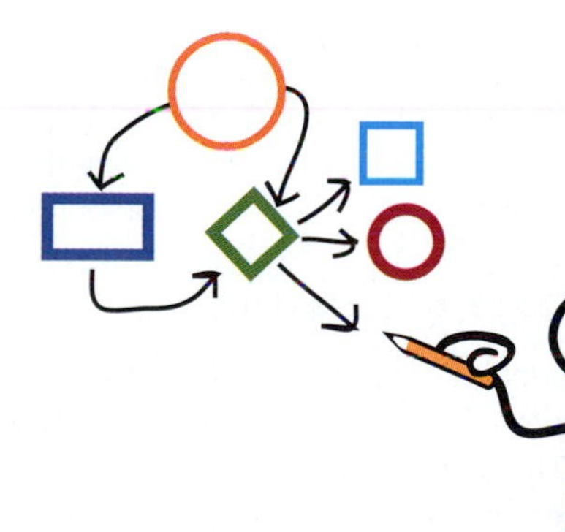

Do It...

5.3: Consider the Currency From a SWOT perspective, what are the opportunities that arise when the currency in a company's home country declines in value relative to other currencies? What are the threats? Limit your response to one page, and be prepared to submit it electronically or present it to your class.

Now Debrief...

- The **exchange rate**, the rate at which one foreign currency is traded for another, is important to businesses that operate globally. Lower exchange rates are good for exporters because they make a country's exports more competitive in the global market.
- The **balance of trade** is the difference between a country's exports and its imports.
- Since the early 90s, the United States has had an increasingly large **trade deficit**—it spends more on imports than it makes on exports. Meanwhile, China has a **trade surplus**; overall, it exports more than it imports.

Concept A
Concept B
Concept C
Concept D

4. Scanning the Trading Environment: Protectionism and Free Trade

In late 2008, the Coca-Cola Corporation offered $2.4 billion to buy out China Huiyuan, China's largest juice company. Several months later, after some negotiations, the juice company rejected the deal. Coke's offer was originally three times the value of the juice company, and, by early 2009, with the decline of the global economy, the deal seemed like an even sweeter option for Huiyuan. Moreover, Coke was one of the few companies with the economic stability to afford such an offer in the global recession. So, why did the juice deal turn sour?

Protectionism: Closed for Business

The rejection was linked to China's recently imposed anti-monopoly laws, which, according to critics, are actually an attempt at trade protectionism.[30] **Protectionism**, the policy of restricting trade through barriers like quotas, tariffs, and other limiting government regulations, has become a loaded issue in an increasingly global economy. Protectionism limits free trade, and although trade barriers throughout the world have been reduced (thanks to the WTO as well as regional trade agreements), some countries remain more protectionist than others.

What does this mean for companies that want to do business with protectionist nations? First, it's important to consider some *motivations* behind protectionist laws and sensibilities:

1. **Balance of trade.** Many nations use protectionist laws to guard against trade deficits. Think back to Boeing's deal with China, in which the company ultimately set up shop in that country to get around certain Chinese government trade restrictions that would have otherwise prevented them from selling their planes in the Chinese market.
2. **Economic circumstances.** In 2008, when unemployment was on the rise, countries became anxious about losing jobs to foreign competitors. As a result, many governments became more protectionist. For example, as part of the 1994 NAFTA negotiations, the United States and Mexico agreed to a program that would allow Mexican trucks to transport cargo in the United States. In early 2009, however, the U.S. government put an end to that program in an attempt to protect U.S. truckers from losing their jobs to Mexican truck drivers. The Mexican government wasn't happy about this decision and decided to put tariffs on 90 U.S. products, thereby raising the costs of these imports and making them less attractive to Mexican buyers.[31]

3. **National security.** National security is sometimes an important motivator behind protectionist policies. For example, U.S. trade laws might limit shipments of goods from overseas until the shipments meet minimum security requirements so that authorities can prevent issues like the smuggling of nuclear or biological weapons into the country.
4. **Sense of patriotism.** Do you remember the intense rivalry between France and the United States shortly after the outbreak of the second Iraq war? Ultimately, the rivalry hampered trade between the two countries. Fueled by a sense of patriotism, many French consumers turned up their noses at American products. In response, in 2005, McDonald's began a marketing campaign in France that emphasized the local nature of its menu items and the use of French produce in its ingredients.[32]
5. **Response to human rights violations.** Consider the U.S. embargo on goods from Cuba. **Embargos** are trade barriers that limit or altogether prohibit trade between one

What are the pros and cons of protectionism and free trade?

country and another. The United States imposed an embargo on Cuba in 1962 as a political protest against the human rights violations by Cuba's communist government. The Cuban Democracy Act prohibits U.S. companies from trading with Cuba.

Of course, *individual businesses* can also choose to limit trade in response to ethical issues. For instance, did you know that when you go to your favorite café and buy a pound of quality coffee for 13 or 14 bucks, less than one dollar of that amount might actually go to the farmers who harvested the beans? The beans are still expensive because often they're sold by intermediaries who buy the coffee from farmers at low prices and then export the product for high profits. The **fair trade movement** has been a reaction against such exploitation, assuring that farmers get a fair price for their produce, supporting small farms instead of large plantations (that might use environmentally harmful processes). Currently, smaller, independent coffee roasters, as well as a number of large chains—including Starbucks, Tully's, and others—are jumping on the fair trade coffee bandwagon.[33]

Subsidies and Dumping

If you have brothers or sisters, you undoubtedly remember the heated arguments of childhood. Sometimes, meetings of the World Trade Organization can sound like an argument between siblings as nations clash over approaches to trade and retaliate against acts of protectionism by other members.

Consider the organization's February 2009 meeting, which took place at a time when member nations were becoming increasingly protectionist. To boost its struggling economy, Russia tried to cut foreign competition by introducing 28 measures to increase tariffs on imports and subsidize its exports. In response, some EU officials reintroduced *subsidies* for dairy exports to help their own farmers compete with falling prices worldwide. **Subsidies**, or government financial assistance paid to certain industries or businesses, help protect domestic products against competition from foreign imports. If the price of imported cheese falls, domestic dairies might only be able to keep up with the lower prices if the government kicks in some cash to help offset the profits the farmers would otherwise be losing. The EU also restricted its imports of U.S. chicken and beef.

In retaliation, the United States implemented tariffs on Italian water and French cheese. The United States also noticed that mattress springs and graphite electrodes imported from China seemed suspiciously cheap. There were cries of **dumping**—the competitive practice of unloading products in a foreign market at prices that are below domestic cost. To protect against dumping, which the WTO considers an unfair competitive practice, the United States created new tariffs to hamper Chinese trade.[34]

Free Trade: Open and Easy

As the previous discussion shows, trade negotiations can get messy. The WTO, made up of 153 member nations that form the bulk of the world's trade, is dedicated to reducing trade barriers and "contributing to economic growth and development" worldwide.[35] In contrast to protectionism, as we've discussed, a **free trade** mentality supports minimizing obstacles (like tariffs and quotas) to encourage the flow of products across borders. Although the WTO supports free trade in theory, member nations may have differing opinions about the way agreements should be carried out. The WTO provides a legal framework to monitor trade agreements between partners and ensure that members are being transparent in their negotiations and trade laws.

Within the WTO, on a more regional level, separate agreements exist between members to reduce trade restrictions even further. As mentioned earlier, since 1993, the European Union has functioned as a single market, applying a standardized system of economic and trade laws to all of its member states and converting (in 16 of its 27 countries) to a common currency, the euro. The greater stability of the union has allowed individual European nations to become stronger contenders in the global economy: The EU, as a whole, accounts for almost one third of the world's GDP.[36]

The EU may be the most complicated of the regional trade agreements (RTAs), but there are a total of 400 RTAs in the current global economy that are set to be in place by 2010.[37] Consider SAFTA, the South Asian Free Trade Area, established in 2004 between Nepal, India, Pakistan, and others. Similar to NAFTA, this alliance plans to remove all customs duties on trade between member nations by 2016.

NGOs: The Counter-Balance to Trade Organizations According to free trade advocates, trade agreements and organizations are raising the standard of living for producers in developing countries, but these transformations can take years to trickle down to a country's lowest-paid workers. The United Nations states that some institution—not fueled by capitalist interests—needs to fill the gaps that are emerging through globalization. The UN developed the term **non-governmental organization (NGO)** to apply to advocacy groups (social, cultural, legal, and environmental) with goals that are primarily noncommercial. A wide range of organizations take the NGO label: Some focus on the environment, others focus on humanitarian aid, and still others work at sustainable development.[38] You're probably quite familiar with some NGOs, like the Red Cross. If you're interested in nonprofit work, the UN's list of designated NGOs is a good place to look.

Do It...

5.4: Describe a Point of View Briefly describe the views typically expressed by protectionists toward an issue like offshoring. Then, write a similar description for free-traders. Then, speculate for a moment what events in a person's life may have led to that person holding those beliefs. Be prepared to submit your answers in writing when you arrive in class. Your instructor may also assign you one of the two roles when you come into class, and you'll be given a chance to debate a team representing the opposing view.

Now Debrief...

- **Protectionism**—government policy restricting foreign trade—is an obstacle for global business.
- Protectionist policies, including tariffs, import quotas, and **subsidies**, are enacted for a variety of reasons, including patriotism, political and ethical issues, national and economic security, and protecting the balance of trade from unfair competitive practices like **dumping**.
- Organizations like the **World Trade Organization** exist to support **free trade** and to arbitrate disputes between trading partners. Regional trade agreements within the WTO include NAFTA, SAFTA, the EU, and nearly 400 others.
- As a balance to trade organizations, **non-governmental organizations** (NGOs)—social, environmental, religious, and cultural advocacy groups—have become increasingly important in a global marketplace.

5. Scanning the Cultural, Legal, Political, and Ethical Environment: Look Before You Leap

Up until the mid-1960s, Pepsi was seen as a cheap alternative to Coke, but in 1963, Pepsi arrived at a successful marketing campaign that transformed its brand image for the better. "Come alive! You're in the Pepsi Generation!" redefined Pepsi as the beverage of the young and trendy.[39] *This campaign is great!* Pepsi thought. *There's a large market in China. Why don't we send our message over there?* What Pepsi didn't take into account was the nuance of translation. When the ads were released on the Chinese market, their advertising claimed: "Pepsi brings your ancestors back from the grave!"[40] Whoops!

This urban legend has circulated around the advertising community for years as a warning against the perils of entering the overseas market unprepared. The moral of the story: Learn about the culture you plan to do business with and collaborate with local experts before jumping into a foreign market. Sometimes, this might simply be a matter of overcoming language barriers.

Even countries that share a language, like Great Britain and the United States, have to be careful about connotations and altogether different definitions of certain words. When the Land's End catalogue was first released in the United Kingdom, the company had to make some massive revisions to capture the market. Words like "pants"—the word for underwear in the United Kingdom—have different meanings on the other side of the Atlantic.

As you can see, as companies expand their markets into different cultures, they must be aware of and adapt to their new market's cultural environment. In this section we'll look at aspects of the global environment companies must scan, including the cultural, legal/political, and ethical environment.

Scanning the Cultural Environment

You may have heard the saying that if you want to learn about water, you shouldn't ask a fish. In this analogy, culture is like water, and people are like fish. When you're surrounded by something, you stop noticing it. You don't imagine there are other ways of seeing the world, simply because you—and everyone you know—essentially see things the same way. This can be a huge challenge, perhaps the *most significant* challenge, in doing business globally.

Although language barriers are generally obvious, differences in customs, worldviews, and nonverbal communication can be harder to understand. However, developing cultural sensitivity to these differences is important if you want to succeed in a global economy. Let's look at a few factors.

Proximity Consider an element of nonverbal communication such as *proximity*, or the closeness in space between two or more people. When you talk to a colleague, you generally stand about three feet apart. Much closer than that, and you'll probably feel uncomfortable. Most of the time, how close you stand is something you don't even think about, because most of the people you interact with come from the same culture you do and have the same sense of comfortable proximity. However, some cultures have "personal bubble" perceptions that are much smaller than the comfort zones of most people living in the United States.

Colors, Signs, and Symbols In the 1990s, a U.S. golf ball manufacturer decided to tap into the Japanese market. Although golf ball sales were great in the United States, the company couldn't figure out why its product wasn't taking off in Japan. As it turns out, the problem ended up being a simple one. The company had been packaging its balls in white packages. In the United States, this color was part of the brand's product recognition, but in Japan, the color white is associated with death and mourning. The balls were sold in packages of four, and four in Japan is a number closely associated with death.[41] As this example illustrates, understanding the symbolism behind colors, numbers, and other signs in your target market is especially important when you consider packaging and labeling.

Other Cultural Customs How many U.S. ads can you think of that emphasize the "fast-acting" effects of a product, or "immediate results"? In the United States, we tend to see time as a limited resource that we need to use efficiently. Many Latin American cultures, on the other hand, think of time as much more fluid. If you're on a business trip to Mexico, some people may trickle into a meeting 30 or 45 minutes past the start time. This is perfectly acceptable; in fact, it is expected in Mexican business culture.

And what about when you leave work for the day? You might offer a general good-bye to your colleagues or friends, but you don't usually get more personal than that. In France, on the other hand, it's bad manners to go without saying a personal good-bye to each person who's still there, whether that's five people or 25.[42]

Another cultural factor to consider is formality. The United States is well known for being a hyper-casual nation. Many other countries, on the other hand, use a greater degree of formality in communications and business interactions. When doing business in Colombia, for instance, it is important to spend time on greetings and social conversation first, before launching into a business meeting.[43] All of these factors, the everyday attitudes and behaviors you take for granted, are worth researching before doing business in another country.

Conducting a Hofstede Analysis of an Overseas Market In the late 1960s, while working as a psychologist at IBM, Dr. Geert Hofstede conducted a study that analyzed differences in worldviews—perceptions, values, and ways of life—in 40 countries and came up with five categories that characterize some of the most important differences.[44] Getting a handle on these concepts will help you grasp a good deal of the cultural and communication differences you might face if you want to expand your business globally.

Power Distance Let's say you make software that helps doctors keep track of patient records, and you want to market your product in France. Your research may show that an ad campaign message emphasizing expert testimony will be fairly successful. However, if you want to expand your business to Switzerland, you'll realize that expert testimony will be less likely to sell software to the Swiss. Why? The answer has to do with **power distance**—how comfortable a culture is with unequal distributions of power. The power distance index (PDI) gauges the degree of power distance and hierarchical structures within a culture. Low-PDI cultures, such as Switzerland, Israel, and New Zealand, place a greater emphasis on independence and self-reliance.

Cultures that are high on the PDI scale tend to set up hierarchies within their cultures. High-PDI countries, such as Malaysia and Mexico, are comfortable with authoritarian leadership, and they value the opinions of experts.[45] So, for instance, if you want to offshore to the Philippines, you should take into account the fact that the leaders in your organization may end up being the folks who have been around for the longest, rather than the ones that you, with your U.S. worldview, might consider to be the most qualified. Take a look at Figure 5.1 to see where several representative nations fall on the PDI.[46]

Figure **5.1** | **Power Distance Index (PDI) Continuum**

Austria – Israel – Denmark – Ireland – Sweden - France - India - UAE - Mexico - Guatemala - Malaysia
←--0--100--→
Low PDI High PDI

Individualism vs. Collectivism There's a Japanese saying that goes, "The nail that sticks up will be hammered down."[47] The United States is home to a highly individualistic culture, where this idea doesn't mean much. In Japan, however, "everyone is part of some collective group, and the group comes first."[48]

These differences in worldview illustrate the opposite ends of Hofstede's *individualism spectrum*. What do the differences mean practically for business? Successful advertising in the United States that emphasizes individualism should not be exported to Japan, and U.S. companies working in Japan must consider this cultural difference to avoid conflict and misunderstanding.

Consider the example of an American consulting company that began to offer IT solutions for Japanese corporations. The company sent in U.S. citizens, Irishmen and women, Turks, Romanians, and Indians to consult with the Japanese corporation, but they didn't provide cultural sensitivity training to their workers. As a result, conflicts arose when employees from individualistic countries began taking control, jumping in to offer solutions when none were asked of them.[49] If you've ever read a job description that included the traits "self-starter" or "highly motivated," you know that these traits are considered desirable in that culture. However, this same behavior may be problematic in a culture like Japan's. Figure 5.2 shows where Japan sits in relation to some other representative countries on the individualism continuum.[50]

Figure **5.2** | **Individualism Continuum**

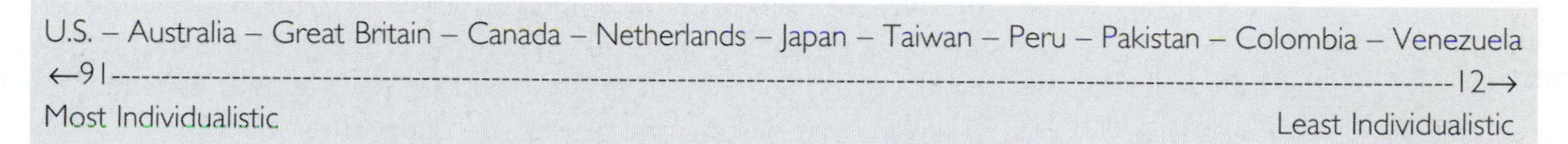

Masculinity vs. Femininity The next time you watch TV, pay attention to the commercials. Do you notice more commercials depicting characters in relationships, or are there more commercials that emphasize success, status, and/or winning?

In Hofstede's analysis, *masculine-oriented cultures* emphasize stereotypically masculine traits, such as heroism, dominance, assertiveness, and competition. So, if you start doing business in Venezuela, for instance, people will expect you to be assertive and competitive in your dealings. "Feminine" cultures, meanwhile, place a higher value on cooperation, consensus, caring, and aestheticism.[51] In cultures with a high masculinity ranking, there is also typically a greater gap between gender roles; these countries tend to be more male-dominated.[52]

Uncertainty Avoidance Did you know that an estimated 75 percent of adults in Great Britain play the lottery at least once a week?[53] It's hard to say for sure, but this *might* be linked to the fact that Britain is an extremely *low-uncertainty-avoidance culture*. According to Hofstede, cultures with low uncertainty avoidance welcome risk and ambiguity. In business, innovations and ideas that push boundaries are encouraged.

In contrast, countries that factor high in uncertainty avoidance have a harder time accepting new ideas. These countries feel more comfortable with ritual, rules, and structure, and they tend to shy away from conflict and uncertainty. In part, these differences are due to a country's makeup: Countries with fairly diverse populations tend to be more comfortable with uncertainty because rituals and customs are more fluid in those places.

The United States ranks fairly low in uncertainty avoidance. In terms of what this means for business, if you're cooperating with companies in countries that have a higher level of uncertainty avoidance, you should adapt your expectations accordingly. Allow time for people to adjust to an idea before you proceed. It can also help to back an idea up thoroughly with facts and statistics to make it clear that the idea is non-risky. Finally, consider involving locals in leadership roles to help reduce unexpected elements.[54]

Long-Term vs. Short-Term Orientation *Short-term oriented cultures* value fast progress and quick solutions. Overspending is more common among businesses in these countries because short-term cultures value immediate results, as opposed to long-term savings. *Long-term oriented cultures*, meanwhile, prefer persevering toward slow results. Thrift is highly valued, and these cultures place greater emphasis on the past and traditions.[55] East Asian countries tend to have the greatest long-term orientation.

If you're doing business in a long-term oriented culture, it's not worth emphasizing the immediate results that customers can get with the product you're offering (e.g., "With this new gadget, you'll be able to increase productivity by 8 percent this quarter!"). Similarly, don't expect business agreements to be reached on the spot. Individuals in long-term oriented cultures prefer to reflect on possible outcomes and proceed methodically.

Scanning the Legal Environment

In 2007, Vetco International, an international oil and gas producer, pled guilty to violations of the **Foreign Corrupt Practices Act (FCPA)** and paid the largest criminal fine in FCPA history—$26 million. Vetco admitted it had violated the FCPA by paying bribes to customs officials in Nigeria that totaled $2.1 million over a two-year period.[56]

The FCPA is a U.S. law that prohibits bribery and requires public companies to use transparent accounting methods. Although the law was established in 1977, it wasn't often enforced until the last few years now that globalization has made relevant the issues the act addresses. Although the United States sees bribery as a legal *and* ethical issue, other cultures tolerate what the FCPA refers to as "corrupt payments." In fact, less than 20 years ago, bribery payments were tax deductible in certain Western European countries. International trade laws now prohibit bribery, but the practice still exists in many countries where it is so built into the cultural structure that officials often let it slide under the radar.[57]

These issues are important to consider for companies doing business in the global marketplace. After all, not only is bribery an ethical issue that socially responsible businesses should take precautions against, but the legal consequences of FCPA violations can also be extremely damaging to a company. Violations of the anti-bribery provisions can result in a $2 million fine for first-time offenders, whereas violations of the internal accounting requirements can bring as much as a $25 million penalty.[58]

Scanning the Ethical Environment

Even when conducting business outside our borders, U.S. companies are required to follow U.S. laws. Although bribery is one concern, there are a host of other legal and ethical issues companies need to consider when operating overseas. For instance, many countries have different policies about child labor, unionization, working conditions, and monopolies. Sweatshop labor—labor conditions where workers are forced to work long hours for low wages, in dangerous conditions—is legal in many developing nations.[59] We've already discussed fair trade practices, but it's worth pointing out that fair trade considerations encompass more than coffee sales. Exploitative labor practices still occur all over the world and even come up in the United States.[60]

An important part of socially responsible business practices includes knowing where your money is going and using discrimination about the business partners you're trading or collaborating with. It all goes back to the triple bottom line. As we discussed in Chapter 3, sustainable companies focus not just on profits, but also how their business affects people and the environment. Consider the Daewoosa factory in American Samoa, shut down after a U.S. Department of Labor investigation in 2003. The owner of the factory was convicted of human trafficking for confining the workers and forcing them to work without pay. More than this, clothing from the factory was exported with a "Made in the U.S.A." label because the factory was located in a U.S. territory. When news of these abuses came to light, the U.S. companies that had been doing business with the factory—J.C. Penney, Kohl's, Sears, Target, and Wal-Mart—received bad press.[61] You can read more about global ethics in Chapter 8.

Scanning the Political Environment

Imagine you work for a company that trades oil in Eastern Europe and you decide you want to invest in a pipeline that will transport oil from Azerbaijan to a Black Sea port in the Republic of Georgia. You've just invested millions of dollars and finished the construction of your pipeline when Russia launches air strikes against Georgia and decides to invade the country. When you began the construction of the pipeline, you realized the political instability of the region was a weakness and even a threat, and now you're faced with the very real possibility that Russia might take Georgia over and seize the part of your pipeline that runs through that territory.

Although the scenario is hypothetical, a Georgia-Russia conflict actually did occur in the summer of 2008, and it's a good illustration of the types of threats U.S. companies face when they expand into politically unstable nations. Businesses must consider the political stability of a region before deciding whether investment in a region is a worthwhile undertaking. Terrorist threats, disease outbreaks, and violent political conflicts are situations businesses may face in many parts of the world. Although cheap labor costs and emerging markets might be an exciting opportunity, it's worth considering whether there are threats in a particular region that outweigh the benefits of doing trade there.

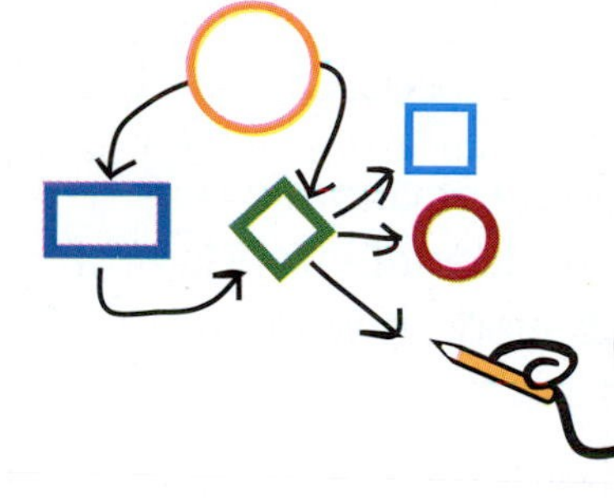

5.5: Prepare for a Business Trip You're preparing for a business trip to a foreign country that you've never visited before. To help you prepare for the trip, you are given the chance to ask five questions of someone who has lived in that region for his or her entire life. What five questions would you ask and why? Be prepared to submit your questions electronically or to present them to your class.

Now Debrief...

- Language differences as well as differing customs, etiquettes, and levels of formality are all important aspects to research before doing business in another country.
- Hofstede's theory identifies five significant factors that shape a nation's worldview: **power distance**, individualism/collectivism, masculinity/femininity, uncertainty avoidance, and long-term/short-term orientation.
- U.S. businesses operating overseas are still subject to U.S. laws, such as the **Foreign Corrupt Practices Act**, which outlaws bribery.
- A business should consider whether its products are coming from countries that allow child labor, unsafe working conditions, low pay, etc., and whether it can avoid these practices among its trading partners.
- Businesses should conduct a situational analysis of the political environment and possible threats, like terrorism or violence, in nations where they plan to operate or invest resources.

Chapter 5 Visual Summary

1. Describe the trends in globalization and how businesses can capitalize on them. (pp. 108–111)

- **Globalization** encompasses the flow of ideas, knowledge, people, trade, business, and culture across borders. Regardless of whether businesses decide to expand their operations overseas or not, the global economy is the economy in which they'll be operating.
- Not only is technology making the flow of information and labor a greater reality, but reduced trade barriers are opening up trade options. It is important to watch global business trends, such as **offshore outsourcing**, to keep up with an environment of rapid change.

Summary: Technological innovation is fueling a more integrated business world, opening up new opportunities and dangers for businesses and consumers alike.

2. Analyze a company's strategies for reaching global markets. (pp. 111–115)

- Before going global, businesses should consider their home country's **competitive advantages**: What trade arrangements and partnerships will give a business the greatest advantage overall in the global marketplace?
- A company that wants to enter the global marketplace must leverage its country's **comparative advantages** over foreign competitors and weigh the risks and rewards of the various modes of entry, which include **foreign direct investment**, **joint ventures**, **strategic alliances**, **licensing**, **franchising**, **importing** and **exporting**, and forming a **multinational corporation**.

Modes of Entry
1. Foreign Direct Investment
2. International Joint Ventures
3. Strategic Alliances
4. Licensing
5. Franchising
6. Importing and Exporting
7. Multinational Corporations

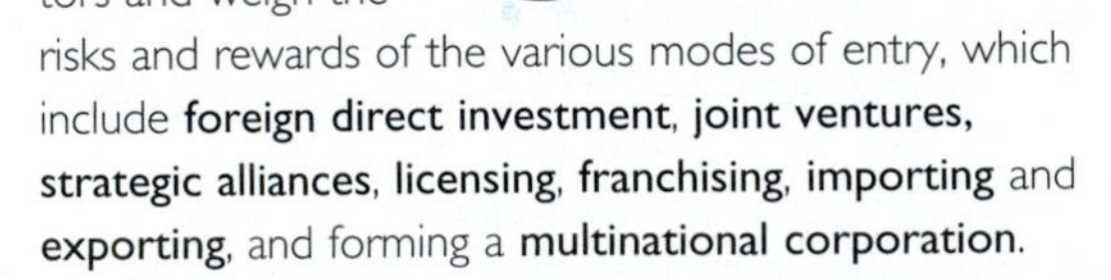

Summary: Different organizations have different needs, and there are a variety of international and domestic business strategies to choose from. Analyzing various trade arrangements and partnerships will help an organization select a strategy that is best suited to its needs.

3. Scan the global economic environment and identify trends and opportunities based on what you discover. (pp. 116–117)

- The **exchange rate** is the amount of any currency you receive when you trade it for another currency. Exchange rates fluctuate constantly based on a wide range of factors, such as inflation.
- Lower exchange rates are good for exporters because they make a country's exports more competitive in the global market. Conversely, higher exchange rates are good for importers because they enable importers to purchase more foreign products at a lesser cost.
- The **balance of trade** is the difference between a country's exports and its imports.

Summary: Global economic conditions can be a major factor in business decisions. Inflation, exchange rates, average wages, and balance of trade need to be considered when scanning the global economic environment.

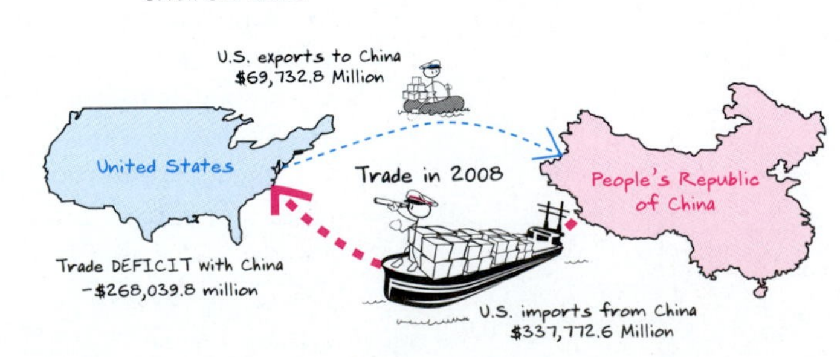

4. Scan the trading environment of a particular region or culture and identify trends and opportunities based on what you discover.

(pp. 118–120)

- When trading with other nations, it's important to keep in mind that some nations are more **protectionist** than others, in an attempt to safeguard their own economies.
- Protectionist measures include tariffs, quotas, **subsidies**, and other government restrictions.
- Organizations like the **World Trade Organization** exist to support freer trade and to arbitrate disputes between trading partners.

Summary: When scanning the trading environment, it is important to truly understand the attitudes of other countries toward trading with outsiders. Some countries might be extremely difficult or impossible to trade with, and the hoops you would have to jump through to do so might mean that the costs outweigh the benefits.

5. Scan the cultural, legal, political, and ethical environment of a particular region or culture and identify trends and opportunities based on what you discover. (pp. 120–125)

- Hofstede's theory identifies five significant factors that shape a nation's worldview: **power distance**, individualism/collectivism, masculinity/femininity, uncertainty avoidance, and long-term/short-term orientation.
- U.S. businesses operating overseas are still subject to U.S. laws, such as the **Foreign Corrupt Practices Act**.

- Ethical labor issues, such as child labor and sweatshops, are important to consider when doing business in a foreign country.
- Businesses should also conduct a situational analysis of the political environment and possible threats, like terrorism or violence, in nations where they plan to operate or invest resources.

Summary: It is vital to understand the cultural, legal, political, and ethical environment of a particular region or culture in which you intend to do business.

Get the most out of what you just read by practicing your skills and actually DOING something with the material! The best place to do this is at **www.mybizlab.com**. Here's just some of what is available to you there:

- Apply your skills in an interactive environment with more **BizSkill** experiences...and see if you have what it takes
- Think critically and talk with your peers on hot business topics in **BizChat**
- Flex your business communication skills and build your own portfolio with the **Communication Plan exercises**
- Watch the chapter material come together with **Just Plain Business** videos
- Study on-the-go with **Audio Chapter Summaries** in MP3 format
- Brush up on the lecture and content with **Audio PowerPoints**
- Discover how well you are doing and see what areas you need to improve on with the **Pre-Tests** and **Post-Tests**

Key Words

These key words and more are also available as flash cards to practice with at **www.mybizlab.com**.

1. Describe the trends in globalization and how businesses can capitalize on them. **(pp. 108–111)**

Globalization (p. 108)
World Trade Organization (p. 108)
European Union (p. 109)
Offshore outsourcing (offshoring) (p. 110)

2. Analyze a company's strategies for reaching global markets. **(pp. 111–115)**

Competitive advantage (p. 111)
Comparative advantage (p. 111)
Collaborative advantage (p. 112)
Foreign direct investment (p. 112)
Joint venture (p. 113)
Strategic alliance (p. 113)
Licensing (p. 113)
Franchise agreement (p. 113)
Importing (p. 114)
Import quota (p. 114)
Tariff (p. 114)
North American Free Trade Agreement (NAFTA) (p. 114)
Exports (p. 114)

3. Scan the global economic environment and identify trends and opportunities based on what you discover. **(pp. 116–117)**

Exchange rate (p. 116)
Balance of trade (p. 117)
Trade deficit (p. 117)
Trade surplus (p. 117)

4. Scan the trading environment of a particular region or culture and identify trends and opportunities based on what you discover. **(pp. 118–120)**

Protectionism (p. 118)
Embargo (p. 118)
Fair trade movement (p. 119)
Subsidy (p. 119)
Dumping (p. 119)
Free trade (p. 119)
Non-governmental organization (NGO) (p. 120)

5. Scan the cultural, legal, political, and ethical environment of a particular region or culture and identify trends and opportunities based on what you discover. **(pp. 120–125)**

Power distance (p. 122)
Foreign Corrupt Practices Act (FCPA) (p. 124)

Prove It

Prove It...

Owner/Investor

Now let's put on one of the BizHats. With the **Owner/Investor BizHat** squarely on your head, look at the following exercise:

You own a large florist's shop, Flora's Flowers, that also offers delivery services and operates out of several storefront locations around town. You've recently decided to expand your business by selling flower arrangements to other local distributors, like supermarkets.

You currently operate a large greenhouse where you grow all of your own flowers, an operation that is fairly time-, labor-, and cost-intensive, and you know that if you expanded your business, you would have to build one or two more greenhouses to produce all the flowers you'd need.

As an alternative, you've considered importing cut flowers from Colombia to add to your floral arrangements. You've heard that Colombia is a major cut-flower exporter, and you think it would be cheaper to buy their flowers than to build the facilities and hire the employees you'd need to grow your own. On the other hand, you're a little worried about possible risks associated with doing business outside the United States.

Conduct a SWOT analysis to help plan your strategy. Make sure to consider political, economic, environmental, and cultural factors that might affect your decision to import. Based on this analysis, would you recommend importing from Colombia or growing the flowers locally?

Flip It...

After doing the SWOT analysis as the owner above, **flip over to the Employee BizHat.**

You're an employee at Flora's Flowers, and you work full time in the greenhouse. Flora has other employees who help with her accounting and marketing or who work in the shop as flower arrangement "artists," but your own job has been limited to the greenhouse since you started working at the company several years ago. You don't mind the work in the greenhouse—it's what you know how to do—but you've recently become worried by rumors that Flora plans to shut down the greenhouse and import her flowers from Colombia.

Come up with some convincing arguments you could offer Flora to persuade her to keep growing her own flowers locally. Assuming Flora doesn't listen to your arguments and decides to phase out the company's greenhouse operations, discuss what some of your options might be. What could you do so you don't find yourself without a job?

Now Debrief It...

As owner of the shop, how do you feel about saving money vs. holding on to your current, trusted employees? Do you feel that it is safer to just go with what you know, or to import from a foreign country? What will you do if you decide to import your flowers, but customers begin to complain that your product is different than it used to be? As an employee in the greenhouse, what arguments can you present to the owner for staying with domestically grown flowers?

Lead:
Vision, Integrity, Change, and Teams

BizSkills invite...

Try It!
There's no better way to learn concepts than to put them into practice. Take your turn in the driver's seat and be a part of actual business decision making by visiting the BizSkill for this chapter at **www.mybizlab.com**.

Now that you've practiced making tough business decisions and seeing the results of your choices in this chapter's BizSkill, it's time to translate those skills into plain English. And if you skipped the BizSkill, go back now!

Chapter 6 Goals

After experiencing this chapter, you'll be able to:

1. Distinguish managers from leaders, and recognize the importance of effective followers.
2. Identify effective leadership, and develop leadership qualities in yourself.
3. Explain how a vision provides direction for an organization, and create a vision for your own career.
4. Describe the importance of change, and be able to lead it effectively and avoid its potential pitfalls.
5. Form effective teams and resolve team issues.

Are you an orange fish or a green fish?

Will the Real Leader Please Stand Up?

If you've ever been in a lab group or worked on a team project, you know that the interactions among team members can often be more interesting than whatever project you're working on. One group member usually takes responsibility to manage the team, set deadlines, and delegate responsibilities, but another group member may emerge as its real leader. While the emergent leader is trying to empower team members and come up with innovative solutions, the manager is focused on completing the task at hand as quickly and efficiently as possible. It's not hard to see that the project manager is getting frustrated with the emergent leader's lack of focus and discipline, while the leader is upset by the project manager's inability to see "the big picture." In the meantime, the team is falling apart because the power struggle is forcing team members to take sides, and nothing useful is getting done in the midst of all the tension.

In a situation like this, it may seem like the conflict is coming from two people butting heads over the same role. But the conflict is actually a function of common misunderstandings regarding leadership and management. In the previous scenario, what would happen if the project manager and the emergent leader stopped struggling to fill the same role and started acting as complements to each other? The project manager's best bet is to get on the same page with the emergent leader and harness his or her ability to innovate, inspire, and motivate. In this chapter, you'll learn the difference between managers and leaders, what it takes to be a great leader, and how leaders provide a vision for organizations, lead change, and form effective teams.

1. Managers and Leaders: A Complementary Distinction

Although many people assume *leadership* is just another word for *management*, the two aren't interchangeable. Think about managers you've encountered who, well, *managed*. They made sure your reports were turned in on time, gave you assignments, and checked that you were adhering to a set schedule. Now think of people who have inspired you to do your job a little better. Maybe these people weren't even authority figures, but peers. This isn't to say managers can't be good leaders, or vice versa; however, there is a clear difference, which you may already understand without even realizing it. Look at the two examples below and identify the manager and the leader.

Can you tell which one is the leader and which one is the manager?

- Jessie began working for a technology company last year, and she has recently begun supervising six members of the research and development team. She likes to plan out her day with a detailed to-do list. The bulk of her day is made up of reviewing proposals and tests and scheduling pitch meetings. Periodically, she also has to handle staff members requesting time off. Overall, Jessie is a good supervisor who gets things done on time and accurately.
- Candace works for the same company as a supervisor in the sales department. She spends much of her time looking at what's being developed and creating ways to pitch ideas to clients. She's excited about the new products coming from the research and development team and is busy figuring out a plan to work with the products in the future. Periodically, she holds strategy sessions with her team to let them know her vision for the future and the opportunities that are coming their way. Employees from all departments come to Candace to discuss their ideas and get her advice. Because of her intuition and instinct, she has been a valuable member of the company.

Based on this information, who's the leader and who's the manager? If you said Jessie was the manager, you're right. Doesn't it feel like Jessie is executing a list of tasks while Candace is developing ideas for the future? Often, this forward-thinking attitude is a good predictor of leadership.

A **manager** typically has formal authority and takes care of four main functions: planning, organizing, directing, and controlling. On the other hand, a **leader** can be found anywhere in the hierarchy of an organization and has the ability to motivate, inspire, and influence the behaviors of other people. In other words, employees listen to managers because they *have* to, but they listen to leaders because they *want* to.

Unlike management, no one is necessarily given the title of *leader*. Is the person in charge really the leader of the organization? Well, it depends. Just because that new intern is fresh out of college, that doesn't mean she can't exhibit qualities such as innovation or intuition in her job. At the same time, a company can have an inspirational leader who can deliver a rousing pep talk at monthly meetings, but is unable to locate his socks in the morning.

The biggest thing that separates leading from managing is the focus on influencing people. Managing—and with it planning, organizing, directing, and controlling—is necessarily focused on process and resources. A manager's job is, after all, to *manage* things, be it people or other resources, and to focus on specific tasks, goals, and objectives.

Employees listen to managers because they *have* to, but they listen to leaders because they *want* to.

Say your department is given a certain amount of hours for a task. As a manager, you're given a team, a budget, and a deadline. Those are your priorities: getting your fellow workers on task to deliver by a certain date. By ensuring the task is completed on schedule and on budget, the manager makes sure the organization receives payment from the customer, brings in a certain level of profit, and is able to continue paying the salaries of its employees. Management is a necessary part of an organization because it is responsible for coordinating activities and getting results.

Most managers' dealings with people are based on how those employees can help achieve set goals. The focus is often on the task more so than on the employee. Leaders, however, really need to know how these employees tick because their ability to motivate and inspire them is one of their primary functions in an organization.

The Importance of Followers

Have you ever watched a flock of geese flying overhead? There is clearly a leader, but each goose plays an important role by flapping its wings and creating an "uplift" for the birds behind it. In fact, because they fly in a V formation with one leader and followers creating uplift, the whole flock is able to fly 71 percent further than had each bird flown on its own.[1]

A *great* leader is both a good manager *and* a good leader.

As is the case with a flock of geese, truly effective leadership is a shared relationship between leaders and followers.[2] This means that success is not only based on the leader; it is also based on the people who are following that leader. The role of a follower is therefore just as important as the role of a leader. Followers can be broken down into two categories: *effective followers* and *ineffective followers*.[3] Effective followers;

- actively support the leader;
- take responsibility for their own success;
- are proactive in determining strategies rather than just reacting to issues;
- understand how to be part of the solution rather than the problem;
- demonstrate assertive behavior rather than passive behavior; and
- hold themselves, as well as others, accountable.

Sometimes, effective followers need to step up and lead, so it's important that they have the same qualities as a leader. However, followers usually use these qualities to support the leader, rather than do the leading themselves. On the flip side of this, ineffective followers:

- sit back, waiting for others to step up;
- have a "me," rather than a "we," focus;
- support decisions based on personal opinion, rather than thoughtful consideration; and
- demonstrate passive behavior rather than active behavior.

As you can see, effective followers don't necessarily need a strong leader to get the job done, but ineffective followers do.

Manager, Leader, or Both?

Now you recognize the distinction between a manager and a leader, and you understand how effective followers are a necessary part of leadership. But it's important to note that being a leader is not better than being a manager (or a follower, for that matter). Both require very similar skill sets to run an organization effectively. The roles are different, but they are not necessarily mutually exclusive.

Good leaders aren't necessarily good managers, and good managers aren't necessarily good leaders. But a *great* leader is both a good manager *and* a good leader.[4] Although the best managers also have leadership qualities, in some cases it's best to let the leaders lead and the managers manage. The most successful organizations employ both managers and leaders, with leaders throughout all levels of the organization's hierarchy.

As you've read about these distinctions, have you felt yourself identifying more with the qualities of a leader or a manager—or both? Think about your work, school, and social life and the leaders you may have encountered there. If you are currently working, is your manager a leader? How does he or she motivate you—or fail to? What about your group of friends—is there someone who everyone else always seems to follow? Try to identify the specific qualities that make this person a leader. As you read more about leadership qualities in this chapter, you'll also see they aren't a result of charisma or other inherent or unattainable qualities you may or may not have. Leadership can be learned, and in the next section, you'll see how.

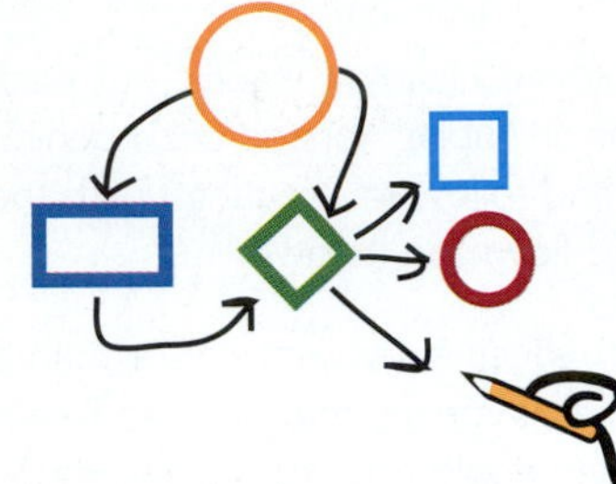

Do It...

6.1: Identify Ideal Leaders, Managers, and Followers On your own, create three lists of qualities that describe the ideal leader, the ideal manager, and the ideal follower. Then share your lists with three other people, and have the team collect all of the qualities for each title that appeared on at least three of the four team members' lists. Now look at the master list you have created for ideal manager, leader, and follower. How many words appear on all three lists? Be prepared to submit your lists electronically or share them with your class.

Now Debrief...

- Leaders and managers are not synonymous. A **manager** has formal authority and takes care of planning, organizing, directing, and controlling to get the job done. On the other hand, a **leader** can be found anywhere in the hierarchy of an organization and has the ability to motivate, inspire, and influence the behaviors of other people.
- Followers are important to leadership because without a team to support them, leaders will not be effective. Followers can be broken down into two categories: effective and ineffective.
- Employees listen to managers because they *have* to, but they follow leaders because they *want* to. The roles are different but complementary, and both are necessary for an organization's success.

2. If You're a Leader, Give Me an "I Five"

If the relationship between leaders and followers is so crucial to leadership, how do leaders get people to follow them? ■ People follow leaders, not because the leaders strive to be followed, but because leaders tend to exhibit qualities that draw others to trust and follow them. While there's no *I* in "team," there are actually five *I*s that are attributed to great leaders. These qualities are *inspiration*, *innovation*, *initiative*, *introspection*, and *integrity*. In this section, we'll look at these qualities, and we'll also discuss ways in which you can develop leadership qualities in yourself.

Inspiration

As an employee or student, what inspires you? After 2008's financial market collapse, U.S. billionaire businessman Warren Buffett's investment company, Berkshire Hathaway, reported its worst financial year ever, turning a net profit that was less than half of the company's bottom line in 2007. Despite the bleak financials, however, Buffett rallied his employees and shareholders, telling them that the United States' and Berkshire Hathaway's best days still lay ahead. He inspired his followers by reminding them that the United States had faced worse challenges before, including the Great Depression and World War II, and always came out strong.

> "If your actions inspire others to dream more, learn more, do more and become more, you are a leader."
>
> **—John Quincy Adams,** Sixth President of the United States

Buffett's confidence in the ability of Americans to overcome adversity provided an inspirational example, not just to employees and shareholders, but to everyone hit hard by the market crash. An *inspirational* leader is passionate about the company's vision and mission, and, as we discuss later in the chapter, is able to share that passion so others have it, too. Effective leaders understand that if employees believe their work has purpose and meaning beyond the tasks they perform each day, they will be more invested.

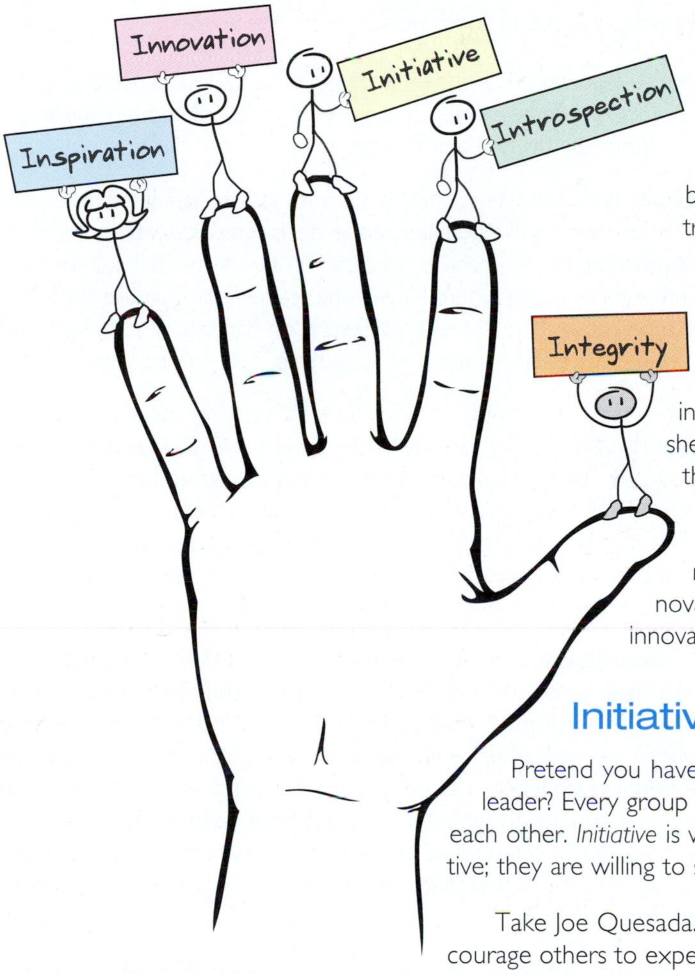

Innovation

How important is *innovation* to leaders? According to a 2005 survey, 53 percent of business and technology leaders claim innovation is the biggest factor in a successful business.[5] Without innovation, companies stop growing and progressing. Consider Nike. Nike was born because of innovation. Company founder Bill Bowerman was a track and field coach who experimented with running shoes. He created the first shoe sole used by Nike with his wife's waffle iron. The shoe was appropriately called the "Waffle Trainer."[6]

Company leaders, like Bowerman, are the people responsible for coming up with new goals and vision, also known as innovation. There is no such thing as a visionless leader, because he or she wouldn't be considered a leader in the first place. This implies, then, that to be a leader, you have to possess an entrepreneurial mindset. Great leaders innovate because this is how one effects change. They are never satisfied with the status quo and are always looking for new and better ways to get things accomplished. (Excited about innovation? We'll talk more about how entrepreneurial leaders thrive on innovation in Chapter 7.)

Initiative

Pretend you have a group assignment: Are you willing to step up and be the group leader? Every group needs some sort of leader. If not, all you do is sit around looking at each other. *Initiative* is what gets someone to step up to the challenge. Leaders have initiative; they are willing to step up, act independently, and take control of the situation.

Take Joe Quesada. As an artist at Marvel Comics, Quesada took the initiative to encourage others to experiment with new styles of writing and art that took antiquated storytelling techniques and replaced them with the more contemporary "language" of television and film. He also used his personal connections to bring new writers and artists from outside comics to the company, such as filmmaker Kevin Smith. In 2000, he became the first artist ever to become editor-in-chief. Quesada has continued to lead and embrace changes in the comic genre. Having the kind of initiative that Quesada possesses can separate a true leader from a follower.

Which of the five Is do you think is most important?

> People follow leaders, not because the leaders strive to be followed, but because leaders tend to exhibit qualities that draw others to trust and follow them.

Introspection

Are you an introspective person? Being *introspective* means a leader can adapt to how a certain situation or person needs to be led. Part of being an introspective leader is having **emotional intelligence**, which is a set of skills that help people better communicate with themselves and the people around them. By being emotionally intelligent, leaders are better able to get people to work toward a common goal.[7] Take some time to answer these five questions about yourself to gauge the various dimensions of your own emotional intelligence:[8]

1. Are you *self-aware*?
2. Can you *manage your emotions*?
3. Do you *motivate yourself*?
4. Are you able to *understand and empathize* with other people's emotions?
5. Do you possess good *social skills*?

Don't make the mistake that emotional intelligence is simply about being a nice person. Rather, for leaders, emotional intelligence is about understanding others, being persuasive, handling disagreements, and getting people to focus positively on their work.[9]

Part of being an introspective leader is also understanding all the various *leadership styles* and knowing how to select the most effective one for a given situation. Although there are many leadership styles, leaders often fall into three basic categories:

1. **Autocratic leaders** typically tell employees what to do and how to get it done, usually without soliciting feedback from others. They make all the decisions and watch over their employees very closely. Autocratic leaders can be necessary in situations that call for such leadership, such as in an emergency room where having one leader calling all the shots can be useful. If all the information required to solve a problem is on hand, time is limited, and employees are already well motivated, the autocratic leadership style can be appropriate.

2. **Democratic leaders** work with employees to find the best way to complete the job while maintaining final authority. Being a democratic leader means that you value the opinions of the others in your group. That's why democratic leaders surround themselves with skillful employees. This is a useful leadership style when both the leader and employees know about the task and can work together to come up with the best decision. Democratic leaders get the best of both worlds: they empower others, and their decisions are better informed because of the input of their fellow employees.

3. **Free-reign leaders** (or *laissez-faire leaders*) are "hands-off" leaders who allow others to have complete freedom in their work environment. Such leaders provide their followers with the materials they need to accomplish their goals, but little to no direction. Because all authority is handed over to the employees, employees are responsible for the outcomes of the work. Although the free-reign leader can get a bum rap, there is a time and place for this style. For example, say you are thrust into a management position for a task you know nothing about. If employees understand what's going on, who are you to tell them what to do? The hands-off approach can therefore be helpful when employees are knowledgeable, self-motivated, and trustworthy.

To be effective, leaders need to be flexible and know when to apply the right leadership style in a particular situation. Sir Richard Branson, chairman of the Virgin Group, is a good example of a leader who uses various leadership styles to good effect. Although he has a strong personality, he has learned the importance of the free-reign style, stepping back and allowing others to run the company. Considering the Virgin Group comprises over 40 different companies, being able to delegate is a necessity for Branson.

While Branson makes liberal use of the free-reign style, he also incorporates the democratic style into his leadership. Branson writes letters to many of his employees, keeping them up-to-date on his activities and encouraging them to speak up with their questions and comments. To facilitate communication, Branson gives out his home address and phone number to his employees so that they can always reach him. Branson's unique combination of free-reign and democratic leadership styles helps employees feel empowered and motivated, a crucial ingredient in the massive Virgin Group's continued success.[10]

Integrity

We've talked about inspiration, innovation, initiative, and introspection, but there's one very important "I" left in leadership: integrity. According to American Express CEO Kenneth Chenault, *integrity* is the foundation on which true leadership is built. Integrity isn't just about speaking truthfully—real integrity requires a leader's words to be consistent with his or her actions, and vice versa. Leaders with integrity also need to have the courage to maintain that consistency. When your integrity is tested, do you have the courage to stay true to yourself?[11]

Organizations whose leaders don't match actions with their words leave their companies open to backlash from customers, and that can have a big impact on the bottom line. For example, in March of 2009, the public was in an uproar when news broke that several executives at financial insurance giant AIG received multi-million dollar bonuses after receiving government bailout money. Although these contracts were technically legal, AIG executives didn't show a lot of consistency with their company's core values by accepting the bonuses.[12] The actions of a few executives tarnished the whole company's reputation.

Customers aren't the only group looking for integrity in leadership—employees also look for integrity from their leaders. An organization's leaders are the organization's moral compass. If a scandal erupts in the CEO's office, it's more than likely that a lack of morale will find its way down the company ladder. This is why leaders must play a major role in establishing the moral climate of the organization and in determining the role of ethics in the organization. We'll discuss integrity and ethics in much more detail in Chapter 8.

Developing Leadership Qualities in Yourself

Leadership is not just an inherent quality that some people have and some people don't. It can be honed and developed. To become a better leader, you need to ask yourself some tough questions, allow those who know you best to answer those same questions about you, and open yourself up to coaching and mentoring from people who have more experience than you.

Put Yourself on the Witness Stand

The following questions relate back to the five *I*s we just discussed. To develop your own leadership skills, take some time to answer them about yourself:

1. Do you get people excited about anything? If so, what? How? If not, why not?
2. What are you passionate about? When is the last time you were really emotional about a situation or event?
3. What do you tinker with in life? In other words, what parts of your life are you constantly trying to improve or enhance?
4. Do others come to you for advice when they're trying to do something new?
5. What activities do you accomplish, almost daily, with little or no guidance or motivation from others?
6. How often do you adjust your style or approach in a situation to accommodate the circumstances or signals you sense from others?
7. How often does your honesty cost you something important? When is the last time you had to sacrifice something to uphold the truth?

Time for the Cross-Examination Maybe you are, as Clint Eastwood once said in the movie *Dirty Harry*, "a legend in your own mind." You aced the questions on the previous page, and you're feeling pretty good about your five *I*s. Let's see how your answers hold up to a second opinion.

Take the list of seven questions that you answered about yourself, and give them to someone who not only knows you well, but who will also tell it like it is. Your toughest critic is actually your best resource at this point. Invite him or her to answer these questions about you, and take time to listen—really listen and understand—to what he or she thinks. Good leaders are confident enough in themselves and their ability to change to allow this kind of critical evaluation. In fact, some of the best leaders engage in what's called a 360° evaluation in which everyone around them evaluates their performance on a regular basis.

Mentor with a Leader Establishing a mentoring relationship with a leader is invaluable. Not only can they lead you toward self-improvement and self-satisfaction, they can also help you develop your own leadership potential. One of the best ways to become a leader is to build a mentor-apprentice relationship with a leader who will challenge you to develop the five *I*s in yourself. This relationship will provide you with a formal environment for learning how to be a good leader.

If you aren't able to find a mentor-apprentice relationship, watch people around you. Who inspires you and those around you to be better? Once you've identified someone, identify what it is that makes this person a good leader. What about him or her is inspiring? You may also want to read about leaders who inspire you.

You'll put yourself in a great position to become a better leader in every aspect of your life if you take time to evaluate yourself, allow others to evaluate you, and pursue a mentoring relationship with someone who has the experience and values to which you aspire. Leadership isn't something you have to be born with—you can build it if you're willing to let others help you.

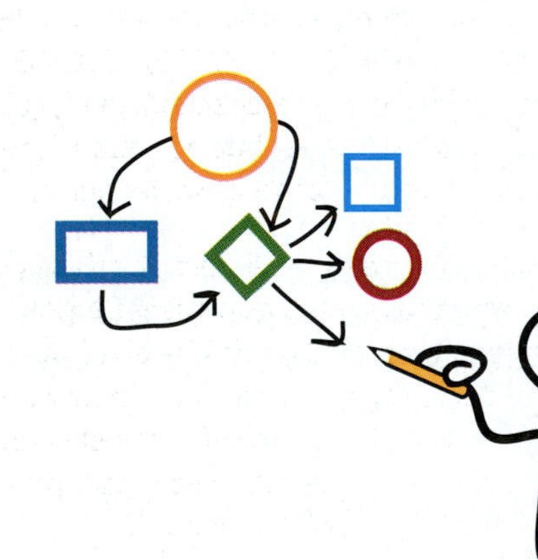

Do It...

6.2: Develop Your Own Leadership Skills Answer the seven questions related to your own five *I*s on the previous page. If you can, have a person you trust answer those same questions about you. Do you feel like you have what it takes to be a leader? If so, what leadership style do you think you would be most comfortable with, and why? Be prepared to submit your responses electronically if your instructor asks you to do so.

Now Debrief...

- Effective leaders have similar qualities: they inspire, innovate, and initiate, and they are introspective and have integrity.
- But even if leaders share these traits, they don't all follow the style of leadership or use the same style of leadership all the time. An **autocratic leader** is a micromanager who typically tells employees what to do and how to get it done. A **democratic leader** works with employees to find the best way to get the job done while maintaining final authority. A **free-reign leader** is a "hands-off" type of leader who allows others to have complete freedom in their work environment.
- You'll put yourself in a great position to become a better leader in every aspect of your life if you take time to evaluate yourself, allow others to evaluate you, and pursue a mentoring relationship with someone who has the experience and values to which you aspire.

3. Thinking About the Future: Having a Vision

What led PepsiCo CEO Indra K. Nooyi to set her sights on transforming a company whose profits were founded on sugary sodas and fatty snacks into a socially and environmentally conscious company selling healthier products and using green technology? Vision. To help make her vision a reality, PepsiCo sold KFC, Pizza Hut, and Taco Bell and soon acquired Tropicana and Quaker Oats. In addition to producing healthier products, Nooyi also wants to produce these products in a more environmentally conscious way, opting for solar and wind power instead of fossil fuels.[13]

As you can see, leaders help establish a vision for an organization. But what is a vision? How is it different from a mission? And how can you set a vision for your own career? In this section, we'll find out.

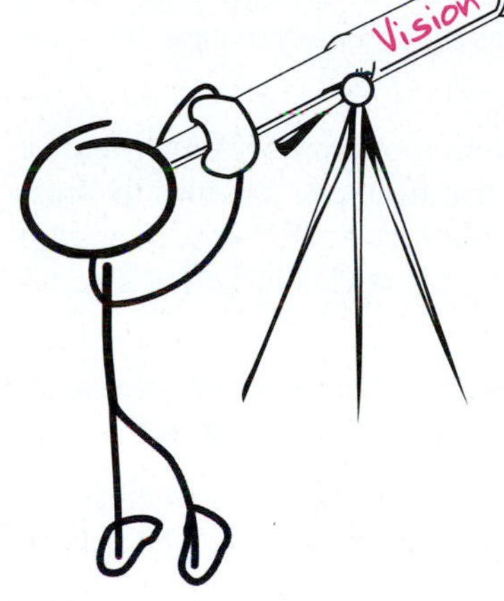

What does it take to make a vision?

Creating a Vision

When you imagine yourself doing various things in the future, you're *envisioning* yourself doing these things. Organizations do this, too, and they convey this image to employees and the world through a **vision statement**—a document explaining where the company wants to go.

Leaders help establish the vision for the organization and are responsible for articulating that vision to everyone else. ■ A vision statement should help motivate, inspire, and excite everyone in an organization. It should also help provide direction and focus to the future. All of this can be done in a few sentences or a few pages, but no matter the length, the vision needs to draw a visual picture of the future that is clear to all stakeholders.

Although *vision* and *mission* are often used interchangeably, they're very different. A **mission statement** is a statement that describes why the company exists as well as its present purpose. Ideally, it is brief, succinct, and easily remembered and referenced on a daily basis by employees to determine, among other things, whether what they are doing today is what they should be doing. To help see the difference, add "-ary" to the end of each. What's the difference between a visionary and a missionary? A visionary is someone who looks to the future to see what's possible, whereas a missionary is someone who is carrying out a task (usually the vision).[14]

Vision statements are sometimes purposely outrageous. In an atmosphere of competition, an organization is most likely to succeed if it is being driven by a vision that is always just slightly out of reach. For example, Amazon.com's vision statement is "to be earth's most customer centric company; to build a place where people can come to find and discover anything they might want to buy online."[15] To be "earth's most" anything is not only unlikely but also immeasurable. And while Amazon.com does offer a wide range of products—from bison burgers to solar panels—offering customers literally "anything" is also exaggeratedly ambitious. However, don't

Translation Guide

In Conversation: *Mission* and *vision* are often used interchangeably in the context of goals, priorities, or plans. For an organization, these are two distinct statements.

In Business Terms: An organization's *mission* describes why the company exists. Its *vision* is an idealized version of how it *sees* itself in the future in relation to its purpose.

Example: Hunger relief agency Stop Hunger Now's mission and vision statements are as follows:

Mission: To provide food and life-saving aid to the world's most destitute and hungry in the most efficient, effective and sustainable manner.

Vision: To end hunger in our lifetime.

think that vision statements are not meant to be fulfilled. The vision statement is the dream, and generally most of us want our dreams to come true.

> ■ A vision statement should help motivate, inspire, and excite everyone in an organization.

So, are organizations with lofty vision statements being ridiculously grandiose? Do vision statements just pay lip service to inflated executives' egos? No, they actually serve a purpose. Consider how a vision statement can affect each of the four hats:

- **Owners/Investors:** Owners can work with an organization's leaders to ensure that everyone is on board with the vision. It's important that the organization's vision aligns with the owners' goals and beliefs.

  Consider Local Harvest Café and Catering, a food service company based in St. Louis. The company's vision of using only local, organic ingredients aligns with the owners' goal of providing high-quality food with minimal impact on the environment. If the owners wanted to become a national brand that everyone has heard of, the company's vision would be very different.

- **Managers**: Managers can use the organization's vision as a tool for motivating people to strive toward an idealized set of priorities.

  In the case of Local Harvest Café and Catering, a manager emphasizes the use of locally grown ingredients over the variety of food offered to customers. The manager may need to limit which dishes the chefs prepare throughout the year depending on which ingredients are available.

- **Employees**: A vivid and inspirational vision can be a potent motivator for employees of an organization.[16] It serves as a consistent guiding force that everyone can turn to when making decisions. If the employees are constantly asking themselves if their decisions are in line with the organization's vision, then the organization can really function as a cohesive unit.

  Employees at Local Harvest Café and Catering must consider the company's vision of sustainability when carrying out tasks like finding suppliers, packaging goods, and disposing of waste.

- **Customers**: Customers can use an organization's vision statement to assess whether the organization is one they want to do business with. They may ask themselves whether the organization's vision aligns with their own priorities and ideals.

  If a customer feels strongly about supporting local businesses or living sustainably, he or she may choose to buy products from Local Harvest Café and Catering rather than a large supermarket.

Your Personal Vision

Think about what might happen if you made a vision statement for your own personal organization: you. In 1984, Madonna famously told Dick Clark that she wanted "to rule the world."[17] In a sense, this was her vision statement. It guided her extraordinarily successful career that has spanned many decades and industries. Although she has never actually been crowned ruler of the world, she has come pretty close to achieving her lofty vision. What are your own career goals, and how might you articulate a vision statement to guide you toward achieving them?

Say your goals are to work for a non-profit organization that helps women who are homeless, domestic violence survivors, or recovering addicts. Your vision might sound something like this:

To improve the quality of life of women and create a supportive community in which they can thrive as self-sufficient individuals.

This vision provides a framework for your career planning, so all of your goals and objectives should align with it. It should help answer the questions:

- What choices should I make?
- How do I want to lead my career life?

It's OK if you never achieve your exact vision. Instead, the vision should help push you in the right direction and show you what is possible.

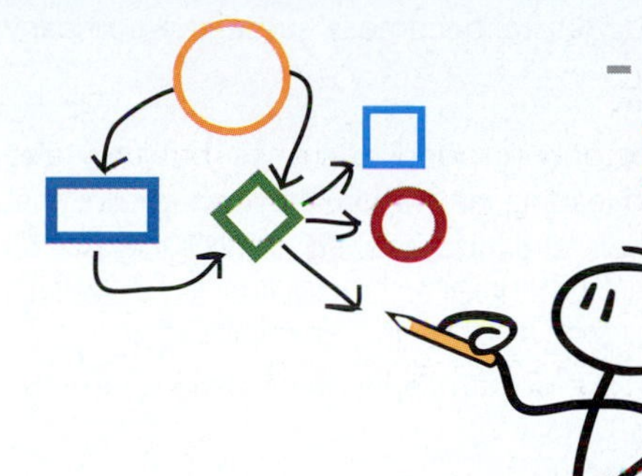

Do It...

6.3: Create a Vision Statement Create a vision statement for yourself that is no longer than one page. Share it with a close friend and invite his or her input. Be prepared to submit your vision statement electronically if your instructor requests it.

Now Debrief...

- A **vision statement** is a statement that explains where the company wants to go. It helps provide direction and focus to the future. A **mission statement** is a statement that describes why the company exists as well as its present purpose.
- *Vision* and *mission* are often used interchangeably, but a vision is an idealized version of how an organization *sees* itself in the future, whereas its mission describes what it *does* to fulfill that purpose in the present.
- Setting a vision statement for your own career can keep your goals focused and communicates them to prospective employers.

4. A Case for Change: Transformational Leaders

Sometimes, employees and an organization's vision statement don't align. In this case, what's a leader to do? This is just one instance when leaders need to know how to lead change and influence reaction to change within the organization as well as outside it.

A leader who inspires and stimulates positive change in his or her followers is sometimes referred to as a **transformational leader**. Change can often be unsettling for people because it means they have to learn about the unknown. People tend to prefer the status quo because predictability and tradition are safe concepts to wrap your head around. There's no fear there. However, transformational leaders understand that change is essential for growth, so they motivate those around them to transform.

Instilling Confidence

Have you ever known someone who really made an impact on you or made you want to change something about yourself? Maybe it was a teacher, a boss, or even an older sibling,-—someone who really took an interest in you as an individual, who stimulated you intellectually, inspired and motivated you, and served as a role model? If so, you know that transformational leaders can be so inspiring that they help instill a sense of self-confidence in others, a confidence that allows others to embrace change because they believe they can handle it. A transformational leader leads others to seeing change as an opportunity in which they can thrive.

Consider Carlos Gutierrez, the former CEO of Kellogg Company. As Gutierrez assumed the role of CEO, the Kellogg Company was struggling to compete in the cereal market. The company needed to adapt to changing customer demands. By tuning into customer needs, rallying employees behind new products, and improving relationships with retailers, Gutierrez helped Kellogg bounce back from its economic struggles to become a successful company once again.

Sometimes, transformational leaders need to not only respond to change, but they also need to actively create it. By looking to the future and leading innovation, they can ensure that the changes that occur are most beneficial for their organizations. ■ Willingness to change is a crucial function of a successful company because it prevents complacency and stagnation, which can be a deadly combination to a business. Good leaders, who thrive in and seek out an atmosphere of change, are the lifeblood of any lasting organization.

Helping Others Accept Change

So, you know the power of change, but how does change happen? And what can good leaders do to make others feel comfortable with change? Often, people won't accept change until they understand how they can benefit from it. According to communications scholar Everett Rogers, people go through a five-step process when assessing their reaction to something new:

Reacting to Change
Step 1: Know
Step 2: Persuade
Step 3: Decide
Step 4: Implement
Step 5: Confirm

Step 1: **Know:** You're aware of the change and basically understand it.

Step 2: **Persuade:** Once you learn more about the change, you form an attitude about whether or not you like it.

Step 3: **Decide:** You actively decide to accept or reject the change.

Step 4: **Implement:** You experience the change.

Step 5: **Confirm:** After you experience the change, you evaluate your decision to adopt it.[18]

The leader's role in this process is to motivate and guide people throughout. Leaders need to get people to see and understand their vision for the future—what they see as "better." They also have to walk people through the change and guide them, making it safe for them to let go of old habits and the present.

Although people tend to follow these five steps when faced with change, their reactions also vary. Whether they're settling into a new job—or even just buying a new television or computer—people tend to either be *innovators*, *early adopters*, *middle adopters*, *late adopters*, or *laggards*. This is important for leaders to understand, because they need to know who their followers are to successfully lead change. Before you read the following, try to guess which one you are—an innovator? Early, middle, or late adopter? A laggard?

- **Innovators:** We all have friends who are always the first to buy the newest gadget. Then, there are those who take it a step farther and actually play a part in *developing* the next big thing. Maybe they beta-test software no one else has heard of or use Apple's iPhone software developers' kit to create a new app. These are the *innovators*. Generally the first 5 to 10 percent of adopters,[19] innovators are quick to embrace change and seek new ways to take advantage of existing technology. Leaders do not have to convince innovators that change is necessary. In fact, innovators actively seek to *be* the change themselves.

■ Willingness to change is a crucial function of a successful company because it prevents complacency and stagnation, which can be a deadly combination to a business.

- **Early Adopters:** *Early adopters* make up 10 to 15 percent of the public[20] and look to the innovators to help figure out whether they want to adopt the innovation or change. For example, if early adopters see that the innovators are pleased with the change or a new purchase, they are more likely to adopt that change or go out and buy the new item themselves. In terms of leadership, this is the group in which many leaders reside.[21] This group is highly regarded for being more cautious than innovators, while also being open to quickly embrace change.[22]

- **Middle Adopters:** Approximately 30 percent of people fall into the category of *middle adopter.*[23] Middle adopters may not be as distrustful of change compared to late adopters or laggards, but they still avoid risk. They are less likely to accept change, simply because they are not looking for change as eagerly as innovators and early adopters are. However, if an innovation or change has positively benefited the first two groups, the middle adopters will likely adopt it.[24] Once something new reaches the middle adopter, it's likely no longer considered new and will have become the status quo. In terms of leading change, if leaders can get middle adopters to accept and embrace change, they are well on their way to success.
- **Late Adopters:** *Late adopters* represent another large portion of society, approximately 30 percent,[25] who follow the middle adopters. Late adopters are reluctant to change, but they generally decide to change so they don't miss out on the next big thing.[26] Because they are risk-averse, late adopters will only take the plunge once they know the water is safe. They hang on to the existing way of doing things out of loyalty for what they have or the fear of trying something different.[27] Leaders trying to create change will therefore have to work harder to get late adopters to accept and embrace change.
- **Laggards:** *Laggards,* about 20 percent of society,[28] are most resistant to change. These are the people who may prefer their VCRs because they don't understand how a DVD player works. Laggards may be isolated from society. When this happens, they have fewer social connections, which can prevent them from seeing the benefit of an innovation or change.[29] In business, leaders must be aware of the risks laggards pose. For example, fear of upsetting the status quo may prevent laggards from investing in newer, better technology, thus, making the company less competitive.

So, after reading this list, were you right in guessing which category you were? If you identified yourself as a leader earlier in this chapter, then you are also likely to be in one of the groups more comfortable with change. If you are slower to come around to change, what do you think a good leader could do to bring you around? The next section explores some of the ways good leaders go about avoiding the pitfalls of change, and ensuring its success.

Avoiding the Pitfalls of Change

So, you understand that change is important to an organization and that effective leaders know how to create and lead that change. What makes a change program fail? Is it because no one wants to change? Is it a result of poor leadership? How can leaders avoid the pitfalls of change?

Why Failure Happens

John Kotter, a recognized authority on leadership and change, put together a list of reasons why failure happens when trying to lead change. See if you agree.

1. **Allowing too much complacency**: *Complacency* is being satisfied where you are and not taking the initiative to grow. When people get complacent, they aren't motivated to change.
2. **Failing to build a substantial coalition**: A *coalition* is an alliance of two or more groups. For change to be beneficial, this alliance needs to be influential enough to get others involved. Many successful change programs involve powerful members of an organization with senior management at their core.

3. **Failing to understand the need for a clear vision**: A clear vision helps rally and inspire employees. Without a clear vision, a change program may break down into various plans without a sense of direction.

4. **Failing to clearly communicate the vision**: Communicating the vision is essential for change because if employees don't understand what's going on, they probably won't be willing to participate in the change.

5. **Permitting roadblocks against the vision**: If people accept a change program, there may still be roadblocks stopping them from fulfilling the vision. Roadblocks include individuals unwilling to change or an organization's structure.

6. **Not planning and getting short-term wins**: To keep and gain momentum for change, it's necessary for leaders to plan for short-term wins. Without this positive reinforcement, many people will give up.

7. **Declaring victory too soon**: It can take years for changes to be truly incorporated into an organization's policies. Declaring victory too soon can cause people to regress back to their old ways.

8. **Not anchoring changes**: Without ingraining a change program into the organization's policies, behavior and values may change as soon as the call for change stops.[30]

Many of the items on the list go back to a company's vision. As we discussed earlier, the vision is important because it gives all employees in the organization a sense of direction and something to work toward. This is where great leaders come in. They not only help create a vision, but they communicate that vision throughout.

Ensuring Success

In order to avoid these mistakes, Kotter[31] also created a change model to help ensure success. To consider this model in context, imagine that you're a business leader at a company that produces a monthly magazine targeted at financial professionals. You see that many other magazines have begun to offer online components, and you believe it's time for your company to follow suit. How can you initiate and implement this change?

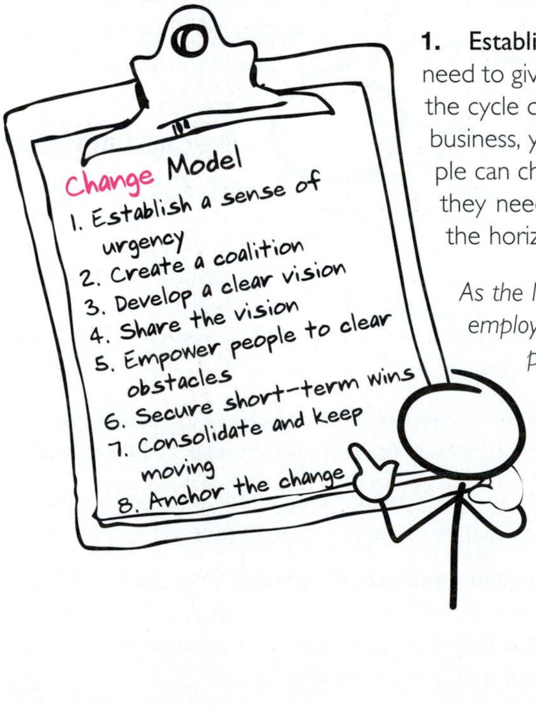

1. **Establish a sense of urgency:** To get people to change, you need to give them a good reason to change. Leaders help break the cycle of complacency and help all employees realize that in business, you have to grow to survive. Leaders know that people can change in the face of a crisis or a great opportunity, so they need to convey this urgency when they see change on the horizon.

As the leader of a print magazine company, you need to show employees that media channels are changing. To remain competitive as a source of financial information, you need to publish content online as well as in print.

2. **Create a coalition:** A strong coalition is vital for a successful change program. At the very least, the coalition should include upper management. Without support, you won't be able to get the program off the ground. Ideally, you'd want the

support of the entire organization, but if you wait for that before going through with a change program, nothing will get done.

Remember the different types of people who embrace change from earlier in the chapter? As the leader of a print magazine company, invite them on your team right away in order for your coalition to grow.

3. **Develop a clear vision:** As discussed earlier, you need a vision to rally and inspire employees to accept change. Without it, an organization may suffer from a lack of focus.

   At your magazine, this means creating a vision that emphasizes the company's desire to reach an increasing number of consumers through online content.

4. **Share the vision:** To get everyone onboard for change, leaders need to communicate their plans, in both words and actions.

   At your magazine, this means having management circulate the vision and incorporate it into staff meetings whenever possible.

5. **Empower people to act:** Employees should feel like they have the ability to embrace a change program. However, to do this it's important to clear their path and make the transformation smooth.

   In the case of the magazine, if employees are hesitant or suspicious of moving content online, have them try the new online magazine for themselves and give feedback. Once exposed to the new format, employees may feel more involved in and accepting of the change, and they may provide useful suggestions.

6. **Secure short-term wins:** Short-term wins are essential for keeping people motivated. If someone told you to change the way you work for the good of the company, but you never saw the results, wouldn't your motivation be negatively affected?

   At your magazine, create a plan to see results within 12 to 24 months; otherwise, some of your supporters may switch teams.[32]

7. **Consolidate and keep moving:** After celebrating a small goal, you may be tempted to take it easy. This can lead to one of the reasons change programs fail that's listed above: "Declaring victory too soon."

   As the magazine's leader, celebrate small victories to reaffirm your team's motivation to accomplishing the overall vision.

8. **Anchor the change:** After going through all of these phases, it's important to cement these changes in the organization's policies. By showing people how the change is working and ensuring management is reinforcing the change, the change is being ingrained throughout the company. It's also important to get employees to connect the implemented changes with the success of the organization.[33]

   At your magazine, this may mean keeping track of the number of visitors to your online magazine to show employees how the company is expanding its reach even as it changes.

It's one thing to be given a list of phases for establishing change, but it's another to see them in motion. In Martin Luther King, Jr.'s famous "I Have a Dream" speech, he declared the "fierce urgency of now" and demanded that America had to change its ways when it came to granting rights to all of its citizens.[34] The time to wait had passed. Those who call for change need to instill a sense of urgency in their followers if they are to enact any change. This speech provided inspiration for generations of people to change and instill that change throughout society.

Do It...

6.4: Create a Change Program Describe a current situation in your job, at school, or with your family, roommates, or friends where some change would be helpful. Describe how you could execute each of the eight phases in the change model for this specific situation. Limit your response to two pages, and be prepared to submit it electronically or discuss it in class.

Now Debrief...

- A **transformational leader** is a leader who inspires and stimulates positive change in his or her followers. Change is necessary for organizations because becoming complacent and stagnant can be deadly.
- Leaders help motivate and guide people toward change. Once a change or innovation is created, people go through a process of knowledge, persuasion, decision making, implementation, and confirmation.
- However, this process doesn't happen for everyone all at once; different people have different ways to get there. Types of people include innovators, early adopters, middle adopters, late adopters, and laggards.
- Many change programs fail. Reasons for failure include allowing too much complacency, failing to build a substantial coalition, failing to understand the need for a clear vision, failing to communicate the vision, permitting roadblocks against the vision, not planning and getting short-term wins, declaring victory too soon, and not anchoring change.
- John Kotter created a model to successfully implement change. The steps in this model are to establish a sense of urgency, create a coalition, develop a clear vision, share the vision, empower people, secure short-term wins, consolidate and keep moving, and anchor change.

5. There's No *I* in *T-E-A-M*

What happens when your professor announces a group project? Often, the room fills up with the sound of muffled groans. Group projects can mean working with people who aren't your friends, and the projects usually require everyone to contribute, so no one can sit back and do nothing. Working with others can be an efficient way to tackle a project, and teams are becoming more and more common in organizations.

As you already know, without solid leadership, a team can be a nightmare of inefficiency. The true mark of a successful leader is the ability to lead a group of people to achieve a common goal. Since a leader is responsible for aligning people to realize his or her vision, it's vital to understand group dynamics and how teams develop. But what is a team? And how does it differ from a group? Any time a collection of people come together and form a relationship to achieve certain goals, then they can be considered a **team**. On the other hand, a **group** is an assembly of people who have a relationship. The difference is that a team has a defined purpose or goal, and a group doesn't.

Teams require a stable structure. They also must recognize themselves as one and operate as a functional unit. Just look at a basketball team. On the court, it's assembled precisely to achieve a goal—winning the game. It is also arranged in a formal structure because each player is assigned a specific position on the team. ■ Teams hold each other accountable for their actions and are selected because of their complementary skills and abilities. Because of this, a team is greater than the sum of its parts.

Creating and leading a successful team doesn't happen overnight. It takes a lot of work. Because so many modern workplaces are focused on teamwork, understanding how to develop a team is very important.

> ■ Teams hold each other accountable for their actions and are selected because of their complementary skills and abilities. Because of this, a team is greater than the sum of its parts.

Stages of Team Development

Teams don't form in a vacuum. Like anything that grows and develops, the formation of a team occurs in stages, and these various stages occur throughout the life of the team. The following is a five-stage model that identifies each stage of a team's development.

Stage 1: Forming. This is the stage in which members first come together and get to know each other. The ground rules of the group are established at this point.

For example, several employees appointed to a professional development committee may come together for an initial team meeting. Once the ice is broken and members understand their standing in the group, the forming stage is complete, and the group moves on to the next stage.

Stage 2: Storming. In this stage, there is a large amount of conflict within the group. Group members may not get along, or they may resist the leader's control.

Stage 2: Storming

In the case of the professional development committee, members may disagree on the company's training needs or how to best conduct training. If this behavior continues, the group could break up. However, these conflicts may also make for a stronger team. If the conflicts can be overcome, the group will move on to the next stage of development.

Stage 3: Norming. This is when the group becomes more cohesive and the individual members begin to feel part of the team. This is the best time to establish the team's vision or mission because the team is building toward a common purpose.

Stage 3: Norming

In the professional development committee, close relationships develop among individual members, leading to a feeling of solidarity for the team.

Stage 4: Performing

Stage 4: Performing. Once a team has settled on a set of expectations and a process for getting things done, they're ready to move on to the performing stage. All the growing pains of starting the team have been worked out, and the team is now ready to get to work. Team members can now devote themselves to achieving their goals. The performing stage is likely to last the longest since it constitutes the whole purpose of forming the team in the first place.

Stage 5: Adjourning

How can you tell if your team has moved to the next stage?

For example, the professional development committee may begin to conduct specific company training.

Stage 5: Adjourning. The fifth and final stage occurs only if the team has completed the mission it set out to do. If there are no other tasks to accomplish, the team may decide to disband.

For example, if the professional development committee has accomplished its goals, it may agree to disband.

At each stage, leaders need to remain aware of what kind of upkeep and damage control may be required to maintain the team's efficiency and cohesion.

Different styles of leadership are also needed at different stages of team development, and team leaders need to understand which style—autocratic, democratic, free-reign, or other—is most effective at each stage. For example, an autocratic style may be needed during the forming stage because it's necessary for the leader to take charge and get things moving in the right direction. However, the take-charge persona of an autocratic leader may not be effective if it is used during the norming or performing stage, which is when feedback and cooperation are needed. An effective team leader is therefore able to adjust his or her style as appropriate.

Avoiding and Resolving Team Issues

After leaders have developed and built a team, they need to put those leadership skills to work again and direct the team. This requires the leader to rally everyone together toward a common goal and keep the ball rolling while avoiding common problems that pop up in teams.

Delegating Tasks The first thing a capable leader needs to do is delegate specific tasks to the right people according to their individual skill set while also effectively explaining and clarifying the task and the goal. Once team members are given tasks, leaders should empower them to become self-motivated. As we discussed earlier, the role of the leader is not to dictate everything team members are supposed to do. Instead, leaders help keep team members focused and motivated. (Want to know more about delegating to team members? Check out Chapter 11.)

Avoiding Groupthink One of the most detrimental situations that can plague any type of group is groupthink. **Groupthink** is the tendency for a team to want to conform in an effort to minimize conflict. You've witnessed this if you've ever been in a group where everyone wanted to get along or everyone agrees with what the first person said. In situations like these, there is a general lack of analysis and critical thinking. Members of a team in a groupthink situation value conformity over evaluating the facts of a situation.[35] Team members may go along with a decision even if it doesn't make sense.

To help prevent this type of situation, leaders must promote independent thinking. During a meeting, the leader may need to draw out individual opinions by asking each team member directly what he or she thinks. The leader may also decide to meet with team members individually before discussing the matter in a group setting.

Encouraging Continuous Learning The most valuable input often comes from team members who can analyze and learn from their work experiences. Leaders can facilitate this type of analysis by encouraging the **continuous learning** approach, which is the process of learning how to learn.[36] Basically, continuous learning refers to learning through life experiences and reflection. Someone who embraces continuous learning would see work as a valuable learning experience. Leaders can adapt this idea by allowing the free flow of information by discussing goals and clarifying the vision. The goal of continuous learning is that knowledgeable team members will be less likely to conform or go with the flow in team situations.

Providing Feedback After the team is organized and thinking independently, it's vital for a leader to provide feedback. Feedback can mean identifying acceptable behavior and encouraging that it continues, or it can mean identifying opportunities for improvement and continuous learning. In order to be effective, leaders have to be specific. For example if you were told, "Overall you do a really good job, but sometimes you don't pay attention to little things," what would you think? Although this gives you an idea of an area you need to work on, it doesn't tell you much else. Now, how would you react if you were told, "Your work on the Peterson project was spot on. The next step is to focus on improving your spelling and grammar"? Isn't this more helpful in correcting a problem area?

When giving feedback, it's also important to keep things professional and focus on the behavior, not the person, giving suggestions for what to do differently. Take the example above. Would your reaction be different if your manager told you, "Your work on the Peterson project was spot on. I also think you should know you're a terrible speller with poor grammar"? That's harsh and unnecessary, right? Also, effective leaders don't wait too long after they notice a problem to provide feedback. Immediate feedback is best.

Do It...

6.5: Distinguish Between Group and Team Select two team projects on which you have worked: one in which you felt good about the project and the people, and one in which you didn't feel good about the project or the people. Quickly list bullet points of what worked or didn't work in each case. Which project fits the term "group"? Which project fits the term "team"? Now, with a partner, compare and contrast your two lists. Be prepared to submit your lists electronically or present them to your class.

Now Debrief...

- A **team** is a collection of people that come together and form a relationship to achieve certain goals. A **group** is an assembly of people who have a relationship. The difference is that a team has a defined purpose, but a group doesn't.
- Teams form in the following stages: forming, storming, norming, performing, and adjourning.
- During the teambuilding process, the leader has the responsibility of delegating tasks, avoiding **groupthink**, promoting **continuous learning**, and providing feedback.

Concept A
Concept B
Concept C
Concept D

Chapter 6 Visual Summary

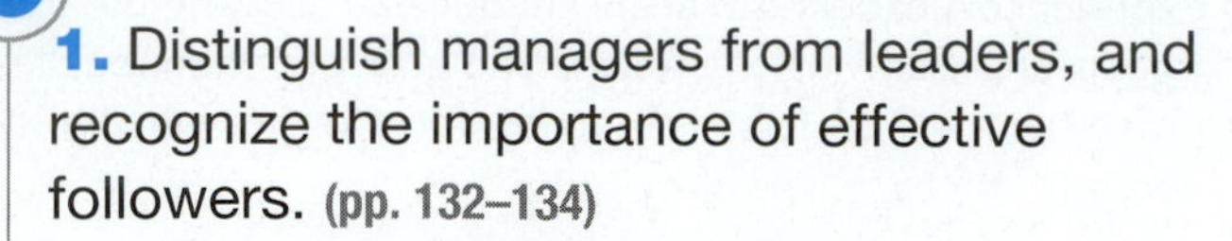

1. Distinguish managers from leaders, and recognize the importance of effective followers. (pp. 132–134)

- A **manager** has formal authority and takes care of planning, organizing, directing, and controlling the organization. A **leader** can be found anywhere in an organization and has the ability to motivate, inspire, and influence the behavior of other people.
- Employees listen to managers because they have to, but they listen to leaders because they want to. People follow the leader, but report to the manager.
- Followers are just as important as leaders because leaders may have trouble being effective without a team to support them. There are two types of followers: effective and ineffective.

Summary: The roles of managers and leaders are different but complementary, and both are necessary for an organization's success.

2. Identify effective leadership, and develop leadership qualities in yourself. (pp. 134–138)

- Effective leaders have similar qualities: they inspire, innovate, and initiate, and they are introspective and have integrity.
- Leadership styles include autocratic leaders, democratic leaders, and free-reign leaders. An **autocratic leader** is a micromanager who typically tells employees what to do and how to get it done. A **democratic leader** works with employees to find the best way to get the job done while maintaining final authority. A **free-reign leader** is a "hands-off" type of leader who allows others to have complete freedom in their work environment.
- Leadership qualities can be developed in many ways, such as by evaluating yourself, allowing others to evaluate you, and pursuing a mentoring relationship with someone who has the experience and values to which you aspire.

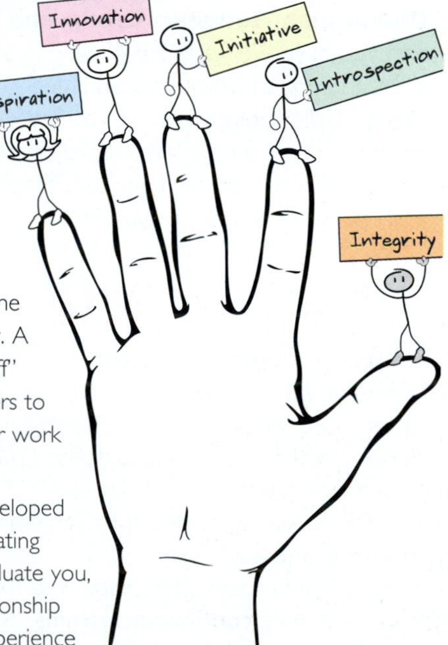

Summary: People follow leaders because leaders exhibit qualities that draw others to trust and follow them. You can develop leadership qualities in yourself in many ways.

3. Explain how a vision provides direction for an organization, and create a vision for your own career. (pp. 139–141)

- A **vision statement** is a statement that explains where the company wants to go. A vision statement should help motivate, inspire, and excite everyone in an organization. It should also help provide direction and focus to the future.
- A **mission statement** is a statement that describes why the company exists as well as its present purpose.
- A personal vision statement can help push you in the right direction and keep you focused.

Summary: *Vision statement* and *mission statement* are often used interchangeably, but they should not be. A vision statement is associated with the future, and a mission statement is associated with the present.

4. Describe the importance of change, and be able to lead it effectively and avoid its potential pitfalls. (pp. 141–146)

- A **transformational leader** is a leader who inspires and stimulates positive change in his or her followers.
- Generally, there is a five-step process that people go through when they come across something new: knowledge, persuasion, decision, implementation, and confirmation. The leader's role throughout this process is to channel his or her inspirational influence by motivating and guiding people.
- However, people don't follow this process at the same time; some people take their time, while others are ready to jump onto new trends right away. Generally, people are innovators, early adopters, middle adopters, late adopters, or laggards.
- Before implementing any type of change, it's good to know the common pitfalls of change programs. The most common reasons for failure include allowing too much complacency, failing to build a substantial coalition, failing to understand the need for a clear vision, failing to communicate the vision, permitting roadblocks against the vision, not planning and getting short-term wins, declaring victory too soon, and not anchoring change.
- To help facilitate change, John Kotter created a model to help ensure success: establish a sense of urgency, create a coalition, develop a clear vision, share the vision, empower people to act, secure short-term wins, consolidate and keep moving, and anchor change.

Summary: Change is essential for growth, so leaders must motivate everyone around them to transform. However, it's important to understand why change programs fail, as well as ways to ensure success.

5. Form effective teams and resolve team issues. (pp. 146–149)

- A **team** is a collection of people who come together and form a relationship to achieve certain goals. A **group** is an assembly of people who have a relationship. The difference is that a team has a defined purpose, while a group does not.
- Teams generally develop in five stages: forming, storming, norming, performing, and adjourning.
- The mark of a good leader is the ability to lead a group of people to a common goal. Because a leader is responsible for aligning people to realize his or her vision, it's vital to understand group dynamics and how teams develop.
- The leader has the responsibility of directing the team. This includes delegating tasks, promoting **continuous learning**, deterring **groupthink**, and providing feedback.

Summary: Because modern workplaces focus on teamwork, it's important for leaders to understand how to develop, build, and direct a team.

Get the most out of what you just read by practicing your skills and actually DOING something with the material! The best place to do this is at **www.mybizlab.com**. Here's just some of what is available to you there:

- Apply your skills in an interactive environment with more **BizSkill** experiences...and see if you have what it takes
- Think critically and talk with your peers on hot business topics in **BizChat**
- Flex your business communication skills and build your own portfolio with the **Communication Plan exercises**
- Watch the chapter material come together with **Just Plain Business** videos
- Study on-the-go with **Audio Chapter Summaries** in MP3 format
- Brush up on the lecture and content with **Audio PowerPoints**
- Discover how well you are doing and see what areas you need to improve on with the **Pre-Tests** and **Post-Tests**

Key Words

These key words and more are also available as flash cards to practice with at **www.mybizlab.com**.

1. Distinguish managers from leaders, and recognize the importance of effective followers. (pp. 132–134)

Manager (p. 132)

Leader (p. 132)

2. Identify effective leadership, and develop leadership qualities in yourself. (pp. 134–138)

Emotional intelligence (p. 135)

Autocratic leader (p. 136)

Democratic leader (p. 136)

Free-reign (or laissez-faire) leader (p. 136)

3. Explain how a vision provides direction for an organization, and create a vision for your own career. (pp. 139–141)

Vision statement (p. 139)

Mission statement (p. 139)

4. Describe the importance of change, and be able to lead it effectively and avoid its potential pitfalls. (pp. 141–146)

Transformational leader (p. 141)

5. Form effective teams and resolve team issues. (pp. 146–149)

Team (p. 146)

Group (p. 146)

Groupthink (p. 148)

Continuous learning (p. 148)

Prove It

Prove It...

Now let's put on one of the BizHats. With the **Employee BizHat** squarely on your head, look at the following exercise:

Imagine you're an intern in the marketing department for a big corporation that you hope to work for on a full-time basis one day. On your first day, you meet your new boss and can't tell right away whether she's a good leader. After working with her for a few weeks, you begin to see a pattern in her working style. Every day, she takes a few minutes in the morning to talk with the interns, either individually or in a group, about tasks that need to be completed that day. She explains the skills required for each task and tries to figure out the best person for the job. Once she assigns tasks, she periodically checks on your progress and suggests how things should be done. You've also noticed that she enjoys chatting with the interns at the coffee machine and the water cooler. Sometimes, she even joins everyone for lunch in the cafeteria. Do you think your boss is a manager or a leader, or both? Why?

Flip It...

After you've decided whether your boss is a manager, a leader, or both, **flip over to the Manager BizHat.**

Imagine you work for a big corporation and are in charge of supervising interns for the marketing department. Part of your job is to show them how the department works and give them tasks to test their abilities. Of the 10 interns you are supervising, you are able to offer three full-time positions with the firm. Even though they are interns, your firm values leaders and is hoping to find the leaders of tomorrow. How will you go about testing the interns to see which are the top three candidates? Will you be looking for anything specific in the tasks you assign them?

Now Debrief It...

Compare the perspectives of the two BizHats described above. Did taking the perspective of an employee describing a manager affect your list of leadership characteristics in the Flip It?

Own:
Entrepreneurship, Innovation, and Forms of Ownership

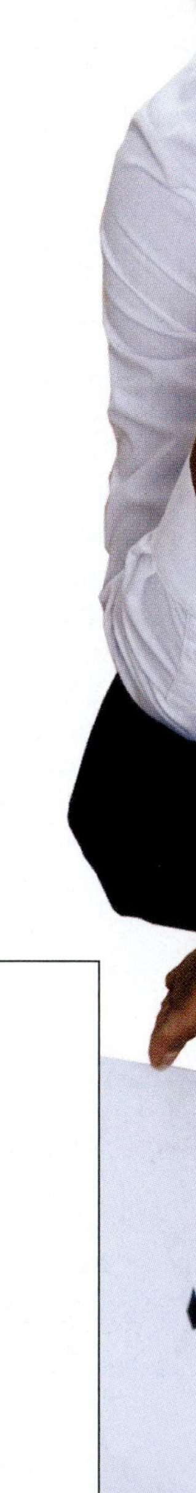

BizSkills invite...

Try It!
There's no better way to learn concepts than to put them into practice. Take your turn in the driver's seat and be a part of actual business decision making by visiting the BizSkill for this chapter at **www.mybizlab.com**.

Now that you've practiced making tough business decisions and seeing the results of your choices in this chapter's BizSkill, it's time to translate those skills into plain English. And if you skipped the BizSkill, go back now!

Chapter 7 Goals

After experiencing this chapter, you'll be able to:

1. Appreciate what it takes to be a successful entrepreneur.
2. Recognize innovation when you see it and justify its effect on the triple bottom line.
3. Conduct a SWOT analysis to identify opportunities and drive decisions.
4. Contrast the different flavors of entrepreneurship and legal forms of ownership and understand the risk/reward trade-offs that each implies.
5. Explain the critical components of a business plan.
6. Locate helpful resources for starting a business, and avoid common mistakes.

Do you have what it takes to be an entrepreneur?

Cooking Up a Business

At first, it was a matter of survival: If you didn't want to end up eating cafeteria food three times a day, you had to teach yourself to cook. And cook you did, graduating quickly from slightly crunchy spaghetti to a full-fledged lasagna that you served up to a few friends who came by for dinner. The more recipes you learned, the more excited you became. Making a cake for your dad's birthday wasn't a chore; it was actually fun, and everyone agreed that the cake was delicious. In fact, you became the go-to chef for all of your family's big events, and your friends started asking you to make your famous sweet potato fries and addictive apple crisp for their Saturday night get-togethers.

You love helping your friends out, and you love cooking (or Web design or writing or playing guitar or skateboarding). But what if your hobby became something more than a labor of love? What if you struck out on your own and turned that hobby into a business?

Starting your own business may sound intimidating, but if there's something in your life you care about doing, and you think other people would be willing to pay you for doing it, you may be on your way to being an **entrepreneur**, a person who takes the risks associated with organizing and managing a new business. With the skills you already have, plus a few pieces of advice you'll find in this chapter, you may be able to turn your passion into the foundation for a successful business.

idea

idea

1. Entrepreneurship: What It Takes

Popular singer-songwriter Ani DiFranco doesn't embrace the label *entrepreneur*—if you're familiar with her lyrics, you probably know she's not the biggest fan of capitalism—but like it or not, DiFranco is a shining example of someone who's turned her talent and her love of music into a successful business.[1] DiFranco has been a musician since she was in her teens, but when she started making her own albums in her early 20s, she didn't want to enlist the help of a major record label. Instead, she started her own company, Righteous Babe Records, in her struggling hometown of Buffalo, New York. DiFranco's music label has taken off right along with her singing-songwriting career, and her entrepreneurial activities have energized Buffalo to the extent that the *New York Times* declared DiFranco "a one-woman urban renewal project."[2]

DiFranco may be a particularly righteous babe, but she's hardly the only young, talented entrepreneur who's found success in unexpected places. Hip-hop beats brought Chris Lighty from the Bronx housing projects to the top of the music industry; Lighty started the record and artist management company Violator in 1990. Violator, which represents such stars as LL Cool J and Missy Elliot, sang a sweet song in 2007 with $11 million in sales. In 2008, Lighty was named one of the top "40 Under Forty" rising stars in business by business publisher Crain's Communications.[3]

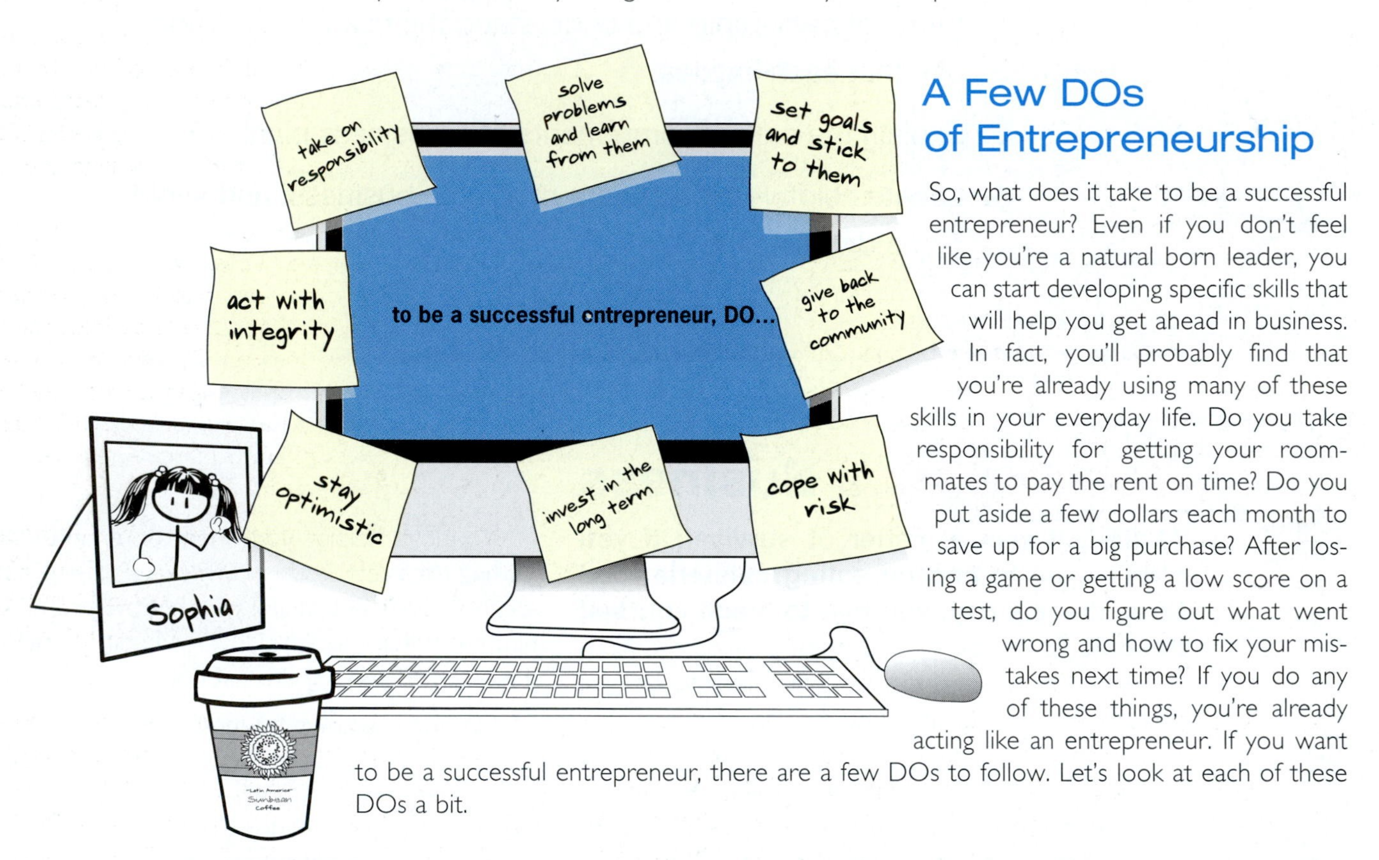

A Few DOs of Entrepreneurship

So, what does it take to be a successful entrepreneur? Even if you don't feel like you're a natural born leader, you can start developing specific skills that will help you get ahead in business. In fact, you'll probably find that you're already using many of these skills in your everyday life. Do you take responsibility for getting your roommates to pay the rent on time? Do you put aside a few dollars each month to save up for a big purchase? After losing a game or getting a low score on a test, do you figure out what went wrong and how to fix your mistakes next time? If you do any of these things, you're already acting like an entrepreneur. If you want to be a successful entrepreneur, there are a few DOs to follow. Let's look at each of these DOs a bit.

DO Take on Responsibility When Larry Page and Sergey Brin met, they were graduate students at Stanford, presumably responsible for the usual things: getting work done on time, reporting to academic advisors, and so on. When they launched the now-ubiquitous tech company Google, however, Page and Brin had to take on a lot of additional responsibilities.[4]

When you're a student or an employee, your teachers and supervisors usually tell you what to do (and, sometimes, how to do it). When you're a business owner, however, no one's standing over you with a to-do list, a syllabus, or a job description. Instead, you have to figure out what needs to be done and either do it yourself or delegate the task to someone you trust. Today, Page and Brin are responsible not only for their own actions, but also for the actions of Google's

> When you're a business owner, no one's standing over you with a to-do list, a syllabus, or a job description.

employees and for the performance of the company as a whole. Taking on that much responsibility can seem overwhelming, but it comes hand in hand with the freedom to do what you think is most important. So, ask yourself: Are you willing to be responsible for yourself and your company?

cope with risk

DO Cope with Risk How do you feel about uncertainty and risk? Starting your own company can be a risky business, especially if you're giving up the security of a regular paycheck for the pursuit of a dream that might not work out in the long run—this is a major drawback to being an entrepreneur. Entrepreneurs know that risk is an inherent aspect of any business, and they don't shy away from taking chances. However, successful entrepreneurs are not extreme risk-takers. Instead, they're *calculated* risk-takers. In other words, after assessing all the risks and weighing all the possibilities, they make sure that their talents exceed any risks they encounter. They write up detailed business plans, carefully obtain the amount of money they need, and proceed only when they know they have a reasonable chance of success.

stay optimistic

DO Stay Optimistic When a friend comes to you for advice about a problem, you probably don't tell her that her problem's unfixable. Instead, you help her brainstorm some creative solutions. That's entrepreneurial behavior in action. Entrepreneurs realize that every business faces hard times and experiences failures, but they put a positive spin on difficult situations and take proactive measures to address those difficulties. Even in the face of a difficult economic climate, entrepreneur Jeff Gebbia wasn't deterred. He felt confident that his line of seat cushions would be successful. He claims that as a small-business owner he has to be his own cheerleader because no one else is going to be. Gebbia's confidence was right on, and since the creation of his company in 2005, sales of his seat cushions have steadily increased.[5]

set goals and stick to them

DO Set Goals and Stick to Them Former college basketball player Katie Kerrigan wanted just one thing: big shoes. She was fed up with the futile search to find dress shoes that would fit her size-11 feet. As a business student, she wrote up a sample business plan for a company that would design and sell stylish women's shoes in larger sizes. It's not too hard to dream about a business you'd like to start, but after graduation, Kerrigan went a step further: She followed up on her business plan and founded KathrynKerrigan.com, which successfully sold shoes to hundreds of tall women desperate for the perfect pump. A few years later, Kerrigan's site was so successful that she opened a retail store as well.[6]

Kerrigan's business was a hit in part because Kerrigan set a goal for herself—sell shoes that tall women can wear—and went after that goal aggressively. Your own goals might range from lofty (be a millionaire by age 30) to eminently achievable (convince 20 friends to order your custom-made earrings), but whatever your goals are, your job as an entrepreneur is to keep your sights set on those goals and work to accomplish them.

solve problems and learn from them

DO Solve Problems and Learn from Them As an entrepreneur, you'll face plenty of roadblocks, and while those roadblocks might be frustrating in the short term, they'll also present you with a good opportunity for learning how to do things better next time. A smart entrepreneur knows the importance of a problem. In fact, a good way to start a business is to have the business be an answer to some type of problem or need. This doesn't have to be complicated—it could be as simple as making something more convenient. Just look at Netflix, the online movie rental service. There are plenty of places to rent movies, but Netflix took convenience to the next level and made renting movies as easy as clicking your mouse.

invest in the long term

DO Invest in the Long Term Where do you see yourself in five years? In 10 years? How are you going to get there? These are good questions to ask yourself if you're planning to start a business (or even if you're not). Entrepreneurs don't work just for that biweekly paycheck; they think about long-term opportunities for their company. Just look at Microsoft. When the company created its own computer science research organization in 1991, it did so to not only stay on top of current technology, but also to look toward the future. One of the primary goals of the organization is to always be looking five to 10 years into the future. This is one of the reasons Microsoft has been able to stay successful in a constantly changing industry.[7]

DO Act with Integrity Oprah Winfrey once said, "Real integrity is doing the right thing, knowing that nobody's going to know whether you did it or not."[8] Acting with integrity in the business world is really no different from acting with integrity in any other aspect of your life. There's a commonly held belief that businesspeople are only "in it for themselves," and too often, we hear stories about greedy CEOs and ambitious employees who end up on the wrong side of the law. But this type of behavior isn't characteristic of most entrepreneurs. On the contrary, cultivating an atmosphere of trust and respect with employees and customers can boost a company's reputation and, by extension, its profits. Successful entrepreneurs are willing to do what they feel is right, even if that means making tough decisions.

act with integrity

DO Give Back to the Community In addition to acting with integrity, entrepreneurs who give back to the community can expect the community to give back to them as well. Look at Mike Ilitch, founder of Little Caesars Pizza. Ilitch was born and raised in Detroit, and when Little Caesars began growing, he started giving back to the community. He initially focused on urban development by revitalizing landmarks and opening fine dining restaurants, but he eventually expanded into professional sports by bringing the Detroit Red Wings back to life.[9] He has also been committed to feeding the hungry. In 1985, he created the Little Caesars Love Kitchen, a traveling restaurant that feeds the hungry and helps provide food after natural disasters.[10] It is ultimately the customer who decides whether a business is successful, and people pay attention to a business's community relationships and charitable acts. This helped propel Little Caesars into a successful franchise.

give back to the community

Do You Have What It Takes? It's time to step back and look at the big picture. How many of these entrepreneurial DOs are you already doing every day? And how many do you think you can take on in the future? You don't need to have been born with a business plan in one hand and a *Wall Street Journal* in the other; if you're willing and able to adopt these skills, you'll have what it takes to be an entrepreneur. And even if you don't plan on becoming an entrepreneur, when you cultivate these skills in your own life, you're giving yourself an instant advantage in the business world.

Do It...

7.1: Identify the Impact What happens when any one of the DOs is missing from an organization? Limit your response to one page, and be prepared to submit it electronically or present it to your class.

Now Debrief...

Concept A
Concept B
Concept C
Concept D

- Successful **entrepreneurs**—people who take the risks associated with organizing and managing a new business—often turn their passions into business opportunities.
- What do entrepreneurs *do,* exactly? They take on responsibility, cope with risk, stay optimistic, set goals and stick to them, solve problems and learn from them, invest in the long term, act with integrity, and give back to their community.
- When you cultivate these skills in your own life, you're giving yourself an instant advantage in the business world.

2. Innovation: An Entrepreneur's Best Friend

Imagine you've put your newly honed entrepreneurial skills to work and started that catering business you dreamed about at the beginning of the chapter. Business is going well, but it isn't always a piece of cake. In fact, cake is your main problem right now. Lots of professional bakers use a smooth, flexible product called fondant to make their cakes' icing look flawless, and your fondant-covered cakes are definitely gorgeous. Unfortunately, though, fondant doesn't taste very good. Your customers love the way your cakes look, and although they wish the cakes *tasted* a little better, they understand that unpleasant-tasting fondant can't be avoided.

■ You don't have to be particularly innovative to be an entrepreneur. Many entrepreneurs are innovation personified: They have a great idea for an improvement they can make to a good, service, or experience, and their customers are happy to pay for that improvement.

Or can it? With a lot of thought and effort, you and your team manage to whip up the world's first fondant that's both attractive *and* delicious. Your customers are thrilled, and the news about your fabulous fondant spreads like wildfire. Soon, your profits are up and your customer base has tripled in size, all because you had an innovative idea.

What's innovation? You might think of it as a unique improvement that earns kudos (and cash) in the market. The goal of innovation is to make a positive change in something so that it increases in value. In some cases, innovative ideas can lead to revolutionary goods and services. ■ Although you don't have to be particularly innovative to be an entrepreneur, many entrepreneurs are innovation personified: They have a great idea for an improvement they can make to a good, service, or experience, and their customers are happy to pay for that improvement.

Innovation isn't simply change; it's change that customers reward with their purchasing power. Check out this example: The cell phone market is a competitive one, and Finnish telecommunications giant Nokia was putting what it thought was a load of innovative features on its phones to stand toe to toe with its competition.[11] However, when Nokia actually interviewed customers about the new features, it discovered that customers found the features confusing and difficult to use. No matter how high-tech a change is, it isn't an innovation if customers can't figure out how to use it! So, Nokia took its customers' advice and innovated differently, adding different colors, easy-to-use features, and other non-techy stuff to their phones. These new phones might not have resembled James Bond's gadgets, but, to Nokia's relief, they caught on with customers.

Levels of Innovation: From Simple to Supersized

Some innovations (like the development of a new surgical technique) are truly life altering, whereas others (like the creation of tasty fondant) are useful on a smaller scale. If you'd like to be an innovator, don't be afraid to dream big, but know that innovation doesn't necessarily require years of research. Maybe you have a plan to start a business that will help college students store their furniture over the summer in dry, safe storage facilities rather than in damp, moldy dorm basements. You'll provide cardboard boxes, packing tape, and scheduled pick-up and drop-off of storage items for a low fee. Could college students come up with this type of innovation? You bet. In fact, students at Swarthmore College in Pennsylvania have done exactly that.[12]

As you look toward entrepreneurship in your own life, you might want to think about the following levels of innovation and decide which level you're most willing and able to target, both now and in the future.

Incremental Innovation A simple improvement in current products or services is called an *incremental innovation*. All that's required for such an innovation is some basic knowledge within the sector or industry. For example, think about software and the different versions of Microsoft Word. The most recent version of Word got rid of traditional drop-down menus in favor of a "ribbon" that controls all of its functions. It also created a preview feature so you can see formatting changes before you make them. These were simple, incremental innovations, and Word remained essentially the same, but first-week sales of the new Microsoft Office 2007 more than doubled compared to its predecessor in 2003.[13]

Disruptive Innovation While incremental innovations simply improve on an existing product, *disruptive innovations* are unprecedented products that transform an industry. A disruptive innovation that you're familiar with is the cell phone. Disruptive innovations are often spurred by new technology, and they're marked by products or services that are substantially different from others in their field. The first cell phone in 1984 was so different from the landline phones that came before it that it created its own new market.

Revolutionary Innovation The largest level of innovation, *revolutionary innovation*, extends past individual products and markets to transform society and create a new way of living. The discovery of a new phenomenon, substance, or concept can give humans fundamentally different ways of getting things done. For example, the Internet is a revolutionary innovation that has fundamentally changed people's behaviors. People spend less time face to face with other people because the Internet fulfills so many of their needs. Now, you don't have to walk outside to get the paper or ask someone for directions. You don't even need to hang out with your friends in person—you can simply chat online.

New Modes of Innovation: It's All About You

> "Innovation distinguishes between a leader and a follower."
>
> **—Apple co-founder Steve Jobs[14]**

It's been a typical morning. You've rolled out of bed, trudged to your computer, and launched your customized iGoogle home page. It tells you that the temperature outside is 56 degrees, you have five new e-mails, your favorite blogs have been updated, and there's a class project due tomorrow (it's listed on your Google Calendar and Google Tasks list). After reading the e-mail, you update your Twitter status before clicking over to Facebook, where you check out some photos your brother posted. You then open iTunes to make sure last night's episode of *Lost* has downloaded.

Congratulations: It's only 9 A.M., and you're already thoroughly steeped in what some people are calling the new wave of innovation. Author C. K. Prahalad refers to it as "the innovation of co-creation."[15] According to Prahalad and others, companies like Google, Facebook, and Apple are changing the nature of innovation by allowing customers to use technology to create unique, personalized experiences. No one else's Google homepage or iTunes library is quite like yours. People like Prahalad are convinced that innovation is no longer a simple matter of creating a unique product and selling it. Now, innovation involves collaborating with customers and taking advantage of widely available, global technologies to help each customer design the exact product that fits his or her lifestyle best.

This isn't to suggest that old models of innovation are irrelevant. Rather, it's meant to show you that you may already be participating in one of the newest and most dynamic forms of innovation. When customers become not only clients but also developers and collaborators, innovation shines in a whole new light.

Innovation and the Triple Bottom Line

Social networking sites such as Facebook and "Web 2.0" tools (such as blogs and virtual communities) that represent the next big thing in innovation are concerned with profits, of course, but they're also very clearly focused on *people*. Remind you of anything? If you said "the triple bottom line," you're right on target. (If you said "nope," you might want to check out the discussion of the triple bottom line in Chapter 3 again.)

Remember that profit is only one leg of the triple bottom line. Companies like Google are concerned with turning a profit, to be sure, but they're also concerned with creating individualized, user-friendly experiences, which means they're focusing on another leg of the triple bottom line: people. Google's tools are designed to enhance people's quality of life, and people aren't required to pay for the privilege of using Google's e-mail service, chat service, or search engine. For many companies, innovation isn't just a moneymaking tool; it's a way of connecting directly to customers and giving them exactly what they want.

How about the third leg of the triple bottom line: planet? As it turns out, innovation is absolutely crucial when it comes to creating a culture of environmental sustainability. If you want to run a sustainable company, how would you ensure that the company's waste was reduced and disposed of properly? How would you ensure that you could connect with people around the world in an efficient, low-cost manner? These questions require innovative answers, and people have come up with innovations that allow companies to go green without breaking the bank.

Getting Innovation Into Your Life

By now, you've heard a lot about how important innovation is to entrepreneurs, but what does it mean for you right now? Fear not: You don't have to be Bill Gates to bring innovation from the business world into your everyday life. Here are some thoughts from Tom Kelly, the general manager of California-based design and innovation consultancy IDEO, about how to prime yourself for innovation every day:[16]

1. **Act like you are a traveler.** When you go to a new place, you're apt to pay attention to small details and see the world in a different way. Even if you aren't going on vacation, you can act like a traveler every day by noticing things around you while you're getting up in the morning, going to class, or heading out to lunch. Write down your emotions and ideas as you observe, because no one is experiencing the world the same way that you are.
2. **Think like an experimenter.** Imagine that you are discovering a new cure for a deadly disease. Be an experimenter, researcher, and discoverer of something brand-new in life.
3. **Be an avid seeker of knowledge.** Every day, a wealth of information is readily available to us, and we just have to absorb it. Learn as much as you can, but while you're learning, be sure to ask questions. Both the information you learn and the questions you ask could give you ideas for innovations that no one else has thought of.
4. **Use all of your brain.** The left side of the brain excels at logic and reasoning, while the right side of the brain is the center of creative expression and emotion. "Left-brainers" tend to be practical, analytical, and good at math and science. "Right-brainers" are more apt to use their intuition, be imaginative, and take risks. Make an effort to embrace both your analytical side and your intuitive side. Innovation requires logic and reasoning, of course, but it also requires imagination.
5. **Remain young at heart.** Reach a happy balance between what you are naturally good at and what people will pay you to do. Most of all, resist other people's attempts to quash your creative and entrepreneurial spirit.

Once you prime yourself for innovative ideas, you need to figure out if the idea is worth embracing. In the next section, you'll learn how to analyze your idea to see if it will be a success.

Do It...

7.2: Innovate a Product Together with a team of two or three students, innovate an existing product (good, service, or experience) of your choice. For example, you may choose to create a better package or improve a feature. Describe your innovation in one page, and be prepared to submit it electronically or present it to your class.

Now Debrief...

- Many entrepreneurs are successful because they embrace innovation, a unique improvement that the market rewards.
- Innovations can range in size and scale from *incremental innovations* to *disruptive innovations* to *revolutionary innovations*.

- The definition of innovation is changing: Companies at the cutting edge of innovation use technology to help individual customers "co-create" personalized content and experiences.

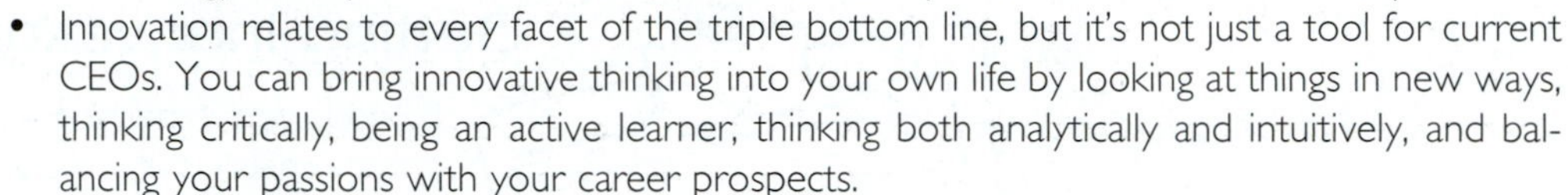

- Innovation relates to every facet of the triple bottom line, but it's not just a tool for current CEOs. You can bring innovative thinking into your own life by looking at things in new ways, thinking critically, being an active learner, thinking both analytically and intuitively, and balancing your passions with your career prospects.

3. Got a Great Idea? SWOT It!

So, you've got what it takes to be an entrepreneur, and you have an innovative idea that you think will knock the socks off your future customers. But will your creativity and determination really help your company be successful? How can you tell if your new business will thrive?

Never fear; SWOT analysis is here! You probably remember SWOT from Chapter 2. As you learned, SWOT can help you identify a company's **S**trengths, **W**eaknesses, **O**pportunities, and **T**hreats. But you can really SWOT anything: new ideas, an industry, even yourself.

Let's say you're deciding what major to pursue in college. You can SWOT that major: What strengths and weaknesses would a degree in English have? How about a degree in physics? Or let's say you're preparing for a job interview: What are your strengths and weaknesses in interview situations? What makes you perfect for this job, and what makes you a less than ideal candidate? What opportunities will help you get the job, and what outside threats do you face?

You get the idea. SWOT can be a handy tool in your everyday toolbox. Furthermore, as we'll discuss in this section, entrepreneurs can use a SWOT analysis to locate new opportunities, find competitive advantages, and make decisions.

The Strategic Balance Sheet

How can an entrepreneur use SWOT analysis to create a competitive advantage? One way is by creating a *strategic balance sheet*. On this sheet, all of the company's pluses (its internal strengths and external opportunities) are listed together, as are all of the company's minuses (its internal weaknesses and external threats). Entrepreneurs can study this sheet to determine

"A pessimist sees the difficulty in every opportunity; an optimist sees the opportunity in every difficulty."
—Sir Winston Churchill[17]

whether the pluses outweigh the minuses. If the pluses are swamped by minuses, entrepreneurs need to think about how they can maximize their pluses, create new pluses, and minimize (or eliminate) the minuses.

Take, for example, this strategic balance sheet for your fictitious catering company:

Strategic Balance Sheet Your Catering Company	
Pluses	**Minuses**
• Food tastes delicious.	• Slightly higher menu prices.
• Staff is well trained.	• Since the company is small, you can't accept all the jobs you'd like to.
• People are looking for companies that use fresh, organic, locally grown ingredients.	• The low-carb craze is slowing down sales of baked goods.

Based on this information, you might decide to look for ways to lower your prices, develop more desserts that aren't so heavy on the carbs, and hire more employees.

Core Competencies Who *are* the employees of your catering company, anyway? Are they Paris-trained chefs, knowledgeable home cooks, or your college roommates who were desperate for jobs? In other words, what *core competencies* do they bring to the business?

Core competencies are skills and areas of expertise that a company's employees possess that are considered better than those of people in other companies within the industry. On a SWOT analysis, these core competencies would be listed in the "internal strengths" category because they make the company competitive and unique.

Core competencies are important to a company because they provide extra abilities when opportunities arise or when the competition tries something different. When companies don't develop their core competencies, they are at a distinct disadvantage because developing those core competencies after the fact takes a lot of time and money.

Core competencies are important not only to business owners but also to employees. What are your core competencies? What unique, valuable skills do you bring to the table? The employees with the most core competencies are usually the most secure when layoffs occur because they're seen as valuable to the company. The woman with the master's degree in computer science and 15 patents to her credit is valuable to the success of her tech company, and the man with the Ph.D. in archaeology is valuable to the success of the natural history museum that employs him. When the heads of these businesses perform SWOT analyses and create a strategic balance sheet, they take their employees' valuable traits and skills into account on the "plus" side of the ledger.

SWOT Is a Constant Process

SWOT analysis isn't a one-time process. There are always new opportunities and threats around the corner. Once you've SWOT-ed yourself through that job interview and landed a good job, are you going to stop looking for opportunities? Probably not. If you like your job, you'll use SWOT to figure out what opportunities are available for you within your company, and if you're less than thrilled with your new career, you might use SWOT to identify opportunities that are a better fit for you.

And you need to keep re-evaluating those threats too. The other potential candidates for the job are no longer a threat to you, but the economic downturn in your industry could be a very real threat to your job. (Time to remind your boss of the core competencies you bring to the company.)

Just like the rest of us, entrepreneurs can use SWOT analysis frequently to identify new opportunities. "Going green" has become particularly popular lately, and companies that manufacture chemical-laden household products might have seen the new "all-natural" focus as a threat. But some of those companies turned that threat into an opportunity by developing "natural" dishwashing detergents and soaps that allowed them to tap into the newly robust green market. In a few years, the allure of eco-friendliness may still remain, but there may be other factors that customers care about more, and companies will have to adjust their products and tactics once again to grab new opportunities and minimize new threats.

Do It...

7.3: Conduct a SWOT Analysis Conduct a SWOT for yourself as a candidate for an internship or full-time career. What are your internal strengths and weaknesses (relative to others who might be competing for the same position), and what opportunities and threats do you face in the market? Limit your response to one page, and be prepared to submit it electronically or present it to your class.

Now Debrief...

- SWOT analysis can be useful for anyone who needs to make a decision, but in particular, it helps entrepreneurs evaluate their employees and ideas, seize opportunities, and think strategically.
- **Core competencies** are skills and areas of expertise that a company's employees possess that are considered better than those of people in other companies within the industry. On a SWOT, these core competencies are listed in the "internal strengths" category.
- SWOT analysis is not a one-time activity, but a constant process that businesses can use to ensure that they are using their employees effectively, taking advantage of new situations, and dodging ever-changing threats.

4. The Flavors of Entrepreneurship and Forms of Ownership

Would you describe yourself as a true revolutionary? Do you have brilliant ideas but tend to drive other people crazy? Would you prefer to work for a boss or be the boss yourself? Does the idea of working from home sound like a dream or a nightmare to you?

If you and a few friends answered each of these questions, each of you would probably come up with different answers. That's because questions like these get at your entrepreneurial style, and not all entrepreneurs are the same. They all have good ideas and a drive to be successful, but in other ways, they're as different as chocolate, vanilla, and strawberry. ■ There are different forms of entrepreneurship based on the degree of control and freedom that the forms provide the entrepreneur, along with the amount of risk, financial commitment, and security they provide. However, once you figure out your "flavor," your job isn't finished. You still have a big decision to make: which form of ownership works best for you?

The Five Flavors of Entrepreneurship

If you go to your local ice cream parlor and ask for a vanilla cone, you know pretty much what you're getting. You've tasted vanilla before; it's safe and delicious. If you go to Japan, though, you might be offered ice cream flavored with *saury*, a saltwater fish.[18] Fish ice cream isn't for everyone, but if you take a chance and try it, you just might find it's your new favorite flavor.

Just like there are different ice cream flavors, there are different "flavors" of entrepreneurship. Some flavors are more traditional, like vanilla; others are more unusual, like fish. In this section, we'll look at each flavor. As you read, think about which type of entrepreneurship might suit you best. Are you a vanilla cone, a fish sundae, or somewhere in between?

Intrapreneur Not everyone is willing to accept the risks associated with being an entrepreneur, but they may still have the drive and innovation to make a difference in their organization. An **intrapreneur** is a person who uses his or her entrepreneurial skills *inside* an organization. You might say these types of people are employee-entrepreneurs. Being an intrapreneur is a low-risk way to flex your entrepreneurial skills. Examples of intrapreneurs range from CEOs of successful companies to managers, to anyone else who wants to show an organization what he or she can do.

If you've ever used a Post-It note manufactured by the company 3M, you've appreciated the work of an intrapreneur firsthand. Many years ago, a 3M chemical engineer named Arthur Fry got frustrated when his paper bookmarks kept falling out of his hymnal at church. Then, Fry had a brainstorm: What if the paper slips had strips of not-too-sticky adhesive along their sides? Fry brought his idea to his bosses at 3M, who encouraged employees to spend part of their time on independent projects like this one, and the Post-It was born.[19]

Social Entrepreneur Sometimes entrepreneurs come up with great ideas that do more than offer an innovative product. **Social entrepreneurs** are people who blend traditional entrepreneurial business development with social objectives for the greater good of society. They act as "change agents," seeking to effect long-term societal change. Whereas traditional entrepreneurs are often driven by a profit motive, social entrepreneurs are more focused on "social value," improving the lives of others.[20] Take social entrepreneur Mimi Silbert. In 1971, she formed the Delancey Street Foundation, a San Francisco-based residential center that provides recovering drug addicts and criminals with a place to learn how to lead drug- and crime-free lives. The organization does not accept government funding or charge its residents; rather, it earns revenue by running over 20 businesses, such as a restaurant and a catering business, that help give Delancey residents marketable skills and train them to become productive members of society.[21] Today the organization has locations in San Francisco, Los Angeles, New Mexico, North Carolina, and New York.[22]

Business Purchaser Perhaps you don't want to work from within a company or don't have an idea for big sweeping change. Another way to become an entrepreneur is to become a "business purchaser" by buying an existing business that's already successful. You don't have to create a business from the ground up; you simply buy it from someone who's already done the foundation work.

Buying a successful, established business definitely has some advantages. If you don't want a lot of risk, for example, this flavor might be for you. However, before taking the plunge, business purchasers should investigate why the owner is selling. Is he retiring? Is she having financial problems? Successful business purchasers are inquisitive, smart, and savvy. Because they're not starting the business from scratch, they have to take care to ensure that every aspect of the business they're inheriting is shipshape.

Franchisee You've probably eaten at a Subway or shipped a package from a UPS Store, but did you know that, if you wanted to, you could run your *own* Subway or UPS Store? It's true, and it's all thanks to franchising.

Here's how it works: The prospective business owner, or the **franchisee**, buys into the business of the **franchisor**, or the business owner who agrees to sell the franchise. The franchisee purchases the right to distribute the franchisor's techniques, products, trademarks, or other relevant items. The franchisee is also given various benefits such as training, advertising, and other support services. In exchange, the franchisor usually gets a percentage of the gross monthly sales and a royalty fee. One of the benefits of franchising is the limited risk involved. Since the franchisor provides training and support, the business owner knows the ins and outs of the business before the doors open.

If you think that franchisee might be your favorite flavor of entrepreneurship, you're in luck—there are myriad successful franchises in the United States. Many of them, such as Pizza Hut, KFC, and Sonic Drive-In Restaurants, are food businesses, but if food isn't your thing, you could run a hotel like the Hampton Inn, a tutoring business like Sylvan Learning Centers, or a hair salon like Supercuts, just to name a few options.[23]

■ There are different forms of entrepreneurship based on the degree of control and freedom that the forms provide the entrepreneur, along with the amount of risk, financial commitment, and security they provide.

Classic Entrepreneur If you're a **classic entrepreneur**, you're one of the original flavors that never goes out of style. Classic entrepreneurs start businesses from scratch and build them into successful, profitable companies. Of course, "classic" isn't a synonym for "old-fashioned." Plenty of tech companies and products of the dot-com boom were created from nothing by classic entrepreneurs with a little creativity and a knack for grabbing on to opportunities.

Classic entrepreneur

A&B Ice Cream

Many classic entrepreneurs start small businesses. **Small businesses**—independently owned businesses that generally have fewer than 500 employees, depending on the industry—are the heart of business in the United States. In fact, 99.7 percent of firms in the United States are small businesses. That's over 27 million businesses.[24] As a result, small businesses generate the majority of new innovative products on the market. That's no small feat!

Many of the big companies you are familiar with today, such as Disney, Apple, Ford, and Hershey Chocolate, started off as small businesses. In fact, classic entrepreneurs started many of these while operating from their homes. These *home-based business owners* run their home business from an office within the home that (for tax reasons) is dedicated only to business pursuits. The home business might be a one-person operation, or the home-based business owner might hire a small number of employees to help out. For instance, Paul Allen and Bill Gates founded Microsoft Corporation. But on April 4, 1975, Allen and Gates were living at 199 California Street N.E. in Albuquerque, New Mexico, having just started the company Microsoft.[25] The house is considered the first place to house Microsoft.

Which Flavor Are You? Now that you've had a look at the menu, answer this: Which entrepreneurial flavor best suits you? For example, if you don't like the idea of being in charge of a bevy of employees, you're probably better off as an intrapreneur than as a classic entrepreneur. Remember, not all entrepreneurs have to operate in the same way or follow the same path; the most successful choose the path that works best for them.

Forms of Ownership

By now, you've determined that you're mint chocolate chip. (Or maybe not, but you have some idea about your entrepreneurial "flavor.") Now that you know which type of entrepreneurship suits you best, you're ready to consider the different forms of ownership you can choose from when you start a business.

Sole Proprietorships When you think about owning your own business, you're probably envisioning a **sole proprietorship**, which is a business that is owned and operated by a single person. Anyone can have a sole proprietorship. When you start your catering business by baking trays of gingersnaps and selling them to your friends for 50 cents each, you're a sole proprietor as soon as you receive that first payment.

Sole proprietorships are the most common type of business because they're so easy to start. There's no special paperwork, and you have complete control of your business. Not only that, but you're truly your own boss. There are also no special tax forms to figure out. When you're a sole proprietor, there is no legal difference between you and your business, so all of the money you generate from your business is claimed on your individual tax returns. And then there's pride; many sole proprietors have a strong sense of pride in themselves and in the businesses they've built.

> "The two most important requirements for major success are: first, being in the right place at the right time, and second, doing something about it."
>
> **—McDonald's founder Ray Kroc[26]**

As a sole proprietor, the good news (and the bad news) is that you're 100 percent responsible for your business. Why isn't this always a pro rather than a con? Well, if a batch of your lasagna makes people sick, you might have a lawsuit on your hands because you—and only you—are liable for that lasagna. (Being **liable** means you are legally obligated to cover the costs or damages your business creates.) Sole proprietors also have **unlimited liability**, which means they're responsible for all debts created by the business. So, if you have a business debt that your business assets can't pay, you may have to sacrifice your personal assets to cover the expense. Worst-case scenario: If you're sued because your food made people sick, you could lose everything you have—your home, car, savings, retirement fund, investments—everything.

Partnerships If you prefer to share responsibility for tasks, rewards, and failures, a partnership may be a better option for you. A **partnership** describes two or more people who share ownership of a business. This means that the partners involved share the profits and the losses. For example, imagine that you enlist your best friend (who happens to be in culinary school) as a co-owner of your catering company. The two of you have just formed a partnership. If your company is a hit, you'll both reap the rewards; if it's a flop, you'll both be down in the dumps.

Why start a partnership? One of the big pluses is money. Partners bring money to the table, so having more people in a partnership translates into starting a business with more money. This is why banks are more likely to lend money to a business with multiple owners—they feel more confident that partnerships will be able to repay loans.

Another perk of partnership is flexibility. Having more hands on deck can give each of you more free time, whether you use that time to increase sales and marketing efforts or take a vacation. Partnerships also allow you to divvy up the work so that each partner can play to his or her strengths. Let's say you hate paperwork, but you love interacting with customers. Your partner actually enjoys paperwork, but he's not great at small talk and selling. In a situation like this, each partner gets to work primarily on the tasks he or she enjoys.

Despite the benefits, partnerships aren't all a bed of roses. Have you ever worked in a group with someone you didn't get along with? If so, you're already acquainted with one of the main drawbacks of a partnership. Before you jump into this type of business, you need to be very particular about the people you choose to work with. If you don't get along with your partner, you might be heading toward disaster. Do you and your partner have similar work ethics? Are your working and communication styles similar (or at least compatible)?

It's especially important for you to trust your business partner because partnerships are another type of business with unlimited liability; if your partner screws up, both of you are held responsible. This is why business partners often create a *partnership agreement* before they enter into ownership together. Creating a partnership agreement forces partners to hash out tough issues before problems arise.

If you've decided to enter into a partnership, you have a couple different options for that partnership's structure:

- **General partnerships** are the default arrangement, in which all partners own, operate, and are fully liable for the business. As you might guess, a **general partner** is someone who owns the business, runs the business, and is fully liable.
- **Limited partnerships** are a little more complicated; they involve a combination of at least one general partner and at least one limited partner. A **limited partner** is simply an investor in the company. Limited partners do not participate in running the business, and they're only liable up to the amount they've invested.

Corporations So, what options do you have if you don't want unlimited liability for your catering company? For starters, you might found a corporation. A **corporation** is a business that is its own separate legal entity, distinct from its owners. It can buy and sell property, and it has **limited liability**, which means that the owners are only liable up to the amount they've invested in the business. This protects owners' and investors' personal assets. If your corporation is liable for something, the corporation's assets are used as payment, and you're not in danger of having to pay with your own savings.

Corporations also look attractive to some entrepreneurs because they can provide credibility to a new business by having "Co." or "Inc." at the end of a business's name. Corporations also have more options when it comes to raising money compared to sole proprietorships and partnerships. Corporations have an easier time obtaining money from banks and venture capitalists, and they also have the option of going public and selling stock. Investors can buy stock in the corporation, generating a lot of money that owners can use to fund the company's growth.

Incorporation may help a company grow and profit, but there are strings attached. Once a company "goes inc.," it faces new hurdles, most of which involve plenty of paperwork. In order to stay transparent, corporations need to maintain records of financial transactions, reports, meeting minutes, and other important details.

There's one other issue to think about before you take the leap and incorporate your catering business: *double taxation*. In a corporation, the business pays taxes on its profits, and shareholders also pay taxes on the income generated from their investments.

Limited Liability Companies (LLCs)

Want to take advantage of the limited-liability benefits of a corporation but avoid double taxation? Maybe you'd be interested in forming an LLC. **Limited liability companies (LLCs)** combine the limited liability benefits of corporations with the tax benefits of partnerships. Although some types of companies, like insurance companies and banks, can't be LLCs, they are an option for many business owners. An LLC might have only one owner (called a "member"), or it might have lots of members; there's no maximum number. Profits from LLCs are reported on investors' personal tax returns, so an increase in profits can raise investors' taxes. Different states have different rules for LLCs, but in general, forming an LLC is a good way to protect yourself from lawsuits against your company while avoiding double taxation.[27]

To clarify the different forms of ownership, see Table 7.1.

Table **7.1** | **Comparing Forms of Ownership**

Form	Advantages	Disadvantages
Sole Proprietorship: owned and operated by a single person	• Easy to start • Owner has complete control • No special tax form • Retains all profit	• Unlimited liability • Pays all taxes • Difficult to raise money for expansion or start-up • No one else to lean on
Partnership: two or more people share ownership	• More start-up money • Flexible • Shared resources • Limited partners: limited liability	• Work ethic differences • Management style variations • General partners: unlimited liability
Corporation: separate from owners; is its own legal entity	• Limited liability • Easy to raise money	• Increased paperwork • Double taxation
Limited Liability Company (LLC): combines the limited liability advantages of a corporation with the tax advantages of a partnership	• No double taxation • Limited liability	• Increased profit can raise personal taxes

Do It...

7.4: Figure Out Your Flavor Which "flavor" of entrepreneur are you most likely to be, and why? Which form of ownership would seem to fit best with that flavor? Limit your response to one page, and be prepared to submit it electronically or present it to your class.

Now Debrief...

- There are many ways to be an entrepreneur, and you can choose the "flavor" that's right for you based on your skill level, your financial goals, and your tolerance for risk. All five flavors of entrepreneurship—intrapreneur, social entrepreneur, business purchaser, franchisee, and classic entrepreneur—are equally valid, but it's important to know which flavor most closely matches your strengths and weaknesses.
- Similarly, there are lots of different ways to be a business owner. You can run a sole proprietorship, partnership, corporation, or limited liability company. The form of ownership you choose for your business will depend on the risks you're willing to take, the amount of control you want to have, and your ultimate goals for the business.

5. A Plan for Success: The Business Plan

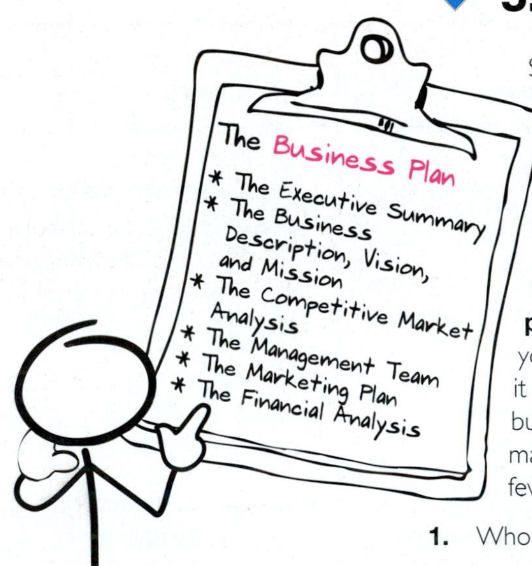

A business plan states your goals and how you plan to reach them.

So, you've performed a SWOT analysis of your new business idea, and it turns out that there are plenty of opportunities ripe for the picking in the catering biz. You've also looked at the options you have for forming your own business. It looks like your new catering company will be able to move from dream to reality. But do you have a plan?

Although there's no single "formula" for success in entrepreneurship, one way to improve your chances of succeeding is to create a business plan.[28] A **business plan** is a detailed, step-by-step plan that distinctly states your goals and explains how you plan to reach those goals. It is a crucial document because writing and researching it help you clarify what you want to accomplish with your business. As you create your business plan, you'll ask (and, ideally, answer) pertinent questions about such areas as marketing, operations, finances, personnel, and long-term development. Here are just a few of the questions you'll need to address:

1. Who is my target customer?
2. Who are my competitors, and what are their strengths and weaknesses?
3. Who should I hire, and what skills should my employees have?
4. How much is launching and sustaining the business going to cost?
5. What are my product offerings, or what are the kinds of goods, services, and experiences I will offer to customers?

In the past, business plans were lengthy, sometimes dull documents with reams of spreadsheets. Today, business plans tend to be shorter and more interesting to read. They must stand out to the banker, chief executive officer, or venture capitalist who may invest money in your venture. Let's look at the elements in a standard business plan.

"The Idea": The Executive Summary

The first part of a business plan, called the *executive summary*, is pretty much what it sounds like: a summary of the main points of your plan. The summary should include a brief description of the business, identify goals and objectives, and let the reader know what the business is seeking from potential investors, bankers, or partners, and how their investment in the company will benefit them. When you write an executive summary, be clear, concise, and compelling—and avoid technical jargon that might alienate your readers.

Above all else, you want the executive summary to convince potential investors that your idea is brilliant and that your business will be a success. If readers aren't impressed with the executive summary, they won't read any further. Here's how an executive summary for your catering business might begin:

> *Sweet Tooth Foods is a catering company that brings vibrant local flavors and first-class service to customers throughout southern New England. . .The company has already secured contracts with new customers and is looking to increase its customer base in the near future. . .*

"The Company": The Business Description, Vision, and Mission

After you give your readers an executive summary of your plan, you'll want to provide a few basic details about your business. Among other things, this section should state the business's legal name and form, its location, its vision and mission statement, and the products it provides.

Legal Name and Form What's in a name? Maybe more than you think. A company's legal name isn't always the same as its commonly used name. For instance, the legal name of IBM is actually International Business Machines Corporation. In a business plan, it might be stated as *"International Business Machines Corporation, doing business as (dba) IBM or I.B.M."*

This section should also state the legal *form* of your business, whether it's a sole proprietorship, a partnership, a corporation, or an LLC.

Location Choosing a location for your business may seem simple, but it's actually one of the most influential factors in determining the success of your business. Your business plan should include a description of the location, such as a physical description and a list of the pros and cons. You should also include a demographics analysis of the area that enables potential investors to understand the types of customers you will be catering to.

If you haven't decided on a final location yet, your business plan should include a list of potential sites along with the pros and cons of each.

Vision and Mission Statements As you learned in Chapter 6, a company's *vision* explains where the company wants to go. Including the company's vision is not only helpful for investors, it also helps unify and motivate employees toward a common goal.

In addition to explaining the company's long-term vision, it's a good idea to include the *mission statement*, which explains the present purpose of the company along with specific goals. Don't get too bogged down by specifics here. Rather than explaining that your catering company's purpose is to cook pasta for exactly seven minutes before plating it, covering it with homemade marinara sauce, and serving it to wedding guests, you might want to stick with the following:

> *Our mission is to improve our customers' quality of life by providing fresh, healthy food and courteous, caring service.*

We'll discuss mission statements in more detail in Chapter 9.

Products What services or experiences does your company provide? What goods do you sell? How will your products benefit the customer? It can be tricky to list specific details about your company's products without overwhelming readers, but with a little work, you can strike a balance between specificity and brevity.

For your catering company, you certainly don't need to list every item on your company's menu. Instead, describe the company's products and give a few specific examples:

> *Sweet Tooth Foods will provide pre-cooked meals to customers' specifications. Our services include a preliminary menu consultation with the head chef, a tasting session, linen and china rental, and up to eight hours of on-site service before, during, and after the event. Customers may choose from a full and varied menu of appetizers, meat and vegetarian entrees, desserts, and beverages.*

"The Opponents": The Competitive Market Analysis

In any competition, it's helpful to know what you're up against, and business competition is no exception. In this section, you'll explain who your competitors are, describe their strengths and weaknesses, and point out how your own company is poised to be successful in the market. (This is a great place to include the results of the SWOT analysis you performed earlier.) In the process of identifying the competition, it is necessary to identify the *market niche*—or subset of the market on which your product is focusing—that has been left open and not addressed by the competition.

For example, the direct competition to your new catering company will include other catering companies in the area. How much do they cost? What services do they provide? Is their food any good? And how do your costs and services stack up?

You'll also need to analyze other aspects of your market to give investors a clear idea of how your company will fit into the big picture. How are local restaurants doing, and what information do they give you about food service? How is the catering industry performing as a whole? You'll want to point out the strengths, weaknesses, opportunities, and threats that your competitors face, and you'll need to convince readers that your own company's strengths and opportunities will give you a good shot at success in the market.

"The Players : The Management Team

People are the essence of an organization, and the quality of your management team will be a deciding factor in your success. When investors and lenders look into your business plan, they'll be especially interested to see your management team's qualifications. This section therefore lists the key people in your company and explains their roles.

At the top of this list is the founder: you. As the founder, you'll most likely serve as a top management person, such as president or chief executive officer. In addition to your key management team, include members of the board of directors, if there is one, members of any existing advisory boards, and specialists or consultants. Any people who are essential or necessary to your operations, such as a scientist performing critical research, should also be listed. You'll want to describe each team member's education, experiences, successes, and strengths.

In addition, you may want to state the management style you plan to accept as your company's culture, and explain how that style will add value to your company and is necessary for its success. For example, the style of management at Yahoo! has been described as "laid-back" and "relaxed," not caring what employees wear to work as long as they deliver their services to customers.

"The Buyers": The Marketing Plan

Wouldn't it be nice if you proclaimed your company open for business and, as if by magic, customers immediately flocked to your door? Unfortunately, in real life, you'll have to forego magic in favor of a solid marketing plan. So, what goes into a marketing plan? Here are a few questions you'll need to address in this section:

- What are the strengths and weaknesses of your product?
- What message do you want to convey to your customers? How will you convince potential customers that your company or product will meet their needs?
- How does your product stack up against the competition?
- How will sales take place? Will you have sales people? Will you have a brick-and-mortar store or a Web site for conducting sales?
- What are you forecasting in terms of sales and units sold?
- Once you've made a sale, how will you ensure that your customers return?

Your answers to these questions will depend on the type of business you're starting and on your target clientele. For example, if you want your catering company to cater weddings, you might target brides- and grooms-to-be by advertising in wedding magazines and on Web sites like www.theknot.com.

"The Money": The Financial Analysis

Your innovative ideas may sound great, but how's your company doing when it comes to money? Potential investors will want to see some hard numbers, so you'll need to present a financial analysis as part of your business plan. Not only will your financial records tell investors how you're doing and what to expect in the future, the plan also gives *you* information to help plan for the future.

Your financial analysis should be down-to-earth and practical. It should include projections for funding, income, and expenses. Explain to the reader how you came up with these numbers, such as researching trends in the industry. It's also a good idea to provide different scenarios for the future, such as best- and worst-case.

In addition, remember the cash flow statement and income statement from Chapter 1 and the balance sheet from Chapter 2? All of these statements or estimates of them should be included in this section of your business plan. Before sending it out, double- or even triple-check your numbers to make sure everything adds up. Incorrect calculations can make a very bad impression on potential investors.

A Business Plan for Life

You've probably figured out by now that, if and when you decide to launch your own company, your business plan will be crucial to your company's success. But what if you aren't starting your own company right away (or ever)? Should you bother to care about business plans?

Well, you don't have to care *passionately* about them—that's a lot to ask, after all—but you should know that anyone who has a plan in life can learn a thing or two from the business plan model. That's because business plans are all about thinking critically, looking ahead, and making sure you have all the tools you need to succeed ahead of time.

Try applying a business-plan frame of mind to your post-college life. What are your own personal vision and mission statement for your life? Maybe you want to devote your life to helping people who are less fortunate than you are, or you want to share your love for music with the world. What concrete steps are you going to take in order to achieve that mission? How are you going to make money, and what are your short- and long-term plans for spending that money? What opportunities and strengths will help you rise above your competitors? You're the president and CEO of your own life, and a little careful planning will help you steer yourself toward success.

Do It...

7.5: Create a Business Plan Imagine that you're about to enter the job market, positioning yourself for a promotion or trying to break into a different career, and apply the business plan components described above to write a business plan outline for You, Inc. Limit your plan to two pages and use bullet points to highlight the key points. Be prepared to submit your outline electronically.

Now Debrief...

- If you're starting a business or heading down a new path in life, you'll need a **business plan**—a detailed, step-by-step plan that distinctly states your goals and explains how you plan to reach those goals.
- The executive summary summarizes the main points of the business plan.
- Next, the business plan should include basic information about the business, such as its legal name, form, location, vision and mission statement, and product information.
- A competitive market analysis helps a business know what it's up against.
- The management team should also be listed on the business plan, so potential investors can review the team's qualifications.
- Finally, the business plan should include the marketing plan and the financial analysis, so people can see how you're going to get your business noticed and keep it running.

6. Where to Find Help Starting Your Business

Let's say you've started practicing your entrepreneurial DOs, you've come up with an innovative idea and analyzed it using SWOT, you've figured out your flavor of entrepreneurship, you know which type of ownership is best for you, and you've created a business plan to turn your dream into a reality. What's next? For some, it's time to get out there and start a business!

Feeling a little daunted? That's understandable; starting a business is intimidating, especially if you don't have much experience or if you're entering a tough economic climate. But there are resources out there that can give you the support you need to start a company of your own, whether that support is legal, financial, structural, or emotional. And while you'll probably make mistakes, there are a few steps you can take to avoid the most common traps that trip up new entrepreneurs.

Finding Funding

Aside from getting a traditional bank loan, where do you go to get funding? Let's look at some other sources for financing.

Personal Sources If you have assets of your own, you might finance your business through cash or through an equity loan on your house or other valuable possessions. If, like many people, you don't have the assets to self-fund your business, you might want to search for business partners who can afford to help you get the company off the ground. If you don't feel awkward asking friends and relatives for help, you could consider them as another source of funding. (Just keep in mind that if the business goes south, so could your relationships, so tread carefully.)

Outside Sources Wealthy individuals may provide capital for your business if they think the venture has a good chance for success. These generous folks are called **angel investors**, or business angels, but they don't invest out of the goodness of their hearts. They want some level of ownership in the business. **Venture capitalists** are another source of funds. These professional money managers might be interested in investing their clients' money in your promising new business in exchange for partial ownership and a high return on the investment. You might also want to contact a stockbroker or investment banker. These individuals often know of wealthy individuals looking to invest in start-up companies.

For start-up companies, funding is also available from state and federal programs designed to assist start-up companies. Finally, *Entrepreneur* and *INC* magazines often list possible financing sources and are good resources for budding entrepreneurs wishing to see how others have financed their businesses.

Finding Help

Sure, you need some money to get your company started, especially if you're a first-time business owner, but you also need some good, sound advice. Fortunately, there are plenty of places you can turn to for help—and even more fortunately, many of these resources are cheap or free. Table 7.2 lists some helpful free and low-cost resources. As noted above, *Entrepreneur* and *INC* also provide helpful resources. Let's look at some other sources in more detail.

Table 7.2 | **Free and Low-Cost Resources for Starting a Business**

Resource	Description
Small Business Administration (SBA) www.sba.gov	Independent agency that assists, counsels, and protects small-business interests
Small Business Development Centers (SBDC) www.sba.gov/aboutsba/sbaprograms/sbdc/index.html	Branch of the SBA, with offices located nationwide, that provides assistance in all areas related to small business
Service Corp of Retired Executives (SCORE) www.score.org	Nonprofit association composed of experienced volunteers who spend time counseling and mentoring small-business owners
National Association of the Self-Employed (NASE) www.nase.org	Nonprofit organization that provides benefits and resources for self-employed and micro businesses, such as day-to-day support and buying power
U.S. Chamber of Commerce Small Business Center www.uschamber.com/sb	Online library full of information for small-business owners, along with small-business "toolkits" that offer advice about hiring, sales, marketing, and other key entrepreneurial activities

Small Business Administration Resources The **Small Business Administration (SBA)** is a government agency that helps get businesses up and running and also provides training and loans to keep the businesses going.[29] Visit the SBA online at www.sba.gov and check out their Start-Up Assessment Tool. After a short registration process, you can take free, self-paced, 30- to 45-minute courses on the site.[30] If you prefer to work in the non-virtual world, you can visit one of the SBA's many district offices to find information that's relevant to your own state and locality.

The **Service Corp of Retired Executives (SCORE)**, a nonprofit organization that's part of the SBA, is dedicated to helping entrepreneurs in all aspects of their businesses.[31] It has nearly 400 chapters and around 11,800 volunteers (with about 600 different business skills) throughout the United States and its territories. These volunteers are retired and working executives, corporate leaders, and small-business owners willing to donate their time to further the cause of entrepreneurship. Since 1964, SCORE volunteers have helped over eight million entrepreneurs. The organization also offers online learning, business templates, how-to articles, low-cost workshops, and a large resource library. You can check out SCORE's Web site at www.score.org.

The SBA also runs the *Office of Small Business Development Centers (SBDC)*, a network of about 1,100 branch offices that provides counseling, training, and technical assistance in many aspects of small-business management. Many of the centers are on or near university and college campuses. If you go to an SBDC office with a simple draft of your business plan and plenty of questions, it can help you develop your business. Take a look at the SBDC locator map, found on the SBA's Web site, to find an office near you.

Industry Conferences and Trade Shows What can you do to get yourself and your business out in the real world? If you go to an industry conference or a trade show, you'll get to network with others in the biz, hear the latest industry news, and meet people in your area who could wind up becoming your customers.

- To find a conference near you, point your Web browser to AllConferences.com, which offers calendars for a wide range of business-related conferences.
- Looking for conferences related to a specific industry? A quick Internet search can probably help you find what you need. (For example, ConferenceGuru.com can give you plenty of details about technology conferences.)
- Finally, if you'd like to attend a trade show, go to TSNN.com for a comprehensive list of upcoming events.

Incubators If you don't have a business space or an office staff, or if you're looking for additional support for your start-up, a business incubator might be able to help you. **Business incubators** provide a wide range of management support services and resources for newly minted entrepreneurs, including shared office space that several start-ups can use simultaneously to reduce overhead costs. Incubators generally provide office equipment, meeting rooms, and a fee-based business support staff to answer phones and perform other basic administrative work.

These incubation sites are usually geared toward entrepreneurs who can't afford to set up their own business space or don't want to work out of a home office. For a new business, an incubator can be a great short-term solution. To find a business incubator in the United States or internationally, visit the National Business Incubation Association at www.nbia.org.

Avoiding Common Mistakes

Even with expert help and advice, chances are good that you're going to make some mistakes when you start your business. Let's look at some common errors entrepreneurs make. By being aware of these mistakes, you will hopefully avoid them.

1. *I don't know how to run a business!* An entrepreneur may have a good idea for a new business but may lack the necessary experience to make the business a success. Not having experience in finance or management can cause an entrepreneur to make poor decisions that may be detrimental to the business.
2. *I have too much debt!* Starting a business can cost a lot of money. Often, entrepreneurs don't have this money in cash, so they take loans or use credit to get started. These resources generally charge interest, so debt can add up so fast that the business can't recover.
3. *I was overly optimistic about my cash flow projections!* Some entrepreneurs expect their cash inflows to be higher than they actually are, leading to cash flow problems.
4. *I incorrectly forecasted my sales channels!* Some entrepreneurs miscalculate which sales channels will be available and find that those that are available are inadequate or too small to generate the volume of business they need.
5. *My operating expenses forecast was unrealistic!* Some entrepreneurs underestimate just how much it will cost to create their product and run the company, especially when it comes to salaries, benefits, and marketing budgets.

Do It...

7.6: Prevent Common Mistakes Pick any three of the sources of help for business start-ups described in this section, and for each, explain how they could help prevent some of the mistakes that entrepreneurs often make. Limit your response to one page, and be prepared to submit it electronically or present it to your class.

Now Debrief...

- Personal sources of funding for start-ups include an equity loan, business partners, and friends and relatives. Outside sources of funding include angel investors, venture capitalists, and government sources.
- Opening a small business can be daunting, but resources are available to provide support. Inexpensive or free resources include Small Business Administration resources, industry conferences, trade shows, and business incubators.
- One way to help your business succeed is by avoiding common mistakes such as lacking experience and accumulating too much debt.

Chapter 7 Visual Summary

Leadership Vision | Chapter 6: *Lead* **Chapter 7: *Own*** Chapter 8: *Act*

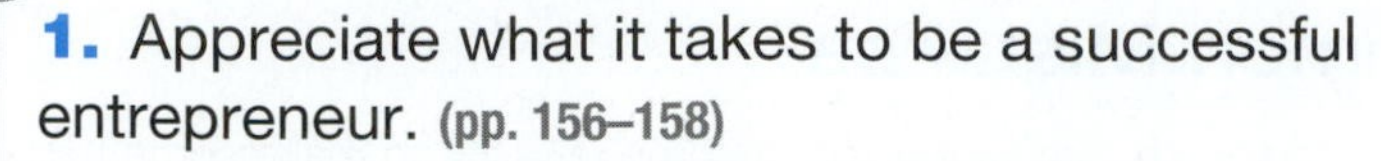

1. Appreciate what it takes to be a successful entrepreneur. (pp. 156–158)

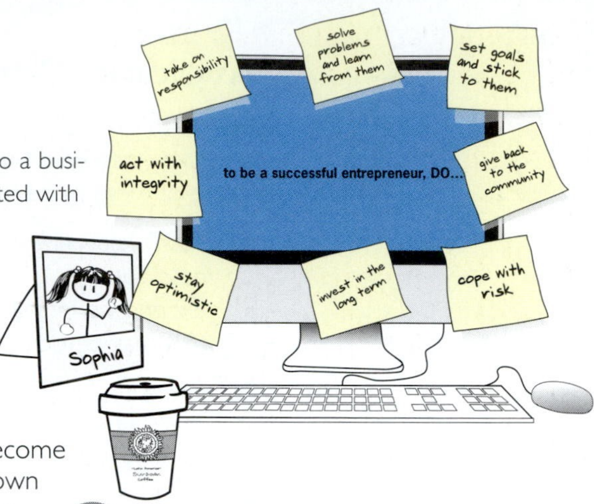

- If you have a passion and can think of a way to turn that passion into a business, you can be an **entrepreneur**, a person who takes risks associated with organizing and managing a new business.
- Successful entrepreneurs don't all share specific character traits, but they do act in certain ways. To act like an entrepreneur, DO take on responsibility, cope with risk, stay optimistic, set goals and stick to them, solve problems and learn from them, invest in the long term, act with integrity, and give back to the community.

Summary: Adopting specific skills are necessary if you want to become an entrepreneur. However, even if you don't want to have your own business, cultivating these skills can give you an instant advantage in whatever you do.

2. Recognize innovation when you see it and justify its effect on the triple bottom line. (pp. 159–162)

- Innovation is a unique change or improvement that the market rewards.
- There are three primary levels of innovation: *incremental innovation, disruptive innovation*, and *revolutionary innovation*. An incremental innovation is a small improvement or change. A disruptive innovation is an unprecedented change that transforms an industry, and a revolutionary innovation transforms society and creates a new way of living.
- Facebook, iTunes, and other forms of social interactive media exemplify "the innovation of co-creation," which some experts see as the next wave of innovation.
- Innovation, especially the innovation of co-creation, is intertwined with each aspect of the triple bottom line. Innovations drive profits, connect companies with the people they serve, and provide eco-friendly solutions to help the planet.
- You can bring innovative thinking into your own life by looking at things in new ways, thinking critically, being an active learner, thinking both analytically and intuitively, and balancing your passions with your career prospects.

Summary: Many entrepreneurs are successful because they have made a worthwhile innovation on an existing product, and customers are willing to pay for the improvement.

3. Conduct a SWOT analysis to identify opportunities and drive decisions. (pp. 162–164)

- You can use SWOT analysis to analyze the strengths, weaknesses, opportunities, and threats that face your innovative idea or your company.
- As an entrepreneur, you can use SWOT techniques to create a strategic balance sheet that illustrates your company's strengths and weaknesses.
- SWOT helps identify **core competencies**, which are skills and areas of expertise that the company possesses that are considered better than those of other companies within the industry.
- Entrepreneurs use SWOT constantly to evaluate new opportunities and avoid threats in their industry.

Summary: SWOT is a good analysis tool for anything, even if it doesn't relate to business.

Strategic Balance Sheet Your Catering Company	
Pluses	**Minuses**
• Food tastes delicious.	• Slightly higher menu prices.
• Staff is well trained.	• Since the company is small, you can't accept all the jobs you'd like to.
• People are looking for companies that use fresh, organic, locally grown ingredients.	• The low-carb craze is slowing down sales of baked goods.

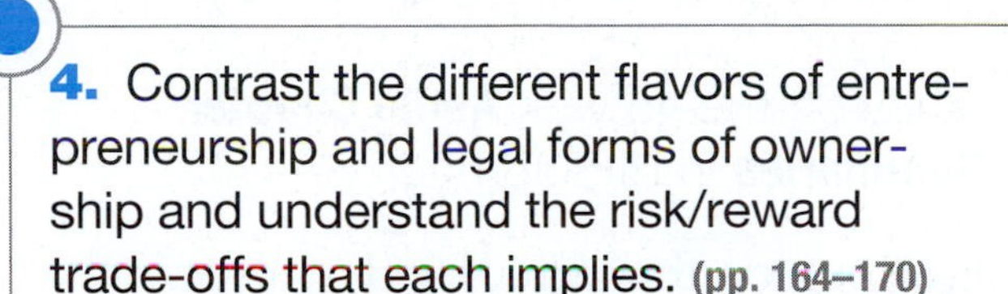

4. Contrast the different flavors of entrepreneurship and legal forms of ownership and understand the risk/reward trade-offs that each implies. (pp. 164–170)

- There are many different types, or "flavors," of entrepreneurship. Not all entrepreneurs are identical, and each person can find the flavor that he or she likes best.
- An **intrapreneur** is a person who uses his or her entrepreneurial skills inside an organization.
- **Social entrepreneurs** are people who blend traditional entrepreneurial business development with social objectives for the greater good of society.
- Business purchasers buy established companies from other people.
- **Franchisees** buy into a business and return some profits to the **franchisor**—the business owner who agrees to sell the franchise.
- **Classic entrepreneurs** start and run their own businesses from scratch.
- There are also several different forms of ownership.
- A **sole proprietorship** is a business that is owned and operated by a single person.
- A **partnership** is shared ownership of a business by two or more people, and it comes in two forms: **general partnerships** and **limited partnerships**.
- A **corporation** is a business that is its own separate legal entity that is distinct from its owners.
- **Limited liability companies (LLCs)** combine the limited liability benefits of corporations with the tax benefits of partnerships.

Summary: Entrepreneurship and ownership are not one-size-fits-all terms. Instead, it's up to you to decide what type of business owner you want to be and what type of business you want to own.

5. Explain the critical components of a business plan. (pp. 170–174)

- A **business plan** states a company's goals and the strategies it will employ to meet them.
- The *executive summary* summarizes the main points of the business plan.
- The business description states the business's legal name, form, location, vision and mission statement, and its products.
- The competitive market analysis describes competitors' strengths and weaknesses, and explains why your company will be successful.
- The management team section lists the key decision makers of the business.
- The marketing plan explains how you're going to promote and sell your product.
- The financial analysis includes projections for funding, income, and expenses, as well as cash flow statements, income statements, and balance sheets.

Summary: A business plan is crucial for a business's success.

6. Locate helpful resources for starting a business, and avoid common mistakes. (pp. 174–177)

- Entrepreneurs can find funding through equity loans, business partners, friends and family, **angel investors**, **venture capitalists**, and other sources.
- The **Small Business Administration** helps get small businesses up and running and provides training and loans.
- **Business incubators** provide shared office space and other forms of support for small start-ups.
- Some common business mistakes include lack of experience and financial mismanagement.

Summary: Starting a business can be daunting, but with the right planning and resources, the term "start-up" doesn't have to be synonymous with "long shot."

Get the most out of what you just read by practicing your skills and actually DOING something with the material! The best place to do this is at **www.mybizlab.com**. Here's just some of what is available to you there:

- Apply your skills in an interactive environment with more **BizSkill** experiences...and see if you have what it takes
- Think critically and talk with your peers on hot business topics in **BizChats**
- Flex your business communication skills and build your own portfolio with the **Communication Plan exercises**
- Watch the chapter material come together with **Just Plain Business** videos
- Study on-the-go with **Audio Chapter Summaries** in MP3 format
- Brush up on the lecture and content with **Audio PowerPoints**
- Discover how well you are doing and see what areas you need to improve on with the **Pre-Tests** and **Post-Tests**

Key Words

These key words and more are also available as flash cards to practice with at **www.mybizlab.com**.

1. Appreciate what it takes to be a successful entrepreneur. (pp. 156–158)

Entrepreneur (p. 155)

2. Recognize innovation when you see it and justify its effect on the triple bottom line. (pp. 159–162)

3. Conduct a SWOT analysis to identify opportunities and drive decisions. (pp. 162–164)

Core competencies (p. 163)

4. Contrast the different flavors of entrepreneurship and legal forms of ownership and understand the risk/reward trade-offs that each implies. (pp. 164–170)

Intrapreneur (p. 165)
Social entrepreneurs (p. 165)
Franchisee (p. 166)
Franchisor (p. 166)
Classic entrepreneur (p. 166)
Small businesses (p. 166)
Sole proprietorship (p. 167)
Liable (p. 167)
Unlimited liability (p. 167)
Partnership (p. 168)
General partnership (p. 168)
General partner (p. 168)
Limited partnership (p. 168)
Limited partner (p. 168)
Corporation (p. 168)
Limited liability (p. 168)
Limited liability company (LLC) (p. 169)

5. Explain the critical components of a business plan. (pp. 170–174)

Business plan (p. 170)

6. Locate helpful resources for starting a business and avoid common mistakes. (pp. 174–177)

Angel investors (p. 175)
Venture capitalists (p. 175)
Small Business Administration (SBA) (p. 176)
Service Corp of Retired Executives (SCORE) (p. 176)
Business incubator (p. 176)

Prove It

Prove It...

Now, let's put on one of the BizHats. With the **Employee BizHat** squarely on your head, look at the following exercise:

Since you were a child, you've always wanted to start your own business. As a kid, you had your own lemonade stands, and you often baked cookies for school fundraisers. Now that you're older, your dream is to open a bakery and sell bread and baked goods from recipes that have been in your family for generations.

You're three years out of college and have $10,000 saved for the job, but you don't think that's enough to get started. Up to this point, you've worked as a dietitian for a corporate food manufacturer, so you have some experience working for a big business. You recently met with a potential investor, who's interested in your business but wants to know more. Put what you learned in this chapter to work and conduct a SWOT analysis. Then, create an executive summary to give the investor.

Flip It...

After you come up with an executive summary for your bakery, **flip over to the Owner/Investor BizHat.**

Imagine yourself as an entrepreneurial consultant/investor who has spent the last 20 years building a successful small business into a multi-million-dollar medium-sized business. You received an executive summary from a young entrepreneur who is only three years out of college and who has only $10,000 to start her business. This is what you know about the entrepreneur and her business:

- She has worked for three years at a major corporate food manufacturer as a dietitian.
- As a child and teenager she always loved to start business enterprises such as a lemonade stand outside her home and making cookies for school projects to raise money.
- Her special interest is making homemade breads and baked goods from recipes handed down from her grandmother.

Considering her age, financial situation, special interests, goals, education, experience, and other such factors, do you think this has the potential to be a successful business? Provide specific feedback. Are you willing to invest your time and money to help develop the business?

Now Debrief It...

Compare the perspectives of the BizHats described above. When you had on the Owner/Investor BizHat, what did you expect from the Employee? When you were wearing the Employee BizHat did you think you had covered everything in your executive summary? Was there anything missing? If so, what?

Act:
Ethics and Corporate Social Responsibility

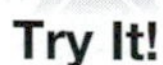

BizSkills invite...

Try It!
There's no better way to learn concepts than to put them into practice. Take your turn in the driver's seat and be a part of actual business decision making by visiting the BizSkill for this chapter at **www.mybizlab.com**.

Start here!

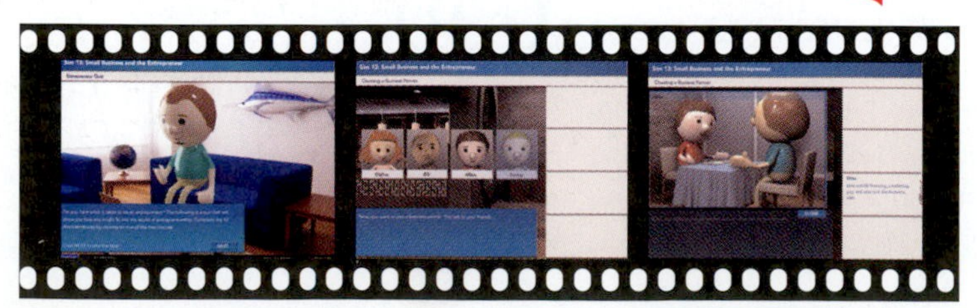

Now that you've practiced making tough business decisions and seeing the results of your choices in this chapter's BizSkill, it's time to translate those skills into plain English. And if you skipped the BizSkill, go back now!

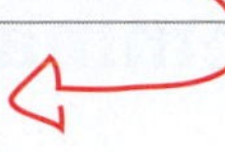

Chapter 8 Goals

After experiencing this chapter, you'll be able to:

1. Appreciate the complexity of the ethical dilemmas you may face in the business world and the need to take a 360° view.
2. Characterize what an ethical organization looks like and the tools that leaders use to create one.
3. Develop an ethical decision-making approach for your career.
4. Identify the specific ethical dilemmas facing different areas of an organization.
5. Justify how ethics are the foundation for a sustainable organization and how companies engage in acts of corporate social responsibility.

Would you fire Martin?

To Fire or Not to Fire?

Martin Cunningham is battling cancer. To keep his life as normal as possible, he has kept his full-time accounting job at Jefferson & Wails. He's worked for J&W for 25 years and has to hold on to his job for just one more year in order to receive full pension benefits. Although the cancer has taken its toll on him, he tries his best to get to the office as often as he can and do the work requested of him.

Rebecca Cramer has worked as an accountant at J&W for seven years. For the past two years, she and her three coworkers have been forced to pick up the slack because Martin isn't as productive as he used to be. She thinks Martin is an amazing person and knows the company has kept him on in good faith, but she and her coworkers are frustrated at having to work nights and weekends because Martin can no longer do his share.

Donald Arnold is the executive director of the accounting department for J&W. Upper management informed him that he needs to downsize his department from five employees to three. Donald has worked with Martin for the past 15 years. He knows that such a drastic cut to the department means he can't afford to keep Martin on staff and overwork the rest of the department even more. But with just one year until Martin is eligible for his full pension, it's a terrible decision. After agonizing over the situation for days, Donald decides to let Martin go.

Although this story was fictionalized for this text, the events actually happened to a real person battling cancer. What do you think Donald should have done? Is it ethical to lay off a company veteran, especially someone who obviously needs full medical benefits and is so close to retiring? Is there a right answer?

1. Ethical Dilemmas

When you first think about ethics, situations like cheating on an exam or getting too much change back from a cashier and keeping it may pop into your head. As the opening story shows, business ethics is often very complicated because there are a lot of competing values and interests, multiple alternatives, and often very sizable consequences to consider.

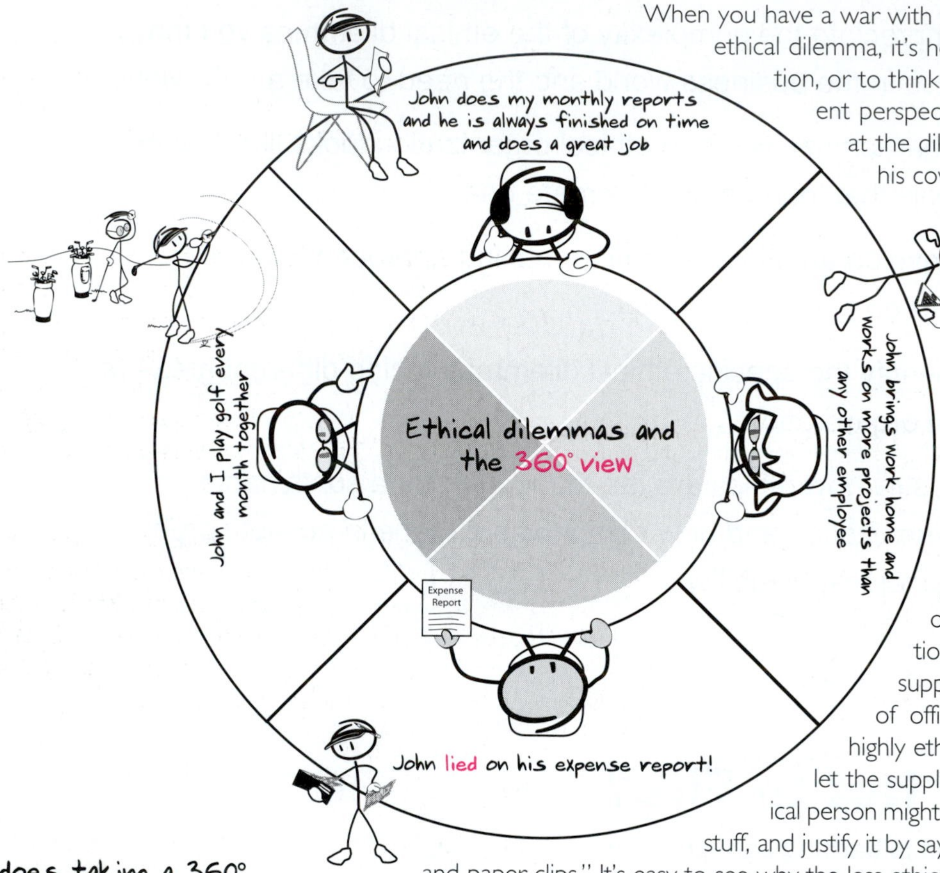

When you have a war with your values, which is the essence of an ethical dilemma, it's helpful to take a 360° view of the situation, or to think about the ethical dilemma from different perspectives. In our opening story, we looked at the dilemma from the perspective of Martin, his coworker Rebecca, and Donald, his manager. Taking the 360° view forces you to slow down, consider another person's perspective, and make a good decision you can live with.

Ethical dilemmas and the 360° view

John does my monthly reports and he is always finished on time and does a great job

John brings work home and works on more projects than any other employee

John lied on his expense report!

Expense Report

John and I play golf every month together

How does taking a 360° view help you make a better decision?

You may think ethics is all about figuring out what's right and wrong, but it's more general than that: **ethics** is the study of human conduct and moral principles. Someone with strong ethics shows a commitment to good human conduct, whereas someone with weak ethics shows more questionable conduct. For example, let's say a supplier accidentally gave you an extra box of office supplies. What would you do? A highly ethical person might notify the supplier to let the supplier know about the mistake. A less ethical person might keep the supplies, rejoice at getting free stuff, and justify it by saying, "Who cares? It's just a box of pens and paper clips." It's easy to see why the less ethical option is an easy one: it *is* only a box of office supplies, after all. But if you look at the situation from all angles, it's not so clear:

- Your coworkers may initially think it's great that you got a free box of supplies; however, they may start to question your ethics on other, larger matters.
- And what would your boss think? If she asks you about the box and you tell her what happened, you end up looking like a thief, and you don't set a good example either within or outside the company.
- Now think about it from the delivery person's perspective. He may not be able to account for the location of the box and could be reprimanded or even fired.
- Also, the supplier will be out the cost of the supplies—and if the company fires the delivery person, it'll have to pay to recruit and train his replacement. The impact of these expenses could be the last straw that convinces the supplier to raise their prices, which would in turn put a dent in *your* company's profits.

Business ethics is often very complicated because there are a lot of competing values and interests, multiple alternatives, and often very sizable consequences to consider.

So, because of a little ethical laziness, you could be partially responsible for damaging the delivery person's job, hurting the supplier's—and possibly your own company's—bottom line, and definitely responsible for messing up your reputation. Now who cares about those free pens and paper clips?

As you would guess, **business ethics** is the study of moral principles and conduct within a business environment. It studies how people behave

"It takes many good deeds to build a good reputation, and only one bad one to lose it."
—Benjamin Franklin[1]

at work, which is not always how they behave in their lives outside work. But is business ethics a contradiction in terms? Many people, especially investors in a company, consider the goal of a business to make profits, and ethics can sometimes hamper this goal.

For example, does a company have an ethical obligation to help needy people even if this assistance will cause the company to lose money? Take drug companies that develop lifesaving treatments for people who are desperate and can't afford to pay for them. In December 2000, the pharmaceutical company Pfizer agreed to send $50 million worth of AIDS drugs to South Africa, free of charge.[2] The drug, fluconazole, treated an AIDS infection called cryptococcal meningitis, which is a deadly brain disease.[3] By supplying two years' worth of free drugs, Pfizer was helping more than 100,000 South Africans stricken by the disease.[4] Pfizer could have instead sold fluconazole only to people who could afford it, but when faced with an ethical choice, the company decided to put immediate profit on the back burner and donate the drug to the victims in South Africa.

As we'll discuss later, often organizations do these kinds of good deeds not only because they're the right thing to do, but because of the long-term effects on the public. For example, by offering drugs for free to those in need, Pfizer garnered a good deal of positive publicity. Many customers prefer to work with companies that have good reputations and that help people. If all other things were equal, would you rather patronize an organization with questionable policies or a socially conscious organization? That's an easy choice. Of course, it's not quite that simple in real life—prices and other factors may affect which company customers choose. Still, a strong ethical foundation can go a long way in helping a business build and maintain a good reputation.

However, it would be naïve to think that the "bad guys" of the business world are always punished for unethical decisions. Many are not even caught, and in some cases, even if they are caught, they are not punished. In fact, some are even handsomely rewarded (think of the early days of the now collapsed energy giant Enron, when company execs were living large). Often, as with the example of Martin Cunningham at the beginning of the chapter, the right answer isn't always clear, so what may be ethical to one person isn't ethical to another.

Do It...

8.1: Take a 360° View Go back to the beginning of the chapter and reread the chapter-opening story ("To Fire or Not to Fire," page 183) and take a 360° view of the situation. If you were Martin's manager, would you fire Martin? Why or why not? Now consider the situation from a coworker's point of view. Would you want the company you worked for to fire Martin? Why or why not? What if you were a customer of the company? What factors would affect your decision? Finally, what if you were Martin yourself? Would you feel it was ethical for you to continue collecting a paycheck at the company? Limit your response to one page, and be prepared to submit it electronically or present it to your class.

Now Debrief...

- **Ethics** is the study of human conduct and moral principles.
- **Business ethics** is the study of moral principles and conduct within a business environment.
- In situations that test your ethics, the right thing to do isn't always obvious.
- Often, when you're having a war with your values, or an ethical dilemma, it helps to try looking at it from all sides—taking a 360° view of the situation.

2. Ethical Organizations: How Do You Know?

Tool 4: A Code of Conduct

People often say you learn the most about people in stressful situations. Businesses are no different—during stressful times, you can often see a business's "true colors." What if you want to know whether an organization is ethical, but there aren't any major issues at the moment that put their ethics on display? In this case, there are other indicators that organizations have an ethical mind-set, some of which we've listed below. Note though that your employer, or potential employer, might not use all the items listed below. Just think of these as tools in a company's ethical toolbox.

Which tool jumps out at you first? Why?

Tool 1: Leaders Setting an Ethical Example

What do you look for in a leader? Whether it's the president or chief executive officer (CEO) of a company or the captain of a softball team, you want someone you trust to make the right decisions and to set a good example. The same is true in the business world. That's why the ethical tone of a company should be set by the men and women at the top of the company's food chain. By having a solid ethical foundation, employees have a better chance of knowing the right thing to do in times of crisis. Two classic examples of what to do and what not to do are the Johnson & Johnson Tylenol crisis and the *Exxon Valdez* oil spill.

Ethics at J&J In 1982, seven people in the Chicago area died after ingesting what they thought were capsules of Tylenol pain reliever. Instead, what they were really ingesting was cyanide. The makers of Tylenol, Johnson & Johnson (J&J), were not responsible for the poisonings; someone had removed containers from store shelves, laced them with cyanide, and returned the bottles to the store. (All of this was before the advent of tamper-resistant seals. In fact, this incident led to stronger safety measures for over-the-counter medications.)

Our Credo
We take full responsibility for our products no matter what the cost
Press Conference

When the news of the deaths broke, the chairman of J&J, Jim Burke, reacted quickly and formed a strategy team. The first item on the agenda was figuring out how to protect the public from danger. The team knew the right thing to do and recalled *every* bottle of Tylenol capsules in the country, even though the poisonings were limited to the Chicago area. This was over *30 million* bottles of Tylenol.[5] Burke knew the *credo*, or guiding principle, of the company was to put people and their well-being before anything else.[6]

Burke's decision to pull all bottles of the drug went against the advice of lawyers and consultants, and many analysts thought the company was finished. However, the company proved everybody wrong by rebounding with stronger safety measures and discounts when its products were relaunched. J&J's management acted ethically because the company's credo had been effectively communicated and reinforced through good practices such as routine ethical "challenge sessions" that helped management fully understand their commitment to the Tylenol brand.

Breach of Ethics at Exxon Not too long after Tylenol was praised for standing by its ethical code, Exxon showed how a company can react when its ethical code is not part of its culture. In 1989, the *Exxon Valdez* oil tanker ran aground and spilled 11 million gallons of oil into Prince William Sound in Alaska. The spill caused tremendous ecological damage to the area and is still evident today.

Exxon's reaction to the crisis was considered inadequate based on the level of damage done. The chairman of Exxon, Lawrence Rawl, failed to act quickly, and the company seemed to ignore the problem for almost a week. When Exxon did act, it tried to shift blame to the captain of the oil tanker, the Coast Guard, and the state of Alaska. Exxon's attempts to contain the spill were not just slow in coming, they were ineffective and poorly planned. In fact, public opinion polling indicated that 77 percent of Americans believed that Exxon had not done a good job of handling the situation. This led many customers to boycott Exxon. The company paid a price, not only in fines, legal settlements, and cleanup costs, but also in goodwill with its customers for its failure to act ethically.[7]

Tool 2: A Focus on More than Just Profits

In Chapter 3, we introduced the notion of *sustainability* and the *triple bottom line (TBL)*, whereby companies focus not just on profit, but on people and the planet as well. Sustainable companies emphasize the importance of creating a successful business while also giving back to people in society and to the environment. Triple bottom line companies look for answers that are in line with all three values and try to do what's best for both the organization and its stakeholders. We'll discuss these concepts in more detail later in the chapter.

Tool 3: A Code of Ethics

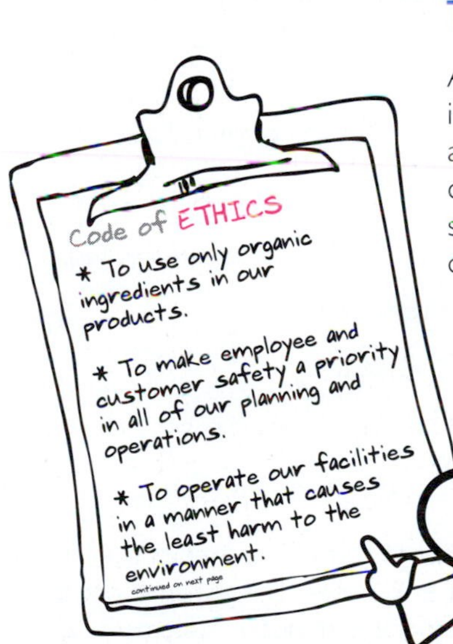

As the old saying goes, "Rome wasn't built in a day." By the same token, you can't build an ethical organization overnight. It takes a lot of planning and work. A business's **code of ethics** is a set of standards established by a company regarding ethical practices. A company may call its code something different, like a credo or a philosophy, or it may embed the code into its mission statement, but whatever it's called and wherever it's found, a code of ethics is a set of standards that employees live by when they are at work.

A code of ethics can act as a preventive measure, aiding employees in making ethical decisions and helping the organization as a whole maintain its moral center.[8] To do this, though, a company's code of ethics has to be more than just for show—it needs to be clearly communicated to employees and actively integrated into the way the company does business. Think back to how Johnson & Johnson prepared its employees to act on its credo.

Where can you find a company's code of ethics? Some companies have a separate publication dedicated completely to explaining the company's code of ethics. For example, the Society of Professional Journalists has a separate code of ethics located on its Web site (http://www.spj.org/ethicscode.asp). The first item in its code is "Seek truth and report it." Within this there are multiple bullets explaining the society's definition of honest and fair reporting. Here is a sample of the list:

- Test the accuracy of information from all sources and exercise care to avoid inadvertent error. Deliberate distortion is never permissible.
- Identify sources whenever feasible. The public is entitled to as much information as possible on sources' reliability.
- Never plagiarize.[9]

Sometimes, a company's ethics policies are combined with another document. For example, Texas Instruments (TI) has a document called "TI Standard Policies and Procedures." Before updating or publishing the document, its policies are reviewed by TI's Ethics Office. So, in this

> "Business leaders should manage their companies by earning reasonable profits through modesty, not arrogance, and taking care of employees, customers, business partners, and all stakeholders with a caring heart."
>
> **—Kazuo Inamori,** Chief Executive Officer of Japanese high-tech ceramics manufacturer, Kyocera[10]

case, you'll find policies relating to ethical dilemmas, such as conflicts of interests, in this document, and not in a separate code of ethics.[11]

A strong code of ethics helps promote public confidence and loyalty. If an organization is doing everything it can to provide the best products to the public and it maintains strong public relations, the organization can retain customers, employees, and stockholders for a lifetime.[12]

Tool 4: A Code of Conduct

Even if you have an up-to-date code of ethics, that doesn't mean anything by itself. The point of creating a code is to guide people in the right direction. Employees may be familiar with the code, but unless they are abiding by the code, it isn't really doing anything for the organization. To help translate these policies into actions, it is vital to establish specific training and procedures for everyone. For most employees, this process begins at an orientation for new hires.

A **code of conduct** is exactly as it sounds; it conveys to employees how an organization wants them to act, or conduct themselves, in the workplace. This is different from a code of ethics in that ethics helps guide employees to make appropriate decisions. A company code of conduct is similar to the policies on academic honesty that you're probably familiar with from your school. The main goal of a code of conduct is to let you know what you should and shouldn't do. The code breaks down specific issues relating to the workplace and specifically states the proper behavior expected from everyone every day. Codes of conduct generally cover things like dress code, confidentiality, discrimination, and policies regarding receiving gifts and using company property.[13]

For example, the codes below could apply to almost any organization:

Employee Conduct

- Swearing, drinking, fighting, and all other unprofessional activities are prohibited.
- Sexual harassment or harassment of any kind is prohibited.
- Using company property for personal matters is prohibited.

Client Relations

- Employees cannot accept client gifts or favors from clients for any reason.

On paper these codes are just words strung together to form lifeless sentences. The key is to get these words to mean something in the eyes of employees. This dynamic occurs when codes are translated into everyday practices. Company mottos and mission statements are useful here because they're generally short and to the point. The Ritz-Carlton hotel chain has a short and sweet motto that cuts to the core of what the company is about: "We are ladies and gentlemen, serving ladies and gentlemen." Not only does this convey good service, but it can also make employees feel proud and inspired. People in the service industry are often taken for granted and dismissed easily, but this motto conveys self-respect to the employee, as well as the feeling that every employee is just as good as someone paying $600 for a night at the luxury hotel.

Tool 5: Ethics Training

Having an ethical company is more complicated than saying, "Here's a list; do the right thing." After all, situations aren't always black or white, where one choice is clearly right and the other is clearly wrong. Employees need to be prepared to

■ Having an ethical company is more complicated than saying, "Here's a list; do the right thing."

interpret the "shades of gray." That's where ethics training programs come in. During an **ethics training program**, an employer is trying to teach employees the appropriate way to act when encountered with an ethical dilemma. The challenge with ethics training is that it is difficult to teach someone exactly what to do when he or she is experiencing an ethical dilemma. Although formal training and distribution of an organization's code of ethics are useful, it is ongoing policies and procedures that help employees continue to abide by the code.

Tool 6: Ethics Management Program

Let's say a company has all the ingredients in place—a code of ethics, a code of conduct, and ethics training. Now it's time to throw all of these ingredients into the pot and blend them into an ethics management program. An **ethics management program** establishes and maintains company-wide policies that explain and demonstrate acceptable behavior and decisions. When organizations institute ethics management programs, employees should be on the same page in terms of vision and day-to-day policies.

A company's ethics management program may involve ethics training seminars, or it may be incorporated as part of employee performance appraisals. When employees are evaluated on the basis of their ethical conduct, they have a strong incentive to make sure they do the right thing on the job. The management program is often customized to fit the organization. If you work for an auto body shop, for example, you wouldn't use exactly the same ethics management program as a retail store.

It bears repeating that for any ethical program to work, the people in charge need to support and model the program. For example, Caterpillar, a major manufacturer and distributor of machinery, utilizes an ethics management program that starts at the top and works its way down. Chief Ethics and Compliance Officer Ed Scott says, "our leaders work to ensure that our Values In Action [Caterpillar's worldwide code of conduct] are part of everyday life at Caterpillar." As an international company, Caterpillar makes sure that its code of ethics is spread to its foreign offices. It has an annual ethics assessment and questionnaire that is translated into 14 languages and is a requirement for every employee. Indeed, Caterpillar has built an ethical reputation over the years, and the current company leadership strives to maintain this reputation. In fact, Caterpillar was selected as one of the 2009 World's Most Ethical Companies by the Ethisphere Institute, an international think tank dedicated to promoting business ethics.[14]

Tool 7: Ethics Committees

Making decisions for a company is never a one-person operation. The leaders of a company often need to gather input from other people before taking action—especially when it comes to ethics. That's why some businesses set up a formal ethics committee to oversee and implement ethics policies. An ethics committee helps a company reflect its values through everyday policies. If an ethics committee decides to commit to helping the environment, you'd expect to see recycling receptacles through the area. Or, if the committee decides to focus on customer service and satisfaction, you'd expect to see policies regarding phone calls or customer interaction.[15]

Your Own Code of Ethics and Conduct

You've seen how companies establish a code of ethics and a code of conduct. Does that mean that employees just sit around and wait for the company to tell them how to act? Of course not. Every day, you make choices about how to behave based on your own informal, unwritten ethical code. But as an individual, it can be helpful to write down this personal code of ethics and conduct so that you can more carefully follow it in your life and career. Your code may include such things as the beliefs you value and the behaviors you will follow, such as not cheating or stealing. No matter whether you write them down or not, critically thinking about your own ethics will help you make decisions that are better in line with your values, both on a personal and professional level.

Do It...

8.2: Write Your Own Code of Conduct Write a code of conduct for your own life and career. Capture your entire code on one page, and be prepared to post or submit it electronically or present it to your class.

Now Debrief...

- It's important for businesses to establish an ethical tone. To help them do this, there are various methods they can use: a sort of "ethical toolbox" consisting of a number of tools.
  1. Leaders of the organization set an ethical example, doing the right thing as a model for employees.
  2. The organization focuses on more than just profit.
  3. A **code of ethics** is created.
  4. A **code of conduct** is followed.
  5. An **ethics training program** may be offered in some cases.
  6. An **ethics management program** may be instituted to establish company-wide ethics policies.
  7. An ethics committee may be formed to give ethical advice.
- A company does not have to use all of these tools to be ethical, but these tools provide solid guidelines.

3. Making Ethical Decisions

In an ethical organization, every member of that organization must be an ethics manager. In this section, we'll look at some approaches to making ethical decisions, and then we'll establish a step-by-step process to help guide you through an ethical dilemma. Let's start by looking at some informal approaches to making an ethical decision.

Informal Approaches to Making Ethical Decisions

You probably know that going through the drive-through isn't the best way to get a healthy meal, but it is often the easiest. The same is true for making ethical decisions—sometimes, making an unethical decision may be the easier road to travel. However, there are several quick checks you can perform to assess whether you're headed down an ethical path:

1. Before you follow through with any decision, check out your stomach. Any butterflies there? If you feel uncomfortable with a decision, it might be time to reevaluate what you're about to do.[16]

2. Another quick way to test whether you're on track with a decision is to consider what your boss or mentor might do in the same situation. Think about someone you know and respect. What would he or she do in your shoes? It might even be worth having a conversation with your boss or mentor about the situation.

3. Another quick ethical check is to imagine what you would feel like if your decision were to appear on the front page of *The New York Times* or on your Facebook profile. How would you feel about your decision if it were publicly known?

Formal Approaches to Making Ethical Decisions

Aside from these informal methods, there are also formal approaches that require you to really think critically about a situation.

Utilitarianism

Do the ends justify the means? This is the question posed by utilitarianism. **Utilitarianism** is a philosophical principle that approaches a decision, whether ethical or not, by focusing on the best interests of the majority of the people involved. This emphasizes the *end product* of a decision, not the process it takes to get there. Problems can arise, however, because some utilitarians believe the end result justifies *whatever* path was used to get there.[17] When using this method, it's important that you don't completely overlook the path taken. If you do, you may be entering questionable ethical territory.

One idea of utilitarianism is that all benefits and drawbacks are quantifiable and can be boiled down into numbers. For example, let's say a manufacturer of high chairs for babies realizes a defect in the high chair that causes the tray in front of the baby to come loose if the baby moves around too much. If the tray becomes loose, the baby can potentially fall out of the chair. To fix the problem, it will cost the manufacturer $9 per chair to recall and replace the tray and bracket that connect to the chair. So far, the manufacturer has already produced 750,000 chairs. This means the total cost of repairing the defect is $6.75 million (750,000 × $9 to repair each chair).

After testing the chairs, the manufacturer realizes only 1 in 100 chairs have the defect, which is equivalent to 7,500 chairs. Let's say the company estimates the cost of an injury to a baby at $50,000. If the manufacturer doesn't fix the defect, the potential cost of injuries is $375 million (7,500 chairs × $50,000 per injury). The cost of the recall is substantially lower than the potential cost of injury ($6.75 million compared with $375 million), so it makes sense for the manufacturer to fix the problem, which is also good news for the babies involved.

Although this example had an obvious conclusion, what if the cost of injury had been *less* expensive than the cost of fixing the repair? Is it ethical for a company to sell high chairs that are potentially dangerous for babies? Also, is it acceptable to put a price on an injury or, in some cases, on a life? There is no definite yes or no answer to this. These are just examples of the uncomfortable decisions that businesses sometimes have to make.

Cost-Benefit Analysis

The high-chair recall scenario above is an example of a cost-benefit analysis. A **cost-benefit analysis** is used in budgeting and planning to compare the total benefits of a project against the cost of going through with a project.

Let's say a corporation is interested in volunteering to build a park in a busy urban area. Figuring out the cost is fairly easy; the company needs to buy the land, sod, flowers, hire workers, etc. But how can a company figure out the benefits of a project like this? Some benefits are intangible: aside from the aesthetic beauty it brings to a neighborhood, the company is creating a safe place for children to play and a family to spend time. How much is that worth? And although this may be a philanthropic project, the corporation may get publicity from local news stations, which could generate interest and potential revenue. In addition, the philanthropic project may qualify the corporation for some tax breaks from the government.

Business leaders must consider issues like these before jumping into a costly project of any kind. This analysis helps not only figure out the best action to take, but it also helps leaders decide whether action is necessary in the first place.

Moral Rights Principle Of course, costs and benefits aren't the only issues to take into account. There is also the **moral rights principle**. Moral rights (often called human rights) are basic fundamental rights everyone possesses, such as the right to be free and to be treated equally. In 1948, the United Nations created a formal document called *The Universal Declaration of Human Rights*. Because the perception of moral rights varies, this declaration has helped reduce squabbling over what actually constitutes moral rights. Followers of the moral rights approach believe there are actions that are either right or wrong, and there are basic moral principles that should not be violated, even for the greatest good of the majority.

For example, most people would rather pay less than more for a good. However, according to the U.N. *Declaration*, it's not morally right to obtain inexpensive goods if they're produced through the use of sweatshops (manufacturing centers with inhumane working conditions and excessively low wages) or if the company doesn't follow other ethical guidelines in their production. If the only way to create cheap goods is through sweatshops or other unethical means, then people shouldn't be able to buy these goods. A utilitarian may argue that many people are benefiting at the expense of a few laborers, so it justifies the decision. However, someone who believes that moral rights should hold some sway in business would claim that any violation of these rights is wrong.

Universalist Principle You've heard of the Golden Rule: Do unto others as you would have them do unto you. The **universalist principle** has similarities to the Golden Rule in that, before making a decision, you ask yourself if the decision would be fair for *everyone* in all circumstances. If so, then ask yourself how you'd feel if the decision was applied to you. Let's say you run a shoe business. You currently manufacture your product in the United States and make a pretty good profit, but your family is telling you to manufacture overseas because it's much cheaper. Then imagine you're the U.S. worker who will lose your job to someone overseas so your boss can make more money—does that seem right to you? Probably not. However, as the business owner, you may not be too worried about the U.S. workers, because your business is healthy and you're living comfortably.

Virtue Principle Let's look at the previous example again. If you're the shoe business owner, what if personal feelings come into play? What if you feel empathy for the U.S. workers who are trying to support their families? You might be hesitant to move production overseas and take away their jobs, even though it would be the best move financially. This is where the virtue principle comes into play. The **virtue principle** looks at a person's character. It involves figuring out which course of action relates to good moral character. Supporters of the virtue principle believe that good moral character can help guide someone toward a morally appropriate decision. This relates back to one of the informal ethical checks discussed earlier: What would your mentor do in your shoes? If you suspect that decision A is the moral decision, then you'd probably make decision A. Showing good moral character or following in the footsteps of someone you consider to be moral helps you figure out the best thing to do.

Distributive Justice Making ethical decisions isn't just about what philosophies or principles you hold. Let's look at something more practical: distributive justice. The **distributive justice principle** focuses on distributing benefits throughout society based on what's fair—basically, that people should receive fair benefits in relation to the work they do, or the burden they take on. One common example of distributive justice is salaries. Let's say Jeremy and Alison work for the same company and have the same duties and salaries. However, Jeremy works longer hours and produces more work per hour than Alison, so theoretically shouldn't he get paid more than she does? This approach is usually not strictly practiced, although this may help you explain why your coworker who does the same job as you makes less (or more) than you do. Generally, it acts more as a guide in distributing benefits fairly throughout an organization.

Table 8.1 sums up the formal approaches to ethical decision making we've discussed. Next let's look at a step-by-step approach.

Table **8.1** | **Formal Approaches to Ethical Decision Making**

Approach	Definition/Description	Example
Utilitarianism	• Focuses on the best interests of the majority • Believes that benefits and drawbacks are quantifiable • Focuses on whether the ends justify the means	Before recalling a faulty baby high chair, a company may compare the estimated cost of injury to the cost of recalling every chair.
Cost-Benefit Analysis	• Used in budgeting and planning to compare the benefits of a project against its cost	A corporation may weigh the cost of building a new park with the benefits of building the park.
Moral Rights Principle	• States that actions are either morally right or wrong, and that there are basic moral principles that should not be violated	Customers may refuse to buy products that were made by sweatshop workers because it goes against their moral beliefs.
Universalist Principle	• States that before making a decision, you need to determine whether the decision would be fair for *everyone* in all circumstances	A business owner may need to decide whether moving production overseas would be fair to his or her employees.
Virtue Principle	• Involves determining which course of action relates to good moral character	People might make a decision based on what they think their mentor would do in the same situation.
Distributive Justice Principle	• Focuses on distributing benefits to individuals fairly according to the burdens they take on	An employee who works more hours and produces more per hour should be paid more than a less-productive worker.

A Step-by-Step Approach to Making an Ethical Decision

Although the previous approaches may help steer you in the right ethical direction, it's helpful to have a concrete process to follow when faced with an ethical dilemma. Let's say you're a supervising editor for a magazine. You've just found out your best writer plagiarized from another publication last year. You're the only one who knows. What should you do?

1. When an ethical dilemma arises, your first step should be to get all the facts. Start by stating the issue as you know it in one or two sentences. Then ask yourself questions such as: (a) What do I know? (b) What are the hidden elements that are not obvious or are difficult to discuss? This is an important step—you can't make a good decision if you don't know all the facts.

- *In the example of the writer who plagiarized, are you sure this is the only time she plagiarized? Try to figure out if there is anything you don't know. What do you know about the other publication the writer plagiarized from? Why weren't you able to catch the plagiarism when it happened?*

2. Next, you need to consider who your decision will affect. Take a 360° view and consider the dilemma from multiple perspectives.
   - *Will your decision affect just you? Your coworkers? Your manager? Investors? Customers? If you fire this writer for plagiarism, how will it affect the company? What if you don't fire the writer? What does that mean for your magazine? Is it possible the story might leak and the entire magazine might come under fire? If this happens, shareholders and readers may question other stories. What if you find other plagiarized material?*
3. After figuring out all the major pieces of the puzzle, you need to continue to gather more information and research similar instances.
   - *Are there similar situations in your organization or in another that can shed light on the subject? If so, research and learn all you can. What was the outcome? Was it successful? How was it similar? How was it different?*
4. Take as much information as possible and use the formal decision-making approaches discussed earlier to come up with potential solutions.
   - *For example, the virtue principle would require you to look inward for an answer to the dilemma. If you allow this person to continue writing for the magazine, what does that say about you? It may say you don't want to rock the boat and are worried about what other people will think. On the other hand, it may say that by giving the writer another chance, you are embracing forgiveness.*
5. After seeing all of your potential solutions, choose the best decision and look at it again from different perspectives. Look back at the four BizHats and how they will be affected by your decision. Also consider the triple bottom line perspective, which requires organizations to consider people and the environment in addition to profit when making decisions.
   - *How will your decision about the writer's plagiarism affect the four BizHats? Will it impact society at large? Or the ethical culture in your office? Your reaction to plagiarism may set a precedent in your company and directly affect similar instances in the future.*
6. Next, take another look at your decision. If you still feel comfortable, implement it.
   - *In the case of detected plagiarism, you may decide to keep working with the writer or you may decide to fire her.*

Clearly, arriving at a decision is not an easy process. But by following these steps, in most cases you should be able to decide on a course of action you and your business are comfortable with.

No matter what your decision, there will be consequences you should be prepared for. In the case of the writer who plagiarized, you would need to determine whether your decision caused any problems inside or outside the office. If so, you would want to look at your decision again and see if there was a better solution you could apply should the dilemma reoccur.

Ethics Showdown: What to Do When Your Ethics Conflicts with Company Ethics

Sometimes, personal ethics conflict with the actions or vision of employers. It can be minor—perhaps there is a disagreement with the termination of a coworker—or it can be major, such as discovering a cover-up within the organization. Here are a few suggestions for what you should do if you find yourself in the middle of an ethical struggle.

If you see someone doing something you believe is inappropriate:

- Give your coworker the benefit of the doubt. There may be something innocent going on that you don't know about.
- It may be helpful to check your employee handbook and see if your company has any policies dealing with the situation.

- Approach your manager to get more information on what you should do. This gives your manager a chance to address the situation.
- If you don't think your manager handled the situation effectively and if you think the situation warrants it, your next step would be to contact your company's human resources department in private.

Again, if this doesn't work, you should *carefully* consider taking the problem further up the chain of command. Using good judgment is key, as not all matters need to be taken up the corporate chain.

In extreme cases, if the company does not address the issue internally and the behavior is very serious—such as embezzlement or fraud or if customer health or welfare is on the line—you may consider contacting someone on the outside, such as the board of directors or a newspaper. If you speak out against an organization or publicize something unethical, you may be called a whistleblower. **Whistleblowers** are employees or former employees of an organization who allege misconduct by the organization.

You may have heard of the famous whistleblower case of Jeffrey Wigand and the tobacco industry, dramatized in the 1999 movie *The Insider*. Wigand was the director of research at Brown & Williamson, then the third largest tobacco company in the United States, and made $300,000 a year.[18] In the mid-1990s, Wigand went public with his accusations against the tobacco company. Wigand claimed executives knew all along that nicotine was addictive. He also claimed executives manipulated the effect of nicotine by adding chemical additives to tobacco products. Not surprisingly, Wigand was fired, but his ordeal wasn't over. Anonymous callers threatened his family, and his wife eventually filed for divorce. Afterward, he wasn't able to find a corporate job, so he ended up teaching high school science for a tenth of what he used to earn. Do you think he did the right thing? Wigand's testimony before Congress was one of the most damning indictments against the tobacco industry. However, the tobacco industry is still going strong, while Wigand's life will never be the same.

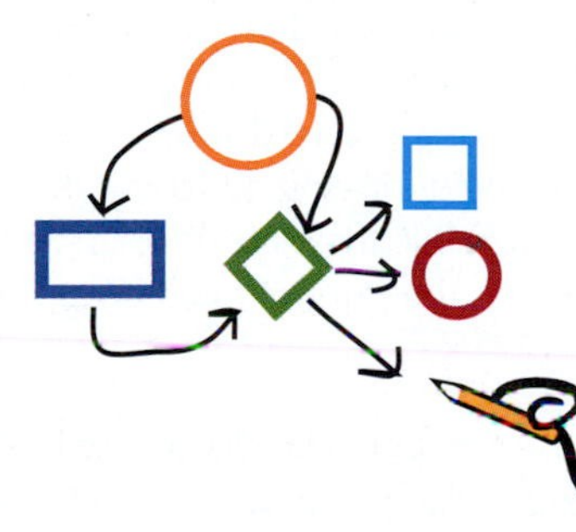

Do It...

8.3: Walk Through the Ethical Decision-Making Process Go back to the beginning of the chapter and reread the chapter-opening story ("To Fire or Not to Fire," page 183). Then, describe how Donald Arnold might walk through each of the six steps of the ethical decision-making process to arrive at a final decision about how he will downsize his department from five to three, and whether Martin Cunningham should be one of the employees to be let go.

Now Debrief...

- Facing an ethical dilemma head-on can be stressful and uncomfortable. However, there are approaches available to help you make a decision.
- Informal approaches include the butterflies-in-the-stomach, what would a mentor do, and front-page news tests.
- More formal approaches include **utilitarianism**, **cost-benefit analysis**, the **moral rights principle**, the **universalist principle**, the **virtue principle**, and the **distributive justice principle**.
- Another way to help you figure out a dilemma is to follow a step-by-step approach: 1. Get all the facts; 2. Consider who your decision will affect; 3. Research similar instances; 4. Use the formal decision-making approaches to come up with potential solutions; 5. Choose the best decision and look at it again from different perspectives; 6. Take another look at your decision; and if the decision still seems good, implement it.
- Employees or former employees of an organization who allege extreme misconduct by the organization to outside sources are referred to as **whistleblowers**.

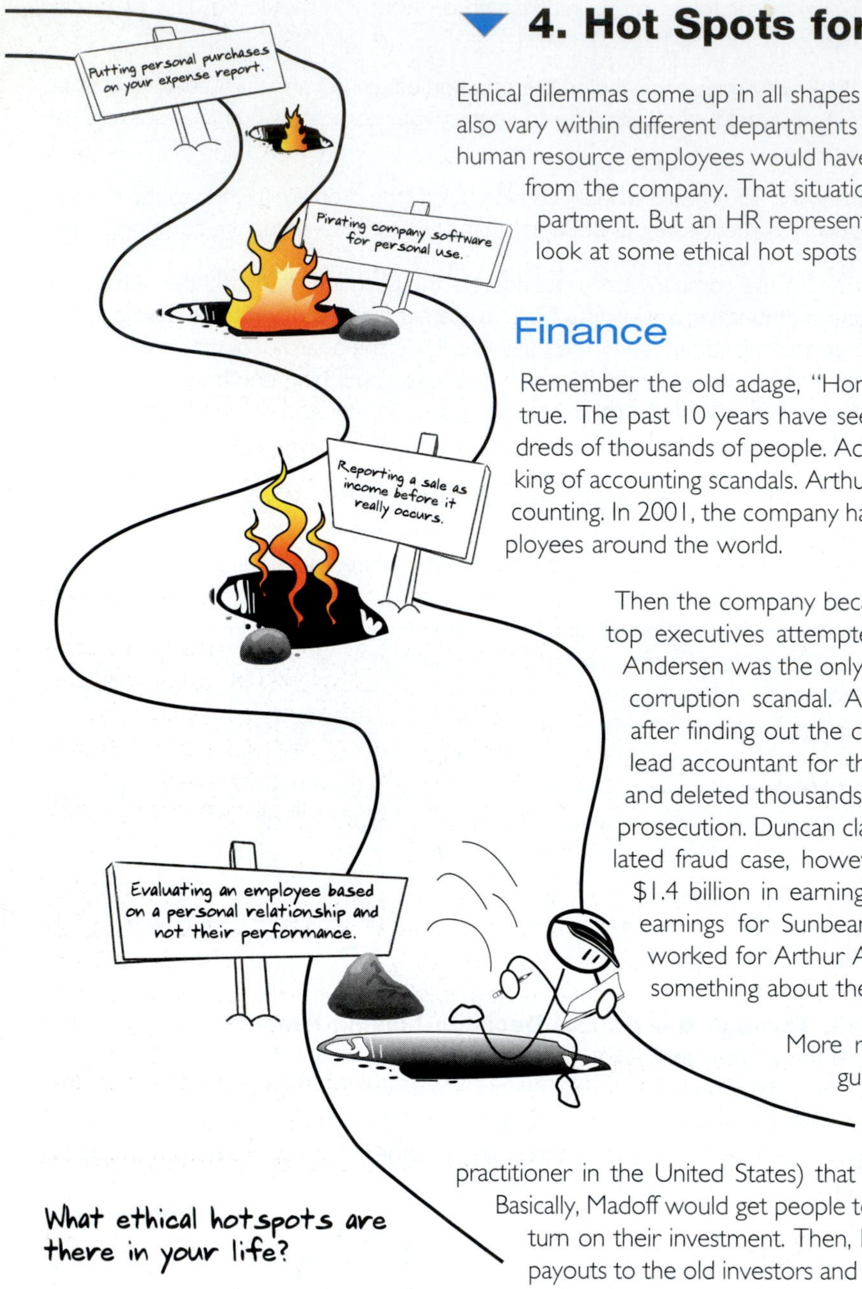

4. Hot Spots for Ethical Dilemmas

Ethical dilemmas come up in all shapes and sizes. Not only do they vary by profession, but they also vary within different departments of an organization. For example, it's not very likely that human resource employees would have the opportunity to hatch a scheme to embezzle money from the company. That situation would be more likely to occur in the accounting department. But an HR representative may act unethically when it comes to hiring. Let's look at some ethical hot spots found in organizations.

Finance

Remember the old adage, "Honesty is the best policy"? In accounting this is especially true. The past 10 years have seen accounting fraud and scandals that have misled hundreds of thousands of people. Accounting firm Arthur Andersen may take the cake as the king of accounting scandals. Arthur Andersen was a huge power player in the world of accounting. In 2001, the company had over $9 billion in revenue with more than 85,000 employees around the world.

Then the company became embroiled in the infamous Enron debacle, in which top executives attempted to cover up losses to protect stock prices. Arthur Andersen was the only outside auditing firm of Enron and had taken part in the corruption scandal. Arthur Andersen's misdeeds don't stop there. The day after finding out the company was being investigated by the government, the lead accountant for the Enron account, David Duncan, shredded documents and deleted thousands of e-mails—destroying the paper trail that could lead to prosecution. Duncan claims he was simply following orders. This was not an isolated fraud case, however. Arthur Andersen was also involved in overstating $1.4 billion in earnings for Waste Management and inflating $110 million in earnings for Sunbeam.[19] This is not to say that all the accountants who worked for Arthur Andersen were unethical, but the level of fraud does say something about the culture of the company.

More recently, in 2009, businessman Bernard Madoff pleaded guilty to 11 felony charges—including securities fraud and money laundering—after running an elaborate Ponzi scheme (named after Charles Ponzi, its most notorious practitioner in the United States) that bilked thousands of investors out of their life savings.[20] Basically, Madoff would get people to give money to his company by promising them a big return on their investment. Then, he would take money from new investors to make huge payouts to the old investors and repeat the process over and over. When Madoff's crimes were finally discovered, countless lives were ruined. Among his victims were director Steven Spielberg and the owner of the New York Mets.[21]

Government agencies like the *U.S. Securities and Exchange Commission (SEC)* were created to help protect investors from situations like these and to make sure the playing field in the securities industry is level and fair. To help consumers gain trust in the market, the government created the SEC in 1934, during the Great Depression. Two factors that led to the stock market crash in 1929 were unreliable information and abuse of financing.[22] The two primary goals of the SEC are to have publicly traded companies provide honest information to the public and to have people who are involved in securities, such as brokers and dealers, put the interest of the investor first. With these two concepts in place, the public is able to make an informed decision for themselves.

One of the laws the SEC enforces is the **Sarbanes-Oxley Act**, which is officially called the *Public Company Accounting Reform and Investor Protection Act of 2002*. The act was created as a reaction to the collapse of mega companies such as Enron and WorldCom. The goal is to protect investors from fraudulent accounting practices. It stipulates financial responsibility by the CEO and the CFO (Chief Financial Officer) of the company, internal audits, and independent outside audits.

Putting personal purchases on your expense report.

Pirating company software for personal use.

Reporting a sale as income before it really occurs.

Evaluating an employee based on a personal relationship and not their performance.

What ethical hotspots are there in your life?

When auditors process financial statements, they need to follow *generally accepted accounting principles (GAAP)*. In Chapter 1, you learned how these principles act as guidelines for accountants for preparing financial statements—sort of like rules in a soccer game. The point of having the principles is to make sure reported information is true. Outside parties, like stockholders, need to trust that the information they receive is accurate. These guidelines help make sure reports are consistently accurate and that inaccuracies are caught, whether they're deliberate or not. Basically, GAAP tries to keep accountants honest and ethical.

Not all accounting scandals are splashed across the news, however. In fact, they may not be very scandalous at all. Here are some common dilemmas accountants face:

- At what point is a sale a sale—that is, when should a sale be recorded as revenue on an income statement?
- I'm a private accountant; is it unethical for me to work for competing companies?
- What should I do if a client asks me to "cook the books"—misrepresent financial data—to cover up some one-time expenses that will only end up alarming investors and hurting the company in the long run?

Human Resources

You've seen how a few bad apples in the accounting department can wreak havoc on a company. But that's not the only department that can act unethically. For example, consider human resource (HR) employees. HR employees have a part in hiring, firing, salary, and discipline decisions. They're also involved in situations regarding harassment, confidentiality, and general grievances throughout the organization. In other words, there are many opportunities for unethical behavior. HR employees assist in handling other people's ethical dilemmas, but there are also challenges that HR employees themselves face.

The hiring process provides many opportunities for HR employees to act unethically. Although an HR employee may not interview a potential candidate, that person probably reviews résumés and forwards them to the appropriate department. If inclined, an HR employee could easily discriminate against candidates based on background, experience, or even names and only pass along résumés they like or of people they know.

In addition to this, here are a couple more common dilemmas HR employees have to deal with:

- I found inappropriate comments and pictures on an employee's social networking account. What should I do?
- I heard from another coworker that a supervisor is dating his supervisee. What should I do?
- My supervisor told me that he would give me a bonus if I didn't report a payroll "mistake." What should I do?

Marketing

When a commercial pops up on your TV, you probably don't think about how much planning and careful consideration went into making it. Yet marketing employees face plenty of tricky ethical issues when deciding how to advertise. Although most adults can see through faulty claims, often children cannot. Children might see a fun tiger talking to them and being friendly, but they don't understand the cereal being advertised is full of sugar. Situations such as these can lead to murky ethical choices. Although children are consumers and have some say in what their parents purchase, is it responsible to promote directly to them?

Marketing isn't all about advertising though. Here are a few more common ethical dilemmas marketing employees face:

- How far should I go to uncover information about a competitor? Is posing as a customer and calling my competitor's toll-free number unethical?

- One of my favorite customers asked for a special deal that I wouldn't offer other customers. Should I do it to get the sale?
- Our brochure lists a product feature we thought would be included with the product, but is not. Should I correct the brochure, or hope no one notices?

Management

As a manager, how far would you go to keep your employees productive and your business profitable? Consider this: if you were on the board of directors for a company and discovered that another board member was leaking company secrets to the press, how far would you go to figure out who was leaking the information? Would you try to access e-mails the board members sent? Would you physically follow board members and their families? Go through their trash? This last question may seem funny, but this exact scenario happened at technology giant Hewlett-Packard (HP).

In 2005, HP board members began seeing company secrets popping up in some of the country's most prominent papers—secrets that included the future direction of the organization and confidential discussions about purchasing other companies. HP was determined to find out the source of the leak—and they broke several laws trying to do so. A few months later, the chairman of the HP board, Patricia Dunn, was indicted, along with private investigators, for spying. What had they done? Investigators had obtained Social Security numbers for board members, employees, and reporters to access their personal phone records. This scheme, known as *pretexting*, involved investigators pretending to be someone else to get the telephone company to grant them access to private information. This allowed the investigators to create online accounts that contained phone logs for the people under investigation.[23] Aside from pretexting, investigators physically followed people, went through their trash, sent hidden software in e-mails to further facilitate spying, and discussed planting spies in the newsrooms that were reporting the leaked information. Not only were these practices unethical, many of them were also illegal. HP's leadership claimed they were able to identify the person who created the leak, but can this end result justify the methods used to get there?

Here are more ethical dilemmas management faces:

- What's okay to charge on a business trip? I don't feel like I get paid what I deserve. Is it okay to expense non-business-related items to make up for this shortfall?
- A friend of mine works for me. Is it inappropriate that I treat her differently from her coworkers, given that she is my friend?
- I'm managing projects for two competing companies right now. Is this unethical?

Information Technology (IT)

Even though many IT workers may not work directly with clients and employees, they still have access to plenty of confidential information. Whenever a person is in a position to know a lot about someone or something, that person has a great responsibility not to misuse or abuse that power.[24]

If you're an IT person, part of your job is to make sure people don't access inappropriate sites, like illegal file-sharing sites. You can either block access to specific Web sites or monitor who's looking at what. Or, you can do a little bit of both. But, how much is too much? When does monitoring morph into surveillance?

It's the same with employee e-mail. Your company's IT department may monitor its employees' e-mail usage to make sure they're not goofing off. As an IT employee, is it ethical to read other people's e-mails? If so, how many e-mails can be read or monitored before it's considered inappropriate? The funny thing about ethics is that there is no all encompassing "right" or "wrong" answer. Often, it's up to the judgment of the person asking the question.

In addition to issues surrounding surveillance, IT people may also ask themselves:

- Does the fact that private information is accessible make it ethical to access it?
- Some employees save personal documents on their computers. Is it ethical to view these documents?
- What data belongs to an employer, and what data is private, on an employer-provided workstation?
- Do employees have a right to know the degree to which they are being monitored?

Global Ethics Issues

With so many different countries and cultures around the world, sometimes things can get lost in translation. We covered some global ethical issues in Chapter 5, but we delve deeper into this topic here.

In the United States, you might give someone a thumbs-up sign to show happiness or approval. But if you flashed a thumbs-up to someone in the Middle East, well, let's just say it wouldn't make anyone too happy. In some cultures, the thumbs-up is considered obscene.

In the same vein, business ethics can vary from culture to culture. With so many different beliefs and cultures working together throughout the world, there are bound to be differences. Often, you hear about ethical problems involving multinational corporations. A *multinational corporation*, as it sounds, is a corporation that has assets, including facilities, in at least one other country outside of its home location. The corporation gets involved with many different belief systems and cultures. Generally, hundreds or thousands of people across the world work together in these types of organizations. That is a lot of people who have very different beliefs about what is and isn't ethical. Imagine you have a cleaning business. It's much easier to clean one room than to clean all the houses on the block, right? Let's also say that one of the homeowners isn't as strict with what it means to be clean. This may give you an opportunity to slack off. This means you could clean that house much faster and make the same amount of money. What an opportunity! This can mirror international business operations. If one country isn't as strict with regulations, this can lead to ethical problems.

Take for instance the Alang ship graveyard in Gujarat, India. This area used to be home to pristine, sandy beaches and clear water, but now it's a giant scrap yard for ship breaking. After ships have worn down, many of them go to this beach to be ripped apart and recycled. Every year, approximately 300 ships go to Alang to be dismantled, amounting to three million tons of steel.[25] There are no formal records at the shipyard, but estimates suggest as many as 30 to 40 thousand laborers work at the yard, and that 20 percent of families in the area depend on the shipyard for their livelihoods.[26]

To people in neighboring cities, Alang represents a modern-day boomtown. This keeps the supply of cheap labor steady. It isn't until the workers get to the shipyard that they see how hard and dangerous the job is. There are no high-tech utilities or equipment, like electricity or machines; laborers use their hands, hammers, chisels, and blowtorches to break the ships apart. As the men work, fumes from burning steel and paint are everywhere. Not surprisingly, many men develop respiratory problems. Additionally, many of the ships contain asbestos and toxic chemicals that the men must work around. Doctors in the nearby Red Cross hospital also say that workers experience high levels of malaria, cholera, and leprosy.[27] The laborers often live in horrible conditions because the owners of the shipyard do not provide homes, electricity, or running water. Aside from this long list of dangers, the actual job of ship breaking is dangerous; falling steel and burns often prove fatal. With all of these drawbacks, why do you think Alang is allowed to remain in business?

Some experts blame the West. Many of the contaminants and pollutants of these ships are banned by international law, but in some areas these laws are ignored in order to generate profits.[28] There are many dirty jobs in the world that someone has to do. Business people know this, and they also know the cheaper the better. Many Western nations send their ships to Alang because they get the best deal, and because environmental and labor laws in their own countries would not allow the same practices. If a ship graveyard popped up in the United States, the cost would be significantly higher because of required safety standards. Areas like Alang, though, are lax in enforcing a code of standards regarding pay and safety. This can lead dishonest businessmen in multinational corporations to manipulate the system and take advantage of more favorable laws, taxes, and standards to increase their profit margins.

Situations like the one at Alang have caused many people to believe that international policies need to be created and enforced. The Caux Round Table (CRT) is an international organization focused on promoting morality and sustainability in the workplace.[29] In order to guide businesses in the right direction, the CRT has developed a set of ethical principles that it believes can translate to organizations all over the world. Incidents like the recent global financial crisis and Bernie Madoff's Ponzi scheme highlight the need for concrete ethical practices and transparency in business. The seven basic principles of the CRT include:

1. Respect stakeholders beyond just shareholders;
2. Contribute to economic, social, and environmental development;
3. Respect the letter and spirit of the law;
4. Respect rules and conventions;
5. Support responsible globalization;
6. Respect the environment; and
7. Avoid illicit activities.[30]

Working together internationally is no easy task, but if companies can follow some basic ethical principles, international business can flourish and still be ethical.

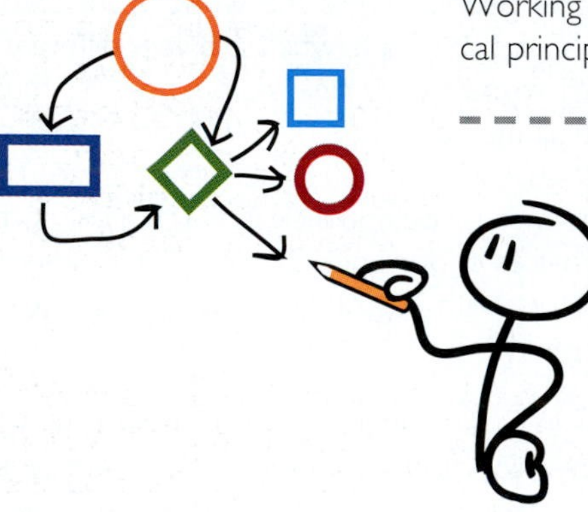

Do It...

8.4: Identify What Went Wrong Read the following examples of ethical lapses and describe, in 25 words or less each, which step(s) of the ethical decision-making process outlined on pages 193–194 was omitted, thus causing the situation to occur.

1. A consumer group presents evidence that a company inappropriately sold customer information they obtained from its Web site to other companies who wanted to target the same customers.
2. The HR department in an organization hires a lesser-qualified candidate because he is in a personal relationship with a member of the hiring committee.

Now Debrief...

- Ethical dilemmas or misconduct can take place anywhere in an organization, from entry level to CEO.
- Each department, area, or function has different hotspots where unethical and/or illegal acts are most likely to occur. For example, members of the accounting department may face dilemmas regarding fraud; human resources, discrimination; marketing, manipulation; and management and IT, spying or invasion of privacy.
- Other conflicts can be created a world away. Multinational corporations have assets, including facilities, in at least one other country outside their home location. This brings together many different belief systems and cultural norms. Because of this, international organizations like the Caux Round Table have been created to promote morality and sustainability in the global workplace.

5. Corporate Social Responsibility and Sustainability: Working Together for People, the Planet, and Profit

When it comes to business ethics, the story isn't over yet. Sure, ethics are important to business owners and employees. But what about everybody else? If businesses hope to be successful, they need to look at the bigger picture and figure out how they can have a positive effect on the world around them.

■ CSR is putting ethics into action. It's when a company "walks the talk."

In fact, as a result of sound ethical practices, there are now strict rules on child labor and safety measures. Anti-trust laws, which prohibit unfair practices and monopolies, also help level the business playing field and instill fairness in business. Additionally, unions and government agencies help establish good working conditions for employees. These positive results of business ethics are known today as corporate social responsibility. **Corporate social responsibility (CSR)** involves an organization looking beyond its own self-interest to consider the interests of society. This means the organization is responsible for its impact on shareholders, the community, and the environment. ■ CSR is putting ethics into action. It's when a company "walks the talk."

Sustainability and the Triple Bottom Line

One important part of CSR is sustainability. As we discussed in Chapter 3, *sustainability* is a company's capacity to create profit for its shareholders today while making sure that its business interests are also in the best interests of the environment and other stakeholders. A company that uses resources irresponsibly and doesn't have a solid plan for the future probably isn't going to stick around very long. Thus, sustainable business organizations have an eye on both the present and the future.[31] As mentioned earlier, the traditional bottom line for business was profit. However, to remain sustainable, companies must focus on the *triple bottom line* of people, planet, and profit, combining economic success with responsible social and environmental activities. In fact, the triple bottom line is slowly becoming the gold standard for measuring sustainable businesses.[32]

Focus on People

So what is the point of corporate social responsibility and sustainability? In part it is to help people. ■ The triple bottom line approach to sustainability suggests that when businesses benefit, the benefit echoes throughout society—people have jobs and therefore money to buy goods, establish a home, and ensure a higher standard of living. Just think back to the crash of the U.S. housing market in 2008. Unsustainable practices led to the near-collapse of both the real estate and financial industries, and many people lost their jobs and their homes as a result.

■ The triple bottom line approach to sustainability suggests that when businesses benefit, the benefit echoes throughout society.

A focus on people also leads to *corporate philanthropy*—social programs and charitable donations made by businesses that have a tangible impact on people's lives. Take, for example, the Target Corporation. It gives 5 percent of its income to communities, equaling about $3 million a week. This money is spent on various charitable and educational programs, as well as the "Target House," a home for families of children being treated at St. Jude Children's Research Hospital in Memphis, Tennessee.[33]

However, as we mentioned in Chapter 3, companies with a triple bottom line focus do not just consider external customers and stakeholders. They also focus on their internal customers, individuals who work for the organization. By taking good care of their employees (or team members, as they are called at Target), providing health insurance and many other benefits, sustainable organizations are working to ensure a happy, loyal workforce for the long term.

Focus on the Planet

You have undoubtedly heard of things "going green." In fact, environmentalism is considered one of the most important movements since the end of World War II.[34] The prospect of dwindling natural resources and climate change has caused a lot of businesses to develop more environmentally sustainable practices.

How do companies actually go about adopting more sustainable practices? Two very basic ways are eco-efficiency and eco-capitalism. The idea behind eco-efficiency was created in 1992 by the World Council for Sustainable Development. *Eco-efficiency* means "producing more with less."[35] The goal is to produce more goods or services using fewer resources. This means reducing waste and improving efficiency. As many companies that have focused on eco-efficiency have found, doing more with less can lead to a competitive advantage due to an increase in resource productivity.[36]

Another emerging idea that promotes sustainability is eco-capitalism. *Eco-capitalism* is the idea that "natural capital" exists through natural goods such as renewable and nonrenewable resources, and that capital is valuable for human consumption. Strategies and products that promote eco-capitalism are good for the environment, and some are also cheaper alternatives compared to traditional products. For example, New Jersey's TerraCycle Inc.'s first product was organic plant food made from worm waste. The company took worm waste, processed it, and turned it into a product that renews natural capital.[37] The company now sells a variety of environmentally friendly products of all kinds.

Focus on Profits

Sustainability sounds great, but achieving it is no easy task. Think of it from your own perspective. As an individual, you may have your own triple bottom line. You may want to be environmentally friendly and give back to the community—but how can you give back if you can barely afford to pay your own rent? Without money, stuff can't happen. This is why making money, or profit, is one of the three bottom lines, and the other two can't exist without it. In business terms, **profit motive** refers to a company's desire to make more money than it spends. It is the motive to do something for profit. You can probably relate to that. If a neighbor asked you to rake the leaves in his front yard for nothing, you probably wouldn't want to do it. How about if your neighbor offered you $20? You'd probably feel more motivated.

■ Focusing on sustainable business practices, both from a social and environmental point of view, can provide companies with a competitive edge, leading to long-term profits and sustainable success.

So does being ethically responsible pay off? The *Wall Street Journal* conducted a test to see how much people were willing to pay for one pound of coffee that came from a company perceived to be ethical, a neutral company (the control group), or a company perceived to be unethical. Take a minute to think about how you would respond in this situation. If you knew a company made something the "right" way, how much would you favor it? How much would you avoid the unethical company? Would you even buy the unethical company's coffee?

The results were interesting. The mean price that people were willing to pay for one pound of the ethically produced coffee was $9.71. It was $8.31 for the control group, and $5.89 for the unethically produced coffee.[38] People were willing to pay nearly four dollars more for the coffee from the ethical company than from the unethical one. This is just a hypothetical situation, but it gives a strong indication that being ethical can lead to greater profits for a company. Indeed, as we've discussed, ■ focusing on sustainable business practices, both from a social and environmental point of view, can provide companies with a competitive edge, leading to long-term profits and sustainable success.

Walking the Talk

The TBL is the new gold-standard in ethical, sustainable business. but some companies choose to go well above and beyond the TBL. In 1992, Gary Erickson founded Clif Bar to produce organic energy bars. Just eight years later, he was offered $100 million for his company.[39] But Erickson loved what he did so much that he turned down the offer. Seem crazy? Not necessarily. Unlike the majority of businesses, Clif Bar has not gone a single year without a profit, and it has never had to borrow from venture capitalists. So what makes Clif Bar different from most companies? Instead of focusing on short-term profits, Erickson believes in focusing on five key sustainability initiatives: planet, community, people, brands, and business.

If you think it's just a gimmick, think again: The company works to make its employees healthier and happier with flexible scheduling, paid sabbaticals, company-sponsored classes, and a state-of-the-art fitness center. It also provides a concierge service so employees can complete errands during the day, and it allows employees to bring their children and pets to work. The company also sponsors a volunteer program, encouraging employees to volunteer on their own time or through company-sponsored events. If all those perks aren't enough to convince you that Clif Bar is onto something, consider the fact that the company uses environmentally friendly packaging, incorporates organic ingredients into its products, and even uses energy from a wind farm in South Dakota. Skeptics might argue that Clif Bar doesn't need to go to such great lengths to do nice things for their employees and the community. Technically, they're right. (Does bringing your dog to work *really* help you create a better energy bar?) However, while Clif Bar's benefits might be a bit unorthodox, they help make the company sustainable and attractive to employees, investors, and consumers alike.

For-Profit and Non-Profit Partnerships

A potential new trend in CSR is partnerships between non-profit and for-profit companies, which can be mutually beneficial. In 2005, the CEO of Groupe Danone, Franck Riboud, met with Muhammad Yunus, founder of Grameen Bank, a bank dedicated to helping poor people around the world get loans. The two created Grameen Danone Foods, which is helping to feed fortified yogurt to hungry children in Bangladesh. Grameen Danone earns back the total cost of operations and gives 1 percent of the profit to investors. The remaining profit is funneled back into the company. Aside from feeding hungry children, the company also provides jobs for the people of Bangladesh by creating Grameen Danone factories across the country.[40]

The exciting part of this project is that the partnership between profit and non-profit is something that other local and international companies may follow to help a worthy cause. In the future, this could help change the corporate structure as we know it into a more socially responsible and mutually beneficial system.[41]

Do It...

8.5: Capture Sustainable Business Practices Together with a partner, go out for a walk in your neighborhood's business district with a digital camera or your cell phone camera. Take pictures of at least three readily observable business practices and classify them as either not sustainable or sustainable. Write a 25-word or fewer description below each photo to justify your classification. Be prepared to submit your photos and comments as one file to your instructor, if requested.

Now Debrief...

- **Corporate social responsibility** involves an organization looking beyond its own self-interest to consider the interests of society. This means the organization is responsible for its impact on shareholders, the community, and the environment.
- One important part of CSR is sustainability. To remain sustainable, companies must focus on the *triple bottom line* of people, planet, and profit, combining economic success with responsible social and environmental activities.
- Two ways to promote sustainability are eco-efficiency and eco-capitalism. *Eco-efficiency* involves producing more products using fewer resources; and *eco-capitalism* is the idea that natural capital exists in nature and that this capital is valuable for human consumption.
- Ethically focusing on profits is an important part of remaining sustainable. In business terms, **profit motive** refers to a company's desire to make more money than it spends.
- To help encourage CSR, some for-profit and non-profit companies are working together and creating partnerships that may one day impact the corporate structure we know today.

Chapter 8 Visual Summary

Leadership Vision | Chapter 6: *Lead* Chapter 7: *Own* **Chapter 8: *Act***

1. Appreciate the complexity of the ethical dilemmas you may face in the business world and the need to take a 360° view. (pp. 184–185)

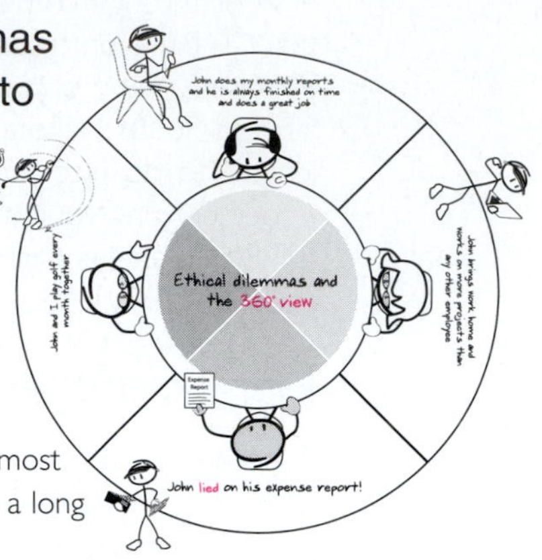

- **Ethics** is the study of human conduct and moral principles.
- **Business ethics** is the study of moral principles and conduct within a business environment.
- When having an ethical dilemma, it's helpful to consider the situation from different points of view.
- Sometimes, companies need to do the right thing, even if it isn't the most profitable. However, in the long term, a strong code of ethics can go a long way toward generating profit.

Summary: The business world is full of difficult situations that can call ethics into question. It's important for a business to consider the outcomes of its actions and the impact these actions will have on the greater world.

2. Characterize what an ethical organization looks like and the tools that leaders use to create one. (pp. 186–190)

- To help you figure out if an organization is ethical, it's helpful to look in the organization's ethical toolbox. Tools include:
- Tool 1: Leaders in an organization set an ethical example.
- Tool 2: Ethical organizations focus on the triple bottom line of people, planet, and profit.
- Tool 3: A **code of ethics** sets standards regarding ethical practices.
- Tool 4: A **code of conduct** conveys to employees how the organization wants them to act in the workplace.
- Tool 5: **Ethics training programs** help teach employees the way the organization wants them to react in an ethical dilemma.
- Tool 6: An **ethics management program** helps establish ethical values, codes, and policies.
- Tool 7: Ethics committees oversee ethics programs.

Summary: Creating an ethical organization is a difficult process. By implementing these tools, an organization can go a long way toward promoting ethical behavior.

3. Develop an ethical decision-making approach for your career. (pp. 190–195)

Making an Ethical Decision
1. Get all the facts.
2. Consider who your decision will affect.
3. Continue to gather more information.
4. Use decision-making approaches to come up with potential solutions.
5. Choose the best approach and look at it again from different perspectives.
6. Take another look at your decision and implement it.

- Informal ways to tell if you are about to do something unethical are the butterflies-in-the-stomach, what would a mentor do, and front-page-of-the-newspaper tests.
- Formal approaches to decision making include **utilitarianism, cost-benefit analysis,** the **moral rights principle,** the **universalist principle,** the **virtue principle,** and the **distributive justice principle.**
- Another way to figure out a dilemma is to follow a step-by-step approach: 1. Get all the facts; 2. Consider who your decision will affect; 3. Research similar instances; 4. Use the formal decision-making approaches to come up with potential solutions; 5. Choose the best decision and look at it again from different perspectives; 6. Take another look at your decision; and if the decision still seems good, implement it.
- People who allege misconduct and speak out against something going on in an organization are sometimes referred to as **whistleblowers**.

Summary: Learning to prevent unethical decisions before they are made is a valuable skill for your career.

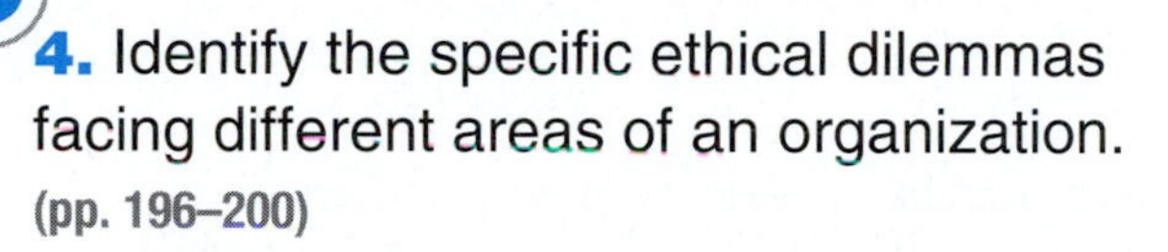

4. Identify the specific ethical dilemmas facing different areas of an organization. (pp. 196–200)

- Specific departments within an organization can face ethical dilemmas that other departments may not have to deal with.
- The accounting department needs to be aware of the potential for fraud and theft. Because of past scandals, agencies like the SEC, legislation like the **Sarbanes-Oxley Act**, and guidelines such as GAAP work to keep accountants honest.
- HR employees take part in hiring, firing, salary decisions, and discipline, which opens the door for many potential ethical dilemmas.
- The marketing department must be aware of manipulative or inaccurate messages.
- Management needs to keep a business productive and profitable, but must be mindful to do it in an ethical way.
- IT employees must be careful not to abuse the power they have through monitoring and surveillance.
- Globalization further complicates ethical issues because people with different beliefs and cultures work together.

Summary: Each department in a business is subject to ethical dilemmas in forms specific to that department's line of work. Conducting international business can create ethical problems, as some cultures may disagree about what is and is not acceptable business behavior.

5. Justify how ethics are the foundation for a sustainable organization and how companies engage in acts of corporate social responsibility. (pp. 201–203)

- **Corporate social responsibility** involves an organization looking beyond its own self-interest to consider the interests of society.
- To remain sustainable, companies must focus on the *triple bottom line* of people, planet, and profit.
- The triple bottom line approach suggests that when businesses benefit, these benefits disperse throughout society. This is simply because when business is good, businesses have more money to spend on helping people.

Summary: It is beneficial to businesses to support a triple bottom line of profit, people, and the environment. This also benefits the world at large.

Get the most out of what you just read by practicing your skills and actually DOING something with the material! The best place to do this is at **www.mybizlab.com**. Here's just some of what is available to you there:

- Apply your skills in an interactive environment with more **BizSkill** experiences...and see if you have what it takes
- Think critically and talk with your peers on hot business topics in **BizChat**
- Flex your business communication skills and build your own portfolio with the **Communication Plan exercises**
- Watch the chapter material come together with **Just Plain Business** videos
- Study on-the-go with **Audio Chapter Summaries** in MP3 format
- Brush up on the lecture and content with **Audio PowerPoints**
- Discover how well you are doing and see what areas you need to improve on with the **Pre-Tests** and **Post-Tests**

Key Words

These key words and more are also available as flash cards to practice with at **www.mybizlab.com**.

1. Appreciate the complexity of the ethical dilemmas you may face in the business world and the need to take a 360° view. **(pp. 184–185)**

Ethics (p. 184)

Business ethics (p. 184)

2. Characterize what an ethical organization looks like and the tools that leaders use to create one. **(pp. 186–190)**

Code of ethics (p. 187)

Code of conduct (p. 188)

Ethics training program (p. 189)

Ethics management program (p. 189)

3. Develop an ethical decision-making approach for your career. **(pp. 190–195)**

Utilitarianism (p. 191)

Cost-benefit analysis (p. 191)

Moral rights principle (p. 192)

Universalist principle (p. 192)

Virtue principle (p. 192)

Distributive justice principle (p. 192)

Whistleblowers (p. 195)

4. Identify the specific ethical dilemmas facing different areas of an organization. **(pp. 196–200)**

Sarbanes-Oxley Act (p. 196)

5. Justify how ethics are the foundation for a sustainable organization and how companies engage in acts of corporate social responsibility. **(pp. 201–203)**

Corporate social responsibility (CSR) (p. 201)

Profit motive (p. 202)

Prove It

Prove It...

Now, let's put on one of the BizHats. With the **Manager BizHat** squarely on your head, look at the following exercise:

You just started working for an insurance company as a manager in the HR department. In order to help gauge the culture in the office, your boss introduced you to everyone as a salesperson, not an HR rep. After you questioned your boss about these tactics, she still wanted to be secretive, so you went along with the plan. Because people don't suspect you are monitoring their behavior, they go about their jobs as they usually would.

Soon after you start, you begin small talk with the employees to get more information about what their work life is like. You start to realize that many employees are acting unethically. They are taking home supplies, using their computers for personal use, fudging expense reports, and providing overall poor customer service. However, although you feel their behavior is unacceptable, they do have some legitimate complaints. What are five things you would do to improve the ethical behavior at the company?

Flip It...

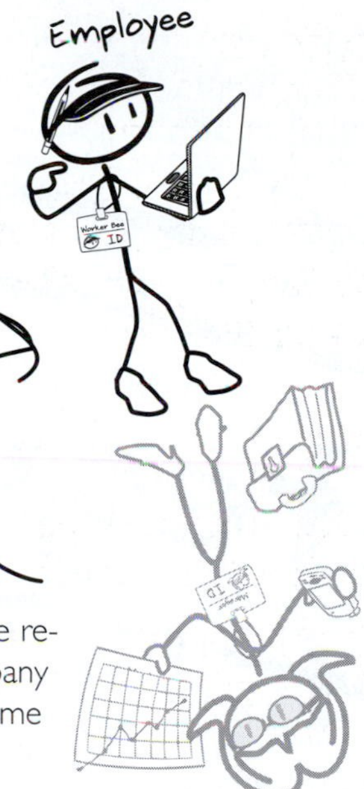

After you've decided how to improve the ethical behavior of the company as the Manager above, **flip over to the Employee BizHat.**

You are now an employee at the insurance company described above. Your manager held a meeting to introduce a new salesperson to the company. The salesperson was nice enough. She made small talk by the watercooler and seemed interested in getting to know everyone. However, a few weeks later, your manager holds another meeting to let you know the salesperson isn't who they said she was. She is really a new manager in the HR department who the company hired to look into employee behavior and satisfaction. Your manager is really upset at the report he received, so now everyone is in trouble. How would you feel if the company revamped its conduct and ethics policies using these tactics? What if some of the changes implemented benefited employees like you?

Now Debrief It...

Compare the perspectives of the two BizHats described above. How did taking up the perspective of the Employee change your view of the situation you first considered from the Manager's perspective? Is there a right or wrong answer in this situation?

Plan:
Roles, Mission, Strategy, and Plans

BizSkills invite...

Try It!
There's no better way to learn concepts than to put them into practice. Take your turn in the driver's seat and be a part of actual business decision making by visiting the BizSkill for this chapter at **www.mybizlab.com**.

Now that you've practiced making tough business decisions and seeing the results of your choices in this chapter's BizSkill, it's time to translate those skills into plain English. And if you skipped the BizSkill, go back now!

Chapter 9 Goals

After experiencing this chapter, you'll be able to:

1. Differentiate the types of skills needed and responsibilities found at each level of management.
2. Justify why having a mission statement and measurable goals is important to an organization and to you.
3. Compare the different types of planning and identify their value to an organization.
4. Explain what tools managers use to create effective plans.
5. Demonstrate how managers plan for and manage risk.

How do you plan for success?

Not Your Average, Everyday Manager

Gemma volunteers at a local animal welfare charity. The charity needs to raise money for a new block of kennels, so Gemma offers to organize a charity auction to help raise the funds. First, she makes a checklist of everything she'll need to do. The checklist indicates that the event will require a lot more time and effort than Gemma had anticipated, so she calls friends to help her. She delegates responsibilities to each of her friends and gives them a time frame in which to complete their tasks. With everyone working on assigned tasks and following Gemma's plan, the charity auction is a success.

Alex decides to host a dance to celebrate end-of-term exams. He posts hundreds of flyers around campus to promote the dance. Alex plans on charging a five-dollar cover and estimates that at least 100 people will attend. He figures he can spend $200 on food and still be able to afford a DJ. When only 30 people show up to the dance, Alex is not just out of pocket at the end of the night; he also has one angry and unpaid DJ.

Neither Gemma nor Alex would describe themselves as managers, yet this is the role they are taking on. If you've ever planned a family outing or organized a party, then you too already know a bit of what it's like to be a manager. As Alex's story shows, not all managers are efficient. So, what makes a good manager, and how can effective planning help you become one? In this chapter, we'll find out.

1. Wanted: Skilled Managers at Every Level

How would you spend your day if you were a manager?

How do you imagine a typical day in the life of a manager? If you have visions of strolling into the office mid-morning for a board meeting, followed by a long, leisurely corporate lunch, think again. Most managers work an average of 60 hours per week,[1] and the pace is intense. Rather than taking part in lengthy brainstorming sessions, a manager's day is filled with brief, fragmented activities, half of which are completed in less than nine minutes. Only 10 percent of activities take more than an hour to complete, and work sessions at one's desk last an average of 15 minutes.[2] ■ Being a manager is less like a walk in the park and more like a series of short, intense sprints around the office.

Managerial Levels and Skills

So, you know a manager's day is often hectic, long, and fast-paced, but what kinds of managers are there and what skills do different managers need? And if you're interested in becoming a manager, would you be a good one?

Table 9.1 shows the basic categories of management. As you can see, you find managers at all levels in an organization: at the top of a corporate hierarchy, near the middle, or near the bottom in a section or department. In most large organizations, the number of managers at each level decreases as you move up the hierarchy, so that fewer managers are at the top levels and more managers are at the bottom. Some smaller companies have just a few managers playing multiple roles, but there is usually a management hierarchy even in a small organization.

Table 9.1 also shows the skills that managers at the different levels most often focus on:

- *Conceptual skills* involve planning and developing abilities. For example, a manager would use conceptual skills to design a new product line or marketing plan.
- *Interpersonal and communication skills* are based on working with people and getting ideas across. Managers with people skills might be in charge of motivating employees and communicating with them.
- *Technical skills* are the skills and abilities needed to get a job done. First-level managers often possess the technical skills to successfully complete the jobs they manage.

Table **9.1** | **What Management Level Is Right for You?**

	Skill Focus	Management Focus	Time Focus	Number of Direct Reports	Spending and Control of Resources
Top Manager	Conceptual, big picture skills	Planning	The long-term future	Few	A lot
Middle Manager	Interpersonal and communication skills	Organizing and controlling	From one quarter to a year	Few to many	Varied
First-Level Manager or Supervisor	Technical skills	Directing	The immediate present	Varies	Minimal

One important thing to note is that regardless of where they fall within the management hierarchy, managers at each level use all of these skills to some extent to be successful.

Why It Matters Looking at Table 9.1, where do you see yourself? Are you a big-picture thinker? If so, you may be suited for a top management job. A people person? Then maybe a mid-level management position is right for you. Do you have specialized technical knowledge, like a background in engineering? Then perhaps being a first-level manager would be right for you. If you currently have a manager, where does your manager fall on the table? Does his or her skill set match the level of management he or she possesses?

> Being a manager is less like a walk in the park and more like a series of short, intense sprints around the office.

Table 9.1 also tells you a lot about and the activities and decisions that consume a manager's day. For example, you see that top-level managers are often focused on long-term planning, have few people reporting directly to them, but have responsibility for delegating many resources (such as money and time). Middle managers are more involved in the long-term organizing and controlling of the company's resources, and lower-level managers focus on directing employees in the here and now.

Knowing what different managers do at different levels of management is important in many ways. It can help you know whether to seek a promotion, for example, or whether to accept one. Have you ever heard the saying that a person in a company rises to the level of his or her own incompetence? This idea, referred to as the "Peter Principle,"[3] is the notion that employees get promoted until they no longer do their jobs well—that is, until they rise up in the organization to the level of their own incompetence. So, it's important to know what your skills are, what you like to do, and what a management job looks like before you seek or accept a promotion.

And even if you're not interested in ever becoming a manager yourself, in every company, from small to large, from for-profit to non-profit, it's important to know who runs the company, who reports to those people, what their responsibilities are, and what they focus on. We discuss the different levels of management in this chapter on planning because they are the people who create the plans that a company follows. The plans these managers create will vary by their level within the organization. The next few sections will describe these levels of management in a bit more detail.

Top Managers

Top managers, sometimes referred to as *senior managers* or *executives*, are at the highest level of management. The **chief executive officer (CEO)** is generally the highest-ranking manager in the organization. In some companies, the CEO reports to the *board of directors*, which is a group of elected or appointed individuals who oversee the activities of the company.

CEOs have very few "direct reports," or people reporting directly to them. These typically include the *chief financial officer (CFO), chief operational officer (COO), chief information officer (CIO),* and other executives with titles such as *executive vice president*. You'll sometimes hear people refer to "C-level" as a general reference to any executive whose title starts with a "C." In large organizations, this can include the previously mentioned CEO, CFO, COO, and CIO, as well as the *CMO (chief marketing officer), CTO (chief technology officer),* and others. Although top managers may not have direct supervision of large numbers of staff, they have the final say for a particular division or geographical region, for example.

What Top Managers Do Top managers do not typically manage the day-to-day aspects of a business. Instead, they focus on long-term planning and making policies for the organization, and they often appoint and review the performance of those managers reporting to them.

As we discussed in Chapter 6, they're also responsible for creating a *vision* for their organization. Top managers are conceptual thinkers who ask and search for the answers to questions such as "Where does the company want to be in five years?" and "What new opportunities or challenges face us, and how can we take advantage of them?" And as we'll discuss later, top managers focus on strategic planning by setting goals such as "We will expand the business by acquiring small accounting firms in Los Angeles during 2010." In sum, top managers make the ultimate decisions regarding large-scale factors affecting the company. Their focus on long-term planning helps steer the company toward its envisioned path.

Becoming Top Management How do you get to be a CEO? Most top managers have a lot of management experience, either with the organization they work with now or with a different one. In large organizations, top managers have usually moved up the ranks of management, sometimes being "groomed" for such positions. Along the way, they've gained the experience they need to do their jobs, and most have an advanced degree like an MBA. But some top managers are entrepreneurs who have started their own companies and called the shots from day one. Take Reed Hastings, founder and CEO of Netflix. Hastings plays an integral part in deciding the direction in which the company will go, planning ahead for when newer technologies eventually replace DVDs.[4]

Middle Managers

What do you think of when you think of the term "middle managers"? Although **middle managers** fall beneath CEOs in the organization's hierarchy, their jobs are essential to the success of the business. Most middle managers are responsible for carrying out the policies, plans, and strategies set by top management—they do so by setting goals, organizing, and controlling the people, time, money, and other resources within their department. They have titles like *marketing manager, regional manager*, and so on. Although their jobs require a variety of skills, the focus of their work is often on people skills, especially for those managers who oversee various departments and have many people reporting directly to them. This is especially true because more and more work in organizations is done in teams, which requires middle managers to flex their people skills.

Communicating Up and Down Because they're more involved in the day-to-day aspects of the company, middle managers often "communicate up" to the top managers they report to and offer them suggestions and recommendations based on their experience. You've probably seen *The Apprentice*. Donald Trump is clearly the CEO of the show, and his son and daughter play the role of middle managers, acting as the "eyes and ears" for their father by providing him with firsthand information he can use (or not, as is often the case) to decide who gets fired that week.

Of course, because middle managers have a number of people reporting to them, they also "communicate down"—which, once again, emphasizes how important people skills are for them. And because their jobs include carrying out the goals set by top managers, part of being a middle manager is motivating employees. We'll discuss the different ways that managers motivate people in Chapter 11, but the point is clear: You can't have bad people skills and successfully motivate people.

Becoming a Middle Manager How do you become a middle manager? Like top managers, middle managers usually work their way up in the company or are hired from the outside with comparable industry knowledge. Usually, they have a business degree or an equal level of experience. In some organizations, middle managers receive less financial compensation than the people who work for them. This is particularly true in sales, where the sales managers often make less than the salespeople themselves, who collect healthy commissions. So, why would anyone take the job of middle manager if this is true? Because it's often a pathway to higher management opportunities in the organization, and because management can offer intangible rewards that match someone's skills and interests.

First-Level Managers/Supervisors Do you remember your manager at your first job? Maybe it was in an office, or maybe at a pizza shop or a video store. He or she was probably a first-level manager or supervisor. **First-level managers** (or **supervisors**) are people in charge of running usually a single department (or store) on a daily basis: directing the workflow, assessing problems, and directing employees. They often have job titles like *office manager*, *store manager*, and so on. They're the ones who assign you your work, monitor your progress, and provide guidance. You address them with questions and problems, or report things like taking a sick day. As an employee, you have the skills needed to accomplish your work, but first-level managers have more experience and often know how to do your work better than you do.

Technical skills are not the only skills required of first-level managers. They report directly to middle managers, and so, like them, first-level managers have to learn how to communicate both up and down the organization's hierarchy. Also, like middle managers, they help motivate employees to accomplish the company's goals, so having people skills is crucial to their success.

Becoming a First-Level Manager How do you become a first-level manager? Many are promoted from within when they are seen as having promise. With luck, hard work, and the right skills and education, first-level managers can work their way up to become a CEO. Take James Ziemer, former CEO of Harley-Davidson. He worked his way up from a job as a freight elevator operator to become part of the accounting department before landing a job as a CFO. From there, he advanced to his role as president and CEO until he retired in 2009.

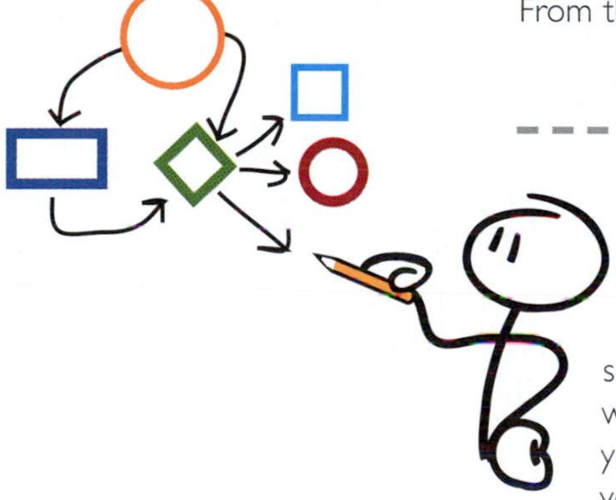

Do It...

9.1: Determine the Skills You Need Pick a management position in a company you might like to have in the future and write it down. Then, list the skills that would be required of you in that position. Looking at Table 9.1, what would your management and time focus be? How many direct reports might you have? Does this sound like a management position that would appeal to you? Be prepared to submit your list electronically or present it in class.

Now Debrief...

- Managers are found at every level of an organization. There are three levels of management: top level, middle management, and first-level management.
- **Top-level managers,** like the **CEO,** are responsible for looking at the "big picture," focusing on long-term planning, and creating a vision for the organization.
- **Middle managers** are those managers responsible for carrying out the plans and policies set up by top-level management. They require strong people skills because they often have many people reporting directly to them, and they have to motivate their employees.
- **First-level managers** are in charge of running a single department or store. They direct the workflow, assess problems, and oversee employees. First-level managers have strong technical skills as well as good people skills. They report directly to middle managers.

2. Creating a Mission Statement, Pursuing Concrete Goals

"A good hockey player plays where the puck is. A great hockey player plays where the puck is going to be."

—Retired hockey player Wayne Gretzky[5]

Imagine sitting in an interview room. Your suit is pressed, your résumé is well organized, and you know that you're perfect for the job. The interviewer turns to you and asks, "What do you want to do with your life?" Do you have an answer ready, or is your mind completely blank? Whether you're interviewing for a position as a top manager or starting out on the lowest rung of the corporate ladder, a good, solid answer tells the interviewer that you have direction and are working toward particular career goals.

Similarly, companies need to know where they're heading in order to succeed. A *mission statement* defines the purpose of an organization and addresses its values and ethical principles. From this, the organization can create concrete goals to help it achieve its mission statement.

Mission Statements for Organizations

In Chapter 6, we discussed how top leaders in a company, often in conjunction with employees, work to create a *vision* for the organization. A company's vision explains where the company wants to go. A vision statement should help motivate, inspire, and excite everyone in an organization and should provide direction and focus to the future.

So how is a mission statement different from a vision? As we discussed in Chapter 6, a **mission statement** focuses on the here and now; it defines what endeavor the organization is engaged in (the nature of the business), who it intends to serve (customers and stakeholders), what needs or benefits it will focus on, and how it will address those needs. The mission statement is usually created by top managers and provides the reason the company exists. Every employee should be able to repeat or explain the mission briefly and easily. The mission forms the company's current plans and guides day-to-day decision making and resource distribution.

Although an organization does not need to achieve its vision to succeed, it *must* achieve its mission statement or it is out of business. In fact, every company, no matter whether it's a sole proprietorship, partnership, non-profit organization, or large corporation, needs a mission statement.

Types of Mission Statements Mission statements vary widely across companies. Some companies have a mission statement that succinctly sums up their business. Take, for example, Google. It has a mission "to organize the world's information and make it universally accessible and useful."[6] The American Diabetes Association's mission statement is also short and to the point: "To prevent and cure diabetes and to improve the lives of all people affected by diabetes."[7] Although concise, both of these statements effectively describe the purpose of the respective organizations. Compare this to the following mission statement from Bayer: "We have set our course for the future."[8] It is unclear from this statement what Bayer's corporate purpose is, so many would say this is not a successful mission statement. What do you think?

Short mission statements such as Hershey's—"Bringing sweet moments of Hershey happiness to the world every day"[9]—are often expanded in other places, such as the company Web site. Hershey's Web site outlines what its mission statement means to all its stakeholders:[10]

- Consumers: Delivering quality consumer-driven confectionery experiences for all occasions
- Employees: Winning with an aligned and empowered organization . . . while having fun
- Business Partners: Building collaborative relationships for profitable growth with our customers, suppliers, and partners

- Shareholders: Creating sustainable value
- Communities: Honoring our heritage through continued commitment to making a positive difference

There are also companies whose mission statements are not so succinct. See for example ice-cream maker Ben & Jerry's mission statement, shown in Figure 9.1. Although it is longer than some, it addresses the triple bottom line of people, planet, and profit that we have referred to throughout the book. The vision of the company, on the other hand, is "to use the power of our business to change the world for the better."[11] That vision is ambitious and rousing, and it may never be fully accomplished, unlike the mission, which the company accomplishes daily.

Why Mission Statements Matter

Why is knowing a company's mission statement—and knowing whether the company actually walks the walk and talks the talk of its mission—important? Let's look at it from the perspective of the four BizHats:

- **The Owner/Investor Hat:** As an owner/investor in a company, you want to know what a company's mission statement is before you put your money on the line. Does the company pursue a mission you support? Does it actually make good on its mission statement through its actions?
- **The Manager Hat:** As a manager, it's important to know the mission statement of the organization you work for because your understanding of your company's purpose will guide your actions—from your planning to your prioritization choices. A manager at Ben & Jerry's will probably make different decisions than a manager running a large conglomerate ice-cream factory.
- **The Employee Hat:** As an employee of an organization, it is vital that you understand its mission so you can see whether your values are compatible with the company's fundamental goals. Take, for example, the Ben & Jerry's mission. If you're deeply passionate about the environment, Ben & Jerry's may be the ideal place for you.
- **The Customer Hat:** Finally, from a customer standpoint, knowing a company's mission statement can help you decide where to spend your dollar. For example, after reading Ben & Jerry's mission statement, would you be more or less likely to buy their ice cream?

So, how can you find a company's mission statement and determine whether an organization really walks the talk? The first part is easy: Most companies' mission statements are on their Web sites. Often, as mentioned earlier, the Web site also details how the company goes about achieving its mission.

Let's take Dallas-based Southwest Airlines as an example. Its mission statement states that the company is dedicated "to the highest quality of Customer Service delivered with a sense of warmth, friendliness, individual pride, and Company Spirit."[12] That's the company's mission statement, but does it really deliver on its promise? Looking a bit more into the company, you'll find that Southwest has received a number of awards; for example, in March 2009, it was ranked seventh in Fortune Magazine's Top 50 Most Admired Companies in the World.[13] Combine this information with personal experience. Have you or your friends had good experiences

Figure **9.1** | **Ben & Jerry's Mission Statement**

Ben & Jerry's Mission

SOCIAL mission
To operate the Company in a way that actively recognizes the central role that business plays in society by initiating innovative ways to improve the quality of life locally, nationally and internationally.

PRODUCT mission
To make, distribute and sell the finest quality all natural ice cream and euphoric concoctions with a continued commitment to incorporating wholesome, natural ingredients and promoting business practices that respect the Earth and the Environment.

ECONOMIC mission
To operate the Company on a sustainable financial basis of profitable growth, increasing value for our stakeholders and expanding opportunities for development and career growth for our employees.

Source: http://www.benjerry.com/activism/mission-statement/mission-statement.gif.

with Southwest? By doing a bit of sleuthing you'll be able to decide whether Southwest's proclaimed dedication to customer service is just lip service or the real thing.

Your Personal Mission Statement Have you ever seen the 1996 film *Jerry Maguire*? Tom Cruise plays a sports agent who realizes he's lost track of what's important to him. He writes a personal mission statement, stressing the value of personal relationships. By the end of the film, he has his own fledgling business, the respect of his clients, and a loving family. Although a personal mission statement doesn't always guarantee such results, it can help you establish what is important and stick to it. Just as mission statements provide companies with direction, they can also help individuals focus on their goals.

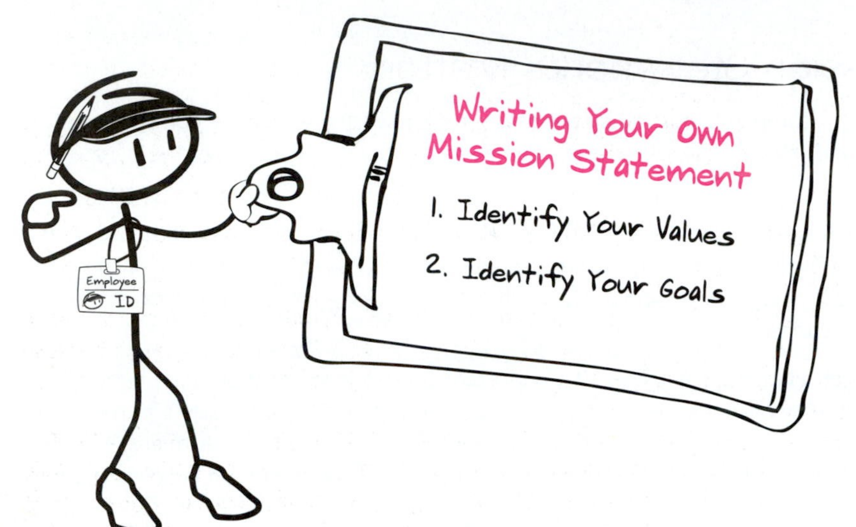

So, how do you go about writing a personal mission statement? The key is to keep it short—no more than two sentences—and to make sure it is easily memorable. Try this simple process:

1. **Identify Your Values:** What is most important to you in life? Do you care more about financial success or a good work-life balance? Are you looking for a position that enhances your appreciation and understanding of various cultures, or do you prefer to be proactive within your own community? List your personal ethics and values.
2. **Identify Your Goals:** Where do you see yourself in three years' time? How about five? What career goals do you want to accomplish? List your short-term and long-term goals.

Once you have established your values and goals, you're ready to write your mission statement.

Take Lisa, who values earning power. She is extremely ambitious, and wants to pursue a career in sales once she finishes her MBA degree. Her mission statement may read, "My personal career mission statement is to become one of the top sales people in a pharmaceutical company within the next three to five years." Lisa's statement is concise, easily memorable, and focuses on a particular goal.

■ To be successful, managers and employees alike have to translate their mission statement into concrete and measurable goals.

It's also important to make sure that your personal mission statement ties in with what your company is hoping to achieve. If you're planning on becoming the company's top software developer as your company is hoping to offshore its software development in the next year, it's time to reassess your goals. Evaluate your personal career mission statement every year to make sure that you're still heading in the direction you intended.

SMART Goals for Organizations

We've discussed how having a mission statement is important to both an organization and employees who work for it. But a mission statement isn't just miraculously realized. ■ To be successful, managers and employees alike have to translate their mission statement into concrete and measurable goals. Setting written goals means you know where you're going, what you have to do, and when. One acronym often used in the business world to describe effective goals is SMART: **SMART goals** are Specific, Measurable, Attainable, Relevant, and Time-based.

SMART Goals Are Specific To be useful, goals need to be specific. This means they have to be well defined and clear. For example, compare these two goals:

1. Reduce expenses for all departments across the board.
2. Reduce travel expenses by 10 percent within the sales department every quarter in 2010.

From a manager's perspective, it's clear that goal 2 is more useful in that it will better shape planning, resource allocation, and decision making. And as an employee, if you know that the department has a goal to reduce travel expenses by 10 percent every quarter, how might it affect your own actions? You may, for example, opt for a cheaper flight or a less ritzy hotel.

SMART Goals Are Measurable SMART goals are also measurable. Let's take the case of Tom, whose doctor told him he was in danger of a heart attack because of his weight. Tom's neighbor Joe is also overweight, but two years later, Joe is still "working on it." Tom instead takes his baseline weight and figures out a plan to improve it. After meeting with a dietitian and joining a gym, he plans to lose two pounds a month for 15 months and get his weight down from 230 pounds to 200.

In our business example, you have a specific goal to reduce travel expenses by 10 percent in 2010. But to be useful, this goal needs to also be measurable. Part of this requires that we break down the goal into quantifiable parts. For example, if you want to reduce travel expenses, you would first measure the status quo (the baseline amount that the department currently spends on travel each quarter), and then track the department's progress each quarter and compare the results to the baseline. If the number has dropped 10 percent in one quarter, the goal has been reached for that quarter.

To test whether a goal is measurable, ask the questions How much? or How many? Vague goals such as "reduce expenses across the board" or "get in shape" are unmanageable because they show no measurable, quantifiable progress.

SMART Goals Are Attainable What goals are within your reach? If Tom sets a goal of losing five pounds instead of two pounds monthly, he would get to his goal earlier, but could he sustain it for the long term? What's the point of a quick, superficial weight plunge and then gaining it all back? Tom is able to attain his goal because he sets a realistic target to shoot for. Similarly, goals in business should be attainable by most employees. For example, if a call center wants to increase productivity by 30 percent, it may set attainable goals for its employees, such as the number of calls that each employee must make in a week.

SMART Goals Are Relevant Tom's mission is to lose weight. His program of diet and exercise is relevant to his mission. In business, goals must also serve a purpose that help achieve the company's vision and mission. The call center's vision may be to become the leader in sales, and increasing its productivity is just one goal that can help it achieve that vision.

SMART Goals Are Time-Based What would happen if Tom planned to lose 30 pounds without giving himself a time frame? He would most likely lose focus well before reaching his target weight because he would not have a deadline to work toward. In business, providing a time frame helps employees concentrate on completing a goal before a set date. This time frame should give employees enough time to complete a task, but not so much time that they lose focus.

SMART Goals for Your Own Career How can SMART goals help you? Creating your own goals is a good way of making sure that you're on target to accomplish your personal career mission statement. Let's take Lisa's statement as an example. Her mission is to "complete my MBA degree and to obtain a sales position at one of the top five pharmaceutical companies by this date one year from today." Her goals are to:

1. complete her MBA; and
2. obtain a sales position at one of the top five pharmaceutical companies.

By assessing whether these goals are specific, measurable, attainable, relevant, and time-based, Lisa can judge whether she is on track to achieve her mission statement. For example, to test whether her second goal is relevant, Lisa may want to research the qualifications needed to work at one of the top five pharmaceutical companies. Is an MBA sufficient, or would she require some initial work experience to help achieve her goal?

SMART goals are part of the **Management by Objectives (MBO)** method of management, which relies on defining objectives for employees and then evaluating their performance based on the objectives that have been set. By creating goals that align with your company's goals, you can better your chances of career progression. Let's say that Lisa finishes her MBA and gets a job at PharmTech, one of the top five pharmaceutical companies in the United States. PharmTech is looking to expand its client base by 15 percent in the next two years. One of Lisa's personal career goals is to make 10 new client contacts within the next year. If she accomplishes her goal, she will help PharmTech achieve its own goal, which will put her in good stead for future raises or promotions.

Do It...

9.2: Create a Mission Statement and SMART Goals for Your Career Create a personal career mission statement and list five SMART personal career goals. Limit your response to two pages, and be prepared to submit it electronically to your instructor or to discuss it in class.

Now Debrief...

- A **mission statement** focuses on the here and now and defines what endeavor the organization is engaged in, whom it intends to serve, what needs or benefits it will focus on, and how it will address those needs.
- Mission statements are not only helpful for businesses. Creating a personal career mission plan can help individuals focus on attaining their goals, by helping them establish their priorities.
- Managers and employees translate their company's mission statement into concrete goals. Effective goals are **SMART**: **S**pecific, **M**easurable, **A**ttainable, **R**elevant, and **T**ime-based.

3. Planning: Failing to Plan Is Planning to Fail

"It is always wise to look ahead, but difficult to look further than you can see."

—Sir Winston Churchill[14]

You're off camping for the weekend. Your mission is to hike a 20-mile trail, and you have specific goals about when you want to reach particular checkpoints. You're good to go, right? Well, not if you haven't planned out your route. An organization can craft a mission statement and create SMART goals, but none of this means anything if there isn't a plan in place for achieving those goals.

Just as there are different levels of management, so too are there different levels of planning—*strategic, tactical*, and *operational*. We'll discuss these levels of planning in this section, as well as why it's important that you also participate in planning on these levels in your own personal career.

Strategic Planning: Pointing the Way

Once a business has developed a mission statement and set its goals, it must determine a way to accomplish those goals. **Strategic planning** involves determining the long-term goals of the organization, Knowing where the company wants to end up in the future is the primary role of top management. At the strategic planning stage, managers discuss broad questions such as:

- Which customers will we serve?
- What products or services will we offer?
- Which geographical area will we cover?

Managers formulate long-term (two-, five-, or 10-year) plans to see where the *entire* organization is headed and what they can do to get there. Every member of top management has to buy in to the strategic plans and sign off on it from the start, or "take ownership" of them.

Who's Involved in Strategic Planning? Since you can't create a product or provide a service without people and other resources, human resources planning is closely tied to strategic planning. A company needs to ensure that it has the people, skills, and talents it needs to achieve its goals.

Top financial professionals also play an essential role in the creation of a strategic plan. When a company decides to follow a particular path, for example, by extending its services into a new geographical area or by developing a new product to compete with a competitor, it is the role of the chief financial officer (CFO) to manage the expenses for the plan. It is also the CFO's job to develop short-term and long-term financial forecasts to ensure that the strategic goals are viable.

It's also important to note that although strategic planning is the focus of top management, lower levels, including employees, can be beneficial to the process by providing input as the strategic plan is developed. After all, everyone must work together—managing up, down, and across the organizational chart—toward specific goals if the strategic plan is going to work.

Tactical Planning: Setting Up Road Signs

In **tactical planning**, middle managers develop a short-term (usually around one year) plan that aligns the right company resources with the strategic plan established by top management. For example, if a company's strategic plan is "to establish software sales presence in Spain and Portugal within the next decade," the tactical plan would then break that plan down to a shorter time frame and assign appropriate resources to make the plan happen. This could include financial resources, human resources, the right data, legal clearance, coordination, and other logistical necessities. For this reason, tactical planning is usually tightly integrated with the annual budget process.

Operational Planning: Paving the Nitty-Gritty Path

What level of planning would you be best suited for?

Finally, in **operational planning**, specific individuals within specific departments develop a plan for how they will carry out the specific tasks, activities, and responsibilities they are assigned based on the tactical plan. The work is then allocated to specific departments that will execute their part in breaking down the plan to current schedules. For example, let's say that the software company branching out in Spain and Portugal initially decides to supply several stores in Lisbon and Madrid. An operational plan may include the specific number of products being shipped on a certain date and the physical process involved in shipping them.

A Case Example: Planning at Trader Joe's

Figure 9.2 shows an example of how a mission statement may play out in the different levels of planning using Trader Joe's, a privately owned grocery store. Beginning as a specialty neighborhood grocery store in southern California in the 1950s, Trader Joe's now has more than 300 stores nationwide. Part of the company's success can be attributed to its careful planning process—it selectively chooses its store locations based on population density, the educational level of the customer, and distribution efficiencies.[15]

Figure **9.2** | **Planning Case Example**

Mission Statement:
"At Trader Joe's, our mission is to bring all our customers the best food and beverage values to be found anywhere, and the information to make informed buying decisions . . ."[16]

Strategic Plan:
To expand in the Midwest by opening 10 stores

Tactical Plan:
Open six stores in Wisconsin, Michigan, Indiana, and Ohio in different phases through a five-year period; assess and open possibly four more in the Cleveland to Columbus area or in the area that offers the most sustained profitability

Operational Plan:
One of many; as an example, new members, both management and retail workers, have to be trained and integrated into the store's culture.

The Importance of SWOT in Planning

In Chapter 2, we discussed *SWOT analysis,* in which a company evaluates all the factors that can help or hinder it from achieving its objective—the company's internal strengths and weaknesses, as well as external opportunities and threats. As you learned, SWOT analysis is a major part of company planning and strategy formation. For example, say you work for a company that manufactures sneakers. A change in government policy lifts restrictions on trading with countries in the Middle East, giving your company a new opportunity to increase its overseas market share. However, without a plan in place to capitalize on that new opportunity, it will never become a possibility.

You can also use plans to turn threats identified through the SWOT process into opportunities. For example, the owner of a small store may view the development of a nearby strip mall as a threat. However, the strip mall also has the potential to bring many new customers into the area. If the small store plans ahead, it may be able to provide a product that is not available at the strip mall, while benefiting from the increased traffic the new shops will bring.

Planning for Your Career

How can you benefit from the different levels of planning? Think back to your personal mission statement and career goals. They might seem out of reach to begin with, but if you break them down into long-term, short-term, and immediate plans, you'll have a solid strategy in place to help you reach them. Also keep in mind that an important part of strategic planning is revising your plan to adapt to the changing environment.

Do It...

9.3: Create Your Own Plan Break down your personal career mission statement and goals into a five- to 10-year strategic plan, a one-year tactical plan, and an immediate two-week operational plan. Be prepared to submit your plans electronically or to discuss them in class.

Now Debrief...

- To help them reach their goals, companies rely on three levels of planning: strategic, tactical, and operational. **Strategic planning** involves determining the long-term goals of the organization. Top management, including HR and finance managers, collaborate on the direction the company will take by formulating two-, five-, or 10-year plans.
- **Tactical planning** involves developing short-term (one-year) plans about which elements of the strategic plan will be implemented, who will implement them, and how they will be implemented. Middle managers allocate appropriate company resources to put tactical plans into place.
- **Operational planning** gets right down to the nitty-gritty details and is used to run daily and weekly operations, such as schedules and standards.
- These three levels of planning can be applied to everyday life, for example, by working out long-term, short-term, and immediate career goals.

4. Planning Tools: The Sharper the Better

When you think of a project manager, do you picture a high-powered businessperson running a multimillion-dollar project? Project management sometimes gives the impression of large-scale projects using the latest technology, megabuck resources, and reams of people. But not all projects are like filming blockbuster movies. Have you ever organized a charity event? Or scheduled an intramural basketball tournament? Congratulations! You're a project manager.

Project managers know that planning is an essential part of successfully running a smooth project. Asking a project manager to deliver a magazine issue on time, on budget, and to the exact specifications without planning is a bit like asking someone to dig a trench with a teaspoon; it becomes a frustrating and inefficient process. Fortunately, there are planning tools that managers can use to make project management an easier and more efficient process.

Tool 1: Action Plans

Jim wants to sell sneakers on eBay. He needs to know about eBay's seller policies, how much he can reasonably expect to get for the shoes, and what costs selling and shipping the shoes will incur. It seems fairly easy, but Jim wants to make sure that he doesn't overlook anything. What should he do?

This is where action plans and timetables come in. An **action plan** is a list of everything that needs to be done to accomplish a specific goal. Action plans list the tasks to be carried out in the order that they need to be done. For example, let's say that Jim is starting a home business selling sneakers on eBay. His action plan might look something like this:

Home Business Action Plan

1. Write a business plan
2. Register as an eBay seller
3. Open a business checking account
4. Obtain business insurance
5. Order initial inventory
6. Post photos and descriptions of products online

Tool 2: Timetables

In the business world, action plans are useful for simple projects. However, if you're working on a more complex project that requires you to finish tasks within a set time frame, you should consider using a **timetable**. Timetables provide a list of completion dates that tell you when each stage of the project is due to be finished.

When creating a timetable, it's usually best to start from the date that the project is due and work backward, listing the tasks in reverse order and filling in the due dates. For example, suppose Jim is commissioned to add a customer's personal design to a pair of running shoes for a big marathon on August 18. Jim can create a timetable to make sure he gets the shoes to his customer on time. His timetable might look something like this:

Personalized Sneakers Timetable

Design finalized: July 15
Shoes completed: July 25
Ship shoes: August 1
Marathon: August 18

Of course, this example is a simple one. Timetables for large projects can be incredibly complex and need special software. For instance, a construction company may use a large timetable to keep track of all the components of constructing a building: when the land needs to be cleared, who will do the work, which part of the building needs to be completed at which time so that electricians, plumbers, painters, and inspectors can work, and so forth. Timetables allow companies to determine how much time they have to complete each task, which helps them plan and prepare for the project as a whole.

Tool 3: Backward Planning

In 1961, John F. Kennedy announced that by the end of the decade, the United States would put a man on the moon. Much of the technology required to do this had not even been invented, and yet the mission was accomplished. How? NASA scientists looked at the final goal and asked themselves "What are all the things we need to do to make this happen?" They used backward planning.

Similar to filling in the dates in a timetable in reverse order, **backward planning** involves starting with your ultimate objective and working backward to outline your plan. This process is much like the supply chain we discussed in Chapter 3: Raw materials travel along a chain of different steps before a final product is delivered to consumers.

Let's use Jim's personalized sneaker commission again. If he knows when the sneakers need to be shipped to the client, he can determine how much time he has for each step. His backward plan would look something like this:

***Jim's Ultimate Goal:* To Deliver the Sneakers to His Client Before the Marathon**

August 18, 2010	Marathon
August 1, 2010	Shoes must be shipped to client
July 25, 2010	Shoes must be finished
July 15, 2010	Personalized design must be finalized

Backward planning is useful in many careers, from teaching (If my student needs to learn these skills by the end of the year, how can I make this happen?) to supply chain management (If I need to deliver 15,000 units by next week, what are the steps I need to take?).

Tool 4: Time Management Matrix

Your inbox is overflowing, the phone is ringing off the hook, and you have people lining up outside your office waiting to talk to you. Where do you start? According to leadership expert Stephen Covey,[17] we should prioritize tasks according to whether they are urgent or non-urgent, and important or non-important, as shown in the **time management matrix** in Figure 9.3. Dr. Covey posits that highly effective people make time for activities that are important but not urgent (Quadrant 2), which enables them to reduce the amount of time they spend on other activities.

For example, let's look at what Jim does:

- His Quadrant 1 activities may include dealing with missed delivery dates and back orders and handling important customer complaints. This quadrant deals with the day-to-day urgent and important issues.
- It's important to focus on the Quadrant 2 activities, which might include increasing marketing efforts or building networks to further his business. None of these activities are urgent, but they are important because they will benefit him in the long term.

Which quadrant do you spend most of your time on?

Figure 9.3 | **Time Management Matrix**

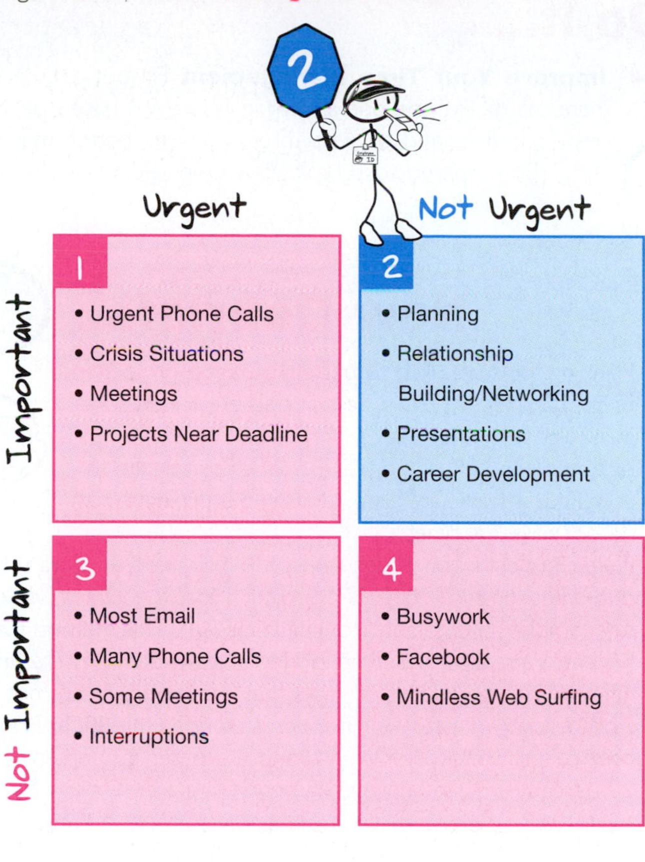

- Quadrant 3 activities are those that might seem important, but are actually more distracting than helpful. Jim may have to answer phone calls, update his seller's page, and deal with interruptions. These activities do not help him complete his work and can make it more difficult to concentrate on the task at hand.
- Still more distracting are activities in Quadrant 4, which are things he might do to avoid work. Surfing the Internet for personal reasons, talking on the phone to friends, or doing busywork are all activities people engage in when avoiding work.

By prioritizing his tasks, Jim can increase his effectiveness and productivity. Similarly, you can use the time management matrix to determine which tasks you perform are most important to getting your work done.

Tool 5: The 80/20 Principle

Another way to prioritize your time is by using the **80/20 Principle** (also known as the *Pareto Principle*). Named after Italian economist Vilfredo Pareto, the idea stems from his observation that 20 percent of people in early 20th-century Italy owned 80 percent of the wealth. In business, his principle spawned many related observations of imbalance between causes and results, such as:

- 20 percent of the employees produce 80 percent of the company's output
- 20 percent of your work can cause 80 percent of your problems
- 20 percent of your customers contribute 80 percent of your revenue

80/20

Some companies use the 80/20 outcomes in their planning process to position themselves for growth and profitability. Meg Whitman, former CEO of eBay, analyzed eBay users and found that 20 percent were responsible for 80 percent of eBay's volume. She used this information to focus on this 20 percent, providing high sellers with special perks such as improved customer service and discounted delivery rates. The eBay PowerSellers program benefits the high sellers by improving their performance, which in turn benefits eBay itself.[18]

So, how can the 80/20 Principle help you? Well, it reminds you to focus 80 percent of your time and energy on the 20 percent of activities that really matter. Reducing time-wasting activities that bring negligible payoffs will help you concentrate on work that is critical. In the long run, this will help you increase productivity, and, by extension, increase your profit.

Do It...

9.4: Improve Your Time Management Fill out a time management matrix like the one shown in Figure 9.3 based on your current schedule and suggest three ways to better manage your time. Be prepared to submit your work electronically or to discuss it in class.

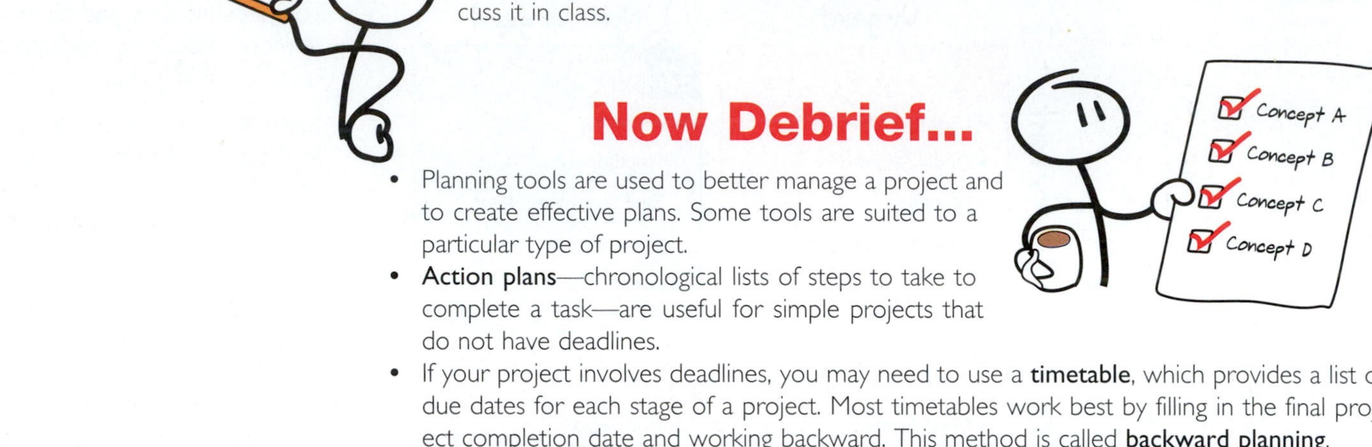

Now Debrief...

- Planning tools are used to better manage a project and to create effective plans. Some tools are suited to a particular type of project.
- **Action plans**—chronological lists of steps to take to complete a task—are useful for simple projects that do not have deadlines.
- If your project involves deadlines, you may need to use a **timetable**, which provides a list of due dates for each stage of a project. Most timetables work best by filling in the final project completion date and working backward. This method is called **backward planning**.
- To better manage their time, project managers may use a **time management matrix**. Highly efficient managers focus on tasks that are important but not urgent.
- Another way of assessing priorities is by using the **80/20 Principle**, which states that 20 percent of the work we do is vital and the other 80 percent is trivial. By focusing on the vital 20 percent, we can improve efficiency.

5. Risk Management: Planning for Problems

When was the last time you got into a car? Chances are, it was fairly recently. Were you worried about your safety? Probably not, because driving is an everyday activity for most of us. But the truth is we take a risk every time we get behind the wheel. In 2006, car accidents were responsible for 42,642 deaths in the United States.[19] Most of us reason that we can minimize the risk of getting into an accident by wearing a seatbelt, driving the speed limit, and staying away from drugs and alcohol when driving. Eliminating the risk altogether by not getting into any motorized vehicle would drastically inhibit our lives (and still wouldn't guarantee longevity).

When it comes to risk management, businesses work in a similar way. Think back to Chapter 2, when we discussed how risk is an inherent and necessary part of doing business—few businesspeople on the *Forbes* rich list earned their millions without taking chances. But just as we can reduce our chances of getting into a serious car accident, managers can also reduce the possibility of serious losses or other adverse effects for their company. As managers plan how their company will achieve its goals, they must factor in the risks involved in each step of the process and the problems they might incur. By determining what could possibly go wrong, they can plan what they are going to do if problems arise. **Risk management** involves:

- Recognizing risk
- Measuring risk
- Planning for risk

- Managing risk
- Monitoring risk

Let's look at each of these in a bit more detail.

Recognizing Risk: One Manager's Loss Is Another's Gain

What is risk? To one person it might be jumping out of an airplane, whereas a more cautious individual might think it involves crossing the street a second before the light turns green. ■ Risk is all about perception, and perception is not always in line with reality. For example, if someone asked you whether it was more dangerous to travel by car or by plane, you would probably say plane. But recall the earlier statistic that there were 42,642 traffic-related deaths in the United States. In 2006, air crashes were responsible for just 755 deaths worldwide.[20]

The Perception of Risk As we discussed in Chapter 2, a *risk* is any circumstance in which the outcome of a decision or action is uncertain. The greater the risk, the larger the difference between a favorable or unfavorable outcome. But people have different perceptions of risk. While one investor may view companies with plummeting stock prices as a risky investment, another may see it as an opportunity to make a lot of money if the stocks recover their value. Remember the SWOT analysis earlier in the chapter? Risks are similar to threats in the sense that they could potentially harm your business, whether through damage to the company's reputation, a reduction in opportunities, or a reduction in options, all of which can result in financial losses.

Risk as Opportunity Many successful managers and companies perceive risk as an opportunity. Take a look at the electric power industry. With the current government discussions about carbon emission controls, electric power companies face serious risks regarding the way they do business. While many of its competitors were scrambling to avoid liability for carbon emissions, General Electric was considering how it might use this potential risk as a business opportunity. In 2005, it launched Ecomagination, an initiative to help meet customer demand for more energy-efficient products. The strategy has proven to be a huge success, with revenues surging 21 percent to $17 billion in 2008.[21]

Measuring Risk: Expecting the Unexpected

We measure risk every day. See if this sounds like a familiar scenario: *My health insurance is due for renewal this month, but I don't think I can afford it. Last year I didn't need to go to the doctor's office, so all that money I spent on insurance was wasted. I'm healthy now, but there's always the chance that something unexpected might happen. Should I take the risk?*

To decide whether to renew your insurance, you might conduct some research, examine the consequences of not having insurance, and look for cheaper options. Businesses work in a similar way. They measure risk by conducting surveys, researching industry *benchmarks* (standards that are used to measure progress), calculating probabilities, and examining the company's current activities. Not all risk is measurable or can even be anticipated, so managers have to prepare to expect the unexpected.

■ Risk is all about perception, and perception is not always in line with reality.

Planning for Risk: Hope for the Best, Plan for the Worst

Imagine that you're taking a trip. Your bags are packed, your flight is booked, and your hotel reservation is confirmed. You're feeling fairly well organized, but what if there is a traffic jam and you miss your flight? What if the airline loses your baggage? What if the hotel has no record of your reservation? If you wrote down a list of everything that could possibly go wrong, you would fill several notebook pages and still not be able to cover everything.

Companies take this perspective when they do business. To minimize risk, they try to identify problems ahead of time, and be sure to have a plan B. They also have plans in place to deal with unexpected crises, should they arise.

Contingency Planning: Having a Plan B

If something doesn't go the way you planned, it's always good to have a plan B. Thinking back to your trip, what would you do if the hotel didn't have a record of your reservation? Keeping a list of alternative hotels and their contact details would give you an alternative course of action.

Contingency planning involves creating a plan of action to prepare a company in case of an emergency or if an anticipated risk takes place. The contingency plan is put into effect to limit the disruption of the emergency to business procedures. This requires preparing an alternative plan in case your first plan doesn't meet the intended objectives. For example, when the space shuttle is due to land at Cape Canaveral to conclude a mission, NASA has a contingency plan in place in the event of bad weather. The shuttle can land in California and the mission will still meet all of its goals. A successful business can plan for and around the problems that occur, keeping a project on schedule and running smoothly.

Crisis Planning: Reacting to the Unexpected

Crisis planning involves reacting to sudden, unexpected changes, such as a natural disaster or a sudden drop in the market. In this case, managers may have to set up ad hoc committees to contend with these risks and use whatever system they have in place to address and communicate their actions. For example, in Chapter 8 we discussed how Johnson & Johnson handled a crisis effectively when bottles of Tylenol were found laced with cyanide. To protect consumers, they immediately pulled 30 million bottles off the shelves and returned to the market with stronger safety measures.

Managing Risk: Making the Tough Choices

Put yourself back in the position of the person deciding whether or not to renew their health insurance. What are your options?

1. You can accept the risk that you might get sick or injured and go without health insurance altogether.
2. You can take out the insurance, which transfers your risk of illness or injury onto the insurance company.
3. You can try to reduce the risk of illness and injury by taking vitamin C every day and canceling those motorcycle lessons.
4. Although you cannot avoid the risk of sickness or injury altogether, you can renew your health insurance and at least eliminate the risk of financial ruin as a result of expensive hospital bills.

To manage risk, companies can also use these four strategies: they can *accept* the risk, *transfer* the risk, *reduce* the risk, and/or *avoid* the risk.

Accepting the Risk

In many cases, companies have no choice but to accept a risk. Police chiefs know that their officers may be in danger on the streets and that their vehicles may be involved in a collision, but there is no way for the department to function effectively without either officers or patrol cars.

In other instances, companies have a choice whether to accept a risk and may decide, after weighing up the potential consequences and possible benefits, that it is worth taking a chance. Launching an expensive product that directly competes with a similar product on the market could potentially have devastating financial consequences if the product fails. However, if it succeeds, the company increases its profits and raises its profile.

Transferring the Risk Just as an individual can take out various types of insurance to cover their financial costs in the event of an accident, injury, or natural disaster, so can companies and nonprofit organizations. A company will almost always take out property and liability insurance, which covers both damage to the property through accident, fire, or theft, as well as any injuries suffered by company employees. Insurance is generally for catastrophic or major risks, rather than for each and every routine or small inconvenience or problem. Other types of insurance include health insurance, disability insurance, workers' compensation, and professional liability insurance.

Reducing the Risk In Chapter 2, we discussed how companies minimize their risk by diversifying their investments. Of course, this is not the only way companies reduce risk. For example, if you have ever had a job, did the company have regular fire and safety drills? Were you shown the correct way to lift heavy equipment? Were you given health advice, or did your company initiate any policies to encourage healthy behavior? If the answer to any of these questions is "yes," then you have firsthand experience of risk reduction in action.

Avoiding the Risk Sometimes, having evaluated all the possible scenarios, organizations decide that a proposed course of action is just not worth the risk. A company might turn down a potentially hazardous job, decide against investing in an unstable business, or reject a proposal to launch a product that may or may not beat the competition.

Monitoring Risk: Reviewing the Choices

Monitoring risk is a no-brainer. Business owners ask their managers to continually follow through with a formal audit or other mechanism to check the progress of actions taken to address risk. Managers must also use SWOT and PEGSET analysis to scan the business environment and to search for outside threats and internal weaknesses.

Do It...

9.5: Create a Contingency Plan Identify several specific risks in your life, such as losing your job, your car breaking down, or losing your ATM card. Create a contingency plan for two of the risks that have the most likelihood of becoming a reality. Be prepared to submit your plan electronically or to discuss them in class.

Now Debrief...

- Risk is a necessary part of doing business, although it can be managed through a process of recognizing, measuring, planning, managing, and monitoring.
- Recognizing risk involves perception, and different people have different perceptions of whether a risk is great or small.
- Measuring risk involves conducting surveys, researching industry *benchmarks*, calculating probabilities, and examining a company's current activities to assess the severity of the risk.
- Companies frequently develop **contingency plans** to plan for potential problems. **Crisis planning** involves reacting to a sudden unexpected development.
- In terms of **risk management**, companies can accept the risk (by default or through choice), transfer the risk (e.g., by taking out insurance), reduce the risk (e.g., through loss-prevention techniques), or avoid the risk altogether (e.g., by not accepting a potentially hazardous job).
- Once a risk has been dealt with, a company will continually monitor the risk and ensure that the current risk management measures are working.

Chapter 9 Visual Summary

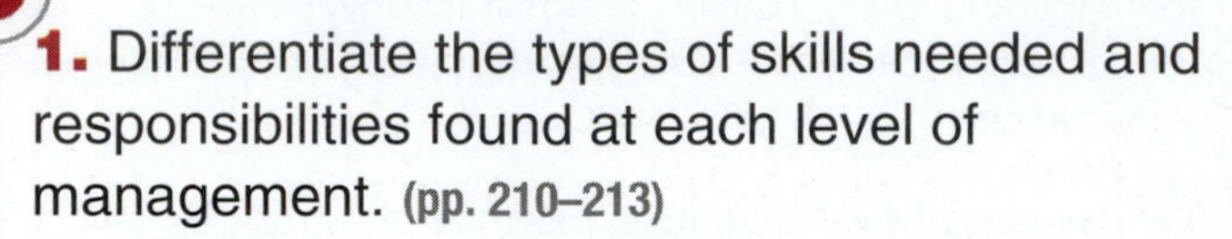

1. Differentiate the types of skills needed and responsibilities found at each level of management. (pp. 210–213)

- There are three levels of management in an organization: top-level management, middle management, and first-level management.
- **Top-level managers** are responsible for long-term planning, making policies for the organization, and appointing and reviewing the performance of managers who report directly to them.
- **Middle managers** are responsible for carrying out the policies and plans set up by top management. They require strong people skills because they need to motivate employees.
- **First-level managers** (**supervisors**) are in charge of running a single department, directing workflow and employees, and assessing problems. They report to middle management.

Summary: There are three levels of management, each with different responsibilities and skill sets. Top managers focus most on conceptual skills, middle managers focus on people skills, and first-level managers use technical skills to complete their jobs; however, each manager needs to use all of these skills to some degree.

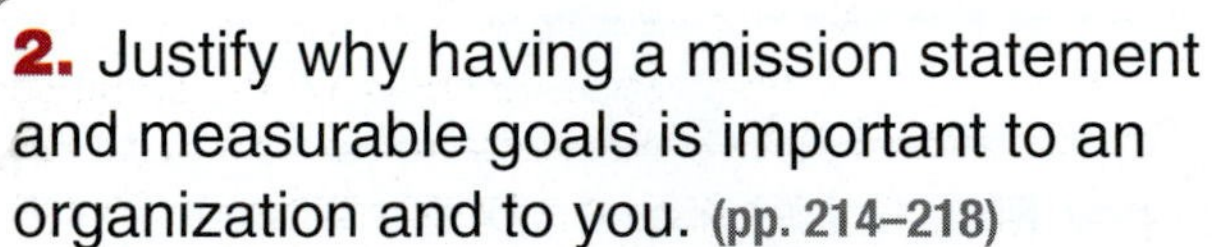

2. Justify why having a mission statement and measurable goals is important to an organization and to you. (pp. 214–218)

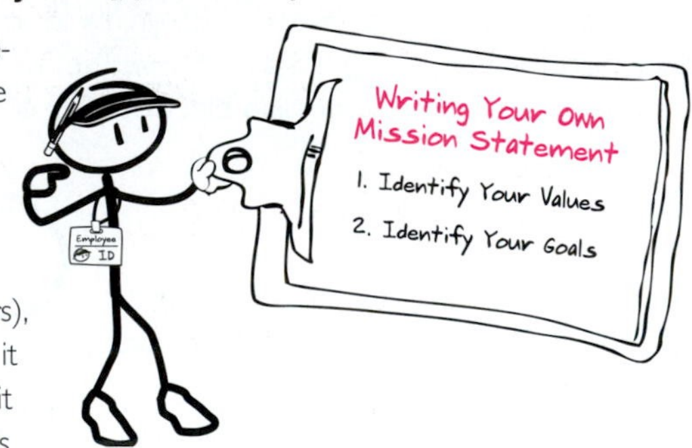

- A mission statement defines what endeavor the organization is engaged in (the nature of the business), whom it intends to serve (customers and stakeholders), what needs or benefits it will focus on, and how it will address those needs.
- To be successful, managers and employees alike have to translate their mission statement into concrete and measurable goals.
- Effective goals are **SMART**: specific, measurable, attainable, relevant, and time-based.
- Creating a mission statement and SMART goals for your own career will help to guarantee your success.

Summary: Businesses use mission statements to create goals that everyone in the company can work toward achieving. Mission statements should be reviewed to make sure that they match a company's current goals. Having up-to-date and realistic goals makes it easier for managers and employees to work toward accomplishing those goals.

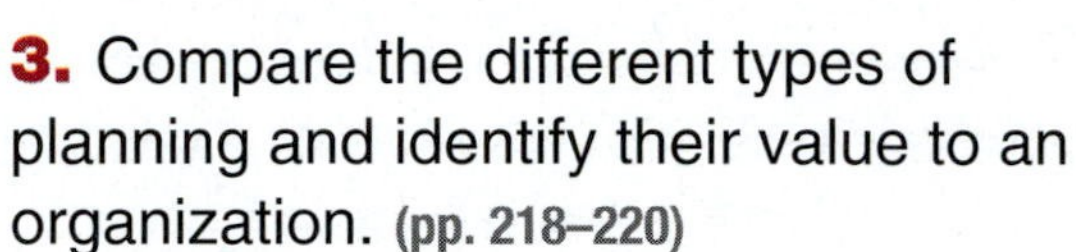

3. Compare the different types of planning and identify their value to an organization. (pp. 218–220)

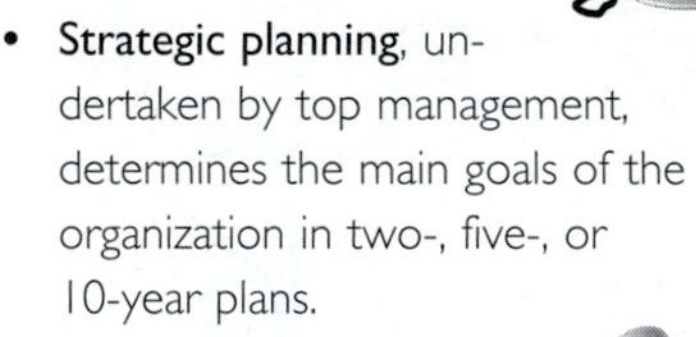

- Organizations use three types of planning: strategic planning, tactical planning, and operational planning.
- **Strategic planning**, undertaken by top management, determines the main goals of the organization in two-, five-, or 10-year plans.
- **Tactical planning**, undertaken by middle management, aligns elements of the strategic plan with the appropriate company resources. Tactical plans are short-term (one-year) plans.
- **Operational planning**, undertaken by specific individuals in specific departments, is used to run daily or weekly operations.
- SWOT analysis is a major part of planning, through which successful organizations attempt to turn potential risks or threats into opportunities.

Summary: Businesses use planning to determine how they will achieve their company goals. Each step of planning divides tasks and resources into smaller portions, making it easier to determine who needs to complete what task within a certain amount of time.

5. Demonstrate how managers plan for and manage risk. (pp. 224–227)

- **Risk management** involves recognizing, measuring, planning, managing, and monitoring risk.
- Recognizing risk involves perception, and different managers and employees have different perceptions and tolerances.
- Measuring risk involves conducting surveys, researching industry *benchmarks*, calculating probabilities, and examining a company's current activities to assess the severity of the risk.
- A **contingency plan** is a backup plan that may be used if the first plan is not successful. **Crisis planning** involves reacting to a sudden, unexpected development.
- Managing risk involves accepting the risk, transferring the risk, reducing the risk, or avoiding the risk.
- Once a risk has been dealt with, it is continually monitored.

Summary: All business ventures involve some sort of risk. Managers plan ahead to make sure that their companies are prepared for any problems that may arise. They use contingency plans to prepare for anticipated risks. They use crisis planning to respond to unexpected problems.

4. Explain what tools managers use to create effective plans. (pp. 221–224)

- Project managers use planning tools to help them deliver a project on time, on schedule, and to the exact specifications.
- Tool 1: An **action plan** is a list of tasks that need to be carried out, in the order in which they should be completed.
- Tool 2: A **timetable** provides a list of completion dates for each task.

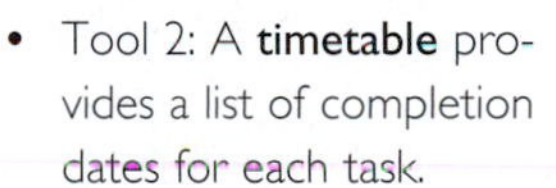

- Tool 3: **Backward planning** is a technique that involves starting with the ultimate goal and figuring out the best way to achieve it by working out each preceding step.

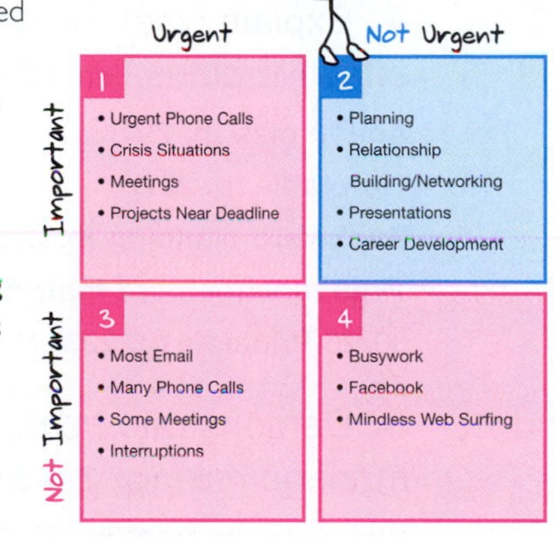

- Tool 4: A **time management matrix** divides tasks into four quadrants—important and urgent, important but not urgent, not important but urgent, and not important and not urgent. Effective managers focus on tasks that are important but not urgent.
- Tool 5: The **80/20 Principle** states that there is an imbalance between cause and effect; 80 percent of output comes from 20 percent of input. By focusing on the effective 20 percent, managers and employees can divide their time more effectively.

Summary: Managers use planning tools to help them create plans that use a company's resources most effectively.

Get the most out of what you just read by practicing your skills and actually DOING something with the material! The best place to do this is at **www.mybizlab.com**. Here's just some of what is available to you there:

- Apply your skills in an interactive environment with more **BizSkill** experiences...and see if you have what it takes
- Think critically and talk with your peers on hot business topics in **BizChat**
- Flex your business communication skills and build your own portfolio with the **Communication Plan exercises**
- Watch the chapter material come together with **Just Plain Business** videos
- Study on-the-go with **Audio Chapter Summaries** in MP3 format
- Brush up on the lecture and content with **Audio PowerPoints**
- Discover how well you are doing and see what areas you need to improve on with the **Pre-Tests** and **Post-Tests**

Key Words

These key words and more are also available as flash cards to practice with at **www.mybizlab.com**.

1. Differentiate the types of skills needed and responsibilities found at each level of management. (pp. 210–213)

Top managers (p. 211)
Chief executive officer (CEO) (p. 211)
Middle managers (p. 212)
First-level managers (supervisors) (p. 213)

2. Justify why having a mission statement and measurable goals is important to an organization and to you. (pp. 214–218)

Mission statement (p. 214)
SMART goals (p. 216)
Management by Objectives (MBO) (p. 218)

3. Compare the different types of planning and identify their value to an organization. (pp. 218–220)

Strategic planning (p. 218)
Tactical planning (p. 219)
Operational planning (p. 219)

4. Explain what tools managers use to create effective plans. (pp. 221–224)

Action plan (p. 221)
Timetable (p. 221)
Backward planning (p. 222)
Time management matrix (p. 222)
80/20 Principle (p. 223)

5. Demonstrate how managers plan for and manage risk. (pp. 224–227)

Risk management (p. 224)
Contingency planning (p. 226)
Crisis planning (p. 226)

Prove It

Prove It...

Now, let's put on one of the BizHats. With the **Manager BizHat** squarely on your head, look at the following exercise:

You work for a graphic design company that creates cell phone covers. Your supervisors are pleased with your organizational skills and ask you to manage a small project. The project requires you to oversee the development of 30 new cell phone covers. Their launch will coincide with the return of a popular reality TV show at the beginning of next year. You will be directly in charge of four of your co-workers throughout the project, even though you all have the same job title.

What planning tools should you use to ensure that the project runs smoothly? Explain how you would use each tool to help you with the project and explain how it would be useful to you and your team.

Flip It...

Now flip over to the **Employee BizHat**. You are an employee at the same graphic design company described above. A co-worker with the same job title as you is in charge of the cell phone cover project you're working on, but he does not have much managerial experience, and the project is not going well. Deadlines are being missed, client feedback is not being passed on to the rest of the team, and there is a very negative atmosphere in the office. What is the best way to handle the situation? How would you help to get the project get back on track? What factors do you need to take into consideration?

Now Debrief It...

Compare the perspectives of the two BizHats described above. How does changing your perspective on the project affect your actions?

Organize: Organizational Structure, Culture, and Employee Recruitment, Selection, and Hiring

BizSkills invite...

Try It!
There's no better way to learn concepts than to put them into practice. Take your turn in the driver's seat and be a part of actual business decision making by visiting the BizSkill for this chapter at **www.mybizlab.com**.

Now that you've practiced making tough business decisions and seeing the results of your choices in this chapter's BizSkill, it's time to translate those skills into plain English. And if you skipped the BizSkill, go back now!

Chapter 10 Goals

After experiencing this chapter, you'll be able to:

1. Interpret and understand an organization chart, and anticipate the role you would be expected to perform in an organization depending on its structure.
2. Detect and recognize an organization's culture in order to make decisions about your career.
3. Use effective recruiting, selecting, and hiring strategies.

How do you organize a successful company?

Organizing for a Purpose

Your alarm goes off at 6:00 a.m. on a Saturday morning. Instead of sleeping in, you drive your sister to swim practice. Since your parents work on Saturdays, it's your job to make sure your sister gets there on time. You're not the only one with responsibilities, though. On weekdays, your father cooks dinner, and your mother does laundry before she leaves for work.

In your neighbor's family, the situation is different. Mr. Spencer works from home and drives his children to their activities. Mrs. Spencer works an irregular schedule but cooks dinner when she can. The children are in charge of laundry. Although this organization works for the Spencers, it probably wouldn't work for your family. At the same time, the way your family assigns duties probably wouldn't work for the Spencers.

Families are organized in different ways based on their sizes and circumstances. For example, families with many children may delegate chores using strict schedules. Smaller families may be more flexible. The location of authority and the lines of communication vary in different family situations as well. In some cases, a parent may impose rules on children without any discussion. In other cases, children have more input.

Like families, businesses are organized in different ways. The organization of a business depends on its size, location, and many other factors. In this chapter, we'll consider how businesses organize themselves and how this affects its organizational culture and human resources.

1. Organizational Structure: Roles of Managers and Employees

Have you ever planned to hold a social event that just never happened due to conflicting schedules, changing plans, or lack of interest? Although friends may agree that a party would be fun, it will never take place without proper organization. Who will bring the food? Who will invite people? As you can see, *planning* to have a party is not the same thing as actually *organizing* a party. This rule applies to business as well.

Chapter 9 discussed the importance of setting goals, developing strategies, and making plans. Goals, strategies, and plans allow employees to prepare for specific projects as well as long-term business endeavors, but they alone cannot achieve results. In addition to creating mission statements, company objectives, and other elements of the planning phase, businesses must establish a framework, or organizational structure, to achieve their goals. In this chapter, we'll explore how organization can help a business create value. First, we'll look at the many different ways in which companies choose to structure themselves. We'll also consider how different organizational structures can affect you as an employee.

Organizational Structure Basics

■ The structure of a business is what makes it click on a daily basis. It is like the organs of your body working in concert to keep you alive and moving. If one of your major organs stopped functioning, your body couldn't perform the way you want or need.

The same applies to business. No structure, no success. While establishing structure, it's important to consider the desired end result. What is it that your company wants to accomplish? What are the goals, mission, and values of the company? The **organizational structure** is the formal configuration of people in an organization that determines the allocation of duties, responsibilities, and authority. Who is responsible for what, and who answers to whom?

The need for organizational structure arises from the **division of labor**, which is simply the breakdown of different specialized roles that employees take on. When creating an organizational structure, a company figures out what roles need to be filled and then decides where to place these roles. For example, a company may decide to place its Legal department within the Human Resources (HR) department. In this case, the legal specialists report to an HR manager. If done properly, the division of labor maximizes productivity. For this reason, organizational structure helps an organization succeed in meeting its goals.

As we'll discuss in this chapter, organizational structure varies according to the type, purpose, goals, and size of the organization. It can be quite simple, as in a business owned and run by one person, or sprawling and complex, as in a multi-location, multi-department, multinational company. In the next few pages, you'll read about various ways that companies are organized. You'll encounter several different ways to describe structure, such as *centralized*, *decentralized*, *flat*, *tall*, *matrix*, and *linear*. Keep in mind that the categories described in this chapter are not entirely independent of one another; a company may adopt elements of multiple structures.

■ The structure of a business is what makes it click on a daily basis.

The Organization Chart and Hierarchy of Authority

Although you can't actually look at an organization with the naked eye and observe its structure, a visual representation of it can be constructed. This representation is known as an **organization chart**, which diagrams the relationships between various departments or employees within an organization. The purpose of an organization chart is to:

1. Describe different types of work or tasks and identify who is in charge of the tasks.
2. Indicate divisions or departments within an organization.
3. Illustrate the relationships between individuals and departments.

Figure **10.1** | **Sample Organization Chart for a Complex Organization**

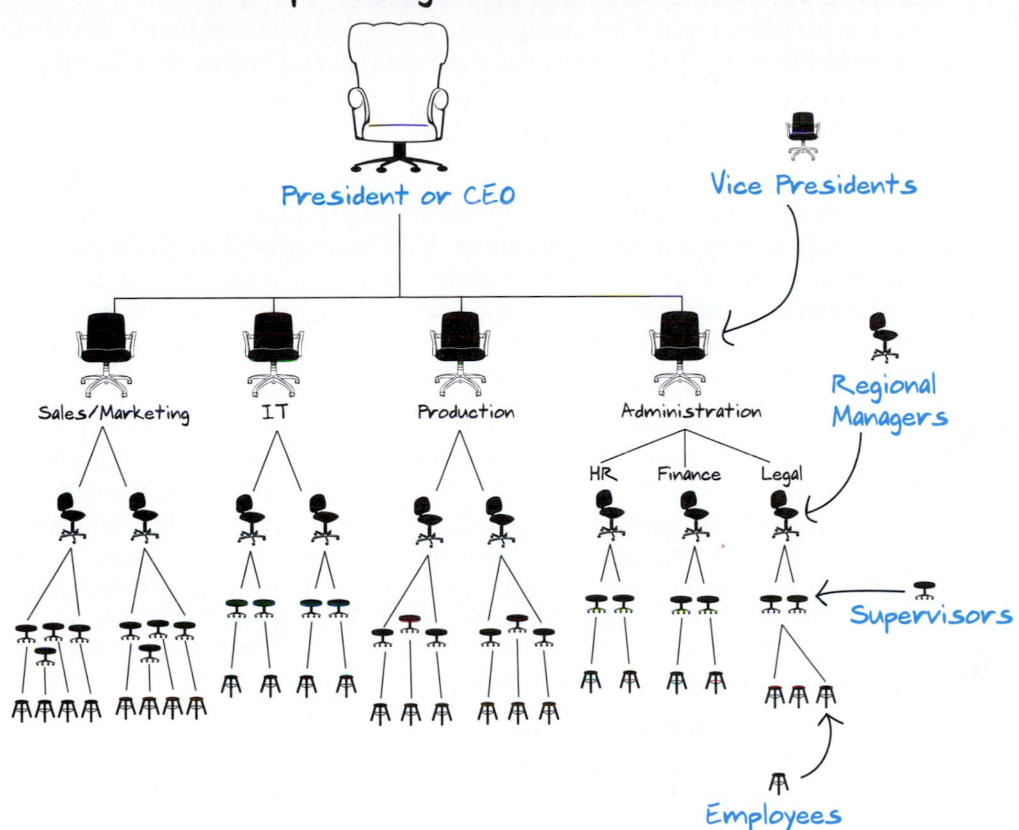

The organization chart also determines the **hierarchy of authority** in an organization. The hierarchy of authority is the official configuration of *reporting relationships*. Thus, employees may look at the organization chart to figure out "who answers to whom."

Figure 10.1 shows a sample organization chart for a large company. As you can see, the president or CEO is at the top of the hierarchy, followed by the vice presidents, the regional managers, and finally the supervisors. These roles fall into the levels of management we discussed in Chapter 9. The president or CEO is a top manager who focuses on the big picture. The vice presidents may be top managers or middle managers, depending on their responsibilities in the organization. The regional managers are generally middle managers who oversee resources for a specific area. Supervisors are lower-level managers who assign employees their work, monitor their progress, and provide guidance.

You can identify the line of authority in Figure 10.1 by following the hierarchy from top to bottom. In general, managers have authority over the employees directly below them in the organization chart. Communication typically occurs between employees and the people directly below or above them in the organization chart. Only in special circumstances do employees "skip" levels and communicate with those further removed from them on the chart.

Centralized vs. Decentralized Structures

Different types of organizational structures determine the roles that managers and employees play. For example, organizations with a **centralized structure** place the decision-making authority in the hands of very few. A highly centralized company relies heavily on the expertise of those leading the company. Decisions are made at the top levels of management and filter down to lower-level employees through the hierarchy of authority. In a centralized structure, it is easier to maintain consistency throughout an organization. In addition, key decisions can be made more quickly because only a few people need to reach a consensus.

A **decentralized structure**, in contrast, spreads authority and decision making down the organizational chart, allowing middle and lower-level managers to make some decisions. A decentralized structure may even leave some choices in the hands of individual employees who do not have the title of manager. This allows employees to be more innovative, but it may also lead to inconsistency. Without enough widespread policies and rules, or enough training and development, a company may become ineffective.

So, is Figure 10.1 a centralized or a decentralized structure? It could actually depict either, depending on whether decision-making authority is concentrated at the top with the president and the vice presidents, or if authority is delegated so that even the low-level supervisors have some decision-making responsibility.

In your business career, you might also encounter the term *bureaucratic* to describe an organization. This term is somewhat related to the term *centralized*. An organization that is strictly

Figure **10.2** | **Sample Flat Organization Chart**

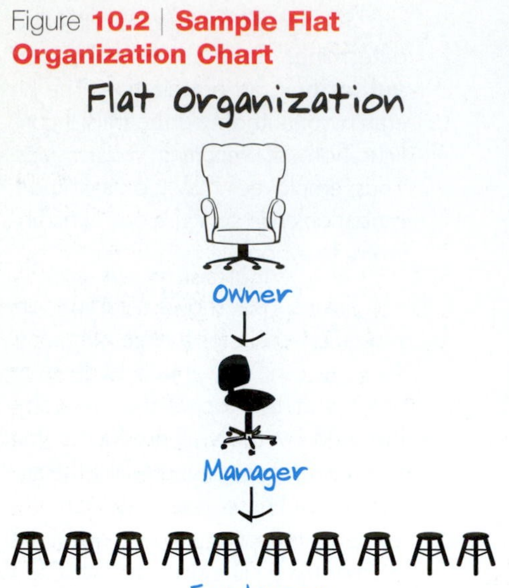

hierarchical, has workers perform highly specialized jobs, has many rigidly imposed rules, and places all authority in the hands of a few top-ranking authorities is known as a **bureaucratic organization**. These days, *bureaucratic* is often seen as a negative term, but in some businesses, it is the best structure to use. A bureaucratic system is most effective for a business that is relatively stable and does not have to face extreme changes.

Flat vs. Tall Organizations

Ever wonder why there are no promotions in your company? One reason could be that there is nowhere to go. If there are 10 technicians, one manager, and the owner of the shop, you're working in a **flat organization**. A flat organization is an organization that has only a few layers of management. In a flat organization, managers tend to have a wider **span of control**; they are responsible for many employees. Consider the flat organization shown in Figure 10.2. The organization has only one manager, who reports to the owner. This manager is responsible for 10 employees.

Flat organizations have several advantages. Most employees are on the same level, which makes it easy to communicate, especially since employees in flat organizations often work in teams. Because there are fewer layers of management, the decision-making process is easier. Flat organizations are also often able to respond to their customers quickly as employees don't have to go up many layers of management to get approval for something. Flat organizations may also have lower employee costs, since they have fewer high-paid managers. However, in flat organizations, the role of lower-level workers may not be clearly defined as so many people work on the same level. Also, there is less room for advancement because the number of management positions is limited.

The flip side of this is a **tall organization**, in which there are many layers of hierarchy, as shown in Figure 10.3. In a tall organization, more layers of management mean fewer employees reporting to each manager. As you can see in Figure 10.3, each manager is directly responsible for no more than three employees. The president or CEO oversees two managers. Each manager oversees two supervisors, who each have three subordinates.

Tall organizations have several advantages. In tall organizations, managers can closely supervise their employees. Also, the role of the employees at each layer is clearly defined. Tall organizations also present more opportunities for advancement, since there are many management positions. Tall organizations do present some challenges, however. The long chain of command means that the decision-making process may be slow. Communication may be more difficult since it has to pass through different layers of management. In addition, tall organizations may have higher costs because managers are often paid more than lower-level employees.

Figure **10.3** | **Sample Tall Organization Chart**

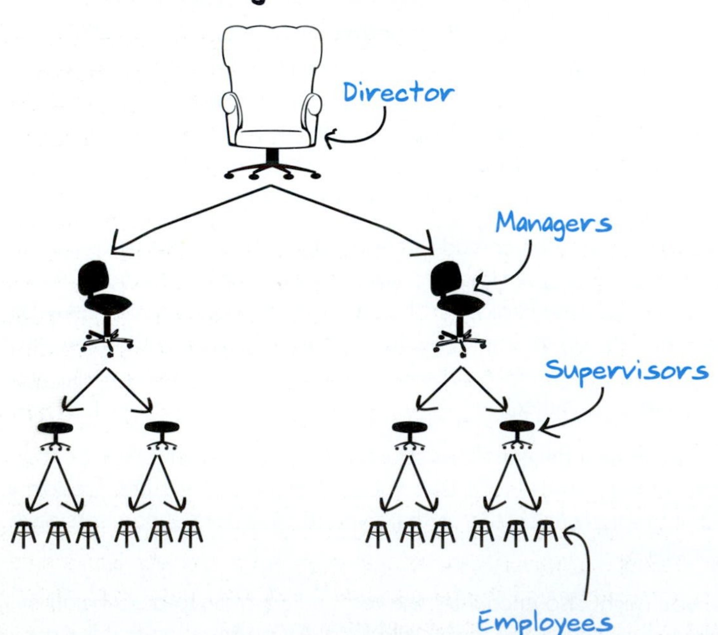

Linear vs. Matrix Structures

There are different ways for organizations to set up the hierarchy of authority. The most basic of these is the **linear structure**. This means that the hierarchy of authority goes down the line from top management to lower-level employees. Each manager is responsible for the positions below, and each employee has only one assigned boss. Linear structure is not exactly the same as centralized structure. In a centralized structure, all authority rests in a limited number of top-level managers. In a linear structure, authority may be more spread out. However, each employee is under the immediate authority of just one manager. Although this design is relatively simple, most organizations have a more complicated structure.

Imagine that you're part of the marketing department. Your marketing manager assigned you to work on Product Z, at the request of the manager of Product Z. You need to take a day off for a dental appointment. Whom do you ask—the marketing manager or the manager of Product Z?

Figure 10.4 | **Sample Matrix Organization Chart**

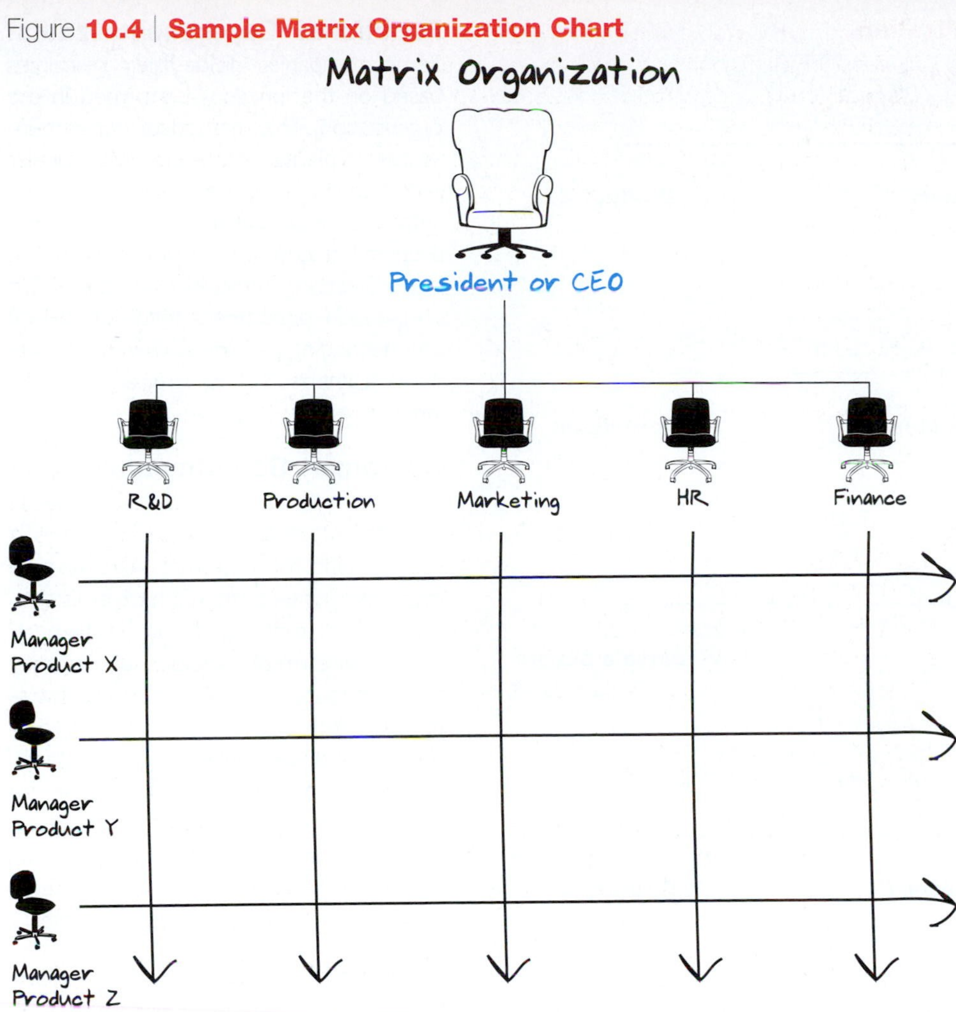

In this case, you may be working in a **matrix structure** with the obvious trait of having more than one boss. It's one way to break a company down into smaller, highly functional units, but it can be a little confusing if specific lines of communication and authority are not established. Figure 10.4 shows an example of a matrix structure. In this structure, employees belong both to a functional department (R&D, Production, Marketing, etc.) and to a specific product team (Product X, Product Y, etc.). In many cases, the functional department manager assigns an employee to a product initially, but then turns over the main authority over the employee to the product manager.

Matrix organizations promote flexible use of human resources. This structure is particularly useful for companies that take on a wide variety of short-term projects. People from different departments can be used temporarily to assist with special projects. This kind of flexibility is great for businesses that need to adapt quickly to changing conditions. If a competitor releases a new product, a matrix organization can set up a rapid-response team to develop a complementary product.

The obvious disadvantage of the matrix system is the frustration faced by an employee with two bosses. Put yourself in that person's shoes. You have two managers to report to, so if the department and project managers disagree or fail to communicate, the workplace is going to be an ugly environment. Another possible negative is that these structures can be expensive in terms of labor costs.

Departmentalization

Imagine you work in the marketing department of a pharmaceutical company. You're responsible for promoting the company's products and identifying new markets. Would your boss ever ask you to conduct scientific experiments for a new drug? Probably not. There are chemists and biomedical engineers who are specially trained for that task. Their function in the company is different from your function, but all of you are important to the company's success.

The division of labor based on function is one form of departmentalization. **Departmentalization** occurs when a company divides its employees into different units, or departments, based on their roles. Each workplace has unique departmentalization needs. For example, a company that relies heavily on computers might need an entire IT department, whereas a single-owner business might be able to accommodate its own computer needs without hiring a full-time IT professional. Figure 10.5 shows some popular forms of departmentalization: by product, function, customer type, geographic location, and process. Let's look at each of these forms in a bit more detail.

Product Departmentalization If a company has several product lines, it may choose to group its resources based on products. Employees with varied skills cooperate to create a certain product or product line. For example, a clothing manufacturer may decide to create separate departments for women's wear, men's wear, and children's apparel. The employees in each department focus on clothing designed for people of a certain age and/or gender.

Figure **10.5** | **Forms of Departmentalization**

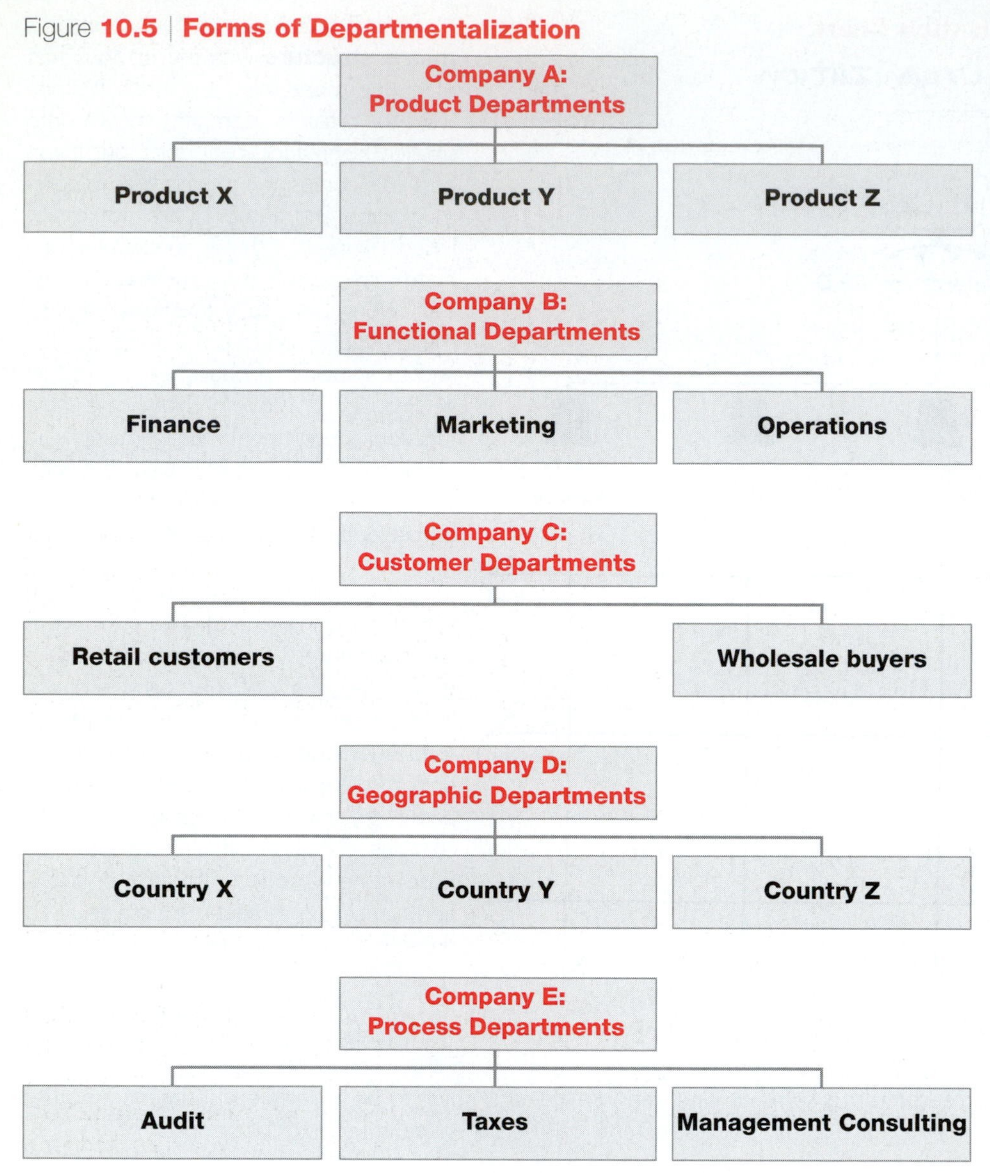

Functional Departmentalization Some companies divide their resources based on the functions performed in the organization. This method of departmentalization places employees with similar skills into the same departments. For example, a large bakery may have food preparation, customer service, and finance departments. Employees in the food preparation department focus on baking and decorating pastries, and employees in the customer service department focus on interacting with customers.

Customer Departmentalization In customer departmentalization, each department in an organization serves a specific kind of customer. Workers in these departments should have skills specialized to meeting these customers' needs. For example, a paper supplier may have a department that serves retail customers and another department that serves wholesale buyers. These departments can be further subdivided, if necessary. For example, within the wholesale buyer department, the company may have smaller departments to work specifically with schools or private businesses.

Geographic Departmentalization What if a company has customers in all different areas of the world? It might not be feasible to ask one department to handle all of these customers. Geographic departmentalization can help an organization provide service in different areas. This type of organization can assign departments by cities, states, countries, or even continents.

Process Departmentalization Supplying products to customers involves many processes. Some companies choose to separate these processes into departments through process departmentalization. For example, when you go to the DMV, there's usually a different line for driver's licenses, titling, and registration. Each process requires different training and skills, which is why the DMV uses process departmentalization. Otherwise, every employee at the DMV would need costly training for each process, and customers coming in for something quick, like a new license photo, could get stuck waiting for employees to finish helping customers with much more involved tasks like administering a driving test.

Adjusting Structure to a Changing Market

Your life is always changing. You meet new friends, get new jobs, and find new places to live. Adapting to these new situations can be challenging, but it's just a part of life. Likewise, modern businesses need to be prepared for **organizational change**; planned or unplanned transformations in the structure, technology, and people that an organization uses. There is nothing wrong with a tried-and-true organizational structure, but sometimes it is necessary to re-evaluate in order to keep up with a changing market.

Take the example of Xerox. In 1990, new CEO Paul Allaire took the reins of a well-established copier company, but found that it was being outfoxed by the competition. Xerox was stuck on the idea of the large, centralized office copier, while new Japanese companies were revolutionizing the market by producing smaller, faster, stand-alone copy units. These new copy machines were selling like hotcakes, leaving Xerox in the dust both domestically and abroad.

Allaire stepped up to the plate to ensure that Xerox would once again become the international standard for copy machines. After studying trends in the technological market, as well as internal structure, resource allocation, procedures, and employee motivation, he developed a new structural vision he dubbed "Xerox 2000." The company changed the way it defined, grouped, and managed its business, with immediate results. For example, the company began to establish close contact with customers to better understand the market. Instead of having orders flow from top managers down, the flow of communication began to move upward, from customers to lower-level employees to management. This allowed employees to respond to customer requests, which resulted in innovative products that satisfied changing customer needs.

The changes at Xerox represent an important trend in business structure. In recent years, many organizations have inverted their organization charts to show that the lowest-level employees tend to be more closely connected to the customer. Although top-level managers have key knowledge and expertise, it's usually the suppliers, technicians, and customer service representatives who interact with customers on a daily basis. These workers hear the customers' praises as well as their complaints, and they are therefore in a position to provide the company with valuable feedback.

Why Organizational Structure Matters to You

When searching for a job, you may consider things like salary, benefits, job responsibilities, and working schedule. Do you ever consider the organizational structure of the business? ■ The structure of a business can greatly affect the opportunities and challenges you encounter at a job.

What Do You Value? Consider the things you value in a career. Do you seek stability? Do you want regular working hours and lots of vacation time? Do you think salary should be based on seniority as well as performance? Or do you seek an exciting and unpredictable work environment that may require some overtime? Do you support performance-based promotions rather than a set pay scale? These questions may help you decide whether you are suited for a bureaucratic organization or not.

■ The structure of a business can greatly affect the opportunities and challenges you encounter at a job.

You'll also want to consider how employees are managed within that business. Do you enjoy working with people who perform different tasks than you do? Do you want to work in a place where your job activities may change quickly? Or do you prefer working with people who share your skills and knowledge? Do you want to have a set role in an organization that rarely changes? In answering these questions, you may determine whether you prefer a matrix structure or a linear structure.

What's Your Best Span of Control? Have you ever put your fingers on the keys of a piano? If your thumb was on the C note, how far could you reach? Five keys? Eight keys? Well, that reach is like the span of control we discussed earlier—how far does your manager's responsibility reach? Five employees? 25 employees?

The span of control in your organization can greatly affect you as an employee. You may find that your boss hardly has time for you. As a manager in a flat organization, he or she may be responsible for more than a dozen employees. You may also feel like you have no chance of getting a promotion, since there is only one manager in the whole organization. If you work at a tall organization, you may find that it takes weeks or months for your salary increase to be approved. In addition, you may have difficulty communicating with people in other departments since your communication has to go through your supervisor.

As you apply to new organizations or move within your current organization, it's important to keep the span of control in mind. If opportunity for advancement is a high priority for you, you may want to work at a tall organization. If quick decision-making and a potentially wider range of duties are important to you, you may want to work at a flat organization.

Line or Staff? Your role in an organization also depends on whether you hold a line position or a staff position. *Line positions* are directly involved in producing or selling a product; they are crucial for the business to function. Engineers, production managers, and marketing specialists all hold line positions. On the other hand, *staff positions* are not involved in producing or selling a product; instead, they directly support line positions. Human resource professionals and legal advisors hold staff positions.

Translation Guide: Line versus Staff

Line: Line employees are directly responsible for the company's product or output. If you're in a line position, you perform an activity that contributes directly to the organization's bottom line.

Staff: Staff are departmental employees who support the line departments. These include legal, tech support, human resources, and others. If you're in a staff role, you support the people in line positions.

Example: If you provide technical support (staff) to the salespeople (line), they will be able to generate more revenue for the organization because they will have the technology tools that help them accomplish their goals.

Your role as a line or staff employee can affect what you get out of a job. Since line positions contribute directly to revenue, they often have higher salaries than staff positions. Also, line positions may have more opportunity for advancement than staff positions, because line positions can make more obvious contributions to a company's profitability. Although staff positions may receive less recognition, they do provide opportunities to gain a deeper understanding of how the business functions. Employees who have held staff positions at some point in their career may gain credibility with colleagues and be better equipped for future challenges.

Do It...

10.1: Choose an Organizational Structure Based on your reading, what sort of organizational structure would allow you to make your best contributions to a company? What sort of structure would be a good fit for your personal career mission? One in which there was centralized or decentralized decision-making? A tall organization or a flat organization? Why? Limit your response to one page, and be prepared to submit it electronically or discuss it in class.

Now Debrief...

- The **organizational structure** of an organization determines the duties, responsibilities, and authority of each employee. Establishing an organizational structure is essential for the success of the goals and strategies set forth in the planning stage.
- In a **centralized structure**, a few top managers have all the authority and make all the key decisions. In a **decentralized structure**, the authority is spread among many employees at different levels.
- Some organizations are set up based on the **span of control** each manager has. In **flat organizations**, each manager has a wide span of control, whereas managers in a **tall organization** have a narrow span of control.
- An organization with a **linear structure** has a chain of command in which each employee has only one supervisor. In an organization with a **matrix structure**, employees report to multiple supervisors.
- Organizations use **departmentalization** to break themselves up into different units. Departmentalization can be based on customers, products, functions, processes, or geography.
- Businesses need to adjust to new technology and changes in the marketplace to stay successful. **Organizational change** refers to planned or unplanned transformations in the structure, technology, and people in an organization.

2. Organizational Culture: Getting a Feel for It

"Every company has two organizational structures: The formal one is written on the charts; the other is the everyday relationship of the men and women in the organization."

—Harold S. Geneen, former CEO of ITT Corporation[1]

We've talked about the importance of organizational structure in the business world. But organization is not the only thing that defines a business. Consider your workplace if you have one. What's life *really* like at work? Do you catch up with colleagues during breaks, or do you spend all your time in a cubicle? Do you feel free to wear jeans and a sweatshirt, or do you arrive each morning wearing a suit and tie?

These elements, along with many others, are part of organizational culture. **Organizational culture** (sometimes referred to as *corporate culture*) consists of the attitudes, values, and norms shared by an organization's members. It determines how people are encouraged to behave at the workplace.

Let's look at an example. MindComet, an Internet marketing/consulting firm, prides itself on being an awesome place to work. Its Web site declares, "Work hard. Deliver. Play Hard." Employees at MindComet take part in a wide variety of activities that make the work experience enjoyable. For example, there is an employee blog dedicated to organizational culture, with entries that feature inside jokes about fellow employees and recaps of company events. Employees are chosen for their expertise and strong work ethic, and they are encouraged to share new ideas. The team is designed to be innovative, creating fresh advertising for major companies.

As for the day-to-day atmosphere in the workplace, there are no cubicles, but there is a lounge that gives free massages to employees. The office has lots of fancy hardware, and ambient music plays from speakers all over the building. Sound like a good place to work? Not only is the environment comfortable and encouraging, but the company also hosts events and outings, including a company retreat to the Bahamas. It is not uncommon for MindComet to include its clients in these events, creating a tighter alliance with the customers they serve.[2]

In short, the organizational culture at MindComet encourages familiarity and a sense of community among employees. Innovation and cooperation are valued over order and independence. However, this organizational culture may not be as effective for other organizations. For example, a prominent accounting firm may not want to encourage casual dress or office-wide music in the workplace, as this may put off visiting clients. In addition, employees may feel that the privacy of a cubicle helps them get their work done and ensures accuracy.

What Constitutes Organizational Culture?

The culture of an organization is what holds it together. It provides stability for all employees and provides the framework for them to get things done. The top of the hierarchy—typically upper-managers and owners—establish the culture. They set the tone for the rest of the workplace. If they emphasize and model teamwork and collaborative decision making, these values will trickle down to the rest of the employees.

Organizational culture affects all relationships in an organization. In an organization that values a rigid adherence to chain of command, lower-level employees may have limited contact with senior managers. In an organization that relies less heavily on chain of command, employees may interact with other employees at several levels. Although some may regard a strict chain of command as oppressive and overly rigid, it can provide consistency and prevent confusion.

At the same time, more open communication paths may allow decision-makers to hear innovative ideas that may otherwise have been filtered out in the chain of command. For example, search engine company Yahoo! encourages employees to make decisions and communicate up the chain of command, even if it means going

A large part of organizational culture occurs beneath the surface.

directly to the CEO.[3] Other companies choose to adhere to more traditional communication channels, in which ideas are presented to direct supervisors and are passed up the chain if the supervisor sees fit.

Although organizational culture can make employees feel like part of a team, it can also exclude those who do not agree with its values. This is especially true in international companies, which have increasingly diverse work forces. For example, America Online (AOL) commissioned a study to uncover employee attitudes toward its organizational culture. This study was commissioned after a series of complaints from female and minority employees about their treatment at work. The study confirmed that these complaints were a sign of a widespread problem. During the study, female and minority employees said that they felt excluded from the "good old boy" network within the company. According to these employees, the exclusive network acted as a "glass ceiling," or unofficial barrier, to prevent them from advancing to leadership positions.[4]

Think of organizational culture as the overall "personality" of the organization. It affects how you'll feel about going to work every day. Will you feel valued? Will you be heavily supervised or given more independence? If you're thinking of taking a job at a particular organization, it's important to know the organizational culture. But how do you do this? Let's take a closer look.

Figure **10.6** | **The Organizational Iceberg**

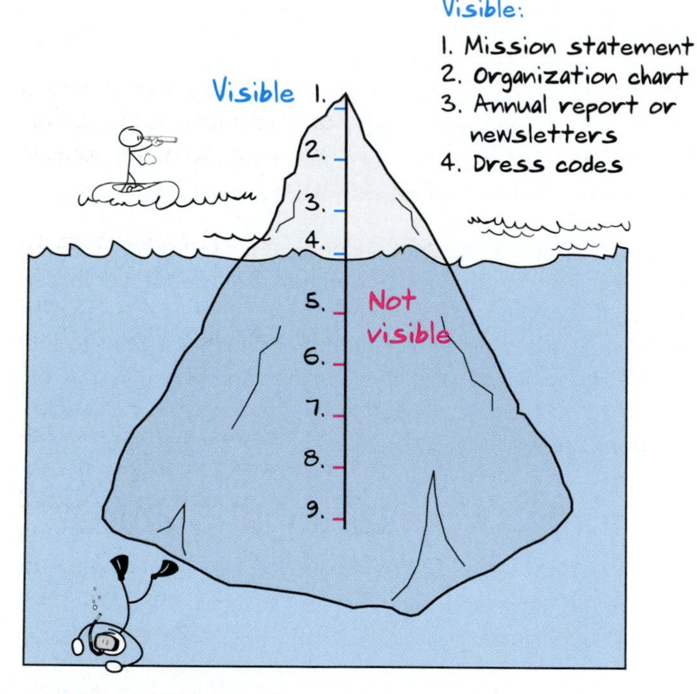

Not visible:

5. Norms
6. Values
7. Employees' perceptions of top managers
8. Identities of informal leaders
9. Relationships

Can you think of any other elements of an organization's culture that may not be visible?

The Iceberg Theory

You've heard the saying, "Never judge a book by its cover." In business, what's on the outside can tell you a few things about an organization, but that's only one part of the story. A large part of organizational culture occurs beneath the surface.

Organizations are sometimes compared to icebergs, because the visible part of an organization is often only a small part of what really goes on within the organization as a whole. As shown in Figure 10.6, the tip of the iceberg includes information you can find out about an organization without working there. For example, an organization may have a mission statement available to the public. It might even have a sample organization chart showing you the formal chain of command. Most organizations publish some kind of annual report or newsletter that provides specific information about the actions of the company. Changes in job titles and descriptions, changes in policy, and new projects are often included in these publications. Other "visible" elements are dress codes and anything else that an outside visitor could see.

But the image that an organization portrays is just the tip of iceberg; the rest of the organization's norms, values, and structures lie beneath the surface, as shown in Figure 10.6. Employees' perceptions of top managers typically fall in this category. In addition, the identities of informal leaders and their relationships with formal leaders are typically below the surface.

To uncover the "submerged" aspects of an organization, you usually have to work within the organization or talk to people who do. By doing so, you discover the true attitudes of employees toward the organization. Do they actually enjoy working there and think it is a good company? Does the organization stand by its stated values and purpose on a daily basis? Who are the informal leaders in the organization? Are they the top managers as shown in the organizational chart, or are there particular employees who step up and really make it all come together? Who influences the president? Who does your manager really listen to? What kind of informal communication goes on? Is the rumor mill running wild, or are employees relatively constrained and respectful?

How to Recognize Organizational Culture

So, how do you recognize the organizational culture of the organization you work for? It's not likely that an organization will send a company-wide memo describing the attitudes and opinions of every worker. Instead, you need to understand organizational culture by paying attention to what is going on around you in the workplace:

- One thing you can do is observe and interact with your co-workers. Make a note of how employees talk or write to each other. Is their tone stiff or friendly? Encouraging or antagonistic? Do co-workers seem to enjoy each other's presence? If there is a lot of tension between employees, it's possible that the organizational culture values competition among employees over collaboration.
- Even the layout of the workplace contributes to organizational culture. Notice how space is used. Where are the offices, and who gets them? How big are the cubicles? What sort of furniture is around? Is there anything on the walls? Do people put personal items, such as photos, on their desks?

These elements can give you important clues about an organization's culture.

Formal and Informal Communication: What's the Story?

Communication is a key ingredient of organizational culture. Imagine the chaos and disorder that would come out of a manufacturing company with no lines of communication. Cancelled orders would still be processed, or orders that needed to be rushed would never get done. In short, a lack of communication leads to a toxic organizational culture.

Organizational culture relies on both formal and informal communication. When you're assessing the culture of your organization, keep an eye out for formal communication. How do supervisors speak to lower-level employees? What's the tone of their conversations? Does your organization have a bulletin board or a newsletter to keep employees informed? If so, what's on it? All of these issues can point to a healthy or unhealthy organizational culture.

The Informal Communication Network

Of course, there's also some communication that takes place "beneath the iceberg." Chatter between employees via online chat, conversations at the water cooler—these are part of informal communication. The **informal communication network** is made up of the informal connections between employees, and it is the pathway through which much information in an organization is shared. Keep an ear to the ground and listen to what employees have to say about the company. What's the latest buzz? What are people complaining or raving about? Is something controversial happening?

For a more direct approach, ask your co-workers how they feel about their jobs. What do they like? What would they change? Who do they consider to be a leader, even if it's not the boss? Would they recommend having their friend apply for a job at the company? Their answers will be revealing about the organization's culture.

The Grapevine

Have you ever head the expression "I heard it through the grapevine"? Maybe you've listened to the classic song by the same name. Information tends to spread by word of mouth through the **grapevine**—casual communications between friends and acquaintances—rapidly reaching the entire organization. Sometimes, the information is valid and can provide valuable insights about people or events within the office. On the other hand, information might also get confused and increasingly inaccurate as it spreads, and nasty rumors can spread this way. The information may sometimes need to be taken with a grain of salt. Still, listening to the grapevine may give you more information about an organization's culture.

Do It...

10.2: Identify Organizational Culture Describe what you think would be the ideal organizational culture for a company you would want to work for. For inspiration, you might want to research *Fortune* magazine's Top 100 Businesses to work for. Limit your response to one page, and be prepared to submit it electronically or discuss it in class.

Now Debrief...

- **Organizational culture** consists of the attitudes, values, and norms shared by an organization's members. A healthy organizational culture encourages and motivates employees, while a toxic corporate culture makes employees feel unappreciated and devalued.
- The iceberg theory holds that the public, formal organization of a company—including mission statements and job descriptions—is just a small part of the whole organizational culture of an organization.
- You can better understand the organizational culture of an organization by observing and interacting with employees as well as noticing how the workplace is laid out.
- The **informal communication network** is the connection between employees, and is the pathway through which most information is shared. The nature of formal and informal communication in an organization can reveal a lot about its organizational culture.

3. Another Brick in the Wall: Staffing the Organization

"If you've really got the right people, and you've got them working together as a team . . . you can make a big difference."

—Steve Case,
former CEO of America Online[5]

Organizational structure and culture are both big parts of an organization, but something's missing: the people. ■ Without people to work and develop structure and culture, there is no organization. In business, organizations are always interested in hiring bright, devoted employees, but it's not that easy to find them. Finding excellent employees is a challenge, as most job openings receive piles and piles of applications. There is an art to finding useful employees, and organizations need to know the methods of finding them. In this section, we'll look at these methods.

Know Who You Are Looking For: Job Analysis

Imagine sitting down to interview a potential employee for an accounting position and immediately deciding that he is too likable not to hire. The employee comes to work for you, but it turns out that he has no idea how to do the job you had assigned him. He is a great people person, but actually knows next to nothing about keeping track of your company's finances. When you sat down to interview him, you were not thinking about the actual requirements of the job; rather, you were looking for someone who you felt you could get along with well.

As this story shows, before you select an employee for a job, you have to know exactly what the job requires— the skills, knowledge, abilities, and experience to get the job done—and then determine which applicant is best suited to fulfill those requirements. When an organization's management sets out to hire employees, they need to keep the organization's mission first and foremost in their minds and hire people who can carry out that mission.

One step in doing this is through job analysis. The purpose of **job analysis** is to document the actual requirements of a job and the work that needs to be performed. This analysis is performed to gain a better understanding of the kind of skills a potential employee needs to fill the position.

■ Without people to work and develop structure and culture, there is no organization.

HR departments are usually in charge of conducting job analysis, as they handle issues of hiring, firing, and assessing employees. There are a few different methods for conducting job analysis. The most common method is interviewing people who currently hold or have held the position, as well as their supervisors. The interviewer or analyst may begin the interview by asking for an overview of duties associated with the positions, and then ask some of the following questions:

- Does someone require special training to perform your job?
- What part of your job is the most time consuming?
- What is the most important part of your job?
- What is the most difficult part of your job?

Directly observing employees in action is another method of conducting job analysis. What is a person with this job doing? What should he or she be doing? Often, analysts use more than one method when conducting a thorough job analysis.

Job Description and Specifications A good analysis will reveal the job description. A **job description** explains what a job entails, such as a list of general duties and responsibilities. This may include:

- the job title;
- a job summary; and
- a list of primary tasks.

The analysis will also establish **job specifications**, which is a list of qualities an employer considers important to the job. A person needs to bring these qualities to the job before they are hired or the qualities need to be identified as part of a training and/or development plan for that person. Job specifications also provide a basis for performance appraisals and give an idea about compensation. As you can see in Figure 10.7, it's basically about figuring out what the person does and what someone who is new will need to know to do the required work. It also sometimes includes how much the position is paid.

Figure **10.7** | **A Sample Job Advertisement that Includes a Job Description and Job Specifications**

Receptionist
Company: Lieberman & Associates
Location: Milwaukee, Wisconsin

Description
Job Title: Receptionist

Summary
The main responsibility of the receptionist is to direct callers and guests to their appropriate destination. The receptionist also provides the first impression of the company for most clients. Because of this, it's important for the receptionist to be friendly and professional.

Everyday tasks
- Welcoming guests
- Answering and directing phone calls
- Coordinating mail
- Conducting general administrative tasks

Specifications
- High school diploma or equivalent
- At least two years' experience working as a receptionist
- Proficiency in Microsoft Office
- Excellent communication skills
- Detail-oriented personality

The Benefits of a Job Analysis Why is any of this important? Isn't it obvious what somebody needs to do on the job?

Well, you may know the basics, but job analysis goes much more in-depth. Having an actual physical document outlining the expectations for each job is invaluable in selecting new, effective employees. By understanding the duties and tasks required on a particular job, you can get an idea of the kind of knowledge, skills, abilities, and other characteristics that a potential employee needs to perform the job well.

The analysis can also uncover changes in technology, working conditions, and other factors that may affect the position in the future. There are professional and legal guidelines in selecting employees, and having a good knowledge of what the position entails helps managers meet these guidelines. (Want to learn more about the laws affecting hiring employees? Check out Chapter 18 at **www.mybizlab.com**.)

Recruiting Employees

It would be wonderful if all workers in the world were hard-working and dedicated to their jobs. But in reality, not everybody is. As a manager or an HR employee, how can you best find those people that are willing to work hard for you? **Recruiting** is the process of creating a pool of potential applicants from which to select qualified people for available jobs.

Internal Recruitment

What is the most reliable place to recruit employees? From the inside, of course. Workers who have already proven themselves within the organization are often the best resource to be recruited for new positions.

Job Posting
* title
* department
* job description
* qualifications
* salary

Internal Job Postings Job openings in an organization are often available for current employees. When an employee accepts another position in an organization, the move is usually upward (a promotion) or lateral (into a different, but comparable position). Posting a notice in the employee break room, sending a group e-mail, and word of mouth are all ways of making employees aware of open positions. The notice typically includes all the information that goes into a job advertisement to the public: title, department, job description, qualifications, and salary.

Although it's not necessary to give current employees first dibs on all job openings, it does help build employee morale to see a fair system of promotion and transfer in place. Internal recruitment is another way of letting employees know that their efforts are appreciated.

Employee Referral Another form of internal recruitment is *employee referral*, in which current, reliable employees recommend people that they know outside the organization for a position. People usually make friends similar to themselves, and (hopefully) their friends will be reliable workers as well. Applicants that are referred by current employees will have more of the inside information about what the job actually requires than people coming in off the street.

External Recruitment

How did you find your first job? Perhaps your parents set you up with a family friend, or you spent the summer sweating it out for a relative's construction company. Most likely, you combed through the help wanted ads in a local paper or on the Internet. Media advertising is the most common form of **external recruitment**—the process of finding job applicants that are outside the organization—that businesses rely on for finding new employees.

Advertisements Ads allow organizations to open up their business to a wide variety of potential employees. Anybody can see an ad and submit an application. Although an organization might receive a lot of applications from unqualified or inexperienced applicants, it will also have plenty of options to choose from.

You can also target a more specific group by advertising in publications that appeal to a certain demographic or publications that are specific to a company's field. Newspaper and magazine ads tend to be relatively inexpensive, while advertising on TV and radio costs more. The high cost of these ads can be considered a disadvantage, but advertising is the easiest way to reach a wide pool of potential applicants.

The Internet One of the most popular forms of recruitment is online. In fact, many companies only accept applications and resumes online.[6] The reason online recruiting is such a hit is because it's inexpensive, fast, and effective. Employers can post an ad to a job search engine, like Career Builder, Monster, or Hot Jobs, and have a pool of candidates the next day. Networking sites, like LinkedIn, are also popular places to search for potential candidates.

Employment Agencies Have you or anyone you know ever signed with an employment or temp agency? Such agencies are a valuable tool in external recruitment for companies. If you need skilled employees in a pinch, an agency can provide you with a database of employees with different skills. Some organizations feel that using temp agencies is a safer way to try out employees, while job hunters often feel it is a good way to try out a variety of organizations and jobs. The drawback to using these agencies is the fee companies have to pay if they end up hiring an employee from

the agency. It is important to negotiate with agencies that the fee will be at least partially refunded if the employee doesn't work out within a certain period of time.

Headhunters There are highly specialized recruitment agents known as *headhunters* who specialize in filling upper-level positions. Headhunters tend to approach qualified people, offering them employment in good positions, rather than relying on long lists of applicants. The cost of getting an upper-level employee from a headhunter is generally expensive.

Job Centers Government-run job centers are a good place to find relatively unskilled employees for entry-level jobs. If you have a lot of lower-level positions to fill quickly, a job center can be just the ticket. The major advantage of using a job center is that it is free for you. You could staff your entire manufacturing department in one fell swoop without having to pay additional recruitment fees.

Direct Contact Direct contact is another method that managers sometimes rely on. This means actually going out into the world to find employees. Companies might visit a job fair, vocational training school, a trade show, or a college to advertise in person. The advantage of doing this is establishing contact with potential employees before hiring them. This improves your company's image, as it shows that you care enough about your employees to go out and meet them before they even work for you. The disadvantages of direct contact are that it is time-consuming and expensive, as a result of the opportunity cost of spending time and money personally recruiting people that could be spent elsewhere.

Who is responsible for making sure the recruiting, selecting, and hiring processes go well?

Walk-Ins Have you ever walked around from store to store trying to find a job? Walk-in hiring is extremely useful for employers looking for unskilled employees. Fast food restaurants and stores rely on this method heavily. It is easy to hire employees either right on the spot or shortly after accepting an application. The disadvantages of this are that it is impossible to anticipate when potential employees may show up. You might find someone that you want to hire, but you have enough people and can't afford more. Chances are if a position opens up three months later, this person already has a job somewhere else.

Selecting Employees

So now you've recruited a nice pile of resumes and applications, and you are sitting at your desk reading through them and trying to figure out whom you should interview and potentially hire. You have been burned in the past by people who you thought would make perfect employees. What is it that you are truly looking for? How can you tell who is going to be a valuable employee and who is not? How do you negotiate a job offer?

Selecting is not just another administrative process; you're forming the workforce that will make the vision of your business come to life. Sure, it's important to carefully read over an application, noting education and past employment history, but actually meeting someone and the impression that he or she makes is the most important part of selecting an employee. You want someone for your business who can go above and beyond the job description, acting as not only a consultant, but also as a salesperson or a leader to others in the company. These intangible qualities cannot be discerned by merely reading an application.

Factors to Consider when Selecting Employees In the past, job experience was the single most important criteria in hiring.[7] Although this quality is certainly relevant today, employers are looking for more in potential hires:

- Today's managers are looking for workers who offer valuable insights, initiative, and diversity. Would you rather have an employee who knew how to do his or her job but never expressed an opinion about how to do things better, or an employee who had to learn on the job but came up with a brilliant idea that changed the way your company does business forever?
- Many employers now believe that a person's behavior, interests, and personality are essential indicators of how well he or she will do on the job. Many companies now use *personality tests* as part of the hiring criteria. These are psychological tests designed to uncover an employee's motivations, code of ethics, and general attitudes toward work and life.
- In addition to personality tests, employers may also check potential applicants' Facebook, MySpace, or other online social networking pages to gauge their personality.

The modern hiring process is complicated, but hiring the wrong employee is a much bigger waste of time and money than spending a lot of both on the hiring process. Someone who does a poor job and has to be fired has cost you not only the salary, training costs, and time you have spent, but also the opportunities that a different employee might have brought to the table. Hiring the wrong person can have a negative effect on your organization's mission, morale—and on your bottom line.

Selecting the Best Employees To make sure you select the best employees, there are some steps you can take:

1. Recruit constantly, even if you don't have a position to fill. It always pays to look forward, and ongoing recruitment leaves you with a variety of qualified candidates for jobs when openings occur. You never know when someone is going to have to leave your company, and it pays to have suitable replacements available.
2. Write an accurate job description and job specification document. A job description thoroughly explains what an employer wants the employee to do, and job specifications explain the qualities that an employer considers important to the job.
3. It's also helpful to consider what would make the best employee for the job. You can do this by:
   - making a list of their qualities and behaviors;
   - determining what makes them best suited for the job; and
   - including these characteristics in the description.

If the position is for a middle manager, how do you want this person to relate to his or her subordinates? If the position is entry-level, how should the employee relate to his or her manager?

The Hiring Process

After reading over applications and deciding which applicants seem best suited for the job, it's time to select a few to interview. The most important things about an interview are how well the interviewee presents himself or herself and how well he or she seems to connect with the job description.

It's also important to consider the overall interview strategy. How many interviews will each applicant have? Who will conduct them? What is the purpose of each one? In addition, you need to know what you want to hear when you start the interview. Use your carefully crafted job description to guide you in your questions, and be sure to listen to and analyze the responses. An employee that meets the characteristics you're looking for in an interview will probably meet the characteristics you're looking for on the job.

Throughout this process, it's important to be mindful of legal issues as well. It's illegal for an employer to base a hiring decision on race, religion, place of origin, age, or disability.[8]

Scoring Potential Employees Many managers score potential employees after reading their application and interviewing them. It's important to be consistent, so the same person should be conducting all of the interviews. Scoring is subjective, but it is a good idea to score a candidate in several areas. One system might be to rate a candidate from 1 to 10 in the areas of capacity to do the job, behavioral preferences in the job, and how well he or she connects with the company team.

Conducting Reference and Background Checks There's one more piece to the puzzle: conducting reference and background checks. This might seem like a logical first step, but if you have truly done a good job feeling out a candidate, a reference or background check shouldn't turn up any surprises.

If you pay careful attention to the hiring process, not only will you have a qualified team of workers, but you should also have a team that you can manage well. You should know what motivates your employees, what they value, and some of the on-the-job characteristics that they have. This information can be invaluable in knowing how to make your team work best.

For Those Sitting on the Other Side of the Desk We've discussed the recruiting, selecting, and hiring process from the perspective of the manager doing the recruiting, selecting, and hiring. But what if you're sitting on the other side of the desk? Want some job-hunting and interview tips? Check out Chapter 19 at **www.mybizlab.com**.

And now that you're familiar with an organization's structure, culture, and employee selection process, you're ready to discuss training and motivating employees, which we'll do in Chapter 11.

Do It...

10.3: Write a Job Description Write a job description and a job specification for a college student. Your instructor may also ask you to do this activity in pairs or teams. Be prepared to submit your responses electronically or discuss them in class.

Now Debrief...

- Organizations aim to hire bright, motivated employees who fit well with the company's mission.
- A **job analysis** describes the requirements of a job and the work that needs to be performed. This information can be obtained through interviews, observation, or a questionnaire. A good job analysis should contain a **job description**, which explains what a job entails, and **job specifications**, which is a list of qualities an employer considers important to the job.
- **Recruiting** is the process of creating a large enough pool of potential applicants from which to select qualified people for available jobs. Recruitment can come from either internal recruitment or **external recruitment**. External recruitment includes using ads, the Internet, employment agencies, job centers, headhunters, direct contact, and walk-ins.
- Selecting the right employees can make the vision of an organization come to life. During this process, it's important to consider job experience, behavior, interests, and personality.
- During a job interview, the interviewer should carefully listen to the applicant's responses to judge how well the applicant sells himself or herself. If an interview goes well, an employer generally conducts reference and background checks.

Chapter 10 Visual Summary

1. Interpret and understand an organization chart, and anticipate the role you would be expected to perform in an organization depending on its structure. (pp. 234–240)

- **Organizational structure**, the formal configuration of people in an organization that determines the allocation of duties, responsibilities and authority, must be aligned with the goals and mission of that organization. The organization structure stems from the **division of labor**, which is the breakdown of different specialized roles that employees take on.
- Having an actual physical diagram of how the organization is supposed to operate, such as an **organizational chart** that diagrams the relationships between various departments or employees, is helpful in avoiding the confusion that can arise in a large organization.
- The **hierarchy of authority**, or the official configuration of reporting relationships, is established on the organizational chart.
- The organizational structure determines the role managers and employees play.
- A **centralized structure** places the decision making and authority in the hands of very few. A **decentralized structure** spreads authority and decision making down the chain of command, allowing middle and lower-level managers to make some decisions.
- A **flat organization** only has a few layers of management that have a wide **span of control**, whereas a **tall organization** has many layers of hierarchy and managers have a narrower span of control.
- An organization with a **linear structure** has a hierarchy of authority that goes down the line from top management to lower-level employees. On the other hand, a **matrix structure** breaks an organization into smaller, highly functional units, so often employees have more than one boss.
- Many organizations use **departmentalization**, which means they divide their employees into different units or departments based on their roles.
- Modern businesses need to be prepared for an **organizational change**, which is planned or unplanned transformations in the structure, technology, and people that an organization uses.

Summary: The organizational structure of a business is what keeps it moving and succeeding while also giving it value.

3. Use effective recruiting, selecting, and hiring strategies. (pp. 244–249)

- Organizations are always on the lookout for bright, devoted employees.
- The purpose of **job analysis** is to document the actual requirements of a job and the work that needs to be performed. Part of good job analysis is figuring out the job description and specifications.
- A **job description** explains what a job entails, whereas **job specifications** are qualities an employer considers important to the job.
- **Recruiting** is the process of creating a pool of potential applicants from which to select qualified people for available jobs. This can be done either internally or externally.
- Internal recruitment includes internal job postings and employee referral. **External recruitment**—the process of finding job applicants that are outside the organization—includes using ads, the Internet, employment agencies, job centers, headhunters, direct contact, and walk-ins.
- Selecting a good employee is the process of conducting a job analysis and recruiting; it is not just dependent on education and prior experience.
- Getting a feel for a potential employee's values and character is an important part of selecting a good hire. This can be done by interviewing the applicant and conducting reference and background checks.

Summary: Carefully conducting the recruiting, selecting, and hiring processes can help an organization put together a qualified team of workers.

2. Detect and recognize an organization's culture in order to make decisions about your career. (pp. 241–244)

- **Organizational culture** (sometimes referred to as *corporate culture*) consists of the attitudes, values, and norms shared by an organization's members. Upper management and owners set the tone for an organization's culture.
- Not only does organizational culture affect the manager/employee relationship, but also the relationships between employees.
- The iceberg theory suggests that there are visible and hidden elements to organizational culture. Visible elements include dress code, office layout, and anything else that visitors could see. Hidden elements include norms, values, and informal leaders.

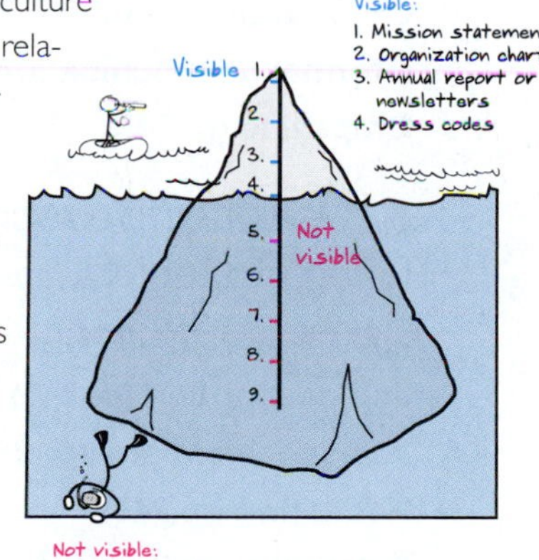

- Employees can recognize an organization's culture by paying attention to the things going on around them.
- The **informal communication** network is the connection between employees, and it is the pathway through which most information is shared.

Summary: Organizational culture provides a valuable framework for employees and also serves as the "personality" of the organization.

Get the most out of what you just read by practicing your skills and actually DOING something with the material! The best place to do this is at **www.mybizlab.com**. Here's just some of what is available to you there:

- Apply your skills in an interactive environment with more **BizSkill** experiences...and see if you have what it takes
- Think critically and talk with your peers on hot business topics in **BizChat**
- Flex your business communication skills and build your own portfolio with the **Communication Plan exercises**
- Watch the chapter material come together with **Just Plain Business** videos
- Study on-the-go with **Audio Chapter Summaries** in MP3 format
- Brush up on the lecture and content with **Audio PowerPoints**
- Discover how well you are doing and see what areas you need to improve on with the **Pre-Tests** and **Post-Tests**

Key Words

These key words and more are also available as flash cards to practice with at **www.mybizlab.com**.

1. Interpret and understand an organization chart, and anticipate the role you would be expected to perform in an organization depending on its structure. **(pp. 234–240)**

Organizational structure (p. 234)
Division of labor (p. 234)
Organization chart (p. 234)
Hierarchy of authority (p. 235)
Centralized structure (p. 235)
Decentralized structure (p. 235)
Bureaucratic organization (p. 236)
Flat organization (p. 236)
Span of control (p. 236)
Tall organization (p. 236)
Linear structure (p. 236)
Matrix structure (p. 237)
Departmentalization (p. 237)
Organizational change (p. 238)

2. Detect and recognize an organization's culture in order to make decisions about your career. **(pp. 241–244)**

Organizational culture (p. 241)
Informal communication network (p. 243)
Grapevine (p. 243)

3. Use effective recruiting, selecting, and hiring strategies. **(pp. 244–249)**

Job analysis (p. 244)
Job description (p. 245)
Job specifications (p. 245)
Recruiting (p. 246)
External recruitment (p. 246)

Prove It

Prove It...

Now let's put on one of the BizHats. With the **Manager BizHat** squarely on your head, look at the following exercise:

You're the division manager for the portable music player division of a major electronics company. You oversee more than a dozen project managers and hundreds of other employees. A new sample line is about to be introduced, and you and the project manager have never seen eye-to-eye in five years of working together. On the first day of the new project, he is already stepping on your toes, telling employees that this is his personal project, and not to report to you if they have any problems. There is a group of mostly new employees involved in the project, and you can see that they are looking up to the project manager as the only authority figure.

How can you make the project manager understand that, yes, this is his project, but that the two of you need to work together on this, as it is your division? How can you best explain the situation to employees without stepping on the project manager's toes? If the project manager still wants to act as though he is in complete control, do you take it your manager? What is the best way to resolve this situation? Do you feel that talking to the employees yourself will offend the project manager?

Flip It...

Now let's flip over to the **Employee BizHat**. You are a new employee at the electronics company from the example above. You have been assigned to work on the new portable music player sample line, and your project manager told you that you only need to report to him. He seems likable enough, but you notice that the division manager seems to have problems with him. When you took the job, you were told that the division manager was the person to report to for administrative concerns, and that the project manager was the person to report to for concerns specific to the project. You don't want to offend the project manager, because he is around you for most of the workday.

What can you do as an employee to stay out of the controversy without compromising your needs? In this situation, to whom do you think you should report? Is it your responsibility to meet the needs of both managers? Who should you go to if the project manager gets upset about you reporting to the division manager? Will you let their disagreement compromise your work?

Now Debrief It...

Now that you've seen the situation from two different perspectives—the division manager and the employee—what's your overall view of the situation?

Direct, Control, Evaluate: Decision Making, Delegating, and Appraising

BizSkills invite...

Try It!

There's no better way to learn concepts than to put them into practice. In the BizSkill for this chapter, you'll learn how to delegate responsibilities based on employee strengths and weaknesses, provide clear timelines and document performance, and set SMART goals—all within the big picture of how to handle firing an employee who is also a friend. Take your turn in the driver's seat by visiting **www.mybizlab.com**.

Start here!

Now that you've practiced delegating responsibilities, setting goals, and firing an employee in this chapter's BizSkill, it's time to translate those skills into plain English. And if you skipped the BizSkill, go back now!

Chapter 11 Goals

After experiencing this chapter, you'll be able to:

1. Characterize your communication style, recognize the communication styles of others, and prescribe how you could work together most effectively.
2. Prescribe the best methods for motivating someone, and explain how you yourself are motivated.
3. Recommend methods for training and developing employees, and know how you can develop your own career.
4. Make good decisions and be an effective delegator or delegatee.
5. Measure the results of your decisions and take corrective action when necessary.
6. Conduct a performance evaluation of someone, and recognize circumstances when someone should be promoted, reassigned, or fired.

What tools work best to direct your company to success?

Wearing the Manager Hat

Jenna Appleton is a project manager in a marketing firm. She manages three people on her team: Caleigh, Owen, and Jodi. Each time a project gets under way, Jenna assigns tasks to the members of her team who are best suited for the job. For example, Jenna knows that Owen wants to become a manager eventually, so she assigns him tasks that carry greater responsibility. If one of her team members has a problem, she tries to find a compromise that will suit everyone's needs. Jenna knows that having a well-run and highly motivated team helps her keep projects on schedule.

You've probably found yourself in a similar situation to Jenna's at one time or another. Maybe you're the organizer in your family, delegating tasks such as laundry and washing up, and negotiating with siblings or children. Managing in the business world isn't all that different. Managers put on their *interpersonal* hats when they play a leadership role or interact with colleagues and employees. They play an *informational* role when they monitor progress or speak on behalf of the organization. And they put on their *decision-making* hats when they handle conflict or negotiate compromises.

In Chapter 9 we focused on the planning aspect of management, and in Chapter 10 we looked at how managers turn their plans into reality by organizing their businesses effectively. In this chapter, we'll discuss how managers direct and motivate employees, control their plans to produce effective results, and evaluate those plans and employees, and how you can do the same.

1. Communication Styles: Managing Personalities

Your best friend calls to tell you she has failed one of her midterm exams. Do you:

A. brusquely tell her to go to her professor and ask if she can retake the exam?

B. feel tempted to interrupt her to tell a detailed story about how you passed your own recent exam?

C. sympathize with her and ask her whether you can do anything to help?

D. barrage her with a series of questions about the content of the exam?

As you'll learn in this section, the answer you give may speak volumes about your *communication style*. Why does a person's communication style matter to managers? Communication styles affect people's interactions in many situations, including those with co-workers. As a manager and employee, ■ understanding your own communication style, as well as that of the people you interact with, can make communication easier and more effective. And as you learned in Chapter 9, interpersonal and communication skills are extremely important to managers, whose job is to plan, organize, direct, and control the people and resources of an organization. In short, knowing how to communicate is vital to *all* employees.

So, what are the types of communication styles? According to the Merrill-Reid model, a frequently used model in management training workshops, we can categorize people according to four personality types.[1] For our purposes, we'll call these four types *directors*, *performers*, *people-pleasers*, and *detailers*. These personality types are closely tied to particular communication styles. Look at Figure 11.1 as we discuss each of these in detail. We'll then discuss how they affect managers and employees.

Figure **11.1** | **Personality Types and Communication Styles: Where Do You Fit?**

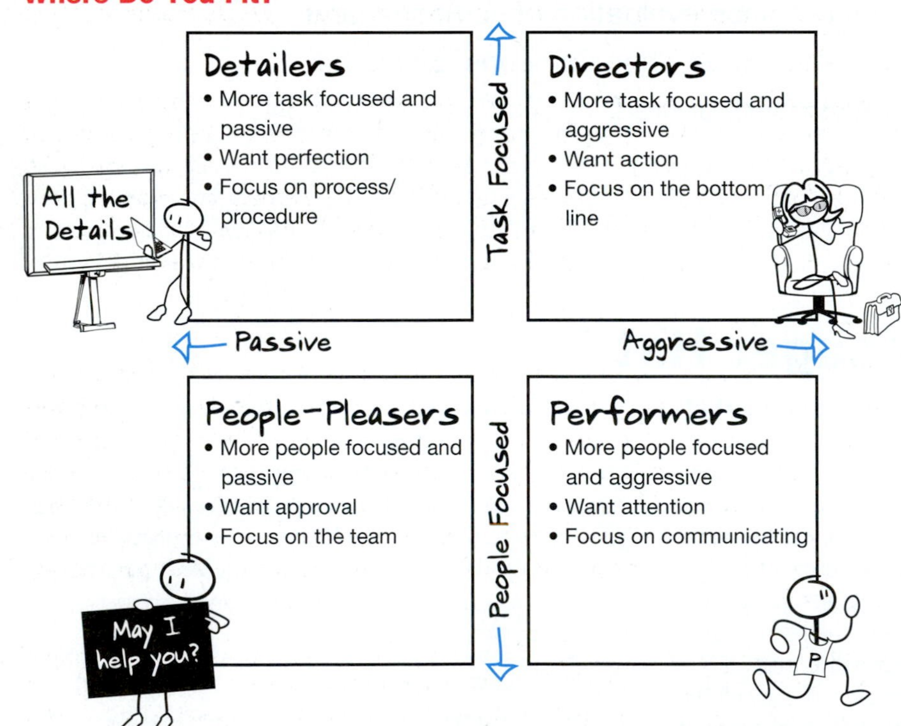

- **Directors: Taking the Lead:** Do you know exactly what you want out of life? Have you had your career goals mapped out since you can remember? Do you thrive on conflict and enjoy hard work? If you answer "yes" to these questions, then you're probably a director. **Directors** are confident decision-makers and risk-takers. In business, they are usually in charge of things—often as CEOs or supervisors within an organization. If you're frequently chosen to be the team leader, and answered (A) in the quiz above, you probably belong in this category.

- **Performers: Natural Born Storytellers:** Do you consider yourself a "people person"? Are you sociable and approachable, but still fairly competitive? Do you relish the chance to launch into a story at any opportunity? If so, you may be a performer. **Performers** are warm, enthusiastic individuals with strong communication skills and a tendency to exaggerate. They may lack the organizational skills necessary to meet tight deadlines, and they may be easily distracted. In business, performers are often found in marketing or sales roles. In the quiz above, if you answered (B), you may be a performer.

- **People-Pleasers: Guaranteed to Be Diplomatic:** Do you avoid conflict? Do you prefer a supportive role to a leadership role? Do you often have difficulty making decisions? If so, you may

■ Understanding your own communication style, as well as that of the people you interact with, can make communication easier and more effective.

be a people-pleaser. **People-pleasers** are kind-hearted, sensitive people who like working with others. They are passive and prefer a collaborative position. In business, people-pleasers are often found in customer service positions because they're very people-focused. In the quiz above, if you answered (C), you probably fit into the people-pleaser category.

- **Detailers: Focused on the Specifics:** Do you like to have all the facts before you make a decision? Are you highly detail-oriented? Do people tell you that you're a perfectionist? If so, you may be a detailer. **Detailers** make great accountants or engineers because everything they do is accurate. Task-focused, rather than people-focused, they may be highly critical and pessimistic by nature. In the quiz above, if you answered (D), you probably fit into the detailer category.[2]

The Management Trick: Putting Some Flex in Your Style

So, what's the point of knowing these different communication styles? It's important not only to know which style you typically lean toward, but also how to best communicate with the other styles. The best communicators are self-aware enough to understand their own communication style, intuitive enough to understand the best ways to communicate with others, and adaptable enough to flex when necessary. Consider the following real-world examples, and think about how each manager might benefit from adapting other communication styles.

Dell as Director Michael Dell runs Dell Computer very efficiently through a director style of management. The company reigns supreme in a low-margin business by squeezing suppliers, having world-class processes, and running a company that doesn't allow for much creativity. For annual employee meetings, the company rents large sports stadiums, and Dell talks about pounding the competition. One executive describes it as "ruthless, macho stuff, and employees loved it."[3]

Would *you* love it? If you're also a director, you probably would. But if you have a different communication style, you might not even be working at Dell. It may seem like a good idea to have a company full of people with the same communication style, but consider the drawbacks. With all independent directors, a company may miss out on the performers' creativity and people-pleasers' sense of teamwork. A group of directors is also likely to be highly competitive, and in their aggressive haste, some of the minutiae that a detailer would have looked out for may fall through the cracks.

Motorola's Galvin as People-Pleaser On the other hand, when Christopher Galvin was chairman and CEO of Motorola in the late 1990s, he brought a different management style to the company by replacing authoritative leaders with more people-oriented managers. But some employees had doubts about Galvin's people-friendly approach.[4] He'd send monthly e-mails to employees describing company activities and explaining his decision making calls. One manager told another that she was tired of Galvin sounding like her dear, sweet dad. She wanted somebody to stand up and lead. In other words, the manager thought Galvin was "too nice."

Can you identify the communication styles in this example? The manager who thought Galvin was "too nice" is likely a director. She viewed Galvin's coddling e-mails as inefficient and unnecessary to getting the task at hand completed. More of a people-pleaser, Galvin may have suffered from focusing too much on how his employees felt to the detriment of efficiently and effectively completing the tasks at hand.

Although the Dell example shows how a company can suffer from a lack a variety in communication styles, the Motorola example shows what happens when two styles clash. So what's the best way to handle this kind of conflict and help an organization benefit from different communication styles working together?

Directors

Flexing

Performers

What does it mean to flex your style?

Style Flexing It's not necessary that anyone change his or her own communication style. Rather, effective managers (and all employees, really) adopt flexing as part of their communication style. *Flexing* means adapting your own style to match the behavior of the person you are communicating with.

Managers need to flex their behavior depending on the situation to make sure that they communicate effectively with others, modifying their own communication style to be more passive or aggressive, or more task-focused or people-focused, depending on the person with whom they are dealing. If a conflict does arise, a manager can use intuitive people skills to determine which communication style would be best to adopt.

- **Flexing Toward Director:** If you're having trouble communicating with a director, he or she may respond with arrogance, bullying, and yelling. To avoid such an unpleasant interaction, try communicating with directors by being businesslike, task focused, and to the point. Acknowledge and support their goals, and you may find that they respond in kind.

- **Flexing Toward Performer:** When the person you're trying to communicate with starts complaining or overreacting to what you're saying, you can be pretty sure you've just stressed out a performer. You can avoid this reaction by allowing him or her to talk, focusing on his or her needs, and being appreciative of that person's strengths and contributions.

- **Flexing Toward People-Pleaser:** Because people-pleasers generally want to keep the peace, sometimes it's hard to tell if they're upset. They may say they agree with you, but when they walk away from the conversation, they fume. Although this response may be difficult to pick up on, one clue may be someone suddenly saying that he or she agrees with you after previously putting up a fight. To ease this communication, try to be sincere and not too formal—people-pleasers tend to be sensitive and care about relationships. Setting concrete goals can also avoid making a people-pleaser feel personally attacked.

- **Flexing Toward Detailer:** The detailer will be less concerned with your personal relationship and is likely to become quiet, negative, and aloof when stressed. You can tap into the detailer's concern for detail by using facts to communicate your detailed expectations. Showing a connection between the detailer's ways, ideas, or practices to your new ideas may provide the transition needed to the detailer, who often doesn't like change.

As you can see, to be an effective manager, you need to be able to effectively get your ideas and information to the people you work with. Of course, effective communicating goes beyond just understanding your own and others' communication styles—managers must also understand the values, points of views, and needs of their diverse groups of employees. Understanding how different people communicate and then effectively adapting to different situations are therefore key aspects of successful communication.[5]

Do It...

11.1: Assess Communication Styles Looking at the four communication styles discussed in this section, which one do you most closely align yourself with, and why? Now choose a friend or co-worker, and assess his or her communication style. To check whether your assessment is accurate, ask the person to read through the description of each communication style and choose the one that best describes him or her. Based on that person's communication style and your own, what approaches would you take to resolve a conflict between you? Be prepared to submit your analysis electronically or to discuss it in class.

Now Debrief...

- Communication styles affect people's interactions in many situations. Understanding your own communication style, as well as that of the people you communicate with, can make communicating more effective.
- Most people tend to have the traits of one of the following four styles:
  - **Directors** are confident decision-makers who like to be in charge of things.
  - **Performers** are people-focused and communicative, and they enjoy teamwork.
  - **People-pleasers** are diplomats who avoid conflict.
  - **Detailers** are detail-oriented and focus on accuracy and high quality standards.
- By flexing your communication in the direction of the style of the person you're communicating with, you can better handle conflict.

2. Motivating Employees

"Motivation is a fire from within. If someone else tries to light that fire under you, chances are it will burn very briefly."

—Stephen R. Covey, Author of *The 7 Habits of Highly Effective People*[6]

What factors have drawn you to a school, a job, even a vacation spot? Are you motivated by a bargain or luxury, freedom or a detailed schedule set by someone else, exciting networking opportunities or job security?

Motivating factors can play a big part in what people choose to do and how well they work. ■ Effective managers know that understanding what motivates employees to work is just as important as understanding the different styles of communication. However, everyone is motivated by something different, and a person's motivations can change over time.

Some people may by motivated by *intrinsic* factors—that is, they enjoy doing the work itself, so the job is its own reward. Other people are motivated by *extrinsic* factors—they enjoy the things they get as a result of doing the work, such as vacations, prestige, or money. A good manager assesses an employee or situation and applies different motivators as needed. In this section, we'll read a few theories that attempt to explain how motivation works to better understand the key role motivation plays in management and to see how you may be motivated yourself.

Maslow's Hierarchy of Needs

Imagine your employer doesn't give you lunch or bathroom breaks and pays you a salary that barely allows you to make ends meet each month. Your job is physically dangerous, and you're always wondering if you might be the next to be let go. How would you feel if your employer tried to make all this up to you by repeatedly telling you that you're doing a great job and inviting you to join in on brainstorming sessions? You might see praise and intellectual opportunities as worthwhile rewards if your physical, safety, and other practical needs are being met. But without satisfying those lower-level needs, your employer's attempts to meet your higher-level needs may seem insulting at best.

■ Effective managers know that understanding what motivates employees to work is just as important as understanding the different styles of communication.

According to psychologist Abraham Maslow's **hierarchy of needs theory**, for people to be effective, needs must be satisfied in a particular order based on how necessary they are for survival. Looking at Figure 11.2, you can see that five basic need types are arranged in pyramid order; the lower-level needs at the bottom must be met before a person can try to satisfy higher-level needs.

Everyone has a different standard for when these needs qualify as being met. A person's standard of living must be met to his or her satisfaction before realistically being able to focus on improving his or her quality of life.

Figure **11.2** | **Using Maslow's Hierarchy to Motivate Employees**

Using the Hierarchy of Needs How can organizations motivate their employees using this theory? Owners and management can consider using wages and compensation plans, role definitions (the status or title of a person within a company), and company activities (such as company picnics and training opportunities) to satisfy the following:

- Physiological needs: sufficient pay, ample breaks for eating and going to the restroom
- Safety needs: a safe working environment, relative job security, health insurance
- Social needs: an environment that generates a feeling of acceptance, belonging, and community—being part of a team
- Esteem needs: expressions of appreciation, rewards for achievements, and increasing levels of responsibility
- Self-actualization needs: challenging and meaningful assignments that spur innovation, creativity, and progress toward long-term goals[7]

Figure 11.2 outlines additional factors corresponding to each of these levels.

Does It Work? It's fine to say that management in an organization should use Maslow's hierarchy to motivate employees, but does it really work?

California-based Joie de Vivre is an example of an organization that has adopted Maslow's hierarchy as its guiding principle. Chip Conley, founder and CEO of the boutique hotel group, attests to how the foundations of Maslow's hierarchy saved his company. In Conley's book, *How Great Companies Get Their Mojo from Maslow*, he explains how all 20 of his San Francisco Bay area hotels suffered when the dot-com bubble burst. While searching his soul, Conley realized that employees want a sense of meaning, and customers want to be transformed. He realized that Maslow's hierarchy of needs would become his "organizing structure for understanding the

You wouldn't expect a manager to motivate an employee by saying, "If you work, we'll pay you." The employee would expect to be paid, even if the manager didn't come out and say it.

aspirational motivations in my workplace and in the marketplace. It would be the road map for the next chapter in my company's history."[8]

Using Maslow as the company's inspiration, Conley refocused his efforts on helping his staff, customers, and investors achieve self-actualization. For his staff, Conley makes sure that they know they are valued. He offers all of his employees—including the cleaning staff—free nights in one of the hotels so that they can enjoy the experience as well. He wants his employees to know that he values them and that he sincerely appreciates the work they do.

For customers, Conley concentrates on great customer service and providing perks meant to make their stay more enjoyable, such as complimentary cakes or small presents for guests celebrating birthdays. Because Conley's business is privately held, he makes sure to meet his investors' needs by only selecting investors who share his vision and goals; in this way, as his company thrives and succeeds in its mission, his investors are similarly benefiting.

Creating peak experiences for employees, customers, and investors fostered peak performance for the company. After applying Maslow's theory, Conley's hotel grew market share by 20 percent (during 2001–2004, a period of big hotel downturn), doubled revenues, was named one of the 10 best companies to work for in the Bay Area, and reduced its annualized employee turnover rate to one-third the industry average.[9]

Herzberg's Two Factors

1. Hygiene Factors: Things employees expect to be in place that do not motivate

2. Motivators: Things that motivate employees when they receive them

Herzberg's Two-Factor Theory

Say you're on a road trip with a friend. You've been driving for 12 hours and decide you're too tired to pull an all-nighter. Just your luck—you see a billboard on the freeway for a hotel that offers in-room spa services, hot chocolate with marshmallows, and a warm cookie served before you go to bed. Sounds great.

But your friend convinces you to drive at least another hour or two, so you pass the exit for that hotel. After two hours, you stop at the next hotel you see. It advertises clean sheets and running water. Are you surprised? Chances are you *expected* clean sheets and running water. Unlike spa services and cookies, clean sheets and running water won't motivate you to stay at a particular hotel. Although spa services and cookies are motivators, the latter are so-called "hygiene" (or maintenance) factors, which means that you *expect* them to be in place. If they were absent, you might leave, but they're not going to motivate you to stay in the way a warm cookie or free wireless service might.

Frederick Herzberg, a behavioral scientist, applied these ideas in his research on employee satisfaction and motivation. He believed that employees expected to receive certain things (such as a salary and bathroom breaks), and that if these factors were missing, employees would be so upset that they would leave. Herzberg's **two-factor theory** labels working conditions as "hygiene factors."[10] These factors do not create employee happiness, but a company's lack of hygiene factors would eventually create dissatisfaction. You wouldn't expect a manager to motivate an employee by saying, "If you work, we'll pay you." The employee would expect to be paid, even if the manager didn't come out and say it.

Using the Two-Factor Theory So how does a manager use the two-factor theory to motivate employees? By using Herzberg's second factor, "motivators." These are things that give someone satisfaction and motivate them when they receive them, such as promotions, bonuses, or educational or other job enrichment opportunities. An effective manager might offer specific motivators to each employee, based on what most motivates that employee to work. For instance, a manager might offer the incentive of promotion to an employee who wants to climb the corporate ladder, and offer additional vacation days to an employee who enjoys traveling. Knowing what motivates your employees is a key part of management.

Does It Work? Some people say Herzberg's two-factor theory is too simplistic and doesn't take into account that some motivators may actually cause dissatisfaction for someone else who doesn't want responsibility. For instance, the employee who likes to travel is given a promotion instead of those extra vacation days. With the promotion come additional responsibilities, which, in turn, could make it harder for the employee to go on extended vacations. On the other hand, Herzberg's simple theory may increase employees' job satisfaction if employers use it to figure out *why* employees are dissatisfied and what might motivate them.[11]

Comparing Maslow's and Herzberg's Models The Maslow and Herzberg models have some similarities, as shown in Figure 11.3. The first three levels of the Maslow model (physiological, safety, and social needs) are similar to Herzberg's hygiene factors. The top two levels in the Maslow hierarchy (esteem needs and self-actualization) are similar to Herzberg's motivators that deal with opportunities, developments, and advancement.

Theory X and Theory Y

How do you feel about work? Do you work because you enjoy what you do or because you have to work? Douglas McGregor explored these two different viewpoints on work and developed two theories that explored how managers view their employees:

- **Theory X** assumes that employees dislike work and responsibility, so they need to be closely supervised.
- **Theory Y** says that employees like work, are motivated, and do not need close supervision to do their work.

How does this connect to motivating employees? Managers who believe that the attitude of their employees toward work is best described by theory X will be relatively controlling, distrustful, and threatening, because they believe such an approach is the best way to motivate employees to work. Managers who believe that theory Y is a better description of their employees will be more encouraging, supporting, and trusting because they know their employees are already motivated to work and simply need the support and encouragement to do a good job. These managers will motivate their employees by working with them to establish and achieve fulfilling goals.[12] Looking at these two theories, which do you believe in more? Which type of manager would you rather have?

Vroom's Expectancy

Have you ever worked hard for something because you believed that you would be well rewarded for your efforts? If so, then you'll appreciate Victor Vroom's **expectancy theory**. Vroom's theory says that employees are motivated when they believe more effort will lead to better job performance, which in turn will lead to rewards they value. According to Vroom, three factors are involved in this process:

1. **Rewards that matter:** Managers need to provide rewards that employees really value. Vroom called the perceived value of the rewards their *valence*.
2. **Confidence in the connection between performance and the rewards:** Employees need to believe that their performance will actually lead to rewards. Vroom called this *instrumentality*, and it simply means that if you perform well, you can trust that you'll be rewarded for it.
3. **Connection between actions and performance:** Once employees know that good performance will be rewarded, they need to understand what specific actions they need to take to yield good performance. Work longer hours? Make fewer errors? Sell more units? The degree to which a manager specifies the actions that equate to good performance creates what Vroom calls the *expectancy*.

Using Vroom's Expectancy Theory How does Vroom's expectancy theory play out in a motivational setting? Let's use Jenna's team from page 255 as an example.

Figure **11.3** | **Comparing Maslow's and Herzberg's Models**

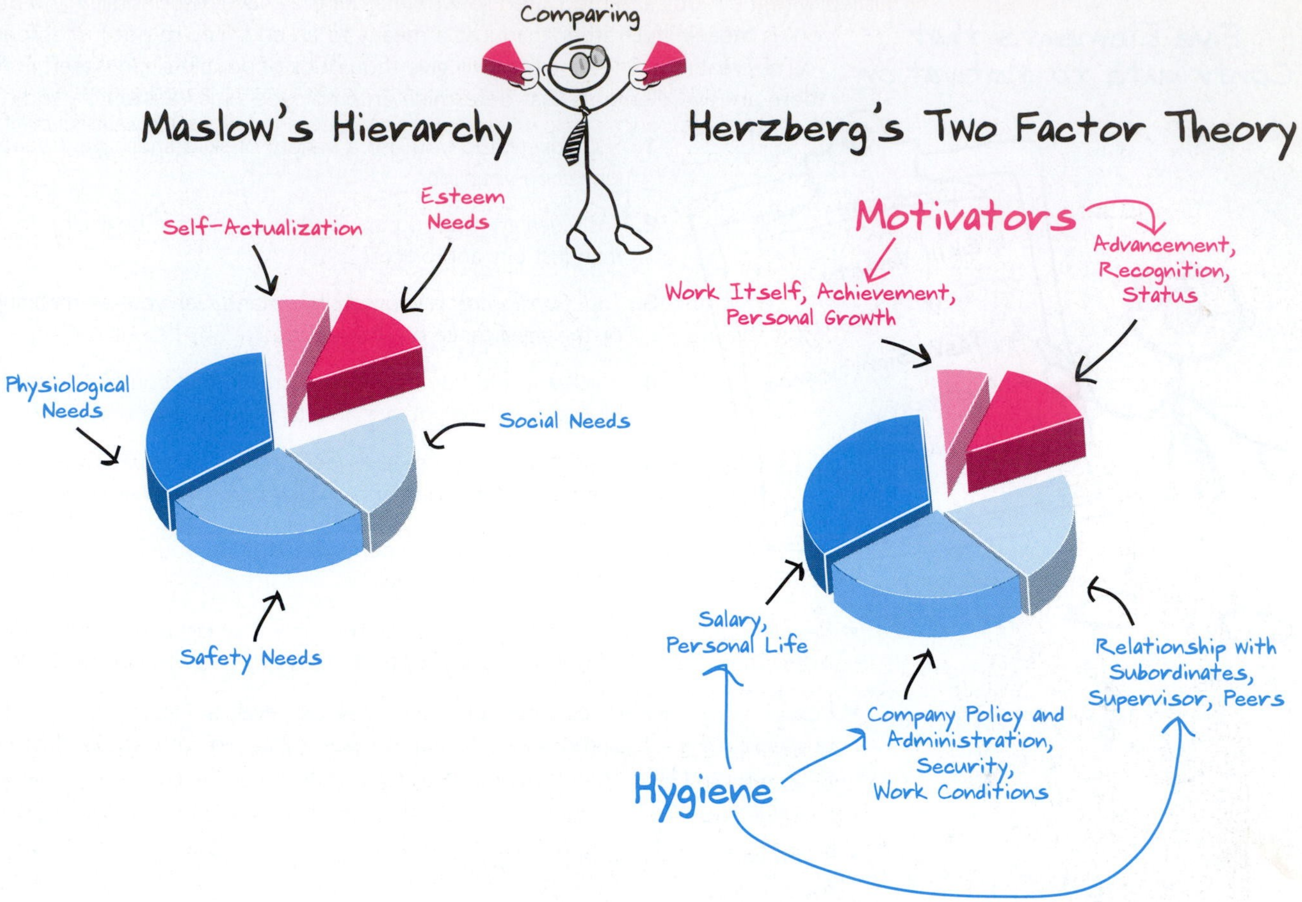

- Jenna knows that Owen wants a promotion, so she offers him more responsibility on their current project. Jenna's decision to offer Owen a promotion fits well with Vroom's theory because Owen has a high *valence* for a promotion.
- If Owen believes that his performance on this project will yield him the promotion, he will have a high degree of motivation to perform well, because he sees the *instrumentality* of high performance in producing a promotion.
- Jenna needs to provide the training and direction necessary so that Owen knows what specific actions he needs to implement to achieve a high level of performance. The degree to which Owen believes that specific behaviors will yield high performance establishes his *expectancy*—or belief—that if he implements those behaviors he will improve his chances of being rewarded.

As you can see, according to Vroom's theory, to be motivated, employees must believe that the reward is worth the work and that they will actually receive that reward when the work is done.

Job Characteristics Theory

Imagine you're looking for a job and see two job descriptions advertised. The first says the job involves repetitive assembly-line work. The second says the job involves creating water filters that will be used to provide clean water in developing areas across the globe. Which job seems more appealing to you? Even though the advertisements could be for the same job, you're likely to perceive the second one as more meaningful because you've been provided with more information about it.

This second advertisement is consistent with J. R. Hackman and G. R. Oldham's **job characteristics theory**. Based on Vroom's ideas, this theory suggests ways to design jobs

so that they are inherently motivating for employees. Employees are more likely to be satisfied with their jobs and motivated to work hard if they have responsibility and believe their work is meaningful, rather than just a means to an end. You're not just soldering metal; you're creating something that will give thousands of people clean water! In this theory, there are five elements that determine an employee's job satisfaction and motivation:

1. *Skill Variety*: Do you use a variety of skills and have a variety of challenges on your job?
2. *Task Identity*: Are you involved in a job from beginning to end, rather than just bits and pieces?
3. *Task Significance*: Is your job important? Can you see meaningful impact or the significance of what you do?
4. *Autonomy*: Do you have autonomy, in that you have certain responsibilities for which you are able to make certain decisions?
5. *Feedback*: Do you receive feedback, which could range from quantitative production numbers to qualitative customer comments?

Think about your own job experiences and ask yourself each question. How many times did you answer "yes"?

- People who say yes to all five questions are probably very highly motivated to stay in that position, and they find the work they do to be satisfying and meaningful.
- People who answer yes three or four times can evaluate their jobs based on which question(s) they answered with "no." For instance, if you think you lack feedback and skill variety, you can talk to your supervisor about trying new tasks and evaluating your work at the end of a project. Your motivation to work increases as each "no" turns to a "yes."
- If you find yourself saying "no" more often than "yes," chances are you're already looking for a new job.

Using the Job Characteristics Theory Have you ever done poorly on a job that you became comfortable with and knew inside out? Then, one day, your manager asks you to work on a project that gives you substantially more responsibility, autonomy, and accountability. You not only complete the job well but you thrive on the work, your achievement, and the recognition. Using the job characteristics theory, managers can let employees assume increasing levels of responsibility and correct their own performance from feedback. What does the business get out of it? Some companies may experience lower absenteeism, reduced turnover costs, and increased employee commitment.[13]

As an employee, using the job characteristics theory can also help you identify areas in your job in which you want to improve, so that you can work with your manager to make that job more meaningful and satisfying.

Do It...

11.2: Determine What Motivates You Use what you've learned about motivation to determine what motivates you. Use the following questions as a guide:

- What three things would motivate you and make you a satisfied employee?
- Which theory best describes how you are motivated?
- What could a manager do to make sure you remain motivated?

Limit your answers to one page, and be prepared to submit them electronically or discuss them in class. Your instructor may also divide you into teams to compare and contrast your answers.

Now Debrief...

- Different things motivate people, and many theories have been proposed to explain why.
- Maslow's **hierarchy of needs theory** states that we are motivated to fulfill basic lower-level needs before we can pursue higher-level needs.
- Herzberg's **two-factor theory** says that hygiene factors can get rid of dissatisfaction, but only motivators can provide real satisfaction.
- McGregor's **theory X** assumes that employees dislike work and need supervision, while his **theory Y** assumes that employees like work and don't need supervision.
- Vroom's **expectancy theory** says that employees are motivated when they believe more effort will lead to increased job performance, which will lead to rewards they value.
- Hackman and Oldham's **job characteristics theory** suggests that employers create jobs that motivate employees by giving them responsibility and a sense of meaningfulness.

3. Training and Developing Employees

"Ray Kroc's genius was building a system that requires all of its members to follow corporate-like rules but at the same time rewards them for expressing their individual creativity."

—John Love,
McDonald's chronicler,
on McDonald's founder Ray Kroc[14]

What university trains 5,000 to 7,000 managers each year and boasts six satellite universities and 139 regional training centers around the world? Hamburger University is tangible evidence of McDonald's commitment to training and developing its employees. Managers are trained in the ways of quality, service, cleanliness, and value, and can even use their HU education as credit toward a two- or four-year degree.

Managers can effectively communicate and provide ample motivation for employees, but without proper training, employees will not be successful at their jobs. Employees can develop skills both in a classroom and on the job, but the benefit of this development is not limited to an employee's own career advancement; skilled and knowledgeable employees are an asset to the organizations for which they work. In this section, we'll look at how managers help employees get the training and development they need to be successful, and how you can develop your own career as well.

Who Needs Training?

When applying for a job, have you ever wondered whether you were *really* expected to know how to do everything in the job description, or whether you'd be given training? One of a manager's important tasks is to identify his or her employees' training needs. Managers do this by assessing the types of employees they have and determining their skill level and needs. Employees can be divided into four main categories:

- **Learners:** You probably work or go to school with people who try really hard, but do not yet have the skills required to advance to high positions within a company. Maybe they are new to the job or to the field, so they don't have much background knowledge to go on. These are **learners**.
- **Leaners: Leaners**, on the other hand, are highly skilled but don't put forth much effort. They are often experienced but require a lot of supervision to get the job done.
- **Life-Support:** Those on **life support** have neither the effort nor the skills, but they may be energized with the right training.
- **Lifters: Lifters** have both effort and skill. They have commitment, intelligence, energy, and stamina—all critical ingredients for organizational success. They are tireless in efforts to figure out something, raise the bar, and inspire others to become part of a winning team.

The Management Connection Once managers identify which category their employees each fall in, what then? The key for managers is to use various training and developing tools to create a plan for each employee:

- provide training and development to support the learners;
- provide strong supervision to the leaners;
- remove or reinvigorate those on life support; and
- develop and hire more lifters.[15]

Taking care of the lifters is a priority for managers not only because they are the most valuable employees, but because they constantly need new challenges. Lifters are the employees that all companies want to recruit.

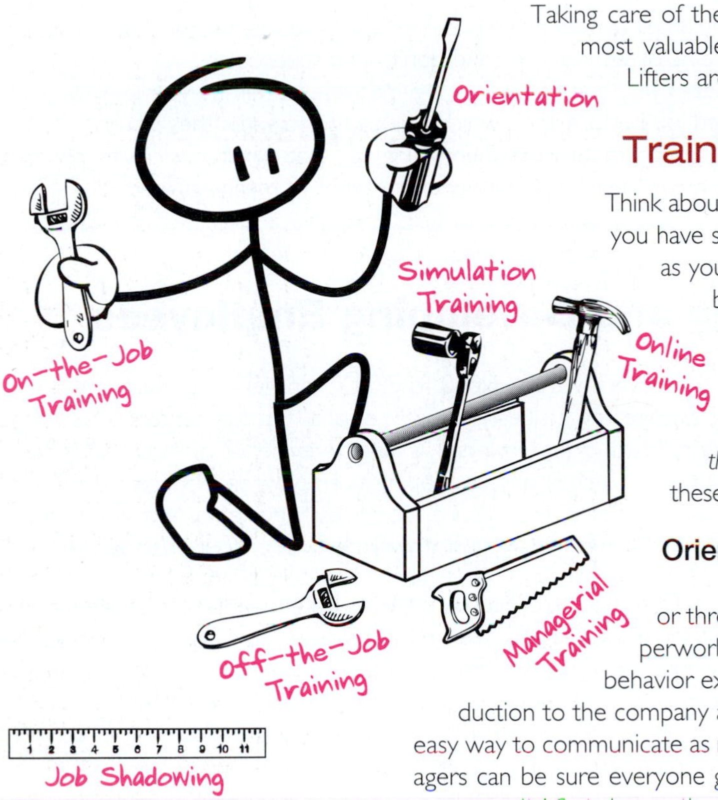

What training and development tools have you used?

Training and Developing Tools

Think about your current or previous job. How did you learn what to do? Did you have several weeks of training, or did you jump in immediately and learn as you worked? Starting immediately and learning as you go may be the best way for a barista to mix coffee drinks, but airline pilots require hours of simulated practice before they actually start flying. *On-the-job training* and *simulation training* are just two training and development tools that managers can use to train employees. Managers can also use *orientation*, *online training*, *job shadowing*, *off-the-job training*, and *managerial training*. Let's take a look at some of these training and developing methods from both perspectives.

Orientation You're the employee, and it's your first day on the job. You head into a conference room, where you and two or three other newbies hear the company's welcome speech, fill out paperwork, and receive instruction about the work you'll be doing and the behavior expected of you. This **orientation** process is the employee's introduction to the company and his or her new job. Companies use orientation as a quick and easy way to communicate as much information as possible to new employees. In this way, managers can be sure everyone gets all the information they need, and they've only taken up the new recruits' first day on the job, allowing the new employees to get right to business on their second day.

On-the-Job Training You're a manager, you need help, and you need it now. You don't have time to train someone in the theoreticals and hypotheticals of what they might encounter once they're actually doing the work. You've decided that **on-the-job training**—teaching employees their jobs by immediately starting them to work, and supervising them until they learn what they need to know—is the right way to go in this situation.

As the employee, how do you feel about on-the-job training? You might feel a lot of pressure being asked to perform without having the necessary training first. You want to impress your supervisors at your new job, but you're worried you'll make embarrassing mistakes as you learn on the go. But you probably also realize that there are some things that you have to learn by doing, and no amount of training and explaining from your supervisor ahead of time is going to help you get comfortable with your tasks. And on-the-job training will also give you the opportunity to show your managers that you're flexible and a quick study, which can only help your position at the company.

Simulation Training For some employees, because of the nature of their work, it might be days, weeks, even months before they begin their actual job. With **simulation training**, managers have employees practice the work they are going to do to familiarize employees with company procedures and any equipment the employees will be using. This helps reduce the risk of injury or damaging expensive equipment, which will save the company money in the long run.

For employees, simulation training is a useful way to make and learn from mistakes. The training may be practiced on different equipment, or it might be specialized computer programming that employees learn online.

Online Training

Online training is just what it sounds like: training that employees receive online. Online training is handy because an employee may be able to access the information from any computer, meaning he or she can do the training either at work or at home.

Online training is handy for employers as well. If several employees need to learn some new skills for a new project, online training is something they can do in their own time at home. Additionally, online training can be cheap: They can make the training program once, and use it over and over again.

Job Shadowing

Another training tool companies may use is **job shadowing**. In this technique, new employees follow and observe an experienced employee to see what he or she does. This type of training is useful because the new employees can see how the job is done before they try their own hand at it.

From an employee's point of view, this training is useful because he or she can get a feel for the job. The experienced employee may act as a mentor, helping the new employee get used to the company and answering any questions the newbie may have. This is also a great way for new employees to meet and form friendships with their co-workers.

Off-the-Job Training and Managerial Training

With the recent economic troubles, more and more people have been going back to school to boost their skills. They may wish to hone their skills so that they can become even more of an asset to their company, or they may be branching out, broadening their skills base as a way to look more appealing to potential employers. This **off-the-job training** is done on their own time, and often at the employee's own expense, although some employers may compensate employees for classes that apply to an employee's role in the company.

Employees may also attend **managerial training** as a way to improve their position within the company—or to score a better job. A company may also send potential managers to management training so that they have the skill set they need when managerial positions become available.

Which Tool Is Best?

Whether you're learning how to brew coffee or how to fly a jetliner, everyone needs some sort of training when he or she first begins a new job. The variety of training and development tools allows companies to choose which training method is best for a position or their line of work. Many companies may use a combination of the approaches to adjust each employee's training and development plan to suit his or her individual needs and goals. The training employees receive not only makes them a more valuable asset to their company, but the skills they learn can help them work toward achieving their career goals.

Developing Your Own Career

Now that you are familiar with the range of possible training tools that companies offer, you're in a good position to identify good opportunities for your own career. It's important for you to look for these opportunities when they're offered in your organization, or create new opportunities by suggesting to your manager how additional training would be good for you and your contributions to the organization.

You should also ask about training opportunities when you interview with an organization. Look for organizations that invest in employee training and development, and consider these opportunities as part of the whole package when you're evaluating job offers. These are just a few ideas of how you can leverage training and development for your career success. For more ideas, check out the Chapter 19 at **www.mybizlab.com**.

Do It...

11.3: Track Your Training Employees undergo training as a way to gain skills that will be helpful for their company and their own careers. Think about your own skills and the training you have undergone. If you are currently not employed, use your college experience as a basis. Divide a piece of paper in half. On the left, list any training or development you have participated in. On the right, list any training you would like and the skills you wish to learn. Under your list, explain how the training builds toward your career goal. Be prepared to submit your work electronically or to discuss it in class.

Now Debrief...

- Training needs vary from employee to employee. **Learners** have high effort and minimal skills. **Leaners** have minimal effort and high skill. Employees on **life support** are lacking in both effort and skill. **Lifters** have high effort and high skills.
- Training methods also vary and include **orientation**, **on-the-job training**, **simulation training**, **online training**, **job shadowing**, **off-the-job training**, and **managerial training**.

4. Decision Making and Delegating

"The most difficult thing is the decision to act, the rest is merely tenacity."

—Aviation pioneer Amelia Earhart[16]

Say you're the CEO of a pet supply store. People can barely distinguish your store from that other one with "pet" in the name, and you want to change that. How do you decide what changes need to be made and how to implement them?

In the 1990s, Brian Devine, CEO of PETCO, decided he wanted to differentiate PETCO from other pet supply companies. The company carefully studied the marketplace. It noticed pet stores with aquariums and fish generated higher foot traffic, so Devine experimented by removing less popular merchandise in stores that were being remodeled and replacing it with aquariums and fish. After doing so, an area of floor space previously accounting for 3 percent of sales suddenly contributed 15 percent.

Devine also placed stores in community-based shopping centers that shoppers visit one to three times weekly rather than those that customers tend to shop once every several weeks, like Home Depot or Costco. PETCO began offering low-cost vaccinations, grooming salons, pet adoptions, dog snack bars, and holiday-themed pictures with pets. PETCO determined that, unlike stores like Wal-Mart, it wanted to avoid being all things to all people. Instead, it focused on filling the empty mid- to high-end niche where pet owners are more likely to consider themselves pet parents. "That decision allowed it to do its own thing and do it better than anyone else without the unnecessary burden of worrying about having to face off daily against cutthroat competition."[17]

Decision making is a big part of running a successful business. We've already learned how communicating, motivating, and training employees can be beneficial for employers and employees alike. Now we'll look at how making decisions and delegating tasks can make a business and its employees more effective.

Decision Making

It's the end of spring semester, and the entire summer is ahead of you. There are several different ways you can spend your summer, but how do you choose what you're going to do?

Decision making is getting results from considering a course of action among several alternatives. It can involve a drawn-out thought process that delays results or on-the-spot decisions that consider the most critical facts on hand.

Think about the decision making involved in planning a major trip, handling emergencies, or deciding how to spend your summer vacation. Think about the options you might have in this last example:

- Take the summer off, but you still need to pay rent for your shared apartment.
- Attend summer school so that you can graduate early.
- Wait tables in a restaurant to help pad your tuition bank account.
- Participate in a New York City internship with low pay and high expenses.
- Work part-time, attend school part-time, and live at home rent-free.
- Attend a family reunion in New Zealand, but the trip will be expensive.
- Volunteer to work in community service with a local youth group.
- Live at home to save money, and look for part-time work when you go back to school.

Think about all the factors you have to take into consideration when choosing how to spend your summer. Can you make your decision alone, or are other people, such as your roommates or family, involved? What about considering costs for summer school and deadlines for the internship and part-time work, reserving a flight to New Zealand as cheaply as possible, or making an early commitment to the community service organization before all the positions are taken? Using an organized approach to decision making can help you get results by looking at key steps and factors in a methodical way.

Deciding Who Has a Say

Take a look at who makes the decision—you alone or you as part of a team? Although individuals do certain kinds of decision making, many companies reach decisions through a consensus method. Team decision making may be preferable because different people and departments may know different relevant information, have different areas of expertise, and represent different interests. Unpopular or controversial decisions may also be easier to swallow if everyone affected by them is part of the decision making process.

Involving too many people in the decision making process can have its drawbacks, though:

- With so many ideas flowing around a conference room table, it's often difficult to stay focused.
- Some people may try to express ideas that would place themselves or their departments in a more favorable light.
- Other times, two or more individuals may engage in power play, each having director communication styles, and will bicker so much that the rest of the team may be demoralized.
- Finally, team decision making is ineffective if the group can't arrive at a consensus or if there is an equal number of votes for each option, arriving instead at a compromise-riddled alternative instead of an optimal course of action.

Decision Making Steps

Regardless of whether your decision is being made individually or in a team, taking an organized approach can give you better odds of having an effective decision making process. Let's use a shoe company that is trying to decide between launching a new women's dress shoe or a new women's casual shoe as an example.

1. **Identify the goal(s) to be achieved and the decision to be made.** In Chapter 9, we discussed how top-level managers form strategic goals that are then filtered from the operational and tactical levels via middle management down to other employees.

   In our example, the goal is to drive revenue growth in the women's foot-care line. The decision to be made is whether a casual shoe or a dress shoe is the best option at this time.

2. **Isolate the facts.** Narrow the focus to the most relevant facts. What are the constraints, such as budget, personnel, and time? Isolating facts may also reveal that a decision will have to be made with limited or incomplete information.

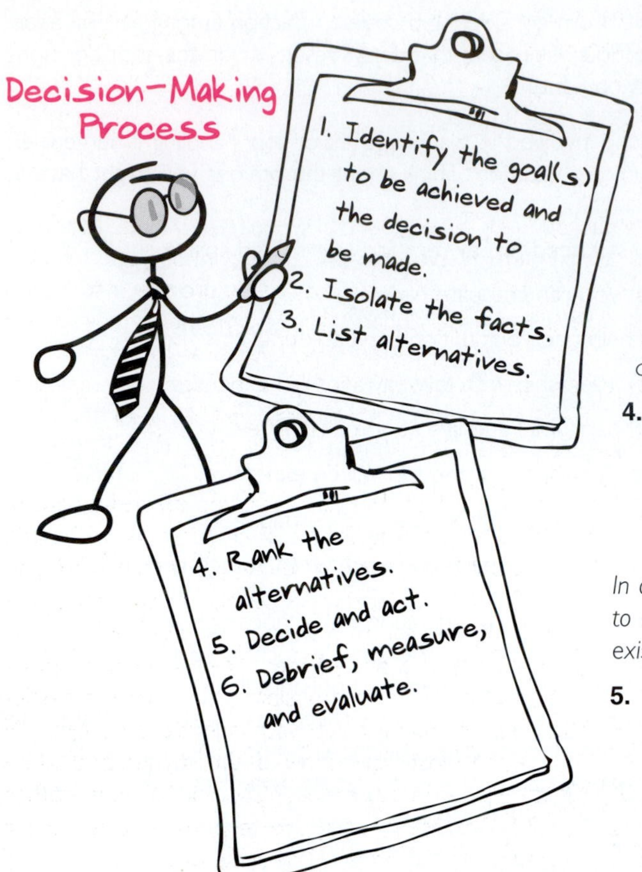

For example, the shoe company may have valuable market research data about women's shoe purchasing trends, retail prices for casual shoes and dress shoes, and projected cost information for manufacturing each type of shoe.

3. **List alternatives.** List as many ideas as possible and weigh the pros and cons of each. Also consider any negative ramifications from not making a decision at all. Then, through a process of elimination, narrow the ideas down to a few that can be considered further.

For example, the shoe company could manufacture its own casual or dress shoes or outsource the manufacturing to lower the unit costs. The company might also consider high-end or low-end lines for either the casual shoe or dress shoe, and compare the profitability and potential sales volume of each.

4. **Rank the alternatives.** Rank your narrowed list of alternatives in order of feasibility, resources, or other important factors. Which alternative is most likely to result in a sound decision for the long term? What is the most realistic alternative for the time, money, and other resources you have, given a particular risk level?

In our example, each alternative identified in step 3 could be ranked according to its potential profitability, relative risk, and compatibility with the company's existing product line.

5. **Decide and act.** Carefully assess the outcome of each decision and determine whether it meets the goal. After selecting the best course of action and justifying it, consider specific details about when it should start, who will be responsible for the project, and when results are expected. Communication and delegation are very important at this stage. Not only are final decisions relayed to managers at different levels, but in many situations, company owners, the board, and shareholders are informed as well.

In our example, the shoe company chooses which type of shoe to launch, who will manufacture it, and how it will be priced and marketed.

6. **Debrief, measure, and evaluate.** After the plan is launched, keep others in the loop with updates. These updates should include measuring the plan's effectiveness and evaluating whether the plan is on track. If the goals of the project change, managers must also be prepared to quickly change course, do some tweaking, or even start from scratch, if warranted.

The shoe company can track the new shoe's performance and compare those results to the original goals for the product launch.

Be the Delegator

Now that a decision has been made, it's time to figure out who will do the work. If you want something done right, you have to do it yourself, right? If you're a manager, you won't have time to get it all done by yourself, and you'll need to enlist some help. **Delegation** is assigning certain tasks to subordinates and giving them the responsibility to carry them out.

Why Delegate? Managers who fail to delegate may become so overburdened with tasks that they don't have time to actually manage anyone or anything or to adequately complete any task. The supervised employees likely won't have much respect or trust for their manager because they feel like he or she doesn't respect or trust them enough to give them responsibilities.

Because managers are usually the ones who have ultimate responsibility for a project, it can be difficult to hand over any control to someone else. It's key for managers to handpick which tasks are really necessary for them to complete and which tasks they can assign to others.

What Should You Delegate? There are a few questions a manager can ask to determine whether delegating is the right choice for a particular task:

- Do I need to be personally involved because of my unique knowledge or skills? If not, is there someone on my team who has specific knowledge or skills that will make him or her particularly good at completing this task?

- Is the task within my major area of responsibility, or will it affect the performance or finances of my division?
- When is the deadline? Is quick action needed? Some decisions require unilateral decision making, but these days the "many hands make light work" ethic is the pervasive thinking.

Effective managers don't just delegate—they empower.

Empowering Others Delegating doesn't mean dumping all of your tasks on other people. Everyone on your team, including you, should have a reasonable amount of work that suits his or her specific knowledge and skills. Once you give someone a task, provide that person with adequate supervision to make sure the job gets done. Although it might be tempting to keep a scrutinizing eye on their work, it's best to avoid micromanagement, as this can stress and demoralize an employee. Instead, be sure to let the employee know what he or she is responsible for and provide support as needed.[18]

What's the difference between delegating and dumping?

This distribution of responsibility is called **empowerment**. The difference between delegating and empowering is like the proverb about the difference between giving a man a fish and teaching him to fish. Delegation is simply giving someone a task to complete, which you, as manager, will oversee and will have to check. Empowerment means giving employees control of and responsibility for running a particular part of the project, with minimal oversight. It's one way to instill ownership in employees, and when people take on ownership, along with it often comes a greater sense of care and responsibility, a greater stake in the outcome, and a sense of pride.

When managers and employees are working together on team goals with respective responsibilities, team efficiency and productivity increase. Moreover, giving subordinates the authority to work solo on a project may also build organization loyalty. Effective managers don't just delegate—they empower.

Be the Delegatee

As an employee, your managers will probably delegate work to you. Not only do you want to fulfill your objectives to potentially rise in the ranks, but you'll gain greater visibility within the company to make that happen. When you have responsibility for a particular facet of a project, there are several things you can do to ensure that things run smoothly:

- If your manager trusts you by delegating a really important project, make sure that you're not going to fail him or her. Bring what you need with you to meetings and to have the most up-to-date information.
- Manage time expectations. If you have a deadline, plan for each day or even each hour so that you can be on track to meet it—and alert your manager as soon as possible if you won't be able to meet the deadline.
- Make a comprehensive review of everything, including events that could cause delays. Show your manager that you can anticipate and respond to possible problems.
- Keep your manager informed with relevant, accurate information. If you do not know a particular figure or the answer to a question, write it down and inform your manager when you find the answer.
- If you encounter a problem, go to your manager with the problem *and* several solutions. Explain which solution you think would be best, and get your manager's final approval on your decision before taking action.

Do It...

11.4: Make a Decision A local gift-shop is losing money and needs to increase its profits to stay in business. The owner needs to decide whether to lay off employees or make some other move to keep its doors open. With the Manager BizHat on, walk through the decision making process outlined in this section and decide what you would do. Now switch over to the Employee BizHat and walk through the same process. Do the two decisions differ? How? Which decision do you think is best? Be prepared to submit your analysis electronically or to discuss it in class.

Now Debrief...

- **Decision making** is getting results from considering a course of action among several alternatives. Managers use decision making processes, either individually or on a team.
- The decision making process includes: identifying the goal(s) to be achieved and the decision to be made, isolating the facts, listing alternatives, ranking alternatives, deciding and acting, and debriefing, measuring, and evaluating.
- After decisions are made, **delegation** is addressed at different levels of management, including the pros and cons of taking a hands-off approach.
- Great managers don't just delegate; they use **empowerment** and give employees responsibility for their work.

5. Controlling and Evaluating Plans and Strategies

Kennedy recently opened up a used book store in her neighborhood. She went through the process of creating a solid business plan, organizing a staff, and getting all the other odds and ends ready for the grand opening. Now that her decisions are in the process of being carried out, what's left for her to do? Can she just sit back and relax? In short, no.

Once decisions are made, the job of an owner or manager isn't finished. Now, Kennedy needs to use her communication and motivation skills to motivate her staff, provide training as necessary, and delegate tasks that would be a better use of another person's time and talents. She also needs to control and evaluate her decisions to see what's successful and what isn't. The results of this process can help her make continuous improvements in the future.

What happens if one of these steps is missing?

Controlling

Controlling someone's work doesn't mean watching over that person like a hawk, nor does it mean outlining every step required for the work to be accomplished. **Controlling** is another function of management that requires managers to create guidelines that ensure an organization is on track to achieve its goals. It is ultimately about monitoring processes, people, procedures, and systems to get feedback for improvement.

Establishing Performance Standards It's impossible for a business to know how it's doing if there are no benchmarks to judge progress. ■ Performance standards, for both employees and the business as a whole, act as the basis for managers to figure out how the business is doing.

As you recall from Chapter 9, many organizations establish standards and objectives using the Management by Objective (MBO) method. This relies on defining objectives and then evaluating success or failure based on the objectives that have been set. For example, before Kennedy opens her business, she may have figured out the maximum profit for different price points. During the evaluation process, this standard can help her gauge her business by seeing whether her profit goal is being met.

■ Performance standards, for both employees and the business as a whole, act as the basis for managers to figure out how the business is doing.

Keep in mind that performance standards should be realistically challenging—neither impossible nor too easy to reach. If they're impossible, it's likely to lower employee and investor morale. On the other hand, meeting standards that employees feel are challenging can boost their morale, as well as increase investor confidence.

Communicating Performance Standards Even though an organization establishes standards, that doesn't mean the job's done. The next step is to make sure these standards are properly communicated to the proper people. Although not all standards apply to all employees, it's important to clearly communicate the ones that do.

One way to communicate performance standards is by having every employee know their job description, which should contain the established standards. Look at the following sample of a job description:

Sample Job Description

Maintain existing client base by servicing and maintaining long-term relationships. Market and sell new company products to clients. Identify, market, and acquire new banking clients through prospecting with bank product managers. Assemble team of new sales associates. Help establish company presence through business activities.

Sounds good, but is anything missing? Which bank product managers will the employee "prospect" with? How many new sales associates are coming in, and exactly how are "business activities" defined? Here's a better job description that incorporates established standards:

Job Description That Incorporates Established Standards

- Maintain existing customer base of 25 to 30 middle-market companies in the northern Seattle area, which is expected to bring in $4 million annual product revenue. Sell new company products to existing client base to bring in $250,000 additional revenue.
- Develop relationships to bring in new client acquisition, producing $500,000 revenue by December.
- Provide on-the-job training to three new sales associates through joint client meetings, servicing existing clients, and routine office work.
- Attend five workshops for additional training.
- Increase company presence in the business community by achieving committee chair status in a prominent business activity, such as the Chamber of Commerce.
- Opportunities for advancement to be discussed upon reviewing year-end results.

With this revised job description, employees will have a much better idea of what performance standards are expected of them.

Evaluating

Once standards have been established and communicated to the necessary people, a lot of the work is done. During the evaluation process, managers judge the performance and assess the outcome. This can be done by taking a look at the established standards and comparing them to the actual performance.

Let's go back to Kennedy. Before she opened her business, she figured out the maximum profit for different price points. After being open a few months, Kennedy can evaluate her business to see where things stand. Do the standards she set months ago align with reality? Once she figures this out, she can create feedback and determine the necessary modifications.

Closing the Loop by Giving Feedback and Making Modifications

Once Kennedy figures out if she's maximizing her profits, she can determine whether changes are necessary to carry out her objective. If no changes are needed, then Kennedy's on the right track. She can take this knowledge and use it to make future business decisions. However, if her business standards and reality don't align, she may need to make an adjustment. To maximize profits, she may have to raise or lower her prices for certain items. This may require her to go back to the beginning of the decision making process. Once she has implemented a change, eventually she'll have to evaluate her business again.

This process of evaluating feedback and making modifications helps identify what was done right and what could have been done better. If things can be done better, a decision needs to be made regarding how things can be improved.

After managers evaluate decisions, they also need to appraise the employees carrying out these decisions. As you'll see in the next section, based on the appraisal, employees are sometimes promoted or fired.

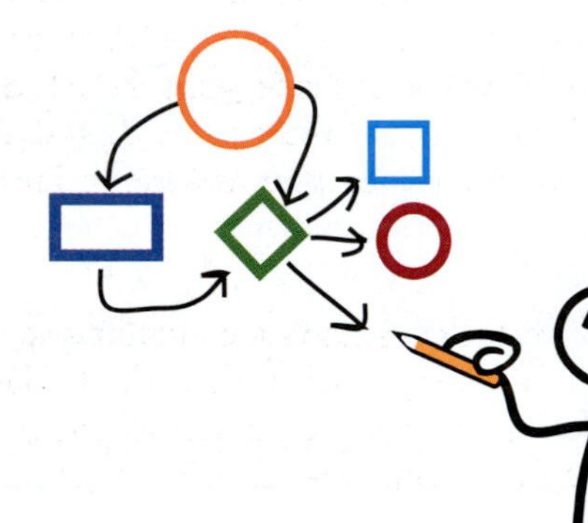

Do It...

11.5: Consider Controlling and Evaluating Think of one of your favorite classes where you felt you learned a lot, regardless of the grade you received. Consider the controlling and evaluating stages, and identify what your professor did that met your needs in each of the stages. Be prepared to submit your response electronically or to discuss it in class.

Now Debrief...

- **Controlling** is another function of management that requires managers to create guidelines that ensure an organization is on track to achieve its goals. It is ultimately about monitoring processes, people, procedures, and systems to get feedback for improvement.
- Performance standards, for both employees and the business as a whole, act as the basis for managers to figure out how the business is doing.
- Once standards have been established and communicated to the necessary people, evaluation takes place. During the evaluation process, a manager judges the performance and assesses the outcome. This can be done by looking at established standards and the organization, and then comparing the results.

6. Appraising, Promoting, and Firing Employees

Rodney has gotten in the door at the company of his dreams. He's loved the past six months, and his mid-year evaluation is coming up. He thinks everything has gone well—he gets along with his manager and co-workers, he's maintained a low but visible profile in the department, and nothing has really gone wrong that *he's* noticed.

What do you think his manager is thinking about when she prepares his evaluation? Has Rodney met measurable performance goals? Has he come up with creative solutions to problems, or is he simply a round peg fitting easily in the round holes without thinking about how things could be done better?

> "How you measure the performance of your managers directly affects the way they act."
>
> **—John Dearden,** former *Harvard Business School* professor[19]

In this situation, Rodney's manager needs to appraise Rodney's work along with appraising how Rodney fits in with the organization's vision. If the organization wants people who are confident and speak up, Rodney's low profile may be an important factor to consider when deciding whether to give him a promotion.

During the appraisal process, managers need to determine what employees are required to do on the job, recognize effective performance when demonstrated, and allow employees to participate in solving any problems that are preventing goal attainment.[20] We'll discuss all of these factors in this section.

Appraising Employees

Once managers have a clear picture of what effective performance looks like, they can accurately appraise employees. Similar to report cards, most companies have an annual or semi-annual formal **performance appraisal** that typically involves evaluations by both the employee and the manager. As you saw earlier, many companies use the MBO method to establish standards. This method also involves appraising performance based on these standards. In some companies this might be just a reaffirmation of the feedback received all year; other times, it might be a lengthy evaluation that contains new information. Typically, an employee writes a self-evaluation, his or her manager writes a performance evaluation, and then the two meet to discuss the reports.

Employee Self-Evaluations *Employee self-evaluations* are similar to what some schools are instituting for student-led report cards: writing down the things that most excited you about learning, some of your perceived weaknesses and what you could do better to understand the material, whether you got along with your classmates, and what contributions you made to better the classroom. Employees would write:

- how they met certain goals;
- improvements needed on projects that missed the mark; and
- how they plan to meet next year's goals in detail.

Basically, an employee self-evaluation is the employee's perception of himself or herself.

Formal Appraisals Managers look at the same areas as employee self-evaluations; however, managers' remarks generally quantify whether standards were met, as well as do some of the following[21]:

1. Give the priority level of the requirement or goal.
2. State the requirement or goal.
3. Write a conclusion as to whether the employee met the requirement or goal.
4. Give comments on the reasons and evidence supporting these conclusions.
5. Record the employee's comments.
6. Jot down notes after the evaluation meeting with the employee.

Note that managers need to have in place clear standards to make an evaluation. In the place for comments, managers must be specific with documentation, be courteous, respectful, show

accuracy, and show documentation for particularly high or low ratings. Good managers will use this time as an opportunity to coach and motivate employees to meet and exceed standards.

Discussing Opportunities for Improvement Throughout the review process, it's also important for managers to be truthful and candid about employee performance. Even the best employee's review is likely to contain criticism. If you are a manager, you can take steps to make sure a performance appraisal is productive:

- Be intentional with your language. Focus on what the employee did well, and then progress to opportunities for continuous improvement: your feedback would begin with "And the next steps are..."
- Be supportive. Understand that being evaluated can bring out emotional sensitivity in both the one doing the appraisal and the one being appraised.
- Be honest and direct. Avoid using meaningless statements to avoid hurting someone's feelings. Focus on observable behavior that he or she can change. Ultimately, being honest might help employees learn from their mistakes.
- Be positive. Communicate to employees that you have confidence in them and their ability to focus on opportunities for continuous improvement.

Constructive criticism can be difficult to take, but both sides of the appraisal need to understand that a productive review ultimately helps everyone involved.

Handling Constructive Criticism Now say you're an employee getting a performance appraisal and your manager has more of a criticism focus. What are some of the ways you can handle this criticism?[22]

- Stay cool, calm, and collected. Don't get defensive, combative, or argumentative.
- If you don't think the review is justified, ask for another meeting to follow up when you're better equipped to respond. Meanwhile, read the review and be honest with yourself—did you actually try to rush a project along because it had too many problems that you couldn't fix? Could you have done more to address some of the issues that cropped up, or were you already thinking about the next project? Use data and other information to show why an outcome was different than what your manager relayed to you. If you're right, make sure your manager documents this on your records.
- Thank your manager for the comments, and communicate that you will use the appraisal as a way to learn, grow, and do better next time.

Whatever hat you wear, performance appraisals are most productive when both managers and employees look forward to them as a chance to check in, catch up, and look for areas for the employee to develop in his or her career.

Promoting Employees

When's a good time to promote someone? Should managers promote someone who has great technical skills but poor people skills? Is there a formula? Should managers promote someone who produces the best team results? How about the technically strong worker who's also a backstabber? Or what about promoting a person who has strong administrative skills but is so-so in understanding in-depth content?

Generally, employees are promoted when companies recognize them for their performance and contributions and a higher-level position opens up. However, as we discussed in Chapter 9, just because someone's a good employee doesn't mean he or she should be promoted. Perhaps an employee is doing such a great job because he or she is most suited for the job he or she currently has, and would not succeed in a promotion.

Identifying Promotion-Worthy Employees

Organizations get the most benefit when good employees who are actually "promotion-ready" do indeed get promoted.[23]

Identifying promotion-worthy employees can be difficult, but they often share some of the following characteristics. Promotion-worthy employees:

- have a demonstrated record of success;
- are willing to take on more responsibility;
- can work without constant or frequent supervision;
- demonstrate leadership and effective followership qualities;
- make decisions that enhance the organization's success;
- have effective people skills;
- have good time management skills;
- have good decision making and delegation skills; and
- have demonstrated success working as part of a team.

When managers are trying to find promotion-worthy employees, they should also be aware of red flags that might suggest certain employees should not be promoted. As noted, some people are content where they are and don't want a promotion. Although managers may think that a certain person is the most-qualified candidate, he or she may not—for personal or other reasons—want to take on any additional responsibilities.

Firing Employees

Appraisals aren't always positive. Sometimes, an employee's performance is not strong enough and he or she needs to be fired. Firing someone is never easy, but it's something that occurs from time to time in all organizations. If an employee is becoming a problem, managers should make sure that the grounds that justify a firing are reflected in the employee's performance evaluation and are backed up by documentation.[24] It's also important for managers to document and discuss work performance so by the time an employee is let go, he or she has had regular and consistent opportunities to improve job performance and work-related behaviors. Terminated employees need to understand exactly why they were let go. Countless examples have been given in which employees sued for wrongful termination and won their cases because nothing in the employees' performance evaluations indicated that they had been performing on a subpar basis.

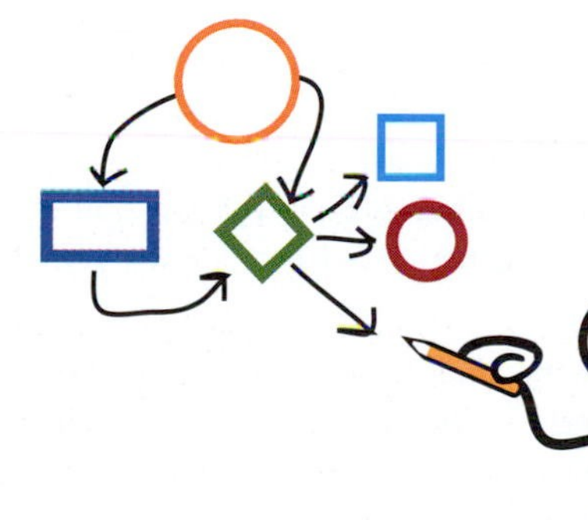

Do It...

11.6: Write Your Own Performance Appraisal Write your own performance appraisal for your effort and performance in this class to-date. Be sure to demonstrate the qualities and elements discussed in this chapter. Limit your answer to 150 words, and be prepared to submit it electronically or to discuss it in class.

Now Debrief...

- A **performance appraisal** is an annual or semi-annual review that typically involves both employee self-evaluations and formal appraisals by managers.
- Employees get promoted when companies recognize performance and contributions. Organizations get the most benefit when good employees who are actually "promotion-ready" do indeed get promoted.
- If a manager decides to fire an employee, it's important for that manager to document and discuss work performance so by the time an employee is let go, he or she has had regular and consistent opportunities to improve job performance and work-related behaviors.

Chapter 11 Visual Summary

Management Perspective | Chapter 9: *Plan* Chapter 10: *Organize* **Chapter 11: *Direct, Control, Evaluate***

1. Characterize your communication style, recognize the communication style of others, and prescribe how you could work together most effectively. (pp. 256–259)

- People can be categorized according to four personality types: directors, performers, people-pleasers, and detailers. These personality types are closely tied to particular communication styles.
- **Directors** are confident decision-makers who like to be in charge.
- **Performers** are people-focused and communicative, and they enjoy teamwork.
- **People-pleasers** are diplomats who dislike conflict.
- **Detailers** are detail-oriented and focus on accuracy and high quality standards.
- Effective managers can adapt their own communication style (or flex their style) to improve their communications with others.

Summary: Communication styles affect people's interactions in many situations. Good communicators understand their own communication style, are intuitive enough to understand how to successfully communicate with others, and are flexible enough to adapt when necessary.

2. Prescribe the best methods for motivating someone, and understand how you yourself are motivated. (pp. 259–265)

- Maslow's **hierarchy of needs theory** suggests that people are motivated to fulfill basic lower-level needs before they can pursue higher-level needs and be truly effective employees.
- Herzberg studied employee satisfaction and motivation and came up with his **two-factor theory**, which breaks down working conditions into hygiene factors or motivators. Hygiene factors are basic work conditions that employees expect to receive, whereas motivators inspire employees to do better.
- McGregor breaks down the workplace into two different viewpoints: **theory X** assumes that employees dislike work and responsibility and need supervision; **theory Y** assumes that employees like work, are motivated, and do not need close supervision.
- Vroom's **expectancy theory** suggests that to be motivated, employees must believe that the reward is worth the work and that they will actually receive that reward when the work is done.
- Hackman and Oldham's **job characteristics theory** suggests that employees are more likely to be satisfied with their jobs and motivated to work hard if they believe their work is meaningful and they have responsibility. The five elements to judge satisfaction are skill variety, task identity, task significance, autonomy, and feedback.

Summary: It's important for managers to understand their employees and apply various motivators as needed.

3. Recommend methods for training and developing employees, and know how you can develop your own career. (pp. 265–268)

- One of a manager's important tasks is to identify his or her employees' training needs. Managers do this by assessing the types of employees they have and determining their skill level and needs. **Learners** have high effort and minimal skills. **Leaners** have minimal effort and high skill. Employees on **life support** are lacking in both effort and skill. **Lifters** have high effort and high skills.
- Training methods vary from place to place, but generally include **orientation**, **on-the-job training**, **simulation training**, **online training**, **job shadowing**, **off-the-job training**, and **managerial training**.
- It's important for employees to look for opportunities already offered in the organization—or create new ones—that will allow them to develop their own careers.

Summary: To be successful, employees need to be properly trained and developed.

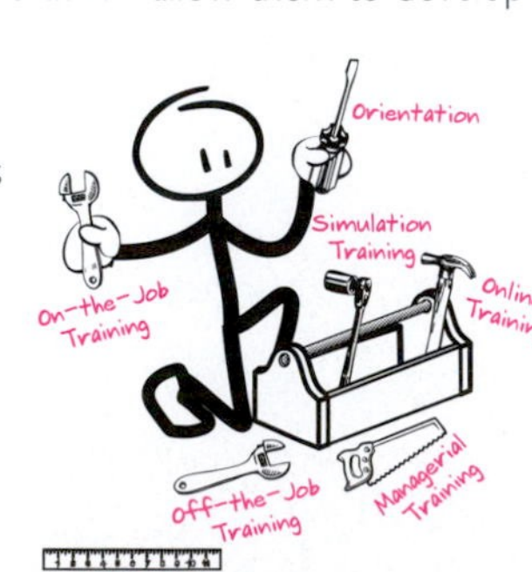

4. Make good decisions and be an effective delegator or delegatee. (pp. 268–272)

- **Decision making** is getting results from considering a course of action among several alternatives.
- Team decision making is important in business; however, it can be easy to lose focus if multiple people are involved. Managers can help keep everyone on track by using an organized approach to decision making. This includes identifying the goal(s) to be achieved and the decision to be made, isolating the facts, listing alternatives, ranking the alternatives, deciding and acting, and finally debriefing, measuring, and evaluating.
- **Delegation** is assigning certain tasks to others and giving them the responsibility to carry them out. This is an important skill to master because managers can become overburdened with tasks that they don't have time to do themselves but are accountable for.
- Great managers don't just delegate, they **empower**, which means giving employees control of and responsibility for running a particular part of a project, with minimal oversight.
- When delegatees fulfill their responsibilities, they may gain greater visibility in the organization or get a promotion.

Summary: Decision making is an important part of a successful business because it involves figuring out the best way to achieve goals. An important part of making decisions effective is delegating.

5. Measure the results of your decisions and take corrective action when necessary. (pp. 272–274)

- **Controlling** requires managers to create guidelines that ensure an organization is on track to achieve its goals. This is done by monitoring processes, people, procedures, and systems to get feedback for improvement.
- Many organizations establish standards using the Management by Objective (MBO) method, which relies on defining objectives and evaluating performance.
- During the evaluation process, managers need to judge performance and assess the outcome. This involves comparing the established standards against the actual performance.
- Managers can provide feedback and make modifications once they have evaluated the situation.

Summary: Managers aren't finished working after they make a decision. They are constantly monitoring the results of a decision, evaluating the decision, providing feedback, and making modifications.

6. Conduct a performance evaluation of someone, and recognize circumstances when someone should be promoted, reassigned, or fired. (pp. 274–277)

- A **performance appraisal** is an annual or semi-annual review that often involves both employee self-evaluations and formal appraisals. During employee self-evaluations, employees identify whether they met certain goals, potential areas of improvement, and how they plan to meet next year's goals. During formal appraisals, managers look at the same areas as employees, but they often quantify whether the standards were met.
- Employees generally get promoted if a higher-level position opens up and their company has recognized their performance and contributions.
- Firing someone can be a very delicate matter. If an employee need to be terminated, it's important that previous evaluations justify the action. If not, an organization can be sued for wrongful termination.

Summary: Companies use performance appraisals to evaluate an employee's performance, which may eventually lead to a promotion or a termination.

Get the most out of what you just read by practicing your skills and actually DOING something with the material! The best place to do this is at **www.mybizlab.com**. Here's just some of what is available to you there:

- Apply your skills in an interactive environment with more **BizSkill** experiences...and see if you have what it takes
- Think critically and talk with your peers on hot business topics in **BizChat**
- Flex your business communication skills and build your own portfolio with the **Communication Plan exercises**
- Watch the chapter material come together with **Just Plain Business** videos
- Study on-the-go with **Audio Chapter Summaries** in MP3 format
- Brush up on the lecture and content with **Audio PowerPoints**
- Discover how well you are doing and see what areas you need to improve on with the **Pre-Tests** and **Post-Tests**

Key Words

These key words and more are also available as flash cards to practice with at **www.mybizlab.com**.

1. Characterize your communication style, recognize the communication styles of others, and prescribe how you could work together most effectively. **(pp. 256–259)**

Directors (p. 256)

Performers (p. 256)

People-pleasers (p. 257)

Detailers (p. 257)

2. Prescribe the best methods for motivating someone, and explain how you yourself are motivated. **(pp. 259–265)**

Hierarchy of needs theory (p. 259)

Two-factor theory (p. 261)

Theory X (p. 262)

Theory Y (p. 262)

Expectancy theory (p. 262)

Job characteristics theory (p. 263)

3. Recommend methods for training and developing employees, and know how you can develop your own career. **(pp. 265–268)**

Learners (p. 265)

Leaners (p. 265)

Life support (p. 265)

Lifters (p. 265)

Orientation (p. 266)

On-the-job training (p. 266)

Simulation training (p. 266)

Online training (p. 267)

Job shadowing (p. 267)

Off-the-job training (p. 267)

Managerial training (p. 267)

4. Make good decisions and be an effective delegator or delegatee. **(pp. 268–272)**

Decision making (p. 269)

Delegation (p. 270)

Empowerment (p. 271)

5. Measure the results of your decisions and take corrective action when necessary. **(pp. 272–274)**

Controlling (p. 272)

6. Conduct a performance evaluation of someone, and recognize circumstances when someone should be promoted, reassigned, or fired. **(pp. 274–277)**

Performance appraisal (p. 275)

Prove It

Prove It...

Now, let's put on one of the BizHats. With the **Manager BizHat** squarely on your head, look at the following exercise:

Imagine that you're an upper-level manager at a sales firm. One of the middle managers, Marla, who has been a long-time, loyal employee, has been slacking off over the past few months. She has been with the company so long that she actually trained you and has helped you with several projects. Although she was hardworking in the past, she now takes extended breaks, often comes into the office late, skips training sessions, and doesn't show the same concern for customer relations that she has in the past. As a result, you've had to ask other employees to stay at the office late to cover her workload and you've received multiple customer complaints about her curt and unprofessional tone. Although Marla has been a middle manager for several years, she fails to look beyond her immediate assignments to do the in-depth planning that is so critical to the company. She's also condescending to the new employees she trains.

How do you address Marla's performance issues? Is a performance evaluation enough, or is it time to let Marla go? What factors do you need to take into consideration before making this decision, and how can you use some of the decision making techniques described in this chapter to come to a conclusion? Write out some of the talking points that you will need to address with Marla for any decision you make about her future with the firm.

Flip It...

Now flip over to the **Employee BizHat**. Imagine that you are one of Marla's co-workers in middle management. How you would speak to her about how her actions are impacting everyone on the team?

Now Debrief It...

Compare the perspectives of the two BizHats described above. How does your management level affect how you speak to Marla? How would the situation change if you were an employee whom Marla supervised?

Discover:
The Marketing Mix, Market Research, and Target Marketing

BizSkills invite...

Try It!
There's no better way to learn concepts than to put them into practice. Take your turn in the driver's seat and be a part of actual business decision making by visiting the BizSkill for this chapter at **www.mybizlab.com**.

Now that you've practiced making tough business decisions and seeing the results of your choices in this chapter's BizSkill, it's time to translate those skills into plain English. And if you skipped the BizSkill, go back now!

Chapter 12 Goals

After experiencing this chapter, you'll be able to:

1. Explain what marketing really is, and use the Ps of marketing to improve your marketing efforts.
2. Take a customer-centered approach in your marketing that includes both external and internal customers.
3. Use marketing research to reveal new insights about customers and markets.
4. Segment markets from one another and identify target markets.
5. Explain the impact of consumer behavior research on marketing strategy, and know how to make educated purchases yourself.

What can you discover about your customers?

The Customer's Story

At a recent doctor's appointment, Donica learns that she has Type 1 diabetes. Although she's concerned, her doctor reassures her that diabetes is treatable with the help of insulin, medical professionals, and state-of-the-art medical devices. Based on her doctor's recommendations, Donica goes to the pharmacy and meets with a specialist who helps her select devices for testing her blood sugar and administering insulin. For the next several weeks, Donica joins an Internet discussion group on diabetes and pays close attention to the ads she sees on TV, the Web, and magazines about diets and other health programs for diabetic people. On one of the Web sites, she discovers that there's a local diabetes support group that meets monthly. To her surprise, she also receives a number of magazines in the mail specifically for people with diabetes. Donica returns to her daily life with some new friends, deeper knowledge about her health and diet, and an appreciation for the medical community.

Although this is a story about health care, it illustrates several facts about marketing, too. First, even though medical professionals, pharmaceutical sales reps, advertising executives, Web site designers, and media professionals all played a role, the customer was always the focal point. Second, the marketing activities in this story were prompted by a genuine customer need that several organizations, both for-profit and not-for-profit, tried to solve. Third, the organizations that provided health care support to Donica had developed products and information that were specifically targeted toward people with diabetes. And finally, the organizations that marketed to Donica were using strategies and tactics that had been carefully developed based on research about people who are living with diabetes. In this chapter, we'll discuss all of these elements, and you'll learn how to build a marketing strategy using these elements as building blocks.

1. Marketing: It's Not What You Think It Is

When you hear the word *marketing*, what do you think of? TV commercials, salespeople, and Internet ads? Many people think that marketing is mostly about sales and advertising. ■ But sales and advertising are only a part of marketing, and they aren't the most important part—the customer is. So, even though you may have had the wrong impression about marketing, you probably know a lot more about it than you might think because you spend a good part of your life in the role of the customer.

The term **marketing** is used to describe the entire range of activities that people in an organization perform to discover customer needs and to provide solutions to those needs through products, including goods, services, and experiences. As customers discover and learn about these products, they make purchase decisions that contribute to the organization's *triple bottom line* of people, profits, and planet, which we've discussed in other chapters.

■ Sales and advertising are only a part of marketing, and they aren't the most important part—the customer is.

This is the first of three chapters about marketing in this book. In this first chapter, we'll describe the activities that make up what is referred to as the "marketing mix." We'll also demonstrate how important it is to have a customer orientation and how marketing research is used to learn crucial information about customers, and we'll look at how organizations carefully select and target the customer markets in which they will invest their time and resources. In subsequent chapters, we'll delve deeper into creating new products and branding, pricing, and promoting them.

Mixing It Up: Marketing Ps

When you hear the word *mix*, you may think of food products like a cake or brownie mix. The term **marketing mix** is used to describe the unique combination of marketing activities that an organization implements to create a product solution to meet customer needs.

The marketing mix has traditionally included what is referred to as **the Four Ps**—*product, price, place,* and *promotion*—to describe the range of activities that has been the central focus of marketers during the era when most products were physical goods sold through retail stores and catalogs. However, we're going to add a few more Ps to your plate in addition to the traditional four. Why? Because the products that are bought and sold in today's marketplace are more likely to be services and experiences than tangible goods, and organizations are focusing on the broader triple bottom line instead of just profits to measure success. Thus, we add *people* and *planet* Ps to your plate to round out your marketing strategy. Let's look at each of these Ps in detail.

What comes to mind when you think of these marketing tools?

Product Think about what you do on an average day. You go to school. You eat. You drive. You hang out with friends. Pretty much everything you do involves products. As we discussed in Chapter 4, over time, products have become more competitive and more complex. As you learned there, *products* can consist of the following:

- *Commodities* are virtually unprocessed products such as fruits, vegetables, animals, grains, and minerals.
- *Goods* are products that are typically developed from commodities, and include items such as clothing, cosmetics, books, and furniture.
- *Services* can be bought and sold just like commodities and goods, but they are intangible and cannot be owned, inventoried, produced, or stored in bulk like goods can. Services also

require the service provider and customer to mutually interact and cooperate far more than goods that can be stored and retrieved from a store shelf.

- *Experiences* also provide an intangible value to customers, but they can be both goods and services, and they directly involve customer participation. Movies, concerts, amusement parks, sky diving, and vacations are all considered customer experiences.
- There is another category of a product that we have not yet discussed: a *transformation* is a set of services that are combined over time to change the inherent nature of a customer, whether by appearance, knowledge, capability, or some other permanent change. Examples of transformations include laser eye surgery, educational courses, and smoking cessation classes.

Not every product fits neatly into one of these categories. Many products are a blend of tangible goods, services, experiences, and transformations. Consider a business like a full-service salon/spa. Customers can purchase goods such as hair products; services such as haircuts; experiences such as all-day packages including a facial, a massage, lunch, and a pedicure; and transformations such as yoga classes or a series of Botox treatments.

Regardless of the product type, as a marketer, you need to know how to identify what customers need and then develop a product that effectively meets that need. If you do, you've developed an item that has *value*—a concept we discuss in more detail in the next chapter—that customers are willing to pay for and keep buying over time, assuming it continues to meet their needs and be perceived as something of value.

At this point you have some kind of a product concept in mind that meets an important customer need. You also have a sense that the product has value in the customer's eyes—it's worth money to them. But how much? That's when the next P, *price*, comes rolling across your plate.

Price

Price is the amount of money that a company charges a customer to buy or use a product. Marketers determine the appropriate price for a product based on four important factors:

1. how much it costs to produce or deliver the product;
2. how much the customer is willing and able to pay for the product;
3. how much the competition charges for comparable products; and
4. whether there are any governmental or regulatory controls on the price.

We refer to these factors as *costs*, *customers*, *competition*, and *controls*, respectively. Setting the right price level therefore requires constant balancing between the organization's motive to make profits, customer preferences and resources, competitive actions, and regulatory restrictions. A company typically cannot make unlimited profits on its products because the other forces need to be accommodated for, but every organization needs to set an adequate price to reap at least some profits. Otherwise, it's not in that company's best interests to continue selling the product.

Marketers have to determine the level of their prices as well as the pricing approach they are going to use. Some products have a one-time purchase price—you buy it, pay for it, and you're done. Other products require monthly or annual rental or licensing agreements, like a monthly Netflix subscription. There are a number of other pricing strategies, which we cover in the next chapter.

OK, so now you have a product that satisfies important customer needs, and you've set the price based on four important factors. Now you have to figure out how to get the product to the customer. Your company might be based in Massachusetts, but your customers might be all over the globe. How do you get your product from you to them? We tackle that question next by looking at the P called *place*.

Place The **place** P refers to designing a process to get the product to the customer where they want it, when they want it, and in the quantity they want it. Marketers often describe the system they design for place as the **distribution system**, and it applies to goods, services, experiences, and transformations:

- If the product is a good, you need to design a transportation and delivery system that moves the product from the place of manufacture to the location where customers want to purchase the product, often in a retail store.
- If the product is a service, you need to design a delivery mechanism to provide that service to customers when and where they want it. Oil changes require physical shops where customers can take their vehicles. Consulting services require consultants to visit with their clients and provide the expertise and help that the customer pays for.
- If the product is an experience or transformation, you need to design an environment, virtual or real, where that experience or transformation will occur. For example, Apple set up the Apple Store where customers can go to download games and other experiential products.

In many cases, the distribution system for a product is one of its primary points of differentiation (often called a *unique selling proposition*) against the competition. For example, AT&T has used the advertising slogan "More bars in more places" to convey its superior distribution system for wireless services. (Want to learn more about how companies distribute products effectively in today's markets? Check out Chapter 16 on **www.mybizlab.com**.)

You've covered a lot of ground to this point: you have a great product set at the right price and delivered in the best way to the customer. What's left to do? So far, you haven't let the customer know what you're offering. You could have the best seafood entrees in your restaurant, but if no one knows that your restaurant exists, it's unlikely that anyone will stop by to eat. So, we have another P to cover, *promotion*, that describes all of the methods you'll use to communicate with your customers.

Promotion Your big day has come—you're graduating from college. The bleachers are full of happy relatives as the joyful graduates crowd onto the field. You, like everyone else, are on your cell phone to your parents trying to help them find you in the crowd. You're in the middle of a sea of graduates who all look the same, so how are they going to identify you? Luckily, you thought of this in advance and you have a pink bunny taped to your cap. No problem—your parents find you immediately.

Companies who are trying to capture the attention and interest of prospective customers face a similar challenge. Not only are there competitive products in the marketplace, but also a zillion advertising messages being pushed out by each company in the hope that their products will get noticed.

The **promotion** P is all about marketing communication. Once you have a great product at the right price and the best method for distribution, you need to establish two-way, interactive communication with your customers so they can learn about your product and your company, and you can learn about them and their needs.

We'll go into detail about marketing communications in Chapter 14. What is important for you to know at this point is that the types of communication you select need to be based on your customer's preferences and habits. You need to reach them in a way that they want to be reached. Otherwise, prospective customers will never notice you in the sea of competitive messages.

More Ps, Please The four Ps we've covered so far have been the traditional components of the marketing mix for a long time. But over time, marketers have added more Ps to accommodate important changes in marketing, from both the marketer's and the customer's perspective. We're not going to discuss every P that has been suggested in the field of marketing; instead, we're going to focus on two additional Ps that are most critical in the current marketing landscape and that are related to the triple bottom line: *people* and *planet*.

People The *people* P involves all the people who are involved in the production and co-creation, service, and consumption of a product, including customers as well as employees—from knowledge workers to front-line employees who serve or deliver. It goes beyond this too and encompasses all of the organization's stakeholders who are affected by the marketer's product or message.

Employees are a particularly important part of marketing's people P. If you're eating out at a restaurant, just think about how a waiter can affect your experience. A rude, standoffish waiter who mixes up your order will leave a bad taste in your mouth, whereas a friendly, attentive waiter can make you want to come back. A company's image can be affected quickly by the impact of just a few employees, so it's important for organizations to acquire and retain competent staff members who will improve product quality and customer service. To ensure excellence with the people P, training, development, and job satisfaction have become very important. This means that human resources and other departments within a company are important partners with the marketing department in delivering an excellent product. Because it's so important, we'll discuss the people P a lot more in the next section, where we focus on the customer.

Planet The environmental impact of a product is influenced by the ingredients used to make it, the byproducts created from the manufacturing process, and the environmental impact from customers buying, consuming, and disposing of the product. How do we become "caring capitalists" and not poison the physical environment in which we do business? We go back to the triple bottom line to make sure that our business strategy is yielding beneficial results not only for the organization's profits, but also for the people we impact and the planet on which we live.

There you have it: the original four Ps plus two more Ps that reflect today's marketing environment. These six Ps comprise the marketing mix that you develop for any product you want to market today. But what about tomorrow, or 10 years from now? Will there be a different mix of Ps that you'll need? We can't predict the future, but by considering how marketing has evolved over time, and is evolving right now, we may be able to predict what marketing might look like.

To Know Where We're Headed, Look at Where We've Been

Let's be honest, if we gave this section the title "The History of Marketing," how excited would you be? Historical accounts are sometimes interesting, but they can also be boring, especially if it's not clear how that history has any relevance for today. So, let's cut to the chase: By taking a quick peek at the historical evolution of marketing, we can better understand why we're focused on the six Ps that we are today, and we just might be able to anticipate what Ps we'll need to think about to succeed in the future.

The Production Era

The first era in marketing is often called the *production era,* and it started around the 1920s. The focus at this point was strictly on the product. If you could make something, you could sell it. Henry Ford cranked out some Model T cars that were all identical, and every one he made was sold. The primary strategy during this era was to become better and better at manufacturing stuff.

The Selling Era Around the 1950s, manufacturing technology enabled companies to actually make more of a product than customers wanted. At this point, you had companies with excess inventory of various products, and they had to figure out some way to convince customers to buy it. This ushered in the *selling era,* during which marketers developed all sorts of interesting strategies to convince customers to buy stuff—and lots of it—often without any consideration of whether the customers really needed it. Unfortunately, a lot of people still relate to this image of marketing, even though this era is mostly behind us.

The Customer Era Between the 1950s and the 1980s, marketers discovered that if they paid a lot of attention to taking care of customers' needs, they could sell more stuff, and do so more profitably. The concept of having a relationship with a customer became the focal issue during the *customer era*, and marketers developed systems like *customer relationship management (CRM) tools* to identify customer needs, communicate with customers, and maintain a relationship marked by trust and loyalty over the long haul. Many firms remain deeply rooted in this orientation today.

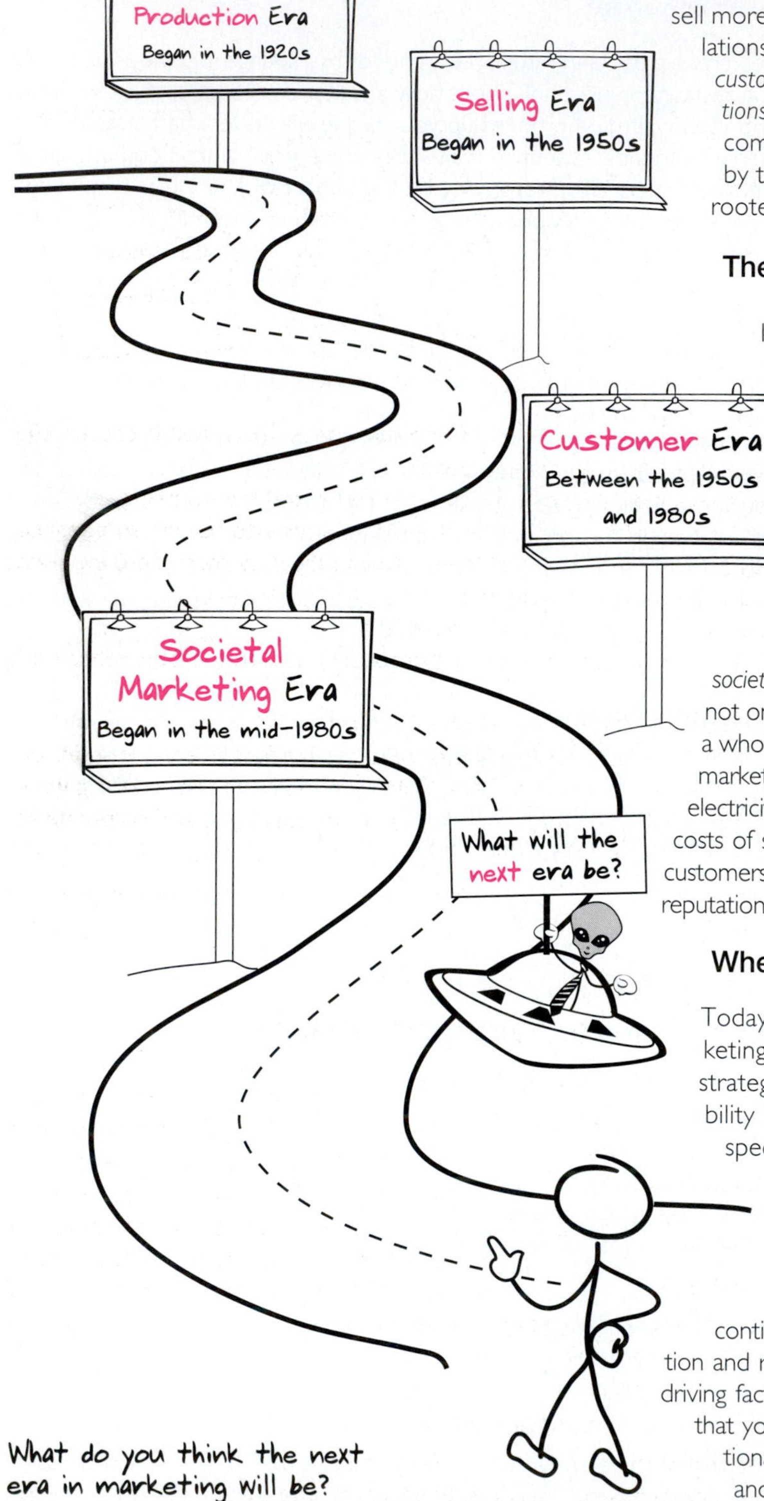

The Societal Marketing Era Over the last 20 years or so, the societal impact of marketing began to emerge, and marketers realized that there are often some unintended and harmful side effects to their success in getting customers to buy and consume, buy and consume. The environment suffered as landfills filled up with bulky product packaging and Styrofoam, society suffered as obesity rates skyrocketed due to the marketing success of such products as fast food restaurants, and some believed that our culture was suffering from an excess of consumerism and gluttony.

As both marketers and customers came to this realization, the *societal marketing concept* emerged. Organizations began to consider not only the needs of their customers, but also the needs of society as a whole. Marketers even discovered how to use their strategies for demarketing, or persuading customers to consume *less* of a product, like electricity and tobacco. Marketers have also discovered the long-term costs of some of their unethical practices that were devastating to their customers' well-being and undermined their organization's integrity and reputation.

Where Are We Now, and Where Are We Going?

Today we're in the midst of an evolution within the societal marketing era. Every organization is challenged to develop marketing strategies that reflect sustainability and corporate social responsibility in every aspect of their business operations, a global perspective, and a marketing communication environment in which the customer, and not the marketer, creates much of the content and dictates the media that they want to rely on to communicate with others.

As we look into the future, we know that marketing will continue to evolve, that the customer will shape how communication and relationships are managed, and that profits will not be the only driving factor to influence an organization's strategy. For you, this means that you'll need to keep your eye on customer preferences, organizational practices, and cultural trends so that you can adapt your skills and knowledge to excel in the era in which you're operating.

Do It...

12.1: Describe the Ps Select two of the marketing eras discussed, and describe which of the Ps was most critical during each. Then, come up with your own name to describe what you expect will be the next era in marketing. Which Ps will you need to be successful during this era? Be prepared to submit your response electronically or discuss it in class.

Now Debrief...

- **Marketing** is the term used to describe the entire range of activities that people in an organization perform to discover customer needs and provide solutions to those needs through products, including goods, services, and experiences.
- The combination of marketing activities that an organization implements to create a product solution to meet customer needs is the **marketing mix.**
- The marketing mix is made up of **the Four Ps**—product, price, place, and promotion. In addition to these, there are two additional Ps: people and the planet.
  - *Products* include commodities, goods, services, experiences, and transformations.
  - **Price** is the amount of money that a marketer charges a customer to buy or use a product.
  - **Place** refers to designing the process to get the product to the customer where they want it, when they want it, and in the quantity they want.
  - **Promotion** includes all of the marketing communication.
  - *People* involves all of the people involved in the production and co-creation, service, and consumption of a product.
  - *Planet* deals with the environmental impact of a product.
- The history of marketing can be broken up into four eras: the production era, the selling era, the customer era, and the societal marketing era. We are in the process of evolving within the societal marketing era due to the marketing strategies of sustainability and corporate social responsibility.

2. Getting Customer-Centered

Whichever marketing era you may be in at the present time or facing in the future, there's one priority you'll always need to consider: maintaining your focus on the customer. It's important, then, to understand what the term *customer* means, who they are, what's important to them, and how they make decisions. If you know all of this about your customers, you'll have a much better chance of designing products and delivering solutions that really satisfy customer needs, and you'll deliver to your triple bottom line.

"This may seem simple, but you need to give customers what they want, not what you think they want."[1]

—John Ilhan, founder of an Australian mobile phone retail chain

External and Internal Customers

Let's start with the meaning of the term *customer*. Remember how the word *product* represented several concepts, including goods, services, experiences, and transformations? Similarly, the term *customer* includes *external customers* and *internal customers*. As you see the term *customer* used throughout this book, keep in mind that the term applies to the full spectrum of customer types. Let's look at them in detail now.

External Customers Individual consumers, businesses (large corporations or small businesses), institutions (like universities, government offices, and hospitals), and non-profit organizations are all **external customers**. Think of external customers as the individuals or businesses that a company develops and maintains relationships with. This definition can also include *suppliers*, who are essential to production and operations.

Building relationships with external customers is extremely important to every organization. Many companies develop goods and services with specific customers in mind. The motorcycle company Harley-Davidson takes the idea of building customer relationships one step further. The company embraces customers as family and plays an active role in customers' lives. Its rich, engaging Web site communicates what every customer wants to hear from a company: "We care about you." The company's sentiment is believable because it's genuine.

Internal Customers If you work for an organization, you'll also discover that there are **internal customers**—individuals and departments within your organization that you have to satisfy and to whom you often need to market an idea or solution. If an organization wants to be successful, it needs to keep its external customers satisfied. But it's equally important for the company to focus on its own human resources, or internal customers. Employees are the backbone of any company and help shape its culture, efficiency, development, and growth. And, of course, sales. Identifying internal customer needs and meeting them is therefore an important goal not just for marketers but for everyone in the organization.

Which are more important, internal or external customers?

Consumer vs. Business Markets

Although there are important differences between the customer types mentioned above, another important distinction is between consumers and businesses. Marketing to consumers requires an entirely different strategy than marketing to businesses, so you'll need to adjust your approach accordingly.

Translation Guide

In Conversation: Often, *consumer* and *customer* are used interchangeably in conversation. However, these do not mean the same thing in marketing terms.

In Marketing Terms: The term *customer* describes everyone who buys products, including governments, for-profit and non-profit organizations, and individuals. *Consumer*, on the other hand, refers specifically to the individuals and households that buy products.

Example: A customer could be a business that purchases 50 computers for its new office, or a student who buys a laptop for school, but only the student is considered a consumer.

Consumer Markets The type of marketing you're probably most familiar with is **consumer marketing** (also referred to as **business-to-consumer or B2C marketing**). Why? Because you're a consumer, and you've experienced firsthand many of the types of marketing tactics that are used to reach and influence consumers. As we'll discuss later in the chapter, consumers sometimes follow a structured, rational approach to making purchase decisions, particularly when they are buying something that's expensive and important (like cars, computers, and college education). However, in most cases, consumers base their decisions on relatively rapid product evaluations that often occur with little or no careful thought.

TV, radio, and Internet advertisements and sales promotions like coupons and rebates are just a few examples of the marketing communication tools that are often used to reach consumers. Why? These tools can reach large audiences at a relatively low cost per customer, and the marketer can provide centralized control over the message that is broadcast through these media. Bottom line: consumers make a lot of purchase decisions every day, and they tend to make those decisions fairly quickly.

Business Markets Even though you're more familiar with companies that market to consumers, you may have a career with an organization that markets to other businesses, or participates in **business-to-business (B2B) marketing**. So, understanding how businesspeople who have the title "buyer" make decisions will benefit you, regardless of your job. As we'll discuss later in the chapter, the business buyer's decision-making process tends to be more formalized and sophisticated than an individual consumer's, because businesses purchase more expensive and complex products, often make larger purchases, and involve more individuals in both the purchase and use of products.

The marketer's role amidst this lengthy and complex process is to be a source of information for the buyer and the other decision makers. In B2B marketing, a personal sales force is often used to provide this expertise.

How Customers Affect Marketing

So, you understand the difference between internal and external customers and between consumer markets and B2B markets. Let's look at an example of how marketing to these different customer groups may play out.

Let's say you're working at a T-shirt print shop that primarily prints T-shirts for youth sports teams, bowling leagues, and other small recreational groups. Because you're always looking for opportunities, you discover an entirely new market for T-shirts: maintenance workers at large companies. You understand the difference between consumer and B2B markets, so you know that your company will have to adjust its marketing approach to comply with a more complex decision-making process. This will require redesigned product brochures, price lists, product samples, and a personal sales force that can personally visit these large companies.

All of your ideas have merit, and they will require money and other resources to make them happen. Who's your customer now? Probably the people in your own organization—your internal customers—who control the marketing budget, the pricing program, and the product design team. You'll need to develop a marketing strategy that helps these important decision makers fully understand your proposal, what you'll need from them to make it happen, and why they would want to invest in it. These decision makers have to see benefits for themselves, their department, and the organization, or they probably won't invest in your ideas.

You'll have to know these people well and understand their needs so you can develop a persuasive proposal that they can support. In essence, you market to them just as you do your external customers. Once you've met the needs of your *internal* customers, you've dramatically improved your chances of success with your *external* customers, so be sure to include both an internal and external customer strategy for any marketing plan you want to implement.

What It Means to Be Customer-Centered

Now that you know a lot more about customers, who they are, what influences their decisions, and how to market to them, let's come back to a basic question: what does it mean to be customer-centered?

It means that every decision that's made within an organization is evaluated through the lens of the customer. It means that the customer always has a seat at the table when the mission is developed, goals are set, strategies are developed, and plans are implemented. It means that the organization changes its structure, its processes, and its policies whenever it discovers that any of these are a hindrance to customers trying to find solutions to their needs. And finally, it means that everyone in the organization—not just the marketing department—considers the customer perspective when making decisions and implementing strategy. Knowing your customer isn't enough—your actions as an individual and your organization's activities have to reflect a customer-centric perspective.

Do It...

12.2: Apply the Ps to Internal Customers Describe how the Ps would apply to internal customers. Do concepts like product, place, promotion, price, planet, and people apply when you are marketing to customers in HR and finance? Limit your response to one page, and be prepared to submit it electronically or discuss it in class.

Now Debrief...

- Businesses that understand their customers have a better chance of designing and delivering solutions to meet customer needs.
- The term *customer* includes both internal and external customers. **External customers** are the individuals and businesses that a company develops and maintains a relationship with. **Internal customers** are individuals and departments within an organization that also have to be satisfied with ideas and solutions.
- **Consumer marketing** (or **B2C marketing**) is marketing to individuals, and **business-to-business (B2B) marketing** is marketing to businesses.
- Organizations adjust their marketing approach depending on their customers. When an organization evaluates ideas through the lens of a customer and considers the customers' perspective, the organization is being customer-centered.

3. Taking Advantage of Market Research

> "We are drowning in information but starved for knowledge."
>
> **—John Naisbitt,** bestselling author of *Megatrends*[2]

By now you get the picture: customers are the most important ingredient to marketers—and to the entire organization. One way to find out more about them is through market research. Just as the name suggests, **market research** *(or marketing research)* refers to organizations gathering relevant information that they can then use to assess marketing situations. This may be a combined effort between members of an organization's internal research and marketing departments, or research may be conducted by specialized external market researchers who consult with the company.

Companies acquire information in order to assess the market and gain a better understanding of their customers, and then use it to make decisions that will generate profits and improve customer satisfaction. When market research is implemented correctly, it is the best way to stay in touch with customers and follow market trends. In this section, you'll learn about the four primary steps of the market research process.

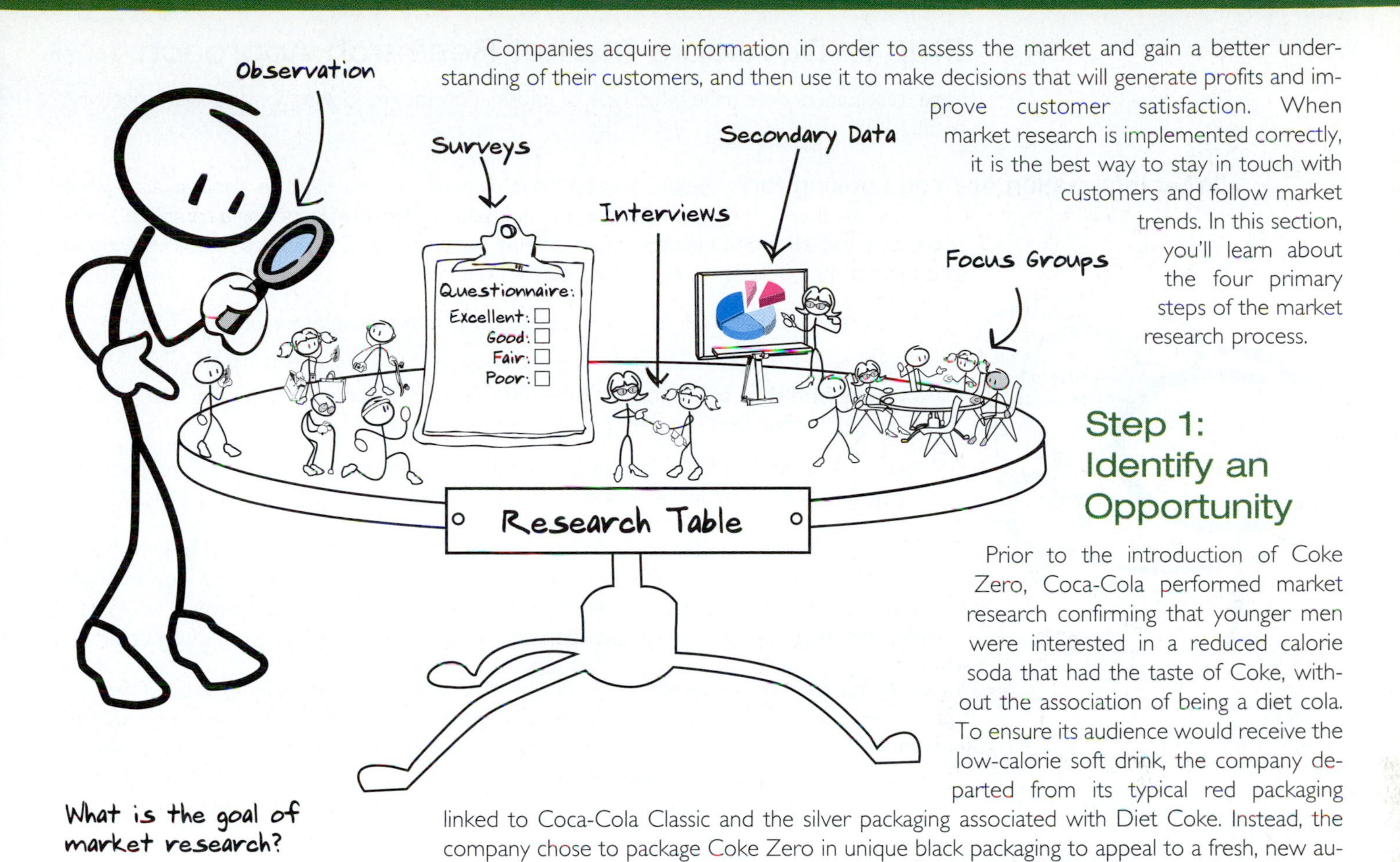

What is the goal of market research?

Step 1: Identify an Opportunity

Prior to the introduction of Coke Zero, Coca-Cola performed market research confirming that younger men were interested in a reduced calorie soda that had the taste of Coke, without the association of being a diet cola. To ensure its audience would receive the low-calorie soft drink, the company departed from its typical red packaging linked to Coca-Cola Classic and the silver packaging associated with Diet Coke. Instead, the company chose to package Coke Zero in unique black packaging to appeal to a fresh, new audience. Paired with an effective promotions strategy, Coke Zero became a success. The market research didn't lie.[3]

Doing market research is a lot like performing scientific research. Before marketers begin, they need to think of a question or set of questions they would like to answer, or a specific problem they would like to try to solve. Basically, you're identifying what you want to know.

To illustrate this practice, let's look at a hypothetical restaurant, Eternal Flavor. Let's say the restaurant's business has been steady and profits have been constant, but two new restaurants are scheduled to open nearby in the next six months. Eternal Flavor needs to figure out what to do to remain competitive and ensure customer loyalty. In order to do this, the owners of the restaurant need to ask themselves some tough questions.

Marketing Questions to Consider Given the information about the new restaurants, the owners of Eternal Flavor may wonder if they are prepared for new competition. Several questions might help them assess the situation:

- How will the new competition affect our monthly revenue? Could the new competition potentially *improve* our own customer traffic and sales volume?
- How can we improve customer satisfaction? Are our customers happy with the current menu selection and prices? Does the restaurant provide an *experience* or just a meal for customers?
- What will the new competition offer? How can our restaurant gain or maintain a competitive edge?

Depending on the answers to these questions, Eternal Flavor can begin thinking about how they are going to get the information they want.

Step 2: Develop a Market Research Approach

Next, researchers determine what type of information they're looking for and figure out who has it.

What Information Are You Looking for? Before you can start researching, you need to know exactly what you're looking for. Are you interested in launching a completely new product or just a modified version of an existing product, like Coke Zero? Are you trying to gauge consumer opinions on a new business venture?

Information can fall into two general categories: quantitative information and qualitative information.

- If you need hard data, or *quantitative information,* you would look at information such as sales volumes, revenue, and supplier costs.
- If you're more interested in figuring out people's thoughts, or *qualitative information,* you would look into opinions, emotions, ideas, and stories.

Before the owners of Eternal Flavor begin gathering information, they've got to know what will help them make decisions. The owners might need to prioritize the information they get based on their research budget or timeline. In this scenario, the restaurant owners could gain valuable knowledge by gathering information on consumer behavior and by soliciting opinions.

Keep in mind that the owners might be able to answer all of their questions, but if they invest too much time and money doing so, they may cancel out any advantages they received from the research. That's why it's important for companies to evaluate *opportunity costs* when performing research. For instance, what could the restaurant do otherwise with the time and money spent on market research? Which strategy will best help the owners achieve their goals in the long run?

Who Has the Information? After identifying what you're looking for, you need to identify where you can find it. In the case of Eternal Flavor, some of the most valuable responders are restaurant patrons who currently visit the restaurant. Researchers may also be able to gain information from people who live or work close by, regardless of whether they've dined in the restaurant before. In addition to seeking information from external customers, the owners should also talk to internal customers, such as Eternal Flavor employees.

Step 3: Collect and Analyze Information

Once you've answered the *what* and the *who*, it's time to consider *how* you will acquire the information you need. Companies have a wide selection of tools and research methods to choose from when picking a strategy. Data is classified based on where it comes from, and is considered either *primary data* or *secondary data.*

- As the name suggests, **primary data** is obtained directly from an information source. Examples include surveys, interviews, observational research, and **focus groups**—organized sessions that solicit opinions and ideas about products from potential customers. See Table 12.1 for more information about these research techniques.
- **Secondary data**, on the other hand, is acquired from resources that have already collected and processed information. Examples include government publications, magazines and journals, and a company's own internal documents, such as financial statements.

In this step, the owners of Eternal Flavor might rely heavily on primary data from surveys, customer feedback, and questionnaires. These methods of data collection are accessible and affordable for a small business to perform.

How Will You Use it? The data's been collected. Now what? Once researchers have collected information from a variety of sources, they assess and analyze it. By doing this, researchers really begin to understand the market and its customers.

Table **12.1** | **Primary Research Techniques**

Method	Description	Pros	Cons
Surveys	Method of gathering information by asking questions to a sampling of people	• Flexible • Easily analyzed • Less expensive than other methods	• People may not be honest • Potential for few responses • May be difficult getting a representative sample
Interviews	Method of gathering information by talking to people and asking them questions	• People can respond in depth • Interviewers can clarify questions	• May be difficult or time consuming to arrange • Potential for dishonest or biased responses • May be expensive
Observational Research	Method of gathering information by observing people's behavior in specific situations	• Can uncover behaviors and habits that customers don't realize about themselves	• Time consuming • Difficult to observe people in the long term • May be expensive
Focus Groups	Method of gathering information by forming organized sessions that solicit opinions and ideas about products from potential and existing customers	• Able to obtain a lot of information • Able to get perspectives on abstract ideas	• Potential for groupthink to occur • May be difficult to find ideal participants or a skilled interviewer

If market research is effective, the findings will reveal valuable information to help inform decision making. For example, the research might provide insights that will affect product or package design, product features, or customer service policies. Some studies might even indicate that a product is likely to fail.

In Eternal Flavor's case, market research may reveal information that the owners can utilize to stay competitive in the market. The owners may already be aware of some information, such as potential opportunities and weaknesses, if they recently performed a SWOT analysis. However, the research may also make them aware of factors such as customer satisfaction. Eternal Flavor may find out that customers would enjoy an expanded appetizer and dessert menu, later hours of operation, and the option to place carry-out orders, but that they like the current portion sizes, ambiance, and quality of service.

Step 4: Identify a Solution

Once a company has obtained all the necessary information it was looking for, marketers and managers are responsible for creating a plan of action to respond to research results. This plan of action sometimes takes the form of a **marketing plan**, which is a document that describes the overall marketing strategy for the entire organization or a specific product. The marketing plan typically provides a SWOT analysis, including marketing research findings; goals for the marketing campaign; how the Ps will be implemented to achieve those goals; and a budget for how the marketing strategy will pay for itself and help the company's triple bottom line.

Although one goal of market research is to improve decision making, companies also use market research to provide customers with a better product. Product improvements ultimately increase customer satisfaction, loyalty, and revenue, so everyone benefits. In this case, Eternal Flavor can decide how best to prepare itself for the market change that is going to result from the openings of the new restaurants.

Do It...

12.3: Describe a Market Research Study Describe a market research study you could design to help you prepare for a job interview. Your goal is to discover an insight about the company that other job candidates don't have. What methodology would you use and what insights would you hope to uncover through it? Be prepared to submit your response electronically or to discuss it in class.

Now Debrief...

- **Market research** is the process of gathering information that organizations use to learn relevant marketing information and to assess marketing situations.
- The four steps of the market research process are:
  - **Step 1: Identify an opportunity:** Researchers come up with questions or a specific problem they would like to solve.
  - **Step 2: Develop a market research approach:** Researchers figure out exactly what they're looking for and who has it.
  - **Step 3: Collect and analyze information:** Researchers acquire the information they need by collecting primary and/or secondary data. **Primary data** includes survey, interviews, observational research, and **focus groups**. **Secondary data** includes government publications, magazines, journals, and financial statements.
  - **Step 4: Identify a solution:** Researchers and marketers create a plan of action to respond to the market research results.

4. Markets Made Easy: Segmenting, Targeting, and Positioning

"The beginning of knowledge is the discovery of something we do not understand."
—**Frank Herbert,** best-selling author[4]

As your graduation date draws near, you begin to wonder what kind of organization you might work for. You'll soon have a degree in finance, so there's a wide range of companies who could benefit from your knowledge and abilities. You stop over at the career center to scan the list of companies that have recently hired finance majors at your college, and you discover that there are over 100 of them. How are you going to narrow your list of choices, and how will you decide which company you will pursue?

Early Saturday morning you load up on coffee and start building a spreadsheet. You list every one of the companies that has hired finance majors in the past, and then you start to sort them by relevant characteristics, such as their location, how big they are, the types of finance positions available in the firm, and what industries they're in.

As you scan the different groups, you eliminate a few because you realize you would never want to work for those kinds of companies, and your list begins to narrow. Eventually, you arrive at a list of 10 companies that you will send your resume to. You'll also keep a close lookout for them at the next career fair. Of course, you know you're not the only graduate pursuing these firms, so you'll be sure to point out to each firm what makes you unique compared to other job candidates.

Organizations use similar strategies to evaluate the potential markets for their products and select the target market they will pursue and in which they will invest resources. This process of identifying potential markets, evaluating and selecting markets to pursue, and then pursuing those markets—often against competitive firms—is the target marketing process that every organization needs to implement to be successful across the triple bottom line.

■ Marketing starts with a customer in mind, and not just any customer—a customer with a need for which he or she is willing to spend money to satisfy. Effective marketing occurs when a company carefully focuses on specific customers from the available market. These potential customers are people who have needs that the company can fulfill with their product. The process of identifying a group of potential customers to pursue, or the **target market**, requires three activities:

■ Marketing starts with a customer in mind, and not just any customer—a customer with a need for which he or she is willing to spend money to satisfy.

1. *Segmenting*, in which you divide the market into clearly distinguishable segments of customers who have similar characteristics that are meaningful for your company and your product.
2. *Targeting*, in which your company carefully selects one or more segments it is going to pursue.
3. *Positioning*, in which you establish your product's advantages over the competition in the customer's mind. This activity is necessary because you're not the only company pursuing that market—some of your competitors are, too.

Although they are presented in a particular order—STP (for segmenting, targeting, and positioning)—they sometimes occur at the same time or in a different order. It's better to think of them as three important activities that have to take place for your company to ultimately determine the optimal target market and how best to position your product in the customer's mind. We'll take a closer look at each activity, with some examples, and then you'll have the chance to practice some STP yourself.

Market Segmenting

Not everyone is going to be interested in a Hello Kitty clock radio or a limited-edition John Denver china dinner plate set. Instead of trying to satisfy all the customers all of the time, businesses focus on satisfying a specific set of customers—customers who have a need or a desire for what is being sold.

Geographic
Demographic
Psychographic
Behavioral
Needs

Segmenting by Needs

Target Market

What other variables could you use to segment a market?

Generally, **market segmentation** is the process of breaking down the overall customer market into smaller groupings of buyers. Companies try to understand their customers by categorizing customers into similar groups based on needs and desires, in addition to particular characteristics. This helps the company better understand the customers' needs, wants, and motivations. By thinking of a pie, you can easily imagine how a market is divided into pieces, or, in this case, segments. Once the market is divided into slices based on one set of parameters, it can be segmented again and again.

Segmentation Variables for Consumer Markets

Consumer markets can be segmented in a number of ways:

- It doesn't make sense to try to sell snowshoes in Arizona, or tractors in New York City. That's why **geographic variables** are sometimes used to differentiate customer markets. So, instead of offering those snowshoes throughout the United States, the company may concentrate on a few regions that receive large amounts of snow, such as Minnesota or Colorado.

- **Demographic variables** used to differentiate segments include age, gender, education level, and socioeconomic status. For instance, a company that sells makeup may focus its marketing efforts on teenaged girls, whereas a luxury car company may focus on older, more affluent consumers.
- **Psychographic characteristics** are also used to help define market segments; these attributes include lifestyle, personality traits, values, and opinions. Psychographic characteristics have more to do with a consumer's reasons for buying. For instance, that luxury car company may create a hybrid line for consumers who are concerned about the environment, focusing on their customers' value for green technology and choice to buy high-end products.

In addition to these categories, there are other ways to segment markets, such as by their behavior and needs.

Segmentation Variables for B2B Markets Market segmentation also applies to B2B marketing; however, the characteristics are specific to organizations instead of individuals. For instance, marketing might focus on characteristics such as the size of a business or the business's industry. By segmenting, or dividing, a large group of buyers into smaller groups, the task of identifying an ideal target market and an effective positioning strategy is simpler and much more focused.

Targeting

Once you've identified several potential market segments that you could pursue through segmentation, you need to pick one or more of these segments to target. **Targeting** requires you to decide which segments you are going to pursue. This allows you to make the most efficient use of company resources by focusing your efforts on customers who have the best potential to be profitable and loyal customers. For example, instead of spending money sending direct mail to every address in New York City to advertise a new exhibit at the Metropolitan Museum of Art, a company could limit the campaign to include the addresses of museum donors or patrons from the past three years (i.e., those individuals most likely to return to the museum).

Picking Target Markets If you have several customer segments that you could pursue, how do you pick the one(s) in which you'll invest resources? Many firms consider three primary criteria when evaluating potential market segments as their target market:

1. **Size and Anticipated Growth:** Organizations generally want to select market segments that are sufficiently large to generate sizable revenues, but not too large to make it difficult for the organization to serve. For example, a small bakery may not be in the game to promote its products to the global market. As firms scan the potential market segments, they're also looking for an appropriately sized segment that offers solid prospects for future growth.
2. **Accessibility:** Once the organization locates some segments that fit its size and growth criteria, another consideration is how easily the market segment can be reached and served. Sometimes, there are large, growing markets that are almost impossible to identify and even more difficult to reach.
3. **Consistency:** As you evaluate the different market segments, you need to consider how well those segments fit your organization's vision, mission, goals, and strategy. For example, if a consumer products firm discovers that a relatively large segment of consumers is using

one of its products for an unsafe activity, the firm should not include this group of consumers in its target market.

All of these factors are essential for figuring out which markets to target. By obtaining this information, marketers can, for example, help determine profitability and whether pursuing a prospective market segment is consistent with corporate objectives, resources, and overall goals. ■ After all, companies can't please everyone, and they don't have the resources to make the whole world their market. They need to make tough choices about which customers they will invest resources on and which they won't.

■ After all, companies can't please everyone, and they don't have the resources to make the whole world their market.

The Costs of Not Targeting Properly Companies spend a great deal of time researching target markets, building relationships with customers, and developing solutions and meaningful experiences for them. Selecting target markets based on informed decisions can result in significant gains, whereas a poor selection can result in devastating losses.

What happens when companies fail to select appropriate target markets? Or what if they eliminate the targeting process from their marketing strategy altogether? If companies select inappropriate markets, they not only forgo revenues by missing the mark, they also waste time and resources. And if companies entirely neglect to select a target market, they waste resources and lose revenues. Why market products to the entire marketplace when viable buyers only make up a small fraction of the market?

Positioning

You've no doubt heard of Match.com, the Web site on which singles vie for attention in hopes of finding a match. In the scope of online dating, there are a limited number of singles that match an individual's preferences, and these single people are only available for a finite number of dates.

Similar to dating, a major part of marketing is making your company's product look better than the competition. Even if no other company offers quite the same product, there is bound to be some level of competition in the market. Something is competing for customers' attention and, consequently, their money. The goal of the marketer shifts yet again; now it is necessary for companies to establish a unique identity that buyers will understand—a foothold, or a position among contenders. This is achieved using positioning strategies.

Specifically, the process by which companies communicate product features and benefits relative to those of competing products is called **competitive positioning**. Marketers use this strategy to create a perception among customers about where their product stands in relation to similar products. Obviously, the goal of competitive positioning is to make your product appear to be better than the competition's product.

To maximize their competitive advantage, singles on Match.com rely on a profile to communicate their personality and interests, among other qualities. Creating a unique profile that attracts viewers differentiates one's self from other singles. This kind of self-promotion is important for gaining interest from dating prospects and represents the concept of competitive positioning. Establishing a competitive position in the marketplace has the same goal for developing a relationship with consumers: "Pick me!"

Figure **12.1** | **Perceptual Mapping**

How would you reposition the items on this map?

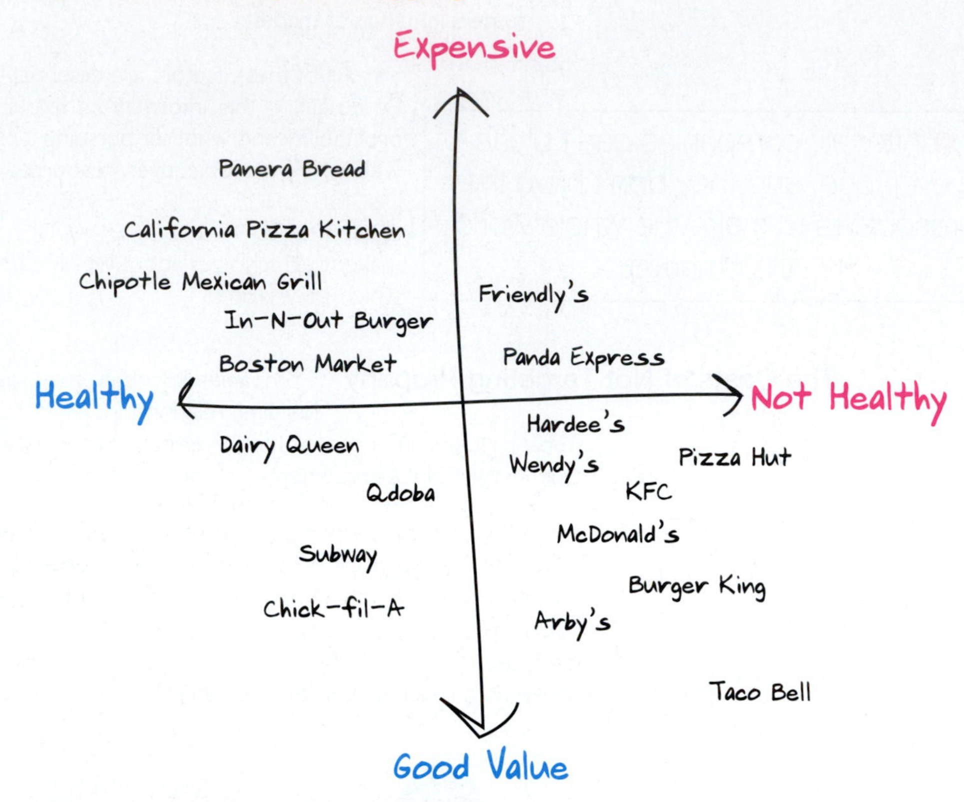

Perceptual Mapping Although competitive positioning makes sense in theory, you may wonder how companies go about achieving it. There are several steps that a business must complete for its marketing plan to be a success:

1. To begin with, marketers assess the competitive landscape to identify how competing products are positioned.
2. Next, they take into consideration key attributes such as price, benefits, features, performance, brand image, customer service, packaging, design, and availability. A technique called **perceptual mapping** (see Figure 12.1) is employed to illustrate how customers perceive existing products, not only in relation to one another, but along a spectrum of product attributes or consumer perceptions.
3. All of this information is used to determine a unique market position, unlike that of competitors, and to establish a clear customer perception about the product. If a product is positioned effectively, consumers will identify it as being of superior value to available alternatives.

For each target market, companies must select a corresponding positioning strategy that is customized for that market.

Repositioning What happens if the target market is no longer responding to your product? Adopting a **repositioning strategy**, a strategy meant to change your targeted market's perception of your product's identity, allows companies to shift customer perceptions of that product. This means that your product is flexible enough to adapt to meet the shifting expectations of consumers.

Although a repositioning strategy provides great opportunities for otherwise stagnant products, it can also be a bit risky. Companies must therefore consider repositioning carefully, as it is best suited for products that are well established, in need of a boost, could benefit from advancing technology, or could extend to new markets.[5] For example, in 2007, high-end women's clothing company Talbots Inc. began developing a comprehensive strategic plan to boost growth and maintain performance. CEO Trudy Sullivan indicated that repositioning would keep the brand "relevant, fresh, and consistent."[6] Although the brand hadn't experienced a decline, the company took a proactive approach to maintain its edge.

Likewise, in 2004, Clearasil launched an ambitious marketing campaign to reach its target market: teenagers. As a departure from the brand's acne-fighting image, the repositioning focused the branding message on building self-confidence through skin care. Marketing strategies associated with this repositioning campaign focused on a new, unified message that revolved around building self-confidence.

Do It...

12.4: Identify Target Markets Either individually or in teams, see how many potential target markets you can identify for a coffeemaker in five minutes. Be sure to use the segmentation variables discussed in this section. Be prepared to submit your list electronically or to discuss it in class.

Now Debrief...

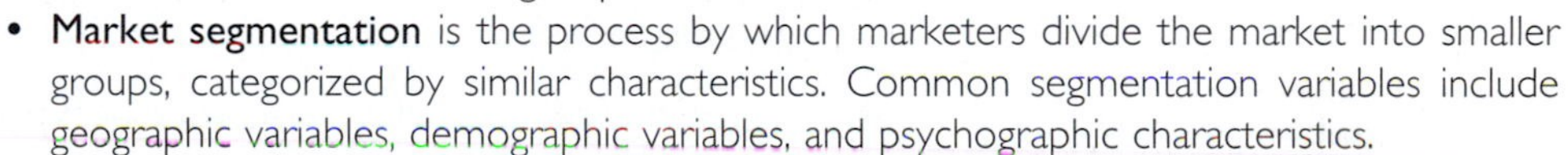

- An organization's **target market** is the group of customers that it focuses on in its marketing efforts.
- To identify a target market, marketers engage in three activities—market segmenting, targeting, and positioning—that help match products and services with customers who are willing to purchase them.
  - **Market segmentation** is the process by which marketers divide the market into smaller groups, categorized by similar characteristics. Common segmentation variables include geographic variables, demographic variables, and psychographic characteristics.
  - **Targeting** involves selecting segments of the market to pursue. Target markets are selected based on a number of variables including size and anticipated growth, accessibility, and consistency.
  - **Competitive positioning** is the process by which companies communicate product features and benefits relative to those of competing products.
  - Under certain circumstances, it might be necessary for an organization to employ a **repositioning strategy**, which is a strategy meant to change the target market's perception of its product's identity.

5. Consumer Behavior

"The aim of marketing is to know and understand the customer so well the product or service fits him and sells itself."

—Peter Drucker, author, professor, and management expert[7]

People can behave unpredictably. You might think you have someone completely figured out, and then he or she does something that smashes the foundation of what you thought you knew about that person. To make sense of why consumers act the way they do, businesses try to determine patterns by studying consumers' habits and spending behaviors. For example, companies can track purchase details such as the date, time, location, and price of purchases, which helps them gain insights that inform marketing strategy. In essence, **consumer behavior** is the

psychology of marketing. Research into consumer behavior seeks to explain how customers feel, think, consume, and make decisions.

When you think about it, every purchase, every transaction, and every experience has a story. For instance, one person may like going to a particular grocery store because it's open 24 hours a day, while another customer may go to that same store because the prices are low and the produce is good, despite two other stores that are geographically closer. No two customers exhibit the same behavior, and even individual customers exhibit a variety of different behaviors from purchase to purchase, depending on the circumstances. In this section, we'll take a look at how and why consumers and business buyers make their decisions, and how consumer behavior can be used from a marketer's point of view.

Consumer Decision Making: It's Simply Complex

A consumer's choice for buying a product may seem irrational at times, but there is often an informal process that you as a consumer go through when you make an important purchase:

1. You determine the need or problem.

   Let's say a close friend is getting married, and you need to buy a gift. Your need or problem is figuring out what to buy the couple.

2. You identify alternatives.

   You want to know what your possibilities are, so you look on their registry for ideas of what they would like. You look at product prices, and whether you can go to the store and buy it or whether you'll have to purchase it online.

3. You look at and evaluate alternatives.

   If someone else is already getting them that vase you wanted to buy, you'll need to look for something else. For example, you can look for other items on their registry within the same price range.

4. You determine which alternative is the best one and make your purchase.

   You may choose to get a set of mixing bowls instead of a mixer attachment because they're a better value and have more uses than the one attachment. Once you make the decision, you either go to the store and buy the bowls, or order them online and have them delivered to the couple's address.

5. You evaluate your purchase.

   Did you make the best purchase possible? Was your choice sound?

Every purchase, every transaction, and every experience has a story.

Of course, consumers don't go through all of these steps every time they buy something—think about the spur-of-the-moment purchases you've made while waiting in grocery checkout lines. Despite this, understanding these basic steps can help you evaluate your own purchasing process and make you more aware of yourself as a consumer.

Analyze Your Own Consumer Behavior Think about some of the purchases you've made recently. Do you typically buy out of convenience, necessity, or impulse? Do you buy a lot of inexpensive items or a few expensive ones? Look at the questions in Figure 12.2 and answer them about yourself. The answers to these questions are the kind of information marketers are looking for—the explanations for why customers behave the way they do. By

Figure **12.2** | **Consumer Behavior Research Questions**

How much do you spend each month?	Do you recycle?
How much do you earn each month?	Do you frequently use coupons?
How far will you travel to shop?	Do you buy full-price items or only shop sales?
What time of day do you like to shop?	Do you enjoy shopping?
Do you shop alone or with friends and family?	Do you pay by credit card, cash, or check most often?
What percentage of purchases do you make online?	What do you do when you're done with a product? Donate it to charity?
Do you typically shop on weekends, weekdays, or both?	Are you interested in paying more for environmentally friendly products?
Do you purchase items as you need them, or to have on hand?	Do you shop for anyone else? Does anyone make purchases for you?

examining the behavior of many people at once, marketers can develop a composite that reveals general patterns and tendencies that are typical for individuals in different markets. For instance, credit card companies track your purchases for trends, Google tracks your searches for trends, and Amazon.com tracks related purchases and tells you what other like-minded customers bought with that item. We'll take a closer look at data-driven decisions in Chapter 15, but for now, suffice it to say that there is no limit to the type and amount of information that marketers use to understand consumer behavior.

Why do marketers care about all of this? By understanding how products are selected, purchased, and used, companies can improve their marketing strategy to entice customers and better meet their needs. To make this possible, companies gather information from a variety of sources to track and understand consumer behavior.

Changing Consumer Dynamics

If you had a job making $12 an hour, and switched to a new job making $17 an hour, how would your shopping habits change? Would you be inclined to spend more money? Less? The same amount? Surely you would find something at least slightly different to do with your newfound wealth. Consumer behavior isn't static—it changes dynamically in response to the marketplace—advancements in technology, changes in the economy, product innovation, and a shift in competitive offerings are just some factors that can influence consumer behavior.

The threat of a recession, for example, alters the way consumers spend or don't spend money, and how they utilize existing resources. Some families might skip a vacation or delay the purchase of a new car, while others may choose to adopt spending habits that affect everyday purchases instead, like taking public transportation once a week instead of driving.

The introduction of innovative products and services and advancements in technology can significantly change consumer spending, too. Think about how the music industry has changed.

Fifty years ago, you would buy records; twenty years ago, those songs were being released on tapes. Fifteen years ago, CDs were the next big thing. With the introduction of a digital file format for music and the rising popularity of sites like iTunes, the way customers acquire, share, and listen to music has significantly changed and is continuing to evolve.

Importance of Understanding Consumer Dynamics Changes in spending habits are important for marketers to track, understand, and respond to. Behavioral patterns can shift within short periods of time, requiring companies to adjust strategies and tactics; if changes in consumer habits are left unnoticed, companies may lose customers over time.

By adapting to shifts in consumer behavior, companies can satisfy consumer needs and maintain financial success. For example, knowing that families skip trips during a recession, hotels might offer unique promotions or partner with airlines to offer extra incentives to budget-conscious families, or create unique opportunities for local and regional tourists instead. To respond to shifts in behavior, companies might, for example, assess whether the demographics of their customers have changed, whether their current pricing model is effective, what competitive threats exist, and whether promotional strategies are generating measurable results.

B2B Decision Making

Earlier we discussed how individual consumers go through an informal process when making important purchases. Business buyers also use a decision-making process, but the process is much more formalized and sophisticated than the consumer process, and business purchases involve a lot more people and far greater sums of money. As you walk through the B2B buyer decision-making process that follows, you'll see similarities to the consumer process, and you also see how it's a more complex and costlier process, too.

What are the differences between this process and your own buying process?

1. The business encounters a problem or need that triggers a search for a solution.

   For example, let's say Boeing decides that it wants to equip all of its aircraft with wireless Internet capability.

2. The buyer seeks information, from within and outside the organization, about all of the possible alternative solutions.

   A purchasing agent or project manager for Boeing meets with the electronics group within the firm and schedules several meetings with wireless network manufacturers and satellite operators outside the firm.

3. Using the gathered information, the buyer critically evaluates each of the alternatives.

   The purchasing agent or project manager carefully compares all the features, advantages, and tradeoffs of the different wireless network options for an aircraft. In doing so, the agent is likely to meet with a range of engineers, financial analysts, and other specialists in the organization for consultation and input.

4. The buyer and any other individuals with purchase authority make a decision and purchase a product.

   Key decision makers within Boeing, including senior executives whose approval is needed for such a significant acquisition, are briefed on the options, and a final purchase decision is implemented.

Table **12.2** | **Comparing Consumer and Business-to-Business Markets**

	Consumer Market	Business-to-Business Market
Market Size	Millions of consumers	Limited number of businesses
Geography	Consumers are spread out across a large area	Businesses may be concentrated in specific areas
Products	Generally standardized	Generally customized
Buyers	The person who will actually use the product	Trained buyers
Sales	Indirect: Consumers often buy from intermediaries	Direct: Businesses often buy from manufacturers
Selling Style	Impersonal: Consumers often look to advertising	Personal: Businesses often use a sales team and personal selling to gain customers

5. The buyer and other individuals who use the product evaluate how well it addressed the problem or need.

Once the wireless/satellite system has been installed, tested, and used on several aircraft, the buyer or project manager solicits feedback from flight attendants, passengers, maintenance personnel, and others who have used or maintained the system to determine how well it has worked and if any problems have occurred.

Table 12.2 outlines the main differences between consumer and B2B markets. As you can see, these differences affect the decision-making and marketing processes greatly.

Do It...

12.5: Document Your Decision-Making Process Recall a recent sizable purchase you have made and describe the stages of the decision-making process you followed. Be prepared to submit your response electronically or to discuss it in class.

Now Debrief...

- **Consumer behavior** research asks questions that can explain the hows and whys of purchase decisions. It generally seeks to explain how customers feel, think, consume, and make decisions.
- When making important purchases, consumers follow an informal decision-making process in which they determine their problem or need, identify alternatives, look at and evaluate alternatives, choose the best one and make a purchase, and then evaluate the purchase.
- Business buyers also use a decision-making process, but the process is much more formalized and sophisticated than the consumer process, and business purchases involve a lot more people and far greater sums of money.
- By understanding consumer behavior, marketers are able to learn new ways to develop, create, and market products.

Chapter 12 Visual Summary

Marketing Savvy | **Chapter 12: *Discover*** Chapter 13: *Create* Chapter 14: *Communicate*

1. Explain what marketing really is, and use the Ps of marketing to improve your marketing efforts. (pp. 284–289)

- **Marketing** refers to the entire range of activities that people in an organization perform to discover customer needs and to provide solutions to those needs through products, including goods, services, and experiences.
- The **marketing mix** describes the unique combination of marketing activities that an organization implements to create a product solution to meet customer needs.
- **The Four Ps** are product, price, place, and promotion. Additional Ps associated with the marketing mix are people and planet.
  - *Products* consist of commodities, goods, services, experiences, and transformations.
  - The amount of money that an organization charges a customer to buy or use a product is the **price**.
  - **Place** refers to the process of getting the product to the customer where they want it, when they want it, and in the quantity they want.
  - **Promotion** deals with marketing communication that includes establishing two-way, interactive communication with customers.
  - The *people* P encompasses all of the individuals who were involved in the production and co-creation, service, and consumption of a product as well as all stakeholders affected by the marketer's product or message.
  - The *planet* P refers to the environmental impact of a product.
- Marketing has evolved over the course of time, from the production concept era, the selling era, the customer era, and the societal marketing era. Currently, marketing is in the middle of an evolution within the societal marketing era.

Summary: The most important part of marketing is figuring out the customer. Marketing is most successful when it takes into account people and the planet in addition to the four traditional Ps.

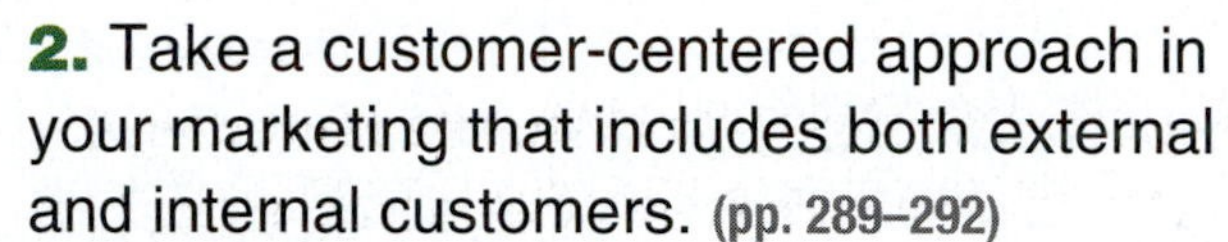

2. Take a customer-centered approach in your marketing that includes both external and internal customers. (pp. 289–292)

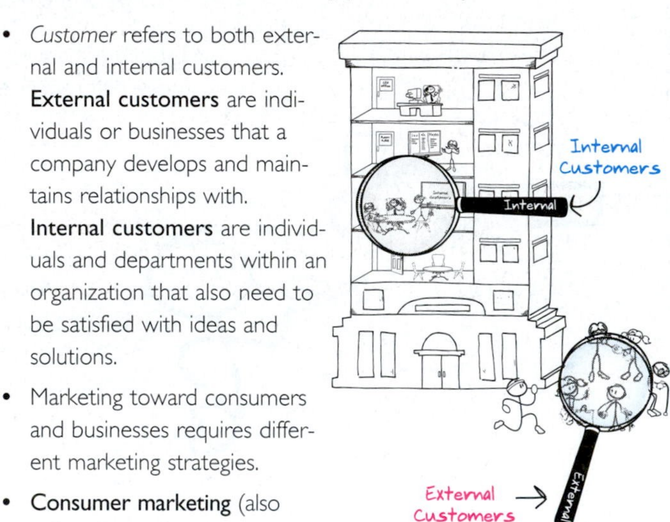

- *Customer* refers to both external and internal customers. **External customers** are individuals or businesses that a company develops and maintains relationships with. **Internal customers** are individuals and departments within an organization that also need to be satisfied with ideas and solutions.
- Marketing toward consumers and businesses requires different marketing strategies.

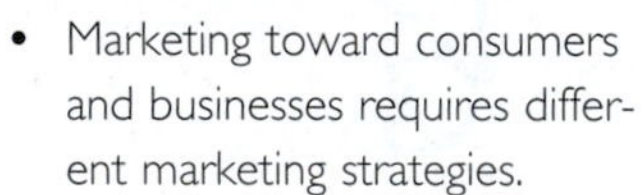

- **Consumer marketing** (also referred to as **business-to-consumer or B2C marketing)** is the process of marketing to individuals who want to purchase products to use. **Business-to-business (B2B) marketing** is the process of marketing to businesses that want to purchase and sell products to other businesses.

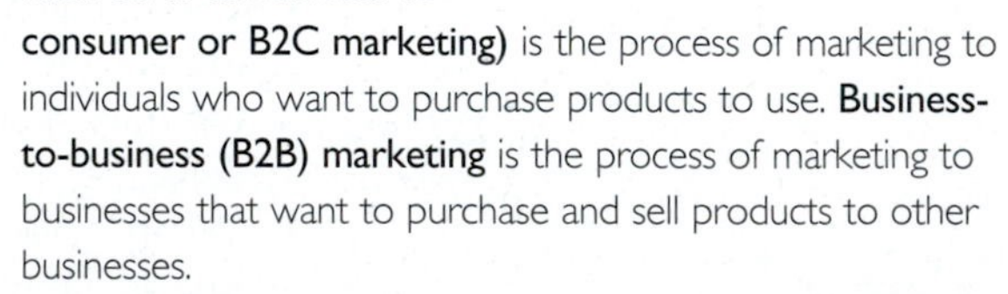

- When an organization is customer-centered, it considers customers when developing a mission, setting goals, developing strategies, and implementing plans.

Summary: By being customer-centered, businesses can better design products and deliver solutions that satisfy customer needs and deliver the triple bottom line.

3. Use marketing research to reveal new insights about customers and markets. (pp. 292–296)

- **Market research** refers to organizations gathering information they can use to better understand their customers, generate more profits, and improve customer satisfaction.
- The market research process includes the following four steps:
- Step 1: Identify an opportunity: Researchers identify what they want to know.
- Step 2: Develop a market research approach: Researchers identify what type of information they're looking for and who has it.
- Step 3: Collect and analyze information: Researchers collect **primary data** and **secondary data.**
- Step 4: Identify a solution: Based on the information collected, companies create a plan of action.

Summary: Market research is used to improve decision making, which ultimately improves customer satisfaction and revenue.

4. Segment markets from one another and identify target markets. (pp. 296–301)

- A **target market** is a segment of a market that an organization focuses on in its marketing efforts.
- The process of breaking down the customer market into smaller groups is called **market segmentation.** These groups are generally broken down by geographic, demographic, and psychographic variables.
- **Targeting** requires an organization to identify which segments it is going to pursue. Targeting allows an organization to make the most efficient use of resources by focusing on potential customers.
- The process by which companies communicate product features and benefits relative to those of competing products is called **competitive positioning.**
- Companies may rethink their marketing strategy and adopt a **repositioning strategy,** which is meant to change a targeted market's perception of the product.

Summary: Organizations segment their market to focus on specific customers who have needs that organizations believe they can fulfill.

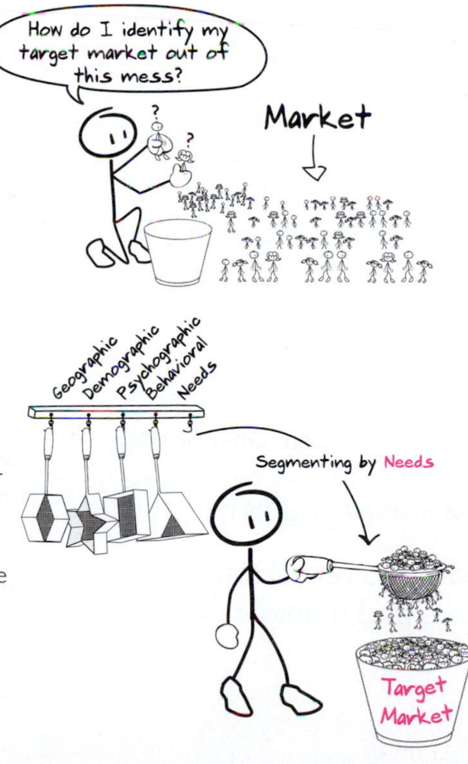

5. Explain the impact of consumer behavior research on marketing strategy, and know how to make educated purchases yourself. (pp. 301–305)

- In essence, **consumer behavior** is the psychology of marketing. Research into consumer behavior seeks to explain how customers feel, think, consume, and make decisions.
- When making important purchases, consumers follow an informal decision-making process in which they determine their problem, search for information, consider alternatives, choose the best one and make a purchase, and then evaluate the purchase.
- Researchers focus on understanding how products are selected, purchased, and used to satisfy customer needs and maximize profit.
- Business buyers also use a decision-making process, but the process is much more formalized and sophisticated than the consumer process, and business purchases involve a lot more people and far greater sums of money.

Summary: Businesses track consumer behavior to determine consumer habits and to adjust their strategies accordingly.

Get the most out of what you just read by practicing your skills and actually DOING something with the material! The best place to do this is at **www.mybizlab.com**. Here's just some of what is available to you there:

- Apply your skills in an interactive environment with more **BizSkill** experiences...and see if you have what it takes
- Think critically and talk with your peers on hot business topics in **BizChat**
- Flex your business communication skills and build your own portfolio with the **Communication Plan exercises**
- Watch the chapter material come together with **Just Plain Business** videos
- Study on-the-go with **Audio Chapter Summaries** in MP3 format
- Brush up on the lecture and content with **Audio PowerPoints**
- Discover how well you are doing and see what areas you need to improve on with the **Pre-Tests** and **Post-Tests**

Key Terms

These key words and more are also available as flash cards to practice with at **www.mybizlab.com**.

1. Explain what marketing really is, and use the Ps of marketing to improve your marketing efforts. **(pp. 284–289)**

Marketing (p. 284)
Marketing mix (p. 284)
The Four Ps (p. 284)
Price (p. 285)
Place (p. 286)
Distribution system (p. 286)
Promotion (p. 286)

2. Take a customer-centered approach in your marketing that includes both external and internal customers. **(pp. 289–292)**

External customers (p. 290)
Internal customers (p. 290)
Consumer marketing (or business-to-consumer or B2C marketing) (p. 290)
Business-to-business (B2B) marketing (p. 291)

3. Use marketing research to reveal new insights about customers and markets. **(pp. 292–296)**

Market research (p. 292)
Primary data (p. 294)
Focus groups (p. 294)
Secondary data (p. 294)
Marketing plan (p. 295)

4. Segment markets from one another and identify target markets. **(pp. 296–301)**

Target market (p. 297)
Market segmentation (p. 297)
Geographic variables (p. 297)
Demographic variables (p. 298)
Psychographic characteristics (p. 298)
Targeting (p. 298)
Competitive positioning (p. 299)
Perceptual mapping (p. 300)
Repositioning strategy (p. 300)

5. Explain the impact of consumer behavior research on marketing strategy, and know how to make educated purchases yourself. **(pp. 301–305)**

Consumer behavior (p. 301)

Prove It

Prove It...

Now let's put on one of the BizHats. With the **Manager BizHat** squarely on your head, look at the following exercise:

You're the marketing manager for a computer company. Your division has been responsible for promoting the company's line of small, inexpensive handheld computers with built-in wireless and long-lasting batteries. Since its launch two years ago, your research has shown that the computer has been popular with business professionals who do extensive travelling. Because of this, most of your marketing has been focused on creating a professional and businesslike image for the product.

Recent fluctuations in the economy have thinned the number of traveling professionals, and the product's sales have begun to decline. As marketing manager, it is your responsibility to boost sales. The company's CEO wants you to scrap all previous advertisements and start from scratch to reposition the product in the changing economic environment. What information would you need before starting a new marketing approach? What issues would you need to address and incorporate into your plan to make this new marketing scheme successful?

Flip It...

Now let's **flip over to the Owner/Investor Bizhat**. You are the CEO of the computer company that sells the handhelds to business professionals. Your marketing research manager has provided you with the preliminary results from the team's research, and they've found that more and more customers are teenagers and college students. What information would you need to present to new investors as you reposition the product line? How could you convince your original investors that their investments in the company are still sound?

Now Debrief It...

Discuss how repositioning a product affects the marketers and the CEO of a company. What information do they need to succeed in their product repositioning? How is the information used in each position?

Create:

Product Innovation, Branding, Pricing, and Value

BizSkills invite...

Try It!
There's no better way to learn concepts than to put them into practice. Take your turn in the driver's seat and be a part of actual business decision making by visiting the BizSkill for this chapter at **www.mybizlab.com**.

Now that you've practiced making tough business decisions and seeing the results of your choices in this chapter's BizSkill, it's time to translate those skills into plain English. And if you skipped the BizSkill, go back now!

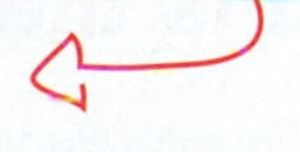

Chapter 13 Goals

After experiencing this chapter, you'll be able to:

1. Recognize how companies use innovation to create and launch new products.
2. Demonstrate how organizations build brands to compete.
3. Devise a pricing strategy to capture a product's true value.
4. Explain why benefits, value, and perception matter.
5. Describe how marketing and innovation affect the triple bottom line.

How's this for an innovation that stands out from the competition?

Innovations and Inspirations

Summer is a tinkerer, and always has been. She's always trying to figure out new, better, and different ways of doing things. The word "conformist" has never applied to her, in any situation. As a child, instead of tying her shoes with the traditional knot, she devised her own, quicker knot that she liked better. As an adult, Summer still has a passion for taking something and making it newer or better. She designs and sews her own clothes, she customizes everything on her computer using open-source software, and she's always helping her friends modify the products they own to suit their preferences and eliminate hassles.

Maybe you know someone like Summer. People like her personify the concept of *innovation*. In this chapter we'll cover a lot of important marketing skills like developing new products, building brands, designing pricing strategies, and creating product value. Although they are sometimes treated as separate and distinct skills, all of these activities can be seen within the context of innovation. As we'll see, truly innovative organizations use branding, pricing, and other elements of their marketing strategies to continually delight their customers with new and better product solutions.

1. Innovation Is the Key

"When you innovate, you've got to be prepared for everyone telling you you're nuts."

—Larry Ellison,

CEO and co-founder of Oracle Corporation[1]

Think about the last time you saw a late-night TV infomercial about the latest product "that will change your life forever." This product probably didn't change your life forever, but it might have been an interesting enough new creation or new angle on an existing product that you at least *thought* about buying it. As we discussed in Chapter 7, you can think of *innovation* as a unique improvement to a product—be it a good, service, experience, or transformation—that earns kudos (and cash) in the market. The goal of innovation is to make a positive change in something so that it increases its value. Innovation can mean creating entirely new products or simply updating existing products.

■ Because innovation often involves taking knowledge about customers and using it to develop products that help solve a particular problem, meet a need, or create a meaningful experience, it plays a key role in the way products are created. And as we'll discuss next, innovating products requires a well-thought-out process. It also requires creativity; businesses must consider how to develop products that meet customer needs without duplicating products that are already on the market.

How Innovation Happens

Take a minute to look at your things and think about the activities you participate in. You'll notice that many of the goods and services that you use are different from what they were, say, 10 years ago. This is due to constant innovation. Not too long ago, caller ID service required a separate device, and it was considered an optional service on a phone line. Now, caller ID technology has been integrated into most telephones and is almost always included as part of a telephone subscription package, offering customers greater convenience and saving them money.

■ Because innovation often involves taking knowledge about customers and using it to develop products that help solve a particular problem, meet a need, or create a meaningful experience, it plays a key role in the way products are created.

Whether you've been introduced to something completely new or you've decided to try an updated version of a good or service from a familiar company, a similar process has gone into its creation. All of the products you know and love—and even the ones you aren't aware of yet—have been subjected to a similar process. For most companies, innovation is the name of the game. Let's look at the step-by-step innovation process.

Step 1: Discover a Need A product can have all kinds of flashy features and gadgetry, as well as a hot marketing campaign, but if it doesn't have a specific use, no one is going to buy it. Figuring out what customers need, or what they think they need, is often the first step in the innovation process. Having such knowledge of needs helps companies come up with new products or refine old ones. How do you discover customer needs?

1. **Perform market research.** As we discussed in Chapter 12, market research is one way in which most companies discover what their customers want and the best way to deliver it to them. This research may take several forms, including surveys, interviews, and focus groups. More recently, technology has enabled market research to include the Internet. In growing numbers, companies are embracing technology in an effort to reach their customers, understand their needs, establish two-way communication, and give them the products they want.[2]

2. **Listen to customer complaints.** A lot of the best information about needs can be found by listening to customer complaints about existing products. Companies can then make modifications to their products that solve these problems. For example, in the past, customers often complained about the difficulty of getting ketchup out of a glass bottle. The

ketchup always seemed to stick in the bottle or fall out in one clump. Heinz responded to this complaint by creating squeeze bottles, which allow ketchup to flow out more smoothly. As one of its more recent innovations, Heinz now offers a ketchup bottle with a wide lid at the base of the bottle, so that all the ketchup sits near the lid and comes out readily when the bottle is opened.

3. **Watch customers use products.** Many companies send their marketing people into the field to observe customers using their products and talking about their experiences with the product. In this way, companies can see what improvements customers may wish to see in their products. This process is also emerging as a major source of new product ideas. Companies with an up-close-and-personal view of their customers' use of their products can identify and develop products for any additional needs their customers might have.

4. **Look to employees for internal inspiration.** In some cases, new products are not based on specific customer needs or complaints. Employees of a company may come up with an idea or a design for a new product on their own. Once the product enters the market, customers then *discover* they have a need for it. This is often the case with technology. Although customers in the 1980s may not have expressed a need for portable phones or personal computers, both of these technologies soared in popularity once they hit the market.

5. **Hire trend-spotters.** Market research is useful, but many of the best ideas come from people who are looking for the next big thing. Professional trend-spotters are always on the lookout for the latest fad or the hottest gadget or service that everyone seems to want. Many marketers rely on a large network of trend-spotters to help them find out what interests potential customers.[3] Marketers are then able to utilize these findings to develop products that match current customer interests.

In addition to these methods, there are additional ways to discover customer needs. For example, some companies review their SWOT or PEGSET analyses and turn potential risks and threats into opportunities for new products. Companies also monitor innovations in other industries or product categories—if it works for others, it might work for them, too. Knowing what a customer wants and needs is the key to creating a successful product. Failure to identify and address existing or potential customer needs can lead to products that fail to sell.

Step 2: Generate Ideas for Solutions

Once you've determined the need for a product, the next step is to *visualize* your product. At this stage of the process, businesses list as many ideas for that product as possible.

- If the product is a *tangible good*, the visualization process involves considering the function and form of the good, brainstorming the desired elements, and conceptualizing how the finished product might look.
- For a *service, experience, or transformation*, the visualization process is a little different. The visualization process for a new cable service, for example, would involve mapping out where the service will be available and listing the steps involved in providing the service, such as drawing up a contract and installing necessary equipment.

Step 3: Screen the Ideas

Once you've come up with a few ideas, it's time to test the marketing waters to see which idea people like most. This part of the process is **concept testing**. Companies use concept testing to evaluate customers' responses to new product ideas. These responses help companies determine:

- whether the products are worth pursuing;
- which products are most likely to sell;
- any flaws the company may have overlooked; and
- potential improvements that would make your product even better.

Concept testing often involves interviews, focus groups, and other qualitative research methods to identify customers' attitudes toward the product.

Concept testing has become increasingly popular in recent years due to the Internet; companies can post images of a potential product online and instantly reach thousands, or even millions, of customers. Customers can then discuss which elements of the product they like and what they think can be improved. Concept testing is an important part of the innovation process because it gives companies a chance to weed out weaker product ideas and develop the products that have the most potential for success.

Step 4: Develop a Complete Product Concept Next, you can concentrate on improving the product that passed your concept testing. In this step, you further develop your product idea by adding more detail to your descriptions.

- By the end of this stage, if your product is a *tangible good*, you have gathered everything you'll need to make a prototype.
- If it's a *service, experience, or transformation*, you have thought out all of your background prep work, as well as how you envision the service, experience, or transformation will actually work.

With your concept fully developed, you can get down to determining how feasible actually producing your product will be by moving on to the next step: creating and analyzing a business case.

Step 5: Analyze the Business Case With your product's concept fully visualized and developed, you need to look at it from a practical point of view. In this step of the process, you analyze your concept to determine how well it might succeed when it hits the market by answering questions such as:

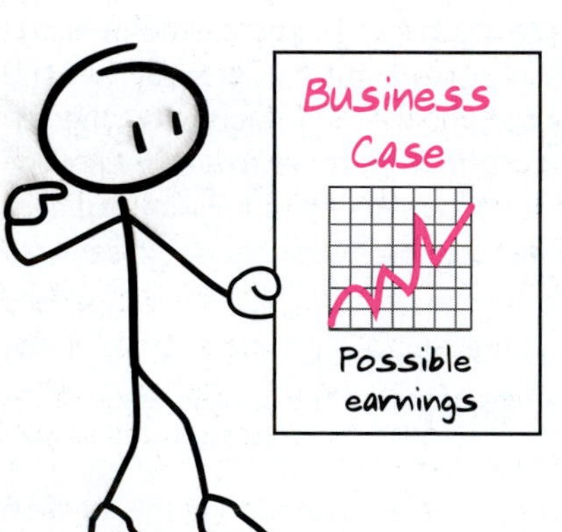

- What is the size of your potential market? Is the market big enough so that an adequate number of people will buy your product?
- Will your product appeal to a wide range of consumers, or is there a specific target audience you are marketing it to?
- How much will customers pay for your product?
- How much will it cost to produce your product?
- How will you transport or deliver the product, and how much will this cost?
- Will the product contribute to your triple bottom line?

Some products, no matter how amazing, will not be successful because they either cost more than what consumers are willing to pay or are too costly for the company to produce and distribute. By creating a realistic business case, you can get a better idea of which products are feasible. This helps you eliminate more of your weaker ideas to concentrate on your strongest and most potential concepts. These remaining concepts then move on to the next stage: developing a prototype.

Step 6: Develop the Prototype Now that you've determined which concepts are most feasible, the next step is to take the concept and create an actual, functioning representation of that product—a **prototype**. This prototype is a working model or representation of what your final product will be.

Say you're planning to introduce a new type of portable MP3 player onto the market. The prototype may not have all of the attributes of the finished product, but it will serve as an example of how the finished product will look and function. From movies to customer service initiatives to sporting goods, all types of products go through this stage as part of the innovation process.

If the product is cutting edge, such as a brand new type of computer technology, a company may choose to apply for a patent at this time. A patent provides an incentive for companies to devote time and resources to developing the product. At the same time, the patent protects the company from competitors taking their designs to create their own versions of that product. (For more on patents and other business law issues, check out Chapter 18 at **www.mybizlab.com**.)

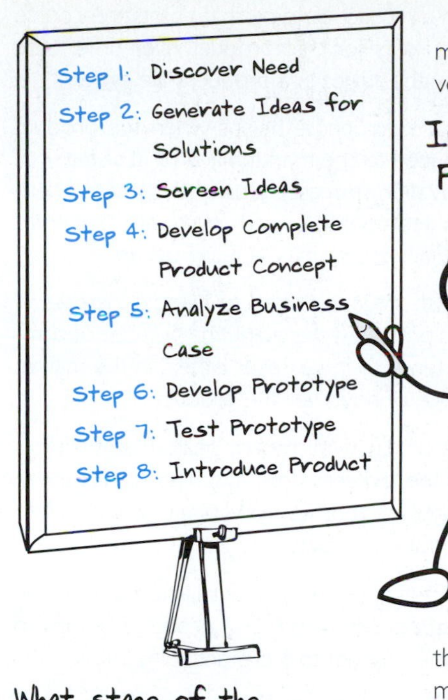

What stage of the innovation process do you think is most important? Why?

Step 7: Test the Prototype

With the prototype completed, you're ready to put your product into the hands of customers for **product testing**. You watch customers to gauge their reactions to the product, and take note of which aspects of the product the customers like, and which aspects need to be improved or removed. There are many techniques for testing a prototype, including video observation, personal interviews, and focus groups. These research techniques involve both quantitative and qualitative analysis of feedback.

Ultimately, the idea is to document the customer's experience with this product. How does it fit into the customer's life? Does it fulfill a specific need? All of the customer feedback a company gathers is noted, analyzed, and then used in improving the product and developing future products. Take the movie industry, for example. Many motion picture companies hold test screenings of their major films to get audience feedback. Twentieth-Century Fox organized test screenings for *Titanic* and *The Simpsons Movie*, among many other films. After the screening, the production team often edits the film based on audience feedback.

This product testing is different from concept testing because customers are no longer thinking about an *idea*—they are testing an actual product. Their reactions to a prototype may be different from their reactions to an image or a description of the product. The product-testing phase can be crucial in determining the success of a product. Focusing on testing the product, modifying it to incorporate customer feedback, and then retesting the product at this stage is likely to result in a finished product that meets your desired specifications, and more importantly, satisfies the customer.

Step 8: Introduce the Product

Finally, after all of your research, testing, and retesting, it's time to release the product and make it officially available to customers. If all of the proper measures have been taken, and the innovation process has been followed thoroughly, the product is likely to be well received and to address the needs of your customers as you had intended.

Innovation and You

So, how does knowing how innovation works affect you? With an understanding of innovation, you can determine possible problems and come up with practical solutions to these problems in almost any situation. You'll be a valuable member to your employer and any other group you're a part of if you can implement this innovation process to solve problems and create new solutions for people's needs. Being innovative is a valuable and desirable quality for a person to have, and it's something you can develop and improve over time by practicing it regularly.

Once a new product innovation has been introduced, it begins to move through the product life cycle, which we discuss next.

The Product Life Cycle

Do you type your papers on an Apple IIe computer? Chances are you don't, as the computer was released in the 1980s and has been replaced with newer versions. Older products become outdated, so they are constantly updated and replaced. As we discussed in Chapter 3, every product

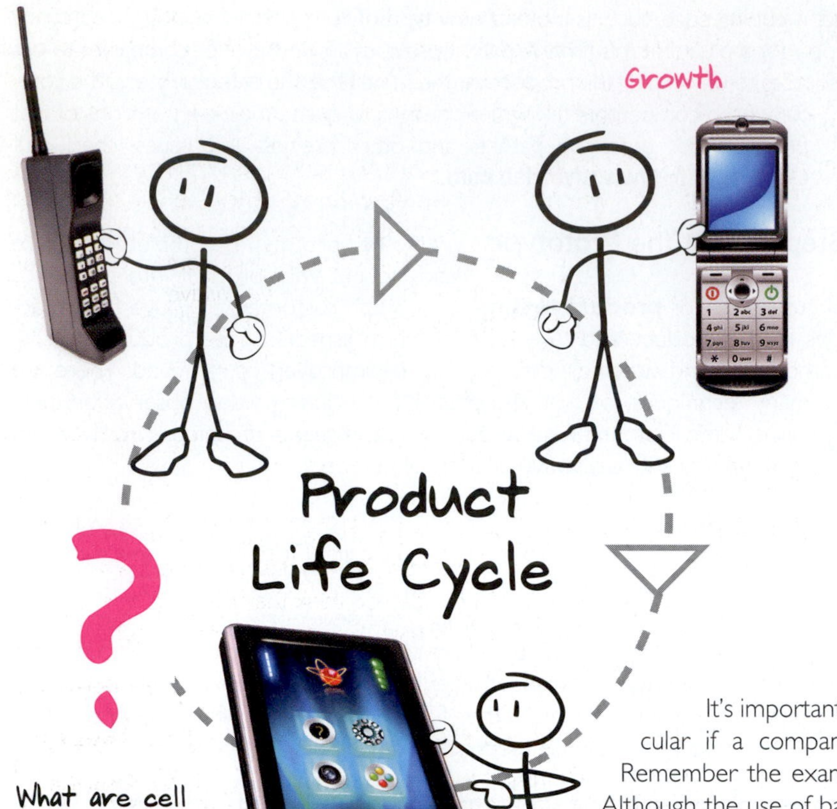

What are cell phone makers doing to prolong the maturity stage or to keep the cell phone from declining?

goes through a *product life cycle* that charts the course of sales and profits for that product over time. Let's quickly review the stages in a product's life cycle:

1. The *introduction phase* begins when the product is introduced to the marketplace (that's step 7 of the innovation process). During this phase, there are few competitors and sales are generally low—in fact, losses may actually occur.
2. The *growth stage* experiences a rapid increase in sales and profits. At this point, the number of competitors tends to increase, as others in the market take notice of how well the product is selling.
3. When a product reaches its peak in sales, it has entered the *maturity stage*. Businesses may try to secure their positions by lowering prices or differentiating their products.
4. The last stage of the product life cycle is in the *decline stage*. Sales are falling, profits may turn to losses, and competitors are dropping off.

It's important to remember that the life cycle of a product can be circular if a company manages to revitalize the product in some way. Remember the example of Arm & Hammer baking soda from Chapter 3. Although the use of baking soda in cooking declined in the mid–20th century, Arm & Hammer repositioned the product as a deodorizer and carpet freshener. As a result, the life cycle of Arm & Hammer baking soda has continued to the present day.

This life cycle can also vary in length, from months to decades. For example, the product life cycle of digital pets, such as Bandai's Tamagotchi, was only a couple of years in the United States. However, the product life cycle of Mattel's Barbie doll began in the 1950s and has lasted several decades.

Why It Matters to Marketers For companies to remain competitive and continue to earn a profit, they need to be aware of where their products are in their respective life cycles and introduce innovative new products when other products are declining. Marketers pay particular attention to the product life cycle to determine which marketing strategies to use.

- For example, during the introduction stage, marketers do their best to generate interest in a product through the use of different types of promotion.
- As the product enters the growth stage, marketers typically lower prices and increase distribution to meet incoming competition and to spur demand from customers.
- In the maturity stage, marketers strive to emphasize the brand name and product differences to build customer loyalty.
- As the product declines, marketers may decide to reduce distribution and advertising.

Of course, there are no strict rules that bind product life cycle stages and marketing strategies. Marketers must make decisions based on each product and its unique situation.

■ Companies that fail to innovate risk being shut out of the market completely.

The Product Mix As an organization continually develops new products, it begins to establish a collection of products that are in various stages of the product life cycle and that satisfy a variety of customers and customer needs. This total collection of products that a seller offers is referred to as a **product mix**. For example, Under Armour's product mix includes backpacks, athletic shoes, and underwear.

The product mix typically includes several **product lines**, or groups of related products. Under Armour offers several lines of footwear, including sandals, running shoes, and soccer shoes. Keeping track of the organization of products in the product mix allows a company to understand how a new or updated product will affect the company's existing merchandise.

In short, companies that are able to introduce new products and update their existing products effectively have a foundation on which to build customer loyalty. They are also able to deliver products relevant to customers' lives and address their current needs and desires. Innovation itself is no guarantee of success, however. It can be hard to come up with new products that are consistently successful. Yet there is no viable alternative to innovation, however risky it is. ■ Companies that fail to innovate risk being shut out of the market completely.

Do It...

13.1: Identify Innovations Select one good and one service that you've seen introduced lately that you believe are true innovations. Briefly explain why you believe they are innovations. Where do you think they reside on the product life cycle? Limit your response to one page, and be prepared to submit it electronically or discuss it in class.

Now Debrief...

- **Innovation** is a process that involves the introduction of new products into the marketplace. It is a unique improvement to a product—be it a good, service, experience, or transformation—that earns kudos (and cash) in the market.
- The process of innovation begins with discovering an existing or potential need. After the need is identified, the company must generate ideas for products that will satisfy those needs. The company must then perform **concept testing**. Customers provide feedback on the company's idea, which will be used to further develop and improve it. After that, the company needs to assess how feasible the product will be. The company then creates and tests a **prototype** of the product, giving them the opportunity to further improve their ideas. When the product finally meets all of the desired requirements, it is released into the market.
- All products have a particular life cycle that they go through. For companies to remain profitable, they must be able to change their offerings as the needs and desires of their customers change.
- As an organization continually develops new products, it begins to establish a collection of products that are in various stages of the product life cycle. This total collection of products that a seller offers is referred to as a **product mix**. The product mix typically includes several **product lines**, or groups of related products.

2. Developing a Brand, Creating a Package

"To succeed in business it is necessary to make others see things as you see them."

—John H. Patterson,
IBM founder[4]

When you turn on the TV to watch one of the cable news networks, do you choose CNN, MSNBC, or Fox? Do you have particular feelings about one of these stations? Maybe one particular station caters to your political opinions, or one show just makes you feel good.

In choosing any product, your choice may have as much to do with branding and the associations that you have developed with the particular brands as it does with the product itself. **Branding** is the way in which a company distinguishes its products from those of other companies. A **brand** is the identity customers associate with a product or company. A brand includes both the company or product's name, such as Dell computers or M&M's candy, as well as its image in the market. Since a brand is largely based on how customers perceive the company or product, it can be hard to define this perception objectively.

But what does branding have to do with innovation? In many cases, a company's brand is one of its primary sources of innovation and differentiation. Products in mature industries like soft drinks and automobiles are so well established that it's often too difficult or costly to develop entirely new products in these categories. It is possible, however, to change how people feel about a product or what they believe about a product through branding, and in some ways this is an important approach for achieving innovation.

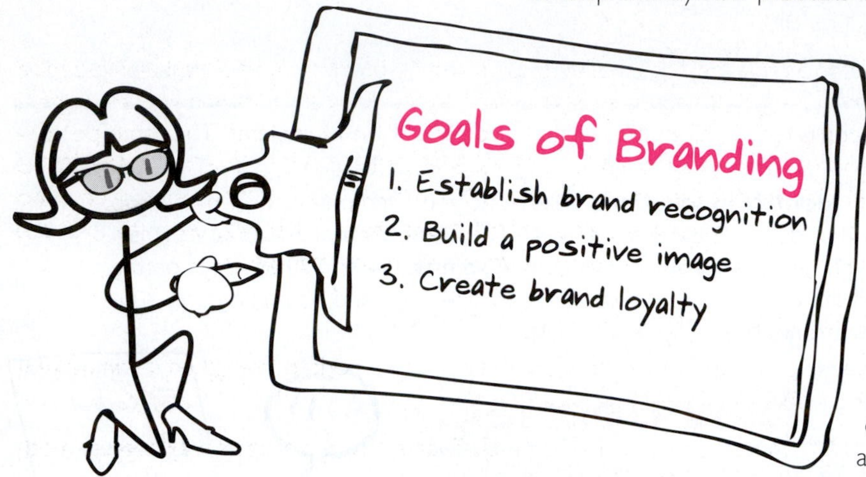

The Goals of Branding

In 2008, Google, Apple, Amazon, Zara, and Nintendo were voted as the best global brands for that year by Interbrand and *BusinessWeek*.[5] Being voted the "best brand" seems like a great accomplishment, but what does a good brand do for its company? What are the goals of branding? Let's take a look at a few key goals here.

Establish Brand Recognition People rely on brands to make decisions. Imagine you go to a vending machine to buy a soda. The machine offers RC Cola, which you don't recognize, and Coca-Cola. If the price difference isn't extreme, you'll probably choose Coca-Cola. Why? Because you recognize the brand. In this case, brand recognition influenced your decision about which soda to buy. **Brand recognition** is the extent to which customers recognize a brand and distinguish it from other brands.[6]

One of the goals of branding is to give customers the impression that a particular product is the only resource for their needs to be met.[7] Naturally, a company would like for customers to seek out its product over others, even if there is little difference between its product and another product. Ideally, customers should be able to recognize a brand and know exactly what they will get from purchasing the product. In other words, customers experience less risk when they buy a brand-name product. For this reason, customers tend to buy products with recognizable brand names over products with generic or unfamiliar brand names.

Build a Positive Image Another goal of branding is to leave a positive, lasting impression on customers. Marketers strive to build brands that link the product or company with positive situations or emotions. For example, some people select one brand of batteries over another based solely on their feelings toward that particular brand. Whether it is a pink, mechanized bunny promoting durability, the stark image of black and copper promoting strength, or the image of an electrified cat promoting power that resonates with the customer, each is an effort by the producers of those batteries to generate positive associations with their brands.

Create Brand Loyalty Most people have brands that they consistently select over and over again. Some people will only drink a certain brand of coffee; others might consistently rely on a particular parcel delivery service or return to the same Web site again and again for news and information. A customer's consistent choice of a particular brand is referred to as **brand loyalty**.

Are you loyal to any particular brands? Why?

One of the goals of branding is to establish the relationships that lead to this type of brand loyalty. One way that companies do this is by rewarding customers in some way.[8] One popular loyalty reward is the frequent flier program offered by many airlines. In this program, with each ticket purchased, customers are awarded a predetermined amount of free air travel that they can use at a future date. If you haven't taken part in that program, maybe you've received a card from a company that enables you to receive special discounts, offers, or premiums each time you spend money on its products. For example, Best Buy offers a Reward Zone card. These and other similar programs are the loyalty methods that companies use to help to ensure that customers will return to their businesses again and again.

Managing Brands

What do you do to create a favorable impression with people in your life? Perhaps you have a good sense of humor that keeps people laughing and feeling happy. Maybe you are a great listener and people feel comfortable talking to you about their problems. The same personality traits apply to brands. ■ A brand creates a personality or an image for a product that dictates how people feel about that product. The employees who establish and promote a brand are called **brand managers**. When you work to improve your personal image, you're actually acting as your own brand manager.

Brand Manager

Brand managers must constantly work to maintain a brand:

- If a certain brand appeals to customers, brand managers work to strengthen it and make it more recognizable.
- On the other hand, if a brand seems to be ineffective, brand managers may suggest modifications or even a complete overhaul.

Brand managers also recognize that powerful brands can sometimes be limiting. For example, the Disney brand is famous for its family movies and its children's merchandise. It has an image of youth and innocence. For this reason, Disney brand managers had to create a separate company to produce non–G-rated movies. They were afraid that movies geared to an older audience would taint the classic Disney brand.

Customers Co-creating Brands In the past, brand managers have gone a long way in the effort to build favorable brand recognition with their products. Generally, it was a one-way conversation. More and more, however, customers are also getting in on helping develop brands. Because of the enhanced level of interaction enabled by the Internet, customers are able to provide input in the process of branding. Some companies have created online forums where customers can log on and discuss products, offer suggestions, and help form the brand in a way that suits their needs.[9] These companies often respond directly to these suggestions, creating two-way communication with their customers.

■ A brand creates a personality or an image for a product that dictates how people feel about that product.

In some cases, companies offer contests asking their customers to create commercials based on their own perceptions of their products. Other companies encourage customers' involvement in branding by asking them to have a say in the products that are created or offering customized products. For example, though blue M&M candies are nothing out of the ordinary today, they didn't even exist until 1995. That's when parent company Mars Inc. launched a nationwide campaign asking customers to vote for a new M&M color: pink, purple, or blue. By empowering customers to get involved and to drive decision-making, the brand boosted its annual sales by 4.7 percent.[10] By building relationships with their customers, companies hope to develop favorable feelings toward their brands.[11]

What to Do When Brand Perceptions Shift

As the business environment and customer needs change, **brand perceptions** can change over time. Sometimes, this happens as a result of a company's own efforts, and other times it happens because of unforeseen external circumstances.

Planned Shifts Kraft Foods is a well-established company in the food industry that has been around for more than 100 years. Due to its long-standing presence, Kraft felt that some of its products might be overlooked because the brand had become so entrenched in the market. In 2009, in an effort to remain in the forefront of the minds of customers and foster growth, Kraft introduced a new brand image for many of its products. The new Kraft logo includes a smile-shaped curve that ends in a burst of shapes, each of which represents a different division of the business. For example, the triangle in the logo is meant to signal Kraft's DiGiorno pizza brand.[12]

Unplanned Shifts Unforeseen circumstances can lead to a change in brand perception, as in the case of Starbucks. Starbucks was initially known for its intimate atmosphere and personalized service, where customers could interact with the staff and with each other in a leisurely way. Because the company wanted to grow and have a broader appeal, Starbucks increased the number of its offerings, which slowed down the service. This affected the Starbucks experience for many customers. The desire for rapid growth—and the way that the goods and services offered by Starbucks changed as a result—changed the perception of the brand. As Starbucks continued to grow, it was seen as less of a destination for a leisurely and personalized experience, and more of an impersonal destination to get a cup of coffee.[13] Although the brand loyalty of the good (the coffee) was still intact, the service and experience components suffered.

■ Depending on the circumstances, it is possible for companies or customers to change a brand's perception.

In the example above, the shift in brand perception was within the company's control. By 2009, during an economic downturn in which customers were becoming increasingly conscious of how their dollars were spent, the perception of the Starbucks brand changed in a different way. Whereas Starbucks was once seen as offering a pricey but high-quality cup of coffee, the perception of the Starbucks brand had shifted to a feeling that there was little value in Starbucks coffee.[14] This shift in brand perception was largely a product of changes in the economy and not due to any changes that Starbucks had made to its brand.

■ Depending on the circumstances, it is possible for companies or customers to change a brand's perception. Businesses perform environmental scanning to stay informed of factors such as these that can negatively affect brand perception. If Starbucks had taken the economic downturn into consideration, perhaps the company could have come up with a strategy that emphasized the value of the brand to counteract the changing economy.

Branding and the Product Life Cycle

Let's say a band has been playing the same songs in concert for the last 20 or 30 years. The band's name is established, and it may always have some kind of fan base, but without shaking things up and standing apart from the competition, the band may never maintain the level of success it once enjoyed. Effective branding is one way to revitalize a product that is nearing the end of its product life cycle. For example, 80s pop group Duran Duran attempted to revitalize their product and change their brand image by collaborating with Justin Timberlake on a new album in 2006. Do you think it worked?

Branding can also differentiate products that are facing tough competition in the maturity stage of the life cycle. Branding is especially important in well-established industries because it is the primary way that companies are able to distinguish themselves and their products from their competitors. The longer an industry has been in existence, the more likely it is that competitors will offer similar products that vary little in comparison.

Think of the premium cable services offered by HBO and Showtime. Each company has been in existence for decades and offers products that are extremely similar: movies and original programs. What differentiates these two companies is their brands. The types of movies and series each company decides to air, the way they present their products, and how customers respond to these efforts differentiate these two brands. HBO and Showtime are constantly trying to outdo each other by releasing hot new series and keeping premium movie service up-to-date and desirable.

Goods Packaging

Service Packaging

Presentation Matters: Packaging

A company's brand is not just built through magazine advertisements and television commercials. Product packaging also helps build the brand. If you walked past a storefront that had a paper sign with the store name written in marker, you probably wouldn't feel compelled to go inside. How popular would Rolex be if the watches came wrapped in tinfoil? Many tangible items have distinct packaging that helps customers distinguish one company's product from another company's product.

Experience/Transformation Packaging

What difference does packaging make to a product?

Packaging for Tangible Goods When you buy something, how does its packaging affect you? Tropicana learned the hard way that packaging matters a lot. In 2009, the company redesigned its popular orange juice cartons to adopt a more streamlined look. The update was not well received by customers and—within the span of less than two months—sales had dropped considerably, losing the company millions of dollars.[15] Tropicana ultimately decided to switch back to its original design, much to the satisfaction of its customers.

As this example illustrates, packaging is an important part of branding. You may think a package's main purpose is to hold or contain a product, but it does much more than this:

1. Packaging attracts a customer's attention.
2. Packaging reflects the type of product that a customer expects to receive.
3. Packaging often improves the function of a product.
4. Packaging protects the product and makes it durable enough for shipping and handling.
5. Packaging lists the contents and the benefits of the product for potential buyers.
6. Packaging addresses consumer safety warnings and warranties.
7. Packaging sometimes lists the price of the product and explains why the product is a good value.

Because packaging is a customer's first encounter with a product, savvy marketers make sure it creates a positive image while also being informative and functional.

Packaging for Non-Tangible Goods When you think of a service, do you think of it as having a package? Packaging and design are not limited to tangible goods. Services, experiences, and transformations are also packaged. From a vacation at a resort to a dinner at a restaurant to a visit to a Web site, each product has a specific manner of delivery to the customer. Think of how a visit to one restaurant will be different from a visit to another. Each is decorated differently and has a different method of delivering the dining experience to its customers. A place like T.G.I. Friday's is packaged as a casual, fun dining experience, whereas an expensive French bistro is packaged as an elegant, refined dining experience.

Consider also a Web site. The packaging of a Web site includes its layout, its color scheme, and its interactivity. A Web site for a financial services firm may use subdued colors and minimal artistic flourishes to emphasize professionalism, whereas a Web site for a day care center may use bright colors and animations to emphasize youth and playfulness.

"Green" Packaging Over the past decade, consumers have shown increased concern over the environmental impact of their shopping and buying habits. Companies have responded by using reduced or recycled packaging. Ever-Green Toilet Paper is now selling its bathroom tissue in a fiber paperboard package rather than in plastic wrapping. All the packaging materials are completely recyclable, which appeals to its eco-conscious customer base. The TJX Companies, such as T.J. Maxx and Marshalls, also focus on recycling. Their distribution centers recycle all the cardboard packaging received from vendors, a policy that helps promote a "green" image.

By constructing an effective, appealing, and lasting brand image, companies are able to interest new customers and generate brand loyalty. The more potent a brand is, the more likely it is to resonate with customers, generate goodwill toward the brand, and result in greater profits. A finely crafted branding strategy can lead to greater customer recognition toward the company and establish a brand as a leader in a particular industry. As we'll see in the next section, branding strategy also determines how a company prices products.

Do It...

13.2: Keep a Brand Log Keep a brand log in which you list every brand you use during a single day. At the end of the day, identify how many of those brands you really care about. Would you be disappointed if these brands were no longer available? Once you've narrowed down the list, consider what makes these brands special. How are they different from other, similar products? How do the companies try to generate brand loyalty? Be prepared to submit your responses electronically or to discuss them in class.

Now Debrief...

- **Branding** is an important tool companies use to establish their products in the minds of customers and distinguish them from other, similar products. A **brand** is more than a logo with a company's name attached to it. A brand is the overall identity that a customer associates with a particular product.
- The goals of branding are to establish brand recognition, to build a positive image, and to establish **brand loyalty**. Companies establish brand loyalty in many ways, such as by offering customer involvement initiatives and various loyalty programs.
- A company's **brand managers** work to widen and maintain a brand's appeal.
- **Brand perceptions** can change over time. Sometimes, this happens as a result of a company's own efforts, and other times it happens because of unforeseen external circumstances.
- Branding is also an important part of the product life cycle and can help differentiate and revitalize brands at different stages.
- Packaging is another important element of branding that can affect the way a product and the brand as a whole are perceived.

3. The Price Is Right: Setting Prices

If you get a job offer tomorrow at a company you really like, how much do you think they should pay you? Your answer will depend on how much you think you're worth. That's YOUR price. You may not have it figured to the dollar, but if a company offered you a job for $10,000 a year, you'd probably decide you're worth more than that. You know your price is higher. Now the question is, how much higher? It depends on a variety of factors, such as your monthly bills (your costs), how much your friends are making at other companies (the competition), and how much you think the company hiring you (the customer) is willing to pay you.

■ Setting the price for a product can play an important role in how well the product is received, how much profit the company can receive, and how the competition will set prices for their products.

When organizations try to develop a pricing strategy for the products and services that they sell, they consider a lot of those same issues:

- How much does it cost to deliver a service or make a product?
- How much is the competition charging for its products?
- How much is the customer willing to pay for what I'm offering?

We'll discuss these issues next.

What Is Price?

A price for an item or service may have many different names. The price you pay for an apartment space, for example, is called rent. The price you pay to work out at a gym is called a membership fee. At school, the price you pay for your education is called tuition. If you've taken out student loans, the price you have to pay for the money you borrowed is called interest. The list goes on and on; but in all cases, there is a price attached to the product, regardless of what it's called.

How do you decide what you're willing to pay for a product?

In short, the **price** is what a company requires from the customer in exchange for a product. Remember from Chapter 12 that price is one of the Ps of the marketing mix. ■ Setting the price for a product can play an important role in how well the product is received, how much profit the company can receive, and how the competition will set prices for their products.

Pricing Strategies

So, how do you set a price on a particular product? You might be surprised to learn that, in many cases, businesses have a lot less control over the final price than you might imagine. Think of the last time you tried to sell your books back to your school bookstore. Almost all students have been upset to discover that they are not offered a price that reflects what they paid for their textbooks when they try to sell them back. This is because, in that circumstance, you are a price taker. As you may remember from our discussion in Chapter 3, a *price taker* accepts whatever the market price is for that product.

Companies that offer distinct or unique products (such as the Apple iPhone) are able to control the price to a greater degree than companies that do not offer such products. Furthermore, companies that have established their brand as being extraordinary in some way (such as Mercedes or BMW) also have greater control in establishing the price.

Pricing Goals When developing a pricing strategy, marketers often consider which goals they are pursuing, such as the following:

1. **Getting a reasonable return or profit:** Prices are usually set so that they allow companies to profit from selling their products.
2. **Building popularity or store traffic:** Sometimes, companies will offer products at prices that are not necessarily profitable to draw in customers and increase profits in the long run.
3. **Creating an elegant image:** Expensive products, like designer clothing, are often priced high to promote an image of wealth and high status.
4. **Aiming for social equality:** Low-priced items are designed so that everyone can afford them.

These goals may change at different points in the product life cycle. When a product is first introduced, marketers may want to build popularity. As a result, they may set a low initial price or offer discounts. Once the product grows and reaches maturity, marketers will most likely set the price higher so that they make a profit.

The Four Cs of Pricing

When considering how to price a product, marketers also consider the **Four Cs**—costs, competition, customers, and controls:

1. *Costs* include everything that you pay for to create your product. Depending on the type of business, costs can vary, but considerations are likely to include production and labor costs, facilities, and, of course, marketing. For any business, it's important to make sure that the costs of running the business are covered.
2. Your *competition* consists of the companies that offer products that compete for your customers. Unless your product is unique in some way or has superior brand recognition, the price you set will need to be in line with your competitors' or you'll lose business.
3. Your *customer* is the individual or organization that will purchase your product. As such, their needs should be addressed when considering price. If you set a price your customers aren't willing to pay, you won't sell your product.
4. *Controls* are any limitations that would affect the price of a particular product. For example, say you own a company that buys and resells tickets for concerts and sporting events. Some states set a limit on the amount that you can inflate the price of a ticket. In this case, the limits set by law are your controls.

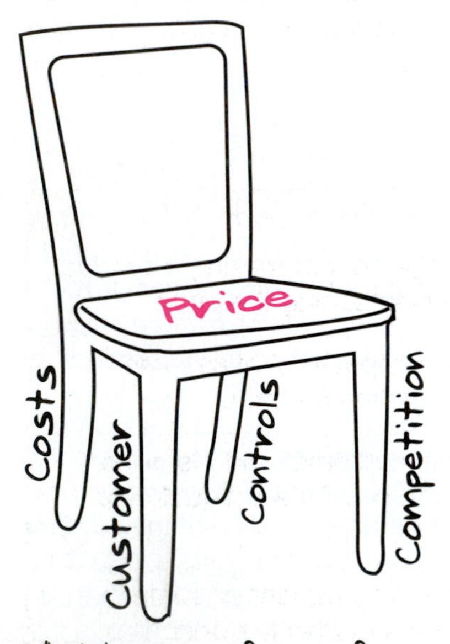

What happens if one of the chair legs is longer or more important than the others?

Selecting a Pricing Strategy

So, you've just developed an incredible new product and considered the Four Cs, and it's time to take it to market. How are you going to set the price? To maximize profits, right? Unfortunately, there are more considerations than just maximizing profits when setting a price. An important step is to select the pricing strategy that seems most suitable for your business and your products—and as you'll see, many relate back to the Four Cs. Let's look at some pricing strategies you have to choose from:

1. **Cost-driven pricing:** This strategy takes the cost of making your product into consideration when setting the price. An example of this is called **cost-plus pricing**, which includes the cost of making the product *plus* any additional money you'll charge for the product. The plus part is what allows a company to make a profit on its product. So, if you

know it costs you $40 to make a product, going by cost-plus pricing would mean that your price would be $40 plus the additional amount you plan to charge for it.

2. **Competitor-driven pricing:** In competitor-driven pricing, the main concern is remaining in the same price ballpark as your competitors. You've probably seen this while shopping around for a new computer or TV at an electronics store. After showing the salesperson an ad for the same product at a lower price at a competing store, he or she may agree to match the competitor's price. Maybe you've noticed that one company will offer a product and then its main competitor will come out with a similar product at the same or lower price. That is competitor-driven pricing at work.

3. **Customer-driven pricing:** As noted above, customers and what they expect to pay for your product helps to establish the price. Cars and homes that are bought at an auction are an example of customer-driven pricing. Those prices are determined by what customers are willing to pay. Another example of customer-driven pricing was when the band Radiohead released their album *In Rainbows* with a price ranging from free to, well, whatever you wanted to pay for it. In this pricing plan, the band decided to allow customers the chance to download their album and pay whatever they felt it was worth.[16]

4. **Control- or regulation-driven pricing:** As noted in our discussion of the Four Cs, the government or some other form of regulation guides this pricing strategy. Price regulations vary by state and may apply only to certain types of businesses. In 2009, for example, legislation was introduced that would limit the amount in fees that a credit card company could charge its customers.[17] In these cases, the price is established, to some

Table **13.1** | **Sample Pricing Strategies**

Pricing Strategy	Description
Cost-driven pricing	Strategy that takes the cost of making a product into consideration when setting the price
Competitor-driven pricing	Strategy that takes competitors' prices into consideration when setting the price
Customer-driven pricing	Strategy in which the customer and his or her expectation of what to pay for a product help establish the price
Control- or regulation-driven pricing	Strategy in which the government or some other form of regulation guides the price
Channel-driven pricing	Strategy that relies on the mode of distribution to determine price
Premium pricing	Strategy in which companies set a high price for a product to distinguish it from the competition and to promote an image of luxury
Everyday low pricing	Strategy in which customers are given the lowest available prices without coupons or special discounts
Penetration pricing	Strategy of attracting new customers by setting a low initial price for a product.
Discounting	Strategy of establishing a price by offering some sort of reduction in a generally established price

degree, by regulation and not by the company itself. The government also regulates the utilities industry. Even though there might be only one or two companies that offer utilities in an area, government regulations ensure that the prices remain reasonable for customers.

5. **Channel-driven pricing:** This strategy relies on the mode of distribution to determine price. You've probably seen an item of clothing that you wanted at a store only to find it available online from the same seller at a lower price. The only difference is how the item is distributed. It can go the other way, too. Sometimes, if you walk into a store, you can find an item at a lower price than if you had purchased it online. If you pick up a pizza from the restaurant, for example, you will often pay less than if you had it delivered.

6. **Other pricing strategies:** There are countless other pricing strategies, including the following popular ones:

   - **Premium pricing** occurs when companies set a high price for a product to distinguish themselves from the competition. This high price promotes an image of luxury and appeals to a wealthier demographic.
   - **Everyday low pricing** guarantees customers the lowest available prices without coupons or special discounts. This pricing strategy appeals to customers who seek bargains, as well as those who do not have time to clip coupons or read about weekly sales. Everyday low pricing is popular with large discount chains, such as Target.
   - **Penetration pricing** is the strategy of attracting new customers by setting a low initial price for a product. This technique may be used to encourage customers to switch brands or to try a new product.
   - **Discounting:** This strategy establishes a price by offering some sort of reduction in a generally established price. You've most likely encountered several discounting strategies during a trip to the grocery store. Buy one, get one free! Buy one, get the second one half off! Maybe you typically pay for your groceries with coupons. These are all discounting strategies that can affect price.

It's important to remember that pricing strategies are often limited by customers' perceptions or by market forces, such as supply and demand. For example, Mazda released its Miata as an inexpensive sports car for teenagers. However, an unexpectedly large number of middle-aged men pre-purchased the car, which significantly increased demand and drove up the price. As a result, Mazda had to change its pricing strategy and marketing scheme to match the market forces.

Staying Ahead of the Curve: Innovative Pricing Strategies

There are a number of opportunities you can leverage in your pricing strategy to achieve innovation. Keep in mind that innovation is about developing new and better ways of doing things and designing new solutions to customer needs or problems. Quite often, customer needs relate to pricing, so your pricing strategy can generate innovative solutions.

Consider the entire rental industry, for example. Today, you can rent cars, furniture, power tools, tents, trailers, and movies, just to name a few. The concept of renting something instead of having to purchase it is actually a major pricing innovation that solved a lot of customer needs.

$5.00 $2.50

How many more units would you have to sell to make up for the lower price?

What are some other pricing innovations?

- Major software companies like Salesforce.com and Google are remaking the software industry by allowing customers to rent their software instead of purchasing it and downloading it on their own computers.

- *Bundling* is another pricing innovation—rarely do you purchase a cell phone without the wireless contract to go with it.

These are just a couple examples of how you can take a look at your pricing strategy and find ways to change it to better meet customer needs. As you can see, innovation is not just about designing new products, it's a way of doing business that continually challenges the status quo and figures out new and better ways to satisfy customer needs and deliver to the triple bottom line. In the next section, we'll see how innovation drives value—or the perceived benefits that customers gain when they purchase various products.

Do It...

13.3: Choose a Pricing Strategy You've just decided to throw your hat into the world of Web design. Using the Four Cs and the information in this section, set a price for your Web design service and explain how you came to that decision. Be prepared to submit your response electronically or to discuss it in class.

Now Debrief...

- Although the name of what customers pay for a product is called many different things, all of those terms refer to the **price**. Many factors affect the price of a product, and in many cases, businesses have less control over price than they would like.
- When developing a pricing strategy, marketers often consider which goals they are pursuing, such as getting a reasonable return or profit, building popularity or store traffic, creating an elegant image, and aiming for social equality.
- When considering how to price a product, marketers also consider the **Four Cs**: *costs, competition, customers,* and *controls.*
- There are a wide array possible pricing strategies, including **cost-driven pricing, competitor-driven pricing, customer-driven pricing, control or regulation-driven pricing,** and **channel-driven pricing**. Other popular strategies include **premium pricing, everyday low pricing, penetration pricing**, and **discounting**.
- Developing innovative pricing strategies helps companies to compete and keep their customers satisfied.

4. Creating Value

So, now that you understand the concepts behind setting a price, it's time to discuss the factors, or benefits, that make purchasing a particular product worth it to customers. **Benefits** are the positive outcomes customers get from using a product. Naturally, benefits differ from product to product—and they can also vary from customer to customer—but the benefits offered by a product are the reasons why a customer seeks it out in the first place. In general, customers want products that

- solve a problem completely;
- don't waste their time;
- provide exactly what they want;
- deliver value where they want it;

- supply value when they want it; and
- reduce the number of decisions they have to make to solve their problems.

These are known as the six principles of "lean consumption." The focus is not on the products themselves, but the process of finding, purchasing, and using these products in daily life.[18] These variables explain why different companies are sometimes able to sell similar or identical products for different prices—they provide more benefits to the customer.

The Value Equation

In commercials, advertisements, and on the news, you always hear about things being offered at a great *value*. But what does value mean, exactly? Value is based in part on perception and in part on an actual, quantifiable measure. A good way to think of value is with this simple **value equation**:

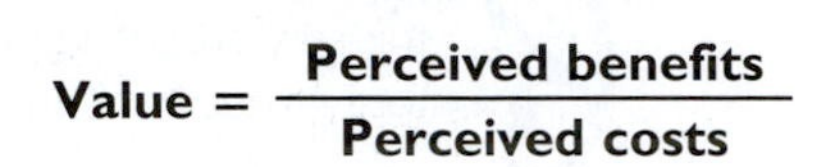

$$\textbf{Value} = \frac{\textbf{Perceived benefits}}{\textbf{Perceived costs}}$$

Employee A's Perception of Customer Need

This value equation helps show you that **value**—what a product is worth to a customer—depends on a cost/benefit analysis performed by the customer. If the *perceived benefits* outweigh the *perceived costs* of a transaction, the customer will theoretically benefit from it. The transaction will add value to the customer's life. If the costs are greater than the benefits, the customer would not benefit from the transaction.

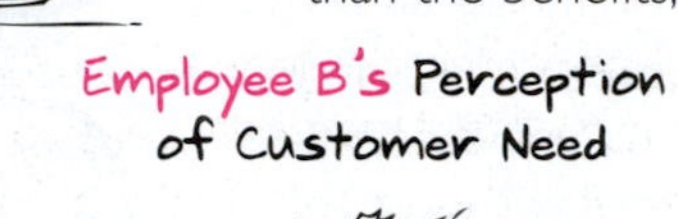

Value-Added Products

In many cases, businesses add value to products in order to attract customers or support higher prices. *Value-added products* are products that are changed or enhanced to become a different product with a higher value. For example, farmers may sell value-added products such as jams in addition to raw fruits and vegetables. Jams are value-added products because they save customers the time and effort of converting the fruit into jam themselves.

Employee C's Perception of Customer Need

Similarly, *value-added services* are services that enhance a core service. Companies often provide value-added services at no extra charge. For example, a telecommunications company may offer the value added service of call waiting if a customer buys a landline calling plan. Services that cater to customer convenience, like free pizza delivery or valet parking, can help enhance the value of a product, regardless of price.

Emphasizing value can be a powerful tool in getting customers to become aware of your product. It is important to remember that the actual price is just one element of the cost of a product for the customer. The tasks of searching for the product, consuming it, and disposing of it all require time and effort. Ideally, all people in an organization add value to the products they offer.

What can happen if perceptions of needs and value are different between the company and the customer?

Perceptions of Value

We've already taken a look at Tropicana and how its packaging update altered the perception of its orange juice and led to diminished sales. Another well-known example is the New Coke disaster. In 1985, Coke introduced an updated version of its Coca-Cola beverage.[19] In one commercial, a well-known Coke spokesperson, Bill Cosby, introduced the product as being "the best-tasting Coca-Cola ever." Unfortunately, a number of customers were outraged at the change in flavor. As a result, sales of the New Coke plummeted and the company decided to reintroduce its former, more familiar Coke. Clearly, Coca-Cola's perceptions of what customers valued (perhaps a change in taste) were not in line with what customers *truly* valued (consistency in their soda flavor).

Value Perception and Brand Perception

As the above example illustrates, a perceived decrease in a product's value can spell disaster for a product. Value perception is strongly linked to brand perception in that both perceptions rely on products meeting the expectations of consumers. When consumers feel that a product falls short of its promised value, they are less likely to purchase that product. However, when consumers feel that a product has increased in value, they are more likely to purchase the product.

Influencing Perceived Value

Companies can influence the perceived value of a product. For example, companies can release a product into the market at a high price and retain that price as long as people perceive that the product has a high value. Some customers are willing to pay a premium because they want the highest-quality product and they want the image that comes with it.

However, perceived value changes over time. To accommodate such changes in perception, one thing that a company may consider is a different pricing strategy. For example, by 2009, the restaurant industry had seen a decline in sales due to the perception that dining out was too expensive. In an effort to change this perception, many casual dining chains like Applebee's and T.G.I. Friday's started offering meals at lower prices.[20]

In addition to changing its prices, a company might also modify where the product is offered, how the product is designed, or how the product is promoted in order to change its perceived value. For example, a business may choose to sell its pastries at coffee shops rather than at gas stations to increase their perceived status.

Do It...

13.4: Analyze the Value of Purchases List three value-added products (goods, services, experiences, or transformations) you have purchased recently. In what ways did the company that created the product add value to it? How did your *perceptions* of the products' value affect the price you were willing to pay for the products? Be prepared to submit your responses electronically or to discuss them in class. Your instructor may also ask you to compare your thoughts with classmates in a small group.

Now Debrief...

- A product's features translate to **benefits** for the customer. Although benefits vary from product to product and from customer to customer, customers seek out products for the benefits they offer.
- **Value** is a combination of the benefits that a product offers in relation to the price, and emphasizing value is one way that companies can get the attention of potential customers. The determination of value, however, is based partially on perception.
- Perceptions are the impressions that a customer has of a particular product, and it is the marketer's goal to create a positive perception of their company's products. Although marketers have their own perceptions of products, the perceptions that the customer develops are much more important because they will be the ones using the product.

How can focusing on the triple bottom line create opportunities for innovation?

5. Marketing, Innovation, and the Triple Bottom Line

When someone asks you how well your business is doing, you're compelled to think of your financial bottom line. Are you rolling in money, or are you just barely getting by? But remember from Chapter 3 that success in business is about more than just profits. ■ Success is based on social and environmental sustainability as well as economic performance.

You could conclude that the triple bottom line emphasizes *obligations* that your company has to fulfill. Trying to do something good for people, profits, and the planet may seem like a lot of responsibility and may even be considered a burden. But there's a different perspective that you might consider. Instead of imposing *obligations* on you, focusing on the triple bottom line can actually create *opportunities* for innovation for marketers and the companies they work for.

Profit-Driven Innovation

Let's start with profits. ■ Every marketing decision will have an effect on a company's financial scorecard. Advertising campaigns, new product development, and price discounts all cost money, and the only justifiable basis for investing in these types of activities is if they generate a financial return. What is sometimes overlooked is the fact that the drive for profitability can actually reveal exciting opportunities for innovation.

For example, retailers like Amazon.com and Wal-Mart have developed a host of innovations in the use of barcode and RFID (radio frequency identification) technologies to reduce the cost of shipping and handling millions of customer orders every day. Another recent innovation is offering cable television service, Internet connection, and landline phone service as part of the same package. One bill for all of your electronic needs is great for you, but how does it affect the company offering these services at a lower price? For one thing, it cuts down on advertising costs, as all the services are combined into one ad campaign. Although providing each service individually would create the most profit in each individual sale, package deals often draw in more customers, leading to more profits. Marketers trying to drive costs out of their advertising campaigns have also achieved significant innovations in digital tools like e-mail campaigns and social media, which we'll discuss in the next chapter.

■ Success is based on social and environmental sustainability as well as economic performance.

Planet-Driven Innovation

Because organizations are now taking the planet into consideration when they develop marketing strategies, they are discovering new ways of differentiating their product and company from the competition. Take a few examples:

- Companies like eco-friendly U.S. company Terra Cycle are using old water bottles to package plant fertilizer made from—of all things—worm poop!
- In the footwear industry, Brooks Sports has just released a completely biodegradable running shoe. Its marketing department promises that the shoe is both durable and

environmentally safe, because, when placed in a landfill, it degrades almost 500 times faster than traditional shoes.

- Multinational consumer product marketers like Procter & Gamble are discovering new packaging innovations that reduce waste, and new detergent formulations that require less water.

These companies are achieving a competitive advantage that is driving business success because they are developing innovations that are beneficial to the environment.

People-Driven Innovation

Similar examples of innovation have occurred because organizations are placing greater emphasis on the social impact of their products.

> Every marketing decision will have an effect on a company's financial scorecard.

As emerging economies such as India and Brazil continue to capture the attention of organizations that are trying to grow their businesses, the importance of developing products that have a positive social impact becomes paramount. Well over a billion consumers in emerging economies earn less than a dollar a day and struggle to find adequate supplies of drinkable water and medical care. Companies that are trying to tap into these huge consumer markets are using innovation to develop products that improve the quality of life in these countries, marketing products ranging from portable water filters, computers powered by hand-driven cranks, and mosquito netting that reduces the occurrence of malaria.

As you consider your own career—possibly in marketing—consider the fact that you could have a direct hand in designing profitable innovations that yield a positive impact on the planet and help consumers around the globe improve their quality of life. The triple bottom line drives innovation, and an effective marketing strategy helps ensure its success.

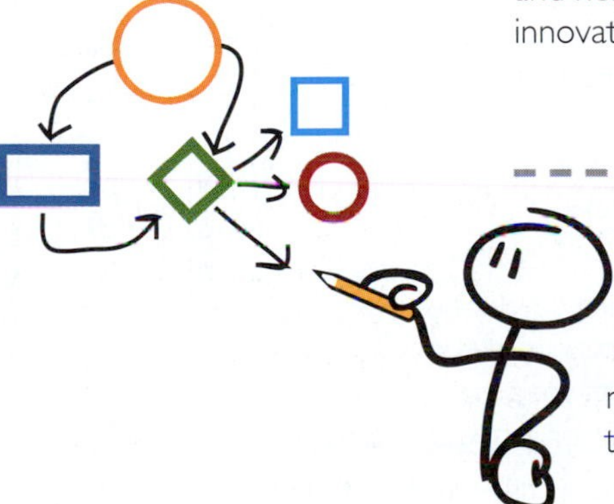

Do It...

13.5: Find Innovation Examples On your own, find an example of a planet-driven innovation and an example of a people-driven innovation not mentioned in the text. Be prepared to submit your responses electronically or to discuss them in class.

Now Debrief...

- The triple bottom line can reveal opportunities for innovation for marketers and the companies they work for.
- Every marketing decision has an effect on a company's financial scorecard. The drive for profitability can reveal exciting opportunities for innovation.
- Because organizations are now taking the planet into consideration when they develop marketing strategies, they are discovering new ways of differentiating their product and company from the competition.
- Similar examples of innovation have occurred because organizations are placing greater emphasis on the social impact of their products.

Chapter 13 Visual Summary

1. Recognize how companies use innovation to create and launch new products. (pp. 312–317)

- Because innovation often involves taking knowledge about customers and using it to develop products that help solve a particular problem, meet a need, or create a meaningful experience, it plays a key role in the way products are created.
- The steps involved in the innovation process are discovering a need, generating ideas for solutions, screening the ideas, developing a complete product concept, analyzing the business case, building a **prototype**, testing the prototype, and launching the product.
- All products move through a distinct life cycle. Products are constantly aging, and, to remain profitable, companies need to introduce innovative new products.
- As an organization develops new products, it establishes a collection of products that are in various stages of the product life cycle and that satisfy a variety of customers and customer needs. This total collection of products is referred to as a **product mix**. The product mix typically includes several **product lines,** or groups of related products.

Summary: By paying attention to customer needs, companies can continue to release innovative products that will sell well and maintain long-term relationships with customers.

2. Demonstrate how organizations build brands to compete. (pp. 317–322)

- **Branding** is the way in which a company distinguishes its products from those of other companies. A **brand** is the identity customers associate with a product or company.
- The primary goals of branding are to establish brand recognition, build a positive image, and create brand loyalty.
- The employees who establish and promote a brand are called **brand managers**. More and more, companies are reaching out to customers and allowing them to participate in the creation of their brands.
- **Brand perceptions** can change over time, for better or worse. Sometimes, this is due to the company trying to change its brand. Other times, this is due to external circumstances.

- Packaging is an important part of branding in helping to establish a product's personality.

Summary: Branding is the entire perception that a customer develops of a product. Any feelings associated with a product are part of its brand name. The goal of branding is to give customers a positive association with your products.

3. Devise a pricing strategy to capture a product's true value. (pp. 323–327)

- What customers pay for your products is called **price**. Setting the price for a product can play an important role in how well the product is received, how much profit the company can receive, and how the competition will set prices for their products.
- When developing a pricing strategy, marketers often consider which goals they are pursuing, such as building store traffic or getting a reasonable return or profit.
- When considering how to price a product, marketers also consider the **Four Cs**—costs, competition, customers, and controls.
- Companies consider the most appropriate strategy for pricing their product, including **cost-driven**, **competitor-driven**, **customer-driven**, **regulation-driven**, and **channel-driven pricing**, as well as **premium pricing**, **everyday low pricing**, **penetration pricing**, and **discounting**, among others.
- Devising new and innovative pricing strategies can improve your company's triple bottom line.

Summary: The price of a product can be the difference between its success or failure in the marketplace. Companies must give careful consideration to the Four Cs and carefully craft a pricing strategy for products at each stage in the life cycle.

4. Explain why benefits, value, and perception matter. (pp. 327–329)

- **Benefits** are the positive outcomes of using a product. Benefits differ from product to product and customer to customer, but the benefits offered by a product are the reasons why a customer seeks it out in the first place.
- The **value equation** shows that **value** depends on the cost/benefit analysis performed by the customer. Emphasizing value can be a powerful tool in getting customers to become aware of your product.

Summary: Positive consumer perception of value adds greatly to the strength of a company's brand.

Employee A's Perception of Customer Need

Employee C's Perception of Customer Need

5. Describe how marketing and innovation affect the triple bottom line. (pp. 330–331)

- The drive for profitability can reveal exciting opportunities for marketing and innovation.
- Because organizations are now taking the planet into consideration when they develop marketing strategies, they are discovering new ways of differentiating their product and company from the competition.
- Similar examples of innovation have occurred because organizations are placing greater emphasis on the social impact of their products.

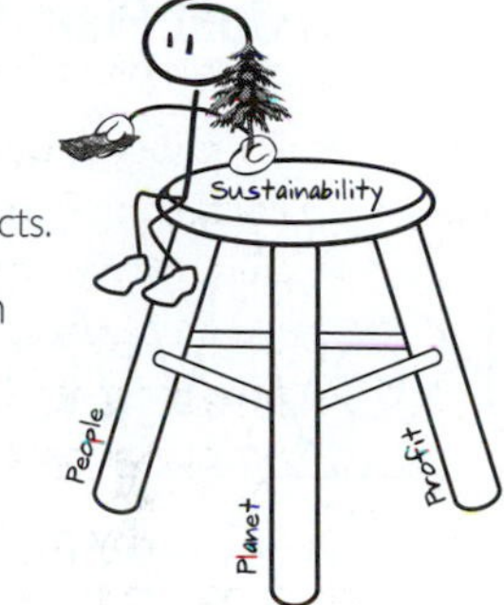

Summary: The triple bottom line can reveal opportunities for innovation for marketers and the companies for which they work.

Get the most out of what you just read by practicing your skills and actually DOING something with the material! The best place to do this is at **www.mybizlab.com**. Here's just some of what is available to you there:

- Apply your skills in an interactive environment with more **BizSkill experiences**...and see if you have what it takes
- Think critically and talk with your peers on hot business topics in **BizChat**
- Flex your business communication skills and build your own portfolio with the **Communication Plan exercises**
- Watch the chapter material come together with **Just Plain Business** videos
- Study on-the-go with **Audio Chapter Summaries** in MP3 format
- Brush up on the lecture and content with **Audio PowerPoints**
- Discover how well you are doing and see what areas you need to improve on with the **Pre-Tests** and **Post-Tests**

Key Words

These key words and more are also available as flash cards to practice with at **www.mybizlab.com**.

1. Recognize how companies use innovation to create and launch new products. **(pp. 312–317)**

Concept testing (p. 313)
Prototype (p. 314)
Product testing (p. 315)
Product mix (p. 316)
Product line (p. 317)

2. Demonstrate how organizations build brands to compete. **(pp. 317–322)**

Branding (p. 318)
Brand (p. 318)
Brand recognition (p. 318)
Brand loyalty (p. 318)
Brand managers (p. 319)
Brand perception (p. 319)

3. Devise a pricing strategy to capture a product's true value. **(pp. 323–327)**

Price (p. 323)
Four Cs (p. 324)
Cost-driven pricing (p. 324)
Cost-plus pricing (p. 324)
Competitor-driven pricing (p. 325)
Customer-driven pricing (p. 325)
Control- or regulation-driven pricing (p. 325)
Channel-driven pricing (p. 326)
Premium pricing (p. 326)
Everyday low pricing (p. 326)
Penetration pricing (p. 326)
Discounting (p. 326)

4. Explain why benefits, value, and perception matter. **(pp. 327–329)**

Benefits (p. 327)
Value equation (p. 328)
Value (p. 328)

Prove It

Prove It...

Now, let's put on one of the BizHats. With the **Employee BizHat** squarely on your head, look at the following exercise:

You are a sales manager for a U.S.-based snack company, and your boss has decided to give you a challenge. You've been put in charge of developing a brand for your company's new breakfast pastry. Your existing snack foods have appealed mostly to families with young children. Your boss informs you that the goal of the breakfast pastry is to branch out a bit and try to gain some new customers. The snack foods you offer have been available for some time, and they have a pretty solidly established brand. What kind of image does your company want to portray with its new breakfast pastry? Is there a specific target audience that you want to appeal to with your brand? How can you make sure that the pastry gains new customers without alienating loyal customers? Describe the steps you will take in creating an effective brand.

Flip It...

After you've looked at situation from the Employee's perspective, **flip over to the Customer BizHat**.

As a supermarket manager, you have noticed that sales for cereals have decreased in the past few years. You are looking for new breakfast products to replace some of the less popular cereals. Describe the type of brand that is likely to get—and keep—your attention.

Now Debrief It...

As an employee, how can you make the new breakfast pastry appeal to the widest possible customer base?

What strategies could you use to attract customers for your new product?

As a customer, how important are brand recognition and the feelings associated with it in buying food products?

Communicate: Promotions and Marketing Communications

BizSkills invite...

Try It!

There's no better way to learn concepts than to put them into practice. Take your turn in the driver's seat and be a part of actual business decision making by visiting the BizSkill for this chapter at **www.mybizlab.com**.

Start here!

Now that you've practiced making tough business decisions and seeing the results of your choices in this chapter's BizSkill, it's time to translate those skills into plain English. And if you skipped the BizSkill, go back now!

Chapter 14 Goals

After experiencing this chapter, you'll be able to:

1. Establish SMART marketing communication goals for a marketing campaign.
2. Select the promotional mix that is best suited for a marketing campaign.
3. Establish a creative strategy and select media vehicles for a marketing campaign.
4. Leverage your customer service strategy to achieve your goals by strengthening customer relationships, satisfaction, and loyalty.

As new forms of communication have emerged, how has marketing changed?

Market Like a Rock Star

After years of late night practices in your friend's garage, your band gets enough money together to rent a recording studio for a day. Feeling like real rock stars, you walk into the studio and cut five songs to a CD. You never sounded better. But, there's just one catch—you need to get the word out to the right people who will buy your music and tell others about it. You don't have the money to run ads, and you don't feel like standing in front of the supermarket with a box of CDs at your feet. The one thing you do have is a lot of friends, and they have a lot of friends. So, you text, e-mail, tweet, YouTube, and Facebook your friends a sample of your band's music and you ask them—beg them—to spread the news about your music. Your friends respond with enthusiasm, and you're amazed to see the downloads start almost immediately. All that time in the garage was worth it!

Whether you're an aspiring rock star or not, this story illustrates a truth about business that makes marketing essential: a successful product requires motivated customers who've been persuaded that your product is worth their time, effort, and money. Marketing communication is used to build relationships with customers, engage their interest in your product, and persuade them to act on that interest. In today's marketplace, you can choose from a lot of different vehicles to transport your message to and from your customers, so you need a solid marketing plan to guide your decisions.

In this chapter, we'll show you how to establish goals for your marketing campaign, and select the best message, promotional tools, and media vehicles to achieve those goals. We'll also show you how to use customer service as an effective strategy to build relationships, trust, and loyalty with your customers that will earn their business for the long term. You'll be able to take what you've learned in this chapter and apply it in any situation—business or personal—that requires effective communication and persuasion.

1. Developing a Message In-line with Marketing Communication Goals

In Chapter 12 you read about how to identify your target audience, and Chapter 13 taught you how to make your product stand out from all the rest. So, let's say you've got a sweet product and you've identified your target market. It might seem like the next logical step would be to dive right in: throw a bundle of money into getting the word out there, right? Well, not quite. You've still got to look before you leap; otherwise, you might as well be tossing your marketing budget down a wishing well and hoping to see results.

In Chapter 9, we discussed how businesses create goals as part of their planning process to help the company determine what it wishes to achieve. Similarly, in marketing, companies focus their marketing and promotions efforts by identifying the purpose or desired effect of their communications. **Marketing communication goals** describe the reaction and response that marketers want to get from the target audience as a result of the **marketing campaign**, or the marketing activities a company engages in to get its product noticed by consumers. This is true for both business-to-consumer (B2C) *and* business-to-business (B2B) communications.

Organizations often use **integrated marketing communications** to send a consistent, unified message across all of their communications, regardless of whether that message reaches customers through advertising, personal selling, the Internet, customer service, or any other means. By using a consistent message and a blend of different types of marketing strategies, organizations attempt to evoke a specific response from their targeted audience.

Types of Marketing Communication Goals

So, why would a company focus on a customer's response to marketing? It all ties back to who your target audience is and what you want to achieve by focusing your marketing efforts on those people. There are four types of goals that marketers will use to get four different types of responses:

1. affective;
2. psychological;
3. behavioral; and
4. relational.

Ultimately, you want to achieve **customer loyalty**—having a customer who returns for business again and again—so you tailor your marketing efforts to encourage repeat customers.

Affective Goals

The clothing company Gap has sourced products from Africa for years, manufacturing goods in Africa and then shipping them to the United States. In 2006, the company decided to start giving back. The Gap (PRODUCT) RED campaign is used to both generate profit and help raise funds for AIDS awareness, treatment, prevention, and research. Half of the profits from sales of the RED line of products are donated to the Global Fund, which helps women and children affected by AIDS in Africa.[1]

Campaigns such as the Gap (PRODUCT) RED campaign that make charitable donations with customer spending are examples of **affective goals** in use. Affective goals aim to make customers feel or associate an emotion with a particular brand or company. In this situation, the company wants to evoke a feel-good emotion from customers who buy its products. Marketing efforts would inform customers that by purchasing a RED product, they are supporting a worthwhile cause and making a difference in the world.

Translation Guide

The distinction between *marketing* and *marketing communication* can get a little fuzzy. In business terms, however, it's important to make a distinction.

Marketing: *Marketing* refers to the range of activities that people in an organization perform to discover customer needs and to provide solutions to those needs through products. Much of this occurs behind the scenes.

Marketing Communication (MC): *Marketing communication* refers to *one part* of the marketing process. It includes all the elements of an organization's communications with its target market.

- *An example of an affective goal might be: "Achieve an association between Gap and charitable giving among 40 percent of the target market by June 2010."*

Psychological Goals You've probably seen the "laptop hunter" commercials where Microsoft gives people money to choose the best computer for their needs. In the commercials, PCs end up being the computer of choice for a variety of reasons. In this case, Microsoft's underlying message to the consumer is that PCs are a better choice than Macs, no matter what your computing needs may be.[2]

In this advertising campaign, Microsoft marketers are more concerned about what customers *think* about their brand as opposed to how customers feel about it. In this case, they are choosing to pursue a psychological goal. **Psychological goals** define what you want your target audience to know, believe, or perceive (i.e., these goals get at customers' attitudes, beliefs, and perceptions). Packaging is often an effective communications vehicle for this message. For example, a cereal manufacturer might include photos of athletes on the cover of its cereal to convey good health and fitness. If the product is a service, like offering legal advice, the people offering that service will dress the part; in this case, by wearing formal business attire.

- *An example of a psychological goal might be: "To achieve more favorable safety perceptions of our brand compared to our closest competitor among 65 percent of our target audience by June of next year."*

Behavioral Goals The next time you get a Sunday paper, take a look at the circulars that come with it. Many of the ads will have coupons that say things like "buy three, get one free" or "get $1 off when you try our new line." The goal of this sort of advertising is to affect your behavior; in this case, they want you to buy three of their products and to try their new product line. **Behavioral goals** define what you want the target audience to do, or at least intend to do.

Which companies communicate along these lines? A good example is a sweepstakes offered by Visa that converts every credit card transaction into a sweepstakes entry. The promotion encourages cardholders to use their Visa card more frequently than usual. Behavioral goals are primarily achieved through promotional offers such as rebates, product samples, or discounts if customers purchase or express interest in a product.

- *An example of a behavioral goal might be: "300,000 new unique visitors will access our promotional Web site by March 2010."*

Relational Goals You work for a company that sends you on overnight business trips at least once a week. Hotel rooms are like a second home for you. When you check in at a particular hotel that you frequent, they remember that you are allergic to down pillows, so the front desk attendant tells you, "We've prepared your room with down-free pillows; is that your preference?" This hotel is showing a high degree of customer service toward you, as you are a frequent customer and your loyalty is important.

What does the hotel hope to achieve by treating you like a VIP? By establishing a higher standard of customer service, this company is forming a positive relationship with its customers, which should pay dividends in the long run. The hotel's goals in this case are **relational goals**: they want customers to know their brand as a friend and trusted partner.

- *An example of a relational goal might be: "Among our target business audience, more than 60 percent will opt in to receive weekly e-mails about our new building projects and specials by January 2011."*

Making SMART Marketing Communication Goals

Is this a SMART goal?

Marketing communication goals ought to have a few key attributes. Remember the SMART goal acronym from Chapter 9? This applies to marketing communication goals as well.

- First of all, the goals should be *Specific*. For instance, a behavioral goal for a company selling toddler toys might be to have 55 percent of parents make two or more toy purchases within 12 months.
- Goals need to be *Measurable*. Once again, "let's make more money" is no good. A measurable behavior goal might be to have 50 percent of your customers return for repeat business by next July.
- Setting goals is pointless if they are not *Attainable*. There's nothing wrong with setting the bar high, but if a business decides it's going to aim for something completely unrealistic (like doubling its profits in the next month), it will only risk disappointment and loss of morale. An attainable psychological goal might be to have 75 percent of customers surveyed say that they associate your product with quality, safety, and sustainability.
- Are your goals *Relevant*? Do your goals also serve a purpose that helps achieve the company's vision and mission? For example, a psychological goal of being viewed as an environmentally friendly company would work well for a company whose ultimate goal is to become a green company.
- Lastly, what is the *Time* frame in which you want to achieve your goals? A relational goal might be to have 25 percent of customers provide feedback of their experiences within 30 days of their purchase.

■ You can choose the goals most appropriate for your marketing campaign by paying attention to who your target audience is and how you want them to react to your marketing.

By using the SMART guidelines and setting realistic goals, an organization can find ways to make its marketing campaign serve its purpose, and serve it well.

The AIDA Model

Although having SMART goals is important, so is having a process to see those goals to fruition. Sometimes, companies use the **AIDA model** as a process to move customers through their SMART goals. AIDA stands for **A**ttention, **I**nterest, **D**esire, and **A**ction. SMART goals specify details that make the goals work; the AIDA model specifies how those goals will be achieved.

1. The first step involves attracting the customer's *attention* to your product. This could mean running ads about your product, or doing a sampling so that potential customers can try your product and be aware of it.
2. The second step involves piquing customers' *interest* in such a way that they want to learn more about your product. Maybe you offer coupons or you have a witty slogan that intrigues your audience.
3. The third step is getting the customer to want (or *desire*) to buy your product. For example, you can make sure your product stands out from the competition by clearly focusing your marketing message on its superior features and value.
4. The final step is *action*, or getting the customer to act and purchase your product, much like the behavioral goal we discussed earlier. For example, you make the product easy for them to purchase by telling them where they can get the product. You can do this by providing a phone number, an address, a Web address, or a store name within your advertisement.

Table **14.1** | **Aligning the AIDA Model and SMART Goals to the Customer Decision-Making Process**

Customer Decision-Making Step		AIDA Goals
Identify a need or problem	Attention	Create brand awareness among 80 percent of the target market by June 2010.
Identify alternatives	Interest	Generate preference for our brand vs. brand B among 60 percent of our target market by August 2010.
Evaluate alternatives	Desire	Create an intention to purchase our product among 35 percent of target market by December 2010.
Make the purchase	Action	Secure 30,000 orders by March 2011.
Evaluate the purchase		Achieve 75 percent repurchase rate among existing customers by June 2011.

Businesses create SMART goals and consider how to walk customers through the AIDA process to get a sense of what they want from their marketing campaigns. Take a look at Table 14.1 to get an idea of how the AIDA process aligns with the marketing communication goals and the consumer decision-making process we discussed in Chapter 12. ■ You can choose the goals most appropriate for your marketing campaign by paying attention to who your target audience is and how you want them to react to your marketing. After that, you can move to the next step: choosing the promotional tools you will use to accomplish these goals.

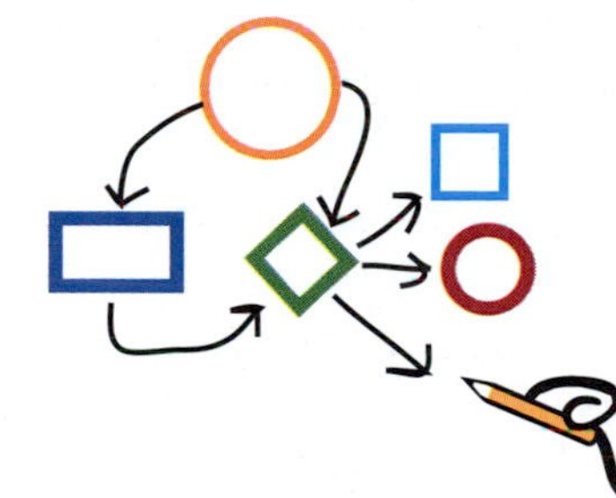

Do It...

14.1: Establish Marketing Communication Goals Write two examples for each type of marketing communication goal discussed in this section, making sure they are SMART (specific, measurable, attainable, relevant, and time-based). Be prepared to submit your goals electronically or to discuss them in class.

Now Debrief...

- **Marketing communication goals** provide an essential foundation for a **marketing campaign**. They describe the reaction and response that the marketer wants to get from the target audience as a result of their marketing communications. Organizations often use **integrated marketing communications** to send a consistent, unified message across all of their communications.
- Marketing communication goals may be:
  - **affective goals**, in which a company wants customers to feel or have an emotional reaction to a company or brand;
  - **psychological goals**, in which a company wants customers to think or associate something with that product or brand;
  - **behavioral goals**, in which a company wants customers to act in a particular way; and/or
  - **relational goals**, in which a company wants customers to trust and relate to their company or brand.
- It is important for marketing communication goals to be SMART: specific, measurable, attainable, relevant, and time-based.
- Some companies consider the **AIDA** (Attention, Interest, Desire, Action) **model** when attempting to accomplish their SMART marketing communication goals.

2. Tools of the Trade: Marketing Tools in the Promotional Mix

Let's say you're the head marketer for a new company that focuses on creating recycled and sustainable products, such as printing paper and disposable paper goods. You've picked your target audience and you have your marketing communication goals in place; now what?

Your next step is thinking about how you will get the word out about your product. What will you say? How will you say it?

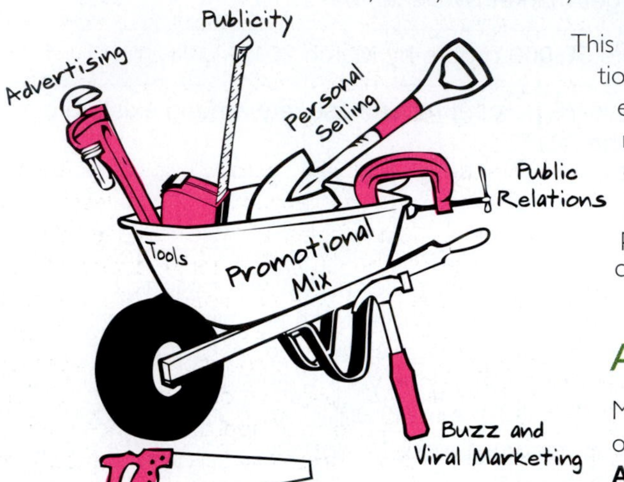

Which tools do you see used most often?

This is where promotion comes into play. **Promotion** is an organization's method of explaining what it offers, garnering customers' interest in that product, gaining their trust in the organization, and motivating them to act. These days there's a veritable smorgasbord of tools available for marketers to achieve their promotional goals. Marketers call this tool kit the **promotional mix**. Marketers can pick and choose the tools from the promotional mix that best accomplish their marketing communication goals.

Advertising

Maybe your preferred method of getting your company's name out there is to buy a commercial slot on TV or the radio. **Advertising** is when a company pays for the promotion of a product. When a company invests in advertisements, it controls the content of its ads in the hopes of achieving a particular marketing communication goal.

Let's use the recycled paper company. Your goal might be to increase the number of corporate customers by 40 percent by the end of the year. To do this, you might buy a page in a business magazine to run an ad that demonstrates office workers using one of your company's recycled products. This paid advertisement allows you to specifically target your audience (corporations and office workers), which should help you accomplish your goal (to increase the number of your corporate customers).

Paid advertising can be an effective way to get your message to a specific target audience. However, television commercials and radio slots can get expensive, and they may not be feasible for small or start-up businesses. Instead, marketers for one of these companies may choose a different tool to promote their product.

Publicity

A company that decides a commercial is beyond its budget may try finding another way to get its name out in the market. Instead of spending money on ad placements, it may decide to sponsor an event that features its products. If a newspaper reporter attends the event and then writes an article about the company, the company is benefiting from publicity. **Publicity** is the information about the company or product that reaches the public in a way that is not paid for or controlled by that company. The newspaper reporter who writes about the company is not being paid by the company to write the article, so any business the company receives because of the article is a result of publicity.

A company might try to use publicity if it has an affective goal. For instance, your recycled paper company might participate in an Earth Day concert as a way to have customers associate your brand with environmental awareness and being a fun and hip company. This event allows you to attract potential customers who are environmentally aware and part of your company's target audience.

Publicity is a cheaper way for businesses to get the word out about their company and product. In addition, customers often trust publicity more than advertising because no one pays for publicity. However, the company has no control over what information is distributed to the public, and it is just as easy to receive bad publicity—such as a poor restaurant review—as it is to receive publicity that will align with the company's marketing communication goals.

Sales and Trade Promotions

Sometimes companies will use short-term activities to boost customer awareness of their products. For instance, when the economy began to slump in 2008, people cut back on spending. To fill their empty tables, restaurant owners began cooking up promotions in response to the economic climate. Domino's Pizza started advertising its "big taste bailout package" promotion: three pizzas for $5 each. The small, startup restaurant Mobatta Crepes in downtown Seattle advertised a new "breakfast bailout": $1 breakfast crepes for a week.

The restaurant used the recession as a marketing hook to bring in customers. **Sales promotions**—contests, sweepstakes, coupons, free product samples, and other "limited-time" offers to attract consumers' attention—are a long-standing component of the marketer's tool kit. Some promotions, like discounts on oil changes or coupons for pizza deals, have a large target market. Both oil changes and pizza are commonly purchased by people across a wide range of consumer demographics. Other promotions may have a more focused approach, concentrating on specific consumers within a larger market. For instance, a restaurant may offer a senior discount promotion in which the breakfast buffet is only $5 for anyone over the age of 70.

However, promotions aren't just limited to communications between businesses and private consumers; **trade promotions** are an important part of B2B marketing strategy. Employee discounts, trade shows, and discounts on items bought in bulk are all examples of this type of promotion.

Suppose your company's marketing communication goal is to have consumers buy two or more of your product at a time. You may choose to run a coupon campaign that gives customers discounts on items bought in bulk. Sales promotions can help bring in business, but they can be costly, too, if they are not targeted to the right market.

Personal Selling

Many organizations, particularly those that sell to other businesses, invest more of their marketing budget on personal selling than any other marketing communications tool. **Personal selling** is when you present your products face-to-face with your customer, whether you're meeting with a prospective customer or doing a follow-up to learn about a customer's experiences. In fact, in many organizations, it is the top salespeople—more than ads or other promotional tools—who attract new customers, secure new orders for products and services, and keep customers satisfied over the long run. Often, a real person or even a team of people are necessary to work with the customer to provide product information and build relationships.

Although personal selling is the most expensive form of marketing communications on a per-customer basis, the investment is often worth the expense. Let's say your recycled paper company's goal is to get more large corporations as customers. You might send a sales representative or a sales team to a potential client to create a company-specific sales plan, showing your prospective client which of your products would best suit their needs, and perhaps offer discounts on selected products for a limited time. Although it might cost your company a fair amount of money up front, a successful business venture could generate a large amount of repeat business for your company in the future.

Public Relations

Forming personal relations with customers is just part of marketing your company's product. You also need to maintain your public image—that is, how your company interacts with all of the other people involved in your company (its stakeholders), including customers, employees, and shareholders. To do this, your company can use **public relations**, the efforts a company undergoes to build and maintain relationships, increase favorable publicity, create a positive company image, and deal with any unfavorable or negative feedback your company receives.

Having good public relations is a key factor to creating and maintaining successful relationships. Public relations are an essential, and sometimes overlooked, part of the marketing strategy. As we mentioned in Chapter 8, socially responsible business practices generate good PR, and good PR generally has a direct impact on profits. Take the recycled paper company, for instance. Let's say a disgruntled former employee claims in a local newspaper article that the company does not really use recycled materials in its paper. The public relations (PR) department in the company could contact the local media and arrange a press conference at the paper plant to refute the claims. The PR department could also e-mail its shareholders and customers to provide documented evidence that it uses only recycled materials. It could also arrange for tours of the plant for school children and their parents during school breaks. By sending a timely, consistent message, the paper company maintains a trustworthy relationship with its key stakeholders.

Buzz and Viral Marketing

Ultimately, companies use these promotional tools to get their name out and promote their products. Whether they choose advertisement or personal selling, a company hopes that it will reach and influence as many potential clients as possible while spending as little money as possible.

Buzz Marketing Perhaps the cheapest way to promote a product is through **buzz marketing**, which is a fancy way of describing marketing information that travels by good, old-fashioned word-of-mouth. For instance, suppose you visit a new restaurant and have an excellent experience: the location is convenient, the pricing is reasonable, the service is great, and the food is fantastic. You tell all of your friends about how great the new restaurant is, inspiring some of them to try it for themselves. They enjoy their dinner so much that they tell their friends, and so forth. And you're probably not the only one who had a good experience. Suppose five other customers go home and also tell their friends, who try it and then tell their friends, etc. Buzz marketing is a fast and virtually free type of promotion that spreads the word about a product without the company having to do anything.

Viral Marketing YouTube videos that seem to become an overnight sensation are part of **viral marketing**—a form of buzz marketing that utilizes the Internet, text messaging, or other social media. For, example, in a recent YouTube video, a group of friends sits around a coffee table with their cell phones pointed inward at a few kernels of popcorn. As the phones sitting on the table all go off at once, there is a spontaneous popping of the popcorn kernels. *Yikes*, you might think. *If that's what cell phones do to popcorn, imagine what my phone is doing to my brain every time I make a call!*

That's just what Cardo, a maker of Bluetooth headsets, wanted viewers to think. Impressed viewers shared the video with their friends, until over 4.1 million people had viewed it. The company eventually came clean about its video "joke," but the buzz undoubtedly made Bluetooth technology a lot more popular. And the cost of making the low-production-quality videos can't have come close to the cost of reaching 4.1 million viewers through traditional promotional media.[3]

Viral marketing, when it works, is one of the sweetest deals a company could hope for. It's practically free, it spreads like wildfire, and by definition it necessitates user involvement. With social networking sites and e-mail list servs, news can spread exponentially within minutes. Viral marketing relies on creating person-to-person "buzz" to increase brand awareness. In fact, if you belong to a social network or newsgroup, you're probably already aware of recent successful viral marketing, such as YouTube video links that have been posted on Facebook.

So, how would your recycled paper company use viral marketing? Let's say your affective marketing communication goal is to further increase your company's fun and hip image among your customers. You might create a video showing office employees using your products to goof off while the boss is away, then post the video in multiple places on the Internet. If you're successful in catching your audience's attention, your company could gain a lot of overnight exposure and popularity. If not, you're only out as much as it cost to produce and post the video.

Choosing the Best Tool

As we've discussed throughout this section, companies pick and choose promotional tools that best help them accomplish their marketing communication goals. A company with an affective goal may not wish to promote a "buy one, get one free" coupon campaign, just as a company with a behavioral goal may not focus on spending its marketing budget on sponsoring events that promote health awareness. By using the proper marketing tools that best compliment your communication goals, you can create a powerful marketing strategy and choose the best types of media to promote your product. Table 14.2 lists the advantages and disadvantages of the various promotional tools.

Table **14.2** | **Advantages and Disadvantages of Promotional Tools**

Tools	Advantages	Disadvantages
Advertising	Companies are able to control the content of their ads as well as specifically target a desired audience.	Television and radio slots, as well as newspaper, magazine, and Web space, can get expensive. This tool may not be feasible for small or start-up businesses.
Publicity	A cheaper way to get the word out about a company or product. Customers also tend to trust publicity because a company does not pay for it.	A company has no control over when or what type of publicity becomes widespread. Bad publicity can have a negative effect on businesses or may not communicate the company's goals.
Sales and Trade Promotions	They provide incentives for customers to take direct action.	Promotions can be costly and may lead customers to wait to act until they receive a coupon offer or special deal. They also have the potential to devalue a brand name.
Personal Selling	Personal selling establishes long-term relationships that may ensure repeat business.	This is the most expensive form of marketing communication on a per-customer basis.
Public Relations	Generally, public relations is thought of as being more credible than advertising. It can also be an inexpensive way of reaching customers.	Like publicity, public relations can be unpredictable because a company doesn't have direct control over the behavior of its stakeholders.
Buzz and Viral Marketing	The cheapest form of promotion, it can spread to a large audience rapidly at minimal cost. It also necessitates active user involvement.	It must be especially catchy and original to motivate users to pass along information without outside incentive. The company also has little control over where, what, when, and to whom the message is sent.

Do It...

14.2: Match Tools to Goals Select one of the marketing communication goals you created for the Do It on page 341. Choose three promotional tools you would use to accomplish this goal, and explain your choices. Be prepared to submit your work electronically or to discuss it in class.

Now Debrief...

- Marketers use the tools in the **promotional mix** as a way to successfully meet marketing communication goals:
  - **Advertising** is a promotional tool in which the company pays to get information about its product out to the public.
  - **Publicity** is a tool in which information about a company is distributed to the public without the company paying for it.
  - **Sales promotions** are short-term or limited time offers, including coupons, discounts, and product samples, meant to draw in customers. **Trade promotions**, such as employee discounts and trade shows, are targeted at other businesses and employees.
  - **Personal selling** is a tool that involves direct face-to-face interaction between a company representative and a customer.
  - **Public relations** is how a company interacts with the world by building relationships, promoting a positive corporate image, and handling any unfavorable rumors or publicity.
  - **Buzz** and **viral marketing** are word-of-mouth marketing tools that are virtually free to the company.

3. Creative Strategies and Media Vehicles: Getting Your Message Out

"In a world where we have too many choices and too little time, the obvious thing to do is ignore stuff."

—Marketing entrepreneur Seth Godin[4]

On April 1st, 1996, a full-page ad appeared in the *New York Times* and six other newspapers across the country, announcing that the Taco Bell restaurant chain had just purchased the Liberty Bell in an effort to help reduce the national debt, renaming the monument the Taco Liberty Bell. People were up in arms. Thousands of Americans called the National Historic Park in Philadelphia to protest, and news about the stunt generated nearly 1,000 media releases before noon that day, when the company announced that the advertisement had been a huge April Fool's Joke.

The upshot of this elaborate joke? Taco Bell's sales increased by over $1 million in the next two days, and the free publicity surrounding the prank was equivalent to the results of about $25 million in advertising efforts.[5] Pretty nifty, considering that Taco Bell only paid $300,000 to run the ads. The company coined the term "publitisement" to refer to the media publicity that allowed Taco Bell to meet its advertising goal: cutting through the general advertising clutter to reach customers in a memorable way and portraying the company as hip, unique, and fun.[6]

These days, innovative marketing campaigns like this one are the messages that stand out. Advertisements are everywhere we go, and more and more, the trick for companies looking to sell us something is to find a way to cut through the racket to make their voices heard. No longer can a company solely rely on the traditional, one-way advertising methods so common to TV commercials (*I'm going to tell you what's so great about my product*) and hope that people will pay attention. The average person on the street is too overloaded with random advertisements to care about or even notice your product. Unless, of course, your message has something truly unique and noteworthy to set it apart.

While the Taco Bell stunt was a brilliant advertising move, David Paine, the founder of Paine PR, the public relations agency that executed the ad, thinks such a trick would no longer be as effective, observing that the general atmosphere today is one of greater caution in believing such things without more evidence.[7] The question for a marketing team is what *would* be successful, given the current environment. Just as companies have to find the best distribution channel to get their product from the point of being manufactured to the point of being consumed (a topic we'll discuss in more detail in Chapter 16), in the same way, marketers need to develop a creative strategy that figures out the best media channels to deliver their message to customers.

Coming up with a Creative Strategy

Marketers will ask themselves, "How can we best present this product as the best choice to fulfill customers' wants and needs?" ■ You have a limited amount of time to get and keep the customer's attention, and at the same time you must differentiate yourself from your competitors. Because of this, you must boil your message down to the core elements. You can start this by looking at your marketing communication goal and determining what you want as a response to your advertising. With your goal in mind, you need to establish a plan for getting these desired results. **Creative strategy** involves figuring out the marketing message and how to get it to your target audience.

During the creative strategy period, the marketing team decides what they're going to say and how they're going to say it. Communicating a message involves more than just words. Think about your personal creative strategy for a minute. When you go on a job interview, you want to communicate professionalism, responsibility, and other qualities that make you come across as employable. Every aspect of your appearance and behavior communicates something about you, whether you're conscious of it or not, and the same can be said of an organization. If a company wants to deliver a certain message about a product, consistency is key, because everything the company does is part of that message.

■ You have a limited amount of time to get and keep the customer's attention, and at the same time you must differentiate yourself from your competitors. Because of this, you must boil your message down to the core elements.

Taco Bell has aimed to portray itself as unique, edgy, and fun to specifically differentiate itself from the plethora of fast-food joints across the country. Their earlier tag line of the 90s, "Nothing ordinary about it," was more recently replaced by the promotional message: "Think outside the bun." The message is essentially the same and has consistently been supported by offbeat and slightly irreverent advertising efforts. The key is that the company uses the right strategy for its message. In other words, the promotional campaign is effective in conveying the image that Taco Bell desires.

The Creative Brief So, how do companies keep their creative strategy consistent? At this stage in the planning process, the marketing team prepares a **creative brief** that captures the essence of the company's message. The brief, usually a document or a presentation, ensures that everyone is on the same page before the company moves forward with its promotional efforts. A creative brief may include something like what is shown in Figure 14.1.

Figure **14.1** | **A Sample Creative Brief**

Explanation	Creative Brief
Here is where you identify the project.	**Project:** New marketing campaign to introduce our new line of bamboo fiber fleece wear
This is the place for some big picture scanning. What's going on in the external environment that might affect your campaign? What conditions *within* the organization will be relevant to consider?	**Background and Overview:** There are currently few competitors who offer clothing that uses bamboo fiber. However, more and more customers are looking for these types of products because they are environmentally friendly and sustainable. Customers are becoming more aware of the environmental costs of clothing production and are cutting back on spending money on many pieces of clothing in favor of buying a few high-quality and environmentally-friendly pieces. Our company will need to evaluate how green our manufacturing process is and change our focus to quality rather than quantity.
Here you briefly state your marketing communication goals. What effect will your communication have on customers? What do you want customers to believe, feel, or do?	**Promotional Goal:** These promotions need to show our company in a trendy, hip, and environmentally friendly setting. We want customers to view our brand as having high quality, while also being responsibly and sustainably produced. We want customers to feel good when they buy our clothing, and we want to form long-lasting relationships with our customers that will lead to repeat business.
Here you state who your promotion is supposed to appeal to and who you want to buy your product.	**Target Market:** Our target market feels strongly about the environment and sustainability. Our target group is mostly teenagers and young adults aged 15–25.
If you had to distill everything down to one message, one sentence, what would it be? This part of the brief is where you write the most important thing you can say to achieve your marketing communication goal.	**Essential Message:** We sell quality products with a conscience; we are always looking for ways that we can better serve the environment and our global community.
People don't usually act a certain way or believe something unless it's for a good reason. Your brief should explore the reasons why your target market should respond the way you want them to.	**Reasons for the Audience to Respond:** Consumers should be moved by the fact that we make sustainable clothing and that we care about the environment. Consumers who are like-minded will want to buy our products because they know we are mindful about how our entire production process affects local and global environments.
Here you identify what you'll need from the people who will be creating the marketing campaign—and when you'll need it. What media are you using for your marketing efforts (a Web site, brochures, TV)? What is your timeline?	**Schedule:** We will need magazine spreads and online advertisements out in public view by the end of July so that we can start promoting our line with other fall fashions. This means we need to start our design process by January, and have final examples done by May. We can do later online promotions on Twitter as the products are released.

Media Vehicles

Part of any marketing campaign is determining how to get your message out to your target audience, and how to get feedback from your customers. **Media vehicles** are the methods you use to get your message out, whether they are print advertising, television commercials, or interactive online platforms. More often than not, marketing involves taking advantage of recently developed technologies and communication methods to reach customers.

Marketing 1.0

In Chapter 12, we talked about the selling era of marketing and how manufacturers needed to convince customers to buy their products. To make their products visible to clients, they used promotional posters and large advertisements in places where there would be the most traffic and potential customers.

Today, billboards are still a common sight along highways and expressways, their messages posted for everyone passing by to read and absorb. Same goes for the ads you see in magazines and direct-mail circulars you get in your mailbox. Marketers who use this type of advertisement want to get their marketing message out to as many people as possible and have a less focused target group. This type of marketing is called **marketing 1.0**.

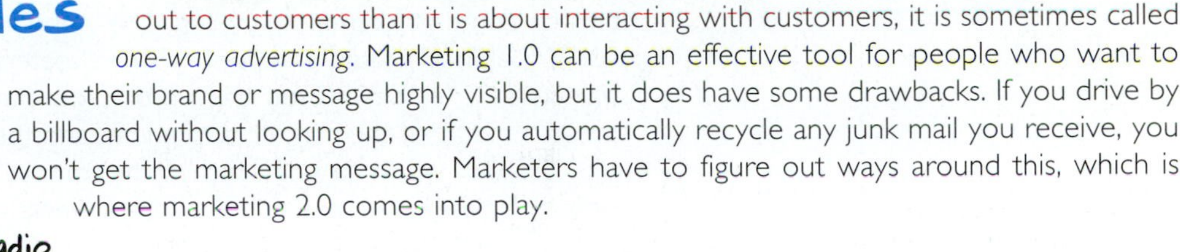

Because the focus of this type of advertising is more about getting the word out to customers than it is about interacting with customers, it is sometimes called *one-way advertising*. Marketing 1.0 can be an effective tool for people who want to make their brand or message highly visible, but it does have some drawbacks. If you drive by a billboard without looking up, or if you automatically recycle any junk mail you receive, you won't get the marketing message. Marketers have to figure out ways around this, which is where marketing 2.0 comes into play.

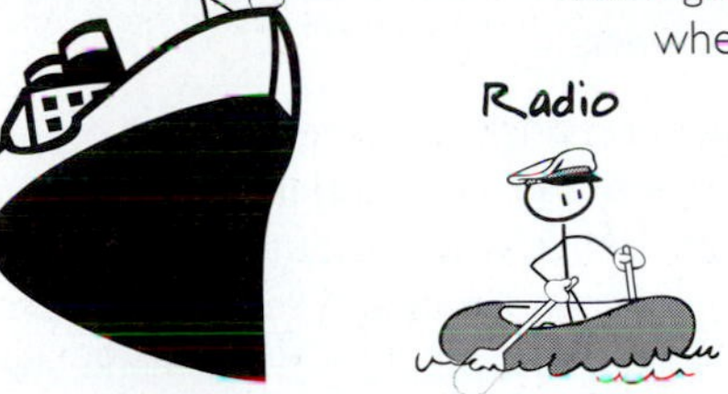

Marketing 2.0 New technology means new ways to market a product. In **marketing 2.0**, marketers use marketing 1.0 ideas with more advanced technology, such as television and the radio. Marketing 2.0 techniques focus on a more targeted audience; marketers can choose to advertise during programs they think their target audience might watch, and have 15- to 30-second commercials on radio stations they think most of their audience might listen to. *Telemarketing* is another 2.0 technique; companies can call up individuals or businesses to play recorded messages to their selected audience.

The 1990s gave rise to an additional form of technology that marketers quickly adapted. With the rising popularity and increasing capabilities of the Internet, marketers found a way to utilize this new marketplace. For instance, how many times have you gone to a Web page with pop-ups ads? How about banners that open a new window when you click them? Similar to the billboards along the road, these types of advertisements are meant to catch your attention and display a marketing message to as many people as possible. They can also be cheaper than renting space on a billboard or placing a commercial during prime-time TV. But what stops someone from closing out of that pop-up or using TiVo to fast-forward through commercials? Marketers needed to find a more effective way to get their message to customers, and so they looked for new ways to utilize this popular technology with so much marketing potential.

Marketing 3.0 One particularly exciting change in communications and information sharing in recent years has been the rise of **Web 2.0**. The term refers to the rise of social networking sites, blogs, wikis, and virtual communities that provide convenient platforms for people to share information and collaborate. Did you know that today the combined population of MySpace and Facebook is greater than the population of the United States?[8] Web 2.0 offers a wealth of opportunity for savvy marketers. These sites are user-driven media, which means that unlike earlier forms of marketing where copywriters simply wrote scripts for advertisements and commercials, in Web 2.0 marketing, users in a social network construct their own content. Taking advantage of these opportunities requires businesses to re-orient themselves to a new marketing mind-set, and that can be both intimidating and challenging.[9]

Just as this new way of thinking about the Internet has been termed Web 2.0, the new marketing mindset inspired by this shift is described by some as **marketing 3.0**. In this type of marketing, customers become active participants in the co-creation of the product, marketing messages about the product, and how the product is used and consumed. Customers who have embraced Web 2.0 tools want to be active friends of a company's brand. This approach can be risky because the marketer surrenders a lot of control over content, design, and process, but it can also lead to much stronger and more enduring relationships between companies and their customers. Let's look at some Web 2.0 tools.

The Internet Many marketers are now using the Internet as a platform for both spreading awareness of their product and interacting with consumers, both of which can be achieved in a variety of ways.

- **Twitter:** Companies are using this fast-paced, network-driven online community as a platform for contests to create buzz and raise brand awareness. One Web site-building company, Moonfruit, hosted a contest where tweeters had to write a short paragraph (140 characters or less) that used the word "moonfruit" somewhere within the text. Word spread throughout the Twitter community, and the company saw a 130-percent increase in its followers within days of launching the contest.[10] Relying on word-of-mouth alone, the company's contest went viral in less than a week.
- **Blogs:** These commentary-driven sites have increasingly become a part of online social networking, as bloggers respond to other bloggers, and Web surfers post their responses to bloggers' messages and share blog links with friends when something sparks their interest. When companies connect with people at the ground level and get their customers to generate positive publicity, they can tap into hugely successful forms of marketing communications. This is something you could add to your company's Web site for little money and with relative ease. Do you think a customer blog feature would help increase your business? At the very least it could make you more aware of what your customers are thinking and saying about your company.
- **Social Networking Sites:** In 2007, the popular social networking site Facebook introduced an advertising system in which companies could create profile pages similar to user profiles. Members of Facebook could now affiliate themselves with brands they loved in the same way they affiliated themselves with friends. In a press release, the networking site explained that the new system "facilitates the spread of brand messages virally through Facebook Social Ads," allowing businesses to join existing conversations and to spark new ones.[11] More recently, the application has been refined to publish user activity on a company's wall, similar to the running news feeds on user profile pages. This allows a brand's followers to connect to an even greater degree than before, providing more opportunity for viral marketing and company visibility.[12]

Cell phones Modern advertising techniques have given jukeboxes a serious facelift. In the old days, you would drop some change into a box and push a button to play a song of your choice. Now, you can text message the name of your favorite song, music video, or sports clip, using Akoo International's new M-Venue application, and the content will be broadcast across the sound systems and onto flat screens at your local bar or burger joint. The take? No longer a couple of quarters. Instead, users give their permission to receive promotional communications and offers in exchange for on-demand access to the service. Now that's creative marketing.[13]

Such cell phone-based forms of interactive marketing have proven quite successful in recent years, as the mobile phone has become practically another appendage for members of the Millennial generation. Opt-in marketing messages for cell phones receive about 10 times the attention that traditional Internet banner ads get.[14] The trick is that users are getting incentives to accept the marketing, whereas much of the other advertising out there comes at them unsolicited. Additionally, this form of marketing helps build customers' trust because people perceive it as more transparent. Take Vodafone's technique of offering free phone minutes or text messages in exchange for voluntary advertising downloads, or Coca-Cola's mobile community, the Sprite Yard. The Sprite Yard offers a social networking venue where people can share content, such as ring tones and short video clips, by opting in to the corporate-sponsored platform.[15]

New Twists on Older Technology Although more and more companies are using newer technologies to promote their marketing message, this doesn't mean they've abandoned older marketing methods. In essence, marketers are finding new ways of using advertising media to greater effect.

- **Billboards:** *Billboards* have been around since the 1860s, but today's digital billboards can switch their messages throughout the day to better target the right audiences: people commuting to and from work during rush hour, stay-at-home parents or retired people traveling mid-day, and a younger crowd out on the town in the evenings. For even finer tuning, some digital billboards are able to detect the radio stations playing in passing cars and display the message that best fits the identified demographic for that station's listeners. This helps marketers use their resources more efficiently: they won't be shelling out the big bucks to display their messages to the audiences who aren't likely to pay attention.[16]

- **Product placement:** *Product placement* is a powerful technique for a company to get its product recognized. When people see their favorite actor using a product in a movie or on TV, they may consider using it, too. What if you could get a screenshot of your Web site to show on a laptop during an episode of CSI? The recognition you could get among the young professional crowd could help springboard your company straight to the top.
- **Plot placement:** *Plot placement* takes product placement one step farther by incorporating a company or brand directly into the plot of the show. In *Project Runway*, for example, several brands have been used as an integral part of the show's plot.

Determining Your Media Vehicles

With all of these different types of marketing available, how do you choose which media vehicle is right for you? It all comes down to your audience. Which form of media are they most likely to use? Chances are, if you're targeting senior citizens, you won't use Twitter to get your word out, just as you wouldn't run commercials for teenagers during a school day. Table 14.3

Table **14.3** | **Advantages and Disadvantages of Various Media Vehicles**

Media	Advantages	Disadvantages
Billboards	• Highly visible	• Less focused target group (for traditional, non-digital billboards) • Easily ignored
Direct Mail	• Can be used to reach specific target audiences • Can offer customers very specific messages and promotions	• Can be expensive • Often thrown away
Television	• Enables a media-rich message that captures attention	• Expensive • Technology such as Tivo allows viewers to skip ads
Newspapers	• Newspapers can be passed from one person to another • Ads can be updated frequently	• Easily ignored • Ads compete for attention with other content
Magazines	• High-quality color ads can attract attention	• Easily ignored • Ads compete for attention with other content • Take a long time to plan and distribute
Radio	• Potential to target to select audiences • Lower cost than some other media vehicles	• Easily ignored • Exposure time is short
Internet	• Potential for interaction with customers • Can be easier to reach target audience • Depending on use, can be inexpensive	• Doesn't always reach desired target audience
Cell Phones	• Opt-in marketing messages receive more attention than traditional methods	• Consumers may react negatively to receiving unsolicited messages on their cell phones

lists the advantages and disadvantages of various media vehicles. Marketers must keep their target audience in mind as they choose the vehicles that will be most effective. In essence, they need to be selective and design a promotional mix that delivers the most bang for their promotional bucks.

Do It...

14.3: Analyze Media Vehicles Watch a television show and identify a particular ad that catches your attention. Describe it briefly, identify who you think the ad's target market is, and explain why it caught your attention. Then, identify two media vehicles besides TV advertising that you think would work to promote the product to its intended audience, and two that would not. Be prepared to submit your work electronically or to discuss it in class.

Now Debrief...

- After companies have determined their marketing communication goals, they use **creative strategy** to decide what their marketing message will be. During the creative strategy period, marketing teams draft a **creative brief** to make sure everyone's on the same page before moving forward with the marketing campaign.
- Companies use different types of **media vehicles** to implement their creative strategies.
- Marketers have used three different approaches to get consumers' attention: marketing 1.0, marketing 2.0, and marketing 3.0.
  - **Marketing 1.0** is a type of marketing in which marketers want to get their message out to as many people as possible, and use media vehicles such as billboards, posters, and newspaper advertisements.
  - **Marketing 2.0** is a type of marketing in which marketers use technology to promote marketing 1.0 ideas. Pop-ups, online banners, telemarketing, and television and radio commercials are all types of marketing 2.0 media.
  - **Marketing 3.0** is a type of marketing in which marketers interact with customers to get a marketing message out. Interactive media such as **Web 2.0** tools promote word-of-mouth advertising as customers participate in writing content.
- Marketers must choose the media vehicles that best suit their creative strategy and marketing communication goals. They can do this by focusing on their target audience and choosing a form of media that their audience is most likely to use.

4. Customer Service: Building Relationships for Better Customer Satisfaction

When someone attempts to communicate with you, isn't it more effective when the person talks with you, rather than at you? This is true in marketing as well. It's a more effective strategy if your organization uses an interactive approach to customer service by asking, "What kind of conversation do we want to have with our customers?" For example, Quicken, a type of personal finance software, hosts an online discussion board where users interact with product experts and other customers to help solve technical problems, generate new product applications, and rant about bugs and crashes.

> Customer service is more than just talking to your customers; it's about interaction with and reaction to the people inside and outside of your organization.

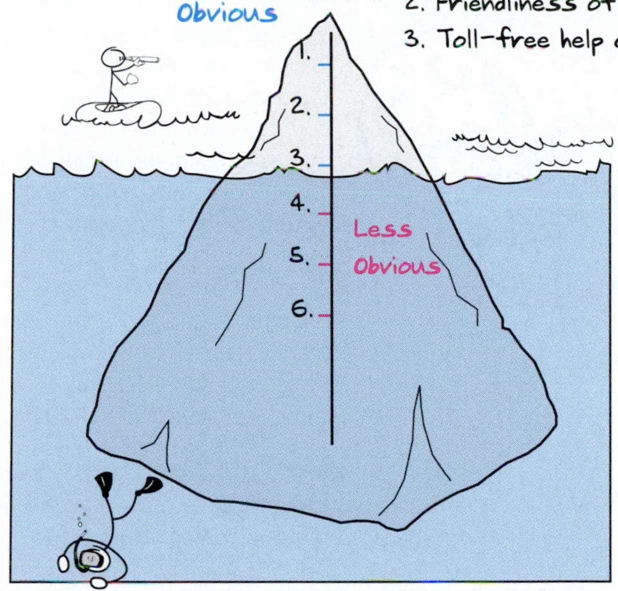

In the same way, isn't it always more fun to do something *together*? Developing a relationship with customers gives your company personality. This is the essence of the experiential approach taken by many companies. They ask the question, "What kind of *experience* do we want to have with our customers?" On Earth Day in 2009, the Jones Soda company invited employees and customers to come into their corporate headquarters to take turns cycling on one of 10 bikes that were set up to generate all the power the company would need to run its operations that day. Customers were invited to get onboard with the company's sustainable energy practice—and sample some free soda while doing it.

As we've discussed throughout the book, developing a personal relationship with customers is the most reliable method of getting them to be loyal to your company. These relationships also naturally spread good publicity about your company. ■ Customer service is more than just talking to your customers; it's about interaction with and reaction to the people inside and outside of your organization. In this section, we'll look at the different ways companies can improve their customer satisfaction by improving customer service and all that it entails.

Communicating with Your Customers

Rumor has it that in 1975, Nordstrom, the upscale department store, wanted to expand its business in Alaska, so the company purchased three store locations from the Northern Commercial Company (NCC), an outfit that sold, among other things, car tires. Shortly after the Nordstrom stores opened, a customer came in with a return. Not realizing that the

NCC department stores had been sold to a new company, the man hoisted a set of tires onto the counter and asked for his money back. Without even batting an eye, the Nordstrom customer service representative asked the man how much the tires had cost, then opened the cash register and handed him the money, inviting him to come back and shop again.[17]

The jury is out on whether this story actually happened or whether it's just an urban legend, but the legend has hung on tenaciously for years as an illustration of Nordstrom's "the customer is always right" service policy. The company, which is known for its customer service, has been around for more than 100 years and is ranked in the Fortune 500. The secret to its success, according to a number of sources, is the value the company has historically placed on relationships with customers. During WWII, when shoe stores across the nation were struggling to get enough merchandise because of government rationing, the Nordstrom family traveled to Midwest manufacturing hubs like Milwaukee and St. Louis to meet personally with shoe manufacturers in an effort to increase their share of inventory. And the efforts proved fruitful; by forming friendships with suppliers, the company made it through tight times when a number of other retailers were shutting down.[18]

Even though the store has drastically expanded since then, they've managed to keep the same spirit, which you might know if you've ever tried to return something at a Nordstrom's store. Because of its customer-driven focus, Nordstrom has many loyal customers.

Customer Service: Getting Feedback and Using It

As marketing communications expert Pattie Simone says, customer service is a business tool that's "obvious, overlooked, and cheap."[19] Businesspeople know that it's always less expensive to hang onto the customers they already have than to put huge efforts into attracting new ones. In fact, bringing in a new customer costs about five times as much as retaining an old customer does.[20] And even more surprising is a fact that applies across industries: if your organization can increase its yearly customer retention by 5 percent or more, your profits will increase anywhere from 25 to 50 percent![21]

The good news is that there's no great secret to building this kind of customer loyalty—it just requires a business to listen to what the customer wants. Think about the last time someone asked you to recommend a good restaurant. You might have mentioned that one restaurant has excellent food but high prices and mediocre service, whereas another restaurant has better prices but a hit-or-miss menu. Your overall evaluation of the restaurant depends on the criteria that are most important to you and how well the place in question meets your expectations in those areas.

Customer report cards and surveys can be good for getting a broad idea of the way customers feel about an organization, but if you want to get more specific—particularly when it comes to discovering positive changes you can make to meet customer needs—other information-gathering methods like focus groups, personal interviews, and careful observations can help.

Moments of Truth Listening to the voice of the customer and then implementing changes in response can put a business far ahead of its competitors.[22] In 1987, Jan Carlzon, president of Scandinavian Airlines, wrote a book he entitled *Moments of Truth*. The book describes the "**moments of truth**" a business faces each time it interacts with a customer. Every interaction, Carlzon wrote, is an opportunity to meet, even exceed, customer expectations—or to disappoint the customer with subpar service. Carlzon concluded that, rather than looking inward, businesses would do better to run customer-driven operations. Since the book's release more than 20 years ago, the concept of moments of truth has gradually been adopted by organizations of all kinds and sizes and has transformed the business world and society at large.[23]

Using Web 2.0 Technologies

Now that people can connect online like never before, consumers can make their opinions about products and services known to both companies and other consumers. Consider the "Verizon Math Fail" video posted on YouTube by a disgruntled customer after his trip to Canada resulted in a higher cell phone bill than he was expecting.

The customer, George Vaccaro, had contacted the wireless company before leaving the country to ask about its pricing policy for Canadian calls and was quoted a price of .02 cents per minute. When he received his phone bill at the end of the month, he was surprised to find that he had actually been charged .02 *dollars*—or 2 cents—per minute. The video is a recording of Vaccaro's conversation with a customer service rep, who insists that there is no difference between .02 cents and .02 dollars, while Vaccaro continues to patiently explain that there *is*. Vaccaro asks to speak with a manager, who gives him the same response.

On YouTube alone, the video generated nearly 2 million views and thousands of comments, with other clients chiming in about their own customer service nightmares. The clip was soon picked up by bloggers and discussion forums across the Internet, and the company still hasn't lived it down: even though the call was recorded back in 2006, two of the top Google search results for "Verizon customer service" *still* pop up with links to this video.

The Upside to Web Exposure On the flip side, savvy marketers can use the social character of Web 2.0 to their advantage. As noted earlier, many successful brands these days offer interactive Web sites where customers can form communities to discuss the company's products. Some companies create wikis—Web sites where users can add, change, and delete the content—in lieu of product FAQ pages. Can't figure out a problem with the new computer software you bought? Log on to the product Web site, and ask a question or read the helpful hints and solutions posted by other customers.[24]

As we noted in Chapter 13, other companies have gone so far as to embrace "co-creation," allowing their customers to help create the brand's message, values, and functions. If you frequent the burger chain In-N-Out Burger, you already understand this concept. The restaurant has a "secret menu" that was built around customer preferences and suggestions. The menu isn't listed behind the counter, but employees have it memorized, and most customers know to ask.[25] The "protein style" burger—a beef patty wrapped in lettuce, hold the bun—was created during the low-carb diet craze. Now, in the world of Web 2.0, it's becoming easier and easier for organizations to tap into customer preferences this way. A company doesn't have to go out of its way to take customer satisfaction surveys; instead, the data can come to them through online discussions.

Using the Feedback Of course, online customer forums can also generate a fair bit of negative feedback (as you learned in the Verizon example). The trick is to allow dissatisfied customers to speak without trying to appease them to shut them up. Their complaints might just get at the heart of something that you've been overlooking. If you change your product or practices based on this feedback, you'll undoubtedly have a stronger product and see a jump in customer satisfaction. Sony discovered a problem with the batteries in its laptops through consumer newsgroups and was able to implement a product recall to replace the batteries so quickly that most customers received the new battery before they even knew there was a problem. Sony turned a problem into an opportunity, thanks in part to an early detection system enabled by customer newsgroups.[26]

Building Relationships: Customer Relationship Management

Keeping a customer happy is not simply gaining information about a customer's service or allowing them to vent in an online chat room about your products. According to marketing entrepreneurs Chip Conley and Eric Friedenwald-Fishman, "A core question every company should ask itself is 'What kind of *relationship* am I building with my customers?'"[27] **Customer relationship management (CRM)**—the strategy a company uses to build and retain relationships with its customers—differs from customer service in that CRM takes a holistic approach to satisfying customer needs and expectations. It's a mind-set that strives to demonstrate customer commitment before looking to boost profits or sales. When there's a problem, rather than looking for a quick fix, good CRM looks to the causes.

For instance, let's say you work in the hotel business. One of your hotel guests, Ms. Lee, has requested a non-smoking room, but there was a mix-up when she made the reservation, and she was accidentally placed in a smoking room instead. When she comes to ask for a new room, the receptionist apologizes and explains that all of the non-smoking rooms have been booked for the night, but he offers to upgrade her to a suite to make up for the hotel's mistake. This is an example of good customer service; certainly it would meet customer expectations.

On the other hand, if your hotel places high value on CRM and your company's relational goal is to build lasting relationships with your customers, you might keep a database in which you track customer behavior and preferences. You might notice in your records that Ms. Lee stayed in your hotel twice in the last year and that both times she requested a non-smoking room. Not only would this help you avoid the mistake of booking the wrong room in the first place, it would also help you to better meet Ms. Lee's needs.

For instance, maybe the last time she stayed with you, she visited the hotel spa. To demonstrate the value you place on the customer relationship, you leave a note in Ms. Lee's room for when she checks in, thanking her for her loyal support of your business, offering a discount for hotel spa services, and asking her for feedback when she leaves.

Supporting Your Staff

Keeping track of your customers' preferences and building lasting relationships with them won't work unless you have a strong team providing those services. And it's no coincidence that the companies that consistently show up in the "best companies to work for" lists are also often the companies with the highest customer satisfaction rates. As we discussed in Chapter 12, increasingly, businesses are coming to accept the fact that strong customer relationships rely on strong relationships with their own employees—their internal customers. Good communication within the company boosts employee morale, keeps all levels of an organization focused on the same goals, increases productivity, and strengthens cooperation between departments and employees.[28]

Employee
Employee ID

Employee empowerment is a key ingredient to excellent internal and external service. Often it's the employees (who work face-to-face with customers), rather than management, who play the strongest role in customer relationship building. And these employees are often in the best position to observe the things that need improvement on the customer service front. If employees at all levels of an organization feel that their roles are appreciated and that their perspectives are respected, then business runs more smoothly, and external customers are more satisfied with their experience.

Take Wegmans Markets, a Rochester-based grocery chain. The company has consistently ranked in *Fortune's* list of top companies to work for—in fact, since 2004, they have ranked in the top five.[29] Not only are Wegmans' salaries and benefits packages at the high end for the grocery industry, but the retailer also offers millions in college scholarships for its employees, and more than half of Wegmans' current store managers began working at the store in their teens as shelf-stockers and bag boys. Allowing all employees to have a say has been part of Wegmans' ethos from the start. Consider the Wegmans' Pittsburgh store whose bakery sells "chocolate meatball cookies," a recipe submitted by one of the store's bakery employees whose Italian family has been making the cookies for generations. If an employee has a suggestion like this, so much the better! The company runs with it.

As a result, Wegmans' employees are well equipped and highly motivated to serve shoppers. The employee turnover rate is less than half of the industry average, and the store consistently outperforms larger grocery chains, both in terms of sales per square foot and profit margins.[30] Socially responsible businesses that demonstrate concern for the community (including their employees, their customers, and their environmental impact) are increasingly the businesses that customers turn to. Businesses whose values are in-line with customer values are the ones that develop the most loyal following.[31]

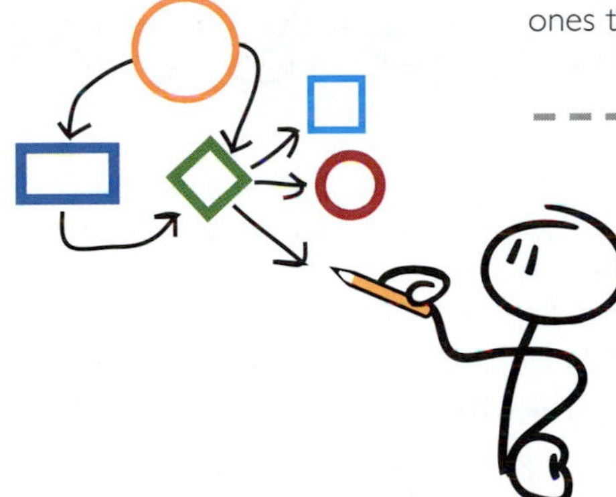

Do It...

14.4: Improve Poor Customer Service With the Customer BizHat on, describe an example of poor customer service you've experienced, such as an unhelpful call center representative. Then, put on the Employee BizHat and determine how the situation could have been improved. Write a brief paragraph detailing what you would have done as the employee had you been in the situation, and what you would do to prevent future problems. Be prepared to submit your response electronically or to discuss it in class.

Now Debrief...

- Strong customer relationships are an essential part of effective marketing. To cultivate customer loyalty, a business must attend to customer service. This includes listening to customers and modifying business practices in response to customer feedback.
- Every interaction with customers is a **moment of truth**; it is an opportunity to meet, even exceed, customer expectations—or to disappoint the customer with a subpar interaction.
- Companies can use Web 2.0 technology to create interactive customer services, such as wikis, blogs, and forums.
- It's much cheaper to keep old customers than it is to bring in new customers, so customer loyalty can have a significant impact on a business's profit margins.
- **Customer relationship management** is the way businesses strategize about building and retaining customer relationships.
- Businesses should also be attentive to the needs of their internal customers. High employee satisfaction often equates to high customer satisfaction.

Chapter 14 Visual Summary

Marketing Savvy | Chapter 12: *Discover* Chapter 13: *Create* **Chapter 14: *Communicate***

1. Establish SMART marketing communication goals for a marketing campaign. (pp. 338–341)

- Marketers must establish **marketing communication goals** by deciding what outcome they wish to achieve from their **marketing campaign**. Organizations often use **integrated marketing communications** to send a consistent, unified message across all of their communications.
- Marketing communication goals need to be SMART, and can be - *affective*, *psychological*, *behavioral*, *relational*, or a mix of these goals. Focusing on goals that best fit your target audience increases the likelihood of ensuring **customer loyalty**.
- Sometimes, companies use the **AIDA model** as a process to move customers through their SMART goals. AIDA stands for **A**ttention, **I**nterest, **D**esire, and **A**ction.

Summary: Marketing communication goals are driven by business goals and what response marketers want from their target audience.

2. Select the promotional mix that is best suited for a marketing campaign. (pp. 342–346)

- **Promotion** is an organization's method of explaining what it offers, garnering customers' interest in that product, gaining their trust in the organization, and motivating them to act. The tools in the **promotional mix** include **advertising**, **publicity**, **sales and trade promotions**, **personal selling**, **public relations**, and **buzz** and **viral marketing**.
- Companies pick and choose promotional tools that best help them accomplish their marketing communication goals.

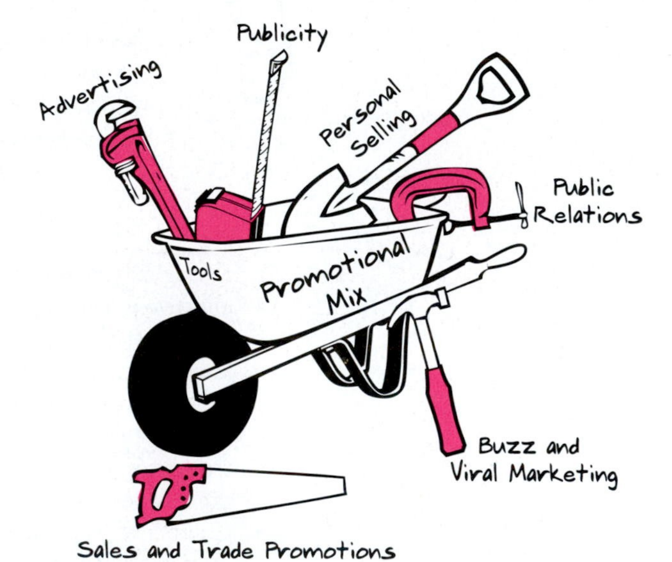

Summary: Once a company has decided on its marketing communication goals, it selects the best promotional tools for the situation.

4. Leverage your customer service strategy to achieve your goals by strengthening customer relationships, satisfaction, and loyalty. (pp. 352–357)

- Companies with strong customer service know that it is important to keep customers happy. Because of this, they collect data to learn about customers' experiences, and use the data they receive to improve their products.
- Customer interactions are **moments of truth** because at each interaction, you can either make the customer happy or unhappy.
- Web 2.0 technology plays a large role in companies learning about customers' reactions to their products.
- Successful businesses work on **customer relationship management (CRM)** to build and retain customer relationships.
- Internal customers are also important; businesses with high employee satisfaction are often high in customer satisfaction as well.

I think I just had a moment of truth!

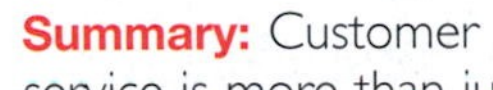

Summary: Customer service is more than just trying to make the customer happy. It is a combination of getting and acting upon customer feedback and building relationships with your customers.

3. Establish a creative strategy and select media vehicles for a marketing campaign. (pp. 346–352)

- Companies use **creative strategy** to decide their marketing message, based on their marketing communication goals and promotional mix tools. They may choose to create a **creative brief** to outline what they hope to achieve with the marketing campaign.
- **Media vehicles** are the types of media that marketers use to get their message out, such as newspapers and television.
- **Marketing 1.0** is a type of marketing in which marketers want to get their message out to as many people as possible, and they use media vehicles such as billboards, posters, and newspaper advertisements.
- **Marketing 2.0** is a type of marketing in which marketers use technology to promote marketing 1.0 ideas. Pop-ups, online banners, telemarketing, and television and radio commercials are all types of marketing 2.0 media.
- **Marketing 3.0** is a type of marketing in which marketers interact with customers to get a marketing message out. Interactive media such as **Web 2.0** tools promote word-of-mouth advertising as customers participate in writing content.

Media Vehicles

Television

Radio

Newspapers

Summary: After choosing the promotional mix of tools, marketers must come up with a creative strategy to implement those tools. They choose different forms of media vehicles to get their message out, depending on their marketing communication goals and their target audience.

Get the most out of what you just read by practicing your skills and actually DOING something with the material! The best place to do this is at **www.mybizlab.com**. Here's just some of what is available to you there:

- Apply your skills in an interactive environment with more **BizSkill** experiences...and see if you have what it takes
- Think critically and talk with your peers on hot business topics in **BizChat**
- Flex your business communication skills and build your own portfolio with the **Communication Plan exercises**
- Watch the chapter material come together with **Just Plain Business** videos
- Study on-the-go with **Audio Chapter Summaries** in MP3 format
- Brush up on the lecture and content with **Audio PowerPoints**
- Discover how well you are doing and see what areas you need to improve on with the **Pre-Tests** and **Post-Tests**

Key Words

These key words and more are also available as flash cards to practice with at **www.mybizlab.com**.

1. Establish SMART marketing communication goals for a marketing campaign. **(pp. 338–341)**

marketing communication goals (p. 338)
marketing campaign (p. 338)
integrated marketing communications (p. 338)
customer loyalty (p. 338)
affective goals (p. 338)
psychological goals (p. 339)
behavioral goals (p. 339)
relational goals (p. 339)
AIDA model (p. 340)

2. Select the promotional mix that is best suited for a marketing campaign. **(pp. 342–346)**

promotion (p. 342)
promotional mix (p. 342)
advertising (p. 342)
publicity (p. 342)
sales promotions (p. 343)
trade promotions (p. 343)
personal selling (p. 343)
public relations (p. 344)
buzz marketing (p. 344)
viral marketing (p. 344)

3. Establish a creative strategy and select media vehicles for a marketing campaign. **(pp. 346–352)**

creative strategy (p. 347)
creative brief (p. 347)
media vehicles (p. 348)
marketing 1.0 (p. 348)
marketing 2.0 (p. 349)
Web 2.0 (p. 349)
marketing 3.0 (p. 349)

4. Leverage your customer service strategy to achieve your goals by strengthening customer relationships, satisfaction, and loyalty. **(pp. 352–357)**

moments of truth (p. 354)
customer relationship management (CRM) (p. 356)

Prove It

Prove It...

Now let's put on one of the BizHats. With the **Manager BizHat** in place, complete the following exercise:

You're the marketing manager at Easy Package, a start-up company that handles shipping and packaging needs for students living on college campuses. The company has recently tried to increase the "greenness" of its operations by switching to all biodegradable packaging materials and by reducing energy consumption at its business headquarters. Additionally, the company has been practicing excellent internal customer service toward its employees for years: great benefits and a strong sense of employee empowerment.

However, up until now the company hasn't done a good job of publicizing its socially responsible practices. You decide to launch a marketing campaign that presents the company as a socially responsible business. Not only do you want to get the word out about the company's values, but you want internal and external customers to feel listened to and appreciated. Unfortunately, the CEO has informed you that you have an extremely tight budget for your marketing campaign. What combination of promotional tools and media vehicles might you use to reach a target market of mostly college students? Why have you chosen these promotional tools and media vehicles? What are some challenges you might face in your efforts?

Flip It...

After you've decided on a marketing communications plan, flip over to the **Employee BizHat.**

You're a shipping specialist (employee) at Easy Package. Management has recently offered an award to the employee who can offer the best suggestions to help improve the company's profile as a socially responsible business, including improving internal customer service and green practices. You've noticed that there seems to be a lack of communication between the shipping department and the customer service department. You've also overheard some customer complaints about the new packaging materials, and you don't think management is aware of the problem. What suggestions might you make to management based on your observations, and why?

Now Debrief It...

As a marketing manager, a large part of the company's image is dependent on your decisions. How will you mold your company's image? Can you think of a way to be socially responsible without seeming like you are just doing it to promote a positive image? As a shipping specialist, do you feel comfortable taking your suggestions to your manager? What can your department do to maintain the company's socially responsible image?

There are even more exciting business topics!

For the following Anybody's Business chapters, check out:

www.mybizlab.com

Glindex

M

Reference Notes

CHAPTER 1

1. Jack Stack, *The Great Game of Business*, Random House, 1994, http://books.google.com/books?id=eN5490tOvRIC, accessed June 3, 2009.
2. Katherine Bell, "Is Transparency Always the Best?" *Businessweek*, April 6, 2009, http://www.businessweek.com/managing/content/apr2009/ca2009047_217089.htm, accessed May 10, 2009.
3. Valerie Jean Mikles, Abstract for "X-ray and infrared spectral and timing observations of galactic interacting binary stars and associated relativistic jets." *Proquest Dissertations And Theses* (2008), January 2009, http://adsabs.harvard.edu/abs/2008PhDT........11M, accessed May 10, 2009.
4. Jack Stack, *The Great Game of Business*, Random House, 1994, http://books.google.com/books?id=eN5490tOvRIC, accessed June 3, 2009.
5. Jack Stack, *The Great Game of Business*, Random House, 1994, http://books.google.com/books?id=eN5490tOvRIC, accessed June 3, 2009.
6. "Benjamin Franklin Quotes," Thinkexist.com, http://thinkexist.com/quotation/if_you_can-t_pay_for_a_thing-don-t_buy_it-if_you/146073.html, accessed May 10, 2009.
7. John Friedman, *The New PR*, p. 31, http://www.scribd.com/doc/297611O/The-New-PR, accessed May 10, 2009.

CHAPTER 2

1. "Paul Clitheroe Quotes - Famous Australian," http://www.woopidoo.com/business_quotes/authors/paul-clitheroe/index.htm.
2. Apple Inc. Balance Sheet, September 2008, *Yahoo! Finance*, at http://finance.yahoo.com/q/bs?s=AAPL&annual, accessed May 14, 2009.
3. Speech, August 10, 1987. http://thinkexist.com/quotation/every_business_and_every_product_has_risks-you/148378.html.
4. "SWOT Analysis - Discover New Opportunities. Manage and Eliminate Threats - Management Training from Mind Tools," http://www.mindtools.com/pages/article/newTMC_05.htm, accessed June, 18, 2009.
5. Ibid.
6. Ibid.
7. Ibid.
8. "Quote Details: George S. Patton: Take calculated risks... - The Quotations Page," http://www.quotationspage.com/quote/2905.html.
9. Marguerite Reardon and Elinor Mills, "Google Unveils Cell Phone Software and Alliance," *CNET News*, November 5, 2007, http://news.cnet.com/google-unveils-cell-phone-software-and-alliance/, accessed April 20, 2009.
10. Miguel Helft, "Google and Amazon to Put More Books on Cellphones," *The New York Times*, February 5, 2009, http://www.nytimes.com/2009/02/06/technology/internet/06google.html.
11. Corporate Diversification, http://www.mgmtguru.com/mgt499/TN8.htm, accessed April 19, 2009.
12. "Daimler-Bend and Chrysler Merge," *The Auto Channel*, May 7, 1998, http://www.theautochannel.com/news/press/date/19980507/press012154.html.
13. "Yum! Brands — The world's largest restaurant company: KFC, Pizza Hut, Taco Bell, A&W All-American Food, Long John Silver's," http://www.yum.com/.
14. John Cassidy, "Going Long," *The New Yorker*, July 10, 2006, http://www.newyorker.com/archive/2006/07/10/060710crbo_.
15. Robert Kiyosaki, *Rich Dad, ...Do Not! What the Rich Teach Their Kids About Money—That the Poor and Middle Class Do Not!* New York: Warner Books, 2000: 35.
16. "Portfolio Diversification," *The Investor*, February 26, 2009, http://monevator.com/2009/02/26/portfolio-diversification/.

CHAPTER 3

1. "Henry Ford Quotes," ThinkExist.com, http://thinkexist.com/quotation/a_business_that_makes_nothing_but_money_is_a_poor/146311.html, accessed May 29, 2009.
2. United Nations, "Report on the World Commission on Environment and Development," http://www.un.org/documents/ga/res/42/ares42-187.htm, accessed April 28, 2009.
3. John Elkington, "Enter the Triple Bottom Line," http://www.johnelkington.com/TBL-elkington-chapter.pdf, accessed April 28, 2009.
4. Booth Moore, "Toms Shoes' model is sell a pair, give a pair away," Los Angeles Times, April 19, 2009, http://www.latimes.com/features/lifestyle/la-ig-greentoms19-2009apr19,0,1059085.story.
5. 3M, Pollution Prevention Pays (3P), http://solutions.3m.com/wps/portal/3M/en_US/global/sustainability/management/pollution-prevention-pays/, accessed April 28, 2009.
6. *Ibid.*
7. Soundview Executive Book Summaries, "The Triple Bottom Line," http://www.sustainableflorida.org/documents/thetriplebottomline.pdf, accessed April 28, 2009.
8. AccountAbility for the WBCSD Accountability and Reporting Work Group, Strategic challenges for business in the use of corporate responsibility codes, standards, and frameworks (Geneva, Switzerland: World Business Council for Sustainable Development, October 2004), http://www.wbcsd.org/web/publications/accountability-codes.pdf.
9. Unilever, "Environmental Sustainability," http://www.unilever.com/sustainability/environment/, accessed April 28, 2009.
10. Milton Friedman, "Capitalism and Freedom," University of Chicago Press, Chicago, Illinois: 2002; http://www.woopidoo.com/business_quotes/authors/milton-friedman-quotes.htm, accessed June 2, 2009.
11. Julie Creswell, "Nothing Sells Like Celebrity," *New York Times*, June 22, 2008, http://www.nytimes.com/2008/06/22/business/media/22celeb.html?_r=1&ref=business&pagewanted=all, accessed May 19, 2009.
12. Don Reisinger, "Nintendo Wii supply finally catches up to demand," *CNET News*, March 20, 2009, http://news.cnet.com/nintendo-wii-supply-finally-catches-up-to-demand/.
13. Helen Joyce, "Adam Smith and the Invisible Hand," *Plus Magazine*, March 2001, http://plus.maths.org/issue14/features/smith/, accessed April 28, 2009.
14. Microsoft Legal Newsroom, http://www.microsoft.com/presspass/legal/default.mspx, accessed April 28, 2009.
15. Alexander T. Tabarrok, "New Policies for the New Economy," *The Independent Institute*, http://www.independent.org/issues/article.asp?id=488, accessed April 28, 2009.
16. SUBWAY, "About Subway," http://www.subway.com/subwayroot/AboutSubway/index.aspx, accessed April 28, 2009.
17. BusinessWeek, "25 companies where customers come first," *MSN Money*, March 2, 2007, http://articles.moneycentral.msn.com/News/25CompaniesWhereCustomersComeFirst.aspx?page=1.
18. Church & Dwight Co., Inc., "Arm and Hammer Baking Soda: Our History," http://www.armhammer.com/history/, accessed April 28, 2009.
19. Robert Weisman, "Demand for hybrids outpaces supply," *The Boston Globe*, June 9, 2008, http://www.boston.com/business/personalfinance/articles/2008/06/09/demand_for_hybrids_outpaces_supply/.

CHAPTER 4

1. Miguel Bustillo, "Retailer Circuit City to Liquidate," *The Wall Street Journal*, January 17, 2009, http://online.wsj.com.
2. Business Cycle Dating Committee, "Determination of the December 2007 Peak

in Economic Activity," National Bureau of Economic Research, http://www.nber.org/cycles/dec2008.html.

3. Christina D. Romer, "Business Cycles," *The Concise Encyclopedia of Economics,* Library of Economics and Liberty, http://www.econlib.org/library/Enc/BusinessCycles.html.
4. "The Unemployment Situation: May 2009," U. S. Bureau of Labor Statistics, http://www.bls.gov/news.release/pdf/empsit.pdf, accessed June 19, 2009.
5. "How the Government Measures Unemployment," *U.S. Bureau of Labor Statistics,* February 2009, http://www.bls.gov/cps/cps_htgm.pdf, accessed June 19, 2009.
6. Ashlee Vance, "Microsoft Slashes Jobs as Sales Fall," *New York Times,* January 22, 2009, http://www.nytimes.com/2009/01/23/technology/companies/23soft.html.
7. "Health-Care Jobs Update: Still Growing," *The Wall Street Journal,* June 5, 2009, http://blogs.wsj.com/health/2009/06/05/health-care-jobs-update-still-growing/.
8. "What is a Dollar Worth?" The Federal Reserve Bank of Minneapolis, http://www.minneapolisfed.org/, accessed April 23, 2009.
9. MGM Mirage, "City Center Announces Scope Changes," *Financial Releases,* January 7, 2009, http://phx.corporate-ir.net/phoenix.zhtml?c=101502&p=irol-newsArticle&t=Regular&id.
10. Tamara Audi, "MGM Mirage Wins a Reprieve on Debt," *The Wall Street Journal,* March 18, 2009, http://online.wsj.com/article/SB123732708930762149.html.
11. Geoffrey Fowler, "Amazon's Sales Surge, Bucking Retail Slump," *The Wall Street Journal,* January 20, 2009, http://online.wsj.com/article/SB123326309581630125.html.
12. "Quote Details: John F. Kennedy: There are risks and... - The Quotations Page," http://www.quotationspage.com/quote/29333.html.
13. United States Congress, *American Recovery and Reinvestment Act of 2009,* http://frwebgate.access.gpo.gov/cgi-bin/getdoc.cgi?dbname=111_cong_bills&docid=f:h1enr.pdf.
14. *Projects in Arkansas, Stimulus Watch,* http://www.stimuluswatch.org/project/by_state/AR&per_page=100, accessed June 19, 2009.
15. Board of Governors of the Federal Reserve System, *Federal Reserve Act,* http://www.federalreserve.gov/aboutthefed/fract.htm.
16. "Factors of Production," *Encyclopedia of Business and Finance,* ed. Allison McClintic Marion and Gale. Cengage, 2001, http://www.enotes.com/business-finance-encyclopedia/factors-production.
17. Philip A. Klein, "Changing Perspectives on the Factors of Production," *Journal of Economic Issues,* 22:3 (Sept 1988), 797.
18. Klein, "Changing Perspectives," 804.
19. Peter F. Drucker. *The Age of Discontinuity: Guidelines to our Changing Society.* New York: Harper & Row, 1969.
20. "History of IBM," *IBM Archives,* http://www-03.ibm.com/ibm/history/history/decade_1900.html.
21. Jessie Scanlon, "Sunflower Sprouts Fresh Stores and Consumers," *Business Week,* July 25, 2008.
22. Rachel Dodes and Sam Schechner, "Luxury-Goods Makers Brandish Green Credentials," *Wall Street Journal,* July 2, 2009.
23. Art Edelstein, "Internet Only Companies Thrive in Online Environment," *Vermont Business Magazine,* http://findarticles.com/p/articles/mi_qa3675/is_200702/ai_n18705462/.
24. http://www.taxindenmark.com/.
25. Morley Safer, "And the Happiest Place on Earth Is. . .," *60 Minutes,* CBS News, http://www.cbsnews.com/stories/2008/02/14/60minutes/main3833797.shtml.
26. Michael Gelb, "For Many Americans, Hard Work Is Badge of Honor," *U.S. Department of State,* http://www.america.gov/st/econ-english/2008/July/20080703151840berehellek0.7706415.html, accessed April 29, 2009.
27. "Government Proposes More Flexible Maternity-Related Leave," *European Industrial Relations Observatory On-line,* http://www.eurofound.europa.eu/eiro/2002/02/feature/dk0202104f.htm, accessed April 29, 2009.
28. "Country Comparison: Unemployment Rate," *CIA World Factbook,* https://www.cia.gov/library/publications/the-world-factbook/rankorder/2129rank.html?countryName=Denmark&countryCode=DA®ionCode=eu#DA, accessed June 22, 2009.
29. "Denmark," *European American Business,* http://www.european-american-business.com/2006/p_51.php, accessed June 23, 2009.
30. "Economy: China," *CIA World Factbook,* https://www.cia.gov/library/publications/the-world-factbook/geos/CH.html, accessed June 23, 2009.

CHAPTER 5

1. Thomas L. Friedman, *The World is Flat,* (New York: Farrar, Straus and Giroux, 2005), 416–417.
2. Thomas L. Friedman, *The World is Flat,* 153–54.
3. Karl Fisch and Scott Mcleod, "Shift Happens," *Slideshare,* http://www.slideshare.net/jbrenman/shift-happens-33834.
4. Karl Fisch and Scott McLeod, "Shift Happens," *YouTube.*
5. Richard N. Haass, qtd. in Marian Salzman and Ira Matathia, *Next Now: Trends for the Future,* (Palgrave MacMillan, 2007), 23.
6. "Profile: World Trade Organization," *BBC News,* March 5, 2009, http://news.bbc.co.uk/2/hi/europe/country_profiles/2429503.stm.
7. "Emerging Economies Report," http://www.emergingeconomyreport.com, July 7, 2009.
8. "User Research Informs Design of Nokia Phones for Emerging Markets," *experiential,* January 22, 2008, http://www.experientia.com/blog/user-research-informs-design-of-nokia-phones-for-emerging-markets/.
9. Fish and McLeod, "Shift Happens."
10. Wendy M. Becker and Vanessa M. Freeman, "Going from Global Trends to Corporate Strategy," *McKinsey Quarterly,* 3 (2006): 16–27.
11. Friedman, *The World is Flat,* 115.
12. Peter Maassen, "Globalization, Internationalization and the Knowledge Society," *Slide Share,* October 8, 2007, http://www.slideshare.net/shanecolvin/globalization-internationalization-and-the-knowledge-society-155979.
13. "Globalization Quotes," *Finest Quotes,* http://www.finestquotes.com/select_quote-category-Globalization-page-0.htm, accessed June 29, 2009.
14. Fish and McLeod, "Shift Happens."
15. Stanley Holmes, "Boeing's Global Strategy Takes Off," *BusinessWeek,* January 30, 2006, http://www.businessweek.com/magazine/content/06_05/b3969417.htm.
16. Greg Johnson, "Mitsubishi Confirms EV-Sharing Deal; i-MiEV to wear Peugeot badge in Europe," *Green Car Advisor,* March 2, 2009, http://blogs.edmunds.com/greencaradvisor/Manufacturers/peugeot/.
17. *Star Alliance,* http://www.staralliance.com/en/meta/airlines/index.html; Jonas, David. "Alliance Execs Discuss Value as Star Turns Ten," *the beat,* June 6, 2007, http://www.thetransnational.travel/news.php?cid=Star-Alliance-Oneworld-SkyTeam.Jun-07.06.
18. "Coke Zero, Shaken, Not Stirred," *License!,* September 16, 2008, http://www.licensing-expo.com/index.php/coca-cola-007-shaken-not-stirred/.
19. Loretta Chao, "IHG to Franchise Hotels in China," January 29, 2008, http://online.wsj.com/article/SB120154569108322845.html?mod=djem_jiewr_hm.
20. Lynn Downey, "A Short History of Denim," 2007, *Levi Strauss & Co.,* http://www.levistrauss.com/Downloads/History-Denim.pdf.
21. Gary Gereffi and Martha A. Martinez, "Torreon's Blue Jeans Boom: Exploring La Laguna's Full Package Solution," *BNET,* April, 2000, http://findarticles.com/p/articles/mi_m3638/is_8_41/ai_62054290/?tag=content;col1.
22. Gereffi and Martinez, "Torreon's Blue Jeans Boom."
23. Office of the United States Trade Representative, "NAFTA Facts," March, 2008, http://www.medey.com/DeyTimes%202008/April/ustr%20nafta%20myth%20vs.%20fact.pdf.
24. Robert E. Scott, "The High Price of 'Free Trade,'" Economic Policy Institute, November 17, 2008, http://www.epi.org/publications/entry/briefingpapers_bp147/.
25. "The Wide, Wide, World of Foreign Trade," *A Pedestrian's Guide to the Economy,* http://www.amosweb.com/cgi-bin/awb_nav.pl?s=pdg&c=dsp&k=24.
26. George Ritzer, *The MacDonaldization of Society,* (Pine Forge Press, 2002), 5.

27. Yuka Hayashi and Joanna Slater, "Japan Economy Quakes Anew As Yen Soars Against Dollar," *The Wall Street Journal*, March 14, 2008, http://online.wsj.com/article/SB120543164157033979.html?mod=djem_jiewr_IB.
28. Hayashi and Slater, "Japan Economy Quakes."
29. Joanna Slater, "Multinationals in U.S. May See Profits Fall," *The Wall Street Journal*, September 6, 2008, http://online.wsj.com/article/SB122065618832205521.html.
30. "Coca-Cola in China Squeezed Out," *The Economist*, March 18, 2009, http://www.economist.com/business/displayStory.cfm?story_id=13315056&source=most_read.
31. Greg Hitt, Christopher Conkey, and Jose De Cordoba, "Mexico Strikes Back in Trade Spat," *Wall Street Journal*, March 17, 2009, http://online.wsj.com/article/SB123723192240845769.html.
32. Shelley Emling, "Protectionist Rhetoric May Frustrate U.S. Firms Doing Business in France," *The Atlanta Journal-Constitution*, November 8, 2005, http://www.redorbit.com/news/technology/299557/protectionist_rhetoric_may_frustrate_us_firms_doing_business_in_france/.
33. "What is Fair Trade Coffee All About?" *Global Exchange*, November 14, 2007, http://www.globalexchange.org/campaigns/fairtrade/coffee/background.html.
34. John W. Miller, "Nations Rush to Establish New Barriers to Trade," *The Wall Street Journal*, February 6, 2009, http://online.wsj.com/article/SB123388103125654861.html.
35. "About the WTO—a Statement by the Director General," *World Trade Organization*, http://www.wto.org/english/thewto_e/whatis_e/wto_dg_stat_e.htm.
36. "World Economic Outlook Database," *International Monetary Fund*, April 2009, http://www.imf.org/external/pubs/ft/weo/2009/01/weodata/weorept.aspx?sy=2007&ey=2009&scsm=1&ssd=1&sort=country&ds=.&br=1&c=001%2C998&s=NGDPD%2CPPPGDP%2CPPPSH&grp=1&a=1&pr.x=50&pr.y=9.
37. "Regional Trade Agreements," *World Trade Organization*, accessed May 11, 2009, http://www.wto.org/english/tratop_e/region_e/region_e.htm.
38. "NGOs—Non Governmental Organizations," *Non Profit Expert*, http://www.nonprofitexpert.com/ngo.htm.
39. "Come Alive!" *Snopes*, February 19, 2007, http://www.snopes.com/business/misxlate/ancestor.asp.
40. Mike Kim, "Advertising Bloopers and Blunders," *5 Star Affiliate Marketing Forums*, http://affiliate-marketing-forums.5staraffiliateprograms.com/marketing-jokes-cartoons-yuk-up/1401-advertising-bloopers-blunders.html.
41. Katherine Toland Frith and Barbara Mueller, *Advertising and Societies* (New York: Peter Lang Publishing, 2003), 36–37.
42. David Hampshire. *Living and Working in France*, http://www.justlanded.com/english/France/Articles/Culture/Social-customs-in-France.
43. Terri Morrison and Wayne A. Conaway, *Kiss, Bow, or Shake Hands*, 2nd ed, 2009, http://www.getcustoms.com/2004XE/Demo/colBusinessPractices.htm.
44. "Geert Hofstede Analysis," http://www.cyborlink.com/besite/hofstede.htm.
45. Katherine Toland Frith and Barbara Mueller, *Advertising and Societies* (New York: Peter Lang Publishing, 2003), 41–42.
46. "Hofstede Scores," http://spectrum.troy.edu/~vorism/hofstede.htm.
47. Sahoko Kaji, Noriko Hama, and Jonathan Rice, *The Xenophobe's Guide to the Japanese* (London: Oval Books, 2004).
48. Kaji, Hama, and Rice, *The Xenophobe's Guide.*
49. Cathy Bernatt, "Managing Cultural Differences": book review, *Creating ...*, http://www.creating.bz/our-reading-circle/managing.html.
50. "Hofstede Scores," http://spectrum.troy.edu/~vorism/hofstede.htm.
51. Frith and Mueller, *Advertising and Societies*, 46.
52. "Geert Hofstede Analysis," http://www.cyborlink.com/besite/hofstede.htm.
53. "United Kingdom," *International Business Etiquette and Manners*, http://www.cyborlink.com/besite/united_kingdom.htm.
54. "Uncertainty Avoidance," *Kwintessential*, http://www.kwintessential.co.uk/intercultural/uncertainty-avoidance.html.
55. Daniel Workman, "Trade Culture Time Horizons," Suite101, January 26, 2008, http://internationalbusiness.suite101.com/article.cfm/trade_culture_time_horizons.
56. Willkie Farr & Gallagher LLC, "Vetco Pays Largest Criminal Fine in the History of the FCPA," February 13, 2007, http://www.willkie.com/files/tbl_s29Publications%5CFileUpload5686%5C2393%5CVetco_Pays_Largest_Criminal_Fine.pdf.
57. Christopher J. Stetskal, "The Foreign Corrupt Practices Act: The Next Corporate Scandal?" *Fenwick & West LLP*, January 28, 2008, http://www.fenwick.com/docstore/Publications/Litigation/sec/Sec_Litigation_Alert_01-28-08.pdf.
58. Stetskal, "Foreign Corrupt Practices Act."
59. *Anti Sweatshop Labor League*, "What is Sweatshop Labor?" February 6, 2006, http://www.geocities.com/whydoyoukeepdeletingme/ASSLLeague.html.
60. "Green America's Retailer Scorecard," Green America, 2009, http://www.coopamerica.org/programs/sweatshops/scorecard.cfm.
61. "Retailer Scorecard."

CHAPTER 6

1. George Ambler, "Leadership Lessons from Geese," original author unknown, http://www.thepracticeofleadership.net/2006/07/18/leadership-lessons-from-geese/, accessed July 12, 2009.
2. J. Thomas Wren, *The Leader's Companion: Insights on Leadership Through the Ages*, New York: The Free Press, 1995, p. 192.
3. Ibid, pp. 194–196.
4. "Managers vs. Leaders: Are they all that Different?" *Fox News*, June 3, 2008, http://www.foxnews.com/story/0,2933,362703,00.html, accessed April 6, 2009.
5. "Innovation Most Critical Factor to Success, Say U.S. Business Leaders; Cisco Innovation 2005 Study Finds Strong Support for Modernizing Health-Care," *Business Wire*, August 10, 2005, http://findarticles.com/p/articles/mi_m0EIN/is_2005_August_10/ai_n14875869/.
6. "Nike's All-Star Sneakers," *Fortune*, http://money.cnn.com/galleries/2008/fortune/0811/gallery.nike_hits.fortune/index.html, accessed June 29, 2009; Karin Klenke, "Cinderella stories of women leaders: connecting leadership contexts and competencies," *All Business*, September 22, 2002, http://www.allbusiness.com/human-resources/employee-development-leadership/387549-1.html.
7. Daniel Goleman, *Emotional Intelligence: 10th Anniversary Edition; Why It Can Matter More than IQ*, Bantam Book: 1995, p. 149.
8. Daniel Goleman, *Emotional Intelligence: 10th Anniversary Edition; Why It Can Matter More than IQ*, Bantam Book: 1995, p. 149.
9. Ibid.
10. "The Importance of Being Richard Branson," http://www.whartonsp.com/articles/article.asp?p=393287, accessed July 2, 2009.
11. "AmEx's Ken Chenault Talks about Leadership, Integrity and the Credit Card Business" *Knowledge@Wharton*, http://knowledge.wharton.upenn.edu/article.cfm?articleid=1179, accessed July 2, 2009.
12. "American International Group, Inc. | Code Conduct," http://phx.corporate-ir.net/phoenix.zhtml?c=76115&p=irol-code_conduct, accessed July 2, 2009.
13. Michael Useem, "America's Best Leaders: Indra Nooyi, PepsiCo CEO," *U.S. News & World Report*, November 19, 2008, http://www.usnews.com/articles/news/best-leaders/2008/11/19/americas-best-leaders-indra-nooyi-pepsico-ceo.html.
14. Hildy Gottlieb, "3 Statements that Can Change the World: Mission/Vision/Values," *Community Driven Institute*, http://www.help4nonprofits.com/NP_Bd_MissionVisionValues_Art.htm, accessed June 26, 2009.
15. AMZN Investor Relations FAQ, http://phx.corporateir.net/phoenix.zhtml?c=97664&p=irol-faq#14296, accessed April 29, 2009.
16. Don Adams, "The Pillars of Planning," *National Endowment for the Arts*, http://arts.endow.gov/resources/Lessons/ADAMS.HTML, accessed April 6, 2009.

17. "Madonna Biography," *Biographies.com*, http://www.biography.com/articles/Madonna-9394994?part=1, accessed June 26, 2009.

18. Everett Rogers, "Diffusion of Innovations," Reviewed by Greg Orr, March 18, 2003, http://www.stanford.edu/class/symbsys205/Diffusion%20of%20Innovations.htm.

19. Todd Rhoades, "Innovators, Early Adoptors, Early/Late Majority, Laggards: Which are You?" *Monday Morning Insight*, December 6, 2004, http://mondaymorninginsight.com/index.php/site/comments/innovators_early_adopters_early_late_majority_laggards_which_are_you/, accessed April 7, 2009.

20. Ibid.

21. Everett Rogers, "Diffusion of Innovations," Reviewed by Greg Orr, March 18, 2003, http://www.stanford.edu/class/symbsys205/Diffusion%20of%20Innovations.htm.

22. Todd Rhoades, "Innovators, Early Adoptors, Early/Late Majority, Laggards: Which are You?" *Monday Morning Insight*, December 6, 2004, http://mondaymorninginsight.com/index.php/site/comments/innovators_early_adopters_early_late_majority_laggards_which_are_you/, accessed April 7, 2009.

23. Ibid.

24. Everett Rogers, "Diffusion of Innovations," Reviewed by Greg Orr, March 18, 2003, http://www.stanford.edu/class/symbsys205/Diffusion%20of%20Innovations.htm, accessed April 7, 2009.

25. Todd Rhoades, "Innovators, Early Adoptors, Early/Late Majority, Laggards: Which are You?" *Monday Morning Insight*, December 6, 2004, http://mondaymorninginsight.com/index.php/site/comments/innovators_early_adopters_early_late_majority_laggards_which_are_you/, accessed April 7, 2009.

26. Ibid.

27. Miguel Helft, "Tech's Late Adopters Prefer the Tried and True, *The New York Times*, March 12, 2008, http://www.nytimes.com/2008/03/12/technology/12inertia.html.

28. Todd Rhoades, "Innovators, Early Adoptors, Early/Late Majority, Laggards: Which are You?" *Monday Morning Insight*, December 6, 2004, http://mondaymorninginsight.com/index.php/site/comments/innovators_early_adopters_early_late_majority_laggards_which_are_you/, accessed April 7, 2009.

29. Everett Rogers, "Diffusion of Innovations," Reviewed by Greg Orr, March 18, 2003, http://www.stanford.edu/class/symbsys205/Diffusion%20of%20Innovations.htm, accessed April 7, 2009.

30. "Kotter Change Phases Model Framework," *Value Based Management*, http://www.valuebasedmanagement.net/methods_kotter_change.html, accessed April 7, 2009; John P. Kotter, *John P. Kotter on What Leaders Really Do*, A Harvard Business Review Book, 1999, pp. 76–91.

31. "Kotter Change Phases Model Framework," *Value Based Management*, http://www.valuebasedmanagement.net/methods_kotter_change.html, accessed April 6, 2009.

32. Kenneth H. Rose, "Leading Change: A Model by John Kotter," *ESI Horizons*, February 2002, http://www.esi-intl.com/Public/publications/22002changemanagement.asp, accessed April 7, 2009.

33. Kenneth H. Rose, "Leading Change: A Model by John Kotter," *ESI Horizons*, February 2002, http://www.esi-intl.com/Public/publications/22002changemanagement.asp, accessed April 7, 2009; John P. Kotter, *John P. Kotter on What Leaders Really Do*, A Harvard Business Review Book, 1999, pp. 90–91.

34. "Martin Luther King Speeches," *MLK Online*, http://www.mlkonline.net/dream.html, accessed April 6, 2009.

35. "Groupthink (Janis), 12 Manage: The Executive Fast Track, http://www.12manage.com/methods_janis_groupthink.html, accessed June 29, 2009.

36. Carter McNamara, "Continuous Learning," *Free Management Library*, http://managementhelp.org/trng_dev/design/cont_lrn.htm, accessed June 29, 2009.

CHAPTER 7

1. Bo Burlingham, "Don't Call Her an Entrepreneur," *Inc.*, September 2004, http://www.inc.com/magazine/20040901/difranco.html, accessed May 6, 2009.

2. Andrew C. Revkin, "Righteous Babe Saves Hometown; A Fiercely Independent Folk Singer's Soaring Career Lifts Buffalo, Too," *The New York Times*, February 16, 1998, http://www.nytimes.com/1998/02/16/nyregion/righteous-babe-saves-hometown-fiercely-independent-folk-singer-s-soaring-career.html?sec=&spon=&pagewanted=all.

3. Crain Communications, Inc., "Crain's 40 Under Forty," http://mycrains.crainsnewyork.com/40under40/profiles/2008/10110, accessed May 6, 2009.

4. Google, "Corporate Information," http://www.google.com/corporate/execs.html, accessed May 6, 2009.

5. Justin Petruccelli, "Optimism Knows No Slowdown," *Entrepreneur*, June, 9, 2008, http://www.entrepreneur.com/startingabusiness/selfassessment/article194606.html.

6. Tamara Schweitzer, "The Bootstrapper," *Inc.*, July 2007,http://www.inc.com/30under30/2007/the-bootstrapper.html, accessed May 6, 2009.

7. Evan Carmichael, "Lesson #3: Think Long-Term," *Famous Entrepreneur Advice*, http://www.evancarmichael.com/Famous-Entrepreneurs/556/Lesson-3-Think-LongTerm.html, accessed June 4, 2009.

8. "Oprah Winfrey Quotes," *ThinkExist.com*, http://thinkexist.com/quotation/real_integrity_is_doing_the_right_thing-knowing/250855.html, accessed April 2, 2009.

9. "Mike Ilitch Biography," *Answers.com*, http://www.answers.com/topic/mike-ilitch, accessed June 4, 2009.

10. "Michael Ilitch," *Ilitch Holdings, Inc.*, http://www.ilitchholdings.com/MediaRoom/LeadershipTeam/MichaelIlitch/tabid/144/Default.aspx, accessed June 4, 2009.

11. Oren Harari, "Does It Matter?" March 2, 2009, http://www.harari.com/blog/index.php?/archives/211-Does-It-Matter.html, accessed April 4, 2009.

12. Swarthmore Storage home page, http://swarthmorestorage.com/index.php, accessed May 6, 2009.

13. Eric Lai, "Office 2007 Sales Off to Faster Start than Last Release," *Computer World*, http://www.computerworld.com/action/article.do?command=viewArticleBasic&articleId=9011237, accessed June 4, 2009.

14. http://www.woopidoo.com/business_quotes/innovation-quotes.htm, accessed June 9, 2009.

15. *CNNMoney.com*, "The Innovation of Co-Creation," http://money.cnn.com/video/fortune/2008/05/22/fortune.reingold.prahalad.fortune/, accessed May 6, 2009.

16. Chuck Frey, "Tom Kelly explains how to cultivate personal innovation for life," *InnovationTools.com*, March 3, 2009, http://www.innovationtools.com/Weblog/innovationblog-detail.asp?ArticleID=1263.

17. http://thinkexist.com/quotation/a_pessimist_sees_the_difficulty_in_every/15269.html, accessed June 9, 2009.

18. "101 Frightening Ice Cream Flavors From Around the World," *Who-Sucks.com*, July 12, 2007, http://www.who-sucks.com/food/101-frightening-ice-cream-flavors-from-around-the-world.

19. John S. DeMott and Rosemary Byrnes, "Here Come the Intrapreneurs," *Time*, February 4, 1985, http://www.time.com/time/magazine/article/0,9171,959877-2,00.html, accessed May 6, 2009.

20. "What Is Social Entrepreneurship?" PBS. http://www.pbs.org/opb/thenewheroes/whatis/, accessed June 16, 2009.

21. "Meet the Heroes," PBS. http://www.pbs.org/opb/thenewheroes/meet/silbert.html, accessed June 16, 2009.

22. "Delancey Street Foundation," http://www.delanceystreetfoundation.org/, accessed June 16, 2009.

23. "2009 Franchise 500 Rankings," *Entrepreneur*, http://www.entrepreneur.com/franchises/rankings/franchise500-115608/2009,-1.html, accessed May 6, 2009.

24. "Frequently Asked Questions," *Small Business Administration Office of Advocacy*, September 2008, http://www.sba.gov/advo/stats/sbfaq.pdf, accessed June 5, 2009.

25. "Albuquerque, New Mexico - Historic Microsoft Headquarters," *RoadsideAmerica.com*, http://www.roadsideamerica.com/tip/13927, accessed April 2, 2009.

26. http://www.evancarmichael.com/Famous-Entrepreneurs/756/The-Burger-King-Ray-Kroc-is-Born.html, accessed June 9, 2009.
27. Internal Revenue Service, "Limited Liability Company (LLC), "http://www.irs.gov/businesses/small/article/0,,id=98277,00.html, accessed May 6, 2009.
28. Rhonda M. Abrams, *The Successful Business Plan: Secrets & Strategies*, Palo Alto, CA: The Planning Shop (4th edition), 2003.
29. Home Web page of the U.S. Small Business Administration, http://www.sba.gov/, accessed April 6, 2009.
30. "Free Online Courses," *Small Business Administration*, http://www.sba.gov/services/training/onlinecourses/index.html, accessed April 6, 2009.
31. Home Web page of SCORE, http://www.score.org/index.html, accessed April 6, 2009.

CHAPTER 8

1. U.S. Small Business Administration, p. 4. October 2007, http://www.sba.gov/idc/groups/public/documents/nc_charlotte/nc_news_respart_news1007.pdf, accessed May 8, 2009.
2. Rachel L. Swarns, "South Africa to Distribute $50 Million in Donated AIDS Drugs," *The New York Times*, December 2, 2000, http://www.nytimes.com/2000/12/02/world/south-africa-to-distribute-50-million-in-donated-aids-drugs.html, accessed May 8, 2009.
3. Mark Schoofs, "Giving It Away," *The Body: The Complete HIV/AIDS Resource*, April 4, 2000, http://www.thebody.com/content/art2773.htm, accessed May 8, 2009.
4. S. Predrag, "Long-Awaited Deal with Pfizer in South Africa," *Bay Area Reporter*, December 7, 2000, http://www.aegis.org/news/bar/2000/BR001206.html.
5. "The Tylenol Crisis," Effective Crisis Management, http://iml.jou.ufl.edu/projects/Fall02/Susi/tylenol.htm, accessed April 14, 2009.
6. "Case Study: The Johnson & Johnson Tylenol Crisis," *Crisis Communication Strategies*, http://www.ou.edu/deptcomm/dodjcc/groups/02C/Johnson%20&%20Johnson.htm, accessed April 14, 2009.
7. William L. Benoit, *Accounts, Excuses, and Apologies*. SUNY Press, 1995. p. 128.
8. Linda Gravett, "How Human Resources Can Help Build an Ethical Organization," *e-HResources.com*, http://www.e-hresources.com/Articles/August2002.htm, accessed March 18, 2009.
9. "Code of Ethics," Society of Professional Journalists," May 19, 2006, http://spj.org/ethicscode.asp.
10. Noah Berger, "Kyocera founder Kazuo Inamori criticizes U.S. CEO excesses," *USA Today*, April 21, 2009, http://www.usatoday.com/money/companies/management/advice/2009-04-19-advice-inamori_N.htm.
11. "Key TI Ethics Publications," Texas Instruments, http://www.ti.com/corp/docs/csr/corpgov/ethics/publication.shtml, accessed April 13, 2009.
12. Carter McNamara, "Complete Guide to Ethics Management: An Ethics Toolkit for Managers," *Free Management Library*, 1997, http://www.managementhelp.org/ethics/ethxgde.htm, accessed March 23, 2009.
13. *Ibid*.
14. "World's Most Ethical Companies 2009." http://ethisphere.com/wme2009/, accessed May 20, 2009.
15. Carter McNamara, "Complete Guide to Ethics Management: An Ethics Toolkit for Managers," *Free Management Library*, 1997, http://www.managementhelp.org/ethics/ethxgde.htm, accessed March 23, 2009.
16. Linda Gravett, "How Human Resources Can Help Build an Ethical Organization," *e-HResources.com*, http://www.e-hresources.com/Articles/August2002.htm, accessed March 18, 2009.
17. "Utilitarianism," *Encyclopedia of Business*, 2nd ed., http://www.referenceforbusiness.com/encyclopedia/Thir-Val/Utilitarianism.html, accessed March 20, 2009.
18. Jeffrey Wigand interview, *60 Minutes*, CBS News, February 4, 1996, Show transcript, http://jeffreywigand.com/60minutes.php, accessed March 25, 2009.
19. "Enron: After the Collapse," *Online NewsHour*, http://www.pbs.org/newshour/bb/business/enron/player6.html, accessed March 25, 2009.
20. Aaron Smith, "Madoff: 'I knew this day would come,'" *CNNMoney.com*, March 12, 2009, http://money.cnn.com/2009/03/12/news/newsmakers/madoff_courtappearance/index.html.
21. "Con of the Century," *Economist.com*, December 18, 2008, http://www.economist.com/research/Backgrounders/displaystory.cfm?story_id=12818310.
22. "Creation of the SEC," The Investor's Advocate: How the SEC Protects Investors, Maintain Market Integrity, and Facilitates Capital Formation, U.S. Securities and Exchange Commission, http://www.sec.gov/about/whatwedo.shtml, accessed March 23, 2009.
23. The Associated Press, "Private Investigator in HP Spying Scandal is Indicted," *International Herald Tribune*, January 11, 2007, http://www.iht.com/articles/2007/01/11/business/hp.php.
24. Deb Shinder, "Ethical Issues for IT Security Professionals," *Window Security*, http://www.windowsecurity.com/articles/Ethical-Issues-IT-Security-Professionals.html, accessed April 1, 2009.
25. Rosie Goldsmith, "Where the ships go to die," *BBC News World Edition*, April 22, 1999. http://news.bbc.co.uk/2/hi/programmes/crossing_continents/317229.stm.
26. *Ibid*.
27. *Ibid*.
28. *Ibid*.
29. "Principles for Business," *Caux Round Table*, http://www.cauxroundtable.org/index.cfm?&menuid=8, accessed March 19, 2009.
30. *Ibid*.
31. World Commission on Environment and Development (WCED). *Our common future*. Oxford: Oxford University Press, 1987, p. 43.
32. "The Triple Bottom Line," *Business and Sustainable Development: A Global Guide*, 2007, http://www.bsdglobal.com/tools/principles_triple.asp, accessed March 27, 2009.
33. Target Community Outreach, http://sites.target.com/site/en/company/page.jsp?contentId=WCMP04-031700, accessed May 27, 2009.
34. John Elkington, "Cannibals with Forks: The Triple Bottom Line of 21st Century Business," New Society Publishers, 1998, p. 45.
35. "Eco-efficiency," *Business and Sustainable Development: A Global Guide*, 2007, http://www.bsdglobal.com/tools/bt_eco_eff.asp, accessed March 27, 2009.
36. *Ibid*.
37. "Eco-Capitalism," TerraCycle Inc., 2008, http://www.terracycle.net/eco_capitalism.htm, accessed April 14, 2009.
38. *Ibid*.
39. Winning Workplaces, "Success Stories: A Values-Based Company," http://www.winning-workplaces.org/library/success/a_values-based_company.php, accessed April 28, 2009.
40. Marjorie Kelly, "Not Just for Profit," *Strategy and Business*, February 26, 2009, http://www.strategy-business.com/press/enewsarticle/enews022609?pg=0.
41. *Ibid*.

CHAPTER 9

1. John Kotter, "What Effective General Managers Really Do" in *On What Leaders Really Do*. Boston: Harvard Business School Press, 1999: p. 149.
2. Henry Mintzberg, "The Manager's Job: Folklore and Fact" In John J. Garbarro (ed) *Managing People and Organizations* (Harvard Business School Publications, 1992) http://www.uu.edu/personal/bnance/318/mintz.html.
3. http://en.wikipedia.org/wiki/Peter_Principle, accessed July 7, 2009.
4. Reed Hastings, "How I Did It: Reed Hastings, Netflix" *Inc.*, December 2005, http://www.inc.com/magazine/20051201/qa-hastings.html.
5. "Quote Details: Wayne Gretzky: A good hockey player... - The Quotations Page," http://www.quotationspage.com/quote/39110.html.
6. http://www.google.com/corporate/, accessed March 2, 2009.
7. http://www.diabetes.org/aboutus.jsp?WTLPromo=HEADER_aboutus, accessed April 16, 2009.

8. http://www.bayer.com/en/mission-statement.aspx, accessed April 16, 2009.
9. Hershey Company Web Site, http://www.thehersheycompany.com/about/, accessed March 22, 2009.
10. Hershey Company Web Site, http://www.thehersheycompany.com/about/, accessed March 22, 2009.
11. http://www.benjerry.com/company/sear/2007/sear07_1.0.cfm, accessed April 16, 2009.
12. Southwest Airlines Web site, http://www.southwest.com/about_swa/mission.html, accessed March 22, 2009.
13. Southwest Airlines Web site, http://www.southwest.com/about_swa/mission.html, accessed March 22, 2009.
14. http://www.planware.org/quotes.htm#13, accessed March 22, 2009.
15. "The Trader Joe's Experience," *Graziado Business Report*, http://gbr.pepperdine.edu/072/tj.html, accessed April 22, 2009.
16. Answers.com Web site, http://www.answers.com/topic/trader-joe-s-company, accessed March 22, 2009.
17. Stephen Covey, A. Roger Merrill, Rebecca R. Merrill, *First Things First: To Live, to Love, to Learn, to Leave a Legacy*. New York: Simon and Schuster, 1994.
18. Joan Magretta and Nan Stone, *What Management Is*. New York: Simon and Schuster, 2002: pp. 175–176.
19. U.S. Census Bureau, http://www.census.gov/compendia/statab/tables/09s1065.pdf, accessed April 23, 2009.
20. U.S. Census Bureau, http://www.census.gov/compendia/statab/tables/09s1036.pdf, accessed April 23, 2009.
21. "GE's 2008 Ecomagination Revenues to Rise 21 percent, Cross $17 Billion," http://ge.ecomagination.com/site/news/press/2008revenuesrise.html, accessed April 24, 2009.

CHAPTER 10

1. "Harold S. Geneen quotes," http://thinkexist.com/quotation/every_company_has_two_organizational_structures/208522.html.
2. "Company Culture :: Fun Corporate Culture, Great Corporate Culture, Productive Corporate Culture, Creative Corporate Culture," http://www.mindcomet.com/company/culture.php.
3. Anthony Vlamis and Bob Smith, "Do You? Business the Yahoo! Way." Capstone Publishing, January 2000.
4. "AOL Employees Complain of Cut-Throat Corporate Culture," *ConsumerAffairs.com*, September 29, 2003. http://www.consumeraffairs.com/news03/aol_employees.html.
5. "Steve Case Quotes - AOL," http://www.afterquotes.com/great/people/steve-case/index.htm.
6. Yuki Noguchi, "Job Seekers Find New Rules of Recruitment," *NPR*, June 17, 2009, http://www.npr.org/templates/story/story.php?storyId=105483848.
7. Ellyn E. Spragins, "Hiring Without the Guesswork" *Inc.com*, February 1992 http://www.inc.com/magazine/19920201/3922.html.
8. "Hiring: Basics Legal Issues for Employers," *TWC*, http://www.twc.state.tx.us/news/efte/i_hiring_basic_legal_issues.html,accessed July 8, 2009.

CHAPTER 11

1. David W. Merrill, and Roger H. Reid. *Personal Styles and Effective Performance*. CRC Press, 1981.
2. Marilyn Manning, "How Effective Is Your Leadership Style?" *The Consulting Team*, http://www.theconsultingteam.com/Articles/howeffectiveisyourleadershipstyle.htm, accessed May 4, 2009.
3. Grzelakowski, *Mother Leads Best*, 10.
4. Moe Grzelakowski, *Mother Leads Best: 50 Women Who Are Changing the Way Organizations Define Leadership*. Chicago: Dearborn Trade Publishing, 2005, 9–10.
5. Merrill and Reid, *Personal Styles and Effective Performance*, 158.
6. *Motivational & Inspirational Corner Web site*, http://www.motivational-inspirational-corner.com/getquote.html?categoryid=56, accessed April 2, 2009.
7. "Abram Maslow's Hierarchy of Needs Theory," *Envision Software, Incorporated Web site*, http://www.envisionsoftware.com/Management/Maslows_Needs_Hierarchy.html, accessed April 4, 2009.
8. Chip Conley, *Peak: How Great Companies Get Their Mojo from Maslow*. San Francisco: Jossey-Bass, 2007, 12–13.
9. Conley, *Peak*, 13–14.
10. "Herzberg's Motivators and Hygiene Factors," *MindTools Web site*, http://www.mindtools.com/pages/article/newTMM_74.htm, accessed April 2, 2009.
11. *Mftrou.com, Management for the Rest of Us Web site*, http://www.mftrou.com/frederick-herzberg-theory.html, accessed April 1, 2009.
12. Douglas McGregor, *The Human Side of Enterprise*. New York: McGraw-Hill, 1960.
13. "Job Characteristics Model," arrod.co.uk Web site, http://www.arrod.co.uk/archive/concept_job_characteristics.php, accessed April 2, 2009.
14. John Love, *McDonald's: Behind the Arches* (New York: Bantam, 1995), 8.
15. James A. Hatherly, *Daring to Be Different: A Manager's Ascent to Leadership*. Belmont, CA: Star Publishing Company, 2003.
16. "Amelia Earhart Quotes," http://www.brainyquote.com/quotes/quotes/a/ameliaearh120929.html
17. Jason Jennings, *Think Big, Act Small: How America's Best Performing Companies Keep the Start-Up Spirit Alive*. New York: Penguin Group, 2005, 147–148.
18. Cari Tuna, "Micromanagers Miss Bull's Eye: Dealing with Every Detail Robs Subordinates of the Freedom to Solve Problems," *Wall Street Journal*, November 3, 2008, http://online.wsj.com/article/SB122566866580091589.html.
19. "How you measure the performance of your managers directly affects the way they act. John Dearden | Dictionary of Quotes," http://www.dictionary-quotes.com/how-you-measure-the-performance-of-your-managers-directly-affects-the-way-they-act-john-dearden/#.
20. Gary P. Latham and Kenneth N. Wexley, *Increasing Productivity Through Performance Appraisal*, 2nd ed. Reading, MA: Addison-Wesley Publishing Co., 1981, 168–169.
21. Amy DelPo, *The Performance Appraisal Handbook: Legal & Practical Rules for Managers*. Berkeley, CA: NOLO, 2007, 111–112.
22. "How to Handle a Negative Review," *eHow* Web site, http://www.ehow.com/how_1000326_handle-negative-review-url.html, accessed April 9, 2009.
23. Donna Flagg, "Promoting Employees: How To Avoid Common Mistakes," *Expert Business Source Web site*, November 14, 2007, http://www.expertbusinesssource.com/blog/1260000326/post/1770017377.html.
24. Amy DelPo, *The Performance Appraisal Handbook: Legal & Practical Rules for Managers*. Berkeley, CA: NOLO, 2007, 30.

CHAPTER 12

1. "John Ilhan Quotes, *Woopidoo! Quotations*, http://www.woopidoo.com/business_quotes/authors/john-ilhan/index.htm, accessed May 13, 2009.
2. Leonard R. Frank, *Quotationary*. New York: Random House Inc, 2001, p. 401.
3. Kate Fitzgerald, "Coke Zero." *Advertising Age*, November 12, 2007.
4. "Knowledge Quotes," *The Quotations Page*, http://www.quotationspage.com/subjects/knowledge/, accessed May 13, 2009.
5. Michael T, "Repositioning mature products." *CNY Business Journal*. http://findarticles.com/p/articles/mi_qa3718/is_199809/ai_n8821039/ September 14, 1998.
6. Vicki M. Young, "Talbots seeks assistance in brand repositioning." *WWD*, October 10, 2007.
7. "Marketing Quotes," *Thinkexist.com*, http://thinkexist.com/quotes/with/keyword/marketing/, accessed May 13, 2009.

CHAPTER 13

1. "Quotes by Larry Ellison :: Finest Quotes," http://www.finestquotes.com/author_quotes-author-Larry%20Ellison-page-0.htm.
2. Salvatore Parise, Patricia J. Guinan, and Bruce D. Weinberg, "The Secrets of Marketing in a Web 2.0 World," *The Wall Street Journal*

Online, February 24, 2009, http://online.wsj.com/article/SB122884677205091919.html.

3. "Messengers of Cool," *TIME.com*, October 17, 2005, http://www.time.com/time/magazine/article/0,9171,1118344,00.html.
4. "John H. Patterson quotes," http://thinkexist.com/quotation/to_succeed_in_business_it_is_necessary_to_make/151515.html.
5. Burt Helm, "Best Global Brands," *BusinessWeek*, September 18, 2008, http://www.businessweek.com/magazine/content/08_39/b4101052097769.htm.
6. Brad VanAuken, "Brand Aid: An Easy Reference Guide to Solving Your Toughest Branding Problems and Strengthening Your Market Position." *AMACOM*, 2003.
7. Karen E. Klein, "A Practical Guide to Branding," *BusinessWeek*, June 9, 2008, http://www.businessweek.com/smallbiz/content/jun2008/sb2008069_694225.htm.
8. Jeff Lipp, "Today's Tip: Using Loyalty Programs to Compete with Big Business," *BusinessWeek*, September 29, 2008, http://www.businessweek.com/smallbiz/tips/archives/2008/09/using_loyalty_p.html.
9. Salvatore Parise, Patricia J. Guinan, and Bruce D. Weinberg, "The Secrets of Marketing in a Web 2.0 World," *The Wall Street Journal Online*, February 24, 2009, http://online.wsj.com/article/SB122884677205091919.html.
10. Judann Pollack, "The Marketing 100: M&M's Kathleen Hiersodt." *Advertising Age*, June 24, 1996.
11. Rob Walker, "The People's Marketing," *Inc.*, August 2004, http://www.inc.com/magazine/20040801/schlitz.html.
12. Elaine Wong, "Kraft Unveils New Brand Identity," *Adweek*, February 17, 2009, http://www.adweek.com/aw/content_display/news/client/e3i0a2ed4a24bf26fb82a8887dd5996d856.
13. John Quelch, "Starbucks: How Growth Destroyed Brand Value," *BusinessWeek*, July 9, 2008, http://www.businessweek.com/managing/content/jul2008/ca2008079_888377.htm.
14. Todd Wasserman, "Hummer, Starbucks Rate Low on Value," *Adweek*, May 11, 2009, http://www.adweek.com/aw/content_display/esearch/e3i6e35e0f4967c742affb2c31025962fb7.
15. David Kiley, "Tropicana Fiasco From Arnell is Gift That Keeps Giving," *BusinessWeek*, April 3, 2009, http://www.businessweek.com/the_thread/brandnewday/archives/2009/04/tropicana_fiasc.html.
16. Josh Tyrangiel, "Radiohead Says: Pay What You Want," *TIME.com*, October 1, 2007, http://www.time.com/time/arts/article/0,8599,1666973,00.html.
17. Jennifer Liberto, "Senate deal on credit card curbs," *CNNMoney.com*, May 11, 2009, http://money.cnn.com/2009/05/11/news/economy/Senate_credit_card_fight/index.htm.
18. James P. Womack, and Daniel T. Jones, "Lean Solutions: How Companies and Customers Can Create Value Together." Free Press, New York, New York, 2005.
19. Todd Leopold, "Advertising builds character," *CNN.com*, August 19, 2004, http://www.cnn.com/2004/SHOWBIZ/08/18/eye.ent.advertising/.
20. Andrew Farnell, "Restaurant Price War Could Starve Fundamentals," *Forbes.com*, March 14, 2007, http://www.forbes.com/2007/03/14/restaurants-price-war-markets-equity-cx_af_0314markets23.html.

CHAPTER 14

1. "Gap Inc. - Our Brands - Gap (PRODUCT) RED ™," http://www.gapinc.com/public/OurBrands/brands_gapred.shtml.
2. Parekh, Rupal. "Microsoft Changes 'Laptop Hunters' Ad After Apple Complains." *Advertising Age,* July 23, 2009. http://adage.com/article?article_id=138117.
3. Christopher Null, "Headset Maker Comes Clean on Cell Phone + Popcorn Gag," *Yahoo! Tech,* June 12, 2008, http://tech.yahoo.com/blogs/null/94863?comment_start=6&comment_count=20.
4. Seth Godin, "Sliced Bread and Other Marketing Delights," *TED,* February 2003.
5. Charles Leroux, "Fools' Paradise: Some of the Greatest April Pranks in History," *The Chicago Tribune,* March 31, 2006, http://www.accessmylibrary.com/coms2/summary_0286-31371252_ITM.
6. Thomas Harris, *Value-Added Public Relations,* (New York: McGraw-Hill, 1999), 102.
7. Leroux, "Fools' Paradise."
8. Tom Hayes and Michael S. Malone, "Marketing in the World of the Web," *The Wall Street Journal,* November 29, 2008, http://online.wsj.com/article/SB122792310060465901.html.
9. Salvatore Parise, Patricia J. Guinan and Bruce D. Weinberg, "The Secrets of Marketing in a Web 2.0 World," *The Wall Street Journal,* December, 15, 2008, http://online.wsj.com/article/SB122884677205091919.html.
10. Dana Mattioli, "Contests and Giveaways Move To New, Fast Terrain of Twitter", *The Wall Street Journal*, July 21, 2009.
11. "Facebook Unveils Facebook Ads," press release, November 6, 2007, http://www.facebook.com/press/releases.php?p=9176.
12. Eric Eldon, "New Facebook Pages Getting Developer Attention," *Venture Beat,* March 9, 2009, http://venturebeat.com/2009/03/09/new-facebook-pages-getting-developer-attention/.
13. Jessica E. Vascellaro and Emily Steel, "Something New Gains With Something Borrowed: Targeted-Consumer Efforts, Typically the Domain of PC Campaigns, Are Now Directed at Mobile Phones," *The Wall Street Journal*, Friday, June 5, 2009, http://online.wsj.com/article/SB124415616442286895.html.
14. Fareena Sultan and Andrew J. Rohm, "How to Market to Generation M(obile)," *MIT Sloan Management Review,* 49, no. 4 (2008): 35.
15. Sultan and Rohm, "How to Market," 40.
16. "The Future of Advertising is Here," *Inc.*, August, 2005, http://www.inc.com/magazine/20050801/future-of-advertising_pagen_2.html.
17. "Return to Spender," *Snopes.com*, January 3, 2007, http://www.snopes.com/business/consumer/nordstrom.asp.
18. Bill Kossen, "Success Came a Step at a Time for Nordstrom," *The Seattle Times,* May 29, 2001, http://community.seattletimes.nwsource.com/archive/?date=20010529&slug=newnordstrom29.
19. Pattie Simone, "A Marketing Tool That's Obvious, Overlooked, and Cheap," *Entrepreneur,* October 27, 2008, http://www.entrepreneur.com/sales/customerservice/article198194.html.
20. "8 Tips to Improve Your Customer Service." http://www.inddist.com/article/166546-8_Tips_To_Improve_Your_Customer_Service.php, accessed May 8, 2009.
21. Anne M. Mulcahy, "The Customer Connection: Strategies for Winning and Keeping Customers," in *The Empire Club of Canada Speeches 2003–2004,* ed. Edward P. Badovinac (Toronto: The Empire Club Foundation, 2005), 447–457.
22. Michael Sullivan, "Retain Customers: Align 'Moments of Truth' with VOC," *Six Sigma,* http://finance.isixsigma.com/library/content/c080416b.asp
23. http://apply-mag.com/mag/farming_moments_truth/, accessed May 8, 2009.
24. Salvatore Parise, Patricia J. Guinan, and Bruce D. Weinberg, "The Secrets of Marketing in a Web 2.0 World," *The Wall Street Journal Online*, February 24, 2009, http://online.wsj.com/article/SB122884677205091919.html.
25. Rob Walker, "The People's Marketing," *Inc.,* http://www.inc.com/magazine/20040801/schlitz_pagen_2.html.
26. "Sony Plans its Own Battery Recall." http://www.cnet.com.au/sony-plans-its-own-battery-recall-339271441.htm, accessed May 8, 2009.
27. Chip Conley and Eric Friedenwald-Fishman, *Marketing that Matters: Ten Practices to Profit Your Business and Change the World* (San Francisco: Berrett-Koehler Publishers, 2006), 1.
28. Donna Earl, "What Is Internal Customer Service?" *Donna Earl Training,* 2008, http://customerservicezone.com/cgi-bin/links/jump.cgi?ID=934.
29. Sharon Linstedt, "Wegmans Stays Among Top 5 the 'Best Places to Work,' *The Buffalo News,* January 22, 2009, http://www.istockanalyst.com/article/viewiStockNews/articleid/2974404.
30. Mathew Boyle, "The Wegmans Way," *Fortune*, January 24, 2005, http://money.cnn.com/magazinesfortune/fortune_archive/2005/01/24/8234048/index.htm.
31. Conley and Friedenwald-Fishman, *Marketing that Matters,* 2.

Sources

Chapter 4, page 86, Based on: CPI Chart Source: Data taken from http://www.bls.gov/cpi/cpid0906.pdf; pages 90 and 91, Based on: How the Govt Makes Money Source: http://theglitteringeye.com/?p=4486.

Chapter 5, pages 114 and 115, based on Top Ten Countries US Exports and Top Ten Countries US Imports http://www.census.gov/foreign-trade/statistics/highlights/top/top0812yr.html; page 117, Based on Balance of Trade Source: http://www.census.gov/foreign-trade/balance/c5700.html#2009.

Chapter 6, page 139, (a) Copyright © 2009 by Amazon.com. Reprinted with permission; (b) Copyright © 2009 Stop Hunger Now. All rights reserved. Reprinted with permission; page 143–144, Copyright © 2009 by John Kotter. Reprinted with permission; page 142, Rogers, Everett, DIFFUSION OF INNOVATIONS. Copyright © Glencoe/Free Press. Reprinted with permission of The Free Press.

Chapter 7, page 161, Frey, Chuck, "Tom Kelly Explains How to Cultivate Personal Innovations for Life," from InnovationTools.com. Copyright © 2009 by Innovation Tools. Reprinted with permission.

Chapter 8, page 200, Copyright © 2009 by Caux Round Table. Reprinted with permission.

Chapter 9, page 214, (a) Copyright © 2009 by Google, Inc. Reprinted with permission; (b) Copyright 2009 American Diabetes Association. From American Diabetes Association. Reprinted with permission from THE AMERICAN DIABETES ASSOCIATION; (c) Copyright © 2009 by Bayer AG. Reprinted with permission; (d) Copyright © 2009 The Hershey Company. Reprinted with permission; page 215, Copyright © 2009 by Ben & Jerry's Homemade, Inc. Reprinted with permission; page 216, Courtesy Southwest Airlines; page 220, Copyright © 2009 by Trader Joe's Company. Reprinted with permission; page 222, based on *7 Habits of Highly Effective People* by Stephen Covey.

Photo Credits

Chapter 1, page 2, Anna Subbotina/Shutterstock; pages 5, 16, Aaron Binaco/Pearson.

Chapter 2, page 30, Sai Yeung Chan/Shutterstock; pages 33, 47, Aaron Binaco/Pearson; page 42, Stephen Chemin/Getty Images, Inc.

Chapter 3, page 54, Dmitriy Shironosov/Shutterstock; pages 70, 73, Aaron Binaco/Pearson.

Chapter 4, page 80, olly/Shutterstock; page 84, Aaron Binaco; page 85, Jupiter Unlimited; page 87, Aaron Binaco/Pearson.

Chapter 5, page 106, R. Gino Santa Maria/Shutterstock; pages 109, 124, Aaron Binaco/Pearson.

Chapter 6, page 130, Christopher Hudson/Shutterstock; pages 133, 137, Aaron Binaco/Pearson.

Chapter 7, page 154, Izabela Habur/istockphoto.com; pages 168, 173, 176, Aaron Binaco/Pearson.

Chapter 8, page 182, Bill Varie/Corbis Yellow/Corbis RF; pages 191, 197, 198, Aaron Binaco/Pearson.

Chapter 9, page 208, Chad McDermott/istockphoto.com; pages 214, 224, Aaron Binaco/Pearson.

Chapter 10, page 232, istockphoto.com; pages 241, 248, Aaron Binaco/Pearson.

Chapter 11, page 254, istockphoto.com; pages 262, 276, Aaron Binaco/Pearson.

Chapter 12, page 282, istockphoto.com; pages 291, 299, Aaron Binaco/Pearson.

Chapter 13, page 310, 316, istockphoto.com; page 316, Techlogica\Shutterstock; page 316, Baris Simsek\istockphoto.com; pages 320, 330, Aaron Binaco/Pearson.

Chapter 14, page 336, istockphoto.com; pages 339, 355, Aaron Binaco/Pearson.